WHY GERMANY NEARLY WON

**Recent Titles in
War, Technology, and History**

WHY GERMANY NEARLY WON

A New History of the Second World War in Europe

Steven D. Mercatante

War, Technology, and History
Robert Citino, Series Editor

 PRAEGER

AN IMPRINT OF ABC-CLIO, LLC
Santa Barbara, California • Denver, Colorado • Oxford, England

Library of Congress Cataloging-in-Publication Data

Mercatante, Steven D.
  Why Germany nearly won : a new history of the Second World War in Europe / Steven D. Mercatante.
     p. cm. — (War, technology, and history)
     Includes bibliographical references and index.
     ISBN 978–0–313–39592–5 (hard copy : acid-free paper) — ISBN 978–0–313–39593–2 (ebook)
  1. World War, 1939–1945—Germany. 2. World War, 1939–1945—Campaigns—Europe. 3. World War, 1939–1945—Campaigns—Eastern Front. 4. Germany—Armed Forces—History—World War, 1939–1945. 5. World War, 1939–1945—Technology. I. Title.
  D757.M397   2012
  940.54'21—dc23   2011043277

ISBN: 978–0–313–39592–5
EISBN: 978–0–313–39593–2

16 15 14 13 12   1 2 3 4 5

This book is also available on the World Wide Web as an eBook.
Visit www.abc-clio.com for details.

Praeger
An Imprint of ABC-CLIO, LLC

ABC-CLIO, LLC
130 Cremona Drive, P.O. Box 1911
Santa Barbara, California 93116-1911

This book is printed on acid-free paper ∞

Manufactured in the United States of America

All maps courtesy of Jason Rea.

Contents

Maps

Tables

Series Foreword

Military historians can be a contentious, feisty lot. There is little on which they agree. The importance of attrition versus maneuver, the relative qualities of "deep battle" and "Blitzkrieg," the command abilities of Patton and Montgomery: put two military historians in a room, and you'll likely get three opinions on any of these questions. And yet there is one thing that unites military historians across the spectrum. Virtually everyone within the field recognizes the crucial role that technology has played in the development of the military art. Indeed, this is almost axiomatic: the very first man who picked up a club against his neighbor was wielding "technology" of a sort. The outcome of wars has been profoundly affected by the technological context in which they were fought. From spoke-wheeled chariots to the M1A1 tank, from blades of Toledo steel to the AK-47, from primitive "bombards" to the MOAB ("mother of all bombs"), the problem of technology has stood at the forefront of military history.

Beyond that unifying proposition, however, problems can still arise in analyzing the precise role of technology. Consider for a moment the impact of the industrial revolution. Just as it transformed society, economy, and culture, it changed the appearance of war beyond all recognition. It was the age of the mass army, "railroads and rifles," and the telegraph. The growth of industry allowed military forces to grow to unheard-of size. In 1757, Frederick the Great triumphed over the French at Rossbach with an army that totaled 22,000 men; at Königgrätz in 1866, well over 400,000 men would be contesting the issue, and Austrian casualties alone, some 44,000 men, would be precisely twice as large as Frederick's victorious host at Rossbach. The railroad allowed these hordes to move, quite literally, 24 hours per day, and the problem of the slow-moving supply column that had bedeviled military operations from time out of mind seemed to have been solved. Moreover, the introduction of the telegraph meant that armies could be kept on a tight leash, even by commanders hundreds of miles away.

For each advantage of the new technology, however, there was a corresponding difficulty. It was soon clear that commanding and controlling the mass army was a huge, even insurmountable, problem. It is generally agreed that Napoleon I had serious problems in this area in 1812 and that he was at his best with armies that totaled 85,000 men or less. It was foolish to expect an army of several hundred thousand men to maneuver nimbly across the countryside, wheel like a company, and whack the opponent a surprise blow in the flank. In fact, getting them to maneuver at all was a stretch. The telegraph was a modern marvel, true, but the vision it offered of total control of far-flung operations turned out to be a mirage. Tied to a static system of poles and wires, it was far more useful to the defender than to the attacker, and it was nearly useless in any kind of mobile campaign. The mass army, then, was a huge body with a small brain and had a very difficult time doing much more than marching straight ahead and crashing into whatever happened to be in front of it.

At that point, a mutual slaughter began. The other great technological advance of the era was introduction of new firearms—the rifled musket, or simply "rifle." It dramatically improved the range and firepower of infantry, and the 1860s would see another breakthrough, the breechloader, which greatly increased rate of fire. With long-range rifles now in the hands of the defenders, assault columns could theoretically be shot to pieces long before they struck home. In place of the old-style assault, there now arose the firefight, with extended skirmish lines on both sides replacing the formations of line and column. It was an "open-order revolution," the logical culmination of tactical developments since the French Revolution. Open-order tactics, however, rarely allowed enough concentration of fighting power for a successful assault. Both sides lined up and fired. There were casualties, enormous casualties, often for little gain. It was the great conundrum of the era. Clearly, technology was not so much a solution to a problem on the nineteenth-century battlefield; it was more like the problem itself.

These are the issues that form the heart of Praeger's new War, Technology, and History series. Books in the series focus on the crucial relationship between war making and technological advance in the past 200 years. During that period, new machines like the rifle, the railroad, and the telegraph (in the nineteenth century) and the machine gun, the airplane, and the tank (in the twentieth) have transformed the face of war. In the young twenty-first century, the U.S. Army has been emphasizing the ways in which information technology can have an even more radical transformative impact.

Historically, armies that have managed to integrate these new technologies have found corresponding success on the battlefield, and their victories have as often as not come at the expense of those who have failed to ground their war-making doctrine squarely in the available technology. The question is, therefore, much wider than a simple list of technical "specs" for various weapons. Books in the series link technology and doctrine—that is, the weapons and the manner in which they were employed on actual battlefields of the day. The series is intended for a wide readership, from buffs and war gamers to scholars and "operators"—military officers and policymakers.

It is hard to argue with the notion that technological change has held the key to understanding military history, and in our contemporary era of information management and smart weaponry, technology continues to change the face of battle. Questions remain, however. Is technology our master or our servant? Are there limits to its usefulness? Does it alter the nature of war, or is war based on timeless, unchanging principles? These are a few of the themes to be explored by the authors—recognized experts all—in this new series. It presents no party line or previously agreed-on point of view. Nor does it offer any simple answers to any of these questions. Welcome to War, Technology, and History.

—Robert Citino

Preface

Conventional wisdom explains German defeat during World War II as almost inevitable primarily for brute-force economic or military reasons created when Germany attacked the Soviet Union and entered into a two-front war. This book challenges that conventional wisdom via three interrelated arguments. First, qualitative differences between the combatants proved more important in determining the war's outcome than have the quantitative measures so commonly discussed in the past. Second, attacking the Soviet Union represented Germany's best opportunity to win a war that, by commonly cited numerical measures of military potential, Germany never should have had even a remote chance of winning. Third, for reasons frequently overlooked and misunderstood, Germany came far closer to winning the war than has previously been recognized.

National Socialist Germany sought to build a self-sustaining European empire capable of challenging the United States of America for global dominance via creating Lebensraum, or living space, for the Germanic people. This was to be done at the expense of eastern Europe's Slavic and Jewish populations. The German armed forces, or Wehrmacht, represented the primary instrument for implementing these strategic goals, a military establishment that early in World War II achieved some of the most stunning victories in modern military history. Thanks to these victories, Germany possessed the surprising opportunity to reshape history as have few other nation-states in the modern era. That said, misunderstandings about not only how the Third Reich built its impressive war machine, but also how and why the war ended as it did have produced a vibrant debate regarding the historical record.

Traditionally, the story of World War II is told as beginning with the infamous German blitzkrieg sweeping through Poland and western Europe, propelled by hordes of Panzers overwhelming their foes. Germany, however, missed its golden opportunity to win the war by ripping out the British jugular at Suez and then taking the Middle Eastern oil fields. Paradoxically, Germany turned on its Soviet ally instead, a decision dooming Germany to defeat in a two-front war as the faceless Soviet colossus used little more than mass alone to overwhelm the Wehrmacht. In this war, described almost exclusively from the German perspective, the narrative virtually ignored the genocidal war of annihilation that the German state and Wehrmacht fought against the Soviet Union. Moreover, this story of the war glosses over how the Wehrmacht's decline and Hitler's failure to secure the bounty of economic resources in the western and southern Soviet Union worked in conjunction with the Red Army's qualitative resurgence to determine the colossal eastern European war within a war. In addition, this narrative posits that Germany never could have secured hegemony over Europe via attacking the Soviet Union. Instead, Germany lost the larger war either once it attacked the Soviet behemoth or, at the latest, with the German defeat before Moscow in 1941, and consequently collapsed in defeat under the sheer weight of numbers.

By forging a new conceptual framework for approaching victory and defeat in a total war context, *Why Germany Nearly Won* challenges this narrative long used to describe Hitler's bid to create a European empire and why he subsequently failed. Simply put, Germany lost the war because it failed to secure the economic resources necessary for fighting a long war that could be found most accessibly within the western and southern Soviet Union. Moreover, had Hitler been able to secure these resources, then the Third Reich could have built its economic and military strength up to such an extent as to have dwarfed the Soviet colossus that ultimately emerged from World War II to confront the United States in a roughly half-century-long Cold War. That said, Germany's chance to forge a self-sustaining European empire ultimately foundered, not only because of its inability to secure its economic future, but also because the Soviet Union and the Western Allies made substantive qualitative improvements to their armed forces at the same time the Wehrmacht lost much of the preexisting qualitative advantages held over its foes.

In an effort to reasonably limit the work's scope, it is not an all-inclusive study. The book remains true to the overriding focus on the Third Reich's thrust for empire in eastern Europe as it dips into detailed studies regarding particular events—to emphasize the overall points driving the book. Part I starts by exploring those economic and military decisions making the Third Reich's genocidal strategic goals possible. This part revisits both the years leading up to the war and the war's initial year by examining the evolution of the prewar German economy and military. Questions posed and answered for the reader in these chapters include the following. How did the Wehrmacht build its formidable fighting power? What were the Wehrmacht's true strengths? What were its weaknesses? What role did the German economy play in shaping early military successes? Why did military events in 1940 play out as they did?

In Part II, the book then delves into the eastern European war, contemporaneously examining the traditions and experiences shaping Germany's Soviet foe and its capacity to resist German aggression. Part II explains for the reader not only why the Third Reich's attempt to conquer the Soviet Union was inevitable, but also why it stood among the more logical decisions in an irrational regime. Nevertheless, Germany's 1941 and 1942 campaigns failed. Why? Did the Third Reich's defeats during this era stem simply from its enemy's numerical strength, or was something else undermining Germany's war effort? Part II's chapters tackle this book's dominant themes, relying on concrete examples from the historical record to bolster conclusions while addressing enduring debates and myths regarding the war. Part II also explores the naval war in the Atlantic and the war in the Mediterranean, examining each theater of operations from within the perspective of how they relate to the larger thesis driving this work. Part II finishes in eastern Europe, where it places into a new construct events that occurred during the pivotal period of the war: from the fighting near Kursk during 1943 through the 1943–1944 battle for the Ukraine.

In Part III, the book returns to the war that Germany fought against the Anglo-American alliance. Part III evaluates the air war over the Third Reich and its impact on the war. Part III also addresses D-Day, Bagration, the combat following these campaigns, and the meaning that these events had for the war. Part III studies these events from a fresh perspective, following the book's analytical framework for exploring the elements that produced military victory during the war. In examining the European war's final year, this work also addresses the question of how Germany hung on for one full year against the world's most powerful nations working in concert to engineer its defeat. Part III explains not only why German military resilience in the face of overwhelming power should have been anything but unexpected, but also how and why the qualitative improvements made by the Red Army and Anglo-American led armies were far more important elements in forging Allied victory than has been previously credited.

Overall, this work offers the reader, whether a layperson, well-read enthusiast, or professional historian, with a unique perspective for understanding how and why World War II ended as it did. *Why Germany Nearly Won* will have met its goals not only if it causes the reader to rethink much of what he or she has otherwise held to be true, but also if it has left the reader with better insight into what we know about the war, the Third Reich, and how the Allies defeated perhaps the most horrific empire in human history.

I have been studying World War II for three decades. During this time, I have enjoyed access to a number of informative resources. Most proximately, and in researching and writing this book, I have had the privilege of drawing not only on the collections of the University of Michigan and Michigan State University libraries but also on the benefits of the interlibrary loan system. In particular, I thank the Brighton Public library, which has brought the best of this nation's library holdings to my doorstep. The support of many colleagues and friends has also proven vital to this project's completion. My editors at Praeger, Michael Millman and Robert Citino, and their publishing teams, have been of tremendous assistance. In terms of developing and testing this work's underlying theories, I am profoundly grateful to Alex Kanous Esq. and my late and dear friend Selwyn Leung, each of whom spent countless hours allowing me to bounce ideas off of them and each of whom provided well-appreciated feedback. My friend, the talented Jason Rea, created the maps as well as several of the tables found in this book. My wife, Denise, not only assisted with creating the numerous tables found within these pages, but has also been a model of patience during the countless nights and days I have spent at work on this book. Without her support, completing this project would have been a much more difficult process. I would be completely remiss if I did not mention my grandfather, Joseph Budzinski, a sergeant in the U.S. Army during World War II; he helped along my very early interest in the war. Finally, I wish to thank my parents, Douglas and Joann Mercatante, each of whom has provided crucial assistance in far too many ways to mention throughout my life, and to whom I am forever indebted.

Key To Military Symbols

Unit Symbols

 Infantry

 Paratroops

Motorized Infantry

Mechanized Infantry

Armour

Artillery

Command Level

II	Battalion
III	Regiment
X	Brigade
XX	Division
XXX	Corps
XXXX	Army
XXXXX	Front/Army Group

Unit Nationality

Unit Command Level

Unit Identification Number

14

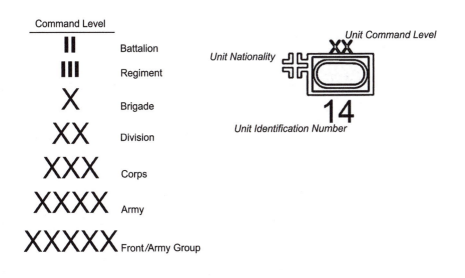

Part I

Chapter 1

The German War Machine on the Eve of War: Myth versus Reality

World War II ended well over 60 million lives in six of the most horrific and brutal years in history. Within this war raged the war in eastern Europe, a war begun by an aggressive and nationalistic German state and a war ranking as the most violent in human history. This war, between Germany and the Soviet Union, decided World War II. Moreover, this war remains the key to understanding how Germany lost a war that at one time it had nearly won. For Americans, accustomed to remembering their own prodigious sacrifice and loss during World War II, the war in eastern Europe, despite its central place in deciding the war, is remembered vaguely if at all. Nonetheless, the war between Nazi Germany and the Soviet Union lasted for 1,418 days of unrelenting intensity and bloodshed. It absorbed each nation nearly in its entirety. From 1941 to 1945, Hitler mobilized 18 million German men and millions of Europeans from other nations.[1] Well over three-quarters of these millions fought against the Soviet Union. At the same time, the Soviet Union mobilized 34,476,000 men and women to fight almost exclusively against Nazi Germany and the other Axis powers.[2] Over any given fortnight during the 1941–1945 eastern European war, the same number of people died in eastern Europe as the United States lost during the entire war against Germany, Italy, and Japan combined. The Soviet Union alone lost over 27 million people—for the most part murdered by the most horrific killing machine in human history, Nazi Germany's Wehrmacht.

During World War II's first three years, Germany regularly defeated the most powerful military establishments on the planet. How Germany won such victories is often ascribed to a variety of reasons. Perhaps the top reason cited for German success is that during the 1930s, the German army had developed a brand-new method for waging war—Blitzkrieg—or lightning war. Nevertheless, the argument that Germany invented a new method of war in the span of a few short years is also patently false. What Germany accomplished in the years prior to World War II was to reestablish a traditional German method for waging war, update it to accommodate the groundbreaking weapons systems fielded during World War I, and consequently come terrifyingly close to securing hegemony over Europe.

THE FRAMEWORK FOR NAZI GERMANY'S MILITARY MACHINE: STRATEGY, TRADITION, DOCTRINE, TRAINING, AND ORGANIZATION

The German army that rolled across Poland's borders on September 1, 1939, had emerged from a long developmental history, predating by centuries the National Socialist regime. The men filling the German ranks in 1939 were the core of what was the world's finest air force (Luftwaffe) and army (Heer), coupled with a noticeably weaker but still dangerous navy (Kriegsmarine); that in combination formed Nazi Germany's armed forces (Wehrmacht). The opportunity for German military planners to create a potent military machine within the brief time following Hitler's ascension to power had arisen primarily for one reason. In the years following the First World War, German military reformers had reestablished a long-standing Prussian/German military tradition, one that they believed offered Germany the best chance to break free from its historical geostrategic constraints. Thus, in examining that Prussian and Imperial German predecessor to the Wehrmacht, we can begin to understand how and why the Third Reich came far closer to cementing a European empire than previously thought.

From the seventeenth century forward, Prussian military leaders, and then the Prussian/German General Staff, grappled with the problems presented by warfare against the multiple enemies surrounding their resource poor and geographically challenged state. The solution, first put into practice by the Prussian army during the seventeenth to nineteenth centuries, was to seek victory via an annihilating first strike delivered by a mobile, qualitatively superior army. Most prominently, the men developing this uniquely Prussian/German method for waging war included Frederick William (the Great Elector), Frederick the Great, Carl Maria von Clausewitz, August Neidhardt von Gneisenau, Gerhard von Scharnhorst, Helmuth von Moltke the Elder, and Alfred Graf von Schlieffen.[3] Several crucial decades during the seventeenth century played a particularly important role in laying the roots for a method of warfare based on mobility—decades punctuated by three separate but equally important battles/campaigns. First was the battle for Warsaw (July 29–31, 1656), when a Prussian army defeated a well-entrenched Polish army by unhinging the Polish positions through maneuver. Second, at the battle of Fehrbellin (June 28, 1675), a Prussian army marched halfway across what would become modern Germany to defeat the imposing Swedish army—at the time regarded as perhaps the best in Europe. The third crucial event sealing the foundation of a military tradition based on moving more quickly and decisively than its foe came during the Winter Campaign of 1678–1679. During this campaign, Prussian soldiers used the mobility provided by sleighs to indirectly decimate and drive the Swedish army from Prussian territory.

During the eighteenth century, Frederick the Great built on the nascent tradition established in the seventeenth century. He strung together a series of victories, including at Rossbach and Leuthen, that swept much larger armies from the field of battle. In addition, at Leuthen, Frederick's armies displayed two key characteristics embodied in the Wehrmacht's future successes. One was the independence enjoyed by the Prussian local commander to make his own decisions in regard to solving the problem of how best to defeat his opponent on the battlefield. This would later become explored as part of a German system of command, known in the Anglo-American world, for better or worse, as Auftragstaktik. Second, Frederick's armies embraced the value of combined arms in defeating the Prussian army's foes. In the decades that followed, the Prussian army developed its approach to warfare. It did so both on the battlefield and in writing—emphasizing the value inherent in mobility, maneuver, combined arms, and the independence of the local commander at the operational and tactical levels. Such a concept of waging war represented an operational tradition focused on defeating an entire enemy army in a war of movement. This was conceptually defined by the Prussians/Germans as Bewegungskrieg.[4]

Despite advancing a coherent approach to warfare seemingly tailor-made to address Prussia's weak position in central Europe, the Prussian army did not always find success. In 1806, Napoleon's brilliantly led, veteran, and far better organized army soundly defeated the Prussian army at Jena. Reform in response to defeat began almost immediately. Scharnhorst played perhaps the pivotal early nineteenth-century role in reshaping the Prussian army. He made two primary contributions. First, beginning in 1810, the Prussian army, at Scharnhorst's urging, opened an Officers War College—the precursor to the latter War Academy. Second, in 1813, he convinced the king to issue a decree whereby each field commander would be assigned a chief of staff, assigned to help guide him in decision making. Prussian commanders soon came to rely heavily on their chief of staff. In creating such command teams, the Prussian army further improved its efficiency and speed of decision making and movement. The Prussian army took quantum leaps forward over competing military establishments.

In the mid-nineteenth century, the next great contributor to the Prussian/German method for waging war had also emerged; General Helmuth von

Moltke, a man who served as chief of the Prussian/German General Staff from 1857 to 1888. Moltke's accomplishments included creating perhaps the first handbook for warfare at the operational level, his insistence on regular war games to test ideas in the field, and his incorporation of the rifle and railroad into the Prussian army. Furthermore, despite facing the daunting command-and-control issues presented by massive nineteenth-century armies, Moltke actively sought to maneuver multiple armies concentrically, to encircle and destroy his foes in what would become gospel for his successors in the German army, namely, the goal of creating a Kesselschlacht (or cauldron battle).[5] Moreover, Moltke advanced the theory that because warfare was uncertain, the local commander would be allowed to pursue the objective created by his superior by whatever means he found most expedient, helping to imbue the Prussian/German army with its deadly battlefield flexibility. Finally, Moltke was more than a thinker. He won tremendous victories in the field, validating many of the Prussian army's approaches to warfare.

Alfred von Schlieffen followed Moltke. Schlieffen added to German doctrine an emphasis on the battle of annihilation, or Niederwerfungsstrategie, also known as Vernichtungskrieg.[6] For Schlieffen, Hannibal's victory at Cannae in 216 BCE, where Hannibal's Carthaginian army of approximately 50,000 men had used deception and maneuver to defeat a Roman army of 80,000 men, was the key example of a battle of annihilation. This belief was shared by most of his peers. Although Schlieffen lacked the war-tested and thus battle-tested field commanders, such as Friedrich Wilhelm von Seydlitz in the eighteenth century or the highly aggressive Gebhard Leberecht von Blücher in the nineteenth century, to actually test out his ideas, Schlieffen did have a General Staff far larger than anything yet enjoyed by his nineteenth-century predecessors. Despite enjoying such an imposing body of work to draw on, imperial Germany's military establishment failed to adequately adapt to growing geostrategic realities and responsibilities. Even as late as 1914, Kaiser Wilhelm II entertained a convoluted military hierarchy, with 48 army and naval officers allowed near constant access to him.[7]

In 1916, after the Verdun debacle of World War I, Lieutenant General Erich Ludendorff and Field Marshall Paul von Hindenburg took command of the German war leadership. Ludendorff's and Hindenburg's primary contribution to the still evolving German method of war was to inject ideology into the mix. Thus, in the years following the First World War, National Socialists and an increasingly radicalized German military establishment embraced total war from Ludendorff's social and ideological perspective. As National Socialist views on total warfare evolved and found acceptance in the 1920s and 1930s German military establishment, Germany rebuilt its armed forces. The Treaty of Versailles had left post–World War I Germany with a seemingly impotent armed forces establishment. Nevertheless, the German military overcame the Versailles restrictions. Just as it had following Prussia's catastrophic defeat at Napoleon's hands, post–World War I German military reformers once again sought to re-create an army emphasizing movement and combined arms. One man in particular played a central role in shaping the Weimer Republic's armed forces into the mold that future expansion built on: General Hans von Seeckt.

THE GERMAN WAR MACHINE'S DOCTRINAL BASE

For the German army, doctrine had always been much more of an art than a science. For example, Schlieffen's loose theoretical planning framework, developed for attacking France in the event of war, met a key component of Prussian/German military doctrine. It relied on officers who viewed war making not as the product of a clearly defined methodology, but as an art impossible to condense into an all-encompassing list applicable to every situation. In the 1920s, Seeckt embraced this traditional German approach to war as a basis for the army's organizing doctrines, published in 1921 as *Command and Combat with Combined Arms*.[8] Seeckt's combat experience, mostly on the German Eastern Front of World War I, had confirmed to him that mobile warfare held the key to German success. Seeckt hammered home the traditional German emphasis on deploying assault armies concentrically, preserving mobility to locate weak points in the enemy defenses, usually the flank. Then the Germans would exploit the enemy weakness by sending the assault and pursuit echelons through and flowing around strongpoints to simultaneously arrive at the critical point on the battlefield known as the Schwerpunkt.

The General Staff that Seeckt clandestinely rebuilt in the 1920s also had its basis in what had come from before. For example, so that staff officers in the Prussian and German army could better serve, in the German army staff officers held equal responsibility with their commander for command decisions, the prospective staff officers apprenticed in field commands.[9] The General Staff officer, well versed in the common operational scheme of maneuver embraced by the Prussian/German army, could advise the local decision-making officer in a manner consistent with the campaign's larger operational goals. This ensured continuity between the campaign's goal and the independent tactical methods used to attain that goal. Meanwhile, at the tactical level, the training priority in Germany's military schools focused on instilling and encouraging in officer candidates the ability to exercise independent thought under extraordinary pressure. Again, this was not a new method of training. For instance, during Prussian training maneuvers in September 1743, combined-arms "mixed infantry-cavalry exercises explored ways to seize a fortified position. The point was not to work out a schema or 'school solution,' but to expose officers and men to the problems involved in these operations."[10] Subsequent course curricula reflected the preference for producing junior officers and noncommissioned officers (NCOs) with a skill set capable of flexibly dictating a battle's flow. To that end, a crucial part of the German training curriculum emphasized training every commander at a level well above his own; that is, a platoon commander trains as a company commander. Therefore, when officers or NCOs were killed on the battlefield, even a junior soldier could quickly step in, take over the unit, and meet the mission goals, thereby maintaining a swift operational tempo.

Seeckt, nevertheless, had failed to comprehensively prepare the German army for twentieth-century warfare, although it was not entirely his fault. One problem within the German General Staff and officer training had begun as the nineteenth century ended. At the turn of the century, officer training had become increasingly technical, with a specialized focus on military history. This made it more difficult for German officers to effectively link the strategic-level political objectives that drove any war with the strategic and operational-level military means used to realize the war's political objectives. In the 1920s, Seeckt only marginally addressed such systemic problems.[11] This meant that though Seeckt and his contemporaries, such as the Truppenamt's Lieutenant Colonel Schleicher and Colonel Joachim von Stulpnagel, actively planned for the creation of a German military establishment that would aggressively wage war with the goal of preparing for the "ultimate battle for world domination,"[12] they (and others like them), in the early to mid-twentieth-century German military high command, essentially abdicated strategic considerations to the nation's political leadership. When the Prussian/German state possessed a leader of enormous talent and skill, this was not a problem, as when Otto von Bismarck unified Germany and cemented the new nation's standing in central Europe. Nonetheless, his wartime twentieth-century successors, Wilhelm II and Hitler, lacked Bismarck's unique talents. Thus, Germany, with a military establishment that could charitably be described at best as one that struggled with strategic matters, fought its twentieth-century wars from a position of ever-increasing weakness—as the field of combat spread to consume not only entire continents but also the globe.

In addition, within the German officer corps itself and, in particular, those responsible for decision making at the operational and tactical level, Seeckt failed to productively address the competing problems and successes produced by the culture of excessive risk taking that was almost bred into German battlefield commanders. Levels of aggression consistently demonstrated in practice—but sometimes at the expense of not only the German strategic focus but also even undermining the chance to engage in the competent staff work and groundwork, most crucially in logistics—needed to sustain the sweeping campaigns that would define World War II. Furthermore, the emphasis on displaying aggression in decision making often would lead to great losses that Germany could ill afford, given its status as a midsize nation. None of this represented a new twentieth-century problem. Throughout Prussian/German military history, a tension had existed within the German officer corps between those who charged into contact with the enemy, and those who reasoned out an approach based on maneuver and minimizing casualties. In failing to come to terms with this tension, Seeckt was not alone. But his omission allowed this philosophical schism to divide the German officer corps in a practical sense. Thus, both Germany's qualitative military strengths and its weaknesses stemmed from past decisions and the tradition imbued therein. This set the stage for the additional building blocks that, for better or worse, formed the Wehrmacht.

TURNING TRADITION AND DOCTRINE INTO PRACTICE AND ORGANIZATION

From 1939 to 1945, roughly 20 million men served in the German armed forces. But only 1 million to 2 million were volunteers. Conscription provided the overwhelming majority of the Third Reich's soldiers.[13] Yet this largely conscript army regularly bested its opponents throughout World War II, especially when fighting on a one-to-one basis and often even when facing far worse odds. The Wehrmacht established such a reputation for battlefield excellence that it is widely regarded today as having been a "professional army." Two elements proved crucial to training the Wehrmacht's men to perform far above and beyond what should have been possible. First, once Hitler took power, leading National Socialists sought to build a youth hardened by ideology, discipline, and strict military-style training. As a result, during the 1930s, paramilitary training organizations sprang up across Germany. By the time an adolescent German male entered the Wehrmacht, he had often already been training for years in not only developing military quality physical fitness, but also such abilities as map reading and marksmanship. In addition, he had learned much about comradeship and group loyalty and had absorbed considerable political indoctrination, all invaluable for creating a disciplined soldier.

National Socialist societal goals, in combination with Seeckt's efforts, accordingly played a critical role in emplacing training regimens that created a second advantage the German army often held over its World War II–era foes—imbuing in the men a fierce dedication to their unit and comrades. The German army typically recruited men from the same geographic area to fight in units raised from that particular geographic area. Thus, German soldiers fought with peers whose families they often knew, and whose values they frequently shared. The parent unit conducted the training via its replacement battalion. Initial training (and follow-up training once a recruit graduated from the replacement battalion to the parent unit) was consistent with larger doctrinal beliefs. Barring promotion, officers and NCOs remained with the same unit, including following recovery from being wounded in combat. All this allowed the World War II German army to continually rebuild shattered units around a stable core. These returning veterans also proved invaluable in strengthening the raw recruits filling in the ranks, greatly increasing combat efficiency. In preserving such traditions, Seeckt's work formed the frame for a military organization that historians to this day refer to as among human history's premier fighting and killing organizations.

Seeckt also helped lay the foundation for one of the greatest strengths maintained by the World War II–era German army. He emphasized NCO and junior officer development in an army limited by treaty in the size of its officer corps. Seeckt cultivated the army's junior-level leadership through creatively exploiting a loophole in the Versailles Treaty that allowed Germany's 100,000-man Reichswehr to field as many NCOs as it wanted. As a result, Seeckt elevated NCO training to a thoroughness and selectivity that defined officer training in other armies. Then, after Hitler took power, the Reichswehr's NCOs became the officer corps for the Wehrmacht. For example, by 1926, the 100,000-man German army had only 36,500 privates. NCOs represented the majority of the remainder, as Versailles allowed only 4,000 true officers.[14]

These well-trained soldiers helped bring to life another key aspect underlying Seeckt's reforms in his belief, like many of his predecessors, in the value of combined combat arms organized into ad hoc mission-specific units. Officers so trained easily "broke up existing units for reassignment into combined arms teams integrating and taking weapons from throughout the larger division and using them in much smaller groups called Kampfgruppen (battle groups)."[15] The practice of forming Kampfgruppen represented a lineage stretching all the way back to Frederick the Great's victories. To that end, Seeckt created a professional core in his army capable of flexibly adapting to almost any circumstance. What's more this was done at a time when many of the world's armies emulated Napoleon's example of massing quickly mobilized conscript armies. The aggressive combined-arms mobile doctrines advocated by Seeckt required not just officers and NCOs but also enlisted men who could fight and think under far more intellectually and physically demanding circumstances than required by those fighting in fixed defensive fortifications. The latter represented the soldier sought by the French army in the 1920s and 1930s. Consequently, Seeckt initiated the world's most arduous training regimes. He trained the German army's men as infantry first, much as in the elite U.S. Marine Corps today. This helped a numerically inferior German army bring great combat efficiencies to the battlefield.

Furthermore, Seeckt took advantage of political developments, especially German ties with the Soviet Union, to expose his men to the newest ideas and train them in using weapons banned by Versailles. For instance, the 1922 Treaty of Rapallo created the means for German weapons manufacturers to join the German military and set up shop in the Soviet Union. Innovation characterized the German military establishment of the 1920s and 1930s.

Officers and men alike were encouraged to study military strategy, history, and tactics—and to think independently. German military training often disregarded the class divisions characterizing the British and French armies of the era. In addition to pedagogical advantages in German training programs, officers gained ample experience and participated in far more large-scale exercises than did their British and French peers. Regular German participation in large-scale exercises also resulted from the organization chosen for the German army, an organization that best implemented the doctrines taught at German military academies and training programs.

The triangular division, divided into three regiments with supporting arms, served as the German army's standard combat formation. German officers traveling to the United States during the 1930s, such as Captain Bechtolsheim of the German General Staff, described the importance of the division within a doctrine based on rapid movement, stating, "Our supreme tactical principle is therefore mobility. Mobility exists down to the organization of the infantry squad. The division, not the Corps is the strategic unit."[16] In combat, the triangular organization often meant two divisional regiments engaged the enemy, with one held in reserve. The reserve aspect was critical to German war making. Even the smallest coherent battle formations, such as squads or platoons, were trained to use reserves—even if this meant only two or three men. Reserves were considered important for a number of reasons, including exploiting opportunities opened up either offensively or defensively, defensively reinforcing a threatened section of the line, or counterattacking an enemy breaking through defensive positions. That said, the triangular model was not dogmatic, German units nearly always enjoyed the freedom to operate outside their table of organization. Although the divisional organizational model proved important, the German army's response to the internal combustion engine would prove even more so.

THE GERMAN ARMY REBUILDS: HOW AND WHY GERMANY CHOSE TO INTEGRATE THE TANK INTO ITS ARMY

Since the end of World War II, competing arguments have held forth all sorts of reasons as to why and how the Wehrmacht forged its early war success. Although German success—and weakness—was mainly the product of centuries of military tradition, the German army forged one important and new advance in the years prior to World War II. What the German army accomplished was to develop, test, and field an innovation rising above all others in terms of transforming the battlefields on which the largest armies in history clashed. This innovation was premised on coupling the promise inherent in the internal combustion engine, as a technology capable of greatly changing how wars were fought, with the logical outgrowth from centuries of a Prussian/German method for waging war. What the 1930s-era German army developed, in short, was a radical new organization of men and machines: the Panzer division ("Panzer" stemmed from the German Panzerkampfwagen, or armored fighting vehicle). The Panzer division grouped the most important combat arms within a single organization capable of flexibly fighting at either the tactical or the operational level. Consequently, the Panzer division enabled the German army to, at times, quite literally run circles around its opponents. We have already examined why tradition meant that the German army of the 1930s was better positioned than its competitors to integrate the internal combustion engine into existing doctrine and tradition. Now let us explore what made the Panzer division such an effective organization, and why it provided Germany the opportunity to achieve unprecedented success during World War II.

The tank had emerged during World War I as an Allied answer to the stalemate brought by trench warfare on the Western Front.[17] Germany also developed tanks during World War I, but did so in only a limited fashion. Unfortunately, for the tank and its enthusiasts, practical experience would be limited. Peace meant that in many countries armored experimentation stagnated. Nonetheless, innovation continued, albeit on a less urgent scale, as military strategists and tacticians debated the new weapon's role in combat. Two schools of thought emerged to lead the debate. One regarded the tank as an adjunct to the infantry and artillery that had formed the backbone for World War I's armies. A second approach for employing armor emphasized massing armored vehicles into cohesive combined arms units to serve as the army's primary offensive weapon system. Individual and isolated thinkers throughout the industrialized world of the 1920s and 1930s enthusiastically backed this idea for employing tanks en masse. These men included Germany's Heinz Guderian and Ernst Volckheim, Russia's Mikhail Tukachevsky, Adna Chafee and Robert J. Icks from the United States, Charles de Gaulle and Jean-Baptiste Estienne in France, and J. F. C. Fuller and G. L. Martel in Britain.

Nevertheless, Germany's unique military tradition created one of the better environments for armored-based doctrines to germinate during the 1920s and 1930s. Throughout the 1920s, German-language military publications wrote of combined-arms formations that, in their earlier incarnations, revolved around horse-mounted cavalry paired with truck-mounted infantry, machine gun sections, and other such supporting arms.[18] When Germany began experimenting with tanks (albeit, given Versailles, these were mock-up tanks), it was, however, not only contemporary writings of the day but also the writings and experiences of Frederick William I, Frederick the Great, Moltke, and Schiefflen that truly paved the way for a return to the past. It was Germany's decision to go beyond the Panzer, and form the combined-arms Panzer division, that ultimately provided the German army with an enormous early World War II advantages over its foes. Moreover, although other armies began creating combined-arms armored divisions, few did so with the balance, flexibility, and focus on exploiting penetrations deep behind enemy lines maintained by the creators of Germany's Panzer division. Furthermore, 1930s Germany stood nearly alone in developing multiple combined-arms divisions capable of operating en masse, or being flexibly broken up to meet any mission. Successfully maneuvering armored units is no easy feat. It requires a well-trained officer corps and advanced communications equipment—all necessary for controlling tanks on a fast-moving battlefield, and all representing qualities found in the 1930s-era German military establishment.

The cavalry and tank possessed clear historical and tactical parallels. The German cavalry produced a talented junior officer core dominating the ranks of early Panzer advocates; Cruewell, Hoepner, Kleist, Mackensen, Manteuffel, and Schweppenburg represented just a few of these men. The German army's tradition of innovative and flexible tactics meant that the cavalry did not hold a stranglehold on armored officer candidates, nor did it stifle armored development, as the cavalry arm did at times in the United States. Moreover, a number of future Panzer leaders came from the infantry. These men included Manstein, Guderian, Rommel, Balck, Hoth, Model, and Thoma. After World War I, German Major Fritz Heigl, an infantry officer, wrote *Taschenbuch der Tanks* (Pocketbook of Tanks), a book that, along with his later publications, influenced better-known German tank advocates. Additionally, senior officers in Germany supported the creation of the panzer divisions. Resistance against the tank was not as strong as some, such as Guderian, would have us believe. The same debates regarding armor the world over thus occurred in the German army. In the German army, however, officers with new ideas enjoyed more influence than did their international peers.

The restrictions imposed on Germany by Versailles meant that early testing in armor theory stemmed from an unlikely source: the motor battalion, or Kraftfahrabteilung. Versailles had allowed each German infantry division to include one Kraftfahrabteilung in its order of battle, ostensibly for transport only. The Germans, however, quickly turned it into a hotbed for experimentation regarding operational motorized and mechanized applications, with Lieutenant Colonel Oswald Lutz and Colonel Alfred von Vollard-Bockelberg playing pivotal early roles in this process. So did Lutz's junior protégé, Lieutenant Heinz Guderian, who took a post with the 7th Kraftfahrabteilung at Munich in 1922. While these men led practical experimentation, Ernst Volckheim, assigned to the Inspectorate for Motorized Troops in 1923, published numerous works that led German doctrinal thought in regard to incorporating the tank into the combat arms and the form such tanks should take: medium sized with a potent gun.

Wilhelm Heye, who in November 1926 replaced Seeckt as the chief of the Army High Command, furthered the tank's cause. So too did Kurt von Hammerstein-Equord, chief of the Army High Command from 1930 to 1934, who focused on realistic war games that also involved the use of motorized formations. In 1931–1932, exercises using dummy tanks, planned and led by Lutz, as inspector of motorized troops, and Guderian, his chief of staff, further incorporated tanks and other combat arms as a coherent whole. In addition, the September 1932 exercises, pitting forces led by Gerd von Rundstedt against those led by Fedor von Bock, furthered the cause of motorizations advocates.[19] With Hitler's election, and his penchant for change, the German army threw itself even more so into developing a nascent armored arm. In June 1934, the German army established the Kommando der Panzertruppen, led by General Major Lutz, with Heinz Guderian as his chief of staff. Germany's first Panzer division began training in July 1935. Because of relentless experimentation, theorizing, and training, the German army consequently enjoyed a tremendous advantage over its prospective rivals.[20]

Ironically, armor represented only a small part of the German army. Nevertheless, the striking power carried by the Panzer divisions far outweighed their small numbers. Each Panzer division was a self-contained army unto itself. For instance, a Panzer division contained engineers to remove obstacles and fight as infantry. Motorized infantry protected the division's flanks, seized the land overrun by the Panzers, and widened gaps in the enemy lines. In this way, artillery and other support formations, such as anti-tank and anti-aircraft units (often used to destroy obstacles), could move up and support the fast-moving Panzer spearheads. In addition, German close air support, most famously delivered by the infamous Stuka—from the German Sturzkampfflugzeug or dive battle aircraft, produced by Junkers, provided direct fire support to the armored spearheads and helped guarantee flank security for the Panzer columns. This was unique to German doctrine. For instance, leading British armored theorists, such as Fuller and Liddell-Hart, mostly ignored the role of close air support in assisting armored divisions.[21]

German military planners emphasized mobility and speed as tools; allowing the Panzers to break through enemy lines and more easily create the Kesselschlacht, or battle that results in a Kessel, literally translated as "cauldron." In German military parlance, this meant a "pocket" of encircled panicked enemy soldiers more susceptible to surrender to the infantry mopping up behind the fast-moving armor. The acknowledged fluidity on the new battlefield—the requirement for quick independent action and decision making—consequently highlighted the largely unacknowledged technical reason for German Panzer success. Another irony (other than the marginal numbers of Panzers) underlying Germany's tank use early in the war was that German Panzers held few advantages in armored protection or armament over rival tanks. Instead German Panzers relyied on superior maneuverability, well-designed commander's cupola's, superb optics, and other such nontraditional determinants of technically evaluating a tank that, nevertheless, prove vitally important in the most crucial elements of tank on tank warfare, that is, being the first one to see, engage, and hit an enemy tank. Thus, this focus on creating technical attributes that could best exploit combined-arms armored doctrine in waging a war of maneuver led to the development of all-too-often-overlooked but equally important technical advantages.

For instance, technical experts, such as Guderian, Fellgiebel, and Lutz, had insisted on equipping each and every German Panzer with a two-way radio. Guderian and Lutz recognized the importance of pairing certain and seemingly disparate technical developments, such as tanks and signals, with past German military teachings and experiences. Although Guderian was a smooth political operator and shrewd self-promoter, he did play a seminal role in building the German Panzer arm. Guderian's views regarding the best practices for using armor were not unique, however, relying heavily on work done by his peers.[22] Processing information in a timely fashion today remains a vital attribute for any successful army. The German army understood this earlier than rival armies did. Integrating technical developments with thorough training enhanced superior command and control, thus allowing Panzer leaders to react on the fly and instantly communicate with other Panzers under their command. All this exponentially increased the Panzer division's operational tempo, and played a critical role in allowing the German army to overwhelm more numerous enemies. In addition, when designing their tanks, the Germans, unlike some of their most significant early war opponents, created enough room in the turret for the tank's commander, gunner, and loader. The driver and radio operator sat in the tank's main body on the tank's left and right side, respectively. Through specializing crew tasks, German tankers accordingly enjoyed important advantages over multitasking enemy tank crews numbering as few as two men and often no more than four. In particular, the commander's liberty to concentrate on directing his tank created a devastating first-hit capability.

The Panzer division represented the essence of an organizational approach based on the traditional seventeenth- to twentieth-century Prussian/German emphasis on movement, flank attacks, concentric encirclements, combined arms, and decisive encirclement battles. Such aggressively taught and practiced doctrine would prove crucial to Germany's exploration of another revolutionary weapons system to emerge from World War I: the airplane.

QUESTIONING THE AIRPLANE'S ROLE AS A WEAPONS SYSTEM: HOW GERMANY ADDRESSED THIS DEBATE

Although it is fashionable to argue the 1939-era Luftwaffe was designed mostly to support the army, the Luftwaffe actually began as a fairly well-rounded institution. That said, there is no question Germany developed its air force with a tactical role in mind. The importance attached to the close support role is evident in Luftwaffe publications, such as *The Conduct of Air Operations, Air Field Manual No. 16*, issued as a field manual for the

Luftwaffe in 1935 and prepared by the Air Ministry, formed in 1934. Seeking to attain air superiority ranked first and, second, *"combat and other air action in support of the army forces on the ground"*(emphasis added), further missions included isolating the battlefield, with a strategic role coming second to last in order of priority in the Luftwaffe's missions.[23] The Luftwaffe's first chief of staff, General Walther Wever, played a key role in not only building a close air support component within the Luftwaffe, including training air liaison officers, but also increasing ties and communication with the army, a vital prerequisite to successful tactical air support.

Effective tactical air support also required technical innovation. Thus, in order to develop a precise hitting arm within the Luftwaffe for supporting the army, the Luftwaffe turned to dive-bombing. Ernst Udet, World War I fighter pilot, was the chief of the Luftwaffe's Technical Office in the mid-1930s. In 1934, he had visited the United States and came away impressed by the U.S. Navy's Curtiss Helldiver dive-bomber. Germany shipped two back for the Luftwaffe. This led to Germany's first true ground support aircraft, the Hs-123, later replaced by the infamous Ju-87 Stuka dive-bomber. In Germany, the tactical benefits provided from dive-bombing fit in well under economic constraints. Effective dive-bombing nevertheless required skilled (i.e., expensively trained) pilots. The technical effort to perfect dive-bombing doctrine moved the Luftwaffe away from strategic aircraft, resulting in research and development gravitating further toward precision bombing. As such, Germany developed a new suite of technologies, such as specially designed bombsights and automatic contact altimeters, to pull the Stuka from its dive with minimal effort from the pilot.

The Spanish Civil War provided Germany the chance to experiment and test airpower applications, producing notable successes, including those involving close support aircraft. During the summer of 1939, the Luftwaffe even set up the world's largest close air support formation. This Nahkampfdivision, or close-combat division, was led by Wolfram von Richthofen and numbered 300 combat aircraft in September 1939. It would later be expanded into an entire Fliegerkorps, or air corps, and play a pivotal role in assisting the German army in its march across Europe. Nevertheless, there was much more to the Luftwaffe's development in the mid-1930s than merely as a tactical air force. For instance, Wever supported creating a viable strategic bombing capability. In January 1934, Field Marshall Erhard Milch, a leading architect of the Luftwaffe, drafted an organizational goal that included nearly one-quarter the Luftwaffe's strength in heavy bombers. German bombers, such as the Do-17 and He-111, were well equipped to hit Germany's closest potential rivals: Poland and France. Regardless, economic dislocations rippling across Germany later in the decade shelved the plan and refocused the Luftwaffe on what seemed at the time more efficient airpower uses, such as those focused on developing dive-bombers.

The Luftwaffe's architects also had long since recognized the great importance that organizational decisions served in building a combat arm from the ground up. Consequently, the Luftwaffe proved well organized for a number of air roles, including operating decisively against opponents lacking its concentrated strength. This represented an outgrowth from German experience during World War I, when Imperial Germany countered its numerical deficiencies in the air by massing its available aircraft. For instance, at the operational level the Luftwaffe turned its hitting power into an organized fist far more potent than the spread out aerial assets fielded by Germany's potential foes. What the Luftwaffe did was group its smaller formations into Fliegerkorps and Luftflotten (air corps and air armies, respectively). On September 1, 1939, there were four of the latter. The Luftwaffe's concentrated air corps and air armies thus allowed it to swarm over more dispersed foes at critical points early in campaigns; in an aerial application of concentrated striking power at the key point on the battlefield, or Schwerpunkt.

In examining the rationale behind creating or rebuilding any military establishment, it is always important to explore more than doctrine or organization and look to actual weapons systems chosen to bring doctrine to life. By March 1936, final testing in Germany had begun on the next generation of aircraft, carrying the Luftwaffe forward into the war. These aircraft included the Me-109 and Me-110 fighters, the Ju-87 dive-bomber, several reconnaissance models, the JU-52 transport, and the Do-17, He-111, and Ju-88 bombers. The development of advanced aircraft across the spectrum, even with prototype four-engine bombers (e.g., the Ju-89 and Do-19) in the pipeline, owed its existence to Wever's vision. He worked with a politically well-connected Hermann Göring, commanding the Luftwaffe, along with Erhard Milch, working on the industrial output side of the process. Together, this triumvirate produced superb initial results. Wever's untimely death from an air accident in June 1936 is widely regarded as irrevocably stunting the Luftwaffe's growth. Nevertheless, by September 1939, the Luftwaffe possessed over 4,300 operational aircraft available for use in combat, with a well-trained pilot cadre to fly these aircraft. The German navy, on the other hand, unlike the German army and air force, trailed its chief European rivals in nearly every possible comparison.

THE WORLD'S MOST POTENT ASYMMETRIC WEAPON

When World War I began, the battleship, evolved from the steam-powered ironclad and dreadnought, had reigned supreme. The Royal Navy led the world in battleship deployment; however, the Imperial German Navy had challenged British supremacy via a naval strategy premised around the battleship and battle fleet.[24] By the end of the nineteenth century, Alfred von Tirpitz (1849–1930), as the secretary of state of the Imperial Navy Department, with Kaiser Wilhelm II's blessing, had launched the Imperial German Navy on a breathtaking expansion focused primarily on building a modern and powerful battle fleet. Tirpitz was undeterred by Britain's technological breakthroughs and prodigious building program. He continued ahead with his own, though he eventually modified his belief in the decisive battle to take into account the deterrent effect that a German battle fleet "in being" offered against the British navy. Tirpitz's fleet-in-being compromise highlighted a salient weakness of any battle fleet. The massive cost incurred in building and maintaining such ships meant that nations only cautiously employed their battle fleets—contrary to the reality that the best weapons are often expendable and affordable. Accordingly, the submarine, an inexpensive weapons systems possessing a long theoretical lineage of its own, emerged during World War I to provide an asymmetric solution for those seeking to challenge the world's naval powers.

Britain's greatest threat during World War I had come from German submarines, or U-boats, (from the German Unterseeboot). Nonetheless, following World War I, German naval planners missed the proverbial boat in regard to further developing the U-boat into a true underwater weapon. Even a full decade after World War I ended, the head of the German navy from 1928 to January 1943, Grand Admiral Erich Raeder, remained heavily influenced by his mentor, Tirpitz. This is not to say that Raeder dogmatically adhered to Tirpitzian strategy. Raeder sought to build a more flexible fleet. But his ideas remained far too centered on building battleships and battle cruisers for carrying out commerce warfare on the high seas.[25]

Raeder spent a significant amount of time during his first 11 years as the Kriegsmarine's commander building the few capital ships that Germany's limited economic resources would allow and planning for massive outlays for more capital ships. He did all this even though Article 181 of the Treaty of Versailles, among other things, had left the post–World War I German navy restricted to a woefully small fleet with almost no realistic short-term chance of challenging the British Royal Navy in the open Atlantic.[26] Moreover, Raeder diverted scarce resources into capital ship construction even as Hitler entered into agreements such as the Anglo-German Naval Agreement of June 18, 1935, a treaty that memorialized German naval inferiority in relation to the Royal Navy. Hitler had supported the agreement at the time; as he hoped to avoid war with Britain while he pursued the establishment of a greater Reich in Eastern Europe. Overall, Raeder's greatest failing was that he seems to have hardly considered how to build a navy that would best support perhaps Hitler's clearest-stated strategic goal; establishing Lebensraum on the European continent first, and only second seriously taking war to the British and Americans. Nation-states require an economy producing advanced weapons systems in considerable quantities if the state is to expand and conquer. Consequently, we next turn to Germany's economic development and analyze the actual form taken by the German military.

HOW PREPARED WAS THE NAZI ECONOMY FOR WAR?

On taking office in January 1933, Hitler lined up Germany's key power brokers to help push the National Socialist agenda forward. On February 3, 1933, Hitler had met with the military leadership to impress on them Lebensraum's importance. He hardly needed to so exercise himself. The senior officer corps not only had long since agreed with Hitler's views, but also worked actively to implement them even without specific direction from party leaders. With the senior officer corps on board, Hitler turned to economic matters.

The National Socialist economy was built on the back of and for two primary interest groups: business interests and the farm lobby. "For businessmen, Hitler's idea of 'living space' blended easily into notions of a 'greater economic sphere' (*Grofsraumwirtschaft*)."[27] The National Socialist Party also gave voice to the 9.3 million German agricultural workers in 1932.[28] Just one year later, this link between Nazi ideologues and the German agricultural industry resulted in the Ministry for Food and Agriculture being headed by a devoted Nazi Party member, Richard Walther Darré. Darré, along with his colleague Herbert Backe, forged a close relationship with Heinrich Himmler and the SS. This relationship played a pivotal role in setting in motion the ruthless and genocidal agriculturally based reordering of eastern Europe's economy in the wake of the German war machine later in the decade.

On February 20, 1933, Hitler, Göring, and the president of Germany's Reichsbank, Hjalmar Schacht, met with 25 of Germany's top businessmen. Schacht solicited enormous sums of money from Germany's largest corporations and industries. With financial backing secured, Hitler set in motion his plans for rebuilding the German war machine. The National Socialist leadership planned to turn Germany's entire population into servants of the war effort. In June 1933, Schacht, Blomberg, Göring, and secretary of the state of the Air Ministry Erhard Milch met and planned to spend the colossal sum of 35 billion reichsmarks on the military between 1933 and 1941 alone. German armaments spending soared higher than the defense spending of any previous peacetime capitalist nation in history. In March 1935, military projects consumed 73 percent of the Reich's financial outlays on goods and services.[29] On December 18, 1933, an announced mobilization plan led to the Wehrmacht taking in 650,000 men in 1935 and 1,200,000 in 1936. This massive peacetime mobilization produced a September 1, 1939, army that featured 2,758,000 men in 102 divisions, an army that had already surpassed the Imperial German Army's size on the eve of World War I.[30]

If this military expansion were to continue, however, Germany needed raw materials and capital, both in extraordinary short supply. These shortages played a central role in the financial crises that wracked the German economy in 1934, 1938, 1939, and 1941. In turn, Hitler consistently regarded conquest as his solution for Germany's economic limits. Hitler viewed the states in central and eastern Europe as both markets for German goods (once Aryanized) and sources for vital raw materials. Germany imported immense amounts of raw materials, including Swedish iron ore, sulfur, timber, and finished products, such as high-grade steel, copper, and ball bearings—all vital for weapons manufacturing. Germany also imported raw materials from other European nations, including from Italy, Hungary (oil), Yugoslavia (bauxite), Romania (oil), Greece and Turkey (nickel and chromium), and Finland (nickel).[31] In addition to imports, Germany relied heavily on enormous domestic coal and steel industries, straining to meet the demands of rearmament and considerable projects to improve transport infrastructure for the military.[32] The cornerstone of Hitler's economic goals revolved around economic self-sufficiency and accumulating resources through trade and outright exploitation of the Balkan countries or via synthetic locally produced materials. Regardless, steel shortages became common; mostly because of the demands placed on refining operations. Blomberg consequently predicted that the German army would not be ready for offensive war until the spring of 1943.[33] Nevertheless, Hitler reiterated that the German economy and military needed to stand ready for war well before 1943, as Hitler was eager to begin his genocidal reordering of eastern Europe. At a 1936 conference of agricultural experts, Darré coldly and brutally laid out the scope planned for a German empire acquired via war:

> The natural area for settlement by the German people is the territory to the east of the Reich's boundaries up to the Urals, bordered in the south by the Caucasus, Caspian Sea, Black Sea, and the watershed which divides the Mediterranean basin from the Baltic and the North Sea. We will settle this space, according to the law that a superior people always has the right to conquer and to own the land of an inferior people.[34]

On November 10, 1937, Hitler explained to his military leadership the time line for creating a new Europe dominated by Germany. According to Hitler, if Germany failed to acquire Lebensraum in eastern Europe, its relative military power would peak in 1942–1943. Thereafter, it could only decline given the rejuvenation of rival nations' armament programs. Consequently, by 1938, the percentage of the Wehrmacht's cut of state funding had climbed from 4 percent, when Hitler took office, to over 50 percent.[35] As a result, the years 1937–1938 featured massive domestic economic dislocations. Raw materials, labor, and capital regularly were available only in short supply. The superheated economy created a situation whereby as early as August 1936, the chief of the General

Army Office, Major General Friedrich Fromm, had predicted a need for war no later than 1940, or else a need to disband much of the growing Wehrmacht.

In addition to the issues posed by basic economics, another problem hindered the Wehrmacht's development. From a strategic perspective Hitler was clearly driving his nation toward a war of expansion in eastern Europe, followed by an anticipated conflict against the United States. Nonetheless, a serious lack of cooperation plagued the service branches. This was coupled to an even worse lack of vision. For instance, in 1934, as the Wehrmacht began picking its primary weapons systems, little thought was given to reigning in Germany's specialist workshop economy and rationalizing its efforts for greater output. In addition, Hitler hardly laid out a consistent path for meeting his goals. For instance, and initially, important actors in the armaments industry, such as the Army Ordnance Office, were told that they had a 10-year window to prepare for war. But then this view of the future was yanked away in 1936, and instead they were put on a four-year path to war. Others, like the Kriegsmarine, were given even less time. For instance, it was only in May 1938 that Hitler informed senior naval commanders that they needed to prepare for a possible war with Britain. This was followed by Hitler's April 1939 repudiation of the June 1935 Anglo-German Naval Agreement, which had seemed to memorialize German naval inferiority in relation to the British Royal Navy. This left German naval planners scrambling to figure out how to address the Royal Navy's overwhelming strength. Such late changes meant not only that the crucial preparation and conversion stage of weapons technology was arbitrarily reduced, and that the Wehrmacht would go to war in 1939 equipped with many obsolete or nearly obsolete weapons, but also that, even worse, the various service branches fought for their own parochial needs. No overall vision for planning and development was imposed on them.[36]

Thus, inadequate amounts of raw materials represented only part of the problem constraining an inefficient German war machine. Take, for example, the Luftwaffe. It rapidly expanded during the years 1932–1938. By the close of the 1930s, well over 250,000 German workers built 10,000 aircraft per year in an industry involving many of the world's largest companies, including Henschel, Blohm & Voss; Siemens; AEG; Bosch; Krupp; Daimler-Benz; BMW; and Junkers. Expansion faltered, however, because of inadequate resources, a deficiency in trained manpower, inefficient manufacturing processes, insufficient investment in industrial machinery, and because competition with other armed forces branches brought aircraft procurement to a crawl. Therefore the Luftwaffe spent the years 1936–1939 converting its frontline strength to second-generation aircraft; even though most such aircraft had been ready for production since late 1936. Germany lost tremendous ground so recently gained over foreign competitors. Production had stagnated in Germany to such an extent that not until 1941 did aircraft production levels reach levels projected for 1939 prior to the cuts in fiscal year 1937–1938.

GERMANY'S EXPANSION 1935–1939

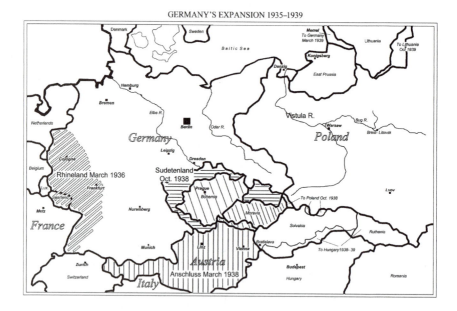

Furthermore, in the late 1930s, the synthetic fuel program, run in large measure by the massive conglomeration I. G. Farben, required even more time if it were to mature. With overseas fuel sources out of the question, the only short-term solution for Germany's fuel problems came from Hungarian and Romanian imports. Neither ever provided enough oil. Germany's economic problems continued only in regard to manpower. Economic output further struggled as Germany drafted military-age men into military service from mines, factories, and fields. German society reeled under the impact brought by expanding the economic base coupled with massive military mobilization. Contrary to past accounts regarding German women in the workforce, Germany exploited female labor, as did many of its rivals, with women representing 37.3 percent of the workforce in 1939.[37] Another way the German economy expanded was through Hitler's diplomatic successes. For instance, the Sudetenland provided unique coal deposits critical to the emerging synthetic fuel industries. Austria also offered new iron ore sources and manufacturing locations. The spring 1939 annexation of the Czechoslovakian rump state and great industrial works in eastern Czechoslovakia brought a windfall of military equipment, allowing Hitler to add three armored divisions and 15 infantry divisions to the Wehrmacht's order of battle. Military-age males (20 to 39 years of age) under German control rose substantially as a result of the seizure of Austria, Czechoslovakia, and Memel, rising from 11.2 million men to 14.3 million men.[38] Thus, Hitler's immense economic effort and diplomatic measures, though falling short in a number of key measures, had created the industrial base to support a world-class military.

WAS THE WEHRMACHT READY FOR WAR?

The 1930s German economy possessed the capability to create a wide variety of war machines. Because of the decisions made well before the war, a framework existed that dictated the Wehrmacht's shape. As far back as the early 1920s, the *Reichswehr* had clandestinely begun rearmament in secret deals not only with German industrialists and the military establishment, but also via work on various prototypical weapons systems in countries such as the Netherlands, Sweden, Switzerland, Spain, and the Soviet Union. Without this work, it would have been virtually impossible for German industry to produce the wide range of weapons that entered mass production in the years immediately preceding the onset of World War II. Thus, when the German economy began its prodigious growth, German leaders engineered the industrial base for rapidly building a broadly but shallowly armed military establishment. Such a developmental framework was necessary until conquest provided the economy with the resources necessary to build a military for fighting a global war. In answering the question regarding German readiness for war, in weighing the strengths and weaknesses of the Wehrmacht in September 1939, examining the choices made in equipping and arming Germany's Panzer divisions offers perhaps the clearest example of the link between German economic output and equipping the Wehrmacht.

During the design/testing process for Germany's medium tanks, Germany built training/light tanks in the interim: the Panzer I, armed with just two machine guns, and the Panzer II, armed with a 20-mm cannon and one machine gun. By the end of 1935, Germany fielded three Panzer divisions, the 1st, 2nd, and 3rd, equipped with nearly 500 light tanks each. The army organized each division's armored complement into four tank battalions in two regiments. Nevertheless, despite its initial organization, for much of the war the Panzer divisions would operationally deploy outside a single standard organizational framework. Mostly, this stemmed from the German emphasis on the flexible combined-arms battle group tailored to specific situations. Beyond the Panzer division, Germany also began fielding a number of other "fast" divisions. These included motorized divisions and, in the fall of 1937, three motorized "light divisions" built from the disappearing cavalry arm. The latter was ostensibly designed to perform reconnaissance, screening, and pursuit operations as an adjunct for the more heavily armed Panzer divisions.

Even without the material taken and used to put together the motorized and light divisions, equipping the Panzer division proved a major problem. On the one hand, German weapons manufacturers designed a slew of armored fighting vehicles for use in the Panzer divisions. For example, in response to the need for infantry to keep pace with tanks, German arms producers developed half-tracked (with two front wheels) armored personnel carriers developed from prime-mover chassis used to pull artillery pieces: the Leichter Schutzen-panzerwagen SdKfz 250 and the superb Mittlerer Schutzenpanzerwagen SdKfz 251, each used to transport motorized infantry, or Panzer grenadiers. German weapons manufacturers also developed a range of Panzerspahwagen, armored reconnaissance cars, for use in the Panzer division's reconnaissance battalions alongside motorcycle mounted infantry. In addition, to control the hordes of Panzers initially envisioned for each Panzer division, approximately 200 specialized command tanks had been built by the fall of 1939.[39] German industry could not possibly equip the rest of the army with such a varied range of vehicles. Thus, horses were employed to tow the bulk of the infantry's heavy weapons, such as artillery and anti-tank guns, with all the difficulties this presented inherent in attending to the care of these large animals. The Wehrmacht would actually use twice as many horses in World War II as the Imperial German Army had in World War I.

By 1939, German economic dislocations, a lack of access to oil and rubber, an immature automobile industry, the concomitant decision to allow specialized heavy equipment companies to help build tanks, and procurement decisions prioritizing weapons systems other than armored fighting vehicles had all led to the Panzer divisions being short of modern armored fighting vehicles in general. Accordingly, 1,445 obsolete Panzer Is equipped Germany's Panzer divisions in 1939, as did over 1,000 similarly outdated Panzer IIs.[40] This was in spite of the fact that as early as the Spanish Civil War, it was obvious that the Panzer II lacked the ability to survive on the modern battlefield. Soviet built T-26 tanks equipped with 45-mm guns that had been supplied to the Republicans regularly bested German Panzer Is and IIs under the command of Colonel Wilhelm Ritter von Thoma and his German contingent fighting with the Nationalists. It was in Spain where Thoma resorted to using 88-mm anti-aircraft guns in an anti-tank role against the Soviet-built tanks, in large part because German tanks could not defeat the Soviet armor.

As war began in 1939, the German army especially missed the more power-fully armed Panzer III and IV medium tanks. Better armament did not, however, mean adequate armament. The Army Ordnance Office's problematic decision to use a 37-mm tank gun in early marks of the Panzer III—related, for logistical reasons, to the previous order to equip German anti-tank units with the 37-mm PAK 35 towed anti-tank gun—handicapped German tank armament well into 1941. Even though the 37-mm cannon possessed an out-standing muzzle velocity, the weapon's small caliber made it difficult to penetrate enemy armor. All this occurred despite the Panzer III's design parameters calling for mounting a superb long-barrel high-velocity 50-mm L/60 gun, equal to anything that Germany's potential enemies deployed in the late 1930s. Although gun barrel diameter is often regarded as the primary determinant in measuring the efficacy of a tank's primary armament, the longer the barrel, the higher the velocity of the round fired from the barrel. The higher the velocity of the shell fired by the tank, the more likely the tank can destroy another tank. Because of the Ordnance Office's decision, the Panzer III, in its most commonly built "D" version of this period, mounted the insufficient, relatively short-barreled 37-mm gun. The Panzer IV possessed thicker armor than the Panzer III but for armament received a low-velocity, short-barrel 75-mm L/24 "infantry" gun. Regardless of their problems, the Panzer IIIs and IVs represented perfectly adequate tank designs inasmuch as they were reliable, maneuverable, relatively easy to maintain in the field, and, most importantly, had been designed to take advantage of the high quality and training of German tank crews standing among the world's leaders as practitioners of combined-arms mobile warfare. By 1939, there seemed no good reason why these tanks should not have equipped the bulk of Germany's Panzer divisions. Nevertheless, a number of decisions, including building up the West Wall, the Plan "Z" naval buildup, and economic shortfalls caused by rampant steel shortages, as well as the inherent inefficiencies of a disjointed German armaments industry, meant that German Panzer divisions went to war woefully deficient in medium tanks.

In addition, Germany's ability to mass-produce medium tanks was limited by another problem, namely, Germany's choice in tank manufacturers. Krupps, MAN, and Henschel carried reputations for producing well-built heavy equipment, such as locomotives. However, locomotive construction in Germany meant highly skilled labor and handcrafting for quality. In addition, armored components needed for a single tank model came from across Germany: Maybach-built engines and Krupps-built guns. In comparison, in the United States, automobile manufacturers, such as General Motors and Chrysler, built tanks from start to finish, providing tremendous economies of scale. Nonetheless, Germany's armored output problems stemmed most of all from steel shortages. For instance, constructing Raeder's battle fleet consumed enormous amounts of steel and skilled labor. It is not a reach at all to argue that Germany went to war in 1939 with obsolete light tanks because Raeder had convinced Hitler to build a battle fleet of dubious use.[41] By 1939, only 98 Panzer III and 211 Panzer IV tanks equipped German Panzer divisions. German tank production during 1939 ground along at anemic levels. Only 249 tanks rolled off German assembly lines during the entire year, numbers dwarfed by the combined output of Allied factories outstripping German armaments manufacturers in virtually all categories of weaponry at a level equaling or exceeding even late war output disparities enjoyed by the Allies over Germany.[42] To round out the 1939–1941-era Panzer arm, Germany therefore pressed into service Czech tanks redesignated as the PzKw 35(t) and PzKw 38(t). This decision made the tenuous supply of spare parts only more difficult to maintain, exacerbating problems revealed during the Anschluss, especially in regard to inadequate armor recovery assets and limited logistical support. Even in the infantry's ranks,

German economic woes meant that 34 of Germany's 105 frontline divisions remained underequipped on the eve of war.[43] Raw materials shortages, such as in copper, were coupled with steel shortages to crimp the production and stockpiling of shells, mines, mortars, artillery tubes, and tank guns. In addition, other problems afflicted the Wehrmacht.

The single greatest weakness inherent in the armed forces of Nazi Germany existed in the command-and-control structure that evolved throughout the late nineteenth and early twentieth centuries and then reached its final structure in the early years of Hitler's reign.[44] During the years between the world wars, military education and most writings in German military periodicals focused on the operational and tactical; little was mentioned of strategic military concerns. Subjects such as economics and political science were virtually ignored,[45] as was, most crucially in a global war, waging coalitional warfare. The Kriegsakademie virtually ignored the subject. Only the short-lived Wehrmachtakademie, from 1935 to 1938, even began examining coalitional warfare, and this organization was founded most notably because of efforts led by War Minister Field Marshall Werner von Blomberg, Army General Walter von Reichenau, and Luftwaffe General Walter Wever. Once Blomberg was removed, the Wehrmachtakademie closed. Therein went, among other things, the Wehrmacht's best chance of producing an officer corps sensitive to the needs of integrating German partners in an effective coalition, a failing that would stand in stark contrast to the overwhelmingly successful alliance maintained by Germany's foes. Overall, Germany's military leadership, though well prepared for making sound tactical and operational decisions, would during WWII prove woefully ill-equipped for marrying operational military goals to overriding strategic military and national goals.

Then, in 1938, Hitler replaced the War Ministry with a military command structure titled the OKW (Oberkommando der Wehrmacht, or High Command of the Armed Forces). In name, the OKW held responsibility for overseeing the individual military services. In practice, however, the OKW offered an opportunity to tighten Hitler's grip over the OKH (Oberkommando der Heer, or Army High Command). The Army High Command had traditionally represented the most powerful and influential command, nonetheless, as result of the OKW's formation only during Germany's war against the Soviet Union would the OKH hold primacy over the OKW in a theater of operations. Otherwise, the OKW had surpassed the OKH in a command sense even though the OKH retained control, for example, over mechanized artillery and heavy engineering equipment as well as the army's personnel department. Add the self-directed Waffen-SS to this mix (though on the battlefield it worked under OKH or OKW direction), and German strategic-level planning degenerated into a horrible amalgam of competing organizations with little centralized direction or coordination. Hitler further watered down his strategic-level command efficiency by appointing easily controlled political hacks to the

OKW's senior levels, men such as General Wilhelm Keitel, OKW chief of staff, and General Alfred Jodl, in command of the OKW Operations Department.

Finally, in 1938, Hitler, in no large part through his own political machinations, drove out the army's existing leadership. This was done despite their near unanimous agreement with Hitler's goals, if not the timing behind achieving them. Hitler appointed officers whom he could better control, including Walter von Brauchitsch, who was appointed to the position of OKH commander in chief despite the fact that he was a vacillator with no great vision for directing the army. In addition, Franz Halder took over as OKH chief of staff. Halder was a talented career staff officer when he replaced Beck in August 1938. Halder, however, had a poor understanding of global and strategic matters, and his grasp of modern operational matters was far more conservative and traditional than that advocated by more visionary men, such as Erich von Manstein. For his part, Hitler took over as supreme commander of the armed forces, retired 14 generals, and demoted 40 others. As supreme commander, Hitler would ultimately prove lethal to Germany's ability to prosecute continent-wide warfare. Nevertheless, Hitler did have some strategic talent and, despite his clear goals for Lebensraum, had an opportunistic streak that provided some measure of flexibility to Germany's strategic orientation. Overall, however, Hitler lacked many characteristics important for leading a nation's armed forces. In particular, he was prone to irrationalism, was impatient, relied on his own inherent prejudices and incomplete information to make snap decisions, and lacked the necessary disposition for working well with his senior military leadership.

The purges and parallel command structures fostered by Hitler and his self-serving senior officers thus played a notable role in undermining the Wehrmacht's efficacy. For instance, the Luftwaffe and Kriegsmarine utterly failed to develop an effective strategy for applying airpower to naval warfare. Instead, in March 1934, Raeder had ordered a shipbuilding program to produce, by 1949, a German fleet comprised of at least three aircraft carriers, eight battleships, eight cruisers, 48 destroyers, and 72 submarines.[46] Consequently, by 1939, even in terms of being ready to fight a short-term asymmetric war against the Royal Navy, the German navy possessed a U-boat fleet only 60 strong and no aircraft carriers. In addition, German torpedo development had stagnated so badly in comparison to other naval power of the era that not until November 1942 did Germany produce a reliable magnetic torpedo for its U-boat crews.[47] Furthermore, the Kriegsmarine's bitter contest with the Luftwaffe was so destructive that Germany began World War II without a dedicated torpedo bomber and thus a nearly nonexistent capability for delivering history's most effective antishipping weapon. That said, the navy was not alone in its failings. All the German service branches failed to coordinate their efforts. The army and navy hardly spoke and planned, much as in World War I. Moreover, even though the Wehrmacht's operational capabilities for waging war across continents and in the maritime realm proved primitive as best, capabilities needed for fighting on the continent had also been relegated to second-class status. For instance, intelligence-gathering operations had been particularly undersourced, compounding an existing bias in German military culture toward the operational. In addition, politics constantly disrupted the development of effective German intelligence-gathering organizations. Finally, arrogance within counterintelligence helped conceal the vulnerability of Germany's much-vaunted Enigma code machines.

Despite the host of economic and military problems cataloged in this chapter, for the reasons explaining the Wehrmacht's strengths, no country ranked better prepared for war than did Germany on September 1, 1939. The commonly believed myth that this preparation arose from an overwhelming preponderance of the best equipment for the world's largest military is, however, simply untrue. In World War II's early years, an underequipped, outnumbered German military, but with a professional core well versed in tradition and doctrine, dominated its opponents.

Chapter 2
The Third Reich Ascendant: The Reasons Why

Between 1933 and 1939, Germany equipped Europe's finest overall military and expanded its borders, population, and industrial capacity, all without firing a shot. In the fall of 1939, however, the uneasy and intermittent European peace ended. It is not the intention of this book to reexamine Germany's 1939–1940 campaigns in detail. Nonetheless, in terms of answering why the Wehrmacht nearly delivered to Hitler the continental empire he sought and why Germany ultimately failed, as well as untangle some of the more pernicious myths used to explain away early war German successes, it is useful to examine the Wehrmacht's performance from September 1939 to the summer of 1940. We start by analyzing the German military performance in Poland, and then take a look at how Germany's political and military leadership, even after the spring 1940 campaign in western Europe, still only partially understood what had produced their success.

EVALUATING THE GERMAN MILITARY PERFORMANCE IN POLAND

Germany crushed an army of 1 million men in only three weeks. On its face, this describes Germany's victory over Poland. In reality, the Wehrmacht's performance ranked as decidedly spotty. The Poles fought extremely hard, and actually held out longer than it subsequently took the Germans to break the French army's back and drive the British Expeditionary Force (BEF) from Europe. Had the British and French seriously challenged the western German border in September 1939, the Wehrmacht may have been dangerously overstretched or worse. Regardless, the Allies left Poland to fight alone. Poland alone against Germany, however, did not necessarily represent a German cake-walk. In August 1939, Poland's army included 30 infantry divisions, 11 cavalry brigades, part of the centuries-old Polish tradition of mounted excellence on the battlefield, and two armored brigades—all told, over 1 million men when mobilized. What's more, the Polish 7TP light tank was, in terms of hitting power, the equal of its primary German foes. Nevertheless, the Poles, with a small industrial base, could field hardly enough tanks of any kind.

The German army invading Poland on September 1, 1939, represented two armies: one modern, mobile, and world class and the other a throwback to World War I. Doctrine meant that Germany concentrated most available Panzers in just two armies. These Panzers would spearhead a massive Moltkean-style double envelopment designed to trap the Polish army in two pockets. General Guenther von Kluge's 4th Army represented the striking power in General Fedor von Bock's Army Group North. Twenty-one divisions and 600 tanks organized into the 4th and 3rd Armies. General Walther von Reichenau's 10th Army spearheaded General Gerd von Rundstedt's potent 36-division, 2,000-tank Army Group South. Rundstedt's Army Group also included the 8th and 14th Armies under Generals Johannes Blaskowitz and Wilhelm List, respectively. The German officer corps overwhelmingly looked forward to an ideologically charged and criminally prosecuted campaign against the hated Jew and Slav. Halder was so excited that he spoke of finishing off the Poles in "three weeks, and if possible, in fifteen days. It will thus be left to the Russians to say whether the Eastern Front will dictate or not the destiny of Europe. In any case, a victorious army . . . will be ready to confront Bolshevism or . . . to launch itself against the West."[1]

The German assault began at 4:45 a.m. on September 1. The Polish air force dispersed prior to the invasion, instead of rising en masse to challenge the Luftwaffe. Accordingly, it saw its numbers quickly whittled down in a mis-guided hope to preserve its striking power. The Polish army fought mostly alone as German planes and artillery pounded the Polish capital, killing over 60,000 of Warsaw's citizens. Then, on September 17, the Red Army's 265,000-man Ukrainian Front and 200,000-man Belorussian Front, commanded by Army Commander First Rank Timoshenko and Army Commander Second Rank Kovalev, respectively, invaded the remnants of Poland. By October 6, 1939, Poland's last centers of organized resistance had surrendered to the German-Soviet partnership. Germany had lost 13,000 to 16,000 dead, and 30,000 to 32,000 wounded. The Polish military suffered 70,000 killed, 133,000 wounded, and 700,000 captured. Approximately 100,000 Polish soldiers escaped into Hungary, Romania, and Lithuania to carry on the fight alongside the Western Allies.

Within occupied Poland, atrocities began almost immediately. From September 1939 to June 1941, Stalin deported over 250,000 Polish prisoners

GERMAN AND SOVIET INVASION OF POLAND SEP. 1939

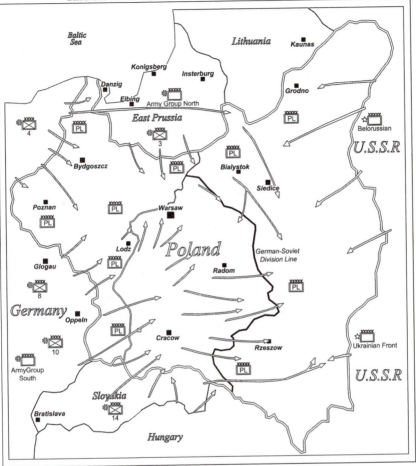

of war and 1 million Polish civilians—sent mostly to the Gulags. Thousands died in transit after being packed into cattle cars with no food and being exposed to disease and the elements. On arriving at the Gulags, and after this nightmarish journey, hundreds of thousands more would die. As for the Soviet occupation policies, in general, murder, torture, kidnapping, massive theft, phony elections, and deportations were everyday occurrences.[2] Then, during the spring of 1940, Stalin authorized the murder of at least 20,000 Polish prisoners of war, intellectuals, and anyone else who Stalin feared might cause unrest.[3] Despite these horrors, Soviet atrocities paled in comparison to German activities.

Within days of the war's beginning, German crimes against Polish civilians, including killing, rape, and looting, had become frequent occurrences. At the same time and in preparation for German settlement, Hitler ordered immediate widespread executions aimed at the Polish intelligentsia. German forces also began depopulating huge swaths of the Polish countryside. By 1942 and as a result of Nazi policies, a fifth of Poland's 35 million prewar population had been killed.[4] For the most part, the leadership and men of the Wehrmacht either participated in the massacres or stood aside and observed. By the end of October, the Wehrmacht, the Einsatzgruppen, and various German security and police services had killed 20,000 people in 764 massacres, with 311 of these the Wehrmacht's responsibility.[5]

Beyond participating in genocide, the Wehrmacht's leadership took the time to examine the military establishment's performance on the battlefield. They found less-than-stellar results. For instance, German infantry all too often relied on German airpower and armor to do the heavy lifting. In particular, wide-ranging Polish light cavalry frequently inflicted stiff losses on the German infantry, especially in daring night rights that shook many a German infantry unit. However, once German armored vehicles arrived on the scene, the Polish cavalry were doomed if they could not disengage. This was the exact fate of the Pomorska Cavalry Brigade's 18th Regiment of Pomeranian Uhlans near the Brda River. German propaganda famously mischaracterized this action as a desperate Polish cavalry charge against German tanks, an image that has wrongfully continued to color history's view of the campaign. As it was Poland's flat and dry plains, and road and rail network provided the infrastructure needed by German motorized units seeking to maintain a quick operational tempo, while the vast majority of Germany's army marched on foot alongside horse-drawn equipment. Accordingly, the two-tiered nature of the German army meant that encircled Poles often either retreated through the gaps between the German armor and infantry or put up stiff resistance against the German infantry. The shallow 300-plus-mile depth of the Polish battlefield masked the full extent of these underlying problems, and alleviated significant logistical troubles already plaguing the German army.

As for the Panzer divisions, even the inadequately armed Poles proved the obsolescence of the Panzer I and II. Depending on the source, Germany lost anywhere from 200 to 674 tanks, 319 armored cars, 195 heavy guns, and 11,000 trucks and motorcycles seriously damaged or destroyed. On September 8 alone, the 4th Panzer Division lost 50 of 120 tanks to Polish infantry and anti-tank guns in Warsaw's streets. The inability of German industry to provide enough medium tanks as replacements prior to the 1940 campaign season magnified these losses. By the spring of 1940, Germany had manufactured only 540 new tanks since the war began, in contrast to Allied and Soviet factories all too often leaving German industrial output in the dust. Moreover, heavy armor output included only 15 of the newly developed assault guns, which were designed to increase the infantry's punch. Furthermore, by the end of the Polish campaign, German ammunition stocks had fallen to dangerously low levels.

Finally, the Luftwaffe had finished the campaign as a nearly spent force, with only enough bombs stockpiled to have lasted another two weeks. Had the Polish been able to hang on, or had the British and French actively supported the Poles, the Luftwaffe may have been nearly combat ineffective by the end of October. Although Poland fielded 390 obsolete aircraft, including only 150 fighters, the Luftwaffe lost 285 aircraft in combat against the well-trained, aggressive, and world-class Polish pilots. German losses included 78 expensive He-111 and Do-17 medium bombers, with a further 279 aircraft damaged.[6] Taken from an original force of 2,200 aircraft, this meant that during a single month's combat, nearly one-quarter the Luftwaffe's aircraft were seriously damaged or lost.[7] The Polish campaign led the German army to institute a rigorous training program even further emphasizing Bewegungskrieg's importance as an organizing principle, and reinforcing the use of the combined-arms Kampfgruppen that had yet again proved highly successful. Consequently, the German army that would invade western Europe in May 1940 would prove to be a much better instrument of war than had its September 1939 predecessor.

GERMANY LOOKS WEST: THE CRITICAL STRATEGIC AND ECONOMIC DECISIONS IMPACTING GERMAN MILITARY POWER IN 1940–1941

Since World War II ended, the German blitzkrieg has been advanced as not only the dominant reason for German military successes, but also part and parcel of German military planning for the 1940 campaign in western Europe. In reality, nothing could be further from the truth. On October 9, 1939, Hitler drafted War Directive No. 6 ordering the OKW (Oberkommando der Wehrmacht, or High Command of the Armed Forces) and the OKH (Oberkommando der Heer, or Army High Command) to prepare Germany's invasion of western Europe. The attack's main blow, as unimaginatively planned by a General Staff that throughout WWII would prove to be far more accomplished in their role as war criminals than they would as masters of war, was set to plow through Belgium, Luxembourg, and Holland into northern France.

In concert with the plan, on December 12, 1939, Hitler ordered artillery and artillery ammunition output to increase by more than eight times. Ammunition outlays were already using 400,000 tons of steel per month, or one-quarter of available steel, in the fall of 1939, and this increase only further hindered the production of the equipment needed to fight a war of maneuver, such as trucks and armored fighting vehicles. Hitler also ordered a further emphasis on Ju-88 production; in preparation for the General Staff's plan to launch the Luftwaffe at England once the German army captured Allied air bases in France along the

English Channel. Consequently, Hitler had reoriented the German economy in a manner inconsistent with the German army's strengths. Instead, and much as during World War I, Hitler had ordered the increased production of mortars, howitzers, and artillery, with a large fleet of Ju-88s standing in for the Zeppelins previously sent against Britain. These decisions, however, though mirroring the advice he received from his senior military leadership, meant that during the war's initial 10 months, artillery, artillery ammunition, and Ju-88 production consumed two-thirds of all resources devoted to German armaments production.[8] These actions, more than any other decision, left the Wehrmacht short of tanks and other armored vehicles, not only in 1940 but also one year later in the vastness of eastern Europe.

Regardless of the economic decisions made during the fall of 1939, many top German generals, in contrast to the subsequent planning for invading the Soviet Union, were highly vocal about holding off on attacking France. Hitler, for his part, was less than impressed with his General Staff's arguments, and on November 23, 1939 Hitler assembled his top military strategists for a conference to "remind them" of National Socialism's goals. Hitler made clear the Third Reich's larger strategic focus on creating Lebensraum in eastern Europe after the western European campaign ended. As for the thought that Germany might need to invade Great Britain provided that France fell, it was hardly considered. On November 15, 1939, Raeder had directed his staff to study the possibility that the Kriegsmarine might need to lead an invasion of Great Britain. But both the army and the Luftwaffe had been less than constructive in assistance. Hitler and the OKW were not even consulted, and the planning fizzled out as the Wehrmacht prepared to invade western Europe.[9]

COMPARING THE OPPOSING ARMIES AND PLANS ON THE EVE OF WAR

In the spring of 1940, Germany faced in Britain and France the world's most powerful combined military and economic powers enjoying levels of armaments output dwarfing German efforts. Consequently, the Wehrmacht would fight Allied strength from a position of numerical inferiority in nearly every measure. Regardless, it would defeat its much larger foes in a matter of weeks. A closer look at the state of the British and French armed forces in May 1940 helps explain why.

Both the British and the French had rebuilt their armed forces during the massive arms race that had preceded World War II. Each did so in a manner complementing the martial tradition found in each nation's armed forces. For instance, Britain addressed the problem posed by its global commitments by substituting firepower for manpower, specifically through revamping a large air force and navy and leaving comparatively meager assets for the British army. Consequently, from September 1939 to May 1940, the British Expeditionary

Force (BEF) conducted no large-scale (multidivisional) maneuvers, staff war games, or communications exercises.[10] As for developing modern equipment, the British army fell far behind its potential foes, particularly in regard to armored warfare. Of Britain's tanks, probably the best was the slow, heavy infantry tank nicknamed the "Matilda." The Matilda's armament featured a 2-pounder gun, equivalent to a 40-mm gun, capable of firing rounds at a muzzle velocity reaching 853 meters per second. Moreover, the Matilda II's frontal armor, at 78 mm thick, provided ample protection against the inadequately armed Panzers. Nonetheless, the ponderous Matilda, all too often grouped with other tanks in stand-alone brigades, contributed to the lack of flexibility and mobility of Britain's armored organizations in comparison to Germany's Panzer divisions. The British, however, enjoyed the support provided by a powerful but fragile ally.

World War I had devastated France. Roughly 1,398,000 French soldiers died during the war. At the front alone, France lost 25 percent of its military-age male population (those 18 to 27 years old).[11] Birthrates plunged as a result; leaving 1939 France with only 4 million men aged 20 to 34. Furthermore, economic depression struck France later than Germany. Therefore, as Germany emerged from its economic malaise France began an economic downturn lasting through most of the 1930s.[12] As for the French army, it was organized as a conscript army whose predominant goal was waging static defensive warfare. This led to many structural issues plaguing the army, including, most notably, training problems. For example, in 1927–1928, conscript service dropped to one year; just enough time to train a soldier in adequately manning a defensive position but not nearly enough for training in the complexities of maneuver warfare. Only in the late 1930s did the French increase the length of conscription service. Moreover, between September 1939 and May 1940, the French army did not train at the large-unit level.

Given French doctrine and tradition, in 1930, French Defense Minister Andre Maginot had received orders to build a series of fortifications from the Swiss border in the French southeast extending north to the plains bordering Belgium. As with most military expenditures, cost overruns and delays exacerbated the Maginot Line's already exorbitant price. Worse yet Marshall Maurice Gamelin led the defensive-minded French army and obstructed reformers, such as Colonel Jean Baptiste Estienne, General Aime Doumenc, and Major Charles De Gaulle. Consequently, France possessed only one armored division as late as the mid-1930s. Even worse, the French army's operations manual, *Instruction sur l'emploi des Chars de combat* (Instructions on the Employment of Battle Tanks), published in 1930, taught that "battle tanks are escort weapons for the infantry."[13] Thus, training and doctrine remained behind the times, as did crucial aspects of otherwise seemingly adequate French tank designs.

In 1940, France deployed many tanks of varied size, quality, and quantity. Of the many tanks equipping the French army, the Somua Company built in early 1940 one of the best-armed and best-protected tanks in the world. With a turret-mounted 47-mm high-velocity cannon, the Somua proved harder hitting than anything in the German arsenal, and it allowed the French tankers to stand off and engage German tanks at ranges beyond the Germans' ability to effectively engage the French. Despite weighing a mere 13 tons, the Somua possessed 60 mm of *sloped* frontal armor, impenetrable to almost all German tanks at anything but the closest ranges. The Somua however also possessed a crippling defect shared by many French designs. Of France's tanks, only the heavily armed and armored Char B1 bis carried even a four-man crew, the Somua possessed a three-man crew, and France's remaining tanks had only two-man crews. The Somua's undermanned turret therefore meant that it was incapable of maintaining the demanding pace of target acquisition, firing, and reloading needed in an era when first-shot kills were rare during fast-paced mobile battle. In addition, French armor lagged significantly behind the German use of signals technology in their Panzers. Similarly overall French training and doctrine in regards to the use of armor hardly paced German efforts. Moreover, in terms of fighting a war of maneuver, not only did the Germans possess a decided edge in doctrine, organization, and training, but even the largest German tank of the era, the Panzer IV, would prove far more reliable and durable than the heavy French tanks.

Despite only slowly coming to grips with the impact of the internal combustion engine on warfare, the Allies actually chose a deployment scheme far more aggressive than tradition may have made seem likely. Given the Maginot Line's defensive strength, and the unfavorable terrain lining the Franco-German border, the Allies believed that a German offensive needed to come through northern Belgium. Gamelin, the Allied commander in chief, based his strategy on leveraging the strong Belgian fortifications with the French First, Second, and Ninth Armies and the BEF moving east to meet a German invasion near the Dyle River defensive barrier in Belgium, with this later extended to reach the Breda river. The Allied defensive plan, however, labored under the burden brought on by two problems. First, the Allies presupposed that German planners regarded the heavily wooded and hilly Ardennes in southern Belgium as impenetrable. Therefore, the Allied command had assigned inadequate defensive forces to the Ardennes. These deployments had been made even though in the late spring of 1938, the then commander of the French Second Army, Major-General Andre Gaston Pretelat, had led a map exercise showing that the Germans could cross the Ardennes and reach the Meuse in only 60 hours, a predication that, as it turned out, would be short only three hours in its accuracy. Gamelin had dismissed the results by arguing that French reserves could take care of backing up the weakly defended Ardennes.[14] The second problem underlying Allied defensive plans related to the first problem; that is, they were predicated on Belgian defensive fortifications buying enough time for the advancing Allied armies to arrive at the front. That said the Allied plan was not particularly poor; rather, it simply had the misfortune of facing a better plan, one far more successfully married to a tradition that embraced waging a war of maneuver.

THE GERMAN INVASION PLAN

Hitler had been prepared to attack France late in 1939 in a plan code-named Case Yellow. Nevertheless, the Polish campaign had left the German army in a particularly dreadful state, with only 541 medium tanks operational by October 1939. Then, on January 10, 1940, a German officer, carrying enough information to give away the focus of the invasion plan, force landed in Belgium because of poor weather. Although such a misfortunate occurrence may have seemed devastating, in reality it helped open the door to a far more creative and explosive plan. On October 25, 1939, General Erich von Manstein authored and proposed a different plan than Halder's unimaginative Case Yellow, one surpassing Schlieffen's operational vision and, no less, the weak OKH effort.

For his part, Manstein had already made two important contributions to the German army. First, prior to the war the army had chosen his plan for expanding its ranks by creating new units from existing divisions. This framework allowed for a remarkable level of flexibility in the years to come.[15] In addition, after his October 1, 1935, promotion to deputy chief of the General Staff, Manstein moved ahead of his more conservative and senior peers in embracing the assault gun as a mobile weapons system providing the infantry with impressive firepower, and the additional mobility needed for the army's preferred method of fighting. Despite Manstein's impressive résumé, the Blomberg and Fritsch scandals brought his career to a screeching halt. This resulted in, among other things, Manstein's demotion and destroyed his chances for becoming chief of the General Staff. This quite possibly was an outcome that had altered history, for had he, rather than the more conservative and less gifted Halder, been promoted, who knows what would have happened with Manstein's operational talent turned loose on the Allies and then the Red Army. Instead, having been marginalized, Manstein was initially deflected by both Halder and Brauchitsch in attempts to have Hitler review his plan over the OKH's version. However, Henning von Tresckow, one of Manstein's former students at the General Staff, was friends with Rudolf Schmundt, Hitler's aide-de-camp. From these connections, Hitler, who had his own reservations about the OKH's plan, first viewed and then, on February 17, 1940, approved Manstein's plan.

Manstein's plan coupled simplicity with deception and concentrated strength to strike a decisive blow. It featured strong German armies attacking into the Netherlands, drawing Allied forces to meet what appeared as the German army's main attack axis. At the same time, the primary strike force would attack through the thinly defended Ardennes and penetrate deep behind the Allied forces advancing into northern Belgium and the Netherlands. On breaking out of the Ardennes, the German armor would turn northwest, driving to the English Channel and trapping the Belgian army, Dutch army, the BEF, and France's best armies in one huge pocket. Rundstedt, commanding the German spearhead (Army Group A), received the bulk of the Panzers and truck-mounted infantry. Bock led Army Group B, receiving several Panzer divisions as he faced the difficult task of taking on the best Allied armies in northern Belgium and the Netherlands while maintaining the illusion that his armies represented Germany's main punch. Meanwhile, the infantry-dominated Army Group C would tie down Allied forces along the Maginot Line and protect von Rundstedt's flank.

In terms of organization and the German operational art, Army Group A represented a significant step forward. German planners massed most of the armor, five Panzer divisions, three motorized divisions, and the elite Grossdeutschland regiment all under General Ewald von Kleist in a single Panzergruppe within Army Group A's 12th Army, formally named Gruppe von Kleist.[16] In addition, the Germans further supported Kleist by stationing General Hermann Hoth's 15th Panzer Corps and its 542 tanks just to his north. Kleist's Panzergruppe, though subordinated to a field army,[17] represented the precursor to the massive groupings of armor that the Germans would launch against the Russians one year later. Germany further concentrated Army Group A's spearhead into five Panzer divisions divided into two Panzer corps. The 41st Panzer Corps, led by Lieutenant General Georg-Hans Reinhardt, could put 436 tanks into the field. Even more impressive, the 19th Panzer Corps, under Guderian, contained the 1st, 2nd, and 10th Panzer Divisions with 818 tanks combined.[18] This represented not only the Panzer army's Schwerpunkt but also the most powerful grouping of armor in the world. Guderian further sharpened the spearhead's tip by concentrating the divisional artillery from the 2nd and 10th Panzer Divisions, along with the 19th Corps artillery, into one massive concentration of firepower: 236 artillery pieces, all supporting the 1st Panzer Division. Accordingly, the 1st Panzer Division represented the Schwerpunkt of the corps, which represented the Schwerpunkt of the army, which represented the Schwerpunkt of the Army Group.[19] The German economy had also provided the German army with lavish amounts of supporting firepower in the form of huge stocks of ammunition built up by Hitler's previous orders.

Both Army Group A and Army Group B received strong support from highly trained elite units. The Luftwaffe's paratroopers were tasked in part with removing the threat posed by the potent Belgian and Dutch fortresses, especially Eben Emael blocking the road west from Aachen. The Germans developed an audacious plan capitalizing on the fort's only real vulnerability: air-delivered infantry carrying highly specialized weapons, such as hollow-charge and shaped-charge explosives to penetrate and destroy the thick armor girding the fort's strongpoints. German planners also liberally deployed paratroopers and other crack troops to seize important bridges over the Meuse River, supplement German air attacks on Allied airfields, and wreak havoc behind Allied lines. As in Poland, the Luftwaffe's first job was eliminating

Table 2.1 Comparison between Allied Forces and German Forces on May 10, 1940[1]

	Manpower[2]	Tanks[3]	Aircraft	Artillery
Allies	4,000,000[4]	4,200	4,469	14,000[5]
Germany	3,000,000[6]	2,574	3,578	7,378

[1]Hans-Adolf Jacobsen and Jurgen Rohwer, eds., translated from the German by Edward Fitzgerald, *Decisive Battles of World War II: The German View*, (Andre Deutsch, 1965), 39; John A. English and Bruce I. Gudmundsson, *On Infantry*, rev. ed. (Praeger, 1994), 59; Adam Tooze, *The Wages of Destruction, the Making and Breaking of the Nazi Economy* (Allen Lane, 2006), 371–72; I. C. B. Dear, ed., *The Oxford Guide to World War II* (Oxford University Press, 1995), 316; Marcel Stein, *Field Marshal von Manstein: The Janus Head: A Portrait* (Helion & Company, 2007), 77.

[2]144 Divisions: 104 French, 22 Belgian, 10 British, and eight Dutch.

[3]3,254 French tanks: six armored divisions, 12 motorized divisions, two armored brigades, and over two dozen independent battalions.

[4]Including 2,240,000 French, 650,000 Belgian, 500,000 British, and 400,000 Dutch soldiers.

[5]10,700 French, 1,338 Belgian, 1,280 British, and 656 Dutch. Tooze, *The Wages of Destruction*, 372.

[6]Stein, *Field Marshal von Manstein*, 77. German manpower was divided into 94 divisions in three Army Groups, including 10 Panzer divisions and seven motorized divisions.

Allied airpower on the ground in attacks designed to leave little to challenge the Luftwaffe in the air. Despite all this, an initial look at the size of the opposing armies painted a picture boding ill for German chances if in fact quantitative measures were the dominant element in deciding World War II.

The Allies fielded 104 French divisions, 10 British (the BEF numbered approximately 450,000 men by April 1940), 22 Belgian, and eight Dutch divisions for a total of 144 divisions (see table above). When these divisions are combined with divisional equivalents, by adding up the numerous smaller independent units, the final tally shows that the Allies had mobilized approximately 7 million men. About 4 million of these men stood in the path of the expected German offensive. These 4 million men faced 3 million German soldiers from a Wehrmacht 5.4 million men strong in the spring of 1940.[20] In addition, the German reserves held another 28 second-tier divisions. As for armor, the Allied armies included 3,254 tanks in the French army alone. All told, the Allies fielded 4,200 tanks, including 300 powerful Char B1 bis and 250 Somua medium tanks. For their part, the Germans could deploy 2,574 tanks in the Panzer and motorized divisions. In the spring of 1940, the German Panzer division possessed an authorized strength of approximately 300 tanks. In reality, each Panzer division had a unique organization and individualized tank complement. Nonetheless, on May 10, 1940, only 349 Panzer IIIs and 278 Panzer IVs equipped frontline German Panzer divisions. The remaining German tanks included the obsolete Panzer I (523 at the front), the Panzer II (955 at the front), the Czech-built 35(t) (106 at the front), and the Czech-built 38(t) (228 at the front), accompanied by 135 command Panzers. To boot, the German frontline units received support from only

7,378 artillery pieces.[21] The Allies could call on far more gun tubes to support their frontline combat units. In only two areas did Germany possess numerical superiority: anti-tank and anti-aircraft guns.

Moreover, though numerically superior, French and British armored divisions lacked the balance of the German Panzer division. In addition, many French tanks were spread into over 25 independent battalions and scattered across the front. All told approximately 1,125 French tanks served to back up the infantry.[22] The fact that the French Division Cuirassee de Reserve (Reserve Armored Divisions) had only recently been formed had a far greater impact in terms of handicapping combat efficiency. For their part, the British armored division was ostensibly larger than its French brethren, authorizing approximately 280 tanks each, but the BEF possessed no intact armored divisions, though 75 of the BEF's 320 tanks consisted of the heavily protected, well-armed Mark II Matildas. Moreover, the 1st Armored Division was due to arrive in France by the end of May. In addition, the Belgians fielded about 270 tanks, and the Dutch could deploy 40 tanks.[23] That said, the Allies deployed 4,469 combat aircraft against 3,578 available German aircraft.[24] On the other hand, most German squadrons included modern combat aircraft that were in a far better state of readiness than the Allied aircraft. Overall and based upon the respective numerical strengths of the opposing armies, the battle should have quickly settled into a long, drawn-out struggle. After all, such an analysis is consistent with the most common descriptions of quantitatively predetermined battlefield outcomes during World War II, especially during its latter years.

Instead, the outmanned Germans not only prepared to invade western Europe but, in the spring of 1940, invaded and seized Denmark and Norway as well. Germany took Denmark in a single day with operations led by the world's first combat airdrops, a series of landings along the coast, and a combined-arms motorized infantry force driving the length of the Danish peninsula. As for Norway, some 9,000 German troops landed up and down the Norwegian coast in the first wave alone, leading to a hasty initial Allied retreat and eventually to the June 1940 evacuation of subsequent Allied reinforcements. Two of the world's largest navies, the British and the French, had failed to stop the relatively puny Kriegsmarine from landing troops almost at will up and down the long Norwegian coast. Nevertheless, the Allies had won one enormous strategic benefit: they had virtually destroyed Germany's entire surface fleet. For instance, Norwegian shore-based gun batteries sank the cruiser *Blucher* on April 9, 1940, and the cruiser *Konigsberg*, also damaged by shore-based gun batteries, went down at the hands of British Skua dive-bomber crews the next day. The list of German capital ships damaged and put out of action indefinitely included the following:

- *Hipper*—damaged in action on April 8, 1940
- *Karlsruhe*—torpedoed by a British submarine on April 9, 1940

- *Gneisenau*—damaged in a surface engagement with the HMS *Renown* on April 9, 1940, and then damaged again by a submarine-delivered torpedo in June
- *Lutzow*—torpedoed by a British submarine on April 11, 1940
- *Scharnhorst*—damaged in action in June 1940

These losses, coupled with the December 1939 loss of the "pocket battleship" *Graf Spee* and the torpedoing of the cruiser *Leipzig* in a separate action—in addition to the February–April 1940 sinking of 12 of the 22 destroyers with which Germany began the war—represented the German surface fleet's near destruction only eight months into the war and crippled future German attempts at maritime-based power projection. On the continent, however, the German army quickly proved its world-class status.

THE FRENCH CAMPAIGN

Early on the mild spring morning of May 10, 1940, the Luftwaffe hammered 83 airfields in Belgium, France, and the Netherlands, quickly destroying 732 Allied aircraft against losses of 125 German aircraft.[25] Meanwhile, though German paratroopers suffered heavy losses to Dutch anti-aircraft weapons, they quickly captured intact key bridges over the Meuse and Maas Rivers. The Dutch government surrendered at noon on May 15. As Germany efficiently subjugated Holland, in the early morning hours of May 10, 85 men from the 7th Fallschirmjager Division swooped in on gliders to capture the Belgian flagship fortress. With Eben Emael neutralized and German possession of several bridges across the Meuse River, Army Group B freely advanced into Belgium. The Allied forces reacted quickly, recognizing the German frontal advance into northern Belgium and the Netherlands as the German invasion's main axis given its sheer speed and destructive power. In total, 35 Allied divisions rushed northeastward to the Dyle River line in northern Belgium between Antwerp and Namur.

Meanwhile, Army Group A's powerful tank heavy spearheads quickly traversed 70 miles of excellent defensive terrain in the Ardennes and then crossed the Meuse River against two poorly equipped and trained French armies: the 2nd and the 9th. Army Group B attacked relentlessly, effectively tying down the Allied defenders on the Dyle River line. Army Group A meanwhile exploded away from the hard-won bridgeheads across the Meuse. The Luftwaffe, enjoying almost total local air superiority, successfully interdicted Allied reinforcements moving toward the area.

Not all went well for the Germans. At times, they experienced heavy tank losses against the French, in one instance, and amidst an intense battle at the town of Stonne, a single French Char B1 bis lit up a column of German armor destroying almost a dozen panzers, but the Allies failed to act quickly enough and with the concentrated force necessary to disrupt the German tempo and

GERMAN INVASION OF WESTERN EUROPE MAY 1940

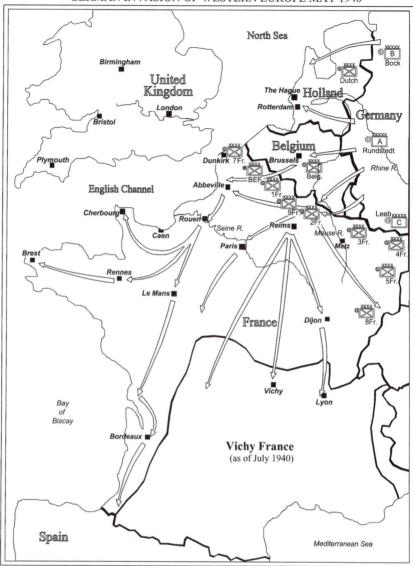

engineer an operational reverse. The highly mobile, fluid, combined-arms teams formed by, out of, and within the individual Panzer divisions overcame latent German inferiorities in tank firepower and protection. Therefore, in using momentum and speed as a weapon unto itself, the Germans achieved the necessary shock effect to destroy the Allied defensive system. Only the OKW's interference, stemming from fears regarding a potential Allied counterattack into the exposed armored flanks, slowed the Panzertruppen. On May 17, the concerns expressed by his command caused Hitler to issue a halt order, though in reality the Allies were incapable of massing the mechanized reserves needed to crush the Panzers. Guderian obstinately and creatively worked around the order but only after crucial delays. Nevertheless, by May 20, German tanks from the 2nd Panzer Division had crossed the Somme River and reached the English Channel at Abbeville. Germany's outgunned, underarmored, quantitatively inferior Panzer and motorized divisions had encircled approximately 1.7 million British, French, Dutch, and Belgian soldiers in an enormous pocket 120 miles long and 72 miles wide.[26]

The British desperately assembled all available ships to rescue the BEF. In the meantime, the same German armies that previously traversed the distance from the Ardennes to the English Channel in mere days sat immobilized. On May 23, Hitler had ordered another halt with his spearheads only about 10 miles from Dunkirk. Hitler's reasoning behind halting his rampaging Panzer armies remains heavily debated to this day, though it appears that Hitler acted on advice received from Göring, Keitel, Jodl, and Rundstedt. Suffice it to say that Hitler—having lacked a clear strategy for dealing with the British since the war had begun and, along with many of his senior military commanders, having misunderstood what they really had created in their Panzer divisions—misjudged his opponent at Dunkirk.

The British rescued approximately 338,226 Allied soldiers, creating an enormous psychological boost at Britain's lowest point of the war. It also denied the Germans a complete strategic victory to match the astounding operational triumph achieved in the preceding weeks. That said, and despite the successful rescue operation, nearly all the equipment Britain brought to France sat abandoned on Dunkirk's beaches or in the French countryside. The British had rescued their army but possessed nothing left with which to equip it. Meanwhile, the Germans had regrouped and turned into the French interior. A new French government, led by Marshall Philippe Petain, formally capitulated on June 22, 1940, at Compiegne. Regardless of the totality of the French defeat, the French soldier had fought hard at times and had done so despite the overall poor leadership and tactics demonstrated by the Allies as a whole. At least 120,000 French soldiers lost their lives in just six weeks of combat. The Belgians lost just over 7,000 dead, the Dutch suffered 3,000 killed in action, and the British lost only 3,457 dead in the campaign, though overall British casualties reached 68,111, including wounded and captured. Germany suffered 49,000 dead and missing and 100,000 wounded, but stood as master over nearly all of western and central Europe.

EVALUATING GERMANY'S OPTIONS
AFTER THE FALL OF FRANCE

Occupation of Belgium, Luxembourg, France, and the Netherlands allowed German forces to loot with abandon, taking 2,170 tanks, albeit with the vast majority unsuitable for use with German armor doctrine, 5,017 artillery pieces, 4,260 locomotives, and 140,000 railcars. Germany also secured enormous stores of raw materials, such as oil, copper, tin, and nickel, as well as 107,841 tons of iron and steel just through 1941.[27] The German occupation of western Europe proved particularly important to Hitler's war effort. For instance, in 1943, raw material supplies from France and Belgium alone fed "37 per cent of German tin consumption, 27 percent of iron ore, 24 percent of bauxite and copper, 16 percent of alumina and lead, and 10 per cent of nickel."[28] Germany's victory meant that Hitler dominated a total landmass only slightly geographically smaller than the United States, but possessing over twice the 1940 U.S. population. Switzerland and noncombatants, such as Spain and Turkey, moved even farther into the German sphere of influence, contributing traded goods, resources, and financing to the Third Reich. Hitler's popularity soared within Germany. In addition, he guaranteed the loyalty of his senior military leadership with massive financial bribes. These were coupled to a wave of promotions that produced 12 field marshals, or seven more field marshals than the Kaiser had appointed during the entirety of World War I. Regardless the German economy, despite reaping considerable gains from military conquest, struggled under reoccurring deficiencies in raw materials, transport, and labor. Insufficient raw material access during 1940, especially coal and fuel oil, had also helped crash the Nazi-dominated western European economies. Moreover, war mobilization meant that Germany's manpower problems only worsened in 1940. Meanwhile, Germany's leadership grappled with strategic concerns presented by Britain's refusal to leave the war.

Hitler had hoped—and expected—Britain to negotiate a peace, as did many within the Wehrmacht's senior leadership and German Foreign Office. Instead, Britain fought on. Therefore, Hitler faced several options, with three having acquired particular status in today's literature as potential war-winning decisions. These options included invading Britain, blockading Britain into submission, or pursuing a Mediterranean strategy. Hitler found none of these choices attractive, though he either made or entertained halfhearted attempts involving all three. Nonetheless, given the fact many today cling to these strategies as having offered Hitler his best chance to win the war, and with many analysts blaming Germany's defeat in the war on Hitler's failure to act on any of these options, we must take a closer look at Germany's ability to carry off any of the aforementioned strategies.

First, the conventional wisdom has long held that Germany could have invaded Britain in the summer or fall of 1940 and knocked the British out of the war. To that end, on July 17, the OKH debuted an invasion plan code-named Sea Lion. This plan anticipated landing in England 260,000 men in 41 divisions. In reality, the 1940-era Wehrmacht hardly had a chance to meet such an ambitious goal, chiefly because naval operations in Scandinavia had decimated the German surface fleet. In June 1940, the Kriegsmarine had available only one heavy cruiser, two light cruisers, seven or eight destroyers, and nine torpedo boats to guard a motley invasion fleet of transports, civilian barges, and small craft.[29] The weak and unimposing German Kriegsmarine could hardly fight off a Royal Navy retaining at least four battleships, three battle cruisers, three aircraft carriers, nine cruisers, and 57 destroyers in the British home waters on June 10, 1940, much less the near equally imposing fleets of British capital ships and submarines cruising nearby in the Atlantic and Mediterranean.[30] The OKH was not ignorant of the Royal Navy's dominance, either, and many within the army's command lacked faith in the ability of the Luftwaffe or the Kriegsmarine to protect their men. The German navy's inability to challenge the British at sea stood obvious to everyone, including Stalin, who, in response to British Ambassador Stafford Cripps's request for help because Germany held complete hegemony in Europe, retorted, "I am not so naïve as to believe the German assurances that they have no desire for hegemony, but what I am convinced of is the physical impossibility of such hegemony, since Germany lacks the necessary seapower."[31] All the same, during the summer of 1940, planning for Sea Lion began moving ahead.

Raeder's staff quickly put together invasion plans that actually fit within available means for delivery; though premised on shaky grounds and with a decided lack of push from above.[32] To offset the Royal Navy's immense superiority, planning for Sea Lion presupposed that German mine belts, coastal artillery, deception, and assistance from the Italian navy would help distract the Royal Navy. This would ostensibly fill in for the Kriegsmarine's inability to provide more than a modicum of protection to even part of the invasion fleet. Problematically for the Germans, the British had already figured out how to defeat Germany's otherwise initially effective magnetic mines. Moreover, the Germans lacked enough mines in stock to seal off the English Channel and lacked the naval power to stop British minesweepers from removing mines as fast as they were laid.

As for coastal batteries, by September 1940 the Germans had built a number of expensive big-gunned coastal batteries in Calais, opposite Dover, at the English Channel's narrowest point. The results achieved by these batteries were hardly encouraging. In one stretch, and despite firing 1,880 rounds at British convoys steaming at five to six knots, the Germans failed to record a single hit. British warships, operating at far higher speeds, were even better protected, and, in a number of raids on German-occupied France throughout 1940, German coastal batteries proved nearly impotent against British warships.[33] Nevertheless, during the summer and fall of 1941, the Italian navy tied down significant British naval assets in the Mediterranean, but, given the inadequacy of the Kriegsmarine's surface fleet, this hardly mattered. In addition, there remains a serious question as to whether the Kriegsmarine could merely transport and supply the invasion force, no less protect it.

The German Naval Staff estimated that they were short, by roughly 1,250,000 tons, of the 2 million tons of shipping in total needed just to move the planned first wave. Even worse, this assumed no serious losses in shipping during the buildup. Such assumptions forced the army to scale down its plans to the point that they hoped to land nine stripped-down divisions in the first wave, minus their artillery and many of their vehicles.[34] Moreover, since Germany lacked the necessary merchant shipping, and had no dedicated amphibious warfare craft, most of the invasion force would be carried on modified river and canal barges and other such commandeered civilian craft. Furthermore, since many of the barges lacked their own propulsion, tugboats would tow the heavily laden barges, barges designed for operating on rivers and canals, not the notoriously rough English Channel, across the channel. Then the tugs would maneuver the barges into place for landing, and then steer them back across the channel to get not only the 1,900 tons per day of supply that the initial landing force would need but in addition the following two planned invasion waves. Of course, the likelihood of this happening assumed that the initial landing force, lacking in artillery, naval gun support, or air support, would survive the first day and night. It also assumed that hardly any tugs and no fewer than a few hundred vessels sank during this process or were destroyed by British defensive efforts.[35]

The odds of the British proving ineffectual at doing even moderate damage to a virtually unguarded invasion force are even more unlikely when one considers an actual circumstance where the Germans tried this stunt, but with seaworthy transportation. During the invasion of Crete in May 1941, some 2,331 German soldiers and their equipment were loaded into 25 steamers protected by only one Italian destroyer in attempting to cross 70 miles of open water. On the same day they left port, three British cruisers and three destroyers found the convoy and sank every steamer but three.[36] To counter Operation Sea Lion, the Royal Navy still held, within 10 hours' sailing time of the planned German invasion route, one battleship, nine cruisers, 56 destroyers, and 40 torpedo boats.[37] The Germans had no real sea-based answer to this force, much less the even greater naval assets that the Royal Navy could deploy on slightly more extended notice. This left the Luftwaffe.

During World War II, naval airpower ascended to primacy over biggunned capital ships, but this had become obvious only later in the war and after a significant shaking-out period in which doctrine, tactics, aircraft, and technologies had all undergone radical improvement. Thus, early war airpower employment at sea had, even as late as the summer of 1940, hardly proved able to hold an edge over warships. For instance, during the

Norwegian campaign, the Royal Navy had been able to operate quite effectively despite the Luftwaffe's regular presence over Scandinavian waters. The Royal Navy had landed and evacuated men mostly where it wanted. Although the British had been thoroughly embarrassed in terms of failing to prevent the German occupation of Norway, while sustaining some heavy losses of their own, the Royal Navy had wiped out the bulk of the German surface fleet in return. Subsequently, at Durkirk, the Royal Navy performed even better in the face of the overwhelming German air superiority, and in spite of the fact that Allied shipping was often forced to remain stationary for long periods of time. The Allies rescued 338,226 men while losing less than 10 percent of the gathered shipping (72 of 848 ships/vessels) to enemy fire, totals including those sunk by German U-boats and torpedo boats.[38] Only four destroyers were lost in total to German air attacks during the Dunkirk operations. Furthermore, two of the four had been completely stationary when sunk.[39] Moreover, by the end of June the Luftwaffe was hardly ready for another major campaign; having lost 1,400 aircraft during the May-June fighting over Western Europe, or a quarter of its May 10th strength.

The Luftwaffe not only lacked time to recuperate but during the summer Kanalkampf—battles fought between the fall of France and the onset of the battle of Britain, fought between the Luftwaffe and British convoys and their escorts operating in the English Channel—the Royal Navy had again fared remarkably well against the Luftwaffe's efforts. Although German aircraft had proved effective in destroying shipping when in port, so much so as to make Dover's port almost inhospitable, German pilots had struggled to hit aggressively maneuvering British destroyers at sea.[40] Even close air support specialists, such as General Wolfram von Richtofen and others with ample experience striking fixed land fortifications, had commented on the difficulty in hitting warships at speed on the open ocean and expressed doubt that they could have protected Sea Lion's invasion force from the Royal Navy.[41] For many of the same reasons as presented above, it is doubtful that Hitler could have blockaded Britain into submission. Even when, in anticipation of Sea Lion, the Royal Navy had stripped away a number of escorts from cross-Atlantic convoy protection, during only one month were German U-boats able to sink even close to half the tonnage that Donitz had estimated would be necessary on a regular basis if Germany were to strangle Britain by sea.[42]

Some have argued a Mediterranean strategy represented Germany's best bet in 1940 in lieu of invading the British Isles.[43] After all, a successful pursuit of the Mediterranean strategy would have sealed off Europe's southern flank, allowed Germany to set up air and naval bases to directly interdict the middle and South Atlantic trade routes, cut the British jugular at Suez, enabled Germany to drive into the Middle East, seize sources of oil production, threaten the southern Soviet Union from across the Caucasus, and threaten the Indian subcontinent. Although this Mediterranean strategy, derived originally from arguments made by Raeder at the time, had continued to attract interest, one basic problem remained. If the Kriegsmarine and Luftwaffe lacked the strategic lift capabilities to ensure successfully crossing the English Channel and maintaining an invasion force in England, and lacked the surface fleet to protect an invasion force attempting to cross a body of water measuring 100 miles at its widest, then how could they adequately support projecting German power into a distant infrastructure-poor region of the world; with none of this taking into account the likelihood that such a strategy would bring the United States, and its imposing navy, into the war?

Moreover, a Mediterranean/Middle Eastern commitment required unique capabilities not only that Germany lacked—including long-range maritime aircraft and carrier-based fleets to provide mobile air support, heavy long-range transport aircraft, naval sealift capabilities, and a large well-protected merchant fleet—but also that Germany would have needed years to create. Furthermore, Germany lacked the oil to transport across the sea, protect, and supply nearly one-third of its available Panzer divisions, the minimal number that was estimated as necessary to secure the Middle East. In addition, solving German problems of projecting power required more than throwing men and equipment at the problem, for the more men and machines that were spilled into the barren desert, the greater the logistical difficulties grew. The Afrika Korps learned this truth in the coming years. In June 1945, German Field Marshal Wilhelm Keitel admitted as much when he described, to his American interrogators, the failures of the Afrika Korps and those of the Italians as based on Germany's inability to supply its forces in Libya and Egypt.[44] Moreover, Keitel's admission further undermines the enduring myth that holds that Germany's best bet for winning the war involved launching a giant German pincer move on the Middle East, an argument continuing today as one of World War II's great counterfactual what-ifs. Furthermore, even if Germany had succeeded, Britain could have continued fighting, particularly if the United States had poured material support into Britain.

Thus, it is perhaps no surprise that, when faced with "options" such as the aforementioned, Hitler, although demonstrating indecision following the French defeat, focused on eastern Europe. Eastern Europe represented the one region of the world that Hitler could quickly conquer and then use its natural resources to fuel the Third Reich's economy and create a self-sustaining continental empire capable of waging global war, all without completely revamping the Wehrmacht. Moreover, if secured, eastern Europe would have been virtually impossible to blockade. In particular if Hitler could seize Ukrainian and Caucasian raw materials, then he could realize the vast economic potential inherent in western Europe's' captive populations and industrial might, potentially making the Third Reich nearly invincible.

Thus, on July 31, 1940, Hitler met with Brauchitsch, Halder, Keitel, Jodl, and Raeder and explained the need to attack the Soviet Union during the

Table 2.2 Soviet versus Middle Eastern Leaders in Oil Production[1]

Country	Oil Production
USSR[2]	35.0[3]
Iran[4]	10.2
Iraq[5]	4.4

[1]Ronald C. Cooke and Roy Conyers Nesbit, *Target: Hitler's Oil, Allied Attacks on German Oil Supplies 1939–1945* (William Kimber, 1985), 22.
[2]Second in the world in 1940.
[3]In millions of tons. Soviet numbers from 1940. Iran and Iraq's numbers from 1938.
[4]Fourth in the world in 1938.
[5]Seventh in the world in 1938.

spring of 1941. Hitler's military leadership in turn began planning the invasion and worked back toward their Führer. Meanwhile, Führer Directive No. 16 on July 16, 1940, had belatedly put forward the German plan to invade Britain. Hitler set September 15 for the invasion date mostly because he insisted that the invasion would happen only if the Luftwaffe could first achieve complete air superiority. In reality, such a task proved beyond the Luftwaffe's abilities, in short because the Luftwaffe, although capable of putting far more aircraft into the battle than the British—on paper the Royal Air Force's (RAF's) odds were daunting with over 1,600 German aircraft, including 1,100 fighters, squaring off against 700 Hurricane and Spitfire single-engine fighters—proved incapable of forcing a decision by itself.

Overall, the critical August–October portion of the Battle of Britain represented a disaster for the Luftwaffe, and a blow to the prestige of the Wehrmacht as a whole. By October 1940, the Luftwaffe mustered only one-third the frontline fighter strength that it held in July 1940.[45] In one final ironic turn for the defeated Luftwaffe, the most proficient Fighter Command squadron during the battle, by claimed kills, was the RAF's 303 Squadron, with 126.5 kills. Polish pilots, equipped by the British with Hurricane fighters, staffed 303 squadron and its sister 302 squadron's ranks, having escaped from Poland the previous fall. Polish pilots ended up with 203 confirmed kills during the Battle of Britain while shooting down an average of 10.5 German aircraft for each Polish pilot lost.[46] By October's end, the Luftwaffe had lost a staggering 1,733 aircraft, including irreplaceable numbers of expensive bombers built in 1938–1940 at great cost to Germany's economy. In contrast, the British lost 915 aircraft, a significant number, but these were almost exclusively cheaply produced fighters. Accordingly, the British Fighter Command patrolled Britain's skies stronger at September's end than in July. Superior British tactics, in particular the use of ground-based radar to detect incoming German raids and marshal Fighter Command's slim resources where needed, and leadership worked just as effectively for the Fighter Command as such qualities had worked for the German army in creating a set of conditions whereby a numerically inferior foe could defeat even a larger opponent. Moreover, the Germans made numerous mistakes, especially in seeking to use airpower as a means to crush the British population's will to fight. This had been a goal from the beginning of the air offensive, but one that the Luftwaffe began almost single-mindedly pursuing at the same moment that it had come close to irrevocably wearing down the RAF's Fighter Command to the point of operational insignificance.

Since World War II's end, many accounts describing the 1940s-era battles in western Europe portray the Wehrmacht as an undefeatable colossus. In reality, the same Wehrmacht, in particular its army, armed mostly with tanks equipped only with machine guns and 20-mm cannon, beat more numerous heavily armed western European armies. Yet, for the more than sixty years since the end of World War II, the primary lessons emphasized from the Allied defeat in France remain firepower and force for the sake of it, rather than the accomplishments wrought from intelligently applied force. Germany won in France because of qualitative military excellence and lost over England because of the RAF's qualitative excellence. Yet only the RAF's defense of Britain is widely noted as the product of superior planning, equipment, and training. As a result, advocates for brute force hold that Hitler was committing a colossal error when he turned on the Soviet Union. Nevertheless,

> even after the occupation of Western Europe, Germany did not have the upper hand in a long war against Britain and America. The chronic shortage of oil, the debility of the European coal mines and the fragility of the food chain, made it seem unlikely that Germany would in fact be able to "consolidate" its conquests of 1940 without falling into excessive dependence on the Soviet Union. Even if this were possible, the combined manufacturing capacity of Britain and America vastly exceeded the industrial capacity currently under German control and this, in turn, spelled disaster in a protracted air war. The German army, on the other hand, had proved its ability to achieve decisive victory against what were thought to be the strongest armies in Europe.[47]

Hitler's monstrous regime thus turned east to face the tyrant Josef Stalin and the Soviet Union. Only Imperial Japan, in its racist Asian war, would match the barbarism—but not the bloodshed—seen in Germany's eastern European campaign, the largest and bloodiest war in human history.

Part II

Chapter 3

Comparing the World's First Military Superpowers on the Eve of War

Today's conventional wisdom argues that the Third Reich's downfall began once it attacked the much larger Soviet Union during the summer of 1941. However, if Germany was predestined to defeat once it attacked the Soviet Union, then how did the Wehrmacht forge a series of epic victories from 1941 to 1943 over a much larger Red Army? If brute force wins wars, why did it take a Red Army over twice as large as its opponent over two years to win back what Germany had seized in just four months? For that matter, how did the Red Army, following some of the most staggering losses in modern military history, then transition to a period when it consistently defeated the German army? This chapter opens our exploration into the 1941–1945 Russo-German war and answers questions such as these by first examining the industrial and military colossus that was the Soviet Union in 1941. Then we turn to the ideologically charged plan that Hitler and his General Staff put together for defeating the Soviet Union, and conclude by evaluating the Wehrmacht in the spring of 1941.

CREATING A BUDDING SUPERPOWER: SOVIET MILITARY AND INDUSTRIAL REFORMS

Well before World War II began, Stalin knew that Russia, with four-fifths of its population rural, needed to modernize to survive. Stalin's beliefs were far from unique. After all, during World War I, Russia could hardly provide rifles for its army, much less field a modern war machine.[1] What was unique was that Stalin relentlessly followed his vision for the Soviet economy. He did so mostly by implementing a series of five-year plans[2] that in 1937 resulted in the Soviet Union lagging behind only the United States and Germany in terms of its rank as an industrial great power. Nonetheless, Stalin built this economic prowess at the expense of his people. He collectivized agricultural work and brought under state control two-thirds of all small businesses in the Soviet Union. Small property-owning farmers classified as wealthy, known as the kulaks, were killed, exiled to Siberian gulags or concentration camps, or forced to work in the factories. Millions of people starved to death, including over 3 million Ukrainians in 1932–1933 alone. Although Stalin's campaign of mass murder represented a central part of his effort to cement his control over the Soviet people, this virtually genocidal economic effort had an additional over-riding purpose: arming and equipping a military establishment second to none. Prior to Stalin, Vladimir Ilyich Lenin had well understood the symbiotic relationship between economic and military strength, and after Stalin took power, so did his chief military leaders, including Red Army Chief of Staff Boris Shaposhnikov and Mikhail Tukhachevsky. Tukhachevsky's May 1928 General Staff Study found that industry and labor would need to mobilize massively, far before actual combat began, if the Red Army were to win a future war against an equally matched opponent. Consequently, by 1940, one-third of Soviet expenditures were going to armaments.

At the same time that Stalin built up Soviet heavy industry, the Workers and Peasants Red Army (*Raboce-krestjanskaja krasnaja armija*), or Red Army, founded in 1918, refined its doctrine and organization.[3] People's Commissar for Military and Naval Affairs Mikhail Vasilevich Frunze and the Red Army's Mikhail N. Tukhachevsky, N. E. Varfolomeev, A. A. Svechin, V. K. Tiandoafilov, and G. S. Isserson stood at the forefront of the world's armored theoreticians and practitioners during the interwar years. The Red Army soon ranked alongside the German army as a world leader in exploring the internal combustion engine's impact on warfare. Clandestine cooperation between the German and Soviet military establishments, beginning in the 1920s, had helped along this development. New training schools and facilities, in places such as Kazan and Lipetsk, produced groundbreaking work in mobile warfare. Each country's military leadership interpreted the results of this work within the prism of their own unique military traditions, conse-quently producing distinctive war-fighting techniques.

The Red Army drew heavily on the Russian army's experiences in the Russo-Turkish War of 1876–1877, against the Japanese prior to World War I, the Russian Civil War, and the war against Poland following World War I. These wars had featured not only Russian-launched massed infantry attacks but also daring Russian cavalry raids that penetrated deep behind the enemy's front lines. In addition, even though by the 1930s there were notable similarities between German and Russian conceptions of the operational art, there were also clear differences. For instance, the Germans saw aircraft as providing the primary punch to clear the path for their motorized spearheads. The Russians viewed artillery as the central component in blasting apart enemy defensive lines. Thus, as early as 1937, the Russians fielded twice as many artillery pieces as did the Germans.[4]

Frunze laid much of the groundwork for the Red Army's doctrinal base. Contrary to German doctrine, he firmly believed that war against modern industrialized nation-states could not be won in a single strike. Frunze thought that victory required an extended effort featuring repeated, relentlessly pursued, massive campaigns. As such, in 1925 and following Frunze's theoretical approach to total war, the Soviet Union began to reorganize its armed forces. Although Frunze died in 1925, cutting short his pioneering work, his peer A. A. Svechin finished his classic military study titled *Strategy*, a work that, as had Frunze, argued that total warfare meant that a future war would be an endurance test. Svechin posited that armies would fight being spread out across vast distances, flowing forward and back across territory, rather than be fixed in place. Accordingly, the Red Army would require the ability to push broadly frontwide against any foe in repeated campaigns designed to exhaust an opponent's capacity to resist. Educational efforts reflected these ideas. By the early 1930s, the Frunze and General Staff academies led officer training at the strategic and operational levels. A proliferating number of specialized academies focused on training junior officers in topics such as military chemistry, military engineering, and war economy.[5]

Marshal Tukhachevsky (1893–1937), a former tsarist lieutenant and a man who would become perhaps the foremost Soviet leader in testing and implementing his and his peer's theories on strategic- and operational-level warfare, followed up on Frunze's and Svechin's work, as did V. K. Triandafilov, who, with G. S. Isserson, published the Red Army's nascent offensive doctrine, *Character of Operations of the Modern Army*, in 1929.[6] Tukhachevsky argued vociferously for creating a professional army, a decision later helping to seal his undeserved fate but done so similarly to Seeckt's conception for a highly trained mobile army. Tukhachevsky, like Seeckt, also emphasized the use of massed armor operating in conjunction with combined-arms operations at ratios ideally well over the traditionally sought-after three-to-one advantage that an attacker needed to best a well-dug-in defender. This was to be done by taking units from relatively quiet areas of the front and concentrating them on decisive sectors of the front. To batter through enemy defensive lines, massed artillery fire would be employed, followed by combined-arms armored infantry combat engineer concentrations. Once the Red Army achieved penetration, mechanized and cavalry units would exploit the gaps thus created and strike into the enemy's operational and strategic rear. Campaigns would feature consecutive and systematic operations. This required extensive logistical preparation. Accordingly, the Red Army sought to create a synergy between army and front-level logistical matters; one reaching the strategic level, including orienting the economy to fight in depth over time.

The Red Army encapsulated its operational-level theories into two doctrines: "deep operations" (*glubokaya operatsiya*) and "deep battle" (*glubokii boi*). Both doctrines are similar; only the operational scope and force size provided the difference. As such, here we use the term "deep operations" to convey the teachings embodied in both. The key to this doctrine is that it was highly aggressive and entirely offensive in nature. Its most important tenets were published in 1933 as "Principals of In-Depth Operation" (*Osnovy glubokoy operatsii*) and tested in maneuvers across the Soviet Union.[7] As for weapons systems, tanks joined artillery as the centerpiece of it all. By 1935–1936, the Red Army was well on its way to ranking as the premier army in the world. Yet within two short years, the modern fighting force emerging under the stewardship of Tukhachevsky, Triandafillov, and their peers had been torn asunder by Stalin.

Beginning in 1937, Stalin eviscerated the Red Army's officer corps with round after round of cannibalistic, politically directed purges. Stalin also imprisoned or killed millions of Soviet citizens. Stalin's primary tool for repression had evolved out of Felix Dzerzhinsky's "Chekas"—a secret paramilitary police force serving a similar role that the Gestapo, the SA, and the SS did in Germany. In 1938, the Chekas became the even more murderous NKVD (People's Commissariat for Internal Affairs). Stalin's police state killed an estimated 776,074 political prisoners. The vast majority, 681,692, were murdered in 1937 and 1938. Another 1,053,829 died in the gulags between 1934 and Stalin's death in 1953.[8] The Soviet military establishment suffered just as did the larger population. Eight members of the Soviet high command were arrested on charges of treason. Included in this group was the father of Soviet armored forces and deputy commissar for defense, Marshal Tukhachevsky. His execution followed thereafter. Summary executions and arrests of military officers continued for years. One-half of all officers in the Red Army were arrested or killed outright. Some argue that the total number put to death stood at 41,218 officers, including the entire high command and most of the Red Army's operational level leadership.[9] Others think that those executed numbered much lower. They place the total number of officers arrested in the Red Army between 1937 and 1939 at 35,000—with 11,000 returned to active duty by 1940.[10] Regardless, of the five marshals in the Red Army, the purges killed three. In the four years preceding the 1941 German invasion, the purges killed 20 army commanders and 64 corps commanders; 15 and 62 men, respectively, held these posts in 1936. Of the 201 divisional commanders in the Red Army in 1936, 131 were executed.[11]

The impact produced by, in particular, the loss of Tukhachevsky, Triandafilov, and Isserson cannot be overstated. The morale and combat efficiency of the Red Army melted. Officer suicide rates climbed dramatically. Junior officers with little experience were rapidly promoted and replaced those killed or forced out. Officers barely over 35 years of age led divisions and corps. Men barely past their 40th birthdays led entire armies.[12] The military academies struggled to replace educators lost to the purges. As late as the fall of 1940, not one of a sample of 225 regimental commanders in the Red Army had graduated from the Frunze military academy, and most of them (200), had been trained only to the level of lieutenant.[13] The Red Army's growth merely exacerbated the purge's deleterious impact. The Red Army grew from around 842,000 men in 1926–1927 to 5 million men in June 1941. This left the Red Army 36,000 officers short. In response, the Red Army drained upperclassmen from officer cadet schools and threw them into leadership roles for which they were nowhere near ready to assume. Simple theories of massed assault substituted for the revolutionary combined-arms skills previously cultivated.

THE RED ARMY ON THE EVE OF WAR

On paper, by 1941, the Soviet Union deployed a huge battle-trained Red Army. For instance, in the Spanish Civil War, the Soviet Union had sent both "volunteers" and equipment. More important, from 1938 to 1939, large-scale battles involving tens of thousands of men were fought against the Japanese. In Poland during 1939, the Red Army skirmished against the Polish army's remnants, learning more lessons regarding deploying large armies in the field. The Red Army also had deployed into the Baltic states and parts of Romania in 1940, gaining similar experience to that acquired by the Wehrmacht during the German occupations of Austria and Czechoslovakia. Finally, there was Finland, and the 1939–1940 winter war.

Stalin had attacked Finland on November 30, 1939, hoping for easy territorial gain. Although isolated, the Finns received ample support from Sweden, a traditional Russian rival. Nonetheless, the Red Army vastly outnumbered the Finnish armed forces. Even so, in a humiliating turn of events, Finnish troops, fighting behind a massive series of fortifications erected in dense swamps and forests and led by Field Marshal Carl Gustav Emil Mannerheim, held off the far larger Red Army for far longer than should have been possible. During the war's first month alone, 18,000 Soviet soldiers, representing half the initial invading army, had been lost as either killed, missing, or captured.[14] The Finns used well-placed roadblocks, hit-and-run tactics led by hundreds of white-clad ski troops, well-timed counterattacks, and an ingenious logistical support network built by plowing roads through the deep snow across frozen lakes. Despite Mannerheim's defensive effort, Stalin had forced Finland to come to terms by early 1940. Brute force had forged a victory though at a grotesque cost in lives: over 126,000 Soviet dead and 300,000 wounded. In addition to these combat deaths, the Red Army's unpreparedness for fighting in the cold meant that frostbite had ravaged poorly clothed Soviet soldiers.[15] Although Finland lost thousands of square miles of territory and suffered 48,243 killed in action, it remained independent.

The winter war, in spite of its short-term costs, may have helped save the Red Army in 1941. Defense Commissar Voroshilov had long since advocated for increasing the time spent training all ranks, especially junior officers. When the results of this inadequate training brutally played out during the winter war, it provided further impetus for his reforms. In addition, Stalin had been impressed by the skilled and well-equipped Finnish ski troops. He not only ordered the Red Army to form similar units but also made available improved stocks of winter clothing and equipment capable of working in the severe cold.[16] Finally, the Red Army had learned another important lesson. Late in 1939, the Finns had ranked among the world's leaders in automatic weapons usage. These weapons included the 9-mm Suomi M-31 submachine gun and an early assault rifle: the 7.92-mm M26 light machine gun. Even though classified as a light machine gun, the M26 proved more similar to the American Browning automatic rifle than a characteristic light machine gun. The Russians suffered enormous casualties fighting Finnish infantry armed with such firepower. In response, the Red Army ordered thousands of light automatic weapons and later used simple but ruggedly built submachine guns to great effect against the Germans.

As the Red Army absorbed what it had learned in Finland, it faced another task greatly inhibiting its ability to field an effective military establishment: its need to integrate the fruits of Stalin's massive reindustrialization into its ranks. In 1939 alone, the Red Army received 10,382 aircraft and 2,950 tanks, a total number of tanks ranking greater than the entire 1939-era German tank park.[17] Meanwhile, following the French defeat, Stavka, the Red Army's high command, had significantly amped up the pace of mobilization. Nearly 3 million men deployed into the western military districts. Tens of thousands of reservists added daily to this considerable ledger. All told, the entire Red Army fielded 5,373,000 men in June 1941. Approximately 4,261,000 men served in the Red Army, 618,000 in the Red Army Air Force, 183,000 in the Air Defense Force, and 312,000 in the navy.[18] To manage the masses of men streaming into the Red Army's ranks, Stavka divided western Soviet Union into districts and echelons as envisaged in Soviet State Defense Plan-41.[19] Each district defined a particular axis of operations comprised of many armies acting in concert under a single commander and capable of independent combat operations, just as in a German Army Group. Overall, the Red Army included 303 divisions, consisting of 198 rifle, 61 tank, 31 mechanized, and 13 cavalry divisions; five independent rifle brigades; 10 anti-tank brigades; 94 corps artillery regiments; 75 reserve artillery regiments; and 34 engineer regiments. From these ranks, by the spring of 1941, about 2.5 million men in 171 divisions equipped with 15,000 tanks had deployed to the western border districts, or first strategic echelon.[20]

The five military districts, swelling with raw recruits early in 1941, would be redesignated "fronts" after the onset of hostilities, and for simplicity's sake, that is how this work will refer to them. In the spring of 1941, and running from north to south, the five fronts included the Northern Front, led by General Popov; the Northwestern Front, led by General Kuznetsov; the Western Front, led by General Pavlov; the Southwestern Front, led by General Kirponos; and the Southern Front, led by General Tulenev. These fronts varied tremendously in composition. The Western and Southwestern fronts were by far the largest and most lavishly equipped in terms of armor. The first strategic echelon had been divided into three operational echelons: the first to defend and absorb an invading army's attack and the second and third to counterattack. Behind the fortifications and millions of men in the first strategic echelon, another 57 divisions in five armies along the Dvina and Dnieper Rivers made up the second strategic echelon. These armies were under Stavka's direct control. The second strategic echelon would exploit gains made by the first strategic echelon's counterattacks and carry the war onto German soil.

Problems existed not necessarily because of this larger framework for deployment but because of poor tactical deployment within each front, reflective of their inexperienced staffs. In addition, the purges had meant that even at the Red Army's top ranks, the turnover proved constant. The Red Army's chief of the General Staff represented a revolving door, going through three men in only three and a half years: Boris Shaposhnikov, from June 1937 to August 1940, and then Kirill Meretskov and G. K. Zhukov in January 1941. Shaposhnikov again took over when he replaced Zhukov after the German invasion.[21] In contrast, Halder held the same post in Germany for four uninterrupted years.

Moreover, Shaposhnikov's defensive plan proved dated by June 1941. The Soviet Union's territorial acquisitions in 1939–1940 had moved the border in some places 200 miles to the west. As a result, a new program of building defensive fortifications began. Shaposhnikov then deployed the bulk of the Red Army in forward positions, split between the old border with Poland and the new border with the German Reich, backed only by limited reserves. The basic defensive plan presupposed that these defensive positions could hold the attacker near the border as the army mobilized, and then launch a massive counterattack that would carry the battle onto the attacker's soil. This defensive plan overoptimistically surmised that any German attack would not be massive and overwhelming but feature a steady buildup, thus providing the Red Army with time to react. Meanwhile, the doctrine that the Red Army trained in and organized for was still Tukhachevsky's, or offensive in nature. One of the greatest problems this created was a lack of realistic training in defensive combat.[22] Furthermore, the training (or lack thereof) meant that junior officers suitable for commanding rifle squads often commanded the crucial combat battalions and regiments. In comparison,

1941-era German officers possessed years of practice and extensive combat experience.

As for the recruits, they often proved hardly up to the tasks presupposed by Soviet doctrine in part because access to education, despite the best efforts of the country, remained spotty. The Red Army suppressed one report that found that many conscripts could not even identify Stalin.[23] Furthermore, the withdrawal of men from agricultural production led to endemic food shortages within the Soviet Union. Accordingly, conscripts not only spent a tremendous amount of time growing their own food and raising livestock in response to the nutritionally deficient food fed to them; but also were shunted to work local fields and assist on collective farms with the harvest. Poor hygiene from the nearly nonexistent supplies of soap and rampant crime also contributed to the conscripts' poor physical condition and poor morale. Moreover, time-consuming ideological training and equipment shortages further short-circuited training efforts. Conscripts often did not even have real rifles to train with, instead receiving wooden replicas for crude training purposes. Finally, half of all Red Army recruits serving in the western border regions had only belatedly received their call to duty in April and May 1941. Over two-thirds had served in the Red Army for less than one year by June 1941.[24]

As for the Red Army's striking power, it had been resurrected in an organizational sense only in 1940. Timoshenko, the new commissar for defense in May 1940 and the newly minted marshal of the Soviet Union, had belatedly begun reforms rehabilitating deep operations and its associated doctrines to better prepare his officers to embrace the flexibility and creativity needed to command large mechanized formations. But it would take years for these reforms to pay off. In addition, there had been almost no organizational continuity when it came to the Red Army's armored formations. In November 1939, the Red Army had disbanded the armored corps and replaced them with 15 motorized divisions and assorted tank brigades, regiments, and battalions. Then, in reaction to the speedy German victory over France on July 6, 1940, Stalin ordered the mechanized corps reformed. Nine were in existence by the end of the year, largely in name only, as they were nowhere near ready for operational use. Another 13 were formed in February and March 1941 and thus were hardly ready when the Germans struck in June. The standard mechanized corps included 36,080 men divided into two tank divisions, one mechanized division, and supporting units. The Red Army subdivided each tank division into two tank and one motorized rifle regiment with supporting elements. Each tank division possessed a table of organization and equipment, or *shtat*, of 11,343 men and 375 tanks, broken down as 63 KV-1s, 210 T-34s, and 102 T-26s and BTs.[25] Unfortunately, most mechanized corps were as much as 50 percent under strength in the summer of 1941. Tank strengths varied widely within the 30 existing mechanized corps (see Table 3.1). Moreover, most of the tanks in the mechanized corps were

Table 3.1 Soviet Mechanized Corps in Western Military Districts on June 22, 1941[1]

Number	Date Formed	Personnel[2]	Tanks
1	March 1940	31,439	1,037
2	June 1940	32,396	517
3	July 1940	31,975	651
4	July 1940	28,098	979
6	July 1940	32,382	1,131
8	July 1940	28,713	898
9	March 1941	26,833	298
10	March 1941	26,168	469
11	March 1941	21,605	414
12	March 1941	28,832	749
13	March 1941	17,809	282
14	March 1941	19,332	518
15	March 1941	33,395	749
16	March 1941	26,920	482
17	March 1941	16,578	63
18	March 1941	26,879	282
19	March 1941	21,654	453
20	March 1941	20,391	94
22	March 1941	24,087	712
24	March 1941	21,556	222
Total		517,047	11,000

[1]David M. Glantz, *Stumbling Colossus: The Red Army on the Eve of World War* (University Press of Kansas, 1998), 155.

[2]Soviet T/O&E (Table of Organization and Equipment) in June 1941 called for 36,080 men and 1,031 tanks per mechanized corps.

older models. Furthermore, the grossly inadequate training provided to the Red Army's tanks crews crippled the mechanized corps efficacy. Tank drivers often received barely one hour of training before sent to active duty.[26] Ammunition and spare parts shortages further reduced hours spent on the training grounds.

Despite such handicaps, the Red Army's tanks typically held advantages in hitting power and protection over most German Panzers. For instance, in 1941 the three-man BT-series Bystrokhodnii tank, based on the American Christie design and manufactured primarily at factories in Chelyabinsk and Kharkov, served as the Red Army's mainstay medium tank, packing an adequate 45-mm main gun. The Christie design emphasized mobility and speed derived from an independent suspension and flexible track design coupled with a lightweight, powerful engine. The biggest technical problems inherent in tanks such as the BT series existed outside the traditional determinants in tank power (i.e., armor and armament). The Red Army's tanks possessed poor command and targeting features, including inadequately designed turrets and nonexistent signals equipment. In addition, older tanks that had been built prior to the mid-1930s, with many still in service in 1941, were almost completely used up as effective weapons. That said, in 1941, the Red Army had begun taking delivery of a tank that could trump anything the German army put in the field: the T-34, a tank widely regarded as one of the finest tanks produced during World War II (if not the finest).

Designed by Mikhail I. Koshkin, the chief engineer and designer at the Kharkov Locomotive Factory, or KhPZ,[27] the T-34 medium tank served as a logical next step in Soviet tank design and marked a tremendous technological leap. No German tank, not even the Panzer IV's early marks, competed well with the outstanding armor and armament equipping the T-34. The Model 1941 T-34's 76.2-mm F-34 gun far outranged any German tank gun in 1941 and penetrated German armor at ranges of 1,000 yards. More important, although the T-34's frontal armor was only marginally thicker than the typical Panzer III or IV of the day, the T-34 possessed sloped armor capable of stopping 45-mm anti-tank gun rounds packing a stronger punch than the standard German 37-mm anti-tank gun. The T-34 also enjoyed two other tremendous advantages over its German rivals. First, the T-34 had been built around the superb V-2 diesel engine developed by Koshkin's deputy, Aleksandr Morozov, an engine that helped give the T-34 a combination of range, reliability, and power unmatched by Germany's medium tanks. For instance, in March 1940, Koshkin and two crews road tested two T-34 prototypes by driving them the entire 420 miles from Kharkov to Moscow and then back to Kharkov via Smolensk and Kiev, a 1,800-mile round-trip in total. This road demonstration led to Stalin's support and the beginning of production on March 31, 1940, at both Kharkov and the Stalingrad Tractor Works.[28] In addition to its reliability, the T-34 was considerably more maneuverable than anything possessed by the Germans, even in less-than-ideal tank terrain, in large part because of its wide track and low ground pressure.

Overall, Russian tank designs, led by the T-34, featured simplicity and ruggedness and proved easy to maintain, hallmarks of Russian weapons systems that invariably were enormously cost-effective investments, bringing just enough to the battlefield to perform their tasks without overburdening the Soviet economy. The T-34 met one of the most important axioms of a good weapons system in that it was entirely replaceable. The loss of even hundreds such tanks at a time was largely inconsequential. In contrast, for the Germans, the loss of an equivalent number of technically more complex and expensively built Panzers most often represented a disaster. T-34s were designed to be run into the ground and then be either cheaply rebuilt, often by cannibalizing other, more heavily damaged tanks, or replaced. There was no need to maintain fleets of expensive service and recovery vehicles manned by thousands of expensively trained mechanics and other such specialists.

Unfortunately for the Red Army, its newest tanks also betrayed their evolutionary roots, and thus incorporated several faults from their heirs. The T-34's two-man turret and lack of a commander's cupola limited the Russian tank crew's ability to target and engage opponents. In addition, the standard T-34 came without a radio, except in commanders' tanks. This made it nearly impossible for multitasking four-man T-34 crews to coordinate in combat. The T-34 also possessed inadequate optics, therefore mitigating some of the advantages provided by the T-34's powerful gun and protection. In addition, the T-34's transmission failed to pace its dependable diesel engine. Moreover, the diesel engines, though reliable, had the propensity to overheat if not handled properly.[29] Finally, perhaps the biggest problem with the T-34 was that it was a new weapon, and its crews needed more time than they would get to familiarize themselves with their new tanks. For its part, the equally modern heavy KV-1-series tank enjoyed even better armored protection than did the T-34, but this came with a price. The KV-1 was slow and heavy, at times operating more as a mobile pillbox than anything else. Furthermore, numbers of each tank were limited. The Red Army deployed only 1,475 of the new heavy KV-1 and medium T-34 tanks near the Soviet Union's western borders in 1941.[30] What is more, the Red Army lacked the German army's wheeled mobility, and if anything the Red Army's logistical situation represented an even bigger mess than it did for the Wehrmacht; for instance, the massive mechanized corps often deployed with as little as one day's worth of supplies. For its part, Germany had amassed over 600,000 vehicles to support Operation Barbarossa versus the 272,600 vehicles that the Red Army deployed in western Soviet Union. Even after the Red Army commandeered over 200,000 civilian vehicles, the Wehrmacht proved better prepared for mobile warfare.[31]

Many of the same problems plaguing the Red Army's ground forces also defined the Red Army Air Force's combat capability. On paper, the Red Army Air Force appeared massive and unbeatable. During June 1941 in the western border districts alone, the Red Army Air Force deployed 7,133 combat aircraft against one-third as many German machines and pilots.[32] Nevertheless, many of these aircraft were obsolete. For example, the Me-109F fighters flown by the Luftwaffe woefully outclassed the I-16 and its 300-mile-per-hour top speed as well as the I-153 biplane, yet 3,400 I-153 fighters rolled off Soviet assembly lines in 1939–1940.[33] Meanwhile, next-generation aircraft matching up well with front-line German aircraft, such as the MiG-3 fighter, LaGG-3 fighter, Pe-2 dive-bomber, and Il-2 *Shturmovik* that entered production during the summer of 1940 but by June of 1941 were nowhere close to replacing the mostly obsolete aircraft equipping the majority of the Red Army Air Force.[34]

The ill-timed Russian military reorganization also meant that the Red Army Air Force began its needed expansion of infrastructure only in the months leading up to Barbarossa. Consequently, it shoehorned a tremendous variety of aircraft models onto ever more crowded airfields, creating a logistical mess and playing directly into Luftwaffe doctrine for attaining air superiority. The Red Army Air Force also made many of the same mistakes that the ground forces had made in allocating inadequate resources to training. This represented a crippling deficiency given that, assuming comparable aircraft technology, pilot training ranks as among the most important measures in assessing an air force's combat readiness. Furthermore, the Red Army Air Force's top leadership lacked experience and dealt with debilitating turnover. The Western Front's air force chief was the 33-year-old General Kopets. P. V. Rychagov served as the 29-year-old head of the air force until reassigned in April 1941 and then later arrested. The chief of the Air Defense Administration, General G. M. Shtern, and the deputy chief of the General Staff for Aviation, General Ia. V. Smushkevich, were also arrested just over one week prior to the onset of the German invasion.[35] In addition, the Red Army Air Force failed to follow Germany's strict adherence to concentrated strength as an organizing principle, at least in the air.

On paper, the Red Army enjoyed several quantitative and qualitative advantages over the 1941-era German army. The June 1941 Red Army, with 5.3 million men mobilizing and 3 million men in the western Soviet Union equipped with approximately 11,000 tanks, 9,100 combat aircraft, and 19,800 artillery pieces and mortars, was far more powerful than the 1940-era Allied army (see Table 3.2).[36]

In addition, the Soviet Union's strategic defensive depth offered the Red Army the chance to learn in combat and absorb mistakes. On the other hand, the Red Army faced the world's premier army on its western border. In examining the Wehrmacht on the eve of history's greatest land war, it will become painfully apparent not only why Hitler came close to securing a National Socialist–dominated Europe but also why his Wehrmacht would have to overcome numerous internal problems if it were to achieve such success.

Table 3.2 Overall Soviet Armed Forces Strength Compared to German Armed Forces Available for Operation Barbarossa on June 22, 1941[1]

	Soviet Armed Forces	German Armed Forces
Divisions	303	135
Personnel	5,373,000	3,750,000
Tanks and assault guns	18,680	3,350
Guns and mortars	91,400	7,000
Aircraft	15,599	2,000

[1]David M. Glantz, *Stumbling Colossus: The Red Army on the Eve of World War* (University Press of Kansas, 1998), 292–95.

OPERATION BARBAROSSA AND GENERALPLAN OST: GERMANY PREPARES A WAR OF EXTERMINATION

By the summer of 1940, Hitler had long since been fixated on the Soviet Union. Most important, from Hitler's perspective, war in eastern Europe best served the Reich's ideological basis for a racial empire that would purify and redeem the Germanic people, a basis driving this renewed attempt at a German-dominated eastern Europe by drawing strength from a racially and ideologically charged atmosphere in Germany. Hitler hoped that by sometime in 1942, his attack on the last continental power remaining in Europe would have produced the Lebensraum (living space) necessary for the German people to engage in the long struggle against the United States. The invasion of the Soviet Union would be the greatest race war in history: the Germanic people against the Slav and "Bolshevist Jew."

Hitler's decision to invade the Soviet Union, as apocalyptic and ideological as he intended it to be, nevertheless, in a military sense, possessed a bit of logic. It meant that the German military could use its greatest strengths in an offensive war of maneuver on the European continent, supported by the world's best tactical air force, against an opponent in the midst of wrenching structural changes to its own military. Germany's alternative options to invading the Soviet Union constituted an unappealing litany of playing to German weaknesses. In particular, a failure to deal with the Soviet Union in 1941–1942 would have meant the Soviet Union would occupy the driver's seat in an Axis alliance where the Red Army and Soviet economy commanded ever greater shares of the fruits of Soviet economic output and resource extraction.[37] As early as 1940, the effects of the Allied blockade had already impacted the German economy, with aid from the Soviet Union one of the primary elements keeping the German economy afloat.[38] Thus, Hitler, at a minimum aware of Germany's own economic problems and seeking to control a resource rich region of his own, made the decision that had always been true to his ideological worldview and ordered the OKH to plan Germany's first true Blitzkrieg campaign.[39] Both the German military and the political establishment reacted favorably to Hitler's decision. On July 3, 1940, Halder set the wheels in motion when he ordered Colonel Hans von Greiffenberg of the OKH (Oberkommando der Heer, or Army High Command) to begin exploring a military option against Soviet Union. Then, on July 4, 1940, Halder took the next step and ordered Lieutenant General Georg von Kuchler, commanding the German 18th Army in East Prussia and Poland, and Major General Erich Marcks, his chief of staff, to begin planning for a war against the Soviet Union.[40]

A German invasion of the Soviet Union, widely acknowledged today as the first step in the Third Reich's eventual defeat, faced several handicaps, including many that were self-inflicted. Perhaps most important, Germany failed to incorporate its Axis allies into the planning for a campaign against the Soviet Union.

Table 3.3 Leading Non-German Axis Armed Forces Committed to Operation Barbarossa[1]

	Finland	Hungary	Romania
Divisions	17.5	2	17.5
Personnel	302,600	44,000	358,140
Tanks	86	116	60
Guns and mortars	2,047	200	3,255
Aircraft	307	100	423

[1]David M. Glantz, *Stumbling Colossus: The Red Army on the Eve of World War* (University Press of Kansas, 1998), 293.

Although individually weak, Romania, Hungary, Finland, Slovakia, and Croatia collectively could have provided a powerful adjunct to the Wehrmacht's efforts in eastern Europe (see Table 3.3). In particular, the German Air Ministry and War Ministry, German industry in general, the Luftwaffe, and the German army all did a particularly poor job of sharing or selling resources, technology, and/or patents with nations that could have easily and locally built German equipment that would have greatly enhanced each Axis nation's military potential.

Among the great failure of the German war effort was not only in coalition warfare in general but also, as noted by military historian Richard L. Dinardo, the reality that there would be no German equivalent to the American-made Sherman tank, jeeps, or trucks that powered the United States and its allies in the war against the Axis. Even minor powers, when well equipped, well trained, and well led, could play a significant role on the battlefield as proven by, if no other country, the impact that Poland's armed forces had fighting for themselves, the Allies, and the Red Army during the entirety of World War II. Thus, had German firms licensed other Axis nations to build, for example, Panzer IVs, 88-mm guns, or Me-109 fighter aircraft, there is little question that such a concerted effort would have enabled the various Axis armed forces to far outperform their otherwise mixed battlefield performance during the war. However, Germany's arrogant and incompetent approach to integrating its smaller European allies into the Axis camp proved the norm. Therefore, perhaps it is no surprise Germany's handling of its strongest ally and Russia's historically most significant rival, Japan, was catastrophic for the Axis war effort.

Japan and the Soviet Union had fought repeatedly during the 1930s, most notably in 1938 near the Soviet port of Vladivostok, and then again in a massive battle in 1939 on the Soviet controlled Mongolian border at Khalkin Gol, Nomonhan, where the Red Army decisively defeated Japan. In August and September 1939 alone, Japan suffered tens of thousands of casualties, including at least 30,000 dead against Soviet casualties totaling 24,000 men, including 6,841 killed and 1,143 missing.[41] The scale of this defeat caused the Japanese to abandon plans to invade Siberia. Therefore, though Japan was unlikely to challenge the Red Army thereafter such a searing defeat, Hitler never asked. Moreover, Germany not only ignored Japan but also actually shunned it diplomatically. Japan, of course, had its own strategic plans. In 1941, the Japanese remained deeply tied down in China and faced a possible war with the United States. Thus, on April 13, 1941, the Soviets and Japanese concluded a neutrality pact. Hitler, on top of ignoring the Japanese, also marginalized what should have been a strong Italian contribution to the Axis war effort. For his part, Mussolini insisted on offering up substantial military assets to support German efforts in Russia even though the Italian army was in a far better position to accomplish Axis goals if it maintained a focus on the Mediterranean theater. As for the Mediterranean, Italian incompetence in the Balkans and North Africa meant that during the winter of 1940–1941, Hitler had been forced to dispatch one of his best generals, Erwin Rommel, with one motorized division and one Panzer division, to defend the Italian colony of Libya rather than participate in the invasion of the Soviet Union.

Hitler's poor coordination with his Italian and Japanese allies exacerbated the problems posed by a fragmented German military command, a second key element undermining German preparations for war against the Red Army. For example, even as Hitler ordered a campaign against the Soviet Union he irresolutely bandied about and either rejected or pursued a series of options throughout the summer and fall of 1940, all in direct contrast to the period of reflection and then preparation for invading western Europe that had occurred almost immediately following the end of the Polish campaign. As a result, at the operational level, there was no great push from above to study the French campaign's lessons, even though the Germans had lost a quarter of their tank strength and suffered over 150,000 casualties in only six weeks.[42] The result of the incessant planning, disjointed command, and frenetic pace was that the German high command operated under tremendous strain and, dangerously for strategic purposes, began to specialize. The OKW (Oberkommando der Wehrmacht, or High Command of the Armed Forces) took over in western Europe and the Mediterranean, and the OKH focused on eastern Europe.

The overburdened General Staff compounded another preexisting problem within the German military establishment: Germany's underfunded and marginalized intelligence network, in particular the army's Fremde Heere Ost, or "Foreign Armies East," produced assessments woefully off the mark regarding the Red Army's size, its regenerative ability, and the fact that the Red Army, circa 1941, was taking on a new generation of weapons systems, including some superior to anything in the German arsenal. Poor German intelligence efforts were part and parcel of an organizational culture that not only glorified the operational over the less glamorous but necessary duties in terms of effectively running complex military campaigns but also often relied on stereotypes and ideologically driven assumptions. This reflected the arrogance that had rippled through the Wehrmacht's ranks following France's quick defeat.

Given the racial inferiority that many in the Wehrmacht assigned to the Red Army's leadership and men, it is no wonder that Marcks, his peers, and Hitler expected the invasion's "shock and awe" to first rip apart the Red Army in western Soviet Union and then, after a quick German march on Moscow, bring down a Soviet government that the Gestapo, for one, had already severely underestimated in terms of its political strength. It was a plan featuring classic Prussian goals of annihilating what was believed to be the bulk of the enemy's field army, thus destroying the enemy's will to fight and consequently leading to a negotiated peace with Germany holding control over almost all the European part of the Soviet Union. The Red Army's miserable performance against Finland in 1939–1940 and a concomitant overlooking of its brilliant performance against the Japanese in August 1939 furthered a belief within the German leadership that the Red Army was far from a first-rank foe. An August 1940 study done by the German General Staff's Military Geographic Branch had concluded that the Soviet Union could capably fight on even after losing Leningrad, Moscow, and the Ukraine. Despite the availability of such information, neither Marcks nor Halder seriously planned for such a contingency.

Nevertheless, war games had demonstrated that speed was essential to meeting the plan's aims and amply demonstrated Germany's difficulties if the Red Army weathered Germany's initial assault. Marcks believed, however, that if Germany could conquer the Ukraine and lock up the Baltic, then Germany would have a good chance of beating its combined enemies regardless of whether the Soviet Union hung on in the war. To that end, he wrote a memorandum considering the possibility of a longer war.[43] Around the same time the OKW's Lieutenant Colonel Bernhard von Lossberg, finished his Aufbau Ost, or "Build Up East," and further Operationsstudie Ost, "Operational Study East." In addition to relying on much of the same faulty intelligence that weakened his peer's planning at OKH and making many of the same poor assumptions, including the belief that Moscow should serve as the campaign's geographic focal point regardless of what this would mean for the Wehrmacht, Lossberg did speculate that the Red Army could possibly withdraw into the Soviet interior, extend the German lines of communication, and then counterattack.[44] Yet the parts of these studies and memoranda pointing out the potential for danger inherent in a plan focused on defeating the Red Army in the field were, for better or worse, marginalized in the larger debate between Hitler and Halder over the campaign's direction, and, then largely ignored as General Paulus began the process of formalizing the plan.

During the years 1941–1942, Germany had every opportunity to secure its position on the European continent. Instead, German planners analyzed Germany's time, logistical, economic, and manpower constraints as demanding an all-or-nothing one-time offensive focused on crushing the Soviet military machine. Although in many ways the evolving plan was consistent with Prussian and then German military tradition, such an envisaged campaign was not only risky but also even reckless given the larger resource and manpower constraints facing Germany. The plan finalized by General Marcks on August 5, 1940, submitted by the OKH to Hitler on December 5, 1940, and memorialized by Hitler in Directive No. 21 on December 18, 1940, bore the hallmarks of a General Staff at the height of arrogance and holding the Red Army in deep contempt, breaking with the previous realism suffusing the plans for the attack on the Allies in the spring of 1940. Hitler grandiosely code-named the invasion Barbarossa after German Emperor Fredrick I Barbarossa, who had led German knights in a series of campaigns against the Muslim armies beginning in the late twelfth century, a campaign taking German troops into eastern Europe and Asia Minor.

Barbarossa's first stage was scheduled to take four months to destroy the Red Army, followed in its second stage with the Soviet Union's collapse and an advance ending 300 miles east of Moscow, Leningrad, and the Volga River. Barbarossa directed its main axis toward the land bridge between the Dvina and Dnieper Rivers in the belief that this would force the Red Army to engage and be destroyed on the approaches to the Soviet capital. Following this initial phase, the plan called for Hitler to decide whether to push to Moscow, move on Leningrad, or move south into the Ukraine. The geographic problems alone confronting the Wehrmacht far exceeded those in any previous campaign; a fact some German planners recognized, though their response would be horribly lacking. As it was Barbarossa's goals were simply astonishing. Its first few months alone involved a campaign seeking to absorb a landmass larger than the United States east of the Mississippi River; with a similar range of varied geographical and climactic features and nowhere near the well-developed infrastructure that existed in the United States. Moreover, it was a landmass that dramatically widened as one moved east, a reality that German planners seemed to willfully ignore in constructing a plan that at least strategically was crafted more by faith and wishful thinking than anything else.

Given geographic issues German logisticians made two key concessions. First, they split the army's truck pool in two. One truck fleet would accompany the fast-moving mobile divisions, providing fuel and other supplies. The other would fill intermediate supply depots set up within the newly conquered territories. Even measures such as these stretched the sustainable operational depth of the campaign's initial stage to only about 350 miles into the Soviet Union, near Smolensk in the front's center. The second concession stemmed from the outcome of Major General Friedrich Paulus's December 1940 war gaming of the German assault plans. Paulus had determined that, for logistical reasons, the offensive would need to pause after three weeks, just before Leningrad, at Smolensk and at Kiev. Only after resupply could the German armies resume a successful advance on a single axis. The capabilities did not exist to adequately support three axes of advance following the initial thrust.[45] Even if German engineers could convert narrow-gauge Soviet rail lines quickly enough to help support the German advance, only three main rail lines existed to supply the 10 German armies invading the Soviet Union. To put this in perspective, German logistical planners traditionally sought, as a rule of thumb, one rail line to support *each army*, not each army group.[46] Furthermore, little thought was given to cross-country mobility, a lack of foresight that the German army would never overcome. Finally, supplies of ammunition and fuel were to be prioritized, the expectation being that German soldiers could feed themselves by plundering and looting civilian food sources, exactly what they would do, with horrific results, for the Soviet Union's civilian population.

Organizationally, German planners solved the primary logistical and geographical problems by creating three separate Army Groups split by the vast Pripet marshes bisecting the front. Just north of the Pripet marshes, Field Marshal von Bock commanded Army Group Center with his primary task focused on destroying Soviet forces within Belorussia. On Bock's left flank, north of the Pripet marches, Field Marshal von Leeb commanded Army Group North. First, Leeb needed to sweep Russian forces from the Baltic states while maintaining loose contact with Army Group Center. Then, after taking Leningrad, the Army Group would wheel southeast toward Moscow. South of the Pripet marshes, Field Marshal von Rundstedt led Army Group South. Rundstedt had orders to crush the Red Army west of the Dnieper River and seize the Ukraine. The heavily industrialized Donets Basin served as an important objective for Rundstedt's command, as did Kiev, the Ukrainian capital. In addition, Rundstedt also needed to support Army Group Center's flank. Furthermore, Germany created Group XXI in the Arctic north, a force numbering 250,000 German soldiers fighting alongside 157,000 Finns. Group XXI had orders to protect the Petsamo iron mines and the Arctic highway, supplying iron and key minerals to Germany, as well as conduct limited advances meant to pressure both the Soviet port of Murmansk and the northern approaches to Leningrad. The German command's lack of professionalism was astonishing. Neither Halder nor Brauschitsch nor any other General Staff officer stepped forward and argued that Barbarossa's goals were too far reaching to be accomplished in a single campaign year. Nor did they argue against the fundamental criminality underlying Barbarossa's primary goals in relation to the murder of the populations in the western Soviet Union.

The Wehrmacht's top officers believed in the strategic goal of creating Lebensraum, welcomed Hitler's rise to power, despised democracy, dismissed the strategic reality that it had been democracies that defeated Imperial

Germany in World War I, and provided Hitler the means to wage a war of extermination through these officers' own willingly applied expertise in the art of war. Hitler invited 250 generals to a secret meeting on March 30, 1941, where Hitler hammered home his murderous ideological worldview. Halder casually and dispassionately recorded Hitler's criminal orders as follows: "Bolshevism is antisocial criminality. . . . We have a war of annihilation [Vernichtungskrieg] on our hands."[47] SS Major General Reinhard Heydrich and the army's quartermaster general, Eduard Wagner, met on March 26, 1941, to plan for the impending genocide.[48] On April 28, 1941, the German Eastern Armies received the results from this meeting, titled "Regulations for the Employment of the Security Police and Sicherheitsdienst in Army Units."[49] The SD and the Wehrmacht facilitated their cooperation by embedding an SD representative with the staff from each German army assigned to Barbarossa.[50] To make sure that there was no misunderstanding among the senior military leadership, the following day Brauchitsch informed them, "The troops have to realize that this struggle is being waged by one race against another, and proceed with the necessary harshness."[51]

Members of the SD and SS served as the point men in this racial war, organized into four Einsatzgruppen (action groups), each the size of an army battalion, labeled A, B, C, and D, with the first three around 1,000 men each and D putting around 600 men into the field. Each action group contained four or five smaller Sonderkommandos (special commandos) der Sicherheitpolizei. The leaders of Barbarossa's armies acted to instill the proper spirit in their men. On April 25, 1941, the 18th Army commander, Colonel General Kuchler, informed his officers that "the aim must be to annihilate European Russia."[52] On May 2, the 4th Panzer Army's Colonel General Erich Hoeppner issued orders to the 4th Panzer Group stating, "Every combat action must be inspired, in concept and execution, by an iron determination to ensure the merciless, total annihilation of the enemy."[53] Meanwhile, Halder and Jodl helped draft a May 13, 1941, order singling out the "special nature" of the enemy and the need for "merciless," "ruthless" action against any guerillas or civilian threats with even "collective measures" justified if individual civilian transgressions could not be punished. This same order granted the Wehrmacht blanket legal protection from any otherwise normally punishable crimes against civilians.[54] In regard to prisoners of war, the laws of war would be ignored, as provided in a June 16, 1941, OKW order.

On June 21, 1941, Heinrich Himmler ordered planning to begin for a massive demographic reorganization of eastern Europe, the core of Lebensraum. Professor Konrad Meyer authored the subsequent plan called "Generalplan Ost." Meyer's genocidal plan, approved by Himmler and Heydrich and to be carried out in conjunction with the Wehrmacht's direct and indirect support, foresaw removing at least 31 million people from Poland, Belorussia, the Ukraine, and the Baltic states—mostly via starvation. This immense loss of life would make available massive agricultural resources to feed the population of Hitler's Reich; with most of these resources to come from the Ukrainian "breadbasket." It was in this manner by which Hitler and his minions sought to leverage for their own needs the Soviet Union's economic and agricultural bounty that otherwise would have been stretched thin in attempting to sustain both Nazi Germany and the Soviet Union had Hitler honored his alliance with Stalin and attempted a different strategy. Overall, this meant that the strategic and operational military and economic goals of the campaign were inextricably bound up with planning to commit mass murder. Barbarossa was only the first step, an enabling step, with starvation, genocide, deportation, and enslavement the subsequent and primary elements of a horrific overall plan. This plan would ultimately see German colonists resettle the "living space" won in eastern Europe—and cement Germany's standing at a global power. Hitler, Himmler, Heydrich, and Meyer all drew inspiration in this horrific plan from the "American example." As described by economist Adam Tooze,

> In the autumn of 1941 Hitler returned repeatedly to the American example in discussing Germany's future in the East. The Volga, he declared, would be Germany's Mississippi. And the bloody conquest of the American West provided Germany with the historical warrant it needed to justify the clearance of the Slav population. Here in the East a similar process will repeat itself for a second time as in the conquest of America; A "superior" settler population would displace an "inferior" native population opening the way towards a new era of economic possibility. Europe—and not America—will be the land of unlimited possibilities.[55]

On May 2, 1941, General Thomas, the OKW's top economic expert, met with representatives of the Reich's ministerial agencies to prepare plans for occupying the Soviet Union. These plans openly accepted the starvation of 20 million to 30 million Soviet citizens to feed the German army from Russian sources and placed the highest priority on securing Soviet grain sources. This war of extermination was set to begin, as it turned out, at the exact moment that the relative combat power of the German army was at its greatest height in relation to the Red Army.

THE GERMAN MILITARY MACHINE IN 1941: POWERFUL BUT FLAWED

The German military machine facing the Soviet colossus in 1941 stood in many ways far more powerful than its 1940 edition. Nevertheless, the Wehrmacht also possessed deep structural weaknesses. For instance, the tremendous expansion in the German army's ranks since Hitler had taken power meant, among other things, that the German army lacked enough trained officers. This greatly impaired the Wehrmacht's combat efficiency, as branches of

Table 3.4 German Armed Forces Strength on June 22, 1941[1]

Field army	3,800,000
Replacement army	1,200,000
Luftwaffe	1,680,000
Kriegsmarine	404,000
Waffen-SS	150,000
Total	7,234,000

[1]David M. Glantz, *Stumbling Colossus: The Red Army on the Eve of World War* (University Press of Kansas, 1998), 294.

the General Staff already relegated to second-class status, such as intelligence and logistics, received disproportionately fewer resources.

Meanwhile, the manpower problems filtered down throughout the ranks, and though the Wehrmacht grew from 5.767 million men in June 1940 to 7.3 million men in the summer of 1941 (See Table 3.4), teenagers reaching military age numbered only about 660,000 per year.[56] Any permanent casualties suffered above this number would come from Germany's labor force, as the German replacement army held only 475,000 men when Barbarossa began.

The manpower deficiency not only meant that the German army was operating on a strict deadline, and would need to be managed carefully, but also guaranteed that the economy would struggle with labor shortages throughout 1941. The labor force's size ranked, along with raw materials availability, as the primary determinants regarding armaments output throughout the war.[57] Even so, the inconsistent 1939–1941 German approach to economic mobilization for the radically different wars represented by a continental war against the Soviet Union on the one hand and a maritime struggle against Britain and the United States on the other also significantly handicapped the German war effort.[58]

Germany's failure is, in this respect, critical to understand when examining economic explanations regarding the Soviet Union's ability to withstand a German attack. Simply put, and as it would turn out, the Soviet Union mobilized more effectively for fighting an all-out land war than did Germany. Ignoring these contextual economic realities fuels the myth arguing that a Soviet preponderance in economic and military strength deterministically decided the war from early on. The arrogance and internal inefficiencies characterizing the German state in 1940–1941 leveled a playing field that was sloping Germany's way, (see Table 3.5) and balanced out the early war military ineptitude displayed by Germany's opponents even as they recognized the importance of a singular economic focus rapidly put into place to help effectuate Germany's later defeat. German economic miscalculations were numerous in the year between France's fall and the onset of Barbarossa. It is not the object of this chapter to examine them all, nor is there space for such an analysis. Nonetheless, as to

Table 3.5 Red Army in Western Border Soviet Military Districts versus Axis Invasion Army on June 22, 1941[1]

	Red Army	Axis[2]	German only
Divisions	174	164	135
Personnel	2,780,000[3]	4,733,990	3,750,000[4]
Tanks and assault guns	11,000	3,612	3,350
Guns and mortars	43,872	12,686	7,000
Aircraft	9,917	2,937	2,000

[1]David M. Glantz, *Stumbling Colossus: The Red Army on the Eve of World War* (University Press of Kansas, 1998), 292–95.
[2]Including German.
[3]3,780,000, including strategic reserves deployable in July/August.
[4]Including 700,000 in Luftwaffe.

one example regarding the negative outcome produced by these mistakes, and given the importance of the German Panzer arm to Germany's successes during the war, let us explore the 1940–1941 German Panzer arm.

In preparing for Barbarossa, German planners recognized that the Panzer divisions would be called on more than ever in Russia's vast interior. Accordingly, on June 18, 1940, Hitler and his General Staff doubled the number of Panzer divisions. They did so, however, without increased tank production to match. Thus, they merely watered down existing unit strength and combat potential—at least that was Guderian's position. Others have argued that Hitler made a logical decision. There was no way that 10 Panzer divisions could be effectively deployed across the entire west of Soviet Union.[59] Nevertheless, more Panzer divisions increased the demand for more Panzers. In lieu of enough new Panzers, obsolete tank models, such as the Panzer II, remained in service long after the tank should have been retired. As late as December 1940, the OKH pushed to increase tank production from the 250-tank-per-month rate during 1940 up to 1,250 tanks per month, but the OKW rejected this request, largely because of the Luftwaffe's and the Kriegsmarine's demands for resources.

Consequently, on the eve of history's greatest land war, and lacking in adequate medium tank production, Germany increased its production of self-propelled artillery and assault guns as a substitute. Assault guns—in German known as the Sturmgeschutz (or Stug III), as Germany initially produced its most common assault guns from the Panzer III chassis—were cheaper than tanks. This was because they lacked expensive turrets, the main gun being mounted on the chassis, and needed a crew of only four instead of the five men in most German tanks. Germany organized its Stugs into battalions, Stug Abteilungen, numbering 18 to 30 guns each.[60] Eventually, Germany would put 100 Stug battalions into the field, but production initially proved slow at 50 per month in June 1941. Originally, the Stug III came armed with a short-barrel L/24 75-mm gun. By 1943, the Stug III and later Stug IV, based on the Panzer IV chassis, mounted powerful L/43 or L/48 long-barrel 75-mm guns. The Stug's powerful armament, low silhouette, and reliable armor protection meant that it ranked as one of Germany's best tank killers. Germany built 9,500 Stug IIIs and 1,000 Stug IVs during World War II with another 1,000 Stug IIIs built mounting 105-mm howitzers, designated StuH, for use against soft targets. In addition to relying on assault gun production in lieu of an adequate main battle tank, Germany tinkered with modifying obsolete tanks for new roles. In June 1941, some 150 Panzerjagers, a Panzer I chassis with a Czech-built 47-mm gun and armored gun shield in lieu of a turret, provided some self-propelled anti-tank punch.[61]

Meanwhile, in terms of its tanks, Germany upgraded the Panzer III with a 50-mm L/42 gun and then replaced it with the even higher velocity 50-mm L/60 gun. As German factories regularly refitted the older Panzer IIIs with L/42 guns and produced new models, this left the Panzer III comparably armed to early model Shermans but still inadequately armed for killing tanks such as the T-34. Over one-third the German army's tanks on July 1, 1941, were Panzer IIIs, making up 327 of the early model Panzer IIIs with 37-mm guns and 1,174 Panzer IIIs with the L/42 and L/60 50-mm guns. Panzer III armor thickness also steadily increased over earlier models. The Panzer III needed the better protection to survive on the battlefield. Nevertheless, the net effect created by increasing the tank's weight was to decrease engine life while increasing fuel consumption at exactly the time the German army could least afford it. The Panzer IV, meanwhile, represented the only tank that Germany possessed in 1941 that was able to accommodate the necessary armament for handling the Red Army's T-34s and KV-1s. Yet on July 1, 1941, only 531 served with the German army. Nearly every past account explaining the first months of the tank war between Russia and Germany has focused on the Russian tank park's overwhelming obsolescence in 1941. Germany, however, had no tank that could effectively compete in hitting power or armored protection against any of the 1,861 T-34 and KV-1 tanks that the Red Army fielded in June 1941.[62] Moreover, because of German involvement fighting in the Mediterranean and occupation duties across Europe, some 460 Panzer IIIs, 128 Panzer IVs, and 127 Stug IIIs available to the German army on June 1, 1941, were not deployed with the German forces preparing to invade the Soviet Union.[63]

All told, the German army had 5,262 tanks in June 1941, but if obsolete models, such as the Panzer I, are discounted, then this total dropped to 4,198 tanks.[64] The German army increased its available Panzers from 2,574 deployed to take France in 1940 to 3,332 for Barbarossa. In addition, most of the new Panzer divisions had a more uniform organization than their 1939–1940 predecessors, with each Panzer division averaging a single Panzer regiment comprised of two Panzer battalions (see Table 3.6). Nonetheless, despite

Table 3.6 Comparison between Soviet Tank Division and German Panzer Division in 1941

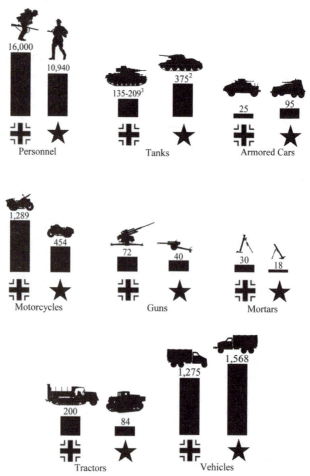

[1]David M. Glantz, *Stumbling Colossus: The Red Army on the Eve of World War* (University Press of Kansas, 1998), 154.
[2]Establishment strength rarely approached this number. An entire Russian mechanized corps in the western military district in 1941 averaged only 550 tanks each.
[3]Reflects actual tank numbers per Panzer division in eastern Europe in June 1941.

the Panzer division's more standardized and streamlined table of organization, many of the newer Panzer formations featured a motley collection of German and captured vehicles, making logistical planning an even worse nightmare. The Wehrmacht would go to war against the Soviet Union while fielding over 2,000 different types of vehicles.

The German army invading the Soviet Union was a far cry from the homogeneously equipped mechanized juggernaut that it has since been made out to be. Yet, all the same in January 1941, the Wehrmacht included approximately 7.3 million men.[65] From this total, the force that was gathered for Barbarossa, including contributions from Germany's Axis allies, numbered 3,600,000 men (3,050,000 of whom were German) against 2,900,000 Soviet soldiers in the western frontier military districts.[66] All told, the Germany army put 180 divisions into the field in June 1941 versus only 143 divisions in May 1940. The majority of the 1941-era German field army was organized in four Armored Groups, Panzergruppen, and seven infantry armies comprising 151 divisions massed on the Soviet borders as members of an undoubtedly lethal but flawed army. These armies included 19 Panzer and 12 motorized divisions equipped with 3,208 tanks, 250 assault guns, 7,184 artillery pieces, and over 600,000 vehicles. Germany's heavy reliance on horses, 600,000 of which had been gathered to help supply and transport the enormous German army, belies the since-ingrained images of the infamous German blitzkrieg. Additionally, the standard German infantry division still relied on 36 horse-drawn, entirely obsolete 37-mm anti-tank guns for defense against enemy armor. Furthermore, the German infantry (and armor alike) lacked enough heavy fire support, with stockpiles of armor-piercing weapons and artillery proving particularly short. Meanwhile, the Luftwaffe, despite its core of veteran airmen, had not recovered from the bloodletting that the British had inflicted on the German aircrews in 1940. Consequently, 200 fewer medium and light bombers assisted the German army in western Soviet Union than during the battle for France.[67] Thus, the Luftwaffe could put only 2,510 combat aircraft into the eastern European skies,[68] though this was also in part because 1,766 combat aircraft were deployed over the English Channel, Scandinavia, or the Mediterranean.[69] Despite these difficulties, for organizational, doctrinal, and other professional reasons, the German army in 1941 represented the world's premier army, wielded on behalf of the Third Reich's violent, racist, and criminal goals.

Regardless of Germany's poor strategic leadership and questionable assumptions in regard to Barbarossa, in comparison to Germany, the Soviet Union came up lacking on a variety of fronts, particularly in terms of economic considerations. Although the Soviet Union possessed a larger population than Germany, vast territorial space, and huge reservoirs of natural resources, poor infrastructure inhibited Soviet economic development. The Soviet Union also possessed a comparatively low gross domestic product, greatly increasing economic costs. German economic advantages held true even given the potential for greater resources provided by the vast Soviet state *unless the Soviets mobilized more efficiently than did the Germans.*[70] Despite the massive Soviet investment in its military, all this investment accomplished was to match Germany's equally prodigious armaments expenditures. In July 1940, Germany was able to equal the combined Soviet and British economic base. Moreover, Germany's steel production, when combined with control over western European steel output, meant that Germany produced 33.4 million tons of steel per year in 1941–1944. In comparison, the Soviet Union only produced 11.3 tons of steel per year during the same period.[71]

Nevertheless, even with German's improved economic position, Hitler, and his senior military leadership, had asked the Wehrmacht to simultaneously defeat the Red Army, occupy a landmass the size of the western Soviet Union, kill off the local population, and completely rebuild the infrastructure and industry necessary to quickly benefit from such a victory. Of course, for its part, Hitler's military leadership not only failed to challenge such expansive goals but also put together a faith-based plan of attack premised on decidedly shaky assumptions, utterly failing to align expectations with the means to achieve them and virtually ignoring the most basic problems of sheer geographic space and logistics confronting the plan as it existed—no less hardly considering what would be needed to be done to preserve the German army's striking power if the Red Army failed to fold up before the German onslaught. Both Hitler and his military leadership thus not only failed to focus their efforts on reasonably attainable goals that would have provided clear strategic benefits to the German war economy, but also plunged forward with a horribly flawed plan even as they looked ahead to a final decision with the United States and Britain. All this handicapped a German military establishment, that if it were wielded with a reasonable modicum of respect for its limitations with a concomitant attempt to preserve its ability to fight a war of maneuver, was ready to lay the framework for Hitler's horrific racial and economic projects. That said, and in spite of its numerous flaws as a plan, Barbarossa, as in France the year before, would once again test the deterministic theories of mass over qualitative measurements of battlefield capabilities. Brute force lost in 1940. Would it carry the day in 1941?

Chapter 4
History's Bloodiest Conflict Begins

On June 22, 1941, Germany invaded the Soviet Union and began the struggle deciding World War II's outcome, a struggle that today's conventional wisdom regards as Hitler's fatal mistake, in some instances, even before Barbarossa began. This determinism has most frequently been bolstered by arguments almost entirely quantitative in nature, ascribing Germany's defeat chiefly to the Soviet Union's size. Regardless, it is this book's contention that, despite its great size, the Soviet Union repeatedly came dangerously close to allowing Germany to seize and secure economic resources that would have provided Hitler with the means to create an almost undefeatable continental colossus every bit the military and industrial equal of the United States of America.

In 1941, only one nation stood as a counterweight to complete German hegemony across all of Europe, the Soviet Union. During 1940–1941, Hitler entertained no other strategic option more likely to grant the Third Reich the freedom to act globally than did Barbarossa. The Soviet Union contained virtually all the economic resources that Germany needed to wage an effective war against an alliance of nations led by the United States. Purported alternative options to invading the Soviet Union in 1941, as argued today, were, for 1940–1941-era Germany, illusory. If Hitler had declined to invade the Soviet Union and another year passed as the Axis alliance retooled for and waged mainly a maritime war against the Anglo-American alliance, one fought across the oceans, seas, and continents marking the epicenter of the classical world, then the opportunity that Hitler held in 1940–1941 to take advantage of the Soviet Union's weaknesses could have slipped by as the Red Army completed reorganizing and rearming. What is more, by 1941, Germany's only reliable short-term potential solutions to domestic economic problems came from either near absolute economic dependence on Stalin's largesse, or the direct acquisition of southern Soviet Union's boundless raw materials. Moreover, many of these raw materials were nowhere near to be found in any kind of readily accessible quantity anywhere in a Middle East that, according to some today, if taken, purportedly offered Hitler his best chance to win the entire war. Such positions are not ones grounded in hindsight.

Within the context of the 1940–1941 era, most military and political experts believed that Germany could defeat the Soviet Union, no less merely accomplish the subsidiary goal of seizing the bountiful economic resources found in the Ukraine and Caucasus. At a dinner on Saturday, June 21, 1941, Winston Churchill was said to have commented, "A German attack on Russia is certain and Russia will be defeated."[1] British military assessments from the era held to the same belief.[2] As for the U.S. analysis regarding the Soviet Union's chances, shortly after Barbarossa began, U.S. Secretary of the Navy Frank Knox advised President Roosevelt, "The best opinion I can get is that it will take anywhere from six weeks to two months for Hitler to clean up on Russia." U.S. Secretary of War Henry Stimson informed Roosevelt that "the Germans would be thoroughly occupied in beating the Soviet Union for a minimum of one month and a possible maximum of three months."[3] U.S. Army Chief of Staff General George C. Marshall concurred, holding that the war would be measured in weeks rather than months.[4]

The consensus opinion expressed by the experts of the day has managed nevertheless to have been turned on its head into a lingering belief today that the Third Reich made its greatest mistake in even contemplating a successful war against the Soviet Union. In part, this is not only because the Third Reich catastrophically lost World War II but also likely because the ideological objectives underpinning Barbarossa and permeating the German General Staff meant that the planning process engaged in by ranking German officers meant vague goals and blind faith in the idea that the Red Army would quickly collapse replaced traditional military standards for planning that, at a minimum, call for bringing together anticipated results with the clear means to achieve those results.

There is no question that Barbarossa's wildly optimistic and unfocused planning undermined its very opportunity for success. Nevertheless, the reality that the summer of 1941 offered the Wehrmacht its best window of opportunity for granting the Third Reich hegemony over the entirety of Europe represents a set of circumstances created as much by Josef Stalin as by anyone else, for, in the late spring of 1941, Stalin undermined the Soviet Union's ability to defend itself to such a degree as to virtually open the country to its own destruction. All this occurred despite the ample warnings that Stalin received as to the danger facing his empire. Thus, when Stalin finally authorized the mobilization that many in his military command had been begging for, it was far too late. Although Stalin's thought process remains elusive, it appears likely that he had a strong fear of a 1941 war with Germany, even going so far as to desperately attempt to appease Hitler, in particular by sending economic assistance up to the date of the actual German attack.[5] A reinvigorated debate, however, continues to this day, revisiting whether the Soviet Union was preparing its own attack on Germany. Nevertheless, most available evidence supports the long-established view that the Soviet Union's belated mobilization had been for defensive purposes. At any rate, early on the morning of June 22, 1941, the Wehrmacht began a string of victories ranking as among the greatest in military history.

Barbarossa opened just after 0300 hours as German Special Forces operations sowed confusion among Soviet border troops and behind the front lines, including cutting telephone lines to a depth of 30 miles into the Soviet Union. Thus cutting the primary means by which the Red Army communicated orders up and down the chain of command in 1941. Command and control promptly disintegrated in the Soviet first strategic echelon. At the same time, thousands of German artillery pieces pounded away at Soviet positions as four entire Luftflotten systematically hammered into the Red Army Air Force. The proximity of the Luftwaffe's aircraft to their objectives meant that the German pilots maintained a remarkable degree of persistence over their targets. For instance, individual fighter-bomber pilots with JG52 reported flying six sorties apiece during the first day alone.[6] On this first day, the Red Army Air Force lost 1,811 aircraft, most on the ground, against only 35 destroyed German aircraft.[7] By the end of June, the Luftwaffe had destroyed 4,614 Soviet aircraft against losses of only 330 German aircraft.[8] In one week, the Luftwaffe had attained total air superiority and a psychological edge over the Red Army Air Force lasting throughout much of the war. Soviet General I. I. Kopets, the Western Front's air commander, shot himself in despair. Stalin furiously ordered many other senior officers of the Red Army Air Force arrested, executing several of them because of the disaster.[9]

Meanwhile, just as the Luftwaffe had caught the Red Army Air Force ill prepared for war, the Red Army's frontline units were either so poorly deployed or distracted that German ground forces easily penetrated Soviet lines. For instance, the NKVD (People's Commissariat for Internal Affairs) and Soviet border guards had spent the weeks leading up to Barbarossa engaged in suppressing a simmering guerilla war in the former Baltic states. Even after battle had been joined, ideological and political priorities distracted significant Soviet military assets. In Lvov, the NKVD reacted to the German invasion by murdering approximately 4,000 people, continuing the record of Soviet atrocities that had marked their occupation of Poland.[10] In addition, across the western Ukraine and Belarus, Stalin's men murdered as many as 100,000 more political prisoners.[11] As the NKVD perpetrated yet another orgy of violence against the people of eastern Europe, the Wehrmacht thundered into the Soviet Union along three immense axes of advance.

OPERATION BARBAROSSA, JUNE 22 TO SEP. 30, 1941

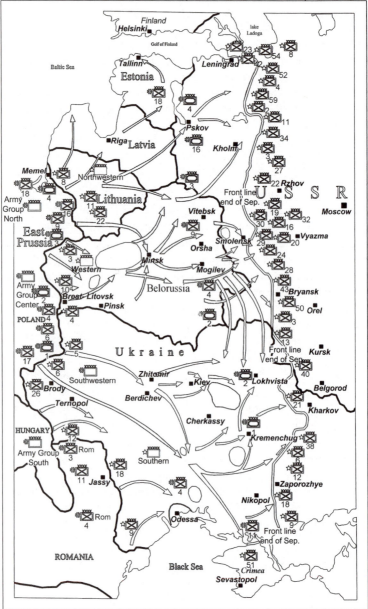

ARMY GROUP SOUTH IN THE UKRAINE

The Carpathian Mountains divided Rundstedt's Army Group South into two wings. Army Group South's southern wing deployed in Romania. It included the German 11th Army, with 175,000 men, and the Romanian 3rd and 4th Armies. That said the Germans had failed to make full use of the initially eager Romanian participation in the war. In particular, German attempts to retrain the Romanian army fell short on a number of levels, with a lack of time and interpreters proving particularly difficult to overcome.[12] Rundstedt's southern grouping initially faced the 320,000-man Odessa Military District under Major General Ivan Tyulenev's command.

Army Group South's northern wing included Panzer Group 1, the German 6th Army, and the German 17th Army, in total some 797,000 men when including support troops and a substantial Hungarian commitment almost one week into the war: the nearly 100,000-man Hungarian Carpathian Army Group led by Major General Ferenc Szombathelyi. All squeezed into the gap formed between the Pripet marshes and the Carpathian Mountains. Rundstedt's northern wing faced a formidable foe: the 870,000-man Soviet Southwestern Front led by Mikhail Kirponos. Kirponos enjoyed several advantages over the Axis forces arrayed against him, including in men, armor, and familiarity with the terrain. The Soviet Southwestern Front's primary striking power resided in its Mechanized Corps: the 8th, 9th, 15th, 19th, and 22nd Mechanized Corps as well as the 8th Tank Division/4th Mechanized Corps. The Soviet units contained varying numbers and quality of tanks, from the 8th Mechanized Corp's 907 tanks down to the 8th Tank Division/4th Mechanized Corp's 258 tanks. All told, the Southwestern Front's mechanized corps contained 3,427 tanks, including 713 medium or heavy tanks, and 513 armored cars. In addition, a veritable who's who of Soviet commanders would be present as part of the Soviet Southwestern Front during the war's first weeks, including Zhukov, as a Stavka representative; Konstantin K. Rokossovsky, commanding the 9th Mechanized Corps, and Mikhail Katukov, commanding the 20th Tank Division.[13]

On the other hand, the German 6th Army, under Walther von Reichenau, and Panzer Group 1, under General Ewald von Kleist, were well led, well organized, and loaded with veteran formations. Kleist's Panzer Group 1 and its 586 tanks, 18 tank destroyers, 36 assault guns, and 54 armored cars served as Rundstedt's spearhead. It featured five Panzer divisions, four motorized divisions, six infantry divisions, one tank destroyer battalion, and two assault gun battalions, all supported by 14 motorized artillery battalions. In addition, some of the German army's leading officers staffed Panzer Group 1, including Kleist; Mackensen, commanding the 3rd Motorized Corps; Heinrici, commanding the 16th Motorized Division; Cruewell, commanding the 11th Panzer Division; and Hube, commanding the 16th Panzer Division. Panzer

Group 1, like its Soviet foes, contained varying numbers and quality of tanks. For instance, the 9th, 11th, and 16th Panzer Divisions all fielded just over 130 tanks each, with 91 Panzer III and IV tanks in each division. In contrast, the 13th and 14th Panzer Divisions could field only 47 Panzer III and IV tanks each. In addition, 219 of Panzer Group 1's tanks were next-to-useless Panzer I and Panzer IIs. That meant that the Germans faced a Soviet Southwestern Front holding a nearly two-to-one advantage in medium and heavy tanks combined, with 278 Soviet heavy tanks against no German heavy tanks.[14]

Therein the numbers game ends and reality sets in. The Southwestern Front was spread across hundreds of miles. In comparison, the Germans had placed their divisions so as to bring overwhelming power to bear in a concentrated fashion. In terms of the primary tactical formation, the battalion, the Germans possessed significant cadres of veteran officers with levels of training and combat experience light-years ahead of their Soviet foes. Moreover, the Southwestern Front's tank units were so deficient in logistical backing, including a horrible lack of spare parts, and so poorly positioned when the war began that Soviet tank breakdown rates reached astronomical levels. For example, the Soviet 8th Mechanized Corps' 300-mile road march to reach the battlefield, at times under sporadic sniper fire from Ukrainian guerillas, meant that when it finally met the Germans, it had already lost half its tanks to breakdowns. In addition, the draftees and other men in the Soviet tank divisions often lacked proper training. In some instances, they did not even share a common language. The 22nd Mechanized Corps' 19th Tank Division included 2,000 men who could not even speak Russian.[15] Endemic equipment shortages included too few trucks and communications equipment, with telegraph the predominant and outdated mode of communication at the army and front level. Finally, on June 19th, Kirponos had been ordered to move his headquarters from Kiev to Ternopol. In transition, when the war began, Kirponos struggled to stay abreast of the fierce fighting that swamped his border defensive forces.

Therefore, on Barbarossa's first day Kleist's Panzers quickly exploited holes blown in Kirponos's defenses by the German infantry. Kirponos responded with aggressive counterattacks directed at the German spearheads. The Germans turned aside these efforts even though many Soviet units performed well, in particular the 87th Rifle Division under Major General F. K. Alabyshev and the 1st Anti-Tank Brigade.[16] Although Kirponos whittled away at the German army's strength, the Red Army paid a heavy price for its inexperience. For instance, when Kirponos called for a concentrated counterattack against Panzer Group 1, to be led by Major General Potapov's 5th Army and some six Mechanized Corps, the rapidly moving German assault armies and the incessant Luftwaffe presence over the battlefield repeatedly threw off the Soviet timetable. Moreover, the Germans nearly always operated in a coordinated combined-arms fashion, representing the hallmark of combat efficiency. For instance, looking only at the 14th Panzer Division's Kampfgruppe

Stempel, we find the 108th Panzer Grenadier Regiment (minus one battalion), the 36th Panzer Regiment (minus one company), a single battalion from the 3rd Artillery Regiment, one battery from the 607th Mortar Battalion, one battery from the 60th Artillery Regiment (both attached from the corps level), one company from the 4th Anti-tank Battalion, the 2nd Company of the 13th Motorized Engineer Battalion, and other smaller supporting units—all combined into one cohesive, exceptionally lethal fighting force.[17]

In contrast, the Red Army's coordination between combined arms proved deplorable. This often resulted in brutally inefficient tactical decisions. Both A. A. Vlasov's 4th Mechanized Corps and K. K. Rokossovsky's 9th Mechanized Corps fought ineffectively in the war's first weeks, even though Rokossovsky and Vlasov were two of the Red Army's better leaders. German air attacks, inadequate motor transport, inadequate reconnaissance, terrible communications equipment, orders from the front level that were frequently countermanded, and poorly trained recruits completely undermined Rokossovsky's and Vlasov's efforts. For example, the Red Army's incomplete tank crew training programs meant that Soviet tank drivers often avoided negotiating difficult but protected avenues of advance, such as those found across reverse slopes of hills or through gullies. Instead, they preferred to drive along hillcrests and other such easily traversable terrain, all too often making them easy targets. In addition, notoriously inaccurate Russian gunnery meant that German tank crews usually achieved critical first hits in combat. Furthermore, Russian tank crews often compensated for their inaccurate fire by moving well within the lightly armed German tank's range, vitiating the significant standoff capabilities offered by the potent 76-mm guns on Soviet T-34s and KV-1s.

Thus, it was perhaps unsurprising that when on the war's first day the Soviet 10th Tank Division and a task force from the 32nd Tank Division counterattacked the German 11th Panzer Division near Radekhov, the Germans claimed 46 tank kills in this engagement.[18] That said, it was still a stiff fight. For example, in one instance, it took 20 hits from German cannon to destroy one T-34.[19] Moreover, following the defeat at Radekhov, Rokossovsky, in particular, fought brilliantly at times. On June 28, he ignored his orders to counterattack. Instead, he massed his artillery and ambushed the German 13th Panzer Division, dealing the Germans a sharp blow and holding his defensive positions for two days.[20] By the time Lvov fell on June 30, Army Group South's headquarters even debated whether their forces could encircle and destroy the Soviet armies defending the western Ukraine. Doubts as to whether Army Group South could meet its objectives were only exacerbated when on July 1, Rokossovsky's 9th Mechanized Corps slammed into the German 25th Motorized Division. Rokossovsky's men, led by Katukov's 20th Tank Division, penetrated some seven miles into the German lines, at times causing heavy German casualties before the Germans forced the 20th Tank Division and its sister 35th Tank Division back to their starting point.

Despite such aggressive counterattacks, by July 9th Army Group South's northern axis of advance had covered 260 miles and had reached to within 90 miles of Kiev. By July 10, the Soviet army in the Ukraine had suffered 241,594 casualties, with 172,323 killed or captured. Material losses totaled 4,381 tanks; 5,806 artillery pieces, mortars, and anti-tank guns; and 1,218 aircraft.[21] Then, on August 3, roughly 100 miles south of Kiev, near Uman, Panzer Group 1 and the German 17th Army encircled the Soviet 6th and 12th Armies. Army Group South had captured another 103,000 men, 317 tanks, and 858 artillery pieces, and two army and seven corps commanders also fell into Axis hands.[22] Rundstedt's feats in the western Ukraine stood all the more remarkable in that he not only faced a deeper and broader front than did any of his peers, but also had needed to deal with the additional complexities posed by integrating two foreign armies into his command. In comparison, to Rundstedt's north, Bock enjoyed the luxury of concentrating two large Panzer groups in a single all-German command on a front only 200 miles wide, an advantage that Bock made spectacular use of as his powerful armored assets shattered the entire Soviet Western Front.

ARMY GROUP CENTER ON THE ROAD TO MOSCOW

Early on the morning of June 22nd, Army Group Center struck from just north of the Pripet marshes. It was by far the strongest attacking German Army Group, and quite possibly the most potent Army Group fielded by any combatant during World War II. Army Group Center included two infantry armies, the 4th and 9th Armies, and the 2nd and 3rd Panzer Groups, in total, 1,180,000 men in 50 divisions. This included nine Panzer and six motorized divisions featuring 1,770 tanks. General Guderian commanded Panzer Group 2, lavishly equipped with roughly 850 tanks and 27,000 vehicles. General Hoth commanded the potent Panzer Group 3, while Field Marshal Albert Kesselring's 2nd Luftflotte, equipped with 1,500 aircraft, flew overhead in support.[23]

Bock's Panzer groups quickly punched across the border, bypassing fortresses such as at Brest-Litovsk, and penetrated deep into the Soviet interior. Despite this success, German infantry, mostly the 45th Infantry Division, spent weeks subduing Brest-Litovsk's defenders, losing 311 killed in action on just the first day, equivalent to almost two-thirds the losses the division had suffered during the entire French campaign, with the combat offering early evidence that perhaps taking on the Red Army would not be nearly as easy as the German had expected.[24] Nevertheless, within hours, the Soviet Western Front's first-echelon armies were in serious trouble. They lacked reserves, were overextended in linear defensive lines with any available armor parceled out piecemeal, and had been forced to negotiate long approach marches with corresponding high rates of breakdowns; all while enduring substantial losses to marauding German aircraft. In addition, the

Soviet 3rd and 10th Armies struggled to reestablish communications with Pavlov's headquarters at Minsk.

Then, on June 28, Army Group Center's twin tank armies, benefiting tremendously from ample air support, closed on the bulk of Pavlov's armies near Minsk. The Germans had formed the initial Kesselschlachts of the campaign. By June 30 and despite desperate and unrelenting Soviet counterattacks, the Germans had completed the encirclement, trapping the Soviet 3rd, 4th, 10th, and 13th Armies. The Soviet Western Front lost 290,000 men as prisoners of war, 4,800 tanks, and 9,400 guns and mortars. Including killed, wounded, or missing, the Red Army had lost over 340,000 men from the 680,000 men serving on the Western Front on June 22.[25] In addition, on June 29, the fortress at Brest-Litovsk had finally surrendered; all told over 7,200 men, mostly from the Soviet 6th and 42nd Divisions. The German 45th Infantry Division had suffered 482 dead and approximately 1,000 wounded during the week that it took to secure an objective that had been expected to fall on Barbarossa's first day.[26] Although it might be argued that taking and clearing a stoutly defended fortress was exactly the kind of operation that could see a blown timetable coupled with unforeseen casualties, for the German army what occurred in executing its bread and butter—the encirclement battle—foretold an even higher cost to come.

German doctrine sought to encircle opponents by surrounding and attacking from all points of the compass and then sealing the encirclement within two rings. The Panzer and motorized divisions, Schnelltruppen, composed the outside ring. After completing the initial encirclement, the Schnelltruppen turned away from the trapped armies and fought off counterattacks while preparing to spring forward again, thereby maintaining the operational initiative.[27] The infantry held responsibility for forming the pocket's inner defensive ring, liquidating the pocket, and blocking Soviet escape attempts. Using infantry to liquidate pockets represented a crucial means to save wear and tear on Panzer divisions. But German infantry frequently struggled to keep up with the fast-moving Panzer groups. When German infantry and armor could work together, the results were impressive, as proven by events near Minsk. Nonetheless, two significant problems had already cropped up to plague the Wehrmacht during Barbarossa's first week.

For one, the Soviet Union's rutted roads and sandy terrain caused German fuel consumption to soar far past preinvasion estimates. Moreover, the foot-marching infantry had lagged far behind the German Panzer and motorized divisions, just as they had during previous campaigns in Poland and France, producing a second problem as gaps reaching at times 190 miles in breadth opened between the infantry and Schnelltruppen, as in the case of the gap that had developed when the infantry finished off the Minsk pocket and then began the march east to complete the Smolensk pocket that the Panzers had begun forming on July 11. Thus, often, the pocket itself featured gaping holes in the German lines, especially initially, and thousands of Soviet soldiers escaped.

German commanders knew what was going on. Nonetheless, the OKH (Oberkommando der Heer, or Army High Command) could not decide whether German forces should focus on a more deliberative wedge-and-pocket approach that would concentrate the Panzer armies and net greater prisoner hauls or pursue a freewheeling deep operational blitz that would shatter Russian armies while forming and, ostensibly, keep the Red Army off balance but lead to looser encirclements. This lack of consensus on what to do in an operational sense, however, was only a symptom of bigger problems afflicting a plan beginning to unravel; as it exacerbated the never-decided issue underlying Barbarossa's strategic purpose, namely, whether to focus on economic goals, as advocated by Hitler, or on classic Prussian goals of annihilating the opposing army in the field, as advocated by the OKH. For that matter, and though the German leadership debated tactics, the campaign's genocidal larger goals were hardly an issue. For instance, the German army marched into Minsk and immediately rounded up and interned 40,000 men between the ages of 18 and 50 and threw them into a prisoner-of-war camp with 100,000 Soviet prisoners of war. On July 7, at the behest of von Kluge, the German army's field police and men from Einsatzgruppen B began shooting approximately 200 men per day—a practice that lasted over two months and left 10,000 bodies in mass graves near the camp.[28]

Meanwhile, although one Soviet counterattack near Bobruisk caused some temporary consternation, the powerful German army group shrugged off the Red Army's efforts. The Red Army's short-lived success at Bobruisk was bookended by Timoshenko's (he replaced Pavlov as Western Front commander) ruinous counterattack at the Sozh River and the utter defeat of the Soviet 5th and 7th Mechanized Corps after counterstriking Hoth's 3rd Panzer Group near Lepel. The Red Army fought hard however, despite being savaged by marauding German ground attack aircraft during their approach marches, the 5th and 7th Mechanized Corps nearly pealed the 3rd Panzer Army from the 2nd Panzer Army and drove the 7th Panzer Division back some 12 miles. Nonetheless, the Germans, led by the 7th, 12th, 17th, and 18th Panzer Divisions, crushed the twin mechanized corps in a massive armored battle lasting from July 6 to the July 11.[29] All told, the Red Army lost 832 tanks in just four days of combat. The scope of the defeat suffered by the Red Army's best-equipped formations shook both Timoshenko and Zhukov.[30] By July 13, the Germans had destroyed or taken 4,799 tanks; 9,427 artillery pieces, mortars, and anti-tank guns; and 1,777 frontline airplanes.[31]

Germany's leaders euphorically reacted to Barbarossa's initial success. Halder essentially declared victory in his July 3 diary entry. Hitler's confidence in victory prompted him to order economic efforts redirected in favor of the Luftwaffe and Kriegsmarine so that Germany could prepare for war against the United States and Britain. By July 20, Army Group Center's Panzer armies had formed the loose outline of another massive, albeit incredibly porous, Kessel just west of Smolensk, ostensibly trapping the Soviet 16th, 19th, and

20th Armies. Nevertheless, the cutoff off Soviet armies put up fierce resistance. It would actually take almost an entire month and 23 of Army Group Center's infantry divisions, along with most of its Panzer and motorized divisions, just to close and liquidate the pocket.[32]

The Soviet leadership ordered relentless attempts to break through to the trapped armies. At the same time, the Red Army threw up new defensive positions farther east. Smolensk was a vital objective, given its role as an important transportation hub on the highway from Minsk to Moscow. Moreover, it sat astride the 50-mile land bridge between the headwaters of the Dnieper and Dvina Rivers, the last great natural barriers before Moscow, still 300 miles to the east. For his part, Bock poorly prosecuted the pocket's formation, and exacerbated the incomplete prisoner haul, when he had ordered both the Third Panzer Army and Ninth Army to track far north in an effort to maintain a tighter front with Army Group North. Guderian made the German problems worse when he struck east without effectively closing the pocket, or providing even a modicum of assistance to the infantry tasked with reducing bypassed Soviet defensive positions. For instance, the city of Mogilev had been turned into a fortress defended by the four rifle divisions from the 13th Rifle Army. They would not surrender until July 27, having held off the German infantry for 17 days. Moreover, Russian snipers and ambushers struck from buildings, forested areas, and even cornfields, inflicting a steady stream of casualties on the German infantry and support units advancing behind the fast-moving Panzers.[33] In addition, near Smolensk, Timoshenko had deployed five armies, including Rokossovsky's new command, the 16th Army, all seeking to crush the German forces and break through to the trapped Soviet armies. Rokossovsky actually maintained contact with the trapped Soviet armies for nearly a week and, along with the efforts made by his comrades, helped 100,000 men escape German captivity.[34] Nonetheless, on August 5, resistance within the pocket finally ended. Another 348,000 Soviet troops marched into German captivity. Again, vast quantities of equipment and munitions had been lost, including over 3,000 tanks and 3,000 guns. That said, Army Group Center had paid a heavy price for engineering this success.

ARMY GROUP NORTH'S INITIAL MONTH OF CAMPAIGNING

On June 22, and striking from eastern Prussia, Army Group North, supported by the relatively small Luftflotte 1, advanced quickly into the Soviet Union and toward Leningrad—over 450 miles to the northeast. Leeb's command found initial success despite the fact that the Soviet Northwest Front, led by General Fedor Kuznetsov, included two of the Red Army's powerful mechanized corps. Moreover, Kuznetsov enjoyed a series of river barriers to aid his defense, a defense further enhanced by the Baltic's narrow defensive front. Kuznetsov also could rely on the Northern Front and Soviet Baltic Fleet's presence in support. Responsible for defending an immense geographic space, from Murmansk and the Arctic Circle south along the Finnish border to Leningrad and the surrounding *oblast* region, the Northern Front included 404,470 men, 7,901 guns and mortars, 1,543 operational tanks, and 1,216 operational aircraft.[35] In addition the 119,645-man Soviet Baltic Fleet included two battleships, two cruisers, 21 destroyers and destroyer leaders, seven destroyer escorts, 68 submarines, and numerous other ships supported by 595 operational aircraft and 2,189 guns and mortars deployed as coastal artillery.[36] All told, and though the Northern Front had to contend with Finnish forces and German forces in Finland, the Northwestern Front had perhaps the strongest proximate supporting assets of any front along the borders of the western Soviet Union. That said, working against its chances was the front's relatively small size in comparison to its peers, with Kuznetsov's command numbering 369,000 men.

The Northwestern Front quickly proved no match for the 641,000 men in the 16th Army, 18th Army, and 4th Panzer Group with Colonel General Erich Hoepner's 4th Panzer Group containing the 41st Corps, under Colonel General Hans Reinhardt, and the 56th Corps, under the talented Colonel General Erich von Manstein. That said, in spite of enjoying superb leadership, because of the armaments procurement decisions made in previous years, the 4th Panzer Army had rolled into the Soviet Union equipped largely with obsolete tanks and a mismatch of French and Czech equipment.[37] Therefore, when elements of the 6th Panzer Division collided with the Soviet 2nd Tank Division of the 3rd Mechanized Corps on Barbarossa's second day, it was to the German tankers' great concern that the Red Army's leadership had liberally equipped the Soviet 2nd Tank Division with T-34s and the colossal KV-1 heavy tank. With their powerful 76-mm guns and 110-mm-thick frontal armor, the Soviet KV-1s could knock out and stand impervious to almost any armor that the German army fielded in 1941. Rumbling forward on June 24, the Soviet tanks crushed everything in their path—in particular pounding the German 114th Motorized Infantry Regiment. Only the concentrated fire from German 88-mm anti-aircraft guns firing armor-piercing ammunition destroyed the mammoth Russian tanks, though some enterprising German soldiers found that five anti-tank mines, combined into one charge, could do the trick as well. Yet despite such hurdles, the veteran German units decimated the Soviet 3rd and 12th Mechanized Corps as the 1st and 6th Panzer Divisions were able to concentrate their efforts against the spread out Soviet attacks. The Northwestern Front's 12th Mechanized Corps alone had seen its tank strength drop in a single week from 690 on the eve of Barbarossa to a mere 50 in running condition. On June 26, Manstein's corps, led by the 8th Panzer Division and German Special Forces, captured crossings over the 300-meter-wide Dvina River at the town of Dunaburg, having traveled 180 miles in only four days. The 8th Panzer Division then fought off in rapid succession attacks from the battered Soviet

21st Mechanized Corps, retreating northeast, and the 27th Army, moving up to reinforce the Soviet defensive front but shocked to find the German army already across the Dvina River; with a yawing roughly 80 mile gap in Soviet lines having opened up near the borders of Army Group North and Center.

Although during Barbarossa's first week Leeb's men had not engineered any massive encirclements, Army Group North's goal, Leningrad, was geographic. Thus, it should have freed Leeb to conduct a quintessential blitzkrieg operation. In such an operation, the goal was not a wedge-and-pocket battle of annihilation but, instead, a deep operational thrust that would use sheer momentum to protect its flanks and deny the Red Army the time to organize a stout defense. Accordingly, the 4th Panzer Group's initial successes had opened up a golden opportunity for Army Group North to advance to Leningrad's southern approaches in one fell swoop, unhinge the Soviet defenses in the Baltic states, and blow through prime defensive terrain that would otherwise have posed a nightmarish obstacle. Nonetheless, Halder, Brauchitsch, and Leeb, in failing to fully comprehend the importance speed of movement and action meant to mobilize mechanized warfare, conservatively argued that it would be better to wait for Reinhardt's Panzer Corps and the 16th Army's infantry. Each lagged 60 to 90 miles behind Manstein. This was in spite of the fact that the only Soviet armies in the immediate area were either tied down fighting the German 16th and 18th Armies or en route to the front and temporarily out of position for much of anything else.

For its part, Reinhardt's Panzer Corps then secured a second crossing site over the Dvina at Jekabpils on the June 28, but he too was ordered to await infantry support. Hitler deferred to OKH and Leeb.[38] For his part, Leeb was a field marshal who, though handicapped by the OKH's less-than-thorough planning for Barbarossa and at times questionable orders, particularly in regard to Halder's virtual obsession with Moscow, was nonetheless out of his element directing a Panzer group. At repeated times throughout Barbarossa Leeb's lack of such experience would undermine Army Group North's efforts as he repeatedly failed to concentrate 4th Panzer Group's efforts or take advantage of opportunities when handed to him; with perhaps no greater mistake coming than in the six-day halt Leeb had imposed on Hoepner's spearheads on the Dvina.

Nevertheless, on July 9, Pskov fell; Army Group North and Luftflotte 1 had not only decimated the Northwestern Front but were only 150 miles from Leningrad. Already, the Soviet armies in the Baltic had lost 90,000 men, 1,000 tanks; 4,000 artillery pieces, mortars, and anti-tank guns; and 1,000 frontline aircraft. Soviet aircraft losses were such that Luftflotte 1 had been able to provide a constant presence over the battlefields, helping to smooth a path for Leeb, whose armies had virtually swept the Baltic states free of Soviet troops in just three weeks. The Red Army's defense had stiffened, bolstered by marshy, densely forested terrain and major rivers cutting north to south across the German line of advance. All the same, on July 14, advance elements from the 6th Panzer Division captured one of two German bridgeheads over the Luga River, the last remaining river barrier before Leningrad, only 60 miles east of the 6th Panzer's positions. Nevertheless, subsequent strong Soviet counterattacks against the German 16th Army contributed to the failure to exploit the bridgeheads. The Northwestern Front's new chief of staff, General N. F. Vatutin, in what would become a hallmark of his superlative wartime leadership, repeatedly used aggressive counterstrokes to sap German momentum. In one instance, Manstein's powerful command, having been redirected south to help fight off further Soviet counterstrokes, fought for its life near Soltsy with its spearhead, the 8th Panzer Division, temporarily encircled and ultimately losing half its tanks in a vicious fight against the Soviet 10th Mechanized Corps and 16th and 22nd Rifle Corps.[39]

Stepping back from Army Group North's effort and examining Barbarossa's overall progress, by mid-July the German campaign appeared to be a phenomenal success. Nevertheless, as each German Army Group rolled deeper into the Soviet Union, ominous cracks had begun appearing in the previously dominant German war machine. Moreover, and contrary not only to initial German expectations but also to the entire military foundation of Barbarossa's premise, the Red Army had not collapsed. Instead, it was inflicting ever increasing losses on German units hard pressed to replace men or machines. Consequently, the Wehrmacht entered uncharted territory as July 1941 wound down. Barbarossa had already become the longest continuously running campaign that the German army waged during World War II, and a campaign whose initial plans and assumptions had become obsolete within weeks of battle being joined, as is so often the case. Therefore, how Germany reacted to the adversity confronting its eastern armies during the summer of 1941 would play a crucial role in determining whether it could secure its hegemony over Europe—but not for the reasons typically advanced today.

THE GERMAN ARMY'S ACHILLES' HEEL
AND HITLER'S STRATEGIC DILEMMA

By early August 1941, the Ostheer, or German army in the east, had taken approximately 1 million prisoners of war. These huge prisoner hauls dominate most contemporary accounts of Barbarossa's first months. Nonetheless, the effort involved in reducing each pocket had not only broken up Barbarossa's operational tempo, and undermined its time lines, but also inflicted a steady toll of casualties on the German army—especially those units involved in pocket-clearing operations.[40] Even worse, as the front increased in breadth, from just over 700 miles to 1,000 miles, German manpower declined. Army Group South fought short 53,000 men, Army Group Center short 51,000 men, and Army Group North short 28,000 men.[41]

Shortages at the front proved emblematic of a larger manpower problem hampering a German armaments industry sputtering along under tremendous raw material deficiencies. As a result, the logistical foundation for Barbarossa, never strong to begin with, had become strained to a near breaking point-with the Red Army's continual resistance and the Wehrmacht's overstretched lines of communication only making things even worse. Meanwhile, as the Wehrmacht burned through fuel at three times its pre-invasion estimates, Soviet oil fields in the Caucasus and a rich bounty of agricultural and industrial assets in the Ukraine beckoned east of its frontline positions. Hitler seems to have recognized the issue, yet he allowed Halder to indulge his obsession with Moscow; and the idea of sapping the Red Army's "vital strength."[42] Although this book does not seek to discuss an idealized approach to fighting a war that had ended half a century ago, the Red Army's resistance and the corresponding lack of a Soviet political collapse meant that as early as August of 1941, the OKH and the OKW (Oberkommando der Wehrmacht, or High Command of the Armed Forces) had to have realized that Barbarossa's original "house-of-cards" assumptions at a minimum stood on decidedly shaky ground, and, in all likelihood, had simply failed to survive the initial weeks of the campaign. To that end, Hitler and his high command debated Barbarossa's direction. In short, the dispute at that time—and the after-the-fact historical arguments based on this debate—have coalesced around two separate viewpoints. Each viewpoint advanced an operational component arguably leading to strategic success.

The first argument doubles down on one of Barbarossa's key assumptions, namely, that the Red Army could be decisively defeated in the field, and posits German troops roughly 220 miles west of the Soviet capital should have massed for one colossal assault on Moscow, ostensibly to draw in the Red Army for one decisive battle of annihilation. Strategically, according to Halder and those in agreement with this view, operational success would have meant not only that Moscow would fall but also that such a fall would have split western Soviet Union in two. Among other things, this would have made Leningrad's defense virtually impossible and potentially led to the collapse of communist rule. At that time, however, no less than today, a strong counterargument postulated that a German thrust on Moscow was fraught with enormous risks as well as questionable in what it may accomplish if for no other reason than the Red Army's regenerative ability, thus calling into question the entire premise of the German army being able to decisively annihilate the Red Army. This has led to a second position.

The second primary argument also featured an operational move leading to strategic success and was also based in part on the actual dispositions of Army Groups Center and South eight weeks into Barbarossa. On August 20, 1941, Army Group Center's easternmost divisions held the Yelna salient just southeast of the Mink-Smolensk-Moscow highway. There, these same divisions were fighting for their very lives against incessant Soviet counterattacks. The remainder of Army Group Center's right flank fell off sharply to the southwest. Meanwhile, roughly 360 miles due south of the Yelna salient sat Army Group South's easternmost divisions at Kremenchug on the Dnieper River. The remainder of Army Group South's left flank trailed off several hundred miles to its northwest. In between these easternmost points of the two German Army Groups existed a vast triangular-shaped geographic space. This space contained the majority of the Soviet army's in the Ukraine, roughly one and a half million men concentrated near Kiev.[43]

Given the positions held by the Soviet Southwestern Front, the second great argument of the time (and since) posited that an attack on Moscow invited disaster unless the German army first dealt with the Soviet Southwestern Front located near Kiev. Moreover, annihilating the substantial Russian armies opposing Army Group South could accomplish much the same in terms of diminishing the Red Army's field strength, as advocated by those pushing for an immediate thrust on Moscow. This leads to the viable strategic option that would have emerged from such an operational success. By eliminating the bulk of the Red Army in the Ukraine, German forces could then redirect their primary effort away from a plan that had already failed to survive contact with the enemy, and, instead seek to seize the crucial economic resources provided, in particular, by the Donbas region and the Caucasus. Hitler was the primary proponent of both aspects of the second argument, one that not only would have offered the opportunity to undermine the Red Army's ability to wage a war of maneuver but also would have immeasurably bolstered the Wehrmacht's concomitant own such ability; all while providing the Third Reich with the resources necessary to cement hegemony over Europe and wage global war. Regardless, the first argument has carried far more weight since the war ended. Nonetheless, a close reading of recent scholarship seems to demonstrate that it appears to have been the far weaker position. The following explains why (and thus, not inconsequently), had Germany vigorously followed up on any operational success that may have flowed from the second option, it may have made its position on the European continent close to impregnable by the end of 1942.

Most German generals involved in the decision-making process during the summer of 1941, including Brauchitsch, Halder, Bock, and Guderian, argued that Germany should have moved on Moscow in August 1941. According to them, and rightfully so in many respects, Moscow represented Stalin's power geographically, economically, politically, and militarily. Several facts, however, challenge these arguments and the postwar "if only the generals had been listened to" arguments dominating the counterfactual literature on the war. Most important is that Army Group Center was not simply sitting unmolested near Smolensk, waiting only for the order to march east. In fact, Bock's Army Group fought against extraordinary pressure brought by the Red Army. This came via repeated and massive counterstrokes that had initially sought to blunt the German advance and rescue some of the Soviet armies caught in the Smolensk pocket, and then had continued with a relentless intensity as the Red Army aggressively sought to drive Germany from the western approaches to Moscow. For just one example regarding the impact that the Red Army's counterpunches had on the German army, we need to examine what transpired from July into September of 1941 near the Russian city of Yelnia.

Late in July, the German 10th Panzer Division and Das Reich SS Motorized Division stood at Army Group Center's vanguard and had settled into a strategically important salient centered around the town of Yelnia. Yelnia offered a superb springboard for launching further attacks toward Moscow. The town sat on high ground and included a crossing over the Desna River as well as an east-to-west rail station. Unfortunately, for the 10th Panzer Division and Das Reich, Stalin, Zhukov, and Timoshenko realized the implications from these prime German positions and relentlessly sought to eliminate the German salient. Nonetheless, the German Panzer and motorized divisions held off seemingly never-ending Soviet assaults. By August 3, however, Guderian had thrown in his only remaining reserves, and both he and Bock screamed for reinforcements. Finally, German infantry, released from finishing off the Smolensk pocket, moved up on August 5, allowing the exhausted German Panzer and motorized divisions to withdraw, but only after having taken a pounding that was emblematic of the larger damage the Red Army was inflicting upon the German army's premier formations.

In turn, Timoshenko wheeled his Western Front farther north to attack the German Ninth Army, and Zhukov's Reserve Front battered away at the beleaguered German infantry now holding the Yelnia salient. The bodies piled up on both sides. From August 30 to September 8 alone, Zhukov and Timoshenko coordinated counterstrokes launched by three Soviet Fronts: the Bryansk, the Reserve, and the Western. Although German losses were heavy and Soviet forces showed initiative, including a daring raid by the Soviet 50th and 53rd Cavalry Divisions, the Soviet casualties remained stunningly high—well over 50 percent on the Western Front alone.[44] The Soviet counterattacks against Bock's armies cost the Red Army dearly. Between July 10 and September 10, the Red Army suffered 486,171 permanent losses in and around the Smolensk pocket and lost 1,348 tanks, 9,290 artillery pieces and mortars, and 903 combat aircraft.[45] The battle for Smolensk, a largely forgotten battle on the Eastern Front (at least the second phase, when the Germans fought for their lives while on the defensive), dwarfs nearly every battle fought in western Europe during the war. Moreover, by September 5, the Red Army had forced the Germans to retreat from the Yelnia salient, the first operational-level withdrawal conducted by the German army during World War II.[46] Overlooking the intensity of the struggle near Smolensk lends credence to the theory that in August 1941, Moscow was sitting ripe for the picking before Army Group Center and bolsters the incorrect beliefs of most of the German General Staff, and its highest-ranking field commanders, that the Red Army could be bested in a classic Prussian battle of annihilation.

A third solution to the Third Reich's manpower problem correctly maintains, both then and today, that if German troops had acted as liberators, then Germany would have greatly simplified the task inherent in pacifying and occupying the western Soviet Union. Hitler rejected such ideas—one of the supreme blunders of World War II but also one entirely consistent with the underpinning political and ideological rationale for a war that the German right wing had been clamoring to wage for over the better part of the previous half century. The subject of this book, however, is not the enormous crimes perpetrated by the Third Reich. Numerous historians have amply documented not only the Third Reich's crimes but also the Wehrmacht's central role in enabling and actively participating in some of the greatest horrors seen in history.

Nevertheless, one point concerning the genocide initiated once Barbarossa began particularly stands out as salient in debunking the argument that following French defeat, the Third Reich would have realistically sought to pursue anything other than an eastern European–centric political, economic, and military strategy. Simply put, policymakers and other elites in the Third Reich supported Hitler's attempt to forge Lebensraum in eastern Europe. Historian Omer Bartov argues convincingly that ranking German officers participated in large part because they shared Hitler's beliefs and dreams regarding a greater Germania ethnically cleansed of Jews and Slavs.[47] Farther down the chain of command, historian Bernhard Kroener has demonstrated that younger German combat officers "identified much more strongly than the older officer generation with social Darwinist ideas of struggle as a form of existence."[48] Finally, the work of American historian Stephen G. Fritz confirmed the impact that virulently racist propaganda had on the average German soldier: "There existed among the troops in Russia such a striking level of agreement with the Nazi regime's view of the Bolshevik enemy and the sort of treatment that should be dealt them that many soldiers willingly participate in murderous actions."[49] For instance, by April 1, 1942, the German army had taken approximately 3.6 million Soviet prisoners of war. In turn, the German army, the SS, the SD, and other security organizations had killed off approximately 2.25 million men, including 600,000 shot outright.[50] Given the historical context summarized above, there was little to no chance that Germany's leaders were about to back off the ideological underpinnings of Barbarossa. The problem was that, by August 1941, this had meant Soviet soldiers, having learned that surrender meant death, often tenaciously resisted against the German invaders.[51]

During Barbarossa's first six weeks, the Wehrmacht had sustained 213,301 casualties, while a mere 47,000 replacements arrived to replace these losses.[52] Meanwhile, German equipment losses climbed ever higher. Regardless of combat losses, armor and other vehicles broke down with a maddening frequency in the summer's dust and heat. In addition, fuel, ammunition, and other critical supplies failed to reach the combat arms in a timely manner. Competent wartime leadership not only is aware of the enemy's strengths and weaknesses but also addresses its own internal weaknesses. The greatest German strength lay in its armored and motorized formations, units that had regularly savaged the Red Army's own mechanized formations. The German army's core, however, was its infantry, and the army's greatest weakness resided in its inherent manpower inadequacies.

This book focuses on analyzing actual historical events to demonstrate how closely Germany came to securing the European continent for National Socialist goals, and why Germany ultimately failed. Nevertheless, it is worth examining two options available to Germany during Barbarossa that could have alleviated much of its problems and that also demonstrate how much, at times, Germany's failures stemmed from internal decision making. Simply put, once the Soviet Union demonstrated that it was not going to simply roll over and die, Hitler and the OKH could have either immediately gone for the economic resources needed to fight a longer war, or consolidated part of the vast eastern European front to ease the burden on the German army's overworked and overstretched infantry divisions. To that end, Army Group North's success during Barbarossa's first month had actually offered the OKH the opportunity to accomplish the latter. Capturing Leningrad, the fourth-largest city in Europe in 1940 and the source of 10 percent of Soviet industrial output, and then shutting down Army Group North's axis of attack for the overall betterment of the German strategic position would have not only denied tremendous resources to the Soviet economy and secured Leningrad's port for efficiently delivering supplies to the front but also released Hoepner's Panzer and motorized divisions to assist the other army groups, all while the remainder of Leeb's command consolidated the German left flank among the dense marshy forests and swamps and countless lakes and rivers crossing the region.

During the summer of 1941, and regardless of Hitler's and the OKH's decisions regarding Leningrad, we can see the bankruptcy in German strategic planning defining the handicaps afflicting Germany's entire war effort. For instance, by late July, the OKH knew that the Red Army was fighting as hard as ever and was hardly evincing signs of collapse.[53] Yet Halder and the OKH's intelligence apparatus continued to underrate the Red Army's defensive strength and regenerative capacity to such an extent that Halder believed not only that the Red Army could be decisively defeated in the field, but also that Moscow could be taken and that the oil fields in Baku could be reached as early as November. This ignored the Red Army's incessant hammering into Army Group Center's front lines near Smolensk, as well as the reality that Army Group Center's struggles in eliminating the Smolensk pocket had proven the rule rather than the exception. Hitler explained to Halder and Army Group Center's leading officers

that Moscow was not as important as seizing the "vital areas" necessary to building Germany's economic strength at the Soviet Union's expense, including the
Ukraine, Leningrad, and the Caucasus. Halder, however, stuck to his guns.[54] All
told, in spite of the obvious need for a substantial revision in plans, the result of
the ongoing debate between Hitler and his military leadership would be that the
July–August Führer Directive Nos. 33 and 34 and their subsequent supplements
set up a situation whereby Hitler and the OKH sought to have it all: Moscow,
Leningrad, the Ukraine, and the Caucasus. Army Group Center's potent, but
fraying, Panzer groups would first be directed north and south to assist in taking
Leningrad and clearing out the Soviet army's massed near Kiev, with Moscow in
play as the primary objective following those operations. Halder had thus won a
pyrrhic victory that, unbeknownst at the time, played a key role in Germany's
defeat. It is entirely possible that had Halder acquiesced to Hitler's wishes for putting economic goals first (since it was highly unlikely that the reverse would have
happened), the Wehrmacht may have turned the southern Soviet Union into a
reservoir of raw materials for guaranteeing the German economy's self-
sufficiency and the Third Reich's stranglehold on Europe.

Consistent with Hitler's insistence on putting Leningrad and the Ukraine
first, OKH ordered Army Group Center to dispatch its 39th Motorized
Corps and 57th Panzer Corps to Army Group North, essentially Hoth's 3rd
Panzer Group, to assist with the strike toward Leningrad; already bolstered
by the arrival of the Luftwaffe's elite 8th Fliegerkorps and its seven Gruppen
of ground attack aircraft and fighters. Problematically, however, Halder's
foot-dragging, as well as delays imposed by the fierce fighting near
Smolensk, would mean that these two powerful corps, which could have
proven effective if working in a concentrated fashion alongside Hoepner's
Panzer group, which in and of itself and to date had hardly operated in a concentrated fashion during the campaign, would arrive independently and subsequently operated mostly in a disjointed fashion; all in direct contrast to
what was to come near Kiev in September.

On August 8, Leeb's spearheads attacked from their bridgeheads over the
Luga River, finally battering through the Russian positions four days later.
Poor leadership and counterattacks from the Soviet 11th, 27th, 34th, and
48th Armies meant that Leeb, instead of exploiting the breakthrough, redeployed the 3rd Motorized Division and Waffen-SS Totenkopf Motorized
Division to rip into the exposed flanks of the Soviet armies threatening
Busch's 16th Army near Staraya Russa. Although by August 25 Manstein's
men had captured 18,000 men and seized or destroyed 200 tanks and 300 guns
and mortars, this was a largely ephemeral victory compared to the larger
rewards that could have been had in moving more decisively on Leningrad.[55]
At the same time, between August 21 and September 9, the German 18th
Army cleared Estonia, captured 9,774 men, and drove the Soviet 8th Army
into a slim bridgehead along the Baltic coast at Oranienbaum. Meanwhile,

reinforcements from the 3rd Panzer Group had linked up with Army Group North after decimating the Soviet 22nd Army near Velikie Luki, taking 30,000 more Soviet prisoners of war. At the same time the German 16th Army, approaching Demyansk and the Valdai Heights, encircled another 35,000 Soviet soldiers and 117 tanks. All told, the reinforced Army Group North had captured tens of thousands of men and hundreds more tanks and guns with the Soviet 11th, 27th, and 34th Armies alone losing over 128,000 men during the final three weeks of August, but, once again, decisions made by OKH and Leeb as well as the Red Army's efforts, had taken the steam from Army Group North's drive on Leningrad. Just as importantly, and as the advance had slowed, Army Group North's casualties had increased. For instance, the German 30th Infantry Division had suffered 1,359 casualties in the freewheeling first month of operations, but during the grind of the campaign's second month had seen its casualties more than double to 2,947 while it had been forced to slug through prepared Soviet defensive positions and fend off ever-increasing counterattacks from Soviet reserve armies granted time to assemble deep within Russia.

In the meantime, a raw materials shortage hung grimly over a sputtering German economy. Oil was far from Germany's only economic problem. Another coal and steel crisis meant that the German army faced its lowest monthly steel allotment since the spring of 1938 at the exact moment that it desperately needed to replace the increasing toll of lost and worn-out equipment in Russia. Despite the fact that the German economy was teetering on the edge of disaster, Hitler's decision to fortify Army Group South's drive in the Ukraine, according to many since, represented for Germany a clear turning point in the war.

The concept of a single turning point as determinative in a series of events as complicated as World War II is difficult to swallow. Moreover, the idea that crushing the Soviet armies assembled in the Ukraine was inherently wrong is even more difficult to believe. In reality, once the Red Army survived Barbarossa's initial blow, the plan, as it existed on June 22, was done. Only after considering the Red Army's costly but aggressive defensive stance can one even think to engage in an in-depth look at a German decision-making process that failed to address the reality that the Red Army was acting in a decidedly different fashion than had been expected, seemed to replace immense losses with ease, was nowhere near collapse, was inflicting punishing losses on Germany's armies, and thus was confounding a German officer corps virtually bred to believe in the primacy of the battle of annihilation.

THE RED ARMY RELOADS

Stalin's initial reaction to the invasion had been to deny it. When that was no longer possible, he gave orders completely out of touch with reality as he mindlessly issued commands to attack and carry the battle off Soviet soil. It even seems that Stalin finally recognized his sheer ineptitude as a leader and was as angry at himself as anyone. "Lenin founded our state," he muttered, "and we've fucked it up."[56] By June 29, Stalin, having slept no more than three or four hours early on the morning that the war began and having worked virtually nonstop since the war's first morning, left Moscow for his dacha outside the capital after reducing Zhukov to tears over the state of the war.[57] Stalin ended up returning to Moscow the next day after being convincing to do so by Beria, Molotov, and much of the Politburo. On his return, Stalin went back to work, and in spite of continuing to make significant military mistakes subsequently put in place perhaps the most powerful command apparatus in the world.

At the top, or grand strategic, level, Stalin organized the State Defense Committee (GKO) comprising Beria, Malenkov, Molotov, Voroshilov, and Stalin—later joined by Voznesenski, Mikoyan, and Kaganovich in February 1942.[58] Stalin served as chairman. Just under the GKO (actually not formed until June 30), Stalin, on June 23, formed the Stavka of the Supreme High Command as a single-body military war command operating at the strategic level. Stavka included Stalin at the top, Timoshenko as the presiding officer, Zhukov as chief of the General Staff, Navy Minister Admiral Kuznetsov, Molotov, and Marshals Voroshilov and Budenny, with Shaposhnikov joining on July 10.[59] Under the overall leadership of Stalin, this single organization stood responsible for directing the Soviet military effort. Unlike the confusion regarding the German OKW and OKH, little doubt clouded Stavka's place in the Red Army's hierarchy.[60] The Red Army's General Staff, essentially tasked with operational-level decisions and coordinating the activities of the fronts, was folded into Stavka.[61] The Red Army's General Staff played a critical role in solidifying the command process at the operational level. For example, General Staff "representatives" would be sent to the front to help plan and direct critical campaigns. Furthermore, staff representatives would also rotate between performing traditional General Staff advisory functions in regard to assisting the local front commanders and would take over individual fronts as needed.

Stalin also set about securing the Soviet interior. He ordered the NKVD to lock down Moscow and the rear areas leading up to and including the operational areas at the front. A heavy emphasis was on keeping the Soviet population in line and under control. In addition, on June 27, the Politburo ordered the evacuation of all state financial reserves, precious metal reserves, and valuable works of art deep into Russia's interior. On July 5, Stalin ordered the Soviet state archives removed from Moscow and sent a further 600 miles east of the Soviet capital. Stalin also effectively manipulated the German invasion not into a war against the Soviet state, a state for which the people justifiably harbored little love, but into a patriotic war to defend the motherland. In a radio message on July 3, 1941, Stalin wrapped his regime in Russian nationalism and defending the motherland as he acknowledged a shared sense of crisis.[62] Stalin made the war his nation's focus in direct contrast to Hitler's attempts to minimize the war's impact on the German domestic population. Stalin also ordered redoubled propaganda efforts to boost the troops' morale. Over 1,000 writers and artists were embedded in the Red Army to provide carefully crafted accounts of military success. Four hundred would die in the intense combat at the front.[63] To further bolster morale at the front, on September 18, 1941, Stalin ordered "Guards" units to be created from units that were performing well in battle.

In addition, and more importantly, Stalin ordered nearly every western factory ripped up and placed onto railcars for transport deep into the Russian interior to the east, and out of German grasp. Those industrial assets that could not be moved would be destroyed in a scorched-earth program. By November 1941, 1,523 factories had been transferred to the Ural Mountains, Siberia, and other locations east of the Volga River.[64] Furthermore, both the United States and Great Britain offered significant economic help, via a massive expansion in the Lend-Lease program to the Soviet war effort. However, the American extension of aid to the Soviet Union came about only after a fierce domestic political battle whereby leading Republicans, such as Herbert Hoover and Robert A. Taft, argued against it on ideological grounds.[65] Others, such as former U.S. ambassador to Moscow William C. Bullitt, were more fatalistic than blinded by ideology and believed that the Soviet Union was doomed no matter what the Allies did.[66]

Churchill also doubted Soviet chances, as did many in his military high command, particularly the chief of the British General Staff, John Dill who believed that the Red Army was almost finished. Nevertheless, they pragmatically sought to help regardless of their beliefs.[67] The British even sought to add to Allied power; by negotiating the release of Polish prisoners of war held in Stalin's gulags, ostensibly to form a new Polish army. Of course, Stalin did nothing to help transport the Polish prisoners. Thus, so began an epic journey, as the emaciated survivors from the gulags, in some cases walking thousands of miles on foot, in August 1941 began assembling to form a new Polish army—tens of thousands died before ever arriving at their assembly camps in southern Soviet Union. At the same time, Stalin extended a peace feeler to the Germans that was offered through the Bulgarian embassy. Stalin offered up Soviet territory, a move that Molotov likened to "a possible second Brest-Litovsk Treaty."[68] Meanwhile, as Stalin accepted British assistance and tentatively wooed the Germans, his army urgently reorganized.

The Soviet leadership mobilized millions of men, completely reorganized the Red Army, created strategic reserves, and reconstituted shattered combat units. Stalin crucially embraced the value in maintaining strong reserves behind the front, providing critical support to his army even as it endured frightful losses. Simplicity served as the order of the day. The Red Army stripped its combat arms of superfluous units and equipment and then refitted them for limited goals. Stavka eliminated rifle and mechanized corps and replaced them with smaller streamlined divisions and brigades that were easier for inexperienced commanders to control. The Red Army parceled out its dwindling tank reserves into brigades or to assist the infantry.

In addition, the Red Army increased the infantry's firepower. It focused on providing ample quantities of cheaply produced but reliable automatic weapons and heavy weapons. Submachine guns designed by weapons manufacturer Shpagin primarily filled the cheap firepower role; the PPsh submachine gun packed a significant short-range punch with its large magazine and became a prized trophy sought by Soviet and German soldiers alike. As for heavy weapons, the Red Army also equipped its infantry with inexpensively produced mortars that efficiently provided additional firepower at the tactical level. Rockets served as another new simple, low-cost, but effective weapon deployed to supplement standard artillery batteries. The Katyusha multiple rocket launching system consisted of a truck with a frame on the truck bed set up to launch a salvo of 192 powerful rockets, each of which weighed 120 pounds. One salvo could saturate a piece of real estate 300 yards deep and 400 yards wide. The weapon made up for being more inaccurate than conventional artillery by providing the Red Army with inexpensively delivered firepower in great quantities that could cover a large target area. Such weapons proved crucial to the success of an army with neither the time nor the means to produce highly trained soldiers absorbed into ranks of crack combat veterans, as occurred in the German army.

LENINGRAD AND KIEV: THE GERMAN ARMY ON THE FLANKS

Meanwhile, as Stalin reorganized, Army Group North's assault on Leningrad had run into the teeth of the city's defenses. In addition, and even worse for the Germans, the Finns had refused to advance past their old borders only 18 miles from Leningrad's northern city limits, thus allowing Soviet reinforcements to concentrate to Leningrad's south and southwest. Nevertheless, on August 24, the Germans cut the rail lines linking Leningrad with Moscow. German forces also encircled Tallinn, and when the Red Army's Banner Baltic Fleet attempted to break out (only 33 of 67 ships made it to safety), Luftflotte I destroyed most of the rest.[69] On September 4, German artillery began hitting Leningrad. On September 8, the Germans completed Leningrad's encirclement with the capture of the Siniavino Heights and the town of Shlissel'burg on Lake Ladoga. On September 9, Reinhardt's Panzer corps began the final assault on Leningrad, penetrating to within six miles of the city before KV-1 backed counterattacks stopped the 1st Panzer Division on the Pulkovo Heights.

Further bolstering the Red Army's defensive efforts was the arrival of Zhukov to replace Voroshilov in command of the Leningrad Front. Zhukov promptly informed the commanders of the Soviet 42nd and 55th Armies defending Leningrad itself that if they retreated, they and their families would be shot. Moreover, as part of the bloody and relentless counterattacks he ordered up in and around the encirclement, Zhukov counterattacked the newly taken German positions on the Siniavino Heights—though failing to break through German lines and reach the city. Then, on September 15, as Leningrad's fate hung in the balance, Hitler ordered Army Group North to reinforce Army Group Center for the drive on Moscow. The opportunity to close out Barbarossa's northern axis of advance was lost.

The Soviet Leningrad Front had survived, albeit at great cost. From the 300,000 men whom it had initially put into the field, it had lost 116,316 as casualties from August 23 to September 30.[70] Four entire Soviet armies were trapped in Leningrad and the Oranienbaum salient—all told, 300,000 men. As for the Germans, Army Group North prepared a blockade of what had been the Soviet Union's second-largest city that would prove medieval in its barbarity. Over 1 million civilians would die of disease and starvation over the ensuing three years as Hitler sought to annihilate Leningrad. At the same time and outside the city, the Wehrmacht and Einsatzgruppen ruthlessly elim-inated the Jewish population in the Baltic states. In September, Army Group North and Einsatzgruppe A murdered 56,459 Jews, including 26,243 women and 15,112 children.[71] Meanwhile, at the opposite end of the front, Hitler's move on the Soviet armies in the Ukraine proved an operational tour de force, producing a success nearly unrivaled in modern military history.

Having turned his Panzer Group south, Guderian, in spite of leading a steadily weakening command due to its already significant losses from the campaign's first months, promptly sliced through the Soviet 40th Army and forced the 21st Army back toward Kiev. With the Red Army distracted by Guderian, Rundstedt shifted Kleist's Panzers to the Kremenchug bridgehead previously won by the 17th Army. On September 12, he launched Panzer Group 1 north to meet Guderian. The Red Army's local front commanders, Field Marshals Seymon Budenny and Kirponos, appealed repeatedly for Stalin's approval to withdraw. Stalin, proving to be his own worst enemy, ordered his commanders to remain in place and replaced those who disagreed with his decision. On September 15, the German armored pincers—Walther Model's 3rd Panzer Division from Guderian's Panzer group, and Hans Hube's 16th Panzer Division from Kleist's Panzer group—linked up 125 miles east of Kiev at Lokhvista.

The Panzers had formed the loose outer ring of an encirclement trapping the entire Southwestern Front, including the 5th, 21st, 26th, and 37th Armies, in a massive Kessel dwarfing even those achieved by Army Group Center in Barbarossa's first weeks. Between September 16 and September 19, German infantry began forming the critical inner ring of the pocket. Meanwhile, to the west, the German 6th Army finished taking Kiev and applied even greater pressure on the trapped Soviet army's. German close air support sowed destruction across the immense pocket, while decimating

Soviet counterattacks launched from outside the pocket.[72] By September 26, the pocket had collapsed. The victorious German armies, totaling one-third of Barbarossa's original number of divisions, had captured over 665,000 men, 884 tanks, and 3,718 guns from six Russian armies representing nearly the entire Southwestern Front and parts of the Southern and Central fronts. Neither before nor since has any army captured as many prisoners in a single battle. Total irrevocable Soviet losses reached 700,544 men from the 760,000 men in the region immediately surrounding Kiev prior to the disaster.[73] The defeat rippled through the very fabric of life, not only in the Ukraine—but also in Europe.

The SD fell on the 930,000 unprotected citizens in and near Kiev, including 50,000 Jews who had chosen to remain from the prewar population of 220,000. Major General Kurt Eberhard of Reichenau's 6th Army, the occupying authority in Kiev, and SS Colonel Paul Blobel's Sonderkommando 4a of Einsatzgruppe C, gathered the Jews from Kiev and the city suburbs. They then initiated a slaughter of epic proportions at the ravines of Babi Yar, murdering 33,771 human beings in total.[74] War and genocide in eastern Europe also provided political cover to Hitler for ramping up the killing at home. On October 15, 1941, Germany began deporting German, Austrian, and Czech Jews. Germany also began constructing gas chambers in a concentration camp in eastern Poland at Belzec. Although there is no evidence as to a single decision leading to the "final solution," the late summer and fall of 1941 bore witness to the Third Reich's march to the industrialized murder of human beings as the Wehrmacht drove ever farther east.

By the end of September 1941, the Wehrmacht had ripped to pieces four of the five Soviet Fronts defending the western Soviet borders on June 22. German Army Groups Center and South held a unified albeit lengthy front line for the first time during Barbarossa, and the Axis army outnumbered the Red Army in the western Soviet Union. The Ukraine stood ripe for the picking, yet Hitler and the OKH redirected the Wehrmacht's flagging efforts back to the front's center for a move on Moscow. Army Group South, instead of triumphantly charging through the massive hole in the Russian lines left by the Red Army's defeat near Kiev, was forced to give up two corps command staffs, one Panzer division, two motorized divisions, and seven infantry divisions to Army Group Center.[75] The delay in the German advance caused by the redistribution of forces, coupled with the 6th Army's need to finish digesting the Soviet pocket near Kiev, subsequently allowed the Red Army to marshal reserves near Kharkov. Accordingly, Army Group South's advance slowed, while further north Hitler's overstretched armies prepared another lunge east.

OPERATION TYPHOON

In Fuhrer Directive No. 35, dated September 6, 1941, Hitler ordered the attack on Moscow to proceed under the code name Typhoon. The attacking armies formed two primary pincers to meet the directive's primary goal for Army Group Center; destroying the Soviet armies massed west of Moscow. Notably, this directive said nothing of taking Moscow per se, but rather of advancing toward it, perhaps indicating Hitler's ambivalence in regard to Moscow as an objective. In the center of the front, Army Group Center's Panzer Group 4 and 4th Army would drive east and north. Guderian's Panzer Group 2 and the 2nd Army struck from farther south, and mostly independently, even though ostensibly once again part of Army Group Center. To the north, Army Group Center's Panzer Group 3 and 9th Army would drive east and south. Furthermore, beyond Army Group Center's area of operations, Hitler ordered that each of Barbarossa's three primary axes of advance be maintained regardless of the reality the logistical base simply did not exist to adequately support such extended simultaneous operations. Moreover, he did so even as he stripped from Army Group North five Panzer and two motorized divisions to further bolster Army Group Center, leaving Army Group North with only two Panzer and two motorized divisions from Schmidt's motorized corps.

Because of the losses sustained by both Army Group North and Army Group South, the army gathered for Typhoon represented on paper one of the most formidable assembled during the war. Bock's command fielded approximately half the German divisions on the Eastern Front (78 divisions), with two-thirds the available armor; 14 Panzer and eight motorized divisions, all organized into three armies, running north to south (the 9th, 4th, and 2nd); and three Panzer groups (the 3rd, 4th, and 2nd). Army Group Center put into the field 1,929,406 men and 14,000 artillery pieces supported by 1,400 aircraft. In particular, Army Group Center's artillery formations were in good shape, having suffered only light losses to date in the campaign. This massive force stood against Soviet armies numbering only two-thirds German strength. Moscow seemingly should have been doomed.

Nonetheless, the Ostheer, though killing, capturing, or maiming 2.8 million men from the Red Army by October 1, had also incurred 518,807 casualties: three times its losses during the six-week French campaign and the rough equivalent of Army Group North having been wiped out in its entirety. Almost one-third of the Ostheer's officer and noncommissioned officer strength had been lost by late September. For an army that relied on its veteran officers to exercise the creativity and flexibility at the tactical level necessary to defeat numerically larger foes, such losses simply could not be maintained. Meanwhile, Army Group Center's Panzer and motorized divisions fielded only about 1,300 tanks. In comparison, on June 22, Panzer Group 3 alone had fielded 840 tanks.[76] Total tank losses in all three Army Groups had reached 30 percent by the end of August with 23 percent more refitting behind the lines and temporarily unavailable.[77] In addition, because Hitler and the OKW were building new formations in western Europe, to guard against the unlikelihood of a British invasion, far too few replacements in men and machines were sent to Germany's eastern armies.

Moreover, beyond the failure to fully concentrate resources in the war's decisive theater were other long-standing problems undermining the German war effort—with logistics ranking as perhaps the most important. Because of the German eastern army's need to transfer armored and motorized units from its flanks to the center of the front, the fraying German logistical network was placed under even greater strain. The German Army Groups were lucky to get even half to two-thirds the daily supplies they needed. There were simply not enough trucks, horses, or aircraft to move supplies from railheads to the front as needed. In addition, the few rail lines in use hardly operated at peak efficiency. For instance, throughout the fall months, winter clothing piled up in Poland. This was because of a variety of reasons, including the slow rate of rail line conversion from the Soviet to the European gauge, bottlenecks far behind the front, and the high priority given to ammunition and fuel.[78] All this meant that Hitler's army prepared to launch a campaign with goals that included conquering an area the geographical size of France with an army, even after receiving reinforcements, smaller than its May 1940 predecessor and to boot all while operating on a logistical shoestring. To defend Moscow, Stalin had gathered 84 rifle divisions, one tank division, two motorized divisions, nine cavalry divisions, and other supporting units and arms, all part of Konev's Western Front, Eremenko's Bryansk Front, and Buddeny's Reserve Front. Unfortunately, these three fronts were spread across 600 miles of north-to-south real estate 200 miles west of Moscow and, even worse, fought from linear defensive positions ill suited to stopping German armor.

Typhoon opened on September 30 with Guderian's 2nd Panzer Group driving east from approximately 60 miles west of Kursk. Guderian split his army into two pincers. Each found immediate success against Eremenko's Bryansk Front, comprised of the 3rd, 13th, and 50th Armies with an additional five-division supporting group.[79] By October 3, part of Guderian's army had penetrated over 130 miles behind Soviet lines and approached Orel, a city of 120,000 and a key road and rail hub in the region. Meanwhile, the other part, in conjunction with the German 2nd Army's eight infantry divisions, distracted the Red Army and Stalin from Typhoon's main weight. On October 8, the 47th Panzer Corps' 18th Panzer Division met the 2nd Army near Bryansk. The two pincers had closed around the bulk of the Bryansk Front. Another 50,000 to 100,000 prisoners of war were taken, depending on the source. Nonetheless, eliminating the pocket once again took time and resources, and many of the surrounded Soviet divisions put up a stiff fight. Resistance within the pocket did not collapse until October 25, thus helping to break Guderian's operational tempo, while inflicting further losses on an army group rapidly running short of both men and machines.[80] Moreover, Guderian's spearheads, charging northeast even as the remainder of his army group crushed the pocket, also had run head-on into a Red Army that still remained Guderain's primary problem.

On the morning of October 6 and near Mtsensk, east of Orel, the 4th Tank Brigade from the 1st Guards Rifle Corps, liberally equipped with T-34s and KV-1s and commanded by Colonel Mikhail Katukov, a man who would go on to even greater fame as one of the Red Army's premier tank army commanders, dealt a sharp blow to the 4th Panzer Division. Although the Germans eventually prevailed, they lost 10 tanks against Soviet losses only half that in the tank-on-tank combat. On November 18, 1941, a special committee arrived at Guderian's headquarters to investigate. This committee included engineers from the Army Ordnance Department (Heereswaffenamt) as well as representatives from Daimler-Benz, Henschel, Krupp, and MAN.[81] The result would be to kick-start Germany's lethargic next-generation medium tank program and ultimately led to the Panzer V "Panther." Meanwhile, at the front, the 2nd Panzer Army quickly fell off schedule as the weather exacerbated the toll taken by the Soviet defensive effort. In other parts of the front, however, and where the Red Army lacked adequate reserves of modern armor, the German attackers won dramatically different results.

On October 2, Army Group Center's main assault opened. It shredded the Soviet defenses. Hoth's Panzer Group 3 had massed 560 tanks in two corps on a front only 50 miles wide and, in conjunction with Strauss's 9th Army, blew open the Soviet defensive front. Hoepner sent a third corps, comprised of one Panzer division and two motorized divisions, through yet another breach in the Soviet lines. Meanwhile, farther south, Panzer Group 4 also split the reserve from the Bryansk Front.[82] Again, Stalin had foolishly massed his men on thinly defended lines with few significant reserves. Again, German armor penetrated deep behind the Soviet lines, as far as 50 miles in just two days. The Russians gamely counterattacked. Konev's Western Front launched the 126th and 128th Tank Divisions, the 101st Motorized Division, and the 126th and 152nd Rifle Divisions into 3rd Panzer's flank.[83] Hoth's Panzer group shrugged it off, crossed the Dnieper, and compromised Konev's entire position.

On October 7, Hoth's Panzer Group 3 and Hoepner's Panzer Group 4, assisted by Kluge's 4th Army and Strauss's 9th Army, closed the jaws of a huge encirclement 135 miles west of Moscow near Vyazma. Tellingly for Barbarossa's ultimate fate, Hoth was forced to stop and await resupply. His tanks and men had already outrun overburdened German logisticians who were straining to support the advance. German infantry again bore the brunt of the effort involved in maintaining the pocket's perimeter, turning aside repeated human wave attacks; albeit at great cost to themselves. Nevertheless, by October 23, the Germans had eliminated the massive Kessel.[84] More than 650,000 Russian soldiers marched into captivity in the twin defeats at the critical railway junctions of Vyazma and Bryansk, roughly matching the German army's historic accomplishment at Kiev. Eight Soviet armies—the 16th, 19th, 20th, 24th, and 32nd near Vyazma and the 3rd, 13th, and 50th near Briansk—had been

BATTLE FOR MOSCOW

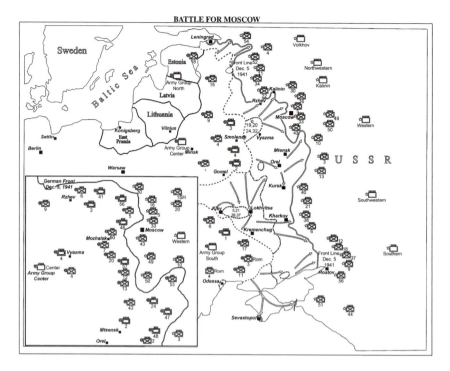

shattered. Soviet equipment losses included an estimated 830 to 1,300 tanks and 6,000 artillery pieces, anti-tank guns, and mortars. On October 1, 1941, the Red Army had assembled 1.25 million men to defend Moscow. By October's end, the German army had captured or killed 1 million of these men.[85] Never before in modern history did a nation suffer such massive defeats in such a short period as did the Soviet Union in September and October 1941. With his armies savaged and dying before Moscow, no strategic reserves immediately available in the western Soviet Union, and a 300-mile-wide hole blown in his front lines, Stalin's empire seemingly faced imminent defeat.

Chapter 5

An Inconvenient Decision Confronts Germany's Masters of War

Germany's twin triumphs at Vyazma and Bryansk marked the end of two successive years at war whereby the Wehrmacht inflicted progressively greater defeats on its foes with hardly any significant reverses in return. This stunning run of success would be unmatched by any other major combatant during World War II. Nonetheless, this string of battlefield accomplishments would, late in the fall of 1941, come to an end at Moscow's very gates. Germany's failure to seize Moscow is widely regarded by today's conventional wisdom as a critical turning point in Germany's war. In reality, how Germany wrapped up Operation Barbarossa would end up mattering far more to the Third Reich's chances for establishing a continental empire than whether Moscow fell in 1941. The following explains why.

DID GERMANY NEED TO TAKE MOSCOW IN 1941 TO WIN THE WAR?

If Hitler's failure to take Moscow represented the fatal blow to Barbarossa, then it is perhaps unsurprising that many of Hitler's generals (and historians heavily reliant on their memoirs) have pointed to Hitler's August 1941 decision to destroy the Soviet armies near Kiev as the fatal delay underlying Barbarossa's failure. Nevertheless, the entire debate and supporting arguments miss a simple point. The actual data and existing historical record show that a successful conclusion to the German campaign against the Soviet Union in 1941, at least one embracing Moscow's fall or as envisioned by Barbarossa's original plan, was unnecessary for Germany to cement its hold on Europe.

To the contrary, in attempting to crush the Red Army in a single campaign season, the Wehrmacht actively undermined its opportunity to secure the Third Reich's future if for no other reason than that, as early as the fall of 1941, it stood hardly closer to defeating the Red Army than it had been on Barbarossa's eve- and thus was nowhere near meeting Barbarossa's essential underlying prerequisite for engineering the Soviet Union's near total collapse. As such, during the fall of 1941, the OKH (Oberkommando der Heer, or Army High Command) and Hitler began planning to revamp the campaign within the Soviet Union from one driven by classic Prussian military goals seeking a single determinative battle of annihilation to a new focus. The objective would be creating the necessary economic base to wage warfare across continents, to be accomplished via seizing the critical economic resources in the Ukraine and southern Russia. Regardless, the OKH and Hitler struggled to reconcile this revision of strategic goals with the state of the German Eastern Front during the fall of 1941.

Identifying a campaign's culmination point is rarely a simple task. In the case of Barbarossa, the difficulty inherent in this task was compounded by unexpected developments, especially a Red Army whose determined resistance had torn asunder Barbarossa's initial assumptions. Although an enduring portrayal of the German officer corps has often been as a pack of hyperaggressive attack dogs, beyond the ability of recognizing when to call off a campaign, the reality was otherwise. Hitler and his military leadership could—and, at times did—make rational decisions regarding when and how to shut down unproductive offensives, even in the wake of their greatest victories. For example, on October 10, Hitler ordered German forces in Finland's Petsamo region near the Arctic coast, to go over onto the defensive. Although such a decision represented the exception rather than the norm, it is emblematic of the fact that the German military establishment seems to have recognized that Barbarossa was approaching a culmination point far short of the campaign's initially unrealistic goals. That said, on the road to Moscow, the German army pressed on. Why?

One reason was that, by the end of October 1941, the Germans had put the Soviet Union in a dreadful strategic position. The Red Army, despite its massive peacetime size, had, for instance, lost six tanks for every German tank destroyed.[1] Inadequate transport, smashed logistics, nonexistent radio equipment, almost no spare parts, and even shortages in rifles proved endemic. Admittedly, not all was doom for the Red Army. Stavka raised new armies on a near weekly basis. Regarding experienced manpower, however, the reserves redeploying west from the Far East—some 27 experienced and well-equipped divisions[2]—represented the last combat-ready forces. Beyond the Red Army's weakness was the even more significant strategic fact that by November 1941, Germany was in control of not only hundreds of thousands of square miles of Soviet real estate, but also approximately 90 million former Soviet citizens from the prewar Soviet population of 171 million people.[3]

Roughly 40 percent of the Soviet Union's labor force had been lost in just five months. In addition, by the late fall of 1941, the Germans had seized or destroyed 47 percent of the Soviet Union's prewar agricultural land, 41 percent of its railroad network and the sources of 62.5 percent of prewar coal output, 68 percent of prewar steel output, and 60 percent of its aluminum output.[4]

During the fall of 1941, Soviet armaments production had correspondingly collapsed. For example, aircraft production fell from 2,329 aircraft built in September to 627 in November. Moreover, this lost output occurred at the exact moment that the Red Army Air Force most needed these replacement machines to counter losses of 21,000 aircraft between June and December 1941.[5] As for the Red Army's ground units, the need to relocate factories had diverted nearly two-thirds of all rail capacity for over three months time and significantly cut into the Soviet Union's previously planned tank output for the year. To boot, a Red Army that had 90,000 guns and mortars on hand prior to Barbarossa was down to 21,933 guns and mortars by December 1, 1941.[6] Ammunition output fell by over half. If not for the tanks and planes redeployed from the Far East, the Red Army would have defended Moscow with scarcely any heavy weapons. Moreover, Stalin's zeal for arresting or executing his failing officers only made the situation worse.

From the German perspective, and regardless of initial planning for the following year's campaign, it consequently must have seemed at the time that one further lunge could have hardly threatened Hitler's position of dominance in his war against Stalin's empire. Nevertheless, data available even at that time show that the Ostheer was in a terrible state in its own right. Overall, Germany's leadership faced several important decisions as October 1941 gave way to November, decisions that in many ways would define the ability of the Ostheer to meet Hitler and the OKH's goals for a 1942 campaign. That said, Germany's incredible 1939–1941 battlefield successes, the confidence that these successes had generated, and Germany's aggressive military tradition also heavily influenced the German decision-making process. Nowhere is this more evident than in two crucial developments that had accompanied and followed the victories at Vyazma and Bryansk. Each of these developments proved pivotal in Moscow's ability to withstand the German onslaught, and the Red Army's ability to inflict concomitantly heavy losses on an overextended Ostheer during the winter of 1941–1942.

First, and perhaps most critically, instead of directly striking the Soviet capital, Hitler and the OKH, riding high after having crushed the Soviet armies west of the capital, ordered Army Group Center to envelop Moscow. To that end, Hitler and the OKH directed significant military assets to move ever farther northeast and southeast of Moscow. Initially, and on some parts of the front, such deployments did not seem problematic. After all, the 3rd Panzer Army's spearheads quickly covered 50 miles to the northeast and by October 14 had taken Kalinin. However, from October 19 to October 29, the overextended 3rd Panzer Army was forced to fend off repeated counterattacks from Konev's new command, the Kalinin Front. These counterattacks were so serious that at one point the Soviet 29th Army had temporarily cut off elements of the German 1st Panzer Division from the rest of the 3rd Panzer Army. In spite of its difficulties one has to wonder what would have happened before Moscow had the 3rd Panzer Army, given the initial speed of its advance, instead been ordered to concentrate its power and advance on a more direct line east in conjunction with its peers in Army Group Center. At the same time and on other parts of Bock's front, the ambitious German orders proved even more ridiculous given the horrific state of German logistical support. For instance, as early as October 3, Guderian's 2nd Panzer Army had started running out of fuel. Guderian's spearhead, having traveled over 120 miles in just a few days, accordingly spent two entire good-weather days sitting in Orel simply because it had to wait for fuel to be brought up, all of which occurred four days prior to the first snows that ultimately turned the roads into a muddy morass.

Beyond issues posed by the ambitious German orders and concomitant lack of logistical preparation for the campaign, however, was an even more fundamental predicament. In October 1941, the Red Army was far from simply lying down and dying before the Wehrmacht. The battles to eliminate the pockets formed at Bryansk and Vyazma took up the better part of October and tied down roughly half of Army Group Center's strength.[7] This had meant that during October's second week, only four Panzer and two motorized divisions had carried forward with the main advance on Moscow. In addition, only two Panzer and one motorized division from Guderian's Panzergruppe had also been able to break free of the pocket battle at Bryansk and advance east on the industrial city of Tula.[8] Moreover, Guderian renewed his drive on Tula only by shortchanging his forces eliminating the Bryansk pocket, and thus once again he had let significant Soviet forces escape encirclement and continue the fight. The decision to pursue a wide-ranging envelopment of Moscow therefore had failed to correlate with the resources available to Army Group Center to meet such an objective. Had the OKH merely concentrated Army Group Center's efforts, even Zhukov concedes that it was unlikely that his forces could have stopped the German army from entering Moscow.[9] Instead, the German army's maneuvering had granted the Red Army much-needed breathing space, which it subsequently put to good use. For instance, by the end of October, some 13 rifle divisions and five armored brigades had arrived from the Soviet interior to bolster the capital's western defenses.[10] These men included the fully trained 15,000-man 32nd Rifle Division from Siberia that, along with the 20th Tank Brigade, would put up a particularly stiff fight in mid-October at Borodino, roughly 60 miles west of Moscow.

Brauchitsch and Halder did as much if not more than Hitler to scatter Army Group Center to all points of the compass and, despite the dogged Soviet resistance on the road to Moscow, pushed Army Group's North and

South forward as well. In so doing, they put further strain on the threadbare German logistical network, strain only made worse as the Red Army launched massive counterstrokes of its own. On October 12, the Leningrad Front, led by Colonel General I. I. Fediuninsky, received orders to commit 70,000 men, 97 tanks (with 59 powerful KV-series tanks), and 475 guns against the 54,000 dug-in German soldiers defending the Schlissel'burg corridor separating the Leningrad Front from Soviet armies to the east. That said, Army Group North's own offensive somewhat preempted the Soviet attack. Regardless, Fediuninsky went ahead, tied down significant German forces near Siniavino, and slowed the German advance seeking to cut the rail lines to Lake Ladoga.

Meanwhile, the 3rd Panzer Army, just south of Army Group North, had finally received authority from the OKH to directly assist the northern pincer of Moscow's anticipated grand envelopment. Only on October 29 did 3rd Panzer Army and the 9th Army defeat a force led by Konev's talented chief of staff, Lieutenant General N. F. Vatutin. All the while, the 3rd Panzer Army shrugged off yet another Soviet counterattack launched on October 24. Meanwhile, by October 25, Army Group North was barely crawling toward Tikhvin, and its goal of cutting Leningrad off from its primary forward supply base. Nevertheless, the operational mess that was the German advance in October and November 1941 was by no means Hitler's fault alone.

Guderian's Panzer Army roamed far to the southeast, as the other pincer for Bock's planned double envelopment of Moscow, while still mopping up cutoff Soviet soldiers and at the same time pursuing operations toward Kursk, moves stretching Guderian's front over 200 miles in breadth. Guderian, down to 271 tanks by mid-October, desperately consolidated his remaining combat power in hopes of battering through Lieutenant General Boldin's 50th Army. Aided by the poor weather, German logistical failings, and active support from the Red Army Air Force, Boldin's men ground down Guderian's Panzer army. A battle group led by Heinrich Eberbach, comprised of the 35th Panzer Regiment, mechanized infantry from the 3rd Panzer Division, and motorized infantry from the Grossdeutschland Regiment, actually made it to Tula, covering over 50 miles in five days. In turn, Boldin's spirited resistance duly evicted the German toehold on the city.[11] At the same time, supply problems, and Soviet counterattacks against Guderian's right flank slowed his advance to such an extent that he was unable to renew his drive to take Tula until November 18. Meanwhile, behind the lines, the Soviet leadership had engineered another massive rebuilding effort.

Early in October, Stalin had reassigned Zhukov from the Leningrad Front to plan Moscow's defense. Zhukov press-ganged over 250,000 civilians into building field fortifications ringing Moscow. Furthermore, he manned the defensive belts with just about anyone he could grab. Nevertheless, on October 19, the Fourth Panzer Army's 2nd, 5th, and 11th Panzer Divisions captured the town of Mozhaisk, ripping the heart from the center of Moscow's primary defensive position. Five German Panzer divisions sat only

60 miles from the Soviet capital. Nonetheless, they had been worn down even more than they had already been by the stiff fighting against Major General Dmitri Lelyushenko's 5th Army at Borodino and Rokossovsky's 16th Army at Volokalamsk. Consequently, the surviving German Panzers had to pause and wait for supplies to be brought forward. At the same time, Kluge directed his 4th Army, with 11 rifle divisions at the front, as if the order had already been given to go into winter quarters. During late October, Kluge only weakly maintained a semblance of an advance despite only minor Soviet pressure against infantry divisions that the German Schnelltruppen desperately needed to assist their own efforts. Meanwhile, Stalin, in response to the thrusts of the German Panzers, and despite Kluge's dithering, desperately ordered another defensive line built several hundred miles east of Moscow. On October 12, Stalin also ordered most of his government to evacuate Moscow for Kubyshev far to the east. In addition, Stalin ordered some 498 factories and industrial works in and around Moscow evacuated east.[12]

As Zhukov took command of the new Western Front, formed from the shattered Western and Reserve fronts, and fed in 90,000 men pulled from reserves and from other fronts into the lines, panicked Muscovites fled the capital by the thousands. Stalin, meanwhile, had been desperately trying to get the British to send direct military support—even asking for British soldiers to fight on Soviet soil.[13] Then, on October 19, Zhukov and Stalin decided to remain in Moscow. They led strenuous efforts to stop the panic spreading throughout the city. Elite politically trusted units, such as the Dzerzhinsky Motorized Division and the Motorized Infantry Brigade of the NKVD (People's Commissariat for Internal Affairs) Special Forces, played a critical role in locking down the capital. The latter unit, the predecessor to the Soviet Spetsnaz, coldly imposed order among the panicked population, including via shooting looters.[14] Of course, the city itself also served as a fortress. The Kremlin, nestled as it was against the Moscow River's banks, had acted as a defensive citadel since the city's founding during the twelfth century. Although the land surrounding Moscow is relatively flat, it features dense forests of pine and birch trees that created further defensive barriers to a German army joining the Poles, French, Tatars, and others who had previously sought to conquer the region. In addition, with reserves pulled from the Soviet interior, the Soviet Western Front saw its armor strength nearly double between October 1 and November 15 with 1,138 aircraft also arriving to support the defense of Moscow. By November 15, the ranks of Moscow's defenders had swelled to 84 divisions and 20 brigades.[15] By November, it was obvious to all, even in Germany, that this war was far from over.

As the Red Army defended the Soviet seat of power, Zhukov carefully marshaled his reserves for a massive three-stage counterattack scheduled for early December. Meanwhile, to play for time, Zhukov remorselessly expended many of the poorly trained recruits west of Moscow. In particular, he ordered them to aggressively defend the important road junctions on Moscow's approaches. Even though the Red Army endured prodigious casualties in these defensive battles, the German army gradually wore down at the same time that the Red Army's striking power grew. By December, the Red Army once again deployed over 4 million men under arms, a staggering total considering that, on November 1, the Red Army had been down to 2.2 million men. The German army in the east, in contrast, had fallen to 2.7 million men from the 3.2 million at Barbarossa's beginning. Although conscripts flowed into the Red Army's ranks, catastrophic equipment losses remained a huge problem. During 1941, the Germans captured or destroyed 20,000 of the Red Army's 23,000 tanks and 41,000 of the 57,000 artillery pieces with which the Red Army began the war in June.[16] On the other hand, Allied convoy PQ-1 had delivered the first Lend-Lease shipment in October 1941, and by the end of 1941, early Lend-Lease aid meant that 25 percent of the Red Army's medium and heavy tanks in service were British tanks.[17]

While the Soviet leadership dug in for yet another defensive stand, the German army faced an additional problem: the weather. On October 7, the first snows fell in northern and central Russia. Intermixed with the fall's incessant rain, the snow turned dirt roads into a quagmire of nearly impassable mud, sucking any nontracked vehicle into its nearly unbreakable grip. The German 2nd Army reported on October 12 that its rate of advance was down to one mile per hour, though this still meant that units such as its own 13th Corps or the 4th Panzer Army's XII Corps were able to cover nearly 50 miles in five days. Nonetheless, the Russian Rasputitsa (muddy season) had arrived. The few all-weather roads in western Russia became strategic objectives necessary to ensure supplies to the front. The rains relentlessly sheeted down. *Panje* carts and *panje* horses, the hardy breed of Russian horses acclimatized to the poor weather conditions, served as virtually the only transportation sources capable of pulling equipment and supplies. Forced labor and German soldiers alike slaved to maintain the few passable roads. Losses from the mud, followed by the first freeze of the winter, proved devastating; the 10th Panzer Division alone lost 50 tanks to the mud that immobilized the tanks and the subsequent drops in temperature that froze them into place.[18] Motor vehicle losses were staggering. In November 1941, the German economy produced 2,752 trucks. During that same month, the German armies in the Soviet Union lost 5,996 trucks.[19] Despite the conditions at the front, on October 19 Halder ordered Army Group Center to prepare to drive on Rybinsk, that is, well north and east of Moscow. German casualties, exacerbated by the inability to maintain mobility, piled up. Approximately 686,000 German casualties had been suffered by October 30—in a testament to the Red Army's considerable and underappreciated capacity for inflicting grievous punishment on the Wehrmacht.

After the war, many historians fixated on the weather as the primary cause for the German inability to take Moscow. In part, this was because of German memoirs claiming that the weather saved Moscow. Nevertheless, the weather was only one of many elements undermining Barbarossa. This is not to say that the weather proved inconsequential, but, rather, and at least in regards to looking at events near Moscow late in 1941, if Hitler and the OKH had managed Army Group Center better, then they likely could have both handled the atrocious weather and reached Moscow despite the Red Army's dogged resistance. Instead, the German advance crawled along until the ground began freezing early in November 1941. In addition, supplies only slowly brought forward by Army Group Center's pitiful logistical support network finally began reaching the frontline troops in quantities adequate to prepare for another thrust later in November.

On November 13, an OKH conference at Orsha fatefully decided the final plans to take Moscow. Halder played the key role in pushing the Wehrmacht forward. The chiefs of staff of Army Groups North and South argued that it was time to stop and refit before renewing operations in the spring of 1942. Bock proposed refocusing Army Group Center's armies more directly on Moscow to the exclusion of other, wider-ranging goals, and then shutting down for the winter. His chief supply officer, Colonel Otto Eckstein, underlined Bock's points in drawing attention to the horrific logistical situation.[20] In choosing to push on, Halder and Brauchitsch likely held several motivations, including the prestige factor in taking Moscow, a fear of the Red Army's ability to rebuild if it were given an entire winter to do so, and the reality that Halder had been deterministically selling to Hitler for over a year the idea that if Moscow were attacked, then the Red Army's "vital fighting strength" would be destroyed defending the capital. Hitler, having never been overly keen on a fight for Moscow, had long since been wavering on the merits of a final push into the Soviet capital over bunkering down for the winter. However, inaccurate intelligence estimates from the OKH had helped to allay some of his fears regarding the Soviet capacity to resist one more German drive on Moscow. Thus, on November 15, mostly because of Hitler, Halder, and Brauchitsch, the final German offensive of 1941 kicked off, seeking to take the seat of Soviet power.

Despite the great weight that military tradition played in directing the German General Staff's decisions, it would be a mistake to ascribe the German decision-making process as deterministically aggressive. After all, in 1940, the German General Staff had originally planned a conservative two-stage offensive into France and the Low Countries; not a single campaign focused on having it all, a la Barbarossa. Therefore, by mid-November 1941, it was not at all unrealistic to have expected an otherwise conservative General Staff to have prepared Germany's eastern army to consolidate its gains, build defensive positions, seek shelter for the winter, and marshal its strength for a final offensive in 1942. Instead, they did the exact opposite, even though by November 1941 the OKH knew that some 20 percent of the June 22 German army's frontline strength in men had become casualties. Even worse, the German eastern army's combat strength, more than 150 divisions on June 22, had fell to the equivalent of 83 full-strength divisions by November's first week. Equipment losses proved nearly as prodigious. For instance, by October 16, the 1st Panzer Division's tank complement had dropped from 154 on Barbarossa's eve down to 79.[21] Not that this was anything new. Following previous campaigns, the Wehrmacht had needed ample time to rest and refit after little more than one month of warfare, let alone four or more months. In addition, not only were the occupied areas of Europe failing to provide the economic support needed by the German economy, in no small measure because of a lack of key natural resources, but within these territories, the first significant signs of resistance and disruption in economic output were emerging.[22]

As for the Luftwaffe, daily attrition and near nonexistent spare parts stores meant that it could barely muster enough aircraft needed for basic air support and reconnaissance. Although during 1941 the Luftwaffe lost only one airplane for every eight Soviet aircraft destroyed, the 2,510 aircraft combat and noncombat losses that the Luftwaffe endured were unsustainable without a pause in operations to rebuild its ranks or receive reinforcement from other fronts; as only one-third of the Luftwaffe was even engaged in Russia by the end of December.[23] Furthermore, Hitler exacerbated the Luftwaffe's problems in Russia when he stripped Kesselring's 2nd Luftflotten from Army Group Center and ordered it to Sicily. Soviet reinforcements streamed into the Moscow defensive zone almost completely unhindered. In addition, between November 15 and December 2, the Red Army would fly five times as many sorties as the Luftwaffe in and around Moscow.[24]

There is a vast body of literature available on the "what-ifs" of World War II and events in and around Moscow in 1941. What these arguments often miss is in addressing the question of the Third Reich's goals. Was Germany trying to defeat the Red Army, or was it trying to secure economic resources so as to cement Germany's position as a continental hegemon? Having never answered these questions in the months leading up to or during Barbarossa, the advance on Moscow continued by its own momentum. Meanwhile, the latest cracks in the Wehrmacht's combat capability had occurred in the area of operations of Army Group North and Army Group South.

After the outstanding success at Kiev, and even with the departure of Guderian's Panzer army and an entire Panzer corps from the 1st Panzer Army, Rundstedt's armies had surged across the western Ukraine. They had been led by the remainder of Kleist's 1st Panzer Army and the 11th Army under Manstein. Manstein had replaced General Eugen von Schobert following his death in a plane crash. Manstein initially focused his army's efforts on taking the Crimean Peninsula. In a bitter five-day battle at the approximately four-mile-wide Perekop isthmus, the 11th Army defeated the first Soviet defensive line. Although suffering heavy casualties in the process, they took 10,000 prisoners, 112 tanks, and 135 artillery pieces and drove the Red Army back to its second defensive line at the Ichoun isthmus.[25]

Nonetheless, on September 26, the Red Army had counterattacked on the mainland. This forced Manstein to send the 1st SS Motorized Division, 30th Corps, 49th Mountain Corps, and 3rd Romanian Army to help the 1st Panzer Army encircle and destroy the attacking Soviet 9th and 18th Armies near Melitopol-Tokmak-Mariupol east of the Dnieper River. This battle of the Sea of Azov ended on October 10 and resulted in the Red Army losing 106,362 prisoners of war, 212 tanks, and 672 guns. Manstein then turned and took the entire Crimean Peninsula, minus the port and fortress at Sevastopol, captured another 100,000 Soviet troops, and did it all by November 16. Also in mid-October, the city of Odessa finally fell to mostly Romanian forces suffering dreadful casualties against stiff Soviet resistance in a siege that had lasted for well over two months. Meanwhile, on October 25, Kharkov, a critical transportation hub and industrial city, fell to Reichenau's 6th Army but the fighting had further drained Army Group South's limited resources. Rundstedt, concerned over his army's flagging strength, met with Brauchitsch on November 3 and insisted that all Army Group operations be halted on the lower Don and Donets Rivers forming the Donets Basin—one of Europe's great industrial regions. Brauchitsch ignored Rundstedt, and instead insisted that objectives as far flung as Stalingrad and the oil fields at Maykop in the Caucasus still needed to be taken.[26]

By November 20, the 1st Panzer Army had captured Rostov on the Don River, but this had only been accomplished via a supreme effort and Rundstedt's Army Group lacked the strength to go farther or even hold to on to Rostov for that matter. On November 22, Timoshenko's 9th, 18th, 37th, and 56th Armies counterattacked the city from its south and east.[27] On November 28, 1st Panzer Army was forced to abandon Rostov. Rundstedt requested permission to pull back to the Mius River, regarded as a strong defensible position, for the winter. Hitler refused in part, agreeing to a withdrawal but to a line east of what Rundstedt had wanted. Miscommunication ensued. The end result was that Hitler believed Rundstedt's further withdrawal to be an act of defiance, and thus Hitler sacked Rundstedt. Reichenau took command, and he promptly requested permission to withdraw to the Mius River. Hitler and Halder belatedly allowed Reichenau to order what Rundstedt could have accomplished under far better circumstances a short time prior.[28]

Meanwhile, Army Group North had driven well east of Leningrad, approached Volkhov, and on November 8 seized Tikhvin; accomplishing all this despite repeated and heavy Soviet counterattacks that invariably resulted in heavy casualties to the Soviet armies involved. During the first week of November 1941 alone, Schmidt's 39th Corps had captured 20,000 men while destroying or capturing 96 tanks, 179 guns, and one armored train. Despite such successes. by mid-November Army Group North's front east of the Volkhov River had dangerously stretched in breadth from roughly 44 miles wide in October to nearly 219 miles wide. Only 10 infantry divisions, two motorized divisions, and two Panzer divisions defended the entire German front between

Lake Ladoga and Lake Il'men. These understrength formations could muster only 120,000 men, 1,000 guns and mortars, and 100 tanks and assault guns. In turn Stavka massed 192,950 men from the Soviet 4th, 52nd, and 54th Armies to hammer the thin German defensive lines, slowly but steadily driving the Germans west in fierce fighting occurring in horrible cold and at times in deep snow. Both sides suffered extraordinarily, but on December 9, Tikhvin was once again in Russian hands.[29] By December 22, Schmidt's two Panzer divisions could put only 30 tanks into the field each, and the 18th Motorized Division had lost 9,000 men.[30] As late as the first week of November, the 39th Corps had been a potent combat formation. Yet because Hitler and the OKH had insisted on maintaining an offensive far past its logical culmination point, Army Group North's striking power had been eviscerated for mere geographic gains subsequently reversed in only one month's fighting.

As the Ostheer suffered its first serious setbacks on its northern and southern flanks, beginning on November 15–16, some 233,000 German men, 1,300 tanks, 1,880 guns, and 800 aircraft hammered away at Soviet forces directly before Moscow, including Rokossovsky's 16th Army and Leliushenko's 30th Army. Temperatures dropped precipitously, leading to rampant frostbite among the ill-equipped German soldiers. German vehicles and weapons ceased to work at minus four degrees Fahrenheit. German locomotives broke down. Logistical support proved hardly adequate for supporting an offensive that featured two pincers —the 3rd and 4th Panzer Army to the north and the 2nd Panzer Army to the south with holding attacks launched by the 4th Army in the center—all seeking to envelop a massive urban area the size of Moscow. Supply trains running east declined by one-third from September 1941 to January 1942. German doctors declared tens of thousands German soldiers unfit for duty, mostly because of weather-related ailments. Available manpower reserves plummeted. Despite all this, Halder planned for Guderian to advance 250 miles to Moscow's east and take Gorki in a continuation of the operational mess that had been Barbarossa.

All the more remarkable in this running litany of the German Eastern Army's increasing weakness is that up to November 1941, and though the Ostheer had endured steep losses in armored fighting vehicles (AFVs), its losses in well-trained and experienced tank crews were only a fraction of what such numbers would otherwise lead one to think. There is little question that German armored fighting vehicle output had been inadequate, with roughly 601 AFVs sent east since Barbarossa began. Nevertheless, when coupled with the remaining 1,490 AFVs at the front, the Germans deployed in the Soviet Union some 2,000 AFVs in November 1941, manned by the world's finest crews. These figures meant that Germany enjoyed a slight quantitative advantage over the Red Army in AFVs and heavy weapons for the first time in the war, coupled with overwhelming qualitative advantages in trained men, organization, and tactical leadership. Nevertheless, the quest for one decisive, sweeping battle of annihilation had allowed the Red Army, a virtually inexhaustible brawler, to draw the fleet-footed, hard-hitting German army into a toe-to-toe slugfest that negated many of the Wehrmacht's advantages.

BARBAROSSA'S DEFEAT

On November 26, German soldiers took the town of Istra, a mere 30 miles northwest of Moscow, and on November 27, Klin fell even as the meager supplies gathered for the German offensive slowly dwindled away–leaving one to wonder how they would have even fought for the Soviet capital once they reached it. On November 28, the Germans crossed the Volga-Moscow Canal at Yakhroma, the last major geographical barrier north of Moscow blocking a German path to encircling the city, and staggered into the outer suburbs of the Soviet capital as they fought off initially weak counterattacks directed at them by the Soviet 1st Shock Army. However, Soviet reinforcements continued to arrive, bolstering the final defensive lines before Moscow, as did an active Red Army Air Force, as further reserves yet assembled behind the lines and prepared to counter the German advance.

On December 1, a patrol from the 4th Panzer Army sneaked through the Soviet 16th Army's lines and reached Khimki, only about 11 miles from the Kremlin, but its parent formation lacked the resources to follow up and exploit this gap in the Soviet lines otherwise protecting Moscow. Despite the reach of the German advance, it had failed to engineer any significant encirclements, therefore allowing the Soviet 16th and 30th Armies to fall back into new defensive positions, including marshy terrain well suited to defensive operations near Istra. Moreover, Kluge had failed to attack at the same time that the 3rd and 4th Panzer Armies had—instead waiting two full weeks to begin on December 1 a meticulously planned offensive 40 miles west of Moscow. What's more Kluge maintained 4th Army's effort for only two days despite meeting initial success—this further allowed Zhukov to shift his forces and reinforce the defensive effort against the 3rd and 4th Panzer Armies. For its part the Siberian 78th Rifle Division proved a particularly tough opponent, stymieing the advance of even the crack 2nd SS Das Reich Motorized Division— worn down as it was by the incessant combat as well as a paucity of supplies.

On November 28, Zhukov and Stavka ordered the 1st Shock Army and the 20th Army, along with heavy close air support, to counterattack the German spearhead. They duly threw the Germans back over the Moscow-Volga Canal on November 29. On November 30, the 3rd Panzer Army followed 9th Army's lead and went onto the defense. On December 2, the 4th Army followed suit as the Soviet lines north and west of Moscow began to stabilize along a front running as close as 20 miles from the capital. Farther south, Halder refused to allow Guderian to pull units out of line to replenish and prepare winter positions.[31] The 2nd Panzer Army, arrayed all around Tula from west, south, and east, pushed on even though the 3rd Panzer Division was

Table 5.1 Decline in Panzer Strength (sample taken from Army Group Center: Panzer Group 3; numbers refer to tanks in running order)[1]

	October 16, 1941	December 1, 1941
1st Panzer Division	79	37
6th Panzer Division	60	4
7th Panzer Division	120	36

[1]Steven H. Newton, *German Battle Tactics on the Russian Front 1941–1945* (Schiffer Publishing, 1994), 53–54.

down to 52 tanks in running order, the 4th was down to 35 operational tanks, the 17th was down to 15 operational tanks, and the rest of the Panzer army was in no better shape (see table 5.1 for more on declining German tank strengths). In spite of such losses late in November, Guderian's 17th Panzer Division actually fought its way into Kashira on the Oka River. They had reached the last natural defensive barrier blocking Guderian's path to envelop Moscow from the south. In response, Zhukov ordered in the 1st Guards Cavalry Corps. Under the cover provided by substantial close air support, it hammered the 17th Panzer Division. Although on December 3 the 24th Panzer Corps cut Tula's rail and road links to Moscow, Guderian's Panzer army could go no further. German divisions existed in name only. Infantry companies fought at platoon strength.[32] Farther north, on December 5, four German armies—the 9th Army, the 3rd Panzer, the 4th Panzer, and the Fourth—sat in an arc arrayed north to south around Moscow's northern and western suburbs. They had been fought to a halt by the Soviet 30th Army, 1st Shock Army, 20th Army, 16th Army, and 5th Army, respectively. German losses had soared ever higher in both men and machines.

It was perhaps this last-gasp drive that had ended early in December that had struck the final blow to Army Group Center's status as the world's finest Army Group, as Bock's command had cannibalized itself for a goal of mythical rather than real significance. As German tanks either broke down or were put out of action in combat, all too often their specially trained tank crews were forced into fighting as regular infantry. Up to this point in the campaign, one of the few bright spots in terms of German losses had been that, in terms of the "specialist" ranks, casualties during Barbarossa had been relatively light, especially in regard to casualties suffered by the actual tank crews. By December, this was no longer true. The technically skilled tank crewmembers were thrown into the meat grinder. They were joined in short order by flak crews, artillerymen, signals specialists, and others who represented the backbone of an effective fighting formation that, if it could be maintained intact, meant that even the extraordinarily heavy losses in the German infantry could be replaced at little loss to the combat effectiveness of their parent unit. On

December 3, the OKH ordered Army Group Center to go over onto the defensive.[33] In any case, the Wehrmacht's final spasmodic efforts quickly became irrelevant on December 5 as Zhukov counterattacked.

Zhukov could not have picked a better time to strike; Bock's Army Group was woefully overextended, lacked any prepared defensive positions, and was caught in the open in temperatures hovering near a meager five degrees Fahrenheit. Army Group Center faced Soviet Fronts holding two-to-one advantages in manpower, albeit inadequately equipped with the Germans holding superiority in artillery and matching Soviet AFV strength. All told, some 1.1 million men, about 800 tanks, and over 7,600 field guns pounded into Army Group Center. Zhukov sought to first stop and then, second, crush the twin salients formed by the German 3rd and 4th Panzer Armies northwest of Moscow and the German 2nd Panzer Army southeast of Moscow. Then his fronts would seek to destroy Army Group Center in its entirety. The Western and Kalinin fronts led the offensive, followed by the South-Western Front on December 6 and the Bryansk Front on December 24.

On December 5, Zhukov's Western Front, led by the 1st Shock Army and also including the 16th, 20th, and 30th Armies, pummeled the 3rd and 4th Panzer Armies. The shock army was a concept that had been kicking around Soviet military circles since the early 1930s. It signified an army designated to lead a primary axis of attack; as such, rather than being an elite army, such as a Guard's Army, a shock army was built for the singular purpose of cracking the enemy's defensive positions. The Red Army, spearheaded by its shock armies and supported by close air support, immediately forced the Germans to give ground. The 3rd Panzer Army had been particularly poorly deployed. Bock had taken away most of its infantry earlier in November, to support the 9th Army, and Reinhardt, whose command featured three Panzer and two motorized infantry divisions, could not pull the Panzer battalions from the line and create a mobile reserve. Consequently, when Zhukov struck, his armies quickly penetrated the German front, forcing the 3rd Panzer Army into a costly retreat, it left behind significant quantities of motorized vehicles and heavy weapons either abandoned or destroyed when they could not be readily freed from the frozen ground. Civilians suffered horribly as the German soldiers not only destroyed equipment they could not take with them, but also torched villages and towns in a scorched-earth campaign—leaving thousands of innocent men, women, and children to face the brutal Russian winter without adequate shelter. On December 7, Hitler allowed both the 3rd and the 4th Panzer Armies to withdraw, but the Germans had reacted far too slowly to Zhukov's counterstrokes. The 3rd Panzer Army was gradually driven west to the Lama River, where it finally halted on December 19 and held its ground until the Red Army launched a new offensive in January. In addition, the 4th Panzer Army and the 4th Army had retreated in good order and filled in the line to the 3rd Panzer Army's south. Meanwhile, on

December 8, Hitler belatedly issued his Führer Directive No. 39, putting the German eastern army onto the defensive. The Germans had some luck in their favor. Zhukov's initial counterattack had merely forced Army Group Center to give ground, as the units that Zhukov was forced to rely on were inadequately equipped and supported for an extended offensive. That said his timing had been exquisite. Such was the state of Zhukov's forces that had Hitler issued his orders only one week earlier, or had Zhukov lacked the nerve to wait until just the right moment, even Bock's weakened Army Group may have stopped Zhukov's initial counterstroke.

Instead, the OKH's decision to pursue Barbarossa far past the point of diminishing returns, and Hitler's concomitant procrastination, meant that Zhukov's modest counterattack rapidly evolved in its second and third stage into an honest chance at destroying Army Group Center. Konev's Kalinin Front and Timoshenko's Southwest Front pushed into Army Group Center's flanks and had met surprisingly weak resistance. Guderian, who had received permission on December 6 to pull in his exposed spearheads and withdraw to better defensive positions, never got the chance to reset. On December 8, Zhukov's Western Front slammed into Guderian's men. Forced into a retreat, shifting and fighting desperately to avoid encirclement, Guderian's army rapidly gave back the land so bitterly fought for and temporarily won over the prior three weeks. The Western Front split the 2nd Panzer Army. The Soviet 1st Guards Cavalry Corps and 22 rifle divisions poured through the gap in the German lines.[34] In addition, the German 2nd Army barely held on. In just six days, between December 9 and December 15, the Soviet counteroffensive had decimated the German 45th, 95th, and 134th Infantry Divisions.

Nevertheless, just as the winter weather played havoc with the poorly clad German soldiers, "General Winter" helped slow the Soviet counterstroke before Moscow. On December 7, winter's first sustained snowfalls began. Up to that point, the weather had varied in its impact on the German and Soviet armies fighting before Moscow, with some German forces badly affected as far back as October, for instance 2nd Panzer Army, while others did not see the first significant bite of winter until later, such as the 9th Army. In December, however, there is no question that the weather had a significant impact on each side of the front line. A frozen snow sea soon covered the vast and empty landscape occupied by Army Group North and Army Group Center. Attackers, Soviet or German, often struggled through deep snowdrifts. Frostbite swept through Russian and German units alike. Although the Red Army clothed its soldiers far better than did the Germans, with thick-padded pants and coats, fur gloves, and hats proving much more common in the Russian ranks, shortages remained.[35] For their part, the Russians remained desperate to get into the German defenses if for no other reason than for the shelter they provided. Communications lines became objectives even more important for attackers in the poor weather, resulting in sustained combat

SOVIET WINTER OFFENSIVE 1941–1942

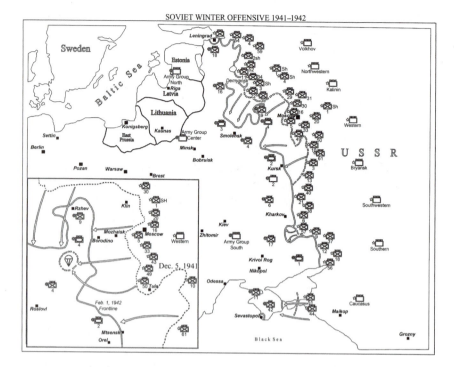

for important railheads and road junctions.[36] German units organized defensive efforts around individual strongpoints, constructed mostly around built-up areas dominating the few roads in the region.[37] They constructed 360-degree hedgehog positions that provided sheltering islands in the vast expanse of snow, mud (with the thaws), and wilderness. The Germans also created artificial depth in the defensive front by staggering strongpoints, and by rationing out combined infantry/artillery positions to the rear.

After visiting Bock's headquarters on December 13, Brauchitsch sought Hitler's acquiescence for a general 100-mile withdrawal to a proposed winter line. Hitler refused. On December 16, he ordered Bock to fight on, while at the same time authorizing the 3rd and 4th Fourth Panzer Armies and the 9th Army to conduct local withdrawals.[38] Brauchitsch, worn down by Hitler, the war, and his failing health, resigned. On December 19, Hitler stepped into the void and declared himself army commander in chief. Hitler further compounded the severe crisis gripping the Wehrmacht when on December 11 he declared war on the United States following the December 7 Japanese attack on the U.S. Pacific Fleet at Pearl Harbor. Given the industrial and potential military might of the United States, there is little question as to the foolishness of this decision. Of course, Hitler had long since—and mistakenly—underrated the United States as a potential foe. Nevertheless, the United States hardly possessed an army ready to become involved in ground combat in Europe. Thus, Hitler still had time to murder and enslave the people of eastern Europe, though, given the Red Army's resistance, his overall plan for slaughtering roughly 30 million inhabitants of eastern Europe as a precursor to the remaining steps in Generalplan Ost could be carried forward only in part, most notably in Leningrad, where over half a million people would starve during the winter of 1941–1942.

Meanwhile, the time to concede Barbarossa's defeat had arrived, with none of its objectives having even come close to being met. By December 1941, Barbarossa had cost the Wehrmacht over 800,000 casualties, including 164,000 dead.[39] December had proven particularly costly in terms of German equipment losses as well as personnel losses. In December alone, Army Group Center lost 496 tanks, 983 artillery pieces, and 800 anti-tank guns.[40] Such waste dwarfed German heavy weapons losses in October, and left an Army Group enjoying dominating November 1941 advantages over the opposing Soviet Fronts in such weapons with a subsequent deficit that it never was able to make up. In examining the historical record, it is hard to conclude that Barbarossa's November continuation did anything else than merely drive the German military into the ground for no additional gain. Even worse, it left the German army vulnerable to a Soviet counterstroke that would prove far more damaging to Germany's prospects for meeting its goals in a renewed 1942 campaign than it needed to be had Hitler and OKH not instead horribly overreached for a goal of dubious importance.

Barbarossa's failure became reality in early December 1941 for a number of reasons, perhaps most important because of the Red Army's capacity to resist, even during defeat, and because of its ability to inflict relentless punishment on a German army unprepared for what such a development meant. The Red Army's effectiveness in wearing down the German armored and motorized forces had in particular upset the campaign's operational tempo, and laid bare the preexisting logistical weakness and incoherent planning that had undermined Barbarossa from the beginning. If, following the defeat of the Soviet armies in the western Soviet Union anything happened other than a complete Soviet collapse, Barbarossa was doomed. Thus, in surviving the heavy German blows, the Red Army had forced the Germans' hand. Although the weather provided a boost to the Red Army at perhaps its worst moment, following the formation of the epic Vyazma/Bryansk pockets on the road to Moscow, its role in Barbarossa's defeat was relatively minor. That said, the Red Army had needed help in stopping Barbarossa's architects from realizing a number of their most important goals. For that, help it could thank Hitler, the OKW (Oberkommando der Wehrmacht, or High Command of the Armed Forces), and the OKH.

Without the poor planning and unrealistic assumptions that undergirded Barbarossa as an operational concept, the Red Army of 1941 could not have prevented any number of catastrophes, including possibly both Leningrad's and Moscow's loss during the summer and fall of 1941. The capture of either would not have won the war outright. Nonetheless, the loss of either city would have been a great blow to Stalin's empire. As it was, the Soviet Union's size had enabled Germany to largely engage in the free-flowing war of maneuver at which it excelled. Nevertheless, the OKH and Hitler reacted poorly to the Red Army's dogged resistance. They never settled on the goals, or the means to achieve them, necessary to avoid allowing the Red Army's ability to frustrate the Ostheer's tempo to become as debilitating as it did. In particular, two crucial debates that plagued the German high command helped fragment the Wehrmacht's efforts during Barbarossa.

The first debate had revolved around what the German army should have done once Barbarossa's first phase ended. Even after this debate was settled, the hard earned victory enjoyed by the significantly weakening German armies east of Kiev was diminished when the 2nd Panzer Army was ordered to march on Moscow in lieu of having Guderian's men strike for economic objectives on the southern half of Germany's eastern front. These resources not only represented the heart of the Soviet economy and agricultural base, but also once put to work for the German economy would have allowed Hitler to wage global war and cement his hold on Europe. The second great debate that had occurred within the German command had been over the means for defeating the Red Army, and/or securing western Soviet Union for German use. The OKH never truly forced its Army Group and army-level commanders to decide on whether to primarily cut up the Red Army thoroughly in wedge-and-pocket operations, or whether it would have been better to pursue a deep operational blitz far into the Russian hinterland. As a result, the German armies executing Barbarossa were frequently ordered to move in as many as three or four separate axes of advance at once. This had greatly assisted the Red Army's ability to push an exhausted German army to the brink of collapse during December 1941.

The optimism and recklessness characterizing Hitler and his General Staff's war making meant that the great gamble had ended in failure. The Red Army and Soviet Union had not collapsed like a "house of cards" but had fought with a determination and aggressiveness much more akin to the ruthless German method of warfare than had been expected. Hitler, for his part, responded to defeat by purging the Eastern Army's leadership, including all three Army Group commanders. Hitler's faith in his own abilities became dangerously blown out of all proportion to his limited talents and capabilities as a military leader. For instance, Hitler greatly shortened the traditional leash given to German officers in creatively interpreting orders and exercising "mission responsibility." Instead of reemphasizing the flexibility and tactical freedom that had proven hallmarks of Prussian and German military success, Hitler began a process that involved rigidly dictating orders to the OKW and the OKH and then passing them down reflexively. Doctrines and training that built the German army into a power house during 1939–1941 fell to the side as Hitler's edicts, particularly those regarding holding ground no matter the cost, all too often took center stage.

In contrast, Stalin and his generals enjoyed a much-improved relationship. Moreover, recently bloodied combat officers stepped into important positions, men such as Konev and Rokossovsky in particular. Born in 1897, Ivan S. Konev, like Zhukov, carried a reputation as a ruthless, hard-driving, aggressive commander, though he only narrowly survived the purges and then the failings of his 19th Army during Barbarossa.[41] For his part, the even-tempered, charismatic, intelligent Rokossovsky ranked among the best generals of any army to fight in the war.[42] Rokossovsky was born on December 21, 1896, in Warsaw, the son of a Polish father and Belorussian mother. During World War I, Rokossovsky served in the Russian cavalry, where, among other awards, he was honored three separate times with the St. George's Cross, one of Russia's top military decorations, and suffered being twice wounded in combat. By 1936, Rokossovsky had risen to command the 5th Cavalry Corps. Nonetheless, he was then arrested during the purges. Released from prison in March 1940, he was quickly promoted to major general. Konev's and Rokossovsky's opportunity to learn during the lean early war years allowed them to improve as combat leaders, much to the German army's detriment.

STALIN OVERREACHES

During 1941, the Red Army lost roughly 5 million men, 20,500 tanks, 101,100 guns and mortars, and 17,900 aircraft, representing 229 divisional-size units wiped from its order of battle.[43] All told, from June to December 1941, the Red Army had lost 20 permanent personnel losses for every German killed in action.[44] In addition, even as late as December, Soviet tactics had been extraordinarily poor, with tanks operating individually in support of broad-front human wave infantry attacks directed directly at German strongpoints rather than around them. Given such losses and problems, other leaders likely would have sought to dig in and regroup—but not Stalin. Instead, he authorized another offensive.

For his part, Zhukov initially approved of a more limited attack on Army Group Center. Zhukov, however, feared that his army lacked enough strength to achieve the broad results that Stalin demanded.[45] Events would prove Zhukov's analysis correct. Nevertheless Zhukov relented to Stalin's demands and agreed that multiple offensives across the front's breadth could pay substantial dividends if only destroying some German armies. Consequently, on January 7, 1942, Stalin launched a massive, frontwide offensive involving nine fronts running from north to south as follows: the Leningrad Front led by Khozin, the Volkhov Front led by Meretskov, the Northwestern Front led by Kurochkin, the Kalinin Front led by Konev, the Western Front led by Zhukov, the Briansk Front led by Cherevichenko, the Southwestern Front led by Timoshenko, the Southern Front led by Malinovskii and, finally, the Caucasus Front led by Kozlov.

On the German eastern front's left flank and beginning on January 10, Army Group North's 18th Army held off the best the Red Army could throw at it. The

Soviet offensive, designed to relieve Leningrad and take the Chudovo-Tosno main supply route, began well, and the 2nd Shock Army penetrated some 50 miles into German lines; however, the 54th Army's advance stalled, leaving the 2nd Shock Army dangerously exposed. On March 15, the Germans cut the base of the salient 2nd Shock Army had driven into German lines, trapping over 50,000 men from the 2nd Shock Army and 59th Army. General A. A. Vlasov was flown into the pocket to try to save the army. After a desperate struggle, however, by June 25, the Germans had eliminated the pocket. The Germans captured Vlasov and 33,000 men and killed an estimated 55,000 Russian soldiers during the struggle; though some 30,000 Soviet soldiers would escape the pocket. All told, between January and June 1942, the Volkhov Front would suffer 403,000 casualties.

To the German 18th Army's south, however, and along the border with Army Group Center, Colonel General Ernst Busch's 16th Army did not fare as well. An epic struggle played out in the snow-blanketed fields and forests near Demyansk. There, on February 8, Kurochkin's Northwestern Front had surrounded 96,000 German soldiers from Busch's command in a 35-mile-wide kessel. Busch's men would ultimately hold out for the remainder of the winter, led by the maniacal defensive efforts of the Totenkopf SS Motorized Division. Then, a relief effort led by Lieutenant General Walter von Seydlitz-Kurzbach, in an operation that lasted from March 20 to April 21, arrived to reopen lines of communication to the trapped German force.[46] Although Seydlitz's men successfully reestablished contact, the encircled men had survived their ordeal in part through aid provided by Luftwaffe supply drops, creating a dangerous precedent. Incredibly enough, German forces never evacuated the pocket completely, and the battles around Demyansk dragged on for a full year. As it was, Germany lost over 265 Ju-52 transport aircraft over Demyansk, destroying the cream of the German air transport arm.

While the 16th Army fought for its life on Army Group North's right flank, Konev's Kalinin Front wreaked havoc on Army Group Center's left flank. The Soviet 4th Shock Army, 29th Army, and 39th Army drove far behind German lines. On January 5, the 3rd Shock Army split Reinhardt's 3rd Panzer Army from the 9th Army's 6th Corps at Rzhev. On January 15, Hitler allowed the bulk of Army Group Center to withdraw, but he demanded Rzhev held. There the 9th Army, under General Walter Model's command, not only successfully checked the Russian advance on January 21, but also then managed to encircle and destroy the Soviet 29th Army, killing or capturing 26,000 men and destroying or seizing 180 tanks—a not inconsiderable number given the state of the Red Army's tank park by this point in the war. At the same time, Belov's 1st Guards Cavalry Corps, supported by three air-dropped brigades and partisans of the 4th Airborne Corps, roamed behind the 3rd and 4th Panzer Armies, creating further chaos across a front that had dissolved in any meaningful sense. Meanwhile, at Sukhinichi, farther south, the 2nd Panzer Army helped free surrounded German forces and also assisted 9th Army in staving off encirclement during the final weeks of January prior to Model's counterstrokes effectively turning the tables on his foe.[47] Farther south yet, the Soviet 6th, 9th, and 57th Armies hammered at Army Group South's 6th and 17th Armies in an offensive that began on January 18, 1942. By January 23, the Red Army had blown open a 50-mile breach in German defensive positions on the Donets River. Unfortunately for the Red Army, its shock armies lacked the logistical support, mobility, and reserves to do much with their success. Consequently, the 1st Panzer Army countered and battered the Soviet attackers back into what became a bulge in the German lines near Izyum. By early March, Army Group South's front had largely stabilized.

As the German and Russian armies remained locked in mortal combat, the Third Reich planned Europe's ethnic future on January 20, 1942, at Wannsee, Germany, with the chilling topic of the "final solution" to the "Jewish problem"—a solution that Hitler had very much accelerated throughout the latter half of 1941 as Barbarossa's failure undermined GeneralPlan Ost's future. Hitler and most of his leading officers ramped up the violence not only against Europe's Jews and Slavs but against others as well. Reprisals had long since become the order of the day for any partisan activities against the Third Reich.[48] The harsh occupation measures meant that resistance hardened. Even in the General-Government territories of eastern Poland, comparatively well staffed with 10,000 Ordnungspolizei and 16,000 Polish and Ukrainian police, there were far too few men to protect the Wehrmacht's lines of communication.[49] Increasing calls for manpower to patrol occupied Europe increasingly sapped the Wehrmacht's frontline strength. Hitler, however, refused to consider alternatives to the mass shootings and executions that characterized the Nazi reign of terror across Europe.

Meanwhile, late in the winter of 1941–1942, Stalin's counteroffensive had degenerated into an increasingly counterproductive exercise. Soviet infantry, lacking the firepower necessary to reduce German defensive positions, were all too often pushed into brutal and useless human wave assaults only weakly supported by tanks spread equally across the front. The lack of armor meant that Soviet cavalry played a critical role in putting pressure on the German positions. In one instance, two entire Cavalry Corps—the 1st Guards and the 11th—attempted to cut behind the German front on the road running from Smolensk to Vyazma.[50] Nevertheless, these units lacked adequate armament and leadership. Inexperienced Russian officers only modestly understood deep operational tactics. Consequently, Soviet divisional strength dropped to 3,000 men on average from starting strengths averaging 8,000 men. German counterattacks created a semblance of a front line, but long, exposed salients served as the norm into 1943. Thus, Army Group Center's front stretched over 900 miles, or equivalent to the distance from Michigan to well into Florida.

By April 1942, the six-month-long battle for Moscow that had begun in September 1941 had ended. The Red Army had suffered 926,000 killed in action defending Moscow and driving the Germans back from Moscow's gates. This number of dead represented more than the British and Americans lost combined, on all fronts, in World War II. Nevertheless, Germany had lost great quantities of war material and heavy weapons; among other things, these losses provided valuable time for relocated Soviet factories to come online and eventually surpass German production. As late as November 1941, the Ostheer possessed over a third of the armor with which it had started Barbarossa, as well as the capacity to retrieve and repair significant numbers of broken-down Panzers behind its front lines. Nevertheless, with the significant retreats forced by the Red Army's counteroffensives during the winter of 1941–1942, by the end of March 1942 the German Panzer and motorized divisions in the Soviet Union had lost this base of strength. Between June 1941 and March 1942, the German army lost 3,100 armored vehicles, 115,000 motor vehicles, 10,400 artillery pieces, and 260,000 horses on top of the 1 million casualties suffered in the Soviet Union.[51] The Luftwaffe was actually weaker than it had been on September 1, 1939, after dropping in strength by 600 aircraft since Barbarossa began.[52] The German army would never completely recover from this bloodletting, and would never again hold the quantitative advantages in heavy weapons and AFVs over the Red Army that it had held in the fall of 1941.

Barbarossa sought to annihilate the Soviet Union in a single campaign, but it failed. This failure, however, did not mean that Germany faced collapse in eastern Europe. In addition, although immense reserves of manpower had fueled the Red Army's resistance, an intense and aggressive defensive struggle waged by the Red Army had played a central role in the Wehrmacht's defeat. Furthermore, even though Hitler had made numerous mistakes, so did his military leadership. Hubris, wishful thinking, poor operational decision making, and fundamental systemic weaknesses in the intelligence and logistical arms of the German war machine had all fueled Barbarossa's downfall. Nevertheless, in terms of the Third Reich's larger war, the United States still stood a full campaign year removed from bringing any real military effort to the war in Europe. Additionally, Britain had suffered devastating losses in Asia to the Japanese and struggled more than ever to defend its empire. Meanwhile, in early 1942, Germany's U-boat campaign in the Atlantic achieved unrivaled success off the U.S. coast.

Discussions regarding the balance of power on the Eastern Front in early 1942 inevitably point to the Soviet Union's enormous geographic size and resources as working against a renewed German campaign. Regardless, and not to minimize Soviet potential, the Soviet Union had been even more blessed with equipment, men, intact industrial might, and resources in June 1941, yet Hitler's armies still had savaged the Red Army. As such, in the summer and fall of 1942, a massive but still raw army would face off yet again against a numerically inferior foe. Nonetheless, the reasons for success and failure on Germany's Eastern Front would prove to be anything but what we have been led to believe.

Chapter 6
Another Roll of the Dice

By the spring of 1942, Germany's strategic options in eastern Europe paled in comparison to those possible the year before. Hitler, however, refused to cede the initiative to a Red Army launching repeated offensives across Germany's Eastern Front. Instead, he commenced an immense strategic-level offensive of his own, one designed not to best the Red Army by seeking to force a single battle of annihilation, as the OKH had sought to do in 1941, but instead, to bring about a solution to the economic problems undermining his war by seizing the resources in the southern Soviet Union—resources that could allow Germany to build a potentially impregnable self-sustaining empire in Europe.

RESETTING THE GERMAN WAR ECONOMY

A number of decisions, issues, and events had worked together to hamstring the German economy in early 1942. Some had been long-standing problems, such as raw materials bottlenecks, shortages in petroleum products, inadequate steel output, and because Germany's otherwise innovative and diverse engineering base regularly struggled to concentrate production on a few war-winning weapons.[1] For example, before the war, the German economy supplied the Wehrmacht with 151 different models of trucks. Yet as late as the spring of 1942, this number had been reduced to a still unwieldy 23 truck models in production.[2] In addition, Fritz Todt, the Third Reich's minister for armaments and ammunition, had faced numerous additional structural problems inhibiting German economic production. Powerful domestic interests worked against each other, hoarded resources, and selfishly curried political favor. The Ministry of Economics, the War Economy Office, and the Four-Year Plan Organization competed at the top of the food chain; farther down the line, 27 other offices contributed to the mess.[3] By 1942, and despite problems such as those cataloged above, Todt had streamlined the convoluted German economic bureaucracy via the creation of Five Main Committees to direct the German armaments effort: ammunition, weapons, tanks, engineering, and general Wehrmacht equipment.[4] As Todt's reforms began to bear fruit, in February 1942 he died in a plane crash. In turn, Hitler replaced Todt with his personal architect, Albert Speer.

Speer lacked economic experience but possessed considerable organizational acumen, and was astute enough politically to work within the Third Reich's top ranks. In addition, Fritz Sauckel, appointed by Hitler on March 21, 1942, to manage Germany's never-ending labor crisis, provided Speer with 970,000 foreign laborers in 1942 alone. Speer routed most of his new workers to army production programs. Accordingly, armaments output climbed. For instance, in 1942, tank production had risen considerably, albeit from anemic 1940 and 1941 levels of 1,460 tanks and 3,256 tanks, respectively.[5] Furthermore, Speer worked to bring the critical parts-supplier industry, 3.8 million workers in 51,000 small firms, in line with the main committees for each armaments sector.[6] He replaced inefficient managers, reorganized the steel industry, and harnessed spare capacity in western European factories, steel mills, coal mines, and other production centers. Furthermore, in 1942, Germany made a 10 percent cut in coal production for domestic use, and centralized control over coal output. Steel production increased, and German productivity doubled within an overall labor force only one-third larger than the year before.[7] Although rationalization had helped, access to improved stocks of critical raw materials also played a key role in increased weapons production.

The 1942-era German army faced an increasingly debilitating problem. Production in important weapons systems had lagged so badly during 1941, and stocks of vehicles had fallen so low, as to dramatically impair its all-important mobility. In addition, fuel, ammunition, horse feed, and other such supplies had been consumed at vastly higher rates than forecast.[8] Moreover, there were not enough trucks, while a lack of rolling stock crippled rail transport. Losses in motor vehicles, prime movers, and horses were so high that in February 1942, Army Group South's new commander, Field Marshal von Bock, reported that the German eastern army was "not combat-ready for a war of movement."[9] This was a damning indictment for an army whose lifeblood was its maneuverability. In response, the German army had speeded development of tracked cross-country transport and towing vehicles: the Maultier (or Mule) and the Raupenshlepper Ost (or Caterpillar Tractor East).[10] Output of both these vehicles rose dramatically throughout 1942, but they provided only a partial solution to the deficiency in prime movers.

Consequently, and even as the 1942-era German economy demonstrated renewed life, Operation Barbarossa's losses had meant that the German army had begun an organizational devolution that ultimately lasted the entire war, one that would see its most important operational unit, the division, slowly cannibalized and weakened. For instance, of the 75 infantry divisions in Army Groups North and Center, 69 had their complement of infantry battalions lowered from nine to six each. Moreover, their organic artillery support fell from four guns in each battery down to three, representing a dramatic loss in indirect firepower. This is also noteworthy in terms of demonstrating how inefficiently the Germans mobilized their economy in comparison to the Soviets. For instance, to rapidly increase firepower, the Red Army had long since been taking delivery of inexpensively produced rockets and mortars as an adjunct to manufactured artillery pieces, moves that the Germans only gradually emulated. In addition, the German propensity to build large-bore anti-aircraft artillery for defending the home front against Allied bombers not only cut into the production of heavy indirect fire weapons for the frontline troops, but also resulted in huge amounts of ammunition diverted to the Luftwaffe. All this created enormous waste. Producing more fighter aircraft instead would have produced far more efficient results given that, on average, for every 16,000 anti-aircraft shells fired, only one enemy aircraft was destroyed.[11] Finally, Germany's Axis allies were just as underequipped as they had been in 1941. Although the 1941-era economic malaise in German-dominated Europe had bought Stalin critical breathing space, the Soviet economy was far from a production juggernaut.

THE SOVIET UNION REARMS

The Soviet Union is often presented during the war in eastern Europe as an overwhelming colossus. The truth is anything but that simple. In 1942, the Soviet Union's gross domestic product (GDP) had declined to only 70 percent of German GDP. Not until 1945 would Soviet GDP once again surpass Germany's.[12] In 1942, Soviet coal output stood at only 23 percent of German coal output, and Soviet steel output only 28 percent of Germany's.[13] Barbarossa also had inflicted tremendous destruction on the Soviet Union's rail and road network, impacting the allocation of raw materials in the Soviet economy, particularly in regard to the distribution of oil from the Caucasus. Difficulties such as these helped cause Soviet crude oil output to fall by one-third from 1941 to 1942. It dropped nearly another 20 percent by 1943.[14] Despite these handicaps, Stalin would wring far greater efficiencies from his hobbled economy than did Hitler from the German economy. Stalin accomplished this feat in large part for two reasons. First, nearly every facet of the Soviet economy went toward producing a few inexpensively produced but reliable and proven weapons systems. Second, Stalin's prewar industrialization programs in such regions of the Soviet Union as the Ural Mountains, Siberia, and Kazakhstan provided a base for readily assimilating western Soviet factories relocated east, and increased natural resource exploitation from these regions. That said, moving factories east had been far from a seamless process. By the summer of 1942, only 54 iron and steelworks, from the 94 in the Soviet Union the previous year, operated anywhere near capacity.[15] Consequently, and as just one example of what this meant for the Red Army, medium tank production had suffered heavily. Although by May 1, 1942, the Red Army could put 4,020 tanks into the field, more than half, 2,025, were light tanks.[16] Though Soviet factories managed to produce 12,553 T-34s during 1942, achieved mostly by squeezing the Soviet population relentlessly and building few other vehicles but tanks, the bulk of this output came later in the year.

Moreover, Soviet manpower losses in 1941 further weakened the Soviet economy. The industrial labor force fell from 8.3 million people in 1940 to 5.5 million people in 1942. By February 1942, the Red Army had lost over 3 million men captured by the Germans, and another 2,663,000 killed in action.[17] In response, Soviet women went to work in the factories at an increasing rate, ultimately constituting three-fifths of the public workforce in 1944. The Red Army also scoured farms for able-bodied men and boys eligible for conscription into the army, but this meant that agricultural output declined dramatically. Without Lend-Lease foodstuffs to compensate for the huge losses in agricultural output caused by German territorial gains, it is entirely possible that by 1944, the Germans would have starved the Soviet Union from the war.

On the other hand, the Red Army took in well over 2 million men per year from 1941 to 1943 alone.[18] In the spring of 1942, and with renewed stores of equipment, more experienced tactical- and operational-level leadership, and greater training time for recruits, the Red Army halted its devolution; and began creating organizations capable of standing up to Germany's murderously effective combined-arms combat teams. For example, on March 18, 1942, rifle divisions received a new *shtat* (table of organization) calling for far more automatic weapons, mortars, and anti-tank weapons than their late 1941 predecessors could rely on.[19] The Red Army also bolstered the effectiveness of the armor and infantry by reorganizing the artillery pieces and rockets rolling off Soviet assembly lines so that the High Command Reserve could concentrate the artillery where needed. Thus began a trend that would remain consistent throughout the war, as the Red Army consistently increased the firepower in its frontline units even while cutting their respective manpower allotment.

The trend toward increased firepower meant that throughout the spring, summer, and fall of 1942, the general of tank forces, I. N. Fedeorenko, who led the Red Army's armored reorganization, set up in total that year 28 tank corps, initially averaging 7,800 men, 98 T-34s, and 70 light tanks each, though its *shtat* would continually be tweaked. Nonetheless, throughout the war, Soviet tank corps remained commensurate in offensive punch to a 1941 era German Panzer division. Additionally, during August 1942, the Red Army also re-created a more manageable and streamlined mechanized corps, 13,500 men and 204 tanks, than its unwieldy 1940–1941 antecedent.[20] Furthermore, on May 25, 1942, the Red Army authorized new tank armies capable of fighting a German Panzer corps on its own terms. Problematically, however, a lack of training time and ongoing deficiencies in communications equipment plagued the first tank Armies.[21] As for equipping the new armored formations, each tank model was redesigned to lower manufacturing costs and increase production.

DUELING PLANS FOR THE SUMMER CAMPAIGN SEASON

Stalin and Stavka had been outfoxed during the spring of 1942 by German intelligence services that created the false impression that German armies were massed near Moscow; thus, they ordered that defensive efforts be concentrated before the Soviet capital. They also ambitiously planned at least six major offensives to be launched across the breadth of the front during the summer of 1942. In particular, Soviet General S. K. Timoshenko, commander of the Southwestern Main Direction, overseeing the Soviet Southwestern and Southern fronts, tapped the 60-square-mile Izyum salient—a bulge projecting into the German lines near Voronezh left over from where Stalin's January offensive had finally ended—as a springboard for a deep operational offensive designed to destroy Army Group South and push to Kiev. In the two fronts spearheading the anticipated campaign massed 640,000 men, 1,200 tanks, 13,000 guns, and 926 aircraft. Stavka had also ordered the Karelian Front to attack the Finns, the Leningrad and Volkhov fronts to rescue the encircled 2nd Shock Army, the Northern Front to hit the German 16th Army, the Bryansk Front to attack toward Kursk in support of the Kharkov offensive, and for the Crimean Front to relieve Sevastopol.[22] These campaigns proved anything but small in scale.

For instance, from January to September 1942, the Leningrad and Volkhov fronts repeatedly hit Army Group North in attempts to lift the German siege on Leningrad and clear the Siniavino heights dominating the approaches to Leningrad. The second Siniavino operation began on August 27, just as Manstein's 11th Army headquarters and four infantry divisions began arriving in the region following their redeployment from Army Group South. Accordingly, and just as in March, the Germans cut off the Soviet penetration and destroyed most of the 2nd Shock Army and the 8th Army, capturing or killing 114,000 men from the Leningrad and Volkhov fronts during the

Soviet offensive, and subsequent German counterattack, against 26,000 German casualties.[23] Farther south, Army Group Center held a winding defensive front between Orel in the south and Lake Il'men in the north. This front featured two massive salients, one held by the Red Army's Kalinin Front, centered near the town of Toropets, and one held by the German 9th Army, centered on Rzhev-Vyazma. In addition, one smaller German salient centered on Demyansk (actually held by Army Group North's 16th Army) abutted the boundary between Army Groups North and Center. On July 30 and August 4, respectively, Konev's Kalinin Front and Zhukov's Western Front attacked the German 9th Army. Konev's front made initial gains, but then was brought to a standstill by German reserves. On August 4, Zhukov struck, blew open the German lines, and committed his mobile group: the 6th and 8th Tank Corps and the 2nd Guards Cavalry Corps. The Germans, with the help of substantial armored reinforcements and questionable Soviet command decisions, stopped the Western Front's counterstroke. Soviet losses reached 500 to 700 tanks, even as Army Group Center weathered an additional attack launched by the Soviet 33rd Army against the 3rd Panzer Army. The primary attacking Soviet armies involved in these offensives—the 20th, 29th, 30th, 31st, 39th, and 41st— began August 1942 with 526,300 men. By September's end, they had lost 344,000 men killed, wounded, missing, or captured.[24]

In the meantime, in July, the Northwestern Front's 11th and 27th Armies attacked, and went nowhere, against Army Group North's 16th Army in its salient at Demyansk. This was followed by an August offensive featuring the 11th and 1st Shock Armies that also turned into a 10-day bloody mess before being called off in the face of stiff resistance, in particular from the 3rd SS Motorized Division. The German army's capacity not only to absorb and defeat each counterstroke, but also to launch counterstrokes of their own, taking 37,000 prisoner of war in Army Group Center's area of operations;[25] highlights the 1942-era Ostheer's considerable destructive capability while on the defensive. Meanwhile, Hitler readied his summer campaign farther south.

The campaign had one overriding goal: seizing the Soviet Union's oil production centers deep in the Caucasus, a task given to Army Group South as laid out in Hitler's Directive No. 41 issued on April 5, 1942. Although this plan, code-named Operation Blau (or Blue), was more focused in scope than Barbarossa had been, it was not nearly focused enough. On the one hand the Wehrmacht would finally seek as its primary goal the acquisition of economic resources that could very well virtually guarantee German hegemony over all of Europe. This represented a very different set of priorities than those of Barbarossa, when the OKH had insisted on attempting to defeat in the field a Red Army enjoying tremendous advantages in time and space as well as abundant reserves. That said, Hitler continued to underrate the Red Army's capabilities and overrate his own army's capacity for conducting offensive operations to such an extent as to once again fail to align expectations with the means to achieve them.

For instance, Directive No. 41 also ordered Army Group North to take Leningrad, with a follow-up assault planned even farther north to sever the Murmansk railroad. Such plans were made in spite of the fact that just in regard to Directive 41's goals in the southern Soviet Union, the German army would not only be logistically hard pressed to take its objectives, but also marginalized the reality that the stakes involved could not have been higher. Anywhere from 70 to 80 percent of the oil used by Soviet industry and the military came from the Maikop and Baku oil fields in the Caucasus,[26] with most coming from the Baku region. Without the Baku oil fields, the Soviet economy would have faced crippling oil shortages, the Red Army's mobility would have been vastly reduced, and Stalin may have been forced to seek an unfavorable peace.[27] It seems that, at the time, the Germans did not fully comprehend the region's importance to the Soviet economy. Nonetheless, both the Allies and the Soviet Union were keenly aware of the significance of the Caucasian oil fields.

Regardless of what the loss of the Caucasian oil fields would have done to the Soviet war effort, they held tremendous potential benefits for the German war economy. Most important, the capture of the Caucasian oil fields would allow Germany to wage a long war with a strong expectation of success. In addition, the oil fields were far better located for German purposes than those found in the Middle East, and they included extensive existing and repairable infrastructure. Thus, once German forces brought the fields online, they could then transport oil overland and, among other things, locally support the entire German Eastern Front. In comparison, any captured oil in the Middle East would have meant the need to create a massive logistical effort and air-sea capability to exploit those reserves. Furthermore, oil was far from the only economic resource available. In southern Russia, there existed a vast bounty of agricultural lands, coal, and iron in the Donbass region, and precious raw materials, such as manganese deposits, in Georgia. Moreover, Operation Blau envisioned German forces reaching and interdicting the Volga River, the Soviet superhighway that carried nearly all of Stalingrad's factory output and raw materials from the south.

Accordingly, Operation Blau offered Hitler the chance to strike a double blow of particular significance in that he could, at a stroke, obtain valuable economic resources, including the abundant reserves of oil in the Caucasus while denying the same to the Soviet Union. If Blau were successful, regardless of what the Soviet rump state did, Hitler could build the Third Reich's economic strength up enough to take on the U.S. colossus in a massive war fought across continents and oceans. No other move available in 1942 offered Germany the chance to so firmly cement a position of dominance over its enemies. For instance, renewing the assaults on Leningrad or Moscow would not have measurably improved Germany's economic situation, nor would they have offered any reasonable guarantees of victory in Europe. It was this unique opportunity for leveraging the

Wehrmacht's strengths to engineer a war-altering success that had made attacking the Soviet Union such an attractive possibility in 1941, and this reality remained true in 1942—regardless of the sheer size of a Red Army that, unless it learned how to fight, would not be able to defeat a German army husbanding its resources and actively waging a war of maneuver.

Approved by Hitler early in April 1942, Operation Blau required Army Group South to first launch a series of operations to clean up its front. Once this was completed, Blau featured a four-tiered schedule of operations. This would start with Blau I, a drive on Voronezh at the Don River; Blau II, a dramatic turn south and planned encirclement at Millerovo on the Donets River; Blau III, a push to Stalingrad on the Volga River; and Blau IV, the drive into the Caucasus. Following its initial phases, Army Group South would be split into two virtually independent Army Groups. Army Group A under Field Marshal Wilhelm List would push into the Caucasus. Army Group B would shield Army Group A's northern flank. Stalingrad's role in the initial plan was of a secondary nature, an objective only in the sense of reaching the Volga and protecting the flanks of the Army Group moving into the Caucasus. Under this plan only after Army Group South secured its northern flank would it redirect its main effort into the Caucasus.[28]

Even though the sequential nature of the plan seemed designed to minimize risks, it still faced numerous challenges. In the spring of 1942, the oil fields at Baku sat approximately 800 miles to the southeast of Army Group South's front lines in the Ukraine. Army Group South therefore needed to destroy the Red Army's regional assets as early in the campaign as possible. This would ensure a speedy advance (assuming proper logistical support), and create enough time to create a defensive front on Army Group South's lengthy and long-exposed northern shoulder. To that last point the plan made significant geographically motivated concessions, including relying for flank security on the liberal use of poorly equipped Hungarian, Italian, and Romanian troops stretched from the Don River to the Caspian Sea. The Romanian commitment to the German-led war against the Soviet Union had increased to 500,000 men in total. For their part, the Hungarians committed the 200,000-man Hungarian 2nd Army, and provided another 50,000 men for occupation duties. Meanwhile, despite the Axis need for Italy to focus on the war in North Africa, Mussolini had sent to Germany's Eastern Front the Italian 8th Army: 229,000 men, 16,700 motor vehicles, 946 artillery pieces, and 90 heavy anti-tank guns.[29]

Another problem undermining Axis operations in the Soviet Union was that despite Barbarossa's horrific intelligence gaffes, Germany had since then made only minor reforms in shaking up its intelligence operations in the east. Reinhardt Gehlen had arrived on April 1, 1942, to lead the German General Staff intelligence organization for the Eastern Front. Nonetheless, just prior to his appointment, in March 1942, Abteilung Fremde Heere Ost, the German army's eastern intelligence arm, had made yet another blunder when it underestimated Soviet manpower reserves.[30] Additionally, the German War Economy and Armament Department also had overestimated Soviet steel and oil output, but grossly underestimated tank, artillery, and aircraft production. Thus, the ill-informed initial German expectation—that if they could wear down the Red Army early in Blau, then they could more easily reach their strategic goals—had a profound impact on how Hitler and the OKH (Oberkommando der Heer, or Army High Command) prosecuted the campaign. One final problem had also cropped up to further undermine Germany's eastern European campaign. German barbarism behind the lines had created a full-scale partisan war not only in the occupied Soviet Union, but even farther behind the lines as well. For instance, the Polish Home Army waged an increasingly active guerilla war along vital German lines of communication.

Nevertheless, in May 1942, the Axis projected considerable power into eastern Europe and numbered 3,580,000 men, 950,000 from Germany's Axis allies, against 5,449,898 men fielded by the Red Army. Army Group South contained the bulk of this strength. It could put 71 German divisions into the field, including nine Panzer divisions and seven motorized divisions with 1,700 tanks and self-propelled guns between the Panzer and motorized divisions, though this was a total some 200 tanks short of authorized strength.[31] In addition, Army Group South could rely on Colonel General Wolfram von Richtofen's elite Fliegerkorps for close air support. From top down, the Army Group enjoyed veteran leadership, from Bock and List to army commanders such as Hoth (4th Panzer Army), Manstein (11th Army), and Kleist (1st Panzer Army). Seven experienced Panzer generals led the Panzer corps spearheading Blau: Geyr, Kempf, Kirchner, Langermann, Mackensen, Stumme, and Wietersheim. Finally, the mobile divisions forming the core of Blau's striking power could also count on proven commanders, such as Breith, Balck, and Hube.

The Soviet Fronts opposing Army Group South included the Briansk, Southwestern, Southern, and Crimean fronts. The Briansk Front's Lieutenant General F. I. Golikov was an established leader, and R. I Malinovsky, commanding the Southern Front, would go on to serve as one of the Red Army's top field commanders. Nonetheless, within these four fronts were 15 field armies commanded by a decidedly mixed bag of generals. The majority lacked the skill and experience of their German opponents. In addition, fully one-third of the 29 tank and mechanized corps commanders in opposition to Army Group South had never held a field command prior to the spring of 1942.[32] Therefore, although the Red Army had retooled, many of the same problems bedeviling it during Barbarossa lurked prior to the onset of Blau.

A BLOODY PRELUDE TO THE SUMMER AND FALL OF 1942

Both the prequel to the German summer offensive and the initial stages in the Soviet spring and summer offensives started in May. The results were uniformly disastrous for the Red Army. Prior to Operation Blau, Manstein's 11th Army defeated Soviet forces on the Kerch peninsula, Army Group South's main body crushed Timoshenko's offensive and countered with its own near Kharkov, and then Manstein captured Sevastopol in early July. During these combined battles, the Red Army lost 540,000 prisoners of war to the Axis armies. Between April and June 1942, the Red Army lost over 780,000 men in total to Army Group South. In comparison, the German army in eastern Europe lost 188,000 men from January to June 1942, meaning that, for every German killed, wounded, or captured, the Red Army endured at least seven permanent losses.[33] Stalin's ambitious goal for turning the tide against Germany in 1942 seemed crushed. Perhaps the only positive to come from the spring occurred when illness caused Shaposhnikov's reign as chief of the General Staff to end in April 1942, with the talented General Aleksandr Vasilevsky replacing him.

The defeat of the May 12 Soviet offensive at the Izyum salient had dealt a particularly tremendous blow to the Red Army. Timoshenko's assault had begun well. It even created a 30-mile hole in the southern part of the Axis lines. From there, however, things went rapidly downhill. Unbeknownst to Timoshenko, he had directed the Southwestern Front's offensive toward German assembly areas for Blau.[34] In addition, Timoshenko waited too long to commit his exploitation force, the 21st and 23rd Tank Corps, and, when committed, their distance behind the front meant that they bogged down on clogged and heavily damaged roads. Moreover, the Soviet staffs lacked the experience necessary to direct their large fast-moving armies, let alone resupply them. Furthermore, German air attacks hammered valuable transportation infrastructure.[35] Meanwhile, Luftflotte 4 also directly supported Kleist's reinforced 1st Panzer Army, spearheaded by General Eberhard von Mackensen's 3rd Panzer Corps. They joined with Friedrich von Paulus's 6th Army to strike deep into the flanks of the Soviet Southwestern Front's attack. On May 22, Mackensen's 14th Panzer Division met up with the German 6th Army's southward-advancing 51st Corps, and Army Group South had caught two entire Soviet armies, the 6th and the 57th; two tank corps, the 21st and the 23rd; a cavalry corps; two independent infantry divisions; and a huge bag of Soviet generals in a pocket running only 10 miles in length and two miles in breadth. The Soviet fronts that were involved lost nearly 300,000 men against 20,000 German casualties. The Southwestern Front commander, along with the commanders of the Soviet 6th and 9th Armies, had been killed, as were nearly every one of the two armies' divisional commanders. The Red Army had lost 1,249 tanks, according to the Germans, or 652 tanks, according to the Russians, and somewhere between 2,026 and 4,924 guns and mortars as well as 540 aircraft.[36]

Stalin desperately barraged his American and British allies to open a second front. The Germans relentlessly launched another drive, this time east, again spearheaded from the south by Mackensen's 3rd Panzer Corps. On June 13, Mackensen met up with the German 8th Corps advancing from the north, and captured another 21,000 Soviet prisoners of war from the battered Soviet 28th Army. On June 22, another German eastward drive, featuring Mackensen's Corps yet again, bagged a significant chunk of the Soviet 38th Army near the Oskol River and 13,000 more Soviet prisoners of war. Regardless, Mackensen's Corps had faced much hard fighting. In particular, the elite Soviet 9th Guards Rifle Division, led by Major General A. P. Beloborodov and supported by the 6th Guards Tank Brigade and 1st Destroyer Division, had caused the Germans substantial trouble.[37] Such defensive efforts proved the exception, however, and the Germans had absolutely mauled the Soviet Southwestern Front.

Meanwhile, in May 1942 in the Crimea, the German 11th Army, with nine German divisions and five Romanian divisions, broke open their months long battle against the Soviet Crimean Front on the Kerch peninsula and the Soviet Separate Coastal Army in Sevastopol. Despite the Crimean Front's size, General Kozlov commanded a force that included 259,622 men, 3,577 guns and mortars, 347 tanks, and 400 combat aircraft, it had failed to best Manstein in nine months of back-and-forth warfare across the Crimean Peninsula. This combat had featured a dizzying array of mobile mechanized warfare, attritional World War I trench-style warfare, daring amphibious assaults and raids, and one of the war's great city sieges.

In the spring of 1942, Manstein broke things open when he had duped Kozlov into misdirecting his defensive efforts. Manstein then concentrated Axis airpower to help his assault elements blast through the southern part of Kozlov's defensive line on the Parpach narrowing, where the Kerch peninsula met the larger Crimean landmass. Manstein also spearheaded his attack with four infantry companies loaded into assault boats. They infiltrated into the heart of the Soviet defensive positions by motoring up a flooded anti-tank ditch under cover of the noise created by the preparatory bombardment. There they surprised the defenders. Once a break had been forged through the Russian lines, the 22nd Panzer Division exploited the opportunity, covered the seven-mile distance to the coast, and enveloped the 47th and 51st Soviet armies. Meanwhile, a brigade-sized Kampfgruppen, featuring two Romanian motorized cavalry regiments, a German reconnaissance battalion, German motorized infantry company, and a German anti-tank company, drove east to Kerch, disrupting Soviet communications and Soviet attempts to assemble a counterthrust. On May 16, German infantry took the city of Kerch. Manstein had captured 170,000 prisoners of war, 258 tanks, and 1,100 guns—against only 7,588 Axis casualties. Manstein then turned his attention on the besieged Soviet forces within the Crimean port of Sevastopol.

Sevastopol possessed formidable defenses dating to the mid-nineteenth-century Crimean War, including three main defensive lines built into bare limestone rock and cliffs studded with concrete bunkers, trenches, heavy gun emplacements, and strongpoints. Manstein, however, had gathered the biggest artillery pieces and mortars ever built to blast through these defensive belts. These weapons included two colossal 600-mm guns and one 800-mm rail gun named "Dora" that could launch shells weighing in at over seven tons each and capable of penetrating 24 feet of concrete from a distance of 24 miles away. Manstein spent nearly an entire month reining unrelenting fire down on Sevastopol's defenders: General I. E. Petrov's 129,000-man 1st Independent Coastal Army. Once the Soviet positions had been heavily degraded, German combined-arms assault teams launched a series of brutal frontal assaults and fierce small-unit actions, eliminating strongpoints individually. On June 28, two German divisions sent by sea outflanked and unhinged the stubborn Soviet defensive positions. Russian resistance collapsed, once again demonstrating how skill, creativity, and the wherewithal to recognize when a critical moment in the battle had arrived, and then adjust aggressively, could defeat even the strongest defensive positions. On July 2, another 95,000 men marched into German prisoner-of-war camps.

From October 1941 to June 1942, the defense of Sevastopol cost the Red Army 156,880 killed, wounded, or missing as well as the 95,000 prisoners of war taken when the port's defenders surrendered.[38] German casualties, though, had also been atrociously high,[39] in stark contrast to German losses during the mobile Kerch clearing operation in May. All told, operations during the spring of 1942 cost the 11th Army 25,000 dead while tying up important rail lines with the ammunition and heavy weapons needed to take Sevastopol.[40] The civilian population in the Crimea continued to suffer horribly, and by April 8, 1942, Einsatzgruppen D had murdered 91,678 people,[41] done with the active support of Manstein's 11th Army.[42] In recognition of his bloody achievements, Hitler promoted Manstein to field marshal. Nonetheless, instead of allowing the 11th Army to cross the Kerch Strait and enter the Kuban, or form a potent operational reserve for Army Group South, Hitler sent the army headquarters, three infantry divisions, one light division, and its heavy artillery to take Leningrad. Hitler then scattered three of the 11th Army's other divisions across the map, leaving the few remaining German and Romanian units with Army Group South.

Because the clearing operations in the Crimea did not end until July, the German summer offensive had been delayed. Meanwhile, Stavka had finally authorized additional reinforcements for the region, in part because of another German intelligence gaffe.[43] Consequently, before Blau I began, Stavka had heavily reinforced Golikov's Briansk Front until it fielded 1,600 tanks in seven tank corps and eight independent tank brigades.[44] Just east of Kursk, Golikov's front faced the German 2nd Army, the Hungarian 2nd Army, and the 4th Panzer Army's 733 tanks and assault guns.[45] Just to the south of these armies sat the Southwestern Front. It had somewhat rebuilt and fielded 640 tanks in four tank corps and 15 independent tank brigades. The German 6th Army served as its initial opponent.[46] Elsewhere, the Soviet Southern Front was weakly equipped in armor, with only eight independent tank brigades.

In opposition, the Axis fielded assorted Romanian, Hungarian, Italian, and Slovakian units; the German 17th Army; and the 1st Panzer Army. Farther south, the all-infantry German 11th Army faced the North-Caucasus Front and Trans-Caucasus Front, each Soviet front being woefully deficient in armor.[47] In addition, the delay in launching Operation Blau had allowed the German tank park to recover to three-quarters its numerical strength on the eve of Barbarossa, and with greater hitting power. Long-barreled 50-mm guns equipped most Panzer IIIs, and high-velocity 75-mm guns equipped the newest Panzer IVs trickling into Army Group South's Panzer and motorized divisions such that most included anywhere from four to 12 of the upgraded Panzers. Army Group South contained 1,635 tanks on the eve of Blau, though only 936 were Panzer IIIs, 156 were Panzer IVs with the short-barrel 75-mm gun, and 121 were Panzer IVs with the long-barrel 75-mm gun.[48] All told, Army Group South's 1.25 million men, 950,000 Germans, including the 11th Army, faced off against 1,715,000 Soviet soldiers. In addition, the Russians held a decided edge in combat-worthy medium and heavy tanks, with 2,300 such tanks facing only 1,327 German medium tanks. In comparison, the Germans could count on a tremendous advantage in airpower: 1,640 machines against only 758 Soviet combat aircraft.

GERMANY'S SECOND GREAT SUMMER OFFENSIVE: STRAYING FROM THE PLAYBOOK

The German assault began on June 28 with a double move on Voronezh. Hoth's 4th Panzer Army and the 2nd Army advanced on one flank, and Paulus's Sixth Army surged forward on the other flank.[49] Spearheaded by three Panzer corps, the German armies met on July 2 deep behind the Briansk and Southwestern fronts' former front lines. In just 15 days, the Panzer spearheads had raced nearly 120 miles, and captured all their geographical objectives on the Don River's western bank. In addition, and in the Voronezh region, they had annihilated the Soviet 40th and 21st Armies, destroyed four of the Briansk Front's seven tank corps, and badly damaged the other three.

Although German forces captured Voronezh on July 6, the Briansk Front and newly formed Voronezh Front had fought fiercely. In an effort to reverse their losses, the Soviet had sent in the newly formed 5th Tank Army, under General A. I. Liziukov, and its 641 tanks in addition to an entire reserve army and numerous tank corps. Yet, even though the 5th Tank Army's ranks included several tough and competent commanders, including General Pavel

Romistrov, who commanded the 7th Tank Corps and later was the 5th Tank Army commander, its combat arms consistently failed to coordinate well or even deploy properly. Hoth's 4th Panzer Army, in conjunction with the Luftwaffe's close air support, simply slaughtered what should have formed a potent threat to the German assault armies. By July 15, the 5th Tank Army had irrevocably lost 261 of the 641 tanks with which it had started the battle one week prior, and, in total, half its tanks were out of action.[50] In addition, the German 2nd, 6th, 4th Panzer, and 2nd Hungarian Armies had opened a cavernous 280-mile gap in the Soviet defensive positions. In response, Stalin ordered General K. K. Rokossovsky to take command of the Briansk Front and Lieutenant General N. F. Vatutin to take over the Voronezh Front.[51]

The German 6th Army and 4th Panzer Army had followed Voronezh's fall by continuing their advance southeast toward Millerovo on the Donets River and toward Kalach on the Don River. They destroyed or severely damaged the Soviet 9th, 21st, 28th, and 38th Armies from the Southwestern and Southern fronts. Meanwhile, on July 7, the German 1st Panzer Army, the 17th Army, and the Romanian 3rd and 4th Armies opened Blau II, ripping apart Soviet defensive efforts before Rostov and capturing the city within just two weeks. Unfortunately, the Germans, relying again on woeful intelligence, had launched two successive encirclement battles by the combined 1st Panzer and 4th Panzer Armies, achieving almost nothing worthy of their efforts. For example, in operations on the approaches to Rostov, Mackensen's 3rd Panzer Corps took 33,000 Soviet prisoners of war against only 251 dead and 1,134 wounded from his command, but as the 1st Panzer Army's spearhead, he had failed to encircle what should have been entire Soviet armies.[52] For their part, Hitler and Halder, disconcerted by the failure to replicate Barbarossa's great prisoner-of-war hauls, had interfered constantly with Bock's ability to develop the German assault toward Rostov and between the Don and Volga Rivers. In retrospect, had Bock been given operational freedom to maneuver it is likely that he could have encircled the Russian survivors straggling east from the first battles near the Don River—regardless of the choice made by Stalin, Stavka, and local Soviet commanders to carry out tactical withdrawals.

For his part, Hitler had arrived at Vinnitsa in the Ukraine. There he set up a command post, code-named "Werewolf," where he would micromanage the campaign. Perhaps his worst decision came quickly when he attempted to have it all at once. Hitler prematurely set in motion an accelerated timetable casting aside the original plans for Blau's third phase. Although Hitler's orders instituted the planned-for reorganization of Army Group South into two army groups, this decision was made even though Army Group South's northern shoulder had not yet been secured. Consequently, Army Group B, under Bock, stood astride the two northern axes of advance near Voronezh and toward Stalingrad. Army Group B initially included the German 4th Panzer Army, the 2nd Army, the Sixth Army, and the Hungarian 2nd Army.

OPERATION BLUE AND DRIVE INTO THE CAUCASUS

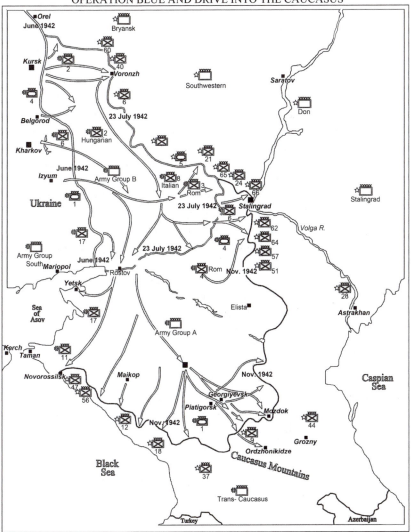

Army Group A, tasked with advancing from the region near Rostov into the Caucasus, under List's command, initially featured the German 1st Panzer Army and 11th and 17th Armies.[53] Unfortunately for List, Hitler broke up the 11th Army, a decision objected to by Halder.[54] Regardless, Hitler, given the great geographical conquests of Blau's first three weeks, overoptimistically believed that the remaining Axis armies in southern Russia carried enough strength to take their objectives. Although List received the 4th Panzer Army shortly thereafter, the untimely diversion of Hoth to the southwest, prior to first advancing to the Volga as envisioned by the original plan, created a huge logistical mess, slowed Sixth Army's advance east, and meant that many Soviet troops escaped encirclements not only along the axis of advance on Stalingrad but also farther south before Rostov.[55] Thus, Army Group A took only 54,000 prisoners during Blau II's first three weeks. Poor prisoner hauls were also exacerbated by fuel shortages plaguing the German Army Groups.[56] At one point in the campaign, the 6th Army wasted eight days sitting because it lacked the necessary fuel to advance. One of the key fundamentals for a German drive into the Caucasus had been severely undermined. Army Group South had failed to destroy the bulk of the Red Army's forces west of the Don River. Meanwhile, Stalingrad sat wide open. It could have been easily taken had Hitler stuck to Blau III's original mandate. Instead, the Soviet Stalingrad Front had been granted the time to set up its initial line of defenses along the Chir and Don Rivers west of Stalingrad.[57]

There were three main reasons for the operational dissonance plaguing the Axis efforts. First, shortly after Blau began, the OKH had realized that the Red Army was stronger than expected. Hitler disagreed. He not only interpreted a June 28 Fremde Heere Ost report on the Red Army's capacity to replenish its ranks and resist in a more optimistic manner, but also was far more ecstatic over the results produced by German victories in the late spring and early summer than had been the OKH. Hitler further undermined Blau's chances for success when he allowed his fears that the Anglo-Americans would invade western Europe to result in his July 9 orders to send two elite SS Panzer grenadier divisions to bolster western Europe's defenses.[58] In addition Hitler ordered other German formations to prepare to transfer west, including the crack Grossdeutschland motorized division.[59] Finally, Hitler's Directive No. 45 dictated that Army Group A move into the Caucasus at the same time that Army Group B captured Stalingrad, with the former plan code-named Edelweiss, rather than after Army Group A's northern shoulder had been secured. This also represented the first time that capturing Stalingrad, in lieu of masking it, had been a part of the plan. Ironically, given Hitler's fears regarding an Allied invasion of western Europe, he would have been better served in more ruthlessly prosecuting the original plans for Blau, at least as it applied to southern Russia. Although counterfactuals are always problematic, it is likely that had Hitler made such a decision, the Red Army would not have been able to stop either Army Group A or Army Group B, and that Operation Blau might have met its goals.[60]

In light of Hitler's changes to Blau, Army Group B comprised the powerful Sixth Army, and the decidedly less potent 2nd Army, along with two weak allied armies—the 2nd Hungarian and 8th Italian—all under General Maximilian von Weichs. All told, Weichs had 37 divisions and 386 tanks against an equivalent Soviet force in terms of manpower, but far more well equipped; with 1,939 tanks. Army Group A included the German 1st Panzer Army, the 4th Panzer Army, elements from the 11th Army, the 17th Army, and the 3rd Romanian Army all arrayed against the weak North Caucasus Front's 253 tanks and 34 divisional equivalents.[61] All told, Blau I and Blau II, between June 28 and July 24, had cost the Briansk, Voronezh, Southwestern, and Southern fronts, and the Azov flotilla 568,347 casualties, including 370,522 killed or captured, out of 1,310,800 men who had fought in these battles.[62] In addition, the Red Army had lost 2,436 tanks, 13,716 guns and mortars, and 783 combat aircraft.[63]

Army Group A represented the linchpin of the German strategic effort. List's objectives included the Maikop oil fields about 180 miles to the south of his positions near Rostov, the Grozny oil refineries nearly 400 miles to the southeast, and the Baku oil fields over 250 miles past Grozny. Incredibly, Hitler was seeking to conquer an enormous expanse containing desert, steppe, the imposing Caucasus Mountains, and a profound lack of transportation infrastructure with initially only four armies (plus supporting elements) and shortly thereafter only three armies. Moreover, these were armies that continued to weaken as they battled to the southeast. The scary thing would be that Hitler nearly succeeded anyway.

List divided his armies into two pincers: Hoth's 4th Panzer Army and Kleist's 1st Panzer Army to the east, with 435 tanks combined, and the German 17th Army and Romanian 3rd Army reinforced with a Romanian Mountain Corps, removed from the disassembled German 11th Army, to the west. Buddeny's North Caucusus Front provided the bulk of the region's defenders. Malinovsky's battered Southern Front could field only 112,000 men, 169 guns, and 17 tanks. After a surprisingly initially tough going, List dismantled Malinovsky's defenses, and sent the Soviet armies before him reeling in retreat. At this point, however, Hitler ordered 4th Panzer Army north to bolster Army Group B's advance on Stalingrad, and therefore likely saved Buddeny's front from total annihilation. In September, List also lost the Romanian 3rd Army to Army Group B. This left him with only the 1st Panzer Army, the 17th Army, and roughly 350 tanks to conquer a landmass roughly equivalent in size to France.

Despite the huge geographic tasks confronting List, Army Group A swallowed up vast amounts of territory, penetrating over 300 miles in mere weeks. By August 10, German forces had captured the Maikop oil fields and put their 6,500-man Petroleum Technical Brigade to work repairing the thoroughly demolished industrial works.[64] Even though List had won impressive victories, from July 1 to August 10 Army Group A had taken 390,000 prisoners of war,[65] he also faced increasingly insurmountable problems stemming from his lack of resources. Nevertheless, on August 30, the 3rd German Panzer Division, from the 1st Panzer Army, crossed the Terek River. Grozny, only 50 miles farther southeast, and thereafter the Baku oil fields on the Caspian seemed within reach. Meanwhile, far to the west of the 1st Panzer Army, the German 17th

Army slugged its way through the prime defensive terrain along the Black Sea's coast—exactly the battle that Germany could ill afford, but could have avoided had Army Group A not lost substantial hitting power after moving into the Caucasus.

As the 17th Army struggled along the coast, the 1st Panzer Army, despite little air support and increasing Soviet resistance, ground ahead and had driven to within striking range of two vital military targets: the Georgian and the Ossetian military roads. Whoever controlled these roads, the only roads in the entire region capable of supporting an army, would control the Caucasus. The stakes could not have been higher. If the Germans pushed through and even blocked the Georgian and Ossetian military roads, then it would have been nearly impossible for the Red Army to maintain its forces in the Caucasus. Almost their entire logistical support network depended on these roads.[66] On October 25, the 2nd Romanian Mountain Division punched through the Soviet 37th Army's defensive positions. In addition, the 13th and 23rd Panzer Divisions crossed the Terek to envelope and eviscerate the Soviet 37th Army, taking 11,000 prisoners of war and blowing open the Soviet defensive front guarding the approaches to the Georgian and Ossetian military roads. By November 1, the 13th Panzer Division's spearhead had advanced to within 10 miles of the Georgian military road and the city of Ordzhonikidze. The 23rd Panzer had closed the Ossetian military road and was within mere miles of shutting down the primary Soviet logistical lines in the Caucasus, and completely isolating the Baku oil fields.

Soviet resistance invariably stiffened yet again, and again the German advance slowed to a crawl. By November 5, however, the 13th Panzer Division had closed to within one mile of its objective. Amidst fierce fighting on November 6, the Soviet 37th Army launched a T-34-led counterattack that ripped into the German lines, temporarily encircled the 13th Panzer Division, and then forced it to retreat. The 1st Panzer Army had run out of reserves, strength, and time while fighting against determined defenders in superb defensive terrain. There is a serious argument to be made that the Germans had mostly themselves to blame for the failure to secure their objectives, for while the German 13th and 23rd Panzer Divisions had ground onward, Hitler and the OKH had dispatched the 16th Motorized Division into a veritable no-man's-land northeast. It drove to within 20 miles of the Caspian Sea, ostensibly on a mission to maintain links between Army Groups A and B, but it accomplishing nothing of strategic value. Had the 16th Motorized Division been instead deployed as part of the 1st Panzer Army's spearhead, could it have proven the difference and allowed the Germans to take the Caucasian oil fields?[67] Meanwhile, as the drama in the Caucasus played out, far to the north, the 6th Army and the 4th Panzer Army had long since begun the battle that many today argue would define the war.

STALINGRAD: AN EPIC BATTLE BEGINS

On July 17, the German 6th Army reached the Chir River, a branch of the Don River, and initiated the battle for Stalingrad when it ran into several units from what would become its nemesis—the Soviet 62nd Army.[68] The region across which the 6th Army fought featured flat, nearly treeless steppe crisscrossed by small ravines and dominated by the parallel north-to-south-running Don and Volga Rivers and their tributaries. The 62nd Army, formed from reserves desperately flung together, represented one of three armies forming the Stalingrad Front on July 22, 1942. Coupled with the 63rd and 64th Armies and the newly forming 1st and 4th Tank Armies, the Stalingrad Front, although raw and inexperienced, was stocked with lavish amounts of armor, some 1,239 tanks in total. It included 550 tanks in the nascent 1st and 4th Tank Armies. The reinforced German 6th Army, with roughly 290 tanks, stood against this imposing weight of Soviet armor.

In addition, to organize Stalingrad's defense, Stalin had sent in new Deputy Supreme Commander Zhukov, along with Soviet Army Chief of Staff General Alexander M. Vasilevsky and political commissar Nikita S. Khrushchev. This was done amidst larger reforms arising from Soviet losses incurred during the spring and early summer. Stalin had virtually shut down agricultural output, and cut back caloric allotments to 750 per day for dependents and only 1,913 per day for heavy workers.[69] He transferred millions of workers into armaments factories where tanks, artillery, and combat aircraft poured off the assembly lines, but with an enormously destructive impact on the Soviet economy. A key element behind Stalin's reformed defensive strategy was his July 28 Order No. 227, the "Not One Step Backward" order. The order read much as a classic Hitler edict on defensive warfare: "Panic-mongers and cowards must be destroyed on the spot."[70] Stalin directed the Red Army to create special ranks of soldiers for the express reason of killing those who ran from German attacks, and he placed them behind the main defensive lines. By April 1943, Viktor Abakumov's "Special Departments" had completed its transformation into the feared SMERSH unit, SMERSH standing for *Smert Shiponam* (death to spies).[71]

Directly facing the elite German 6th Army west of Stalingrad was Major General V. I. Kolpakchi's raw 62nd Army and 42-year-old General Vasili Ivanovich Chuikov's 64th Army. Chuikov was a decorated combat veteran from the Russian Civil War, and a graduate of the prestigious Frunze Academy who had risen through the Red Army's ranks but whose command was horribly inexperienced. The results were inevitable. In a tremendous combined-arms assault beginning on July 24, the German 6th Army penetrated the Soviet 62nd Army's right flank, encircled two Russian infantry divisions, and rolled on to the Don River. The other hammer fell on July 25 as the Germans blasted through the 62nd Army's left flank. Vasilevsky sent in the newly formed 1st and 4th Tank Armies in a desperate July 27 counterattack aimed at saving the 62nd Army. However, active German close air support and superior tactics defeated Vasilevsky's counterattack and decimated all six divisions from the 62nd Army, including the elite 33rd Guards Division.[72] In just eight days, the Stalingrad Front lost half its tanks even as Stavka funneled in hundreds more as reinforcements.[73]

Meanwhile, to stall the main German axis of advance, Stavka had previously ordered the Briansk Front's 5th Tank Army and 40th Army to strike Army Group B's overextended northern flank just west of Voronezh, and for Zhukov's Western Front to strike Army Group Center's 2nd Panzer Army northeast of Orel. Beginning on July 5, Zhukov's 16th and 61st Armies slammed into the 2nd Panzer Army. Nonetheless, poor coordination between arms and the arrival of German reserves doomed the Soviet effort, even though Zhukov's armies held an initial six-to-one advantage in armor.[74] Just to the south, near Voronezh, both the Briansk and the Voronezh fronts launched repeated attacks against Salmuth's well-dug-in 2nd Army. Nonetheless, Salmuth effectively used the 9th Panzer Division to lead a roving mobile reserve that repeatedly hammered the Soviet spearheads and restored his front.[75]

Outside military observers were far from impressed with the Soviet effort. For example, on July 15, 1942, British intelligence prepared a report titled "Possible Action in the Event of Soviet Collapse." This report found that though the Red Army had demonstrated its defensive prowess when dug in, "the Red Army is still not capable of dealing with the Germans in the open terrain of South Russia."[76] Army Group B withstood the Soviet attacks near Voronezh, and by August 8 the 6th Army had taken 57,000 prisoners, captured or destroyed 1,000 tanks,[77] and mauled the four Soviet armies defending Stalingrad's western approaches. That said Soviet resistance meant that the German 6th Army spent over a month clearing the Great Bend in the Don River. Hitler had also been forced to weaken Army Group B's exposed northern shoulder by sending Paulus four German divisions. The ill-equipped Italian 8th Army replaced them on the Don River defensive line.

By mid-August, the reinforcements sent to assist the drive on Stalingrad had transformed the German 6th Army into the most powerful army in the world, deploying 22 divisions and supporting units. In opposition, the Stalingrad Front had dropped from 1,239 tanks on July 22 to 250 tanks, while the Southern Front was down to 200 tanks against roughly 450 German tanks in opposition to both fronts. During the first half of August, Paulus leveraged the rough balance in armored forces to decimate the 1st and 4th Tank Armies and the 62nd Army and then destroy the 4th Tank Army yet again on August 15, while on August 17 defeating a significant Soviet counterattack. Nonetheless, though the Germans relentlessly hammered the Soviet armies across the steppe, Stavka had gained time to rush reserves to the region and

Table 6.1 Soviet versus German Losses on Voronezh and Stalingrad Axes of Operations, June 28 to November 17, 1942[1]

	Casualties	Tanks
Soviet losses	1,200,000	4,862
Axis losses	200,000	700

[1]David M. Glantz and Jonathan M. House, *Armageddon in Stalingrad: September–November 1942* (University Press of Kansas, 2009), 717.

wear down the Germans. If not forced to rely so heavily on superior tactics to compensate for the sheer inadequacy of their own tank guns and armor, the German Panzers may have proved unbeatable. As it was, however, Army Group B battered its way through Stalingrad's outer defensive rings, instilling a demoralizing sense of fear in the Soviet ranks. By the end of August, the 6th Army and 4th Panzer Army had linked up, and the 62nd and 64th Armies had been isolated in Stalingrad, all while the Germans ran the total Soviet losses in the region since mid-July to over 300,000 men and 1,000 tanks (see Table 6.1 for overall Soviet losses).[78]

On August 23, the 16th Panzer and 3rd Motorized Divisions, including 120 tanks and 200 armored personnel carriers, supported by the 8th Air Corps, powered out of a bridgehead over the Don River and raced to the Volga just north of Stalingrad. Stavka and Eremenko, recognizing that the Germans were on the verge of unhinging the entire Soviet defensive effort on the southern half of the front, scrapped together everything they could, including anti-aircraft batteries manned by crudely trained civilians, and rushed them to Stalingrad's northern suburbs. By August 31, the German attempts to break into the city from the north had failed. The German position on the Volga then held on by the slimmest of margins against sustained and heavy Soviet counterattacks launched by recently arrived reserves.

As the bulk of the 6th Army began catching up with its mobile forces, to the south and between August 20 and September 2, the 4th Panzer Army had bulled its way into Stalingrad's southern suburbs. In addition, Hoth, having split the 64th Army, nearly encircled the bulk of the 64th Army as well as endangering a significant portion of the 62nd Army. Yet several mistaken deployments, including by Paulus, let the two battered Soviet armies slip into the relative safety of the city. The Germans suffered another setback when Soviet counterattacks against Army Group B's left wing allowed the Soviet 21st and 63rd Armies to forge important crossings over the Don at Serafimovich and Kletskaia. Major General I. A. Pliev and his 3rd Guards Cavalry Corps played a crucial role in exploiting the initial successes won by the two Soviet armies. Then the German army failed to clear the bridgeheads. The OKH subsequently misread the importance that these bridgeheads would hold to any future Soviet attempts to pressure Army Group B's northern flank.

Despite these minor successes, frustration abounded within the Soviet leadership. Even the new tank corps and tank armies had failed to change the fact that the Red Army had proven unable as of yet to defeat a major German summer offensive. Stalin was furious. He knew Stalingrad's importance to the entire Soviet war effort:

> What's the matter with them (the Red Army's generals), don't they understand that if we surrender Stalingrad, the south of the country will be cut off from the centre and will probably not be able to defend it? Don't they realize that this is not only a catastrophe for Stalingrad? We would lose our main waterway and soon our oil too![79]

If Army Group B took Stalingrad and crossed the Volga, Germany's motorized armies would face little more to stop them than the windswept plains stretching into Asia. In short, the Red Army *had* to stop Germany at Stalingrad. Yet the only thing standing before the 6th Army and the 4th Panzer Army was the beat-up 62nd and 64th Armies. Once again, a massive army bore down on a numerically inferior foe, and Stalingrad's future seemed bleak.

STALINGRAD: A LESSON IN FIREPOWER'S LIMITS

There is no question that the OKH and Hitler had made significant mistakes in how they had directed the campaign in southern Russia. Had the original plans for Blau been followed (instead of the changes made in reality), even leading Russian officers, such as 62nd Army Staff Officer Anatoly Mereshko, admit that their chances would have been nearly nonexistent.[80] Nevertheless, the German 6th Army held enormous advantages over the primary Soviet army defending Stalingrad: the Soviet 62nd Army (see Table 6.2).

Although the battle for Stalingrad has received an enormous amount of attention in years past, most of this attention has come from a German perspective, emphasizing Soviet strength in numbers, the horrors of urban

Table 6.2 German Forces from 6th Army and 4th Panzer Army versus Soviet 62nd Army in Stalingrad on September 3–12, 1942[1]

	Soviet 62nd Army	German 51st Corps, 48th Panzer Corps
Personnel	54,000	80,000
Tanks	115	110
Aircraft	137[2]	550[3]

[1]David M. Glantz and Jonathan M. House, *Armageddon in Stalingrad: September–November 1942* (University Press of Kansas, 2009), 30–31, 84–85, 94–95.
[2]From Soviet 8th Air Army and in operational aircraft on September 3.
[3]From Luftflotte 4 and in operational aircraft in early September.

warfare, and a perspective castigating the very leadership that had brought Germany to Stalingrad. In hindsight, the German war machine rolling toward Stalingrad in August 1942 appeared to be anything but standing on the edge of a disaster. It appeared invincible. It is from therefore a more objective approach that we will examine why the sheer-brute-force advantages enjoyed by the German 6th Army over Stalingrad's defenders, in particular the Soviet 62nd Army, could not produce final success. Yet we will also explore how the battle within the city limits came dangerously close to securing a German victory, and thus how thin the line often stretched between defeat and victory during World War II.

Stalingrad represented a logical place for a Soviet defensive stand. First, if an invader held Stalingrad, then he controlled the approaches to the Caspian Sea, the port of Astrakhan, and the thousands of square miles of steppe that defined a region that had long represented an important trading crossroads. Second, Stalingrad sprawled along the western bank of the Volga River, making laying siege to the city a difficult task. Moreover, Stalingrad represented one of Russia's great industrial cities. Its tractor factory had been converted to tank production in 1941; it boasted one of Russia's oldest artillery factories, the Barrikady, and contained oil refineries, chemical plants, and considerable steelworks.[81] In the fall of 1942, the Red Army turned these huge factory complexes into veritable fortresses of immense proportions. The Red October metalworks, the Barrikady gun factory, and Dzerzhinsky tractor works were each over half a mile long and a quarter of a mile wide.[82] Defensively, Stalingrad also featured a prominent hill dominating much of the northern part of the city, the Mamayev Kurgan, an ancient Scythian burial ground rising 300 feet from the otherwise largely flat landscape. Finally, with one of Paulus's Panzer corps tied down north of Stalingrad, his initial effort to take the city, originally planned to be led by Panzer corps advancing from the north and south of Stalingrad, had devolved into a straight-up west-to-east drive led by a German infantry corps as it thrust into the heart of the city—and the strength of Soviet defenses.

Still, Stalingrad had weaknesses. The Volga River represented less than an ideal place for the Red Army to make a stand, given the need for the Red Army to ship along the river raw materials and oil from the Caucasus into the Russian interior. Moreover, Stalingrad's primary logistical link to the Soviet interior came from a new rail line from Saratov to Leninsk 12 miles east of Stalingrad. This rail line ostensibly replaced those that the Germans had cut during their July and August advance. Thus, to get supplies into Stalingrad, they would have to go by boat across the Volga, under observation from whoever held a long line of hills just to Stalingrad's west and north. Consequently, when on August 23 the Germans entered Rynok, a small suburb just north of Stalingrad, they had captured high ground, allowing them to direct murderous artillery fire down into the city and at the Volga crossings, supply crossings bombarded as well by German aircraft and mortars and even swept by German heavy machine guns. Furthermore, in many places, Stalingrad stood no more than one to two miles deep before reaching the banks of the Volga. Additionally, unlike the byzantine labyrinth that defined many European city layouts, Stalingrad featured many wide streets running straight into the riverbank and providing relatively easy avenues of advance. Finally, Stalin's decision to fight the Germans on the steppe rather than allowing his armies to fade back into the city meant that the Soviet 62nd Army that scrambled into Stalingrad in August was far from the elite force it would become. It was a beaten, bloodied army consisting of a handful of rifle divisions in name only and a smattering of threadbare attached units.

In August 1942, the Red Army had psychologically reached perhaps its lowest point in the war. Soldiers of the Red Army fighting against the Germans in the summer of 1942, such as Anatoly Kozlov, a liaison officer in the 1st Tank Army, spoke for many of his former comrades when he described their despair as near complete in the face of what seemed to be overwhelming German strength. The Germans dominated the skies, possessed far greater mobility, and enjoyed better equipment, particularly in communications.[83] Nevertheless, though General Paulus carried a reputation as a superb planner and a master of organization, he also proved a hesitant field commander. Consequently, at critical points in the battle, when a more engaged, aggressive, and decisive commander may have thrown everything at opportunities as they opened up, Paulus would vacillate. This indecision was possibly critical to the outcome of the struggle, particularly in the crucial battles of mid-September and mid-October.[84]

Sunday, August 23, is often regarded as the day when the battle for Stalingrad formally began as Luftwaffe General Von Richtofen's pilots carpet bombed the city. Before the week ended, the Luftwaffe had murdered over 40,000 civilians—men, women, and children alike.[85] On the ground Paulus pushed home the German assault. German forces destroyed Stalingrad's water supply, electricity, telephone exchange, and rail station. On August 28, a mass panic swept through the city, and the NKVD (People's Commissariat for Internal Affairs) nearly lost control over the population.[86] Looting spread throughout the city. On August 29, however, Soviet reinforcements bolstered Stalingrad's northern defenses. Nonetheless, the 62nd Army was cracking. On September 8, its left front collapsed and completely isolated it from its neighbor armies. Then, on September 12, Vasily Chuikov took command of the embattled 62nd Army.

Chuikov quickly imprinted his authority on the army when, in front of the 62nd Army's entire headquarters, he announced that its location would be only 800 meters from the front lines.[87] Chuikov fought from the front throughout the battle, and this galvanized his men into fighting shape perhaps quicker than anything else he could have done. Having stabilized his army's morale, Chuikov's tactics for combating the Germans were simple but effective. He always sought to throw off the German timetable and disrupt their routine: if attacked, then counterattack. Chuikov fought intuitively. Moreover, his proximity to the front meant that he could speed up his own army's operational tempo to match that of the Germans. Furthermore, Chuikov ordered his men to cling as closely as they could to German positions in order to negate German advantages in airpower and artillery. Chuikov also identified men and officers who were resourceful and innovative and placed them in critical roles, especially in regard to implementing the storm group tactics that would become a core of his army's defensive efforts. Chuikov's tactics meant that, with time, his army quickly evolved into first a veteran army and then an elite one. Chuikov could not accomplish such a turnaround on his own. He relied on a top-notch staff and several superb divisional commanders to help stabilize his command. Foremost was his chief of staff, Major General Nikolai Krylov.[88] At the divisional level, Chuikov could count on capable fighters, such as the 13th Guards divisional commander, Alexander Rodimtsev, and the 37th Guards divisional commander, Viktor Zholudev. That said, it took time for Chuikov to build up his army, and as a result, in mid-September, the 62nd Army faced its first great crisis since being isolated in Stalingrad.

Months of fighting had reduced five of Chuikov's rifle divisions to no more than a few hundred combatants each. Adequate armored support was a dream, and ammunition stores were nonexistent. Meanwhile, his opponent poured it on. During September 1942, the German 6th Army expended some 23 millions rounds of rifle and machine gun ammunition, 750,000 mortar rounds, 685,000 tank and artillery shells, and 178,000 hand grenades.[89] A significant percentage of this deluge came during Paulus's massive September 14 assault. The German attack, heavily supported by ground attack aircraft, took the Mamaev Kurgan, overran most of the city, and in places broke through to the Volga River. Some within the 62nd Army's ranks panicked as the primary ferry crossing across the Volga came under German machine gun fire and relentless Stuka attacks. Chuikov ordered a counterattack on the Mamaev Kurgan, only to see his orders utterly ignored.

Chuikov, recognizing that his army was folding, ordered the just-arriving 13th Guards Rifle Division into the fray. The 13th Guards had been slated to move across the Volga under cover of darkness later that night. Instead, at 2:00 p.m., Chuikov ordered this recently rebuilt and under-equipped division, led by its brave and capable commander, 36-year-old Alexander Rodimtsev, to throw its advance elements, approximately 1,500 men, into the battle. The desperation of such a move becomes obvious when one considers that the Germans held absolute air superiority over the battlefield, and were not only bombing and strafing everything that moved on the broad, fast-flowing Volga—but also directing brutally accurate artillery fire on all the crossing points into Stalingrad. The casualties taken by Rodimtsev's men during the crossing on its face represented a horrific waste of life. Nonetheless, the survivors charged straight into the ferocious German firepower, drove the Germans back from the banks of the Volga, and emboldened the panicking soldiers from the 62nd Army, who, having witnessed an act of unbelievable sacrifice and courage, turned back to their weapons and tore into the Germans. The Russian soldiers had broken the Germans' momentum.

Soviet authorities, seeking to minimize their mistakes, had for decades ignored the truth of what had happened that day, particularly the panic that had swept through the 62nd Army after the German breakthrough. This omission fit in well with postwar German memoirs holding that the 6th Army's fate at Stalingrad was entirely a product of Hitler's decisions, that ignored the 6th Army's overwhelming initial advantages in men and machines over the Soviet 62nd Army, and that disregarded the failings of the German army's operational and tactical leadership. Nevertheless, according to many who were there (Chuikov for one), had the Germans committed even one more battalion to exploiting the initial breakthrough on the afternoon of September 14, then the Soviet position in the city would have been irretrievable.[90]

Undeterred by its setback, the 6th Army launched a series of assaults over the ensuing month; one in particular, on September 22, once again nearly broke Chuikov's defenses. A German night attack on October 1 left the 13th Guards, 10,000 men strong on September 16, down to a few hundred men, but again this crack unit failed to break.[91] Regardless, by September's end, Paulus held most of the city. The 62nd Army's deepest defensive positions had been reduced to the final few blocks before the Volga. Meanwhile, on September 19, Russian counterattacks attempting to relieve the city had failed miserably.

Life within the city limits degenerated into hell on earth. The city burned endlessly, and battle raged to and fro through choking smoke and scattered fires, all accompanied by the dull echo of artillery reverberating through the shattered streets. Disease swept through German and Soviet ranks alike. Clean water had disappeared, and lice and rats flourished in the primeval underworld where men lived and died.[92] The civilian population had it even worse. The 6th Army's Feldgendarmerie (military police) worked hand in hand with the SD to kidnap as many as 60,000 of Stalingrad's citizens; for use as slave labor in German factories. The SD executed another 3,000 within the city, and the German military police and SD pressed Soviet civilians into service assisting the German army. The predatory Germans executed those refusing to help. For those helping the Germans, the Red Army coldly offered no mercy in return, even in regard to children, ordering anyone seen aiding the German army shot dead.[93] This medieval barbarity made a mockery of antiseptic military measures of success.

During October, German soldiers counted victories in hundreds of yards. A Russian sergeant named Jacob Pavlov and his small band of 60 men held out against overwhelming German attacks for nearly two months in a four-story

STALINGRAD

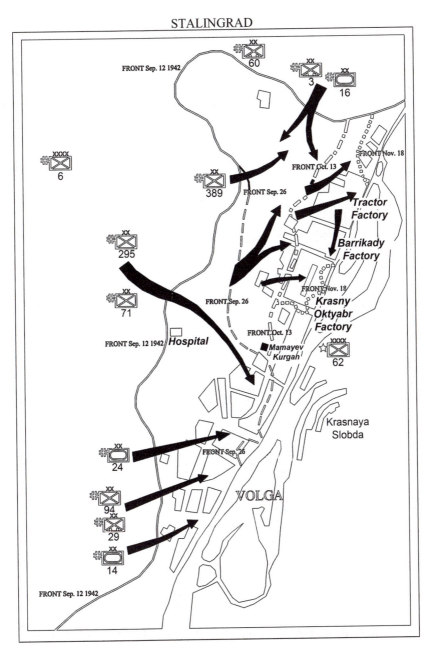

house serving as one part of a series of Russian strongpoints.[94] Combined arms ruled, with the best strongpoints featuring numerous heavy weapons,[95] the 5,000-man 193rd Rifle Division under General Feodor Smekhotvorov proving particularly effective in its defensive efforts.[96] Key buildings or pieces of terrain exchanged hands dozens of times.[97] German troops cleared Stalingrad one block at a time in vicious, bloody, hand-to-hand combat, reducing German advantages in mobility and training to near irrelevance. Paulus continually fed into the city fresh units from his flanks; wearing down his entire army in a war of attrition decidedly playing to Soviet strengths. In a carryover from World War I's Western Front, the sniper regained a prominent position unlike in any other theater during the European war. The Russians elevated their best snipers to hero status and highly publicized these deadly marksmen's exploits. One of the Red Army's best killers was a woman, Tanya Chernova, only 20 years old, who shot dead 80 Germans in three months at Stalingrad.[98] The Red Army's losses in men would prove so severe that by the war's end, approximately 800,000 women had served at the front.[99] As early as 1942, the Red Army's anti-aircraft units, signals units, medical staff, and night bomber squadrons featured increasing numbers of women. Women even served as tank commanders.

For their part, the Germans turned loose a small army of their own snipers, making movement in Stalingrad almost suicidal no matter under what flag a soldier fought. Meanwhile, on October 14, Hitler issued a directive insisting on consolidating and holding the territory captured to date in the German summer offensive, ostensibly as a springboard for a renewed campaign in 1943. With his order, Hitler left open the exposed German flanks outside Stalingrad. Hitler was now gambling. Although German generals had written after the war that the 6th Army had been doomed from almost the moment it entered the city, this was disingenuous. From August into early October, the Red Army had lacked the strength to effectively challenge the 6th Army's exposed flanks. By mid-October, however, Chuikov had held out long enough that a wide range of German generals were forecasting the increasing danger threatening Army Group B's Don River and Kalmyk steppe fronts guarding the northern and southern flanks of the 6th Army and the 4th Panzer Army, respectively. Gehlen consistently pulled his punches however when it came to describing the extent of the threat that the German army faced outside Stalingrad, in all likelihood thus emboldening Hitler to press on. Nonetheless, feeling the pressure, Paulus attacked.

Between October 14 and 17, through sheer will and determination, the 6th Army split Chuikov's command. Five German divisions—over 90,000 men, 2,000 guns and mortars, 300 tanks, and waves of Stukas—forged a path just over two miles wide to the main source of Soviet resistance at the tractor plant and the Barrikady factory. At best, the 62nd Army numbered 50,000 men and 80 tanks. According to those present, it was nowhere near these numbers.[100] German infantry and machine gun teams flowed around the Russian positions, breaking through despite a frenetic defensive effort shocking attackers who thought nothing could have survived the massive air and artillery bombardment that had preceded the assault. Panzers prowled the factory floors, climbing rubble and pouring point-blank cannon and machine gun fire at Russian soldiers fighting with grim determination. The Russian defense flowed flexibly, emphasizing constant small-scale counterattacks in an effort to wear down the thunderous German assault. The bloodshed reached epic proportions. On the night of October 15 alone, over 3,500 Russian wounded were evacuated across the river.[101] By the night of October 14, the Germans had shattered even the best of the defensive positions, annihilating the elite 37th Guards, whose men had fought to nearly the last in a desperate stand within the tractor factory. The 62nd Army staggered under the weight of the German firepower, and the critical hours of the battle had arrived.

At 9:40 p.m., Chuikov, with nothing left to stop the Germans, contacted the Stalingrad Front and requested permission to withdraw his command post across the Volga. Khruschev insisted he remain in the city. It appears that at 1:00 a.m. on October 15, Chuikov was even temporarily stripped of his command. Regardless, Chuikov yet again requested that he be allowed to withdraw. Instead, he received the 138th Rifle Division, and with its support, the lead regiment having crossed the Volga on the night of October 15, the 62nd Army held.[102] For a few brief hours, each commander present may have held the fate of all of eastern Europe in their hands. Had the Russians failed to release the 138th Rifle Division at that time, it is almost certain that the Germans would have driven Chuikov's men into the Volga. On the other side, only on October 23 did Paulus release his reserves: the 79th Infantry Division. Had Paulus released the 79th Infantry either on the night of October 14 or at any almost any time during the morning or early afternoon of October 15, the city would likely have been his.[103]

Undeterred by their previous failures, on November 11 Paulus's 6th Army commenced another huge effort, again across a narrow front, this time three miles in breadth and this time directed at the northern factory district. Paulus stripped his flanks even further bare—combing Army Group B for all the engineers he could find, all in a desperate effort to finish off the Soviet 62nd Army. Five infantry and two Panzer divisions spearheaded by eight pioneer battalions liberally equipped with satchel charges and flamethrowers blasted their way forward backed up by heavy air and artillery support. This mass of men and machines again split Chuikov's command and again reached the Volga. Yet again, Chuikov's men held, launching aggressive counterattacks of their own, inflicting severe casualties on their Nazi tormentors.[104] For instance, in November of 1942, tables of organization and equipment for German infantry, motorized, and panzer divisions called for approximately 15,000 men, 16,000 men, and 17,000 men respectively, yet the fourteen infantry divisions in 6th Army and 4th Panzer Army averaged only 8,533 men, the four motorized divisions averaged 9,896 men, and the four panzer divisions averaged 10,863 men.[105] Meanwhile, as Army Group B was bled white, on the cold hard steppe outside Stalingrad, the 6th Army's poorly protected flanks hung like a gallows over Germany's battered but most powerful army.

Chapter 7
Stalingrad in Context

THE RED ARMY ON THE MARCH:
OPERATIONS URANUS AND MARS

Hitler's role in directing the battle at Stalingrad had become problematic long before November 1942. His public boasting as to the inevitability of German victory only further narrowed the range of military options available to Army Group B. Having divorced the operational progress of his military campaign from its underlying strategic goals, Hitler compounded his errors. Most important, he bet that the Red Army could not exploit either Army Group B's roughly 330-mile-long northern flank running mostly along the Don River between Voronezh and Stalingrad, dependent for its security entirely on the German 2nd Army, 2nd Hungarian Army, 8th Italian Army, and 3rd Romanian Army, or the 4th Romanian Army's overstretched lines protecting the 6th Army's flank south of Stalingrad.

Perhaps unsurprisingly, throughout the late summer and early fall of 1942, Halder had argued incessantly with Hitler regarding Army Group B's dispositions. That said throughout much of the late summer and into the fall, the Red Army had proven incapable of fully taking advantage of Army Group B's poorly positioned armies. Still, as the weeks passed, many in Army Group B and at the OKH (Oberkommando der Heer, or Army High Command) became increasingly vocal regarding the threat posed by a recuperating Red Army. Nevertheless, Gehlen qualified many of his intelligence assessments to such an extent as to understate the threat the 6th Army faced and, once again muddle the message received by Hitler. As for Army Group A, by November 1942, its campaign in the Caucusus had ground to a halt. It could have still done significant damage to Soviet war-making potential, but Hitler and the OKH failed to undermine the Red Army's ability to conduct large-scale offensives by ordering the Luftwaffe to crush Baku's oil refineries and pipelines.[1]

With Hitler myopically focused on Stalingrad, Stavka planned a series of offensives across Germany's Eastern Front. Two assaults served as the campaign's twin centerpieces. These were set to rip open and destroy German Army Groups Center and B at the same time that further attacks struck Army Groups North and A, to be followed late in the winter of 1942–1943 by multiple offensives along all three major strategic axis. Code-named Operation Uranus, the attack that Stavka planned against Army Group B featured a proposed double envelopment of the German 6th Army. Uranus would then lead to a larger offensive designed to destroy Army Group B, code-named Operation Saturn. Red Army Chief of the General Staff Alexander M. Vasilevsky, today recognized as perhaps the best staff officer that the Red Army produced during World War II, played the central role in fleshing out the initial planning conducted by the Soviet General Staff.

At the same time, Zhukov planned an even more massive two-stage effort of his own. Zhukov's Operation Mars served as the match to Uranus, with the German 9th Army the target instead of the German 6th Army, and Operation Jupiter was the complement to Saturn, with the former seeking to destroy Army Group Center. The planned Soviet operations near Stalingrad moved ahead under an improving climate for conducting military operations within the Red Army. Thanks to Stalin's October 9 Order No. 307, for the first time in the war the Red Army enjoyed the autonomy to direct its men where needed without subordination to political commissars. Moreover, training programs had been revamped to emphasize combat skills over political indoctrination.[2] Furthermore, the Red Army had added a new wrinkle to help increase the infantry's firepower in the breakthrough role. It had formed independent heavy tank regiments, with 23 heavy tanks each, as well as independent assault gun regiments. By November 1942, the Red Army could put into the field 6,124,000 men supported by 6,956 tanks and 3,254 frontline aircraft.[3] The Red Army's recuperative powers highlight the absurdity in Hitler's insistence on slugging it out in Stalingrad.

Meanwhile, on September 24, the hostility between Hitler and Halder reached its breaking point. This followed a series of arguments in particular regarding Hitler's assertive role in micromanaging the German campaign in the east, the Red Army's potential, and Hitler's frustration with Germany's war effort.[4] Hitler accepted Halder's resignation from his position as the OKH's chief of staff. In his place, Hitler promoted Lieutenant General Kurt Zietzler, an ideologically driven junior officer lacking the experience needed for such an important position. Despite all this, by November 1942, Paulus had nearly wrested Stalingrad from Chuikov. That said, the almost complete sacrifice of Chuikov's army had borne an incredible bounty for the Red Army.

URANUS AND THE 6TH ARMY'S SACRIFICE: A TURNING POINT IN THE WAR?

At 5:00 a.m. on November 19, Operation Uranus began. Soviet tanks and infantry burst through the loose Axis defensive lines on the snow-covered steppe guarding the 6th Army's northwestern and southeastern flanks. The Red Army had gathered for Uranus 1 million men, 894 tanks, and 1,115 airplanes. The 5th Tank Army from Vatutin's Southwestern Front and the 13th Tank Corps and 4th Mechanized Corps from Eremenko's Stalingrad Front, provided the respective northern and southern spearheads for Uranus. Two cavalry corps, the 8th Cavalry Corps from the 5th Tank Army and 4th Cavalry Corps from the Stalingrad Front's southern pincer, struck outside and parallel to the main thrust to create an outer perimeter to defend against the anticipated German counterthrusts.

Despite receiving frequent warnings of the impending offensive, the Axis forces to the immediate northwest of Stalingrad included only the overstretched Romanian 3rd Army under General Dumitrescu and the German 48th Panzer Corps in reserve. Meanwhile, far to the southeast, Dumitrescu's countrymen in the Romanian 4th Army protected Paulus's right flank in only the loosest sense of the word. The Romanians, including General Ilie Steflea, the chief of the Romanian General Staff, recognized the weakness inherent in their positions. They had complained repeatedly to the Germans.[5] That said, up until November 19, Hitler's gambling with his overextended front lines had largely paid off in the sense that, for over two months, the Red Army had been unable to exploit Army Group B's undermanned defensive front.

In addition, Hitler had been far from oblivious to the 6th Army's poor flank security. For instance, Hitler and Zietzler had formed new units to defend the 6th Army's flanks, though mostly by combing out Army Group B's rear areas for manpower. Other steps taken by Hitler and the OKH included a November 2 order for the Luftwaffe to begin bombing Soviet assembly areas in the Don bridgeheads and behind the Don River. Perhaps most important, on November 3 Hitler ordered the well-equipped 6th Panzer Division and two infantry divisions from France to back up the Romanian 3rd Army and Italian 8th Army. Had Hitler dispatched the 6th Panzer Division even a couple of weeks earlier, a timely arrival behind Army Group B's front lines may have prevented the disaster set to befall the 6th Army. Even without the 6th Panzer Division's presence, the Red Army fielded only 894 tanks in its assault armies against 675 German tanks in and around Stalingrad. This highlights once again how concentrated force could best even near numerically equal foes. Perhaps the most concentrated armored grouping that the Germans relied on for flank security was the weak 48th Panzer Corps. It included the understrength 22nd Panzer Division, part of the 14th Panzer Division, and the 1st Romanian Armored Division backing the Romanian 3rd Army's front. The best unit in the bunch, the worn-out 22nd Panzer could put only 45 tanks into the field. Even worse, Pz 38(t)s and Romanian-manufactured R-2 tanks represented the majority of the 1st Romanian Armored Division's inadequate power.[6]

Consequently, north of Stalingrad, the Soviet 5th Tank Army brushed past a weak and disorganized counterthrust from a 48th Panzer Corps buffeted by initial deployment orders from Weichs, subsequently countermanded by Hitler and Zietzler. The disorganized counterattack saw the Axis Panzer divisions loose all contact with each other, and find themselves forced into fighting for their very survival, let alone stem the Red wave cresting across the steppe.[7] Weichs ordered Paulus to redeploy all his mobile divisions from within Stalingrad to stop the Soviet spearheads. Orders backed by Hitler and Zietzler. Nonetheless, Paulus lacked the fuel to move his Panzers and motorized infantry in anything even remotely like a timely manner. Meanwhile, southeast of Stalingrad, Eremenko's Stalingrad Front, led by the 51st and 57th Armies, dropped the hammer on the Romanian 6th and 7th Corps. Although the German 29th Motorized Division temporarily stalled one Soviet drive, the Stalingrad Front's other attacks met with rapid success.[8] On November 23, the spearheads for the Southwest and Stalingrad fronts, having traveled 70 miles and 50 miles, respectively, met at Kalach to Stalingrad's west. The Red Army had cut off the entire German 6th Army and part of the 4th Panzer Army in a massive pocket.

Paulus sought permission to break out. Nearly everyone at the OKW (Oberkommando der Wehrmacht, or High Command of the Armed Forces) and the OKH agreed. However, Manstein, who had been given command of the new Army Group Don on November 21, comprising the 6th Army, 4th Panzer Army, and 3rd Romanian Army, and Göring, who unrealistically proclaimed that his Luftwaffe could supply the 6th Army, argued otherwise. Whether Hitler allowed Göring's boastful claim to influence him, Manstein's controversial initial opinion, or neither, perhaps with events at Demyansk the previous winter in mind, he ordered Paulus to remain in place. Manstein would change his mind—but too late.[9] Meanwhile, on his arrival in the region, Manstein organized new defensive lines and began assembling reserves needed to free the 6th Army. General Erhard Raus's 6th Panzer Division represented the cream of the German Panzer arm when it arrived near Stalingrad on December 3, 1942. Fresh from refitting in France, Raus's command was superbly equipped with 160 new long-barreled 75-mm-cannon–mounted Panzer IVs and an additional 40 assault guns; all representing more than a match for a typical Russian tank corps. Nonetheless, Soviet pressure forced Manstein to throw the 6th Panzer Division into the fray. Raus's Panzers duly crushed the Soviet 4th Cavalry Corps, but doing so instead of marshaling its strength for the relief effort.

Therefore, though Manstein's Army Group initially shrugged off the Soviet attacks, it only belatedly began an undermanned and difficult relief mission.

OPERATION URANUS

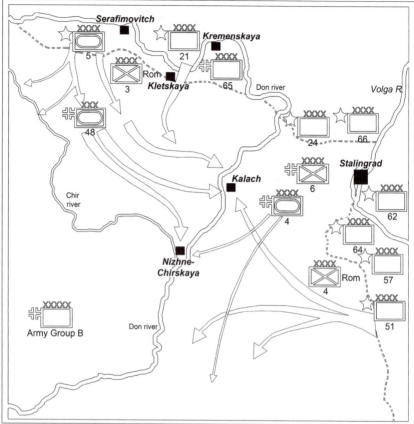

Remarkably, given the gravity of the situation, the rebuilt 4th Panzer Army's 57th Panzer Corps essentially was the relief effort. General Friedrich Kirchner's 57th Panzer Corps comprised the 6th Panzer and worn-out 23rd Panzer Divisions, all told a combined 191 to 232 tanks, depending on the source, along with the 15th Luftwaffe Field Division. On December 12, the 57th Panzer Corps rumbled northeast from the ice-swept fields near Kotelnikovo. The Germans quickly delivered several powerful blows against the Soviet 51st Army in defense. At one point in the battle, the 6th Panzer Division ambushed approximately 40 Russian tanks, and the up-gunned German Panzers easily knocked out 32 Russian tanks in quick succession. Over a two-day period, Raus eviscerated the Soviet 4th Mechanized Corps. Nevertheless, though the Germans pummeled the Soviet tank crews, the strength and persistence of the defensive effort along with incessant Russian counterattacks cost the German relief effort precious time. The 6th Army's chances for rescue diminished with each passing day. Meanwhile, additional problems had also cropped up to overstretch Manstein's Army Group.

On December 7, the Russian 1st Tank Corps had pushed behind the positions of the 48th Panzer Corps on the Chir River. General Hermann Balck commanded the 11th Panzer Division and led the German defensive effort. Balck repeatedly threw back the uncoordinated albeit numerous Russian attacks, including on December 8, when Balck's men destroyed 53 Soviet tanks.[10] Further Soviet attacks on December 17 and 18 left the 11th Panzer Division with only 25 tanks in running condition, but the Panzers found success in again turning the Russian flank, destroying a Russian armored column, and leaving another 65 Soviet tanks shattered on the battlefield.[11] In just two weeks, the 11th Panzer Division virtually single-handedly demolished the Soviet 5th Tank Army.[12] Nonetheless, despite the tactical successes won by the German Panzer divisions, it was not enough. On December 16, the Soviet Southwest and Voronezh Fronts attacked the Italian 8th Army along the Don River. This attack, Operation Little Saturn, represented a scaled-down version of the original Saturn plan, which had called for defeating all of Army Group South. Stavka, grappling with the fact that it held a veritable tiger by the tail, had instead primarily doubled down on its efforts to destroy the 6th Army. The Russian attack on the Don tore through the Italians, left a gaping hole in the Axis front, blew the road to Rostov open, and forced German Army Detachment Hollidt, named after the German commander in charge of the forces in the region, to withdraw.

On December 19 and to the southeast of Hollidt's command, Manstein's relief effort had meanwhile ground forward to within 30 miles of the trapped 6th Army. The Red Army hastily ordered up even more counterattacks against the German units and, bolstered in particular by the Soviet 2nd Guards Army, finally brought the relief effort to a halt. The reasons advanced for the relief effort's failure have resulted in a substantial and lively debate revolving around who on the German side should be held responsible. Nevertheless, choosing whom to assign the blame for 6th Army's destruction perhaps misses the point. The fact that similar debates continue, revolving around any number of potentially war-altering decisions made by various members of the German leadership team, speaks volumes about how, at times, Germany's greatest problems stemmed from within.

Many commentators like to single out a specific event as determinative in the outcome of Hitler's 1942 campaign. Nonetheless, such commentary does a great disservice to our understanding of the war and its outcome. Massive strategic-level campaigns such as Blau, and their outcomes, are simply too complicated to distill down into single definitive turning points. This is even more true in examining how closely Germany came to cementing control over the western and southern Soviet Union's vast economic resources, and thus positioning itself to not only dominate Europe but also survive a global war against a U.S.-dominated alliance of nations.

Therefore, in examining the outcome of the fateful events that unfolded during the last six months of 1942 in the Soviet Union, it is not the idea that had Hitler and the OKH made one fateful decision differently, that they then would have attained Blau's original objectives or, at worst, at least would have put the heel to the Soviet Union's throat. What is most terrifying is that Hitler and his military leadership held numerous and repeated opportunities to make decisions that had they chosen differently *in just a few of these circumstances*, even still allowing for all their other mistakes, that they may very well have altered the course of history. These decision points included the following:

- The abandonment of the original plan for Operation Blau and premature drive into the Caucasus
- Breaking up Manstein's 11th Army following the fall of Sevastopol instead of leaving it with Army Group A or even putting it into theater reserve
- Leaving powerful armored assets in France during the fall of 1942—even after the catastrophic failure of the Allied Dieppe raid in August
- Failing to take Stalingrad on the fly early in September
- Paulus's failure to commit his reserves during either the German 6th Army's mid-September or mid-October assaults in Stalingrad
- The detachment of the German 16th Motorized Division from the drive on the Georgian military road and Ordzhonikidze
- The failure to timely bolster the 6th Army's flanks
- The failure to allow Paulus to immediately break out of the Stalingrad pocket on its formation

Now, given the previous decision making made by Hitler, the OKH, and lower-ranked commanders, it is certainly understandable that many of these mistakes were made, but what is most stunning is that *all* these errors were made. What's more, had any of the central actors on the German side responsible for these decisions even made so much as even a couple of them differently, then events in southern Russia may have unfolded very differently in 1942—with potentially dramatic outcomes for a Third Reich that came horrifyingly close to securing its long-term existence or worse.

Instead, Manstein, having called off the Stalingrad relief effort late in December 1942, faced the monumental task of attempting to safely extricate all of Army Group A from the Caucasus before the Red Army reached Rostov, and potentially unhinged the entire southern half of Germany's Eastern Front. To do so, however, what remained of Army Group B, at that time mostly west of Stalingrad, needed to slow the Red Army's advance toward Rostov. In this assignment, Army Detachment Hollidt's three Panzer and four infantry divisions, plus scattered smaller formations, needed to hold together a 120-mile front and stop the Red Army's 3rd Guards Army, 5th Shock Army, and 5th Tank Army from taking Rostov. Meanwhile, Army Group B's 4th Panzer

Army, four Panzer and motorized divisions, and a single Luftwaffe field division in total, operating just south of the lower Don, needed to hold open not only its own westward path to freedom via Rostov but also so that Army Group A could safely evacuate the Caucusus. Despite the odds, this meager force held off the Soviet 2nd Guards Army and the 28th and 51st Armies. Furthermore it aligned its front with the 1st Panzer Army coming up from the south, thus allowing Army Group A and the 4th Panzer Army to begin filtering through Rostov. On February 2, 1943, Army Group A completed its withdrawal from the Caucusus.[13]

In the meantime, the final role for the formerly proud and merciless 6th Army was to tie down the Soviet armies around Stalingrad. To that end, and even as the 6th Army slowly crumbled, it dealt out considerable death and destruction. All told, Axis forces killed some 485,751 Soviet soldiers in and around Stalingrad—from the 1.1 million killed or wounded during the entire campaign.[14] As for material losses and in just one example of the carnage; from July 25 to December 31, 1942 the Red Army lost 4,862 tanks against Army Group B while German panzer losses totaled around 700 vehicles.[15] What's more, Stalingrad's population suffered 40,000 killed during the battle and another 60,000 dying in the labor camps dotting the Third Reich. Even after the 6th Army had been crushed, the horrors staining the region would continue for years. On December 28, 1943, Stalin and the NKVD (People's Commissariat for Internal Affairs) deported, on charges of collaboration with the Nazi's, nearly 100,000 Kalmyks, descendants of the Mongols who had for centuries otherwise lived south of Stalingrad.[16]

As for the 6th Army's fate, on January 10, 1943, the final Soviet assault on the German pocket began. Paulus officially capitulated on February 2, 1943. Axis losses were staggering; depending on the source, 225,000 to 250,000 men, from an original army totaling 250,000 to 300,000, died or fell into captivity—this figure included the Axis and Russian personnel working with the 6th Army. Germany may have lost more than 200,000 men in total, with over 90,000 captured, according to German sources. According to Soviet sources, they took approximately 120,000 prisoners of war[17] and at least 60,000 killed; some argue that the total actually reached 152,000 killed[18] during the months following the November 19 start of Operation Uranus. For all but 6,000 survivors released years later, surrender ended in death in Stalin's gulags. In addition, by the end of January 1943, the Italian 8th Army had lost approximately 77,000 dead and missing, and the Romanians suffered 140,000 casualties, and the Hungarians 100,000 more.[19]

Hitler had thrown away the initiative regained by the German army during the spring of 1942. For a second straight year, he had taken a viable strategic path toward cementing German hegemony on the continent, for all intents and purposes thereby winning the war, and squandered his opportunity. For two straight years, German mistakes had opened Soviet windows of

SOVIET WINTER CAMPAIGN 1942–1943

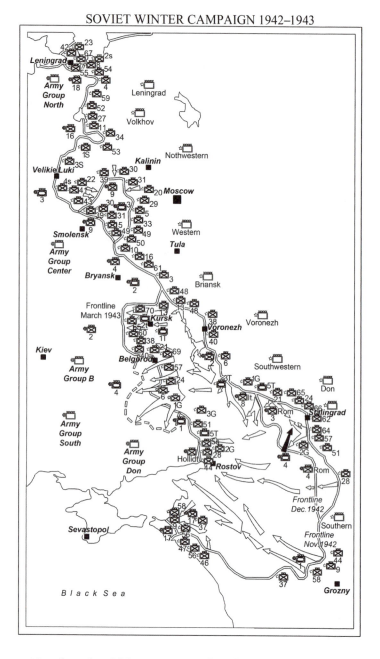

opportunity that should have remained sealed shut. That said, whether Stalingrad represented the beginning of the end for Germany is debated to this day if for no other reason than the outcome of Stavka's other campaigns during the winter of 1942–1943. In regarding these campaigns as a collective whole, we recast the war in eastern Europe. Instead of one specific event during the winter of 1942–1943 representing a decisive turning point, a more nuanced and accurate view of the war emerges: a view of a Soviet 1942–1943 winter campaign that mostly failed to attain its objectives, and one that highlights how the outmanned Axis armies contained a maximal Soviet military effort in large part because of the Red Army's inability to fully close the qualitative gap with a Wehrmacht that, at times, proved its own worst enemy.

OPERATION MARS: ZHUKOV'S WORST DEFEAT PUTS STALINGRAD IN CONTEXT

The November–December 1942 Soviet campaign in and around Stalingrad was just one of four contemporaneous large-scale offensives launched by the Red Army. Zhukov's Operation Mars was the centerpiece. Mars sought to destroy the German 9th Army in the salient that it defended, centered on the town of Rzhev, and then to follow up this victory by annihilating German Army Group Center via Operation Jupiter. On its face, Mars offered a strong chance for success given the immense resources that Stavka placed at Zhukov's disposal. There were, however, notable differences between Mars and Uranus, with perhaps the most important stemming from the German 9th Army's defensive positions and its surrounding support.

The German 9th Army occupied a northeastward-directed bulge in the German-Soviet front only 90 miles west of Moscow: the Rzhev salient. Rzhev had been captured by Army Group Center's 9th Army on October 14, 1941. The Germans had held on to the city despite the Kalinin Front's subsequent and repeated attempts to retake Rzhev throughout late 1941 and all of 1942, including in conjunction with the Western Front during July and August 1942. The Kalinin Front's initial attacks during the winter of 1941–1942 had compressed the German 9th Army into the salient around Rzhev marking its defensive perimeter in November 1942. Even though the salient greatly extended the German front line, the veteran German 9th Army had prepared well-fortified defenses built around the dense forests, extensive swamps, and numerous rivers in the region. Furthermore, General Walter Model, a man whose name became synonymous with defensive excellence during World War II, ably led the 9th Army. In addition, and most critically, Model could rely on ample armored support, unlike Germany's Axis allies on Stalingrad's flanks, with this support including the 3rd Panzer Army.[20]

Working against the 9th Army's chances was that Zhukov had massed for the attack 1,890,000 men, 24,682 artillery pieces and mortars, 3,375 tanks, and 1,170 airplanes within the Kalinin Front, led by Colonel-General M. A. Purkaev; the Western Front, led by Colonel-General I. S. Konev; and the Moscow Defense Zone. The armies that Zhukov assembled for Mars included one-third of the Red Army's manpower and artillery, 39 percent of available aircraft, and nearly half the Red Army's available armor.[21] Overall, nearly twice as many men and more than twice as many tanks were pledged to Mars as for Uranus.[22] Even if one rejects the hierarchical primacy that some attach to Mars, it, and Uranus, possessed complementary objectives, were planned together, and, likewise, both operations included follow-up components scheduled to destroy entire German Army Groups.

The preliminary to Mars began on November 24, when the Kalinin Front's 3rd Shock Army had hit the German 3rd Panzer Army, while the Northwestern Front would hit Army Group North's 16th Army shortly thereafter in the planned first step in Army Group North's evisceration. Meanwhile, on November 25, heavy artillery bombardments hammered German defensive positions across the Rzhev salient, as Operation Mars developed along multiple axes of attack. In one instance, 20,000 men and 100 tanks spearheading the Soviet 31st Army slammed repeatedly into German lines over the course of three days. Nonetheless, the well-dug-in defenders inflicted severe losses on attackers who had seen snow and fog take away their anticipated air support.[23] The German defenses proved so unyielding that they forced Zhukov and Konev to shift the entire primary axis of attack. For his part, Konev seized an opportunity opened by the Russian 247th Rifle Division, supported by 50 tanks, and poured reinforcements through a bridgehead won over the Vazusa River. Yet, determined and cutoff German combined-arms teams from the 78th Infantry Division and the 5th Panzer Division doggedly slowed the Russian advance. Characteristically, the Germans threw together all sorts of unit combinations with their usual tactical effectiveness. Mud and heavy German artillery fire also clogged Konev's chosen axis of advance. He only exacerbated the congestion problems when he rerouted his armies into increasing traffic. The Soviet offensive began to break down.

As the German bled critical momentum from Mars, not all Soviet attacks faltered. The 22nd and 41st Armies, led by Major General V. A. Lushkevich and Major General F. G. Tarasov, respectively, initially enjoyed great success. In just two days, the 41st Army, spearheaded by the 15,200 men and 224 tanks from the 1st Mechanized Corps led by General M. A. Solomatin, ripped a breach in the German lines 12 miles wide and 18 miles deep. At this point in the battle, Tarasov attempted to seize the city of Belyi held by Colonel General Joseph Harpe's 41st Panzer Corps. Kampfgruppen from the elite Panzer grenadier division Grossdeutschland and the 1st Panzer Division also bolstered the German 246th Infantry Division's efforts. Repeated Soviet attempts to take the city foundered in succession. Meanwhile, Lushkevich's 22nd Army saw the initial promise of success wilt away as Grossdeutschland's Panzer Grenadier Regiment spearhead a dogged German defense, halting the better part of two Russian rifle divisions and a brigade of tanks from Major General G. E. Katukov's 3rd Mechanized Corps.

Nonetheless, even as the initiative slipped away, Zhukov remorselessly threw his men against the unbreakable German defensive front. German infantry and Panzer grenadiers in hedgehog-style combined-arms defensive positions fragmented and slowed Soviet attacks, separating the Soviet combat arms and defeating them in detail.[24] In just five days, the Soviet 20th Army alone suffered 58,524 casualties from 114,000 men and lost 200 tanks.[25] The 6th Stalin Rifle Corps lost 20,000 men from the 30,000 men it had sent into battle.

There are several reasons why the 9th Army held off Zhukov's fronts. Perhaps most important, the 9th Army had been backed by the 1st, 9th, and 14th Panzer Divisions and the Grossdeutschland Panzer Grenadier Division. Furthermore, Kluge had ordered the 12th, 19th, and 20th Panzer Divisions to augment the initial German armored concentrations. In concentrating their Panzer divisions, the Germans were able to launch savage and repeated counterattacks. Thus, even though the 9th Army had frequently found itself hanging on for dear life, it largely stopped the best that Zhukov had to throw at it.[26] On the morning of December 7, the Germans counterattacked, hammering Tarasov's 41st Army. Then, led by Grossdeutschland and the 1st Panzer Division from one side and the 19th and 20th Panzer Divisions from the south, the Germans cut off and eviscerated the Russian 6th Rifle Corps and 1st Mechanized Corps. The Red Army lost some 40,000 to 50,000 men.[27] Despite this disaster, Zhukov and Stavka ordered up a fresh round of attacks. On December 11, the Soviet 20th and 29th Armies followed a one-hour artillery barrage with assaults by massed infantry into the strength of German defensive positions. As the Germans methodically slaughtered the Russian infantry, Konev ordered the 5th and 6th Tank Corps in to support the attack. The Soviet armor ran into deeply echeloned anti-tank defenses, and in two days of absolute butchery lost some 200 tanks. Despite the carnage, the attacks continued for three more days before the exhausted Red Army called it off. Between November 24 and December 14 alone, the Germans had inflicted ghastly losses on Zhukov's forces. Mars had cost the Red Army 1,655 tanks destroyed, or nearly 25 percent of the entire Red Army's frontline tank strength in November 1942. Personnel losses during Mars and its complementary operations were equally horrendous and grossly disproportionate to German casualties. Overall, the Red Army endured nearly a quarter of a million casualties in only three weeks of fighting near Rzhev: 70,373 killed in action and 145,031 wounded or sick.[28]

Meanwhile, the Soviet attacks against the German armies that were geographically closest to Model's command, the German 16th and 3rd Panzer Armies, had also run into troubles of their own. Colonel-General P. A. Kurochkin's Northwestern Front's 1st Shock Army and the 11th, 27th, 34th, and 53rd Armies had attacked Army Group North's 16th Army south of Lake Il'men.[29] Marshal Timoshenko oversaw the offensive. Stalin had ambitiously hoped that it would result in the elimination of the German positions at Demyansk, thus opening the front for an ambitious drive to Lake Pskov or the Baltic—cutting off the 16th Army, threatening the 18th Army with destruction, and crushing Army Group North. All told, the Soviet armies held over the defending Germans a three-to-one advantage in men and a five-to-one advantage in tanks. That said, the Soviet armies lacked the ammunition and fuel to sustain a major offensive and faced awful weather conditions, including deeply rutted and muddy roads caused by an unseasonal thaw. The main assault jumped off on November 28 and immediately ran into difficulty, even after artillery had pasted the German positions for 45 minutes. For instance, the terrain broke up armor already dissipated among the infantry. Thus, the infantry could not overwhelm German defenses that were spearheaded by heavy artillery and mortar fire support in addition to well-placed machine guns and minefields; all bolstered by numerous company- and battalion-sized counterattacks. The Russian attacks continued over the ensuing weeks but went nowhere. After regrouping and reinforcing, another attack, on December 23, fared even more poorly as the Germans hit the Soviet army's in their assembly areas with a peremptory artillery barrage. A follow-up effort later in December also failed. All told, the Northwestern Front lost somewhere between 15,000 and 30,000 men[30] and accomplished nothing of significance.

In contrast to the fighting in southern Russia, the Soviet efforts against Army Groups Center and North had been a disaster. Both failures highlighted Germany's prodigious tactical and operational capabilities in facing off against the Red Army's great numerical superiority in men and machines. Not that Mars's impact left Germany unscathed. Approximately 40,000 German soldiers were killed, wounded, or captured in stopping Mars. Nevertheless, the Red Army had suffered over six casualties for each German. What is more, only 23 German divisions had slammed the door on an offensive launched by 83 Soviet divisions in seven armies. Regardless, only Mars was a complete failure. Of the four offensives that the Red Army launched in late November 1942, two had found significant success, one by driving Army Group A from the Caucusus and another, Uranus, destroying the German 6th Army.[31]

Overall, however, and when presenting Operation Uranus in comparison to its sister offensive against Army Group Center, it is apparent that the Soviet Union faced an uncomfortable reality as the winter of 1942–1943 wound down. After nearly two years of warfare, success for the Red Army had proved largely transitory. Likewise, and all too often, it had followed poor German decision making following two successive years at war during which the Germans had owned the summer months. The Red Army's best qualities during this period of the war proved to be its capacity to repeatedly absorb horrific losses, and draw the Germans past their limits. Then Soviet counterstrokes could wear down and ripen German army's for follow-up Soviet offensives during the winter. Had Hitler and his senior war planners recognized this truth, and adjusted accordingly, there was little reason to believe that the same Red Army that had proven incapable of consistently defeating an undermanned German army could drive German forces from Soviet soil. As it was, even after the Red Army had decimated German Army Group B at Stalingrad, and sent the remaining German armies reeling across the steppe, some 65 million people and 850,000 square miles of Soviet territory remained occupied by Nazi Germany.

In regard to the Red Army's capabilities during the winter of 1942–1943, David Glantz, America's foremost expert on the Red Army, noted in particular the Red Army's "inability to penetrate the tactical defenses in the required time period . . . inadequate and inaccurate artillery support during the penetration operation . . . recurring logistical problems which hindered sustained operations . . . difficulty in coordinating tank and rifle units or tank units with other tank units during deep operations."[32] That said, German troops had their own problems. In particular, they fought under a leadership team struggling to grasp the full nature of mobile warfare in the Soviet Union. Hitler and his top generals all too often mandated that German units prepare thinly held defenses tied to the land. In January 1943, few within the German army were ready to apply flexibility and maneuver at the Army Group level in a defensive role. Nonetheless, Manstein would maneuver entire Army Groups across vast distances while on the defensive late in the winter of 1942–1943, and be wildly successful—though against a worn-down opponent. Yet the institutional inertia that he had to struggle against was powerful. In addition, further working against a reliance on mobility as a tool to effectively wage defensive warfare was the German army's increasing demobilization and organizational cannibalization of its prime operational units: its infantry and Panzer divisions.

The primary military lesson to emerge from events in eastern Europe during 1941–1942 was that when the German army concentrated its armored forces, and concomitantly relied on maneuver-based warfare, it was nearly unbeatable—even in facing overwhelming numerical odds. Accordingly, Soviet successes up to early 1943 remained tied to what Germany chose to do, as much as stemming from the direction in which the Soviet Union attempted to steer the war. German failures stemmed from a variety of interlocking elements, including German mistakes—strategic, political, operational, logistical, and so on—coupled with the Red Army's highly aggressive defensive effort and attempts to fight in a deep operational style when on the offensive. The interplay between a Red Army learning to fight, and an organizationally devolving and fragmenting Wehrmacht making just enough mistakes to hamstring its own efforts, thus perhaps best lays the foundation for understanding the state of the war on Germany's Eastern Front during the winter of 1942–1943.

Perhaps no better evidence for this view—one so antithetical to those focusing on the weight of numbers as determinative in the war's outcome—exists than in examining events in southern Russia during January–March 1943. These three months amply illustrate not only the full panoply of elements instrumental in deciding the war's outcome but also the inability of either combatant to grasp the initiative—an inability occurring despite the Red Army's capacity to execute major offensives across Germany's entire Eastern Front, and despite significant German counterstrokes in the Donbass region in February 1943, and near Kharkov and Belgorod in March 1943.[33]

All told, early in 1943, Stavka ordered five major strategic campaigns, composed of many operational-level offensives, launched by nearly every front in the western Soviet Union. These campaigns included Operation Polar Star against Army Group North, seeking to relieve Leningrad and launched by the Leningrad, Volkhov, and Northwestern fronts from February 10 to April 2, 1943. They also included successive Soviet offensives launched against Army Group Center from February 25 to March 21, 1943, aimed at seizing Rzhev, Viazma, Smolensk, Orel, and Briansk and launched by the Kalinin, Western, Briansk, and Central fronts.[34] Additionally, Stavka had ordered every Soviet front in southern Russia onto the offensive.

Of the Soviet offensives launched in southern Russia, Operation Gallop (Skachok) was perhaps the most prominent—given the impact produced by the eventual German response. Gallop began on January 29, 1943, geographically directed at Belgorod, Kharkov, and Kursk with an overall objective aimed at destroying Army Group Don, recapturing the entire Donbas, and driving to the Dnieper River. It would end up coming nowhere close to meeting its expansive goals.[35] This ambitious campaign had been presented by the talented General N. F. Vatutin, the Southwestern Front's commander, to Stavka. It was approved as a double envelopment centered around the Voroshilovgrad region in the Donbas, with the 1st Guards Army and Mobile Group Popov leading the northern pincer and the 3rd Guards Army and 5th Tank Army the southern pincer. In response, Manstein, commanding the whole of the reconstituted Army Group South, the former Army Groups A, B, and Don, fell back before the Russian advance and regrouped his armies.[36] Soviet General Cherniakhovsky's 60th Army, part of Golikov's Voronezh Front, took Kursk on February 8.[37] On February 14, Voroshilovgrad fell, and Vatutin's mobile spearheads drove ever farther west. Major General M. D. Borisov's 8th Cavalry Corps, leading Vatutin's left wing, far outraced his peers.[38] Cherniakhovsky's efforts on the offensive's northern wing and Borisov's deep operations on Vatutin's left wing, however, proved the high-water mark of the Soviet Donbas offensive. On February 17, just after the German army lost Kharkov, and as Soviet tanks approached Manstein's headquarters, the cagy German field marshal remained relatively calm; for he had laid a gigantic trap.

MANSTEIN'S COUNTERSTROKES

In preparation for his counterblow, Manstein had regrouped Army Group South. It included, from south to north, Army Detachment Hollidt along the Sea of Azov. Just north of Hollidt was the 1st Panzer Army, reinforced with the 4th Panzer Army's 48th Panzer Corps. Then farther north, Manstein had positioned the 4th Panzer Army and Army Detachment Kempf, with Kempf defending Kharkov.[39] All told, Manstein had grouped three Panzer corps to encircle and destroy the Southwestern Front's spearheads—Borisov's Cavalry Corps, Popov's Mobile Group, the Soviet 6th Army, most of the 1st Guards Army, and the 1st Guards and 25th Tank Corps.[40] On the morning of February 17, Knobelsdorff's 48th Panzer Corps began Manstein's counter-stroke and quickly encircled Borisov's Cavalry Corps. Meanwhile, Popov's command, ordered by Vatutin to advance, itself came under heavy counterat-tack from the numerically weak but well-positioned 1st Panzer Army. Each of the German Panzer divisions was horribly worn down, the 7th and 11th Panzer Divisions combined being able to put only 51 Panzers into the field.[41]

Regardless of German weakness however, by February 20, Vatutin had recog-nized that his entire front was in supreme danger, as his front's left wing fell apart and his right wing and center collapsed under the weight of Manstein's double envelopment. Stavka failed to grasp the enormity of the change in circumstances and still felt that Vatutin held the initiative. Vatutin knew other-wise. Paul Hausser's SS Panzer Corps—the elite SS Panzer grenadier divisions Das Reich, Leibstandarte, and Totenkopf—had sliced behind the Soviet 1st Guards and 6th Armies. At the same time, the 1st Panzer Army's veteran 7th and 11th Panzer Division, SS Panzer grenadier division "Wiking"—albeit with Wiking able to put only five tanks into the field[42] and the 333rd Infantry Division, along with the Luftwaffe's 4th Air Fleet, providing sustained and effec-tive close air support—defeated Soviet Tank Group Popov in detail and threw back the Southwestern Front in disarray.[43]

Vatutin desperately regrouped and ordered the remainder of his left wing to shore up the even more heavily threatened center and right wing. As Vatutin sought to stem the German tide, the 7th Guards Cavalry Corps disintegrated under the German assault. Manstein threw in the 3rd Panzer Corps, and it attacked Vatutin's beleaguered front late on February 27. Stavka forced Golikov's Voronezh Front to wheel Lieutenant General P. S. Rybalko's 3rd Tank Army and Major General S. V. Sokolov's 6th Guards Cavalry Corps 90 degrees to the south-west, from near Kharkov, in an attempt to relieve the pressure on Vatutin by hit-ting Hausser's SS Panzer Corps. By March 1, however, the exhausted 3rd Tank Army possessed only 80 operational tanks to challenge the potent SS Panzer grenadier divisions—on wide-open terrain no less—where newly established German advantages in long-range gunnery meant that the orders given to Rybalko represented a death sentence. First German artillery, and then the power-ful 88-mm guns on the new heavy Panzer VI "Tiger" tanks attached to the SS Panzer Divisions, and the "long" 75-mm KwK 40 L43 guns on the newest marks of Panzer IVs, ripped apart the Soviet columns. Although the up-gunned Panzer IV and the T-34 stood mostly evenly matched in terms of armored protection, the main armament of the T-34s was not equal to the new cannon of the Panzer IVs.

Moreover, the only chance for a T-34 to defeat the heavily armored Tigers occurred at ranges so close as to be suicidal. Panicked Russian soldiers threw down their weapons and fled as the German tanks cut into their ranks.

The SS Panzer grenadier divisions, equipped with a company of Tigers each, proved particularly effective. In one instance, two Tigers took on a large T-34 formation, destroying over 30 T-34s as the high-velocity 88-mm shells from the new German heavy tanks sliced through the T-34s at ranges far beyond the ability of the Soviet tank crews to effectively retaliate. The SS Panzer grenadier divisions that were arrayed against Rybalko's 3rd Tank Army, equipped with only a smattering of thickly armored and powerfully armed Tigers, were nevertheless more than a match for the Russian tankers. Between March 3 and 5, the SS, with the support of the German army's 48th Panzer Corps, encircled and crushed the 3rd Tank Army's 12th and 15th Tank Corps and four rifle divisions.[44] Manstein then concentrated Hoth's 4th Panzer Army near Krasnomeyshkoye and Zaporozhye's and Hausser's SS Panzer Corps near Krasnograd. All told, the Germans gathered seven Panzer or Panzer grenadier divisions, one motorized infantry division, and four infantry divisions for a counterattack recapturing Kharkov on March 14, and throwing the Red Army completely onto its heels.[45]

Vatutin's Southwestern Front, minus the Soviet 6th Army, had begun the offensive with 265,180 men. Including reinforcements, the Southwestern Front lost 101,733 killed, wounded, missing, or captured from January 1, 1943, to February 22, 1943. In addition, the Southwestern Front lost another 100,000 men between February 23, 1943, and March 8, 1943. As of March 10, 1943, Vatutin reported to Stavka shortages in his front standing at 256,000 men, 1,013 tanks, 1,041 guns, and 5,900 trucks.[46] Moreover, Manstein's counteroffensive did more than defeat the Soviet attacks in the Ukraine. With the Red Army losing another 1,023 tanks and self-propelled guns near Voronezh and Kharkov,[47] Manstein's victory occurred on such a scale as to force Stavka to withdraw armies from redeploying against the German Eastern Front's center and throw them into the battles against Manstein.[48] Meanwhile, the Southern Front, now led by Malinovsky, with five combined-arms armies, a cavalry-mechanized group, and the 8th Air Army, had taken Rostov in early February but then ran into a German defensive wall along the Mius River to Rostov's west.[49] Stavka and Malinovsky had pressured Southern Front's weakened armies to advance regardless of their own diminishing strength. Consequently, on February 23, the 4th Guards Mechanized Corps, that had been gobbling up real estate in the vanguard, was encircled and crushed by German forces led by the 23rd Panzer Division and 16th Motorized Division.[50]

At the same time and well to the north, Stavka had launched another massive offensive against Army Group Center, named Operation Star, and carried out by the Briansk, Voronezh, and Central fronts. Rokossovsky's reinforced Central Front, featuring the exhausted 21st, 24th, 62nd, 64th, 65th, and 66th

BATTLE FOR KHARKOV MARCH 1943

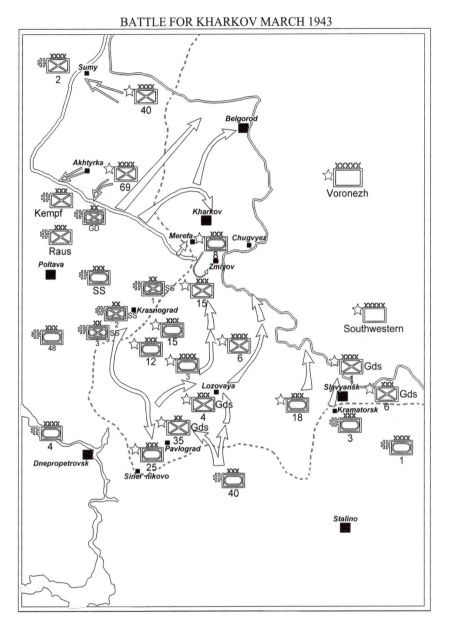

Armies that had finished eradicating the German 6th Army in Stalingrad, had been bolstered by the new 2nd Tank Army under Lieutenant General A. G. Rodin and the 70th Army. Stavka had high hopes for a campaign designed to not only penetrate deep behind Army Group Center but also, in conjunction with the Western and Kalinin fronts, ford the Desna River, take

Smolensk, and complete the encirclement of Army Group Center. Considering what the Voronezh, Southwestern, and Southern fronts were simultaneously attempting to do against Army Group South, these were extraordinarily ambitious goals.

Because of the enormous logistical difficulties involved, the Central Front struggled to redeploy with the speed that Stavka demanded. The Central Front's shock groups, in particular the 2nd Tank Army, had to march some 120 miles just to reach their final assembly areas. They left a trail of broken or bogged-down tanks in the mud. Fuel and ammunition were also in short supply.[51] At the same time, the Western and Briansk fronts saw their attacks run into strong German positions and, from February 22 forward, only painfully battered away against German battle groups, accurate artillery fire, and well-employed tactical reserves. German reserves flowed into the region in part because, on February 6, Hitler had authorized Army Group Center to shorten its lines, including giving up the Rzhev salient.[52] In addition, the Germans enjoyed far superior lines of communication, including numerous intact rail lines. For their part, the Soviet Fronts were advancing across regions featuring horribly degraded rail infrastructure that had never been as strong as that found farther west in areas under German control. Thus, German reserves from farther north and from France had been able to flow into the region with far greater speed then had Soviet armies, particularly Rokossovsky's attempting to redeploy from farther east.[53]

Consequently, by March 1, Manstein's counterstrokes in the Donbas were causing substantial damage and bringing heavy German armored forces farther north.[54] In addition, with the arrival of the German 9th and 4th Armies near Orel during March, and even with the Kalinin and Western fronts pursuing through the Rzhev salient, the steady accumulation of relatively fresh German forces in the region posed a strong threat to the Soviet attackers. Furthermore, the Western Front's 5th, 31st, 33rd, 49th, and 50th Armies had all endured heavy fighting and casualties against the German rear-guard action in the Rzhev salient. These represented substantial losses: 138,577 casualties, with 38,862 men killed, captured, or missing against only a few thousand German casualties.[55]

Therefore, when the Central, Briansk, and Western front finally pressed home their attack on Orel beginning on March 7, and though the Central Front forged several notable successes in the first days, German reserves blunted Rokossovsky's attacks. At the same time, the Briansk Front's attacks went next to nowhere against heavy German resistance—again relying on strong reserves and timely counterattacks. Finally, the Western Front's assault also failed despite having gathered overwhelming numerical advantages. Yet again, German reserves—the 5th and 9th Panzer Divisions and well-planned defensive positions, this time occupied by the 208th and 211th Infantry Divisions—drove Bagramian's shock group back to its start point.[56] Even worse for the Soviet offensive, the German 2nd Army regrouped its forces and thus launched a counterstroke of its own, led by the 4th Panzer Division, that powered into the overextended light cavalry and infantry guarding the Soviet flanks. In addition, Manstein took Kharkov on March 15, and pushed on toward Belgorod on March 17, consequently joining the 2nd Army's push toward the Central Front's rear. In the process, he again crushed the Voronezh Front's 3rd Tank Army, destroyed the 69th Army, and dangerously threatened the 40th Army. By this time, Manstein had defeated two fronts (the Southwestern and Voronezh), badly hammered a third (the Southern), and posed a distinct threat to the Central Front.

Despite the fact that multiple elements contributed to the Red Army's inability to crush Army Group Center, Manstein had played the crucial role in forcing Stalin to cancel the Red Army's attacks against Army Groups Center and South. David Glantz asserts that the impact produced by Manstein's Donbass and Kharkov counteroffensives was "so immense for German fortunes that they had the strategic effect of a full-fledged counter-offensive,"[57] one that Glantz believes saved not only Army Group South but also the entire German Eastern Front. With the mobile armies of the Southwestern and Southern fronts eviscerated by Army Group South's February counterstrokes, Manstein's March follow-up had crushed the Voronezh Front, captured Belgorod, and forced Zhukov to call off the ambitious February–March drive toward Smolensk. Stavka scrambled to respond, including pulling armies from across the front and virtually condemning the ongoing attacks near Orel to failure. In addition, Stavka ordered the potent 1st Tank Army, which had been preparing to strike toward Leningrad with the Northwestern Front, to Kursk. What is more, Stavka also was forced to order the 5th Guards Tank Army, under Lieutenant General P. A. Rotmistrov, to take up positions behind the Voronezh Front. Furthermore, Stavka, fearing the worst following the Manstein counterstroke, and, in reaction it, formed and disbanded multiple fronts as circumstances changed on a nearly daily basis.

On March 14, Manstein had even attempted to convince Kluge to turn his Army Group Center to the south to crush Rokossovsky's armies in the Kursk bulge by meeting Manstein's armies at the salient's base. In retrospect, there is something to be said for Manstein's aggressiveness. The Germans had stabilized the front with relatively fresh reserves, including from western Europe, while much of the Red Army's forces in the region were clearly exhausted.[58] Kluge demurred, however, insisting that his Army Group lacked the strength for such a maneuver.[59] The 2nd Panzer Army duly forced Rokossovsky's men onto the defensive on March 21, and created the northern shoulder of what became the Kursk bulge.[60] Manstein's counteroffensive had meant that not until late 1943 would the Red Army achieve Stavka's objectives otherwise scheduled for completion during the winter of 1942–1943. It is worth noting that in January 1943, Stavka had not only sought to destroy Army Group South with Operation Gallop but also, via Operation Star, begun on February 2, planned to disembowel Army Group Center and drive past Kursk. Thus, much as in November 1942, with Uranus and Mars, late January to early February saw Stavka directing two strategic-level offensives contemporaneously—with Star harkening back to the Red Army's failed attempt to crush Army Group South's left wing in May 1942.

Ironically, because of the strength of the German defensive effort, the Red Army's frontline strength actually declined against the Axis armies in the Soviet Union during this period, mostly from the massive losses incurred at Stalingrad, during Operation Mars, and during the February 1943 campaigns across the entire front. Thus, contrary to popular wisdom, the Red Army did not enjoy an uninterrupted upward curve in its force ratio advantage over the Axis armies following Operation Barbarossa. For example, on November 1, 1942, the Red Army fielded a frontline strength of 6,124,000 men. Yet, by April 3, 1943, the Red Army numbered 5,792,000 men at the front. The Briansk Front endured 134,903 casualties between January 1, 1943, and March 12, 1943. All told, the Kalinin, Western, Briansk, and Central fronts lost 500,000 men in February and March alone.[61] A litany of reasons beyond simply the German army's fighting ability led to such horrendous losses. These included the inadequate employment of combined arms, poor command and control, grotesquely inadequate logistical preparation for offensives, and the failure to adequately reconnoiter German positions and mask the main axis of attack. In part, the weather contributed to the logistical mess, but nevertheless even basic levels of food, fuel, and ammunition often failed to reach the combat battalions. Rokossovsky, in a blistering April 4 report to Stavka, angrily recounted that the numbers of deaths attributable to exhaustion and starvation stood at 114 in the 102nd and 175th Rifle Divisions alone.[62]

Two elements enabled the Red Army to endure the immense casualties and remain on the offensive. First, the Red Army's replacement system operated at peak efficiency in 1943, with replacement units shuttled forward to replace shattered formations on a regular basis. Second, the Red Army regularly press ganged men into uniform as it advanced, and recaptured territories previously lost to the Germans. For instance, the Voronezh Front's 121st Rifle Division numbered 7,025 men on March 25, 1943, with 5,573 of these received as a result of a mobilization conducted shortly after the front recaptured the Kursk region.[63] The 248th Student Rifle Brigade from the 60th Army reported its strength as 2,389 men on March 25, 1943, with the primary reason being the 774 men taken from the recently liberated towns around Kursk, and the conversion of former partisans to full-time soldiers assigned to the unit.[64]

Meanwhile, the Axis army in the east numbered 2,732,000 German soldiers, and another 600,000 allied troops. The Germans had been only marginally able to replenish the eastern army's ranks by calling up approximately

400,000 skilled workers from the factories.[65] In response Germany replaced the manpower lost from its factories with tens of thousands of the approximately 5 million Soviet citizens forcibly deported to work under the appalling slave labor conditions within the Reich. Consequently, by May 30, 1943, the Wehrmacht had never been larger, with 9.5 million men under arms. For his part, Stalin knew that he had gambled and only partially benefited from his attempt to press forward on a broad front. Other than at Stalingrad, the Red Army had failed to attain the goals that Stavka had set for its February–March 1943 offensives. Nor would the Red Army attain Stavka's geographic goal of reaching the Dnieper River until seven months and 3.5 million casualties later.[66]

As the vast drama unfolded across the central and southern sectors of Germany's Eastern Front, the German siege of Leningrad had precipitated yet another Russian attempt to relieve the pressure on the embattled city. The second battle of Lake Ladoga, Operation Spark, opened on January 12, 1943, led by the Leningrad, Northwestern, and Volkhov fronts. Although Soviet casualties had been severe, the Soviet 2nd Shock Army and 67th Army had suffered 115,082 casualties; the Red Army had blasted through the German lines a narrow land corridor roughly four to six miles wide that reached Leningrad. Then, in February, Stavka attempted to crush the bulk of German Army Group North during Operation Polar Star. This campaign saw Stavka attempt an immense deep operational penetration of the German 16th Army's positions far south of Leningrad in the Demiansk region. This Soviet effort planned to include a thrust to the Baltic by a special operational group featuring a full tank army and involved the Leningrad, Volkhov, and Northwestern fronts commanded by Govorov, Meretskov, and Timoshenko, respectively. All through January and February, reinforcements streamed into Timoshenko's Northwestern Front, including the special group of forces Khozin, led by Colonel General M. S. Khozin and featuring the 1st Tank Army, led by Lieutenant General M. E. Katukov, and the 68th Army, led by Lieutenant General F. I. Tolbukhin. Beginning on February 10, the three fronts involved would launch the first in a series of four offensives, all part of Operation Polar Star.[67]

British Historian Evan Mawdsley and American historian David Glantz point out that the Soviet offensives in February 1943 near Leningrad were as ambitious as Uranus in November 1942, according to Mawdsley, and as ambitious as anything else launched by the Red Army in February–March 1943, according to Glantz. Nevertheless, by the end of February, the Red Army's attacks near Leningrad failed to attain their objectives, a failure occurring for a number of reasons. For instance, the Leningrad and Volkhov fronts had been badly weakened by the continuous December–February fighting, including suffering 34,000 dead from the 300,000 men who had begun the Spark offensive in December.[68] In addition, Hitler had allowed his armies to reposition prior to the anticipated Soviet offensive. As a result, the Red Army was forced to restructure its efforts.

It would pay dearly once an abbreviated version of Polar Star reopened in March. Moreover, Stavka undermined the Northwestern Front when it reacted to Manstein's savaging of the Southwestern and Voronezh fronts by redeploying south over three dozen divisions, the 9th Tank Corps, the 1st Mechanized Corps, and the 1st Tank Army.[69]

Furthermore, the Tiger tank–equipped 502nd Heavy Tank Battalion operating with Army Group North had proved quite effective in a defensive role. For instance, in the fierce fighting near Leningrad, the German army knocked out or claimed destroyed 847 Soviet tanks; the 502nd Heavy Tank Battalion received credit for 163 of these kills.[70] Even more remarkably, from January through March, the overextended 502nd Heavy Panzer Battalion never fought as a coherent unit, and, largely because of mechanical breakdowns during this period, not once did the 502nd deploy more than four Tigers in the field at any one time. Incredibly, for each of the six Tigers destroyed from January to March, the Red Army lost 26 tanks. Moreover, of the six Tigers lost few were actually lost in combat, three crews had to destroy their own tanks after being immobilized in unrecoverable situations, including one lost to mechanical failure—an all-too-common occurrence for these otherwise dominant weapons systems.[71]

All told, during Polar Star, the Leningrad and Volkhov fronts threw over 250,000 men against about 80,000 Germans, yet the Russians suffered some 150,000 casualties in February and March alone.[72] The collapse in the Soviet offensives near Leningrad during the winter and spring of 1943, the disappointment near Kharkov, and the defeat hung on the Red Army by Army Group Center meant that, other than Operation Uranus, every other major Soviet offensive during the winter of 1942–1943 fell short of Stavka's stated goals. Moreover, during 1942, the Red Army had suffered a catastrophic 133 percent casualty rate. The Germans, in essence, had destroyed the reconstituted Red Army nearly one and a half times over. Equipment losses had been appalling. For instance, even though 12,553 T-34s had been produced during 1942, the Germans had destroyed 6,500 of them in the same period.[73] Soviet tank crew casualties were so high that women were pressed into service, mostly as drivers. Although only roughly 10 percent of the nearly 1 million women who served in the Red Army from 1941 to 1945 fought in combat roles, the summer of 1943 proved a particularly dicey time for the Red Army. The combination of prohibitive casualties and German control over population centers in the western Soviet Union meant that manpower issues could have become significant. Additionally, Stalin feared for the Soviet Union's economic future at the most simple level, providing food for the men and women slaving in factories or dying at the front. Endemic food shortages in the first quarter of 1943 hampered the shrunken and struggling Soviet economy.

Stalin desperately sought help from abroad. In a letter to Prime Minister Winston Churchill on February 16, 1943, Stalin complained that the Allies were not doing enough. Stalin followed this letter with another on March 15,

1943, again to Churchill, further complaining about delays in opening a second front in France. Meanwhile, Hitler took advantage of the onset of the spring muddy season to retool the German army, and respond to the tightening strategic noose around the Third Reich; a noose tightening not only from Germany's east but also from the warm Mediterranean basin to its south and because of events occurring in the Atlantic Ocean's cold, dark waters to the Third Reich's west.

Chapter 8

The European War's Periphery

A CASE STUDY IN ASYMMETRIC WARFARE: THE BATTLE OF THE ATLANTIC

By the spring of 1943, Nazi Germany and the Soviet Union had fought to a bitter stalemate with neither side truly holding the initiative. Meanwhile, Germany's other fronts had also been far from quiet. These campaigns, fought against the Anglo-American alliance, stretched across vast expanses of open ocean and throughout the Mediterranean basin. Both sides deployed enormous economic and military resources. Yet what is often overlooked is the role played by qualitatively superior doctrine, technology, and leadership in determining victory in both the battle for the Atlantic and during the war in the Mediterranean. Ironically, despite an enduring focus on brute force's role in defeating Nazi Germany, few greater examples from World War II's historical record exists regarding the value inherent in the qualitative over the quantitative in determining victory and defeat in warfare than that gleaned from examining the 1940–1943 war on the periphery of the Nazi empire.

As it is commonly known today, the battle of the Atlantic represented not only the twentieth century's longest naval campaign, but also the longest-running submarine war in history. Admiral Karl Doenitz drove this war via his plan seeking to drive Britain from the war by sinking 750,000 tons of merchant shipping per month, a goal that he never could even remotely consistently achieve. Nevertheless, during the last three quarters of 1940 alone, the Axis sent 1 million tons of shipping to the ocean floor every three months. U-boats did the lion's share of the damage.[1] For instance, during September 1940, German U-boats intercepted British convoys SC7 and HX79, and the radio-directed

U-boat "wolf packs" coordinated their efforts to savage the beleaguered British convoys, sinking 32 ships in total.[2] Much as radio had assisted German Panzer divisions in establishing dominance on land, radio-coordinated efforts at sea also acted as a potent force multiplier.

The North Atlantic's middle passages offered particularly lucrative hunting grounds far beyond the range of the U-boat's greatest enemy: the airplane. However, once the British released adequate numbers of aircraft to Coastal Command, the U-boat crew's job became more difficult. In addition, Allied aircraft also pressured other Axis military assets. For instance, as the spring of 1941 began, the Allies harried the few German reconnaissance and anti-shipping aircraft as well as Germany's few remaining heavy surface warships. The German surface fleet most spectacularly demonstrated its ineffectiveness during May 1941, when the Royal Navy sank the modern and powerful 50,000-ton German battleship *Bismarck*. Severe fuel shortages during the fall of 1941 meant that Germany's surface fleet, including one of the Third Reich's most expensive weapons—the massive battleship *Tirpitz*—floated impotently in harbors across the Nazi empire.[3]

With the German surface fleet largely ineffective, the burden of sinking Allied merchant ships fell on the U-boat fleet. Nevertheless, during the fall of 1941, Hitler scattered his few U-boats across the map.[4] For instance, by April 1942, 19 U-boats patrolled off the Norwegian coast to ostensibly protect against a British invasion. In addition, Hitler and his military command ordered two dozen U-boats into the Mediterranean to support Erwin Rommel's Afrika Korps. There the U-boats sank a mere 2,000 tons of Allied shipping during October 1941.[5] President Franklin Delano Roosevelt's aggressive stance in regard to preparing the United States for war and, more specifically, the U.S. Navy's deployment in the western Atlantic further exacerbated the U-boat's woes. Then, on the morning of December 7, 1941, Japan attacked the U.S. Pacific Fleet at Pearl Harbor, Hawaii, and on December 11, 1941, Germany and Italy declared war on the United States. Hitler's decision, though widely panned for obvious reasons, nonetheless had a certain logic to it—given that Hitler knew about the Americans' German-first focus with or without actual war. Hitler likely also felt that he needed to ensure Japan's commitment, considering Japanese staying power in a war alone against the United States hardly represented a winning bet. On the other hand, even as late as July 1942, Roosevelt came under relentless pressure, including from the U.S. Navy, to give precedence to the war against Japan.[6]

For its part, when war came the United States remained far from ready to defend its waters, let alone carry the fight to Germany. When Fleet Admiral Ernest J. King had taken over the U.S. Atlantic Fleet on December 17, 1940, his command lacked merchant escorts, aircraft, and adequate antisubmarine warfare (ASW) training. In addition, because of poor deployments, it failed to protect the numerous merchant ships traversing the sea-lanes running from the Caribbean and Gulf of Mexico up the U.S. East Coast to the industrial centers in the mid-Atlantic and New England states. In turn, Doenitz, recognizing this weakness, proposed picking off these highly vulnerable, solitary merchant ships plying the inadequately guarded sea-lanes near the American coast. The day after Germany declared war on the United States, Hitler approved Doenitz's plan, code-named Operation Paukenschlag. Amazingly, despite this campaign's underlying importance, and the fact Doenitz's fleet included 91 operational U-boats in December 1941, Hitler made no more than half a dozen U-boats available for carrying the fight to U.S. shores.[7]

Nevertheless, Germany's half dozen U-boats surfaced off the U.S. East Coast early in January 1942 and achieved remarkable successes anyway. In large part, this was because of the sheer laxity of the initial American approach to war, including a failure to institute a convoy system and to black out cities otherwise brightly illuminating American merchant ships cruising along the coast. Furthermore, the U.S. Navy and Coast Guard had assembled only 20 "ships"—mostly Coast Guard cutters and gunboats completely outclassed in speed and armament by a typical German U-boat—to defend the entire 1,500-mile U.S. eastern seaboard. Additionally, the U.S. Navy deployed only 103 operational aircraft to patrol the East Coast from Massachusetts to North Carolina.[8] Facing almost nonexistent ASW efforts, the few U-boats in Paukenschlag's initial sortie thus more than made up for their inadequate numbers. They initiated a two-month-long slaughter of American merchant shipping, sinking 87 ships totaling over half a million tons[9] and efficiently undermined America's greatest strength: its overwhelming economic power. In Britain, Prime Minister Winston Churchill, in a March 12, 1942, cable sent to Harry Hopkins, President Roosevelt's aide, wrote, "I am most deeply concerned at the immense sinking of tankers west of the 40th meridian and in the Caribbean Sea. . . . The situation is so serious that drastic action of some kind is necessary."[10] Shortly thereafter, the U.S. Army Air Force (USAAF) provided nearly 100 medium bombers for ASW duty,[11] and by the spring of 1942, the navy had finally implemented a convoy system off the mid-Atlantic coast.[12]

In response, Doenitz directed his U-boats to the Caribbean. There they again sank Allied merchant shipping at will. In May alone, the Allies lost 115 merchant ships off the American coast, with more than half sunk in the Gulf of Mexico. This distressing figure rose to 122 ships sunk in June, representing over 1 million tons of shipping in May and June, or half of what the Allies had lost in all of 1941.[13] Oil tanker losses were so severe that they threatened to undermine the U.S. ability to project power overseas.[14] In addition, and at the same time, the Germans had also largely succeeded in temporarily shutting down the Arctic Lend-Lease convoys to Murmansk, via the severe damage inflicted to Allied convoy PQ-16 and the virtual destruction of Allied convoy PQ-17.[15]

By the end of 1942, Allied shipping losses to submarines in the Atlantic stood at 5.7 million tons, out of 8.33 million tons lost worldwide. In comparison, that year Allied shipyards produced only 7 million tons of merchant shipping.[16] At the war's beginning, the Allies had possessed a combined merchant fleet grossing 28 million tons of shipping. From September 1939 to March 1, 1943, the Allies had added another 13.5 million tons of shipping to this total, but by March 1, 1943, the Allies had also lost 18.5 million tons.[17] Moreover, Germany produced 121 U-boats during the second half of 1942 and lost only 58, providing Doenitz with 212 operational U-boats in service at the year's end. This was over twice as many as in January 1942.[18] If the Kriegsmarine had merely continued its success rates from the first half of 1942, or, for that matter, from July 1940 through March 1941, when 22 merchant ships went to the ocean's bottom for every lost U-boat, then a vastly larger U-boat fleet may have called into question the Allied ability to project adequate power across the Atlantic—regardless of the Allies' prodigious shipbuilding efforts. Nonetheless, in 1943, the Allied effort at sea turned a corner—and not because of immense Allied economic and military resources per se, but because of the increasing Allied proficiency in using those resources.

WINNING THE BATTLE FOR THE ATLANTIC: ALLIED INGENUITY, TEAMWORK, AND TECHNOLOGY

Nazi Germany encoded its communications via the Enigma machine, a device having originated from a post–World War I design by Hugo Alexander Koch in the Netherlands.[19] These machines were critical to Doenitz's communication with his U-boats at sea. Breaking an Enigma-encoded message required two things: tremendous amounts of work and access to an Enigma machine with the proper settings. The Polish, specifically a group of brilliant students in mathematics from the University of Poznan, laid the foundation for British success in eventually cracking the Enigma codes.[20] Code-named ULTRA by the British, the effort to break the Enigma machines employed hundreds of people centered mostly on a location north of London at Bletchley Park. Nonetheless, the British still needed one final break if they were to crack Enigma, and the Germans duly handed the Allies a glorious opportunity.

On May 8, 1941, the British escort destroyer HMS *Bulldog* drove U-110 to the surface. At this point, the German captain, having ordered the crew to abandon ship, failed to scuttle the U-boat in time, thereby allowing British sailors to come aboard and seize, among other things, German codebooks, charts, and, most important, a complete Enigma machine.[21] The ability to read the German playbook provided a huge boost to Allied ASW efforts, as did increasingly effective technological innovation and teamwork. The development of a range of technologies proved particularly important, including air-to-surface radar, Huff-Duff, high-frequency direction finders used to locate high-frequency radio transmissions by U-boats, and new weapons systems, such as air-launched torpedoes equipped with acoustic homing targeting mounted in Allied long-range Liberator bombers. The pressure that U-boat captains came under resulted from more than Allied technological advances however, for intelligently applied force played an equally lethal role in crippling the German U-boat fleet's effectiveness. Allied ASW assets learned to combine their efforts and integrate new technologies (combining arms as it were) to fix U-boat positions and destroy them. The eventual Allied victory at sea stands as one of the war's great successes, leveraging with an overwhelming reliance on innovation in tactics and technology; a reality perhaps no better demonstrated than during the spring of 1943—when the battle of the Atlantic peaked during one of the war's most dramatic swings in fortune.

Doenitz never deployed a stronger U-boat force as he did in the first five months of 1943. He averaged 116 U-boats per day on station in the Atlantic. Allied problems only intensified when ULTRA intercepts temporarily ceased early in 1943—after the Germans had changed their codes. As a result, during the first three weeks of March 1943 alone, U-boats sent 97 ships to the ocean's bottom, against only seven lost U-boats in return. In one epic battle during March, a huge 40-boat wolf pack savaged Allied convoys HX 229 and SC 122, sinking 21 Allied merchant ships aggregating 141,000 tons of shipping in only four days against the loss of only a single U-boat.[22] Even the normally unflappable British Naval Staff's morale faltered.

Nevertheless, a number of elements came together at this critical phase in the war at sea, allowing the Allies to dramatically turn the tide over the ensuing three months. For one, ULTRA broke the new German codes. In addition, Allied ASW efforts were boosted by the first large-scale Allied escort carrier deployments in a dedicated ASW role, as well as not only the introduction of more new technologies, such as 10-cm radar sets, but also the improvement in availability of existing technologies.[23] In addition, the Allies had redeployed Liberator bombers from the U.S. Army Air Force, the U.S. Navy, and the Royal Air Force Bomber Command, and specially modified them so that the B-24s could fly nearly 20 hours at a stretch, thus helping to close the previously vulnerable mid-Atlantic air gap. Furthermore, the spring 1943 deployment of only six special combined-arms support groups, in part assembled by stripping assets from other duties and consisting of no more than three aircraft carriers, 12 ocean support groups, and initially 40 Liberators on station in the Atlantic, also played a pivotal role in turning the tide.[24] In response, and with U-boat losses soaring as a result of the Allied actions, on May 24, 1943, Doenitz ordered the surviving U-boats to retreat. Although Doenitz continued the U-boat campaign, he never again achieved the success enjoyed early in the war.

For their part, and much as did the Allies, the Germans had been working on advanced technologies of their own. Nevertheless, the Germans failed to aggressively pursue these technologies until far too late in the war. For instance, Germany had long possessed the opportunity to develop and produce true submarines inspired in part by Hellmuth Walter's designs. Once developed, these submarines could travel underwater at combat speeds, featured hulls equipped with stealthy radar-absorbing rubber coatings, and upgraded underwater detection systems capable of tracking multiple targets at distances reaching 50 miles and more.[25] Nevertheless, whether Germany could have rushed these new U-boats into service, even by early 1945, remains questionable. Just as any other radically new weapons system, the world's first true submarines faced a long teething process. German studies back this up.[26] Moreover, mistakes in production and the damage inflicted by the Combined Bomber Offensive on the factories producing parts for the new submarines had only hindered deployment even further.[27] As it was, and despite a massive industrial effort, only six of the new Type XXIII and two Type XXI U-boats ever went on combat patrols, and this came only late in the war.[28] Even worse, the industrial effort behind building the 170 Type XXI U-boats actually ordered by the Kriegsmarine required 40,000 workers and diverted massive quantities of steel that, in comparison, could have instead been used to produce as many as 5,100 tanks during the years most critical (1943–1944) to the Third Reich's survival.[29]

The battle of the Atlantic ranked among World War II's most important campaigns, especially for the Allies, who needed to do more than win the war at sea. The Allies needed to win in such a fashion as to guarantee that the United States and Canada could transfer immense amounts of war material and men across the Atlantic. For its part, as long as the struggle against the Soviet Union continued, Germany did not need to achieve outright victory in the Atlantic but merely delay and undermine the Allied war effort. Yet Germany could not even do that. Allied combined-arms successes as sea effectively mirrored the success enjoyed by German combined arms on land, and could not have highlighted more starkly the failures of German counterintelligence, industry, the Luftwaffe, and the Kriegsmarine regarding integrating their efforts. In particular, the German leadership had proven particularly adept at fatally diluting the deployment of the Kriegsmarine's limited assets. That said, of all the distractions undermining Nazi Germany's war effort, almost none equaled the impact produced by the Axis war in the Mediterranean.

GERMANY AND ITALY: A COALITION OF THE FAILING

World War II's Mediterranean theater tantalizes historians to this day as the source of perhaps the war's greatest "what-if" debates, a debate originally begun by Raeder, Rommel, and other German officers theorizing that had the Axis effort in the Mediterranean and Middle East been coordinated with a Japanese drive into the Indian subcontinent, then the Axis may have won the war. It is this book's contention, however, that the Mediterranean in fact represented a substantial drag on the primary Axis theaters of operation in eastern Europe and the Atlantic Ocean, one primary reason being that Hitler never saw fit to forge a true coalitional war effort with Mussolini. Hitler's largely negligent and reactive approach to Mussolini's own initiatives consequently thrust the Mediterranean theater into a role far more prominent than Germany could support contemporaneous to its considerable military commitments elsewhere. At a time in the war when the Axis should have otherwise held the initiative wherever it wanted, the Allies willingly engaged Germany, and what should have been a troublesome Italian foe, in what became for the Axis a costly and draining struggle on Europe's periphery.

Italy formally joined Germany's war on June 11, 1940, when Mussolini opportunistically declared war on the seemingly defeated British and shattered French states. Within short order, however, Mussolini committed his thinly spread army to fighting the British in North Africa, followed up by a disastrous invasion of the Balkans. Such deployments had amplified the inconsistencies in development within the Italian military and economy that, among other things, had left the Italian army plagued with obsolete equipment and saddled with a poor officer corps. By 1940 Mussolini's overambitious foreign policy had long since overstretched his military. In particular, Mussolini's decision to send the 40,000-man (at its peak in December 1937) Corpo Truppe Volontarie to assist Franco's forces during the Spanish Civil War had weakened the Italian economy at a time when Italy would have been better served modernizing its military establishment. The Corpo Truppe Volontarie, in addition to incurring 12,000 casualties, cost two-thirds the entire Italian military budget between 1935 and 1940.[30] In addition, the Italian military establishment was further burdened by its need to maintain a massive occupation army in East Africa. Moreover, in 1939 and again in 1940, Italy invaded the Balkans. In 1940, Italy also attacked France, invaded Egypt, and sent an aerial contingent to France to participate in the Battle of Britain. Finally, Italy sent an entire army to fight the Soviet Union. All these military commitments overworked an Italian economy and military that could have otherwise provided the primary muscle for a coordinated Italian-German plan of action in the Mediterranean.

In 1936, Italy was a relatively populous European nation of 42 million people. Although lacking access to adequate amounts of raw materials, the Italians had managed to build up strong automobile and shipbuilding industries. Accordingly, Italian production capacities were more than sufficient. The real problem confronting Italy during the war would prove to be the mismanagement of the Axis war effort, and the mismanagement and inefficiency of the Italian industrial base. For example, Italian industry produced enough steel from 1940 to 1943 to have both modernized the army's artillery park and, at the same time, built over 3,000 modern medium tanks. Instead, Italy produced some of the war's worst tanks, and although manufacturing a more-than-adequate 7,000 guns during the same time span, these were mostly obsolete weapons. Meanwhile, the Italian aircraft industry built 10,545 planes from January 1940 to April 1943.[31] Yet most of these aircraft were also obsolete, vitiating what should have been the most powerful air force in the Mediterranean. Furthermore, the Italian automobile industry built more than enough vehicles for Italy to equip several fully motorized divisions for fighting in the North African desert. Nevertheless, Mussolini's overambitious military commitments meant that the Italian North African army's greatest problem, outside of poor leadership and training, was its lack of mobility. Although the Italian military fought marginally more ably than it is often given credit for, it's record during the war has to be considered mediocre at best—in large part because of reasons such as those cataloged above. For instance, the 1940 Italian army in Libya, though numbering 236,000 men, could field only 300 obsolete tanks, 1,500 World War I vintage guns, and 8,000 trucks. In comparison, the British 7th Armored Division alone deployed over 300 medium armored vehicles.

On the other hand, the Italian navy possessed a surface fleet well equipped with fast capital ships. Moreover, the Italian air force possessed a reasonable number of long-range medium and light bombers operating from air bases in Italy, Libya, and Sicily. Nevertheless, once again, numbers proved hardly adequate for producing effective outcomes—in large part because the Italian air force had stagnated during the 1930s as Italian campaigns in Albania, Ethiopia, and Spain ate up 77 billion of the 116 billion lire spent on the Italian armed forces and colonies from 1935 to 1940.[32] Thus, the Italian air force failed to modernize. Only in 1942 did the Italians belatedly narrow Allied technical advantages in the sky, as highly maneuverable and well-powered Macchi 202 fighters appeared in frontline Italian squadrons.

Further working against the Italian and Axis war in the Mediterranean was the British-occupied Maltese island nation, which sat astride the primary shipping lanes in the central Mediterranean; and thereby interdicted Axis lines of communication to North Africa. Malta played a central role in the Mediterranean campaign as fortunes ebbed and flowed for the combatants in the region. If one examines the periods when the Axis maintained their greatest successes against the British army in the North African deserts, these successes closely followed extended operations to denude British air and sea assets deployed from Malta to otherwise logistically strangle the Axis army in North Africa. The Axis, though acknowledging Malta's strategic significance, never allocated enough resources or coordinated well enough to fully neutralize the island. Nothing like the later Anglo-American Combined Chiefs of Staff was even remotely pursued. The result of this systemic failure to even seek more than minimal coordination in military efforts resulted in a series of disasters that crippled the Axis war effort in the Mediterranean from nearly the beginning.

In August 1940, a quarter of a million ill-equipped Italian troops under Marshal Rodolfo Graziani invaded Egypt across its western borders with Libya. Advancing to Mersa Matruh, several hundred miles within the Egyptian border, Graziani halted his army when his supply lines reached their stretching point in front of 100,000 British and Commonwealth soldiers dug in under British General Sir Archibald P. Wavell. Reinforcements from across the British Commonwealth flowed into Egypt, with Wavell's augmented forces consequently spearheaded by the mobile 13th Corps commanded by British General Richard O'Connor. Graziani received no comparable assistance. On December 9, 1940, Wavell's reinforced army struck, and Graziani's forces gave way. Retreat turned into a disastrous rout on February 9, 1941, when Wavell sent a single armored division to cut across the Cyrenaican peninsula, sever the Italian lines of communication, and isolate the Italian army at Beda Fomm. In just two months, the British had advanced over 500 miles and captured approximately 130,000 Italians, 380 tanks, and 845 guns for the loss of only 1,928 killed and wounded.[33]

Amidst the disaster in Libya, Hitler responded by ordering the Luftwaffe's specially trained and equipped antishipping Fliegerkorps 10 to Sicily. The newly arrived German forces badly damaged the British aircraft carrier HMS *Illustrious*, sank the cruiser HMS *Southampton*, and devastated Malta's ports and airfields. In addition, on January 20, 1941, the OKW and Commando Supremo met and belatedly began joint planning.[34] As a result, Italy bolstered its forces in Africa. Furthermore, Germany finally sent to Libya an armored division—the 15th Panzer Division, a motorized division—the 5th Light Division, and Lieutenant General Erwin Rommel in command of what has become famously known ever since as the Afrika Korps.

Rommel landed in North Africa on February 11, 1941, and by March 11, the 5th Panzer regiment had arrived in North Africa; equipped with 120 tanks, including 60 Panzer IIIs and IVs. Rommel promptly attacked. On March 24, he destroyed British positions at El Agheila, sent the survivors reeling into the desert, captured British Generals Neame and O'Connor, and struck east on a 600-mile two-week jaunt to the Egyptian border. That said, in a March 19 meeting at Hitler's headquarters, Brauchitsch and Halder, both immersed in preparing for Barbarossa, had previously informed Rommel that the two divisions from Germany represented all he would get. In addition, Hitler, the OKH, and the Italian commander of the North African theater, General Italo Gariboldi, all had unanimously agreed that Rommel's role in North Africa was purely defensive given a lack of Axis resources, including merchant shipping, and so put him on notice. The August conference in Berlin further saw Hitler, Jodl, and Raeder acknowledge that Libyan port facilities could not support an army in North Africa of a size capable of waging offensive operations to any kind of strategic depth. In Libya, three ports dominated Axis supply efforts, with two, at Benghazi and Tobruk, hardly adequate for supporting even a Panzer corps. Only Tripoli offered a suitable port of supply with the capacity to process 45,000 tons of supplies per month. Tripoli, however, sat over 1,000 miles west of Egypt's border with Libya.[35]

Only a large merchant fleet with ready access to oil and other resources could have effectively supplied a North African army that, given the nature of the desert, required mobility to fight effectively. Of course, Rommel quickly ignored orders based on these realities. Rommel therefore not only cemented his reputation for tactical and operational genius, but also elevated himself to a mythological pedestal almost unique in the annals of twentieth-century military commanders, at least according to some.[36] Others have noted that Rommel merely represented a hyperaggressive personification of the German military tradition valuing mobile sweeping attacks designed to encircle and destroy more numerous opponents.[37] That said, there is little question Rommel proved a highly successful field commander who, among his other talents, fully embraced the value of using combined arms. Regardless of the scope of Rommel's unquestioned abilities, logistics meant everything in the North African desert. Thus, problematically, Rommel's victories often caused him to pursue goals beyond his army's means. For instance, Rommel had followed his spring 1941 victory over Wavell with the first of many pursuits along the lengthy North African coast. Only the defenders at the port and fortress of Tobruk— 12,000 Commonwealth troops, including the besieged 9th Australian Division— slowed Rommel's advance across the Egyptian border, which he crossed on April 14, 1941 regardless. Nevertheless, the British had effectively interdicted Axis shipping; via aircraft stationed at Malta along with surface warships led by British Admiral Andrew Cunningham, who, well informed by ULTRA intercepts, destroyed two Italian convoys bound for Africa, thus forcing Rommel to suspend offensive operations. In turn, Wavell and his freshly reinforced army attempted to relieve Tobruk in an operation code-named Battleaxe. But the British attack, despite quantitative superiority, proved a dismal failure.

Meanwhile, British forces on Malta regularly sank Axis supply ships, and the Axis position markedly deteriorated in the Mediterranean. An uprising in Iraq against the British received only token assistance from the Luftwaffe, while a Royal Navy blockade prevented Germany from assisting Vichy French troops fighting in Syria. The latter subsequently surrendered to the British on July 12, 1941. By the fall of 1941, the combined efforts produced by British aircraft, submarines, and surface warships had caused Axis merchant shipping loss rates to climb over 60 percent. Even though the predations of British convoy raiders sent immense amounts of Axis war material to the sea floor, enough snuck through that, in November 1941, Rommel fielded 414 tanks, 173 German, and nine divisions. The British, however, put over 700 tanks into the field, including 300 American-made Stuart light tanks, 300 Crusaders, 170 Matildas, eight divisions, and over three times the available Axis aircraft. This impressive firepower made up the British 8th Army. In addition, British defenses at Tobruk had been bolstered on August 18 with the arrival of the fresh and highly motivated Polish Independent Carpathian Brigade, comprised of members of the Polish army who had managed to escape from Poland. On November 18, the British Commonwealth forces launched an offensive code-named Crusader. In a running two-week battle,

Rommel repeatedly battered his more numeric British-led opponents. Regardless, several questionable deployments by German officers, including Rommel's ill-advised "dash to the wire," sapped the Axis army's strength. By December 7, Rommel had ordered his worn-out army to retreat. Then, on December 13, 1941, the British hit Axis convoy no. 52. Two ships, hauling 45 badly needed tanks, went under at a time when German tank output barely reached several hundred per month for all theaters.[38]

Rommel, despite the lack of war material reaching his army, avoided encirclement, and finally received badly needed assistance from a reinvigorated Luftwaffe once again protecting the shipping lanes to Libya. Hitler had dispatched Fliegerkorps 2 to Africa from its role supporting Army Group Center in the decisive battles before Moscow. With Fliegerkorps 2 joining Fliegerkorps 10, nearly all of Luftflotte 2 had deployed to the Mediterranean. Consequently, late in the winter of 1941–1942, the Luftwaffe and the Italian air force beat Malta into submission yet again.[39] Meanwhile, German U-boats sank the aircraft carrier HMS *Ark Royal* on November 13, 1941, and the battleship HMS *Barham* on November 25, 1941. Then, in December, the Italian navy sank the cruiser HMS *Neptune* and the destroyer HMS *Kandahar* while damaging another British cruiser and destroyer, driving Cunningham's "Force K" from Malta. In addition Italian frogmen penetrated the harbor at Alexandria on December 19, 1941, sinking a tanker, damaging a British destroyer, and sinking two British battleships.[40] Nonetheless, the British still enjoyed ULTRA's timely insights into Axis deployments. Thus, even as Germany poured air and naval assets into the Mediterranean, Axis shipping losses remained relatively high. Consequently, Germany was forced to redirect oil shipments planned for the Ostheer to instead prop up the Italian navy.[41]

Meanwhile, Rommel, with the logistical situation having improved, rearmed. The Afrika Corps—the 15th and 21st Panzer Divisions—had been folded into Panzerarmee Afrika, which also included the German 90th Light Division as well as six Italian divisions. All told, Rommel had 90,000 men and 561 tanks to work with, but 200 of his tanks were the poorly armed and armored Italian M 13/40s or M14/41s.[42] Moreover, the German tanks included 50 obsolete Panzer IIs and only four new long-barreled 75-mm Panzer IVs.[43] In opposition, Major General Neil Ritchie's 8th Army included 100,000 Commonwealth soldiers, well equipped and deployed in depth west of Tobruk. U.S. Lend-Lease aid meant that the British 1st and 7th Armored Divisions featured 316 American-built tanks, including 167 of the powerful if unwieldy American M3 "Grant" tanks armed with a hull-mounted 75-mm gun and turret-mounted 37-mm high-velocity gun.[44] Ritchie could field 700 tanks. Furthermore, and because of ULTRA, when Rommel decided to attack, the British knew it was coming. Nonetheless, Ritchie failed to concentrate his armor, thus undermining his army's position in an otherwise well-fortified defensive line.

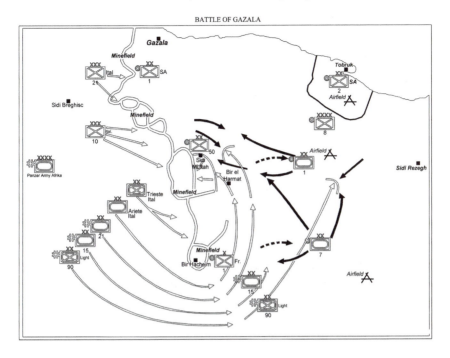

BATTLE OF GAZALA

On May 26 at 2:00 p.m., the Italian 21st and 10th Corps struck the northern portion of Ritchie's positions. Rommel feinted with his fast mobile units to draw off British strength. During the early morning hours on May 27, he then flanked Bir Hacheim to the south with the German 15th and 21st Panzer Divisions and 90th Light Division, along with the Italian 20th Motorized Corps, comprised of the Trieste Motorized Division and the Ariete Tank Division, grouped together into a powerful armored fist. Although the British inflicted heavy losses on the Axis forces, and at one point had cut off a significant portion of Rommel's command, the British had also committed their armor poorly. Therefore, they could not take advantage of Rommel's predicament. Rommel accordingly gathered his armor and struck west, capturing 3,000 men, 90 tanks, and 100 guns. Having reopened a supply line to bring up fuel and ammunition, Rommel then defeated several convoluted and overly intricate British counterattacks. Each counterattack broke apart on fortified Axis positions featuring dug-in armor, anti-tank weapons and artillery backed by savage counterstrokes launched by the German Panzer divisions. Meanwhile, an intense battle raged at Bir Hacheim, where the 1st Free French Brigade and a brigade of Jewish soldiers put up a 10-day defensive battle against the German 90th Light Division, the Italian Trieste Division, and ample German close air support. Nevertheless, on June 11, Rommel resumed his principal attack. By June 21, the British forces began retreating. Tobruk fell, and British Commonwealth casualties skyrocketed to nearly 100,000 men, including 60,000 prisoners of war.[45] Germany once again stood at a crossroads.

MEDITERRANEAN END GAME

During World War II, the German decision-making process all too often smoothed the path for Allied and Soviet military establishments initially making egregious mistakes of their own, but proving adaptable and resilient enough to beat the powerful war machine that Hitler had built. Few times during the war proved more poignant in highlighting the strategic tightrope that both Germany and the Allies walked than during the summer of 1942. Following Rommel's June 1942 victory over the British 8th Army, the German-led command decided between several options. These ranged from the conservative, such as doubling down on the strategy of protecting Italian interests in Libya, to a daring thrust on the extensive British port facilities at Alexandria and the Suez Canal. A middle-ground choice, also reflective of the original defensive rationale behind the German deployment in Libya, was an invasion of Malta, a move that by June 1942 had been long since planned and that if successful could have significantly reduced but, given a lack of oil,[46] not eliminated the enduring Axis logistical weakness in the Mediterranean. Malta's seizure also would have made it easier for the Axis to bog down the Allies in Africa, keep Italy in the war, and allow Germany to focus on its death match against the Soviet Union.

Nevertheless, Hitler backed Rommel's move on Suez, doing what many strategists and military leaders would have advocated—moving to finish a defeated enemy before he could recover. All the same, the drive on Suez allowed British air and naval forces stationed at Malta to recoup from the German spring offensive as Axis military assets were redirected from suppressing Malta to supporting Rommel's move into Egypt. Accordingly, by August 1942, the British yet again were effectively interdicting Rommel's lines of supply. Furthermore, the 8th Army eluded Rommel's attempts to force a decisive battle at Mersa Matruh, albeit only after losing another 8,000 prisoners of war—mostly because of Rommel's adroit maneuvering. The 8th Army's retreat finally ended at El Alamein, the last natural defensive position west of Alexandria's important naval base and deep-water port. The massive Qattara Depression to the south, and the coast to the north, meant that the Germans could not outflank the British positions at El Alamein. With its flanks protected, the 8th Army threw back repeated Axis attacks that began on June 30, and continued throughout the summer.

Meanwhile, a massive Allied resupply effort in August replenished Malta's battered defenses. British and American aircraft based on Malta then relentlessly attacked Axis ports, cutting Tobruk's cargo-processing capacity in half.[47] Lieutenant General Bernard Law Montgomery took command of 8th Army and, forewarned by ULTRA, threw back Rommel's latest offensive during the battle of Alam Halfa. Following his success at Alam Halfa, Montgomery inexorably built up his forces, receiving a shipment of 300 new M4 Sherman medium tanks from the United States. Montgomery's approach to campaigning has been heavily criticized since the war's end and could best be characterized as deliberate. It may have in part reflected the fact that Montgomery knew that his country lacked the manpower reserves to afford costly mistakes. As it was late in 1942, manpower shortages caused the British army to break up the 8th Armored Division and the 44th Infantry Division.

By the end of October, Montgomery was ready to strike. He deployed 230,000 men against 124,000 Axis soldiers (82,000 German), 1,500 aircraft against 350 Axis airplanes, 2,311 artillery pieces against 1,368 Axis guns, and 1,230 tanks against 490 Axis tanks. The Axis armor park included only 30 of the Panzer IVF2 "specials" equipped with the long-barreled 75-mm guns competitive against the 8th Army's Sherman and Grant tanks.[48] In October 1942, the 8th Army deployed from north to south the infantry-heavy 30th Corps and the 13th Corps. To exploit penetrations anticipated by his assault divisions—the 1st South African, the 2nd New Zealand, the 9th Australian, and the British 51st Highland—Montgomery held his 3rd Corps, the 10th Corps, and its armored divisions in reserve.[49] For his part, Rommel had situated his infantry in deep, linear, heavily mined defensive positions. Rommel deployed the Axis armor to the north and south in pairs: the 15th Panzer with the Littorio Armored Division behind the north defensive shoulder and the 21st Panzer with the Ariete Armored Division behind the southern defensive shoulder.

On the night of October 23, at 10:40, Montgomery began his offensive, code-named Operation Lightfoot, with a massive artillery barrage and bombing raids under the bright full-moon light.[50] Near nonexistent stocks of Axis artillery ammunition dictated a negligible response to the initial bombardment. More important, Rommel's dire fuel reserves limited his mobility and ability to effectively counterattack, a situation only made worse when on October 26 the British sank two Axis merchant ships carrying a combined 4,000 tons of fuel and 1,000 tons of ammunition. Moreover, ULTRA intercepts again allowed Montgomery to read Rommel's playbook. Despite such Allied advantages, Axis forces contained the initial penetrations, and easily defeated one effort in particular by the British 10th Armored Division seeking to springboard off the initial lodgments won in Axis lines by the infantry. With his initial break-through attempts having been stymied, Montgomery doubled down on his effort to wear down Rommel's forces. Ultimately, the battle lasted two weeks, until, with only 20 operational tanks left against Montgomery's 600, Rommel finally received permission to withdraw on November 4, 1942. Axis casualties totaled over 30,000 men. All things considered, the Axis forces had fought well,

EL ALAMEIN OCT. 22, 1942

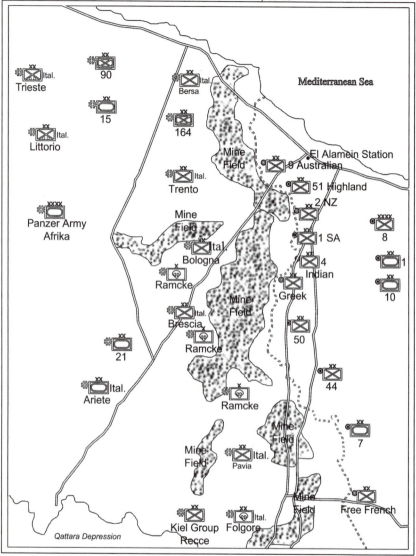

including the often maligned Italian infantry.[51] Rommel ascribed his defeat as stemming from logistical failings and British air and naval superiority, and for the most part was correct in his assessment. The 8th Army, though enjoying the benefits of overwhelming material superiority and ULTRA intercepts, had also fought well, particularly the British artillery and sappers; whose efforts proved crucial in breaking the Axis defensive positions. On the other hand, Montgomery's subsequent pursuit of the Axis across the desert proved painfully slow, and enabled Rommel's exhausted army to avoid complete destruction. Regardless, events on the distant Atlantic North African coast had further altered the balance of power on the continent even more in favor of the Allies.

Code-named Operation Torch, on November 8, 1942, three independent naval task forces landed Allied troops simultaneously at Casablanca in Morocco, with approximately 25,000 American troops under Major General George S. Patton Jr.; Oran, with 18,500 American troops under Major General Lloyd R. Fredendall; and Algiers in Algeria, with 9,000 American and 11,000 British troops under American Major General Charles W. Ryder. The only significant sustained resistance against the landings came at Casablanca. There, Vichy French troops initially fought hard against Patton's men before being ordered by French headquarters to stand down.

On November 28, 1942, Rommel flew to the Wolfshanze to request that Hitler allow the Axis forces in North Africa to evacuate. Instead, Kesselring and Hitler decided to make a fight of it, in part because Hitler worried about the impact that losing North Africa would have on his Italian ally's involvement in the war. Axis reinforcements secured the key Tunisian ports of Bizerte and Tunis. Meanwhile, the German army occupied Vichy France. Although Allied forces, approaching from the west, had penetrated into Tunisia within weeks after landing in North Africa, by the year's end the Germans had managed to stabilize their positions 30 miles west of Tunis. Axis forces in Tunisia were led by Colonel General Hans-Jurgen von Arnim and his nascent 25,000-man 5th Panzer Army. The Luftwaffe deployed over 1,220 combat aircraft and 673 transport aircraft to supply and provide close air support for the Axis armies squeezed into Tunisia.[52] While German reinforcements flowed into North Africa, the German 6th Army slowly starved to death at Stalingrad, and Manstein's relief effort stopped short several dozen miles from the 6th Army's perimeter. In addition, Hitler reassigned several Panzer divisions to France despite the fact that existing German forces in France had defeated a small-scale Allied landing at Dieppe in August 1942. These questionable deployments dovetailed on a poor decision to allow Göring to create "field divisions" from excess manpower in the over-million-man Luftwaffe. Had the Germans retrained the men wasted in the poorly performing Luftwaffe field divisions and incorporated them into existing units, in 1943 alone the army could have brought roughly 100 divisions up to full strength.

In the meantime, as Hitler and his command fumbled about, in January 1943 the Allied principals met at the Casablanca Conference and cemented their plan to defeat Germany. Most important, and despite numerous objections from the U.S. Joint Chiefs, the Allies reached an understanding that invading France was impossible in 1943. Churchill's persistent lobbying meant that plans to knock Italy from the war jumped up the Allied priority list, with an operation to invade Sicily planned for the summer of 1943. However, the Allied commander, American General Dwight D. Eisenhower, first needed to boot Axis forces from North Africa. To that end, he placed British Lieutenant General Sir Kenneth Anderson in direct control over the western Tunisian front with three corps under his command: the American 2nd, the British 5th, and the French 19th. On paper, the Allies seemed overwhelmingly strong. In reality, the British 5th Corps really resembled nothing more than various disjoined parts from different divisions. Moreover, the woefully underequipped French 19th Corps could hardly provide a competitive presence on the battlefield. Only the American 2nd Corps possessed adequate striking power. But the green American troops represented an untested commodity against a strengthening Axis army in Tunisia.

By February 1943, over 140,000 fresh Axis troops, mostly German, had arrived in North Africa. Rommel argued that the buildup was madness given Allied air and naval superiority in the Mediterranean. In December 1942 alone, Germany lost 54 tanks, 111 guns, and 964 vehicles within 32 Axis merchant ships sunk by Allied forces. Even with several hundred transport aircraft deployed to the Mediterranean, Axis logistical efforts proved completely inadequate.[53] Despite his lack of enthusiasm for remaining in North Africa, Rommel moved to organize an attack. His counteroffensive ultimately resulted in one of the greatest defeats suffered by the U.S. Army during the twentieth century. As bad as Rommel's counteroffensive, known today as the battle for Kasserine Pass, went for the Americans, it could have been a lot worse. The split Axis command in North Africa meant that Rommel and von Arnim bickered constantly, and fought for control over resources. Kesselring brought the two German generals together on February 9, 1943, and the three hammered out a plan. Arnim was to attack into western Tunisia and penetrate the Faid Pass to the north. Rommel's spearhead would advance from the south to take Gafsa. Rommel sought to seize the huge Allied supply dumps at Tebessa and from there be in position, at only 100 miles from the coast, to drive north and force the Allied armies in western Tunisia to withdraw or be lost. Arnim, however, remained fearful of such a bold plan. He sought a more limited attack. The failure to iron out the differences between these two commanders would prove fatal to the German plans.

American General Fredendall's 2nd Corps opposed Arnim and Rommel.[54] Fredendall made numerous mistakes. Most important, he deployed his troops in isolated outposts on the heights of key passes and spread his reserves thinly, attempting to defend nearly 100 miles of real estate with only Combat Command A (CCA) and Combat Command C of the U.S. 1st Armored Division and one French division. An American combat command roughly equaled a brigade in size. Although similar in some respects to a German Kampfgruppe, the American combat command was formed from a single division. Fredendall had further spread CCA's battalions between widely separated *djebels* (hills) bracketing the Sidi-Bou-Zid Road. The wide spacing between the American battalions meant that mutual support for the defensive positions proved almost nonexistent.

On Sunday, February 14, 1943, the 10th Panzer Division began the German offensive by skipping past the American 168th Regimental Combat Team, and then pounding into CCA. Although American reserve battalions launched a brave counterattack, CCA disintegrated under the German pressure. By the day's end, one-third of the 1st Armored Division's striking power had melted away, with 1,500 men and well over 100 tanks and other armored vehicles lost. The German troops took Gafsa the following day and began their move on Kasserine. The remaining elements from the 1st Armored Division moved to intercept the German advance near the Faid Pass. The American counterattack began terribly. First, German Stukas broke up the attacking forces as they sat in their assembly areas. Then long-range fire from German artillery and anti-tank guns picked apart the American frontal assault as it moved across open land, followed by a prompt German counterattack. Most of the American troops fled in panic, with one armored battalion completely annihilated. In just two days, the Americans lost over 3,000 soldiers, and the equivalent of half an armored division.

Arnim meanwhile had moved reconnaissance units forward to Sbeitla, creating a renewed panic among the Americans, who again fled in disorganized confusion. Farther south, Rommel, advancing from Gafsa, scattered the American forces that his men encountered and captured the airfield at Thelepte, where the retreating Americans destroyed 30 of their own aircraft on the ground. Rommel was ready to go for broke with a deep thrust designed to take apart the entire Allied front in Tunisia. Arnim refused. Rommel repeatedly appealed to Kesselring for help. Kesselring met with Hitler in Rastenburg, but the decisive moment had passed. Rommel pushed on, and by the day's end on February 20, had seized Kasserine Pass. Allied reinforcements arrived, however, and blocked Rommel's attempts to move any farther. The Americans stopped the 21st Panzer Division cold on the road to Le Kef, where American infantry from the 1st and 34th Divisions held strong positions well supported by artillery. Meanwhile, 20 miles west of Kasserine Pass, well-dug-in American infantry, again heavily supported by artillery, checked the 10th Panzer Division's advance. At the same time, on February 21, the 10th Panzer's remaining units met a wall formed by British infantry supported by 50 tanks and once again by American artillery.[55] Kesselring subsequently approved Rommel's request to call off the offensive. During the battle for Kasserine Pass, over 7,000 Americans were killed, wounded, or captured from the 30,000 Americans who fought in the eight-day battle. The Americans lost 183 tanks, 104 half-tracks and 208 artillery pieces. Germany suffered only minimal losses: 1,000 casualties, including only 201 dead and 20 permanent tank losses.[56]

BATTLE OF KASSERINE PASS

The German attack rattled the Allied command. The British openly questioned the competence of American commanders. All too often, American armored units deployed in piecemeal repeated early war errors made by the British and French.[57] The American Army Air Force also performed miserably.[58] German combined arms meant that the American anti-tank doctrine, which advocated using independent tank destroyer battalions, proved ineffective. And it came under heavy criticism from American field commanders. In response, Eisenhower shook up his command. On March 7, 1943, he put General George S. Patton in command of the 2nd Corps. Patton ranked among the war's most controversial figures. However, there is no questioning his drive and aggressiveness. Eisenhower also promoted the quietly competent Major General Omar N. Bradley, who eventually took over the 2nd Corps, as the first step in a steady rise through the ranks mirroring the stable hand with which he led. British officers Admiral Cunningham and Air Marshall Tedder commanded all naval and air forces, and American Major General Carl Spaatz led the Northwest African Air Force. Eisenhower also placed British General Sir Harold Alexander in command of the entire Allied 18th Army Group comprising the 1st and 8th Armies as well as the U.S. 2nd Corps and the French 19th Corps.[59] Although other men took on important roles, Eisenhower, Bradley, Patton, Alexander, Clark, Montgomery, Tedder, Spaatz, and Cunningham remained the key Allied figures throughout the European war's remaining years.[60]

As for the Axis, they had not only wasted the opportunity opened by Rommel at Kasserine, but also maneuvered a quarter of a million soldiers and huge stores of equipment and supplies into a dead end. They were trapped between two powerful armies, and reliant on a logistical chain perpetually in crisis. Arnim actually surmised that the odious Axis supply situation meant that Eisenhower did not even need to attack his army, as the Axis forces in Tunisia would starve by July.[61] On March 9, a sick and dispirited Rommel left Africa for good. The Allies launched a series of powerful blows from east and west. They forced the Axis armies back on Tunis, despite the German's skillful use of terrain and reserves. The Americans improved weekly. On March 23–24, Patton's men carved the counterattacking 10th Panzer Division to pieces near El Guettar. On May 6, 1943, Anderson launched a massive assault that finally broke through the shrunken Axis defensive perimeter and finished off the Axis army in Tunisia. Axis losses reached 238,243 soldiers; inaccurate records show that German prisoner-of-war estimates fall between 102,000 and 160,000 men.[62]

Hitler's and Mussolini's armies in North Africa had fought for nearly three years. It is no stretch to argue that they accomplished little more during these years than undermining the primary Axis effort in the Soviet Union, all while suffering 620,000 casualties. In comparison, the Allies suffered 260,000 casualties, including 220,000 British, 20,000 French, and 20,000 Americans.[63] In addition, severe Axis equipment losses in the Mediterranean hobbled Hitler's war. Between November 1, 1942, and May 1, 1943, alone, the Luftwaffe lost 2,422 aircraft, including 888 single-engine fighters, 117 twin-engine fighters, 128 dive-bombers, 734 bombers, and 371 transports.[64] The British, in engaging the Axis in North Africa, had maneuvered their opponents into an arena representing the one place where the British, and then the American army, could engage the Germans without having to face the Wehrmacht's strength on the European continent. In addition, the Allies had put pressure on the Axis that the British in particular likely could not have equally exerted anywhere else from 1940 to 1943. Although the German forces deployed to North Africa remained comparatively small in comparison to the powerful army in Russia, this in no way takes away from the fact that an entire veteran Panzer corps, led by an operational maestro such as Rommel, could have possibly provided the difference between victory and defeat in any number of situations that arose on the Eastern Front during 1941–1943.

The Allies followed up their victory in North Africa with a July 1943 invasion of Sicily.[65] The Italian campaign that followed not only drove Italy from the war in September 1943 but also tied down significant German military assets. Nonetheless, it remains hotly debated as to who benefited most from this arrangement or, for that matter, who suffered least. On the one hand, Allied operations in Italy caused Germany to siphon off significant forces that otherwise could have been deployed in eastern Europe, particularly during the critical months following the German attack at Kursk. In addition, the Allies caused 536,000 German casualties against 312,000 Allied casualties. Yet Germany thwarted overwhelming Allied material superiority, and fought a two-year withdrawal up the Italian peninsula that lasted until the war's final days. For instance, German troops held one defensive line south of Rome for six months, most famously in the battles around Monte Cassino.

Perhaps the best argument in support of the Allied decision to invade Italy comes from General Marshall himself. Marshall argued the Allies needed to conduct the Sicilian and Italian campaign if for no other reason than to maintain pressure on Germany and keep Russia in the war. In addition, and even though the Americans had spent a significant portion of their first year in the war attempting to convince the British that they should invade France sooner rather than later, an invasion prior to 1944 likely could have been catastrophic for the Allies, especially given what had happened at Dieppe, during Torch, at Kasserine Pass, and particularly in considering the Luftwaffe's strength in 1943. Before the Italian campaign even began, however, one of the war's great decisions had confronted the OKH and Hitler: how to approach the summer campaign season in eastern Europe.

Chapter 9

Seizing the Initiative: The Sword versus the Shield

THE STATE OF GERMANY'S EASTERN ARMY IN THE SPRING OF 1943

The winter of 1942–1943 had not been a particularly good one for the Wehrmacht. By the spring of 1943, the German army in the Soviet Union could put only 2.7 million men into the field, a total roughly half a million men understrength. In addition, the German army had lost an entire year's output of arms and equipment.[1] Moreover, at the same time, and unlike years past, Allied pressure in the Mediterranean and on Nazi-occupied Europe had required an ever greater diversion of Axis resources away from eastern Europe. The German economy's failure to mobilize as effectively as its foes had further hindered the Axis strategic position in the war. Yet despite all this, the Wehrmacht had at times dominated eastern Europe's early 1943 battlefields. In large part, this had been because of its preeminent ability to still effectively wage a war of movement.

At the same time, however, the German army struggled to maintain this all-important mobility. This struggle stemmed from a number of reasons, including an attempt to address one of the Red Army's more significant qualitative advantages over the German army, namely, tanks more heavily armed and better protected than anything in the German arsenal. To that end, Hitler and German tank manufacturers had, prior to 1943, initiated the development of tanks possessing far greater hitting power and armored protection than almost any other army's tanks. The clash of armor on the 1943–1945 battlefields thus would come to represent a clash of armored philosophies. The Germans moved away from the production of relatively reliable, modest-sized tanks that reflected the German army's traditional doctrinal emphasis on fighting a war of maneuver. At the same time, both the Red Army and the Allied armies doubled down on manufacturing tanks that could be easily manufactured, and that were reliable and logistically friendly. For instance, the Sherman tank could be relatively easily produced and shipped in great quantities across the ocean to fight what was thought to likely be a fluid mobile war against the army that had invented the blitzkrieg. As for the Soviets, they had concentrated limited economic assets on producing a few dependable weapons systems that could fight the sweeping war of maneuver called for by Soviet war-fighting doctrines. Therefore, even though late-war German tanks would reign supreme in terms of firepower and armored protection, the high rates of fuel consumption and the mechanical unreliability of the new Panzers only further accelerated the German army's movement away from waging mobile warfare.

All this occurred despite the fact that early in 1943, the newly upgraded Panzer IV "G" and "H" models, mounting a high-velocity L/48 75-mm gun and having heavier frontal armor, at 80 mm thick, had begun appearing. By the end of 1943, the Germans had produced 3,073 of these tanks.[2] The newest Panzer IV, which proved a handful for the T-34/76, was economically inexpensive to build, robust, reliable, and not unduly burdensome to Germany's threadbare logistical network. Moreover, and given the damage inflicted on Soviet armor in years past by well-trained German tank crews demonstrating superior tactics, even when all too often fighting from what amounted to poorly armed and protected Panzers, such tanks could have proven just the answer the German army needed toward redressing the advantages in hitting power and armored protection of the T-34—without abandoning the emphasis on mobility that had brought the German army its greatest successes.

Nevertheless, despite the qualities of the newest marks of the Panzer IV, including its ability to match up well with the T-34, it had gained a much bigger peer late in 1942. The Panzer VI "Tiger," mounting the dreaded 88-mm high-velocity gun as its primary armament and with 100-mm-thick frontal armor, could penetrate any enemy tank at standoff ranges reaching over one mile without fear of being destroyed by Soviet or Allied tank guns. Nevertheless, each Tiger tank included 26,000 parts, needed 300,000 man-hours to build, and, fully outfitted, cost as much to build as roughly three Panzer IV medium tanks. In addition the Tiger also took far longer to manufacture. To make matters worse, substantial operating costs plagued the Tiger, including massive fuel and oil consumption. In addition, the Tiger demanded ample service time to remain in operating condition, caused by the increased wear and tear that the heavy vehicle put on its drivetrain—hardly representing a tank well adapted to survival on eastern Europe's free flowing battlefields. Toward that end, German designers had also developed another new tank. One much closer to embracing everything a balanced tank should possess, but one still very much flawed in 1943.

The Panzer V "Panther," Germany's new medium tank, owed much to the superb T-34 that had spurred its development. The German Army Ordnance Department (Heereswaffenamt) had, since 1938, led the tentative effort to produce a new medium tank. Accordingly, Daimler-Benz and MAN (Maschinenfabrik Augsburg—Nürnberg) had submitted proposals for producing Germany's next-generation medium tank. Nonetheless, for a number of reasons, including a pledge that the MAN design could go into production earlier than the Daimler-Benz design, the MAN design won out. MAN subsequently rushed to make good its promise on a quick delivery. This decision would go on to play an important role in the countless mechanical problems that plagued the otherwise imposing new tank.[3] The Panzer V was armed with one of the war's finest tank cannon, a long-barreled high-velocity 75-mm L/70 gun designed by Rheinmetall-Borsig. This weapon was capable of penetrating well over 100 mm of armor at 1,000 meters. Though the tank weighed approximately 45 tons; in part this was because of its thick, well-sloped frontal armor. Hitler had wanted 250 Panthers ready for combat operations by May 12, 1943. But with the Panzer III and IV still in production, as well as development work on a "Panther II," there were not enough resources available to both meet his goal and iron out the many problems with the vehicle. In particular, the front-wheel transmission and engine, designed for a lighter tank, labored under the enormous strain produced by the tank's heavy gasoline engine and belated augmentation of the vehicles' armored protection. Furthermore, it was not until the winter of 1943–1944 that many initial design problems, including a shot trap between the Panther's turret and hull, had been resolved. As it was, the Panther's mechanical issues had long since been representative of such problems afflicting the entire German armored fighting vehicle (AFV) park. A plethora of designs in production meant that inadequate stocks of spare parts existed for resolving field maintenance problems[4] among ever more varieties of assault guns and self-propelled artillery and anti-tank guns. All of which were fielded by a German army whose 1943-era Panzer divisions consequently and consistently put far fewer numbers of tanks into the field than called for by their tables of organization and equipment.

Guderian, having been recalled to service on February 17, 1943 as the inspector general of armored troops, recognized the greater issues afflicting the German tank park and demanded that the newest marks of the Panzer IV constitute the main short-term striking power for the German Panzer arm. As it was, the Panther's problems were so great that in June, the first 250 produced had to be rebuilt. Additionally, German planners, such as the Army Ordnance Office, had shot themselves in the foot not only in underestimating the need for modern tanks but also in arbitrarily changing factory orders between vehicle models.[5] This meant that one factory so afflicted switched between the production of the Panzer IV, Panzer I, Panther, StuG IV, and various armored recovery vehicles before receiving final orders to

Table 9.1 Panzers per Panzer Division during the War[1]

Date/Total Panzer Divisions[2]	Authorized/Actual Panzers per Division
October 1935/3	561
May 1940/10	320
October 1940/21	190/160
October 1941/24	190/145: In combat on the Eastern Front, these numbers regularly dropped far lower.
1942/27	175/135: In combat, rarely averaged even 135 "runners."
1943/32	175: Actual strength far lower. Army Group South averaged 50 Panzers per division in July 1943.
1944/38	135: The nine Panzer divisions in France on June 6, 1944, averaged 80 Panzers each; Eastern Front Panzer divisions averaged even fewer.
1945/42	Panzers per division in 1945 rarely climbed over 50 in running condition.

[1]Robert M. Citino, *The Path to Blitzkrieg: Doctrine and Training in the German Army, 1920–1939* (Lynne Rienner Publishers, 1999), 231; *The German Armored Army*, prepared by the Military Intelligence Service War Department, Washington, DC, Special Series No. 2, August 10, 1942, unclassified July 13, 1987; Karl H. Theille, *Beyond Monsters and Clowns: The Combat SS: De-Mythologizing Five Decades of German Elite Formations* (University Press of America, 1997), 90; James F. Dunnigan and Albert A. Nofi, *Dirty Little Secrets of World War II* (William Morrow, 1994), 147; Roman Johann Jarymowycz, *Tank Tactics from Normandy to Lorraine* (Lynne Rienner Publishers, 2001), 105. See also Samuel W. Mitcham Jr., *Hitler's Legions: The German Army Order of Battle in World War II* (Stein and Day, 1985).

[2]The total number of divisions shown include Waffen-SS Panzer divisions.

produce the StuG IV, changes that meant that the manufacturer produced 150 fewer AFVs than it could have during that time.

Guderian was able to alleviate some of the mess by canceling several poorly designed weapons. In addition, he advanced a number of other recommendations, including, among other things, an insistence on the army's need to maintain an armored reserve deployed behind the front lines. This would leverage efficiencies created by increasing armor serviceability and repair while maintaining greater numbers of Panzers in a state of combat readiness. He also revamped training programs for German tank crews, making them even more realistic, especially in gunnery skills and live-fire "battle runs," with a heavy focus on testing the speed of target acquisition and accuracy of fire against both stationary and moving targets.[6] The training heavily emphasized teamwork, problem-solving skills, and communication and went well beyond what the typical Soviet tank crew received.

Despite Guderian's reforms, Hitler and the OKH (Oberkommando der Heer, or Army High Command) played yet another role in further undermining the German army's flexibility, in part because they all too often took the Panzer out of their Panzer armies. For example, during Operation Barbarossa,

Table 9.2 Combat Equivalency Comparison between Standard German/Soviet Fighting Organizations in 1943–1944[1,2]

German	Soviet
Infantry division	Two rifle divisions
Panzer battalion	Tank brigade
Panzer division	Tank corps
Corps	Army
Army	Front
Army Group	One to three fronts

[1]See William M. Conner, *Analysis of Deep Attack Operations: Operation Bagration, Belorussia 22 June–August 1944* (Combat Studies Institute, 1987), 17–18, and Roman Johann Jarymowycz, *Tank Tactics from Normandy to Lorraine* (Lynne Rienner Publishers, 2001), 301.

[2]U.S. divisions carried even greater equivalent firepower/combat power against their German competitors and Soviet peers. For example, a standard 1943–1944 U.S. infantry division with its regularly attached support units equaled a 1944 Soviet mechanized corps and surpassed a 1943–1944 German Panzer grenadier division. A standard 1944-era U.S. armored division equaled a German Panzer corps in tanks and surpassed even a 1945 Soviet Tank corps in men and tanks. See also Ronald Andidora, *Home by Christmas: The Illusion of Victory in 1944* (Greenwood Press, 2002), 29, and Trevor N. Dupuy, David L. Bongard, and Richard C. Anderson Jr., *Hitler's Last Gamble: The Battle of the Bulge, December 1944–January 1945* (HarperCollins, 1994), 407.

Germany had deployed four full Panzer armies each featuring massive concentrations of armor. By early 1943, only two Panzer armies consistently fought together in a manner whereby their structure matched their imposing name.[7]

Moreover, the German infantry and artillery arms had fell further behind in the arms race between the Red Army and the Wehrmacht. For example, in 1943, most German infantry carried obsolete carbines, the K-98, as their primary weapon. This was even though Germany had introduced the world's first true assault rifle, the Sturmgewehr, into small-scale production in 1943 but not into mass production.[8] In addition, the German economy could not produce the newest model of armored infantry fighting vehicle designed by the army— the fully tracked Katzchen—without pretty much ceasing existing half-track production prematurely. As it was, during the Kursk campaign, the half-track–equipped Panzer grenadiers not only enjoyed substantial cross-country capabilities, but also suffered far lower casualties than the truck-mounted or foot-marching infantry.[9] In terms of indirect fire, the German army was perhaps even worse off. Mortar production and field artillery production were either concentrated in obsolete weapons or marginalized, such as in regard to artillery tube production; where priority went to the Luftwaffe's immense numbers of anti-aircraft batteries. Finally, the German and Axis military establishments had still failed to rationalize armaments production in a few commonly shared weapons systems.

As for his strategic approach to the war in eastern Europe, Hitler planned to put Germany's eastern army onto the defensive in 1943, though only after a limited summer campaign. Hitler explored several options. Ultimately, he decided to follow up on an idea first proposed by Manstein on March 10, 1943, an attempt to pinch off an approximately 150-mile Soviet held salient, projecting into the German lines north of Kharkov and south of Orel, surrounding the battered Soviet city of Kursk. The open terrain in the region favored the attacker, though the salient offered several geographic strongpoints, including numerous gullies and valleys as well as several rivers and hills. Code-named Operation Zitadelle (Citadel), the German attack on the Kursk salient called for a double envelopment of the Soviet forces within the salient to be forged by striking from the salient's base on the northern and southern edges. Zitadelle offered a number of potential benefits for the German war effort, including the chance to eliminate several Soviet armies and provide time so that the army could build up its reserves, all while consolidating the Third Reich's hold on Ukrainian raw materials.

Meanwhile, the Russian command team put in place their plan for the summer campaign season. They were led by Chief of the General Staff Vasilevsky; General Aleksei Antonov, who in December 1942 had joined the General Staff's Operations Directorate; and Zhukov. The plan put together by this triumvirate was accepted by Stalin at an April 12 meeting in Moscow. It recommended reinforcing the Central and Voronezh Fronts near Kursk to first stop the German summer offensive and second, once the anticipated German offensive had been defeated, launch a series of Soviet offensives. Intelligence, including from ULTRA and Soviet spies, backed Zhukov's assessment regarding German intentions at Kursk. Although the decision to hand the initiative over to the Germans has been lauded in hindsight, what is often forgotten is that at the time, Stalin had made an extraordinarily risky decision. During the previous two years of warfare, the Red Army had consistently failed to stop assaults launched by smaller groupings of Panzers, no less the mechanized armies the Germans were deploying on the open steppe near Kursk. Stalin therefore left almost nothing to chance as he assembled 22 rifle armies and five tank armies around Kursk, efforts noticed in turn by the Germans.

At a May 4 meeting in Munich, German aerial reconnaissance photos demonstrated clearly to Hitler, and others present, that the Soviets were preparing massive defensive fortifications, including huge minefields, tank ditches, and anti-tank and artillery positions in depth in and around the Kursk salient. Hitler ordered further delays to strengthen Army Group Center, a decision recommended by Model and also influenced by Guderian's objections to the operation as drawn up. Meanwhile, even though after what amounted to a three-month lull in operations on the German Eastern Front had resulted in the creation of two very powerful armored groupings—in the form of the German 9th Army and 4th Panzer Army, the best chance to pinch off the Kursk salient had passed.

The Red Army already had 20,000 guns and mortars emplaced in the Kursk salient along with 6,000 anti-tank guns and over 40,000 mines as well as thousands of miles of communications wire. The latter allowed local Soviet

Table 9.3 Red Army versus German Army in Kursk-Orel Region on July 4, 1943

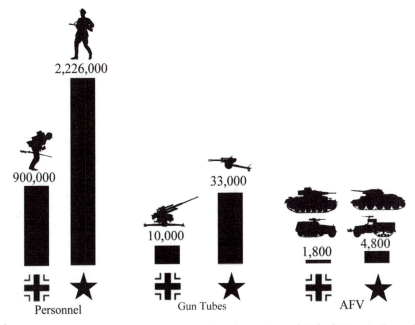

2,226,000

900,000

33,000

10,000

1,800

4,800

Personnel   Gun Tubes   AFV

[1]David M. Glantz, *When Titans Clashed: How the Red Army Stopped Hitler* (University Press of Kansas, 1995), 165.

commanders to issue orders with a timeliness going far beyond that achieved in past responses to German assaults. Furthermore, the Red Army had assembled numerous anti-aircraft formations that subsequently would play an important role in hindering German ground attack aircraft seeking to replicate the past year's success—when they had inflicted grievous losses on Soviet armored units.

In addition, and unlike during March, when the Germans enjoyed the benefit provided by relatively fresh regional reserves, the Red Army had not only rehabilitated the bulk of its forces, but also assembled powerful regional reserves of its own. These included, most prominently, the Steppe Front, commanded by Colonel General Konev and spearheaded by General Rotmistrov's 5th Guards Tank Army. The Red Army Air Force gathered some 1,000 combat aircraft comprising the 16th Air Army in the salient's northern sector, along with the 2nd Air Army's 881 combat aircraft assembled to support the Voronezh Front in the Kursk salient's south.[10] Furthermore, the Red Army and 300,000 civilian workers constructed eight defensive barriers at Kursk, with these barriers reaching their deepest, nearly 30 miles in depth, at the salient's base.[11] The primary thrust of the Red Army's efforts was on stopping the German armor. To that end, the Red Army created numerous armor-destroying strongpoints, *protivotankovye opornye punkty*, that brought artillery, anti-tank guns, mortars, and automatic weapons together in bristling arrays of weapons and fortifications; the strongest of these featured as many as 30 anti-tank guns in superbly camouflaged positions, though most contained six to 12 anti-tank guns. For instance, in the Soviet 69th Army's defensive sector, its rear defensive line alone contained 19 such strongpoints to bolster just three rifle divisions—with many Soviet rifle divisions being assigned their own Destroyer anti-tank regiments of roughly 20 anti-tank guns each. Just as in years past, at Leningrad, Moscow, and Stalingrad, the German army had let an initial weakness in the enemy positions slide by. Instead, and despite the concerns of numerous high-ranking officers as well as of Hitler himself, German forces prepared to attack an enemy ready and waiting at his point of greatest strength.

Although Hitler expressed reservations about the planned assault, he still gave it the green light. Nevertheless, his senior military advisers deserve ample criticism. They had presented no unified front coalesced around any palatable existing alternatives in reaction to the obvious Soviet defensive preparations near Kursk. For instance, since the Red Army obviously knew where the Germans intended to attack, why not shift the attack axis to the much weaker Soviet defenses in the salient's western tip? (an idea to which Manstein belatedly seems to have come around in June).[12] Such a strategy provided German forces an opportunity to achieve a quick breach of defensive lines otherwise oriented outward along the salient's length. It would have forced the Stavka to commit its armor reserves in a head-on clash against the concentrated firepower of the rejuvenated German Panzer arm. This idea was something that Guderian had previously advocated in May, and had Zitadelle been so modified it would have brought about a clash that the Red Army might easily have lost. Zeitzler, however, failed to back such changes to the plan; in part because by mid-June he believed that it would have taken too much time to engineer such a shift.[13]

In May 1943, Germany possessed another compelling reason for calling off or dramatically modifying Zitadelle: Axis defeat in Africa. The German losses in Tunisia included six divisions, three of these being Panzer divisions. These losses, on top of the 26 German divisions destroyed at Stalingrad and thereafter in southern Russia, were even more vexing because the German delay in attacking at Kursk had occurred in part to allow Germany's newer and more powerful tanks to equip the assault armies. Beginning late in 1942, however, OKW (Oberkommando der Wehrmacht, or High Command of the Armed Forces) had reinforced the Mediterranean theater of operations with a Panzer division as well as over 50 Tiger tanks. If instead Axis forces had withdrawn from North Africa, even as late as following the February 1943 battle of Kasserine Pass, they would have freed up additional armor to support Zitadelle. This is not to say that another Panzer division and several dozen more Tigers would have guaranteed success at Kursk. However, from January to February 1943, a single company of Tiger tanks from Schwere Panzer-Abteilung 502, deployed near Leningrad, had knocked out 25 percent of the Soviet tanks destroyed during those months by the entire German 18th Army, and accomplished this feat even though it could put no more than nine Tigers into the field at any one time. Moreover, given the success subsequently enjoyed by the Tiger tanks at Kursk, at a minimum the presence of another heavy tank battalion could very well have tilted the scales enough to have left German forces in better position to parry the Soviet counteroffensives following Zitadelle.

THE RED ARMY ACCELERATES ITS TRANSFORMATION

For his part, Stalin was deeply concerned over his army's prospects for successfully stopping a German summer offensive. In a letter to President Franklin Roosevelt on June 11, 1943, Stalin harshly criticized the Allies for delaying opening a second front in France. Meanwhile, Stalin left nothing to chance in preparing his armies to face the third German summer offensive against his country. The Red Army had noticeably strengthened each individual unit's firepower, and had distributing ample quantities of anti-tank weapons throughout its ranks, including new weapons such as the *RPG-43* anti-tank grenade. To further protect against German armor, the high-velocity 57-mm M1941 anti-tank gun also finally reached the Red Army's anti-tank units in appreciable numbers.[14] In regard to indirect fire support, the revised *shtat* for each rifle division called for its regiments to receive not only more but also more powerful mortars. Moreover, the infantry could count on direct armored support from armored units such as independent tank regiments, numbering 20 to 40 tanks, and heavy breakthrough tank regiments—numbering around 24 tanks each.[15]

Additionally, an improved esprit de corps had also taken hold in the Red Army. In part, this had stemmed from the formation of Guards Armies, but also developed because of accelerated procedures for awarding military decorations—with many decorations coming with privileges in pay, rations, or travel.[16] Moreover, the tactical- and operational-level leadership of the Red Army had been significantly bolstered by the increasing presence of tens of thousands of experienced combat officers turned out by stiffened training programs, the return of tens of thousands of previously wounded and combat experienced officers to the front, and the culling of ineffective leaders during the prior two years.

In the air, new single-engine fighters by Yakovlev and other manufacturers meant that the Red Army Air Force's aircraft technically matched up well with Germany's frontline fighters. The premier Soviet ace during the war, Ivan Kojedub, flew a La-5, and later a La-7, in amassing his 62 kills and reputation as being among the war's best pilots. The Red Army Air Force's growing cadre of veteran pilots proved capable of giving even Germany's best a run for their money. The Il-2m3 Shturmovik close support aircraft also proved highly effective in the close air support role. It was adept at dishing out the punishment, and could famously take it as well.

Furthermore, hundreds of thousands American-made jeeps and trucks provided the Red Army with mobility and logistical support. Already, 183,000 sturdy, reliable trucks and light vehicles had reached the Soviet Union by the middle of 1943.[17] Millions of tons of Lend-Lease food, explosives, and industrial supplies further helped keep Russian factories humming, and the Red Army in the field. Lend-Lease also supplied enough tanks so that in June 1943, some 61 of 256 Soviet tank brigades were fully or partially equipped with American-, British-, or Canadian-built tanks.[18] For instance, of the 351 operational armored fighting vehicles equipping the Soviet 6th and 7th Guards Armies in June 1943, fully 121 were Lend-Lease–provided Stuart, Lee, Matilda, and Valentine tanks. Additionally, the Allies provided over 2,000 locomotive engines, over 20 times the Soviet Union's 1942–1945 production of such engines. The Allies also delivered most of the railway cars that the Red Army used in 1942–1945. Moreover, the recapture of southern Russia had meant the regained use of regional rail lines and the Volga River, the loss or interdiction of each having greatly impeded the distribution of oil and thus degrading the Red Army's mobility during the fall and winter of 1942–1943. Therefore, during the late spring and early summer of 1943, the Red Army was able to build reserves and accumulate great quantities of war material to support operations in the Kursk and Kharkov regions, something that it could hardly do only months earlier and that in part had contributed to German late-winter successes.[19]

The vast amounts of war material produced by the greatest industrial nations on earth continue to attract considerable attention from many historians when they attempt to explain how and why Germany lost World War II, and thus influence a conventional wisdom based in part on the power and weight of sheer numbers to explain the outcome of the greatest war in history. Even in recent decades, the historical narrative is punctuated by widely acclaimed historians who have proven far from outliers in looking at the sheer productive capacity of the Allied nations as determinative in the war's outcome—historians such as John Ellis, who in 1990 went all in on the brute-force thesis for explaining the war's outcome. In 2000, Bevin Alexander, in his popular book theorizing how Hitler could have won World War II, railed against Hitler's decision to attack the Soviet Union and its immense resources, including economic, in lieu of exploiting what Alexander believed to be better opportunities elsewhere. Today, historians such as P. M. H. Bell, who devoted an entire chapter of his 2011 book on the 12 turning points of World War II to describe how crushing Allied advantages in material output during World War II's mid-to late years proved crucial in deciding the war, contribute to the myth that German defeat during World War II was based largely on brute-force economic or military reasons created when Germany entered into a multifront war against the Allies.

Bell's work is particularly illustrative because much of it otherwise thoughtfully goes beyond defaulting to quantitative-based arguments in explaining the war's outcome. Yet, when he turns to the economics of the war, the centerpiece of his chapter on the "battle of the factories" is a series of tables showing that late in the war, the Allies overwhelmingly outproduced Axis factories and thus, as long as the Allies held serve in other key determinants of success, that this sheer weight of war material had proved decisive in shifting the balance of power against the Axis. Ironically, the author's own tables show that in 1941, Germany faced similar numerical odds against Britain and the Soviet Union, and yet this early period of the war is one characterized by Axis military triumph and geographical conquest. Given the consistent Allied advantages in armaments output throughout the war, and vast difference in outcomes during the war's major periods, if the Allies were to overcome a Wehrmacht they otherwise had struggled to survive against in the field, let alone best with any kind of consistency, then something else had to happen for the Allies if they were to win the war other than to merely double down on producing ever greater numbers of war machines.

For instance, in terms of the Soviet war effort, qualitative determinants ultimately proved more important than did the quantitative in powering the Red Army's resurgence, with organizational decisions being one such source of qualitative improvement. A good example of this came on January 28, 1943, when the Soviet State Defense Committee issued Decree No. 2791calling for the reorganization of tank armies drawing their strength from the Red Army's 34 tank and 13 mechanized corps.[20] The new tank army contained two tank corps, one mechanized corps, two tank destroyer regiments (20 76-mm guns each), two mortar regiments, two anti-aircraft regiments, two self-propelled artillery regiments (with nine Su-76s and 12 Su-122s in each), a Guard mortar regiment, and reconnaissance elements. Though this brought the tank army's size up to approximately 46,000 men, 648 tanks, and nearly 700 guns and mortars;[21] more important, these changes continued the trend within the Red Army of organizing its units toward effectively applying firepower and combined arms on the battlefield. These changes continued the evolution of the Red Army away from an early war reliance on massed infantry heavy assaults, or the use of sheer numbers of armored vehicles packed into mechanized corps made far too unwieldy by their size.

Nonetheless, on a technical basis, and in regards to the actual equipment used by the Red Army only marginal changes were made to the T-34, in the Model 1943 T-34/76, with these modifications proving inadequate for competing with Germany's newest AFVs. In particular, the T-34/76's F-34 main gun could not penetrate the Panther's frontal turret armor at all, and could penetrate its frontal glacis armor only at a distance of 300 meters. Conversely, the Red Army had joined the German army in embracing the assault and self-propelled gun. Both the SU-85 and the SU-100 proved effective anti-tank weapons; with their low frames, sloped armor, and, in the SU-100's case, a potent 100-mm anti-tank gun. In addition, the SU-122 and SU-152 provided further mobile firepower. In terms of training, however, the Red Army's armored units regularly faced the same persistent problems that they always had. For instance, tank training schools provided only highly abbreviated basic training programs, comparing unfavorably with the training that the Germans provided their tank crews.[22] Furthermore, even though Soviet tank production proved tremendous, Soviet tank losses were equally staggering. From 1943 to 1945, the Red Army lost, on average, just over 1,000 T-34s per month.[23]

That said, the increasingly heavy weaponry and armor weighing down German Panzers meant that the T-34/76's existing advantages over the 1941–1942 German tank park in terms of efficiency, reliability, and mobility had only strengthened. For instance, the T-34/76 used only a quarter of the fuel that a Panther needed to travel one kilometer, and only half the fuel needed by a Panzer IV to travel the same distance. From the perspective of operational readiness/reliability rate, a T-34 tank battalion commander could count on a 70 to 90 percent "runner" rate. In contrast, a 1943-era German unit equipped with Panther Ausf "A" or "D" model tanks was lucky to maintain one-third of its tanks running in the field. It is not a stretch at all to state that in 1943, had the German army concentrated on producing the latest marks of the Panzer IV, a tank roughly as reliable as the T-34/76, and had the Red Army, even one with twice as many tanks as the Germans, been forced to fight with tank battalions averaging the rate of breakdowns they had endured in 1941, the war may have unfolded very differently than it did.

For Zitadelle, the Germans had massed 900,000 men, 3,155 armored vehicles, and 9,966 guns and mortars in Model's 9th Army—part of Army Group Center under Field Marshal Gunther von Kluge on the salient's north and Manstein's Army Group South, deployed to Kursk's south, spearheaded by the 4th Panzer Army under Hoth. Only 200 Panthers and 135 Tigers, divided into 75 Tigers in Heavy Tank Battalions 503 and 505 and one company of Tigers each to the Gross Deutschland Division and SS Panzer Grenadier Divisions Leibstandardte, Das Reich, and Totenkopf, numbered among the 2,700 German tanks, assault guns, and self-propelled guns. Over 2,600 German aircraft supported the attack, representing the last great German air-power concentration in the war.Nevertheless, and though the Germans had gathered 50 divisions in the Kursk region, Hitler's prior decision to rebuild the 20 lost Stalingrad divisions in France meant that German forces at Kursk would fight a full 45 infantry battalions short of their establishment strength. As a result, Panzer divisions would all too often be forced during the battle to perform tasks otherwise better filled by the infantry, with significant ramifications for its outcome.

In opposition, waited 1,087,500 Soviet soldiers, 3,275 armored vehicles, and 13,013 guns and mortars in the Central and Voronezh fronts, under General Konstantin Rokossovsky and General Nikolai Vatutin in the north and south,

Table 9.4 German Order of Battle for Citadel Offensive, July 1, 1943[1,2]

Army Group Center
Ninth Army
335,000 men, 590 tanks, and 424 assault guns[3]

20th Army Corps	23rd Army Corps	46th Panzer Corps	47th Panzer Corps	41st Panzer Corps	8th Army Corps (Hungarian)	9th Army Reserve
45th Infantry	7th Infantry	78th Assault	2nd Panzer	18th Panzer	102nd Infantry	10th Panzer Grenadier
72nd Infantry	216th Infantry	31st Infantry	6th Infantry	86th Infantry	105th Infantry	12th Panzer
137th Infantry	383rd Infantry	102nd Infantry	9th Panzer	292nd Infantry	108th Infantry	4th Panzer
251st Infantry		258th Infantry	20th Panzer			203rd Security
						221st Security

Air support: Luftflotte 6

Army Group South

Fourth Panzer Army
223,907 men, 925 tanks, and 104 assault guns

2nd SS Panzer Corps	48th Panzer Corps	52nd Army Corps
1st SS Panzer Grenadier	3rd Panzer	57th Infantry
2nd SS Panzer Grenadier	11th Panzer	255th Infantry
3rd SS Panzer Grenadier	167th Infantry	332nd Infantry
	Grossdeutschland Panzer Grenadier	

Army Detachment Kempf
126,000 men, 344 tanks, and 155 assault/self-propelled guns

42nd Army Corps	3rd Panzer Corps	11th Army Corps
39th Infantry	6th Panzer	106th Infantry
161st Infantry	7th Panzer	320th Infantry
282nd Infantry	19th Panzer	
	168th Infantry	

Air support: Luftflotte 4

[1]David M. Glantz and Jonathan M. House, *The Battle of Kursk* (University Press of Kansas, 1999), 283–89; Nik Cornish, *Images of Kursk History's Greatest Tank Battle July 1943* (Brassey's, 2002), 217.

[2]All ground units listed are divisional in size. Note that there were numerous brigades, detachments, and other smaller units included in the German order of battle not listed herein but included as part of each listed army's total strength.

[3]All tank and assault gun totals are based on listed totals of on-hand strength rather than the actual numbers of "runners" or vehicles actually available for combat operations, which varied considerably from unit to unit and on a day-to-day basis.

Table 9.5 Red Army Order of Battle for Kursk Defensive Operations, July 1, 1943[1]

Central Front 711,575 men and 1,785 tanks self-propelled guns	Voronezh Front 625,591 men and 1,704 tanks and self-propelled guns	Steppe Front (Reserve) 573,195 men and 1,639 tanks and self-propelled guns
13th Army	6th Guards Army	5th Guards Army
48th Army	7th Guards Army	27th Army
60th Army	38th Army	47th Army
65th Army	40th Army	53rd Army
70th Army	69th Army	4th Guards Tank Army
2nd Tank Army	1st Tank Army	5th Guards Tank Army
Air support: 16th Air Army	Air support: 2nd Air Army	Air support: 5th Air Army

[1]David M. Glantz and Jonathan M. House, *The Battle of Kursk* (University Press of Kansas, 1999), 290–335; Nik Cornish, *Images of Kursk History's Greatest Tank Battle July 1943* (Brassey's, 2002), 218.

respectively. In addition, Colonel General Ivan Konev's Steppe Front in reserve to the east numbered 449,133 men, 1,506 tanks and self-propelled guns, and 6,536 guns and mortars.[24] Never before—nor since—has the world seen such a concentration of men and material as that assembled by the Wehrmacht and the Red Army in July 1943 near Kursk.

KURSK: REVISITING ONE OF HISTORY'S MOST CONTROVERSIAL BATTLES

The largest battle in history's most destructive war began at 1600 hours on July 4, 1943, when German assault battalions from Manstein's Army Group South began a reconnaissance in force. On July 5, the assault's spearheads followed amidst a torrential downpour. Focke-Wulf 190-A-fighter bombers, Stukas equipped with wing-mounted 37-mm cannon, and Henschel 129 B2 tank destroyers equipped with 30-mm automatic cannon hammered the Soviet defenders. On the other hand, Soviet Shturmoviks also regularly prowled the sky, and Soviet aircraft would become even more active as the battle went on. In order to penetrate the thick Soviet defensive anti-tank fronts, the German armored spearheads formed wedges, or Panzerkeil, led by heavy Tiger tanks where possible. The plodding and methodical offensive tactics allowed the German armor to slug through the thick defensive belts. But, from the first hours of the attack German infantry and armor alike suffered continuous and, especially for the infantry, heavy losses to mines, artillery, Soviet close support aircraft, and automatic weapons.

On the Kursk salient's northern face, Model's 335,000-man 9th Army began its attack at 0430 hours on July 5. Model made uneven progress against Rokossovsky's Central Front. This was despite the fact that Model's 9th Army deployed 478 tanks and 348 assault guns in six Panzer divisions, one Panzer grenadier division, 14 infantry divisions, and several independent battalions. Model had controversially decided to retain most of his armor in reserve, leading with his infantry instead. Consequently, Model's infantry endured dreadful casualties. In addition, Model missed one of the few chances his army had to win a breakthrough in the stiff Soviet defensive front. With three Panzer divisions, an assault gun detachment, a heavy Panzer battalion, and a single infantry division the German 47th Corps represented Model's most powerful assault corps.[25] The 505th Heavy Panzer Battalion, attached to the 6th Infantry Division, plowed through the Soviet defensive positions and lit up Rokossovsky's tanks one after another. Within hours, the Germans had torn asunder the Soviet 15th Rifle Division's positions and threatened to unhinge the first defensive belt. Instead, Model stuck dogmatically to a plan calling for releasing his mechanized divisions in a trickle rather than an armored torrent. Consequently, the 2nd, 9th, and 18th Panzer Divisions did not move up to attack until July 6—Zitadelle's second day—and the 4th Panzer Division did not move up until the evening of July 6.[26] Model had let pass the initial opportunity provided by the combined-arms Tiger and infantry teams.

In contrast, Rokossovsky had quickly moved up ample reinforcements of his own. These included the 1st and 13th Anti-tank Brigades as well as the 21st Separate Mortar Brigade, an artillery brigade, and over 350 aircraft. Moreover, General Pukhov, commanding the 114,000-man 13th Army, committed from his reserves the 27th Guards Tank Regiment and 129th Tank Brigade and every combat engineer he could find. Rokossovsky also ordered immediate counterattacks in response to a German advance that threatened to take the important defensive hub at Ponyri Station. On July 6, the Russian 16th Tank Corps and 17th Guards Rifle Corps crashed into Model's Panzers. Rokossovsky later threw in three more Russian tank corps. Hundreds of Soviet and German tanks and other armored vehicles met in one of the great armored battles in history. On the Soviet counterattack's first day, the Tigers from the 505th Heavy Tank Battalion shattered the 16th Tank Corps.[27] Russian mines, however, and the Tigers' ever-present mechanical problems, meant that operational readiness in the unit's Tigers varied considerably from day to day. In addition, the Tigers could not on their own defeat the superbly prepared and well-supported Soviet defensive positions. Model bogged down in the second Soviet defensive line. By July 10, 1943, his offensive had failed. With Model's defeat, the German offensive's best chance for anything resembling a victory would come on the Kursk salient's southern face.

Manstein's assault armies included the 223,907 men in Colonel General Hermann Hoth's 4th Panzer Army, General Walter Kempf's 126,000-man independent detachment, and in reserve the 112 tanks in the 17th Panzer Division and the 5th SS Panzer Grenadier Division Wiking, grouped together

BATTLE OF KURSK

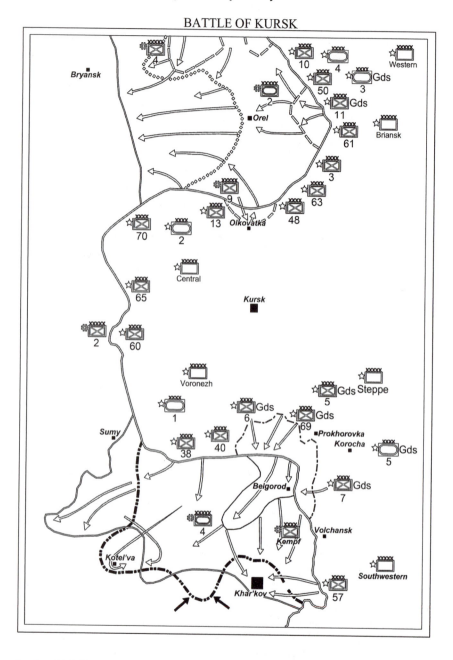

in the 24th Panzer Corps. Hoth concentrated his striking power in General Otto von Knobelsdorff's 61,692 man 48th Panzer Corps: 535 tanks and 66 assault guns split between the elite Grossdeutschland Panzer Grenadier Division and the 3rd and 11th Panzer Divisions. The formidably equipped

Grossdeutschland included 46 Tigers and 34 Sturmgeschutze along with 67 Panzer III/IVs.[28] In addition, the 39th Panzer Regiment, assigned 192 Panthers in two battalions, had been attached to Grossdeutschland as an anticipated powerful breakthrough or shock formation.[29] The equally potent Waffen-SS Panzer divisions in Paul Hausser's 73,380-man 2nd SS Panzer Corps deployed just south east of Knobelsdorff. The 2nd SS Panzer Corps fielded in its three divisions a total of 259 tanks, including 42 Tigers, and 95 assault guns.[30] In terms of combat power, the 2nd SS Panzer Corps and 48th Panzer Corps each ranked every bit the equal of a Soviet combined-arms army. In addition, Army Detachment Kempf sat to the right (east) of Hoth's Panzer army. Kempf's striking power was concentrated in General Hermann Breith's 3rd Panzer Corps (6th, 7th, and 19th Panzer Divisions [299 tanks], 168th Infantry Division, and 503rd Heavy Tank Battalion [45 Tiger tanks and an assault gun detachment]). All told, Manstein's Panzertruppen deployed 1,081 tanks and 376 assault guns supported by 1,100 German and Hungarian aircraft in the German 4th Air Fleet.[31]

Given the awesome power of the 2nd SS Panzer Corps, and in spite of the strength of the defensive effort, on the first day it managed to shatter the 6th Guards Army's 1st defensive belt and approach the second belt. Nevertheless, for its part, the 48th Panzer Corps, with Grossdeutschland facing the 6th Guards Armies' right wing, failed to pace its peers in the SS. In part this was because in response, Vatutin had ordered up Lieutenant General M. E. Katukov's massive 1st Tank Army, reinforced with the 2nd Guards and 5th Guards Tank Corps: over 40,000 men and 1,046 tanks, mostly T-34s, and self-propelled guns—all meant to support 6th Guards Army's second defensive belt.[32] Although German losses ebbed and flowed in the face of Vatutin's reinforcements, which also included his infantry reserves committed to the battle on July 6, and echeloned defensive positions, German control over the battlefield often allowed repair teams to bring Panzer divisions back up to a healthy strength for the next day's advance. Nevertheless, Vatutin, like Rokossovsky, launched numerous counterattacks that played a crucial role in throwing off the German assault's timetable. In particular, relentless counterstrokes brought the 48th Panzer Corps to a halt and, crucially, prevented Hoth from repositioning Grossdeutschland to support a long-planned-for final push against the Soviet strategic armored reserves farther east. In addition Vatutin's aggressive defensive effort, particularly via a massive counterattack launched on July 8, also forced 2nd SS Panzer Corps to expend considerable efforts repositioning its Kampfgruppen and modifying its route forward.

During this time, the long-awaited Panthers had made a disastrous combat debut when committed, along with Grossdeutschland, to an overclogged battlefield on a far-too-narrow front. Twenty of the 39th Panzer Regiment's Panthers broke down on the initial 21-mile road march from the railhead to the final assembly area. Just over 24 hours later, only 50 remained operational.

Four tanks did not even leave the assembly area, as internal fuel leaks led to fires, immobilizing them. Many others were lost when they ran into a muddy ravine on the first day. There, and because the final drive on the Panther Ausf. D was so underpowered, when the tanks reversed, they overheated and even had teeth sheared off drive sprockets as they attempted to back out.[33] Then, on July 7, the 39th Panzer Regiment ran into the 3rd Mechanized Corps of the 1st Tank Army dug in along the Pena River. Halted by obstacles, including a minefield, the Panthers were engaged by 60 dug-in T-34s, losing 27 Panthers against Soviet losses of 30 T-34s, in the first major tank engagement fought between the two primary contenders for the title of the war's best tank. More important, a 4th Panzer Army that had been expected to have broadly broken through the entirety of the 6th Guards Armies defensive zone on day one had managed only one breakthrough. Thus, within the first days of the offensive, its timetable had already been completely upset. On the other hand, in just two days of combat, Manstein had forced Vatutin to commit the Voronezh Front's reserves, representing the Red Army's operational reserves for the Kursk salient's southern face. For the Germans, this was of a profound significance, for even if Zitadelle failed to encircle the Soviet fronts in the Kursk salient, as originally envisioned, a primary secondary goal of crushing the Soviet operational and then strategic reserves remained.

Meanwhile, the 2nd SS Panzer Corps fought 10 miles to the east (the right flank) of the 48th Panzer Corps, methodically punching through the successive Soviet defensive belts and further chewing up Soviet operational tank reserves—as well as Vatutin's ever-weakening rifle divisions. By July 8, the 2nd SS Panzer Corps reported that it had destroyed 121 Soviet tanks against only 17 permanent losses of its own. Moreover, and though suffering heavy infantry casualties, the SS had largely defeated the 6th Guards Army's primary defensive belt as well as forging a penetration in its second defensive belt; plus was maneuvering toward an anticipated meeting with the Soviet strategic tank reserves.[34] Kempf and his 3rd Panzer Corps, east of the 2nd SS Panzer Corps, also slowly plowed ahead against brutal resistance from, in particular, the 7th Guards Army and in the face of increasing Soviet air attacks. By July 11, Kempf had ground through key Soviet defensive positions held by the 305th and 107th Rifle Divisions, and chewed up over six miles of real estate. By early on July 12, he had closed to within 15 to 18 miles of the railway junction at Prokhorovka, at that time also being approached by the 2nd SS Panzer Corps.

Vatutin was well aware that his armored losses had reached a critical stage, and that Soviet operational reserves on the southern facing of the Kursk salient had been decimated. Although Manstein was nowhere near generating the speed necessary to cut off the Soviet fronts in the Kursk salient, his 2nd SS Panzer Corps was progressively defeating Soviet defensive lines that had taken months to prepare. In addition, even though the Voronezh Front had managed to contain the bulk of the German effort, on July 9 the 48th Panzer

Corps had realized its greatest success to date during the offensive, having penetrated the second defensive belt and, even worse, from Vatutin's perspective, having done so despite the previous commitment of all the Voronezh Front's operational reserves. With the Voronezh Front's position predicated on its ability to hold the three primary defensive belts, questions arose regarding its ability to continually launch the aggressive armor heavy counterattacks that appeared to be the primary reason it had otherwise earlier impeded 48th Panzer Corps. Moreover, the 2nd SS Panzer Corps' deep penetration into Vatutin's front, and mounting infantry and anti-tank gun losses, meant Zhukov feared that the Germans could break through.

In response, on the night of July 8–9, Zhukov, Vasilevsky, and Vatutin agreed that the 5th Guards Tank Army under P. A. Rotmistrov should move up along with the 2nd and 10th Tank Corps. In addition, Stavka also ordered the 5th Guards Combined Arms Army, under Lieutenant General A. S. Zhadov, to move up: the Red Army was now committing significant forces from its strategic reserves. Stavka further reshuffled both the defensive effort and the dispositions of the Soviet reserves. Meanwhile, on July 9, Hitler allowed Manstein to order his reserves, the 24th Panzer Corps, to the front. On July 11, Manstein, Hoth, and Kempf met regarding the impending clash. Everyone knew the stakes involved. Stalin demanded constant reports from the front and intently oversaw what was happening, given that the 4th Panzer Army had already severely bloodied Katukov's 1st Tank Army.[35] As it was however such Soviet losses were far from in vain. Vatutin's aggressive counterattacks against the 48th Panzer Corps had meant that the 2nd SS Panzer Corps stood alone in the reinforced 5th Guards Tank Army's oncoming path.

The battle of Prokhorovka really comprised a series of battles, loosely connected by their geographical proximity to the town's west. Hemming in these battlefields were a railway embankment, numerous ridgelines, and several rivers. The fighting spread beyond a single physical location. Historians to this day debate the tank numbers present on the primary battlefield where the 2nd SS Panzer Corps met the 5th Guards Tank Army. The best estimates of German tank strength on hand generally hold that the three Panzer grenadier divisions forming the SS Panzer Corps deployed 294 tanks and assault guns, with only 15 Tigers in total.[36] As is unfortunately usual when regarding the war in eastern Europe, the Soviet numbers remain ill defined. That said, the most reputable sources state that the 5th Guards Tank Army deployed approximately 826 operational tanks and self-propelled guns broken down as; 463 T-34s, 301 T-70 light tanks, 25 Churchill medium tanks, and 37 SU-76 and SU-122 self-propelled guns. Given less than the entire 5th Guards Tank Army deployed to fight the SS near Prokhorovka, and, given that only some of the German units in the region met the 5th Guards Tank Army's charge, most estimates hold, in the aggregate, that roughly 500 German and

Soviet tanks and self-propelled guns met on the primary battlefield of approximately three square miles.[37]

Rotmistrov had planned to deploy most of his tank army west and southwest of Prokhorovka, leaving not much more than the 5th Guards Mechanized Corps to move up just behind his shock force—all told four entire tank corps in the vanguard. Rotmistrov, however, never got the chance to carry out his attack as planned, for on July 11 the 2nd SS Panzer Corps savaged Rotmistrov's 2nd Tank Corps and the elite Soviet 9th Guards Airborne Division, thus having already overrun the 5th Guards Tank Army's planned-for jumping-off point for the counterattack. Even though Zitadelle had been contained in a strategic sense, events were overtaking a Soviet command that constantly had to readjust the location and timing of the commitment of a significant part of the Soviet strategic tank reserves. Moreover, the 69th Army's 48th Rifle Corps was facing the threat of encirclement, while, at 0400 hours, word reached Rotmistrov that Kempf had broken through to the south, forced the 35th Guards Rifle Corps to fall back, as Kemp's men pushed to within only 12 miles of Prokhorovka. This caused Vatutin to order Rotmistrov to dispatch a substantial part of his 2nd Guards Tank Corps and 5th Mechanized Corps to meet Kempf. Although his odds for success had narrowed considerably, with a third of his remaining tanks light T-70s, Rotmistrov still had in his first echelon the better part of the 18th, 29th, and 2nd Guards Tank Corps. Of these formations, roughly 348 tanks from the 18th and 29th Tank Corps deployed in depth on a roughly four mile wide front to spearhead his blow against 140 to 150 tanks of the 2nd SS Panzer Corps.

On July 12th the 1stt SS Panzer Grenadier Division Leibstandarte stood at the forefront of a wedge-shaped deployment near the bend in the Psyol River. Deployed to its east was the 2nd SS Panzer Grenadier Division Das Reich and to the west the 3rd SS Panzer Grenadier Division Totenkopf. The Soviet counterattack's Schwerpunkt—the 31st and 32nd Tank Brigades from the 29th Tank Corps—fell on the 1st SS Panzer Grenadier Division, which had deployed its lead Panzer IVs on a slope in hull-down positions. Although past accounts have described a massive meeting engagement, it was in reality only these attacks on the 1st SS Panzer Grenadier Division that came closest to resembling such a melee. Elsewhere, the 2nd SS Panzer Corps was ready and waiting for the Soviet counterattack, having constructed a deadly defensive network featuring interlocking fields of fire from a dense plethora of heavy weapons.

Consequently, within minutes of the beginning of the Soviet counterattack, German tanks, assault guns, anti-tank guns, and artillery sent one T-34 after another up in flames. Within a few hours the first Soviet echelon had largely been defeated, even as the surviving Soviet tank crews charged forward with reckless abandon. In a wild battle at point-blank range, the more numerous Soviet tanks finally began inflicting punishment in return. Nevertheless, by the day's end, of the tanks and self-propelled guns from the 5th Guards Tank Army that participated in the counterattack on July 12, over 50 percent had been knocked out, some 350 tanks and self-propelled guns—with over 220 Soviet tanks and self-propelled guns left smoking on the battlefield as irrevocable losses. All told, a 5th Guards Tank Army that could put well over 800 tanks and self-propelled guns into the field on July 11 could field only roughly 400 such vehicles on July 13. In contrast, Hausser's SS Panzer Corps had not only temporarily resumed its advance, but also could still put 251 tanks, assault guns, and self-propelled guns into the field, having suffered approximately 20 irrevocable losses. Nevertheless, the remainder of Konev's Steppe Front approached the battlefield with several hundred tanks. In addition, Vatutin's additional counterthrusts against the 48th Panzer Corps to the west of the 2nd SS Panzer Corps, and his efforts against the 3rd Panzer Corps to the southeast of the 2nd SS Panzer Corps, had together forced the German command to halt the offensive.[38] Manstein disagreed and sought to continue the assault, overoptimistically believing that it might have been possible to finish smashing the Russian armored reserves; even though three of the five Soviet tank armies in the region were mostly rested—and at or near full strength. However, though there was much hard fighting ahead on the southern face of the Kursk salient; the Soviet 69th Army's 48th Rifle Corps lost over 15,000 men in a small pocket briefly forged by the 2nd SS Panzer Corps and 3rd Panzer Corps following Prohorovka, a massive Soviet counteroffensive having begun near Orel further prompted Hitler to order Manstein to wind down Zitadelle—a general retreat began on July 16, ending on July 23 at the original front lines from three weeks prior.

The Red Army paid a heavy price for stopping the German attack at Kursk. Most sources state that it had suffered 177,847 casualties, and some estimate that casualties reached 300,000 men, all while losing 1,614 tanks and self-propelled guns, 3,929 guns and artillery pieces, and 459 aircraft. In comparison, German tank losses were not as severe as previously estimated, with anywhere from 270 to 323 tanks and self-propelled guns totally written off, depending on the modern source.[39] Regardless, Germany's 49,822 casualties, for an army already short of infantry, represented a real problem.

Table 9.6 Soviet and German Forces Committed to Kursk Operation and Losses[1]

	Soviet	German
Men committed	1,910,361	780,900
Men lost	177,847	49,822
Tanks and self-propelled guns committed	5,128	2,928
Tanks and self-propelled guns lost	1,614	323

[1]David M. Glantz and Jonathan M. House, *The Battle of Kursk* (University Press of Kansas, 1999), 275–76, 345.

Zitadelle did not break the German army's back. That would come in the following year. What Zitadelle meant was that for the first time in the war, a large-scale multiarmy German offensive had failed to break free of the tactical area and reach its opponent's operational depth.[40] In addition, by controlling the battlefield, the Red Army returned hundreds of recovered and repaired tanks and assault guns to their parent formations, greatly enhancing available combat power, including through the use of captured and repaired German armored vehicles.[41] For instance, during 1943, Soviet factory number 38 in Gorki rebuilt 1,200 captured German AFVs into Su-76 self-propelled guns.[42] More important than whether Zitadelle could have been ended better is answering the question as to what caused Zitadelle's failure. Traditional arguments have pointed to Soviet fortifications and mistakes made by German leadership. Both played a role, but the first was far more important. The depth and elasticity of the defenses constructed by the Red Army had allowed its units to avoid being annihilated in the open. Instead, they were often able to fall back into succeeding defensive zones—where reinforcements moving up from behind buttressed their strength, all of which denied the Germans the chance to develop the necessary speed to make Zitadelle a success. Furthermore, Rokossovsky's and Vatutin's aggressiveness in conducting an active and mobile defense had also played an important role in stopping the German offensive.

In addition, before Zitadelle had even ended, and on July 12, Rokossovsky had launched his five-army Central Front in conjunction with General M. M. Popov's Briansk Front (433,616 men and 847 tanks and self-propelled guns) and General V. D. Sokolovsky's Western Front (189,062 men and 735 tanks and self-propelled guns) at German positions near Orel in an offensive codenamed Operation Kutuzov. The Soviet armor assigned to the offensive included General P. S. Rybalko's 3rd Guards Tank Army, with its 731 tanks and self-propelled guns, and General V. M. Badanov's 4th Tank Army, with its 652 tanks and self-propelled guns, the 20th and 25th Separate Tank Corps, and the 2nd Guards Cavalry Corps.[43] Coordinated partisan attacks, 1,460 in July alone, ripped apart rail lines needed to support the German front.[44] Within a week of the beginning of the assault, the Russian offensive had penetrated over 40 miles into German lines.

In response, Kluge rushed four Panzer divisions north. In one notable engagement that began on July 20, the 8th Panzer Division, and supporting forces, stopped the entire 3rd Guards Tank Army.[45] On August 5, Russian troops nevertheless fought their way into Orel. Regardless, the battered German armies were able to stabilize the front. By August 18, Army Group Center had inflicted 429,890 casualties on Rokossovsky's men and destroyed 2,586 tanks. This represented more than one-quarter of the Soviet tank strength across the entire Eastern Front.[46] On the other hand, between July 11 and August 20, the German 9th and 2nd Armies suffered a staggering 89,688 casualties. Moreover, permanent German losses of 371 tanks and assault guns in the Orel salient, worse than German armored losses during

Zitadelle, had left Army Group Center hard pressed to replace its material losses no less its substantial losses in manpower.

THE SUMMER AND FALL OF 1943 IN EASTERN EUROPE: HOW GERMANY IRREVOCABLY LOST THE INITIATIVE

Overall, on the German Eastern Front's north and center, where the terrain was conducive to defensive operations, the German Army Groups spent the late summer and fall of 1943 only slowly giving ground. In particular, Army Group North defeated several Soviet offensives. These included the Leningrad and Volkhov fronts' fifth offensive at Siniavino, an offensive that began on July 22 but failed to accomplish much of anything—while leaving 79,937 men dead, wounded, captured, or missing from the 253,300 men who had begun the attacks. Not until September 1943, and the Sixth Siniavino Offensive, did the Red Army finally break the German hold on the crucial high ground east of Leningrad. This was accomplished in a well-led operation conducted by General N. P. Simoniak's 30th Guards Rifle Corps that nevertheless cost his command and the Soviet 8th Army another 70,000 casualties. That said, and all told, the German defenders of the less than imposing Siniavino Heights, at roughly 160 feet above sea level, had held their ground for two years despite repeated efforts by numerically far superior Soviet armies to defeat them.

As for Army Group Center, during Operation Suvorov, the Western Front hit the 4th Army, and the Kalinin Front, under Eremenko, hit the 3rd Panzer Army. These attacks led to the German loss of Bryansk, followed by Smolensk's fall on September 25. Nevertheless, the Soviet armies advanced at only a glacial pace in the face of fierce German opposition. Even on October 6, when Eremenko's 3rd and 4th Shock Armies annihilated the Luftwaffe's 2nd Field Division, German close air support and the arrival of the 20th Panzer Division, 129th Infantry Division, and 505th Heavy Tank Battalion fatally slowed the Russian advance. Then, on November 2, Eremenko's 1st Baltic Front, formerly the Kalinin Front, again attempted to split the seam between the 3rd Panzer Army and Army Group North. Nonetheless, mud came to the German defense and knocked the wind from 1st Baltic Front's otherwise successful advance. The front stabilized into early December.[47]

Meanwhile, and most importantly, following Zitadelle's defeat the Red Army had relentlessly sought to destroy Army Group South and eject the Wehrmacht from its hold on Barbarossa's greatest prize: the Ukraine. During 1941, it had taken Army Group South just four months to overrun the Ukraine, capturing 205,000 square miles and 40,000,000 people. From August 1943 to April 1944, the Red Army fought the second battle for the Ukraine, a battle ranking among the most epic, important, and poorly understood of any during the war. The scope of the campaign was vast. Millions of men and thousands of tanks and aircraft clashed across hundreds of miles, almost without pause, for eight unrelenting months. Mobility proved crucial to its outcome, as freewheeling mechanized clashes defined the fight for the Ukraine. To that end, the Red Army and its mechanically sound medium tanks, backed by fleets of Lend-Lease trucks, held crucial advantages over a Wehrmacht that it could not consistently best in previous years—no matter how many "waves" of men and machines it had blindly thrown at the Germans.

On July 17, Soviet armies had opened the Ukrainian campaign by attacking German defenses on the Mius River. This attack resulted in horrific losses for the attacking Soviet armies, but tied down the SS Panzer Grenadier Divisions Totenkopf and Das Reich, which Manstein had directed south, thereby opening up Army Group South's front for the main blow. Moreover, Soviet anti-tank gun fronts inflicted heavy losses on the 2nd SS Panzer Corps even as it crushed the Soviet bridgehead over the Mius during three days of fighting beginning on July 30. Although having taken 18,000 prisoners of war, the SS armor had been weakened by the fighting, and was poorly positioned for what was to come.

On August 3, Vatutin's Voronezh Front, supported by the Steppe Front, struck just south of the Kursk salient in Operation Rumiantsev. Zhukov had wanted Rumiantsev to begin two weeks prior, or immediately after Zitadelle had been stopped. But it had taken weeks to rehabilitate the 1st Tank Army and 5th Guards Tank Army following Zitadelle. With the tank armies rebuilt, over 800 T-34s in the 1st Tank Army and 5th Guards Tank Army slammed into the German lines on a narrow 12-kilometer-wide front west of Belgorod. Hoth's Panzer army, just one month earlier the most powerful ever assembled by the Third Reich, had been reduced by Manstein's and Hitler's redeployments to only three Panzer and four infantry divisions. Therefore, Vatutin's and Konev's forces rapidly penetrated the 4th Panzer Army's lines.

Retreat proved costly for the German army. The 19th Panzer Division's newly attached Panther battalion was forced to blow up 72 of its Panthers because they had been under repair when the Russians struck. As it was the best reliability that Panzer battalions equipped with Panther Ausf. D models could achieve during 1943 hardly averaged better than 25 percent. The represented a stunning waste of industrial resources that did much toward leaving German Panzer divisions disastrously shorthanded during perhaps the most crucial months of the war. The Panthers that actually were in running condition on August 6 destroyed 17 T-34s from the Soviet 31st Tank Corps without loss. But as the battalion retreated, 16 of 27 operational Panthers broke down on a 60-mile road march. On August 8, and as he rushed reinforcements north from the Mius Front, Manstein argued for receipt of heavy reinforcement, or for withdrawing his Army Group from the Donets region. Hitler shot down his arguments. Manstein railed against this decision in his memoirs, but he had played a crucial role in weakening the 4th Panzer Army. In addition,

Hitler had every reason to seek to hold onto the Donets Basin; it was the prime remaining European source for a potentially significant increase in German iron output. A primary reason that Germany had been able to increase its steel production since Speer's takeover of the armaments industry had been because of the supply of manganese ore from the occupied parts of the Soviet Union, including from Nikopol and Krivoy Rog in the Ukraine.[48] In the months that would follow, and as German access to important raw materials found in northern and eastern Europe diminished, such as raw materials necessary to manufacture high-quality steel, the results would show up at the front; where brittle steel plates would reduce the stopping power of armor on German AFVs by as much as 20 percent.

Although Rumiantsev had started well for the Voronezh, Steppe, and Southwestern fronts, having decimated three German infantry divisions in the offensive's initial days, in battles lasting from August 8 to 25, the Soviet fronts suffered grievous losses. For instance, on August 20, the 3rd Panzer Corps and 24th Panzer Corps trapped the Soviet 4th and 5th Guards Corps west of Kharkov. Although the German Panzer corps lacked the strength to hold the pocket, the Germans took 32,000 prisoners of war.[49] The Soviet assault ground on however, and reached its climax on and following August 21 in a savage fight to decide Kharkov's fate, as the 5th Guards Tank Army sought to envelop the city. The German defenders, however, comprised of infantry and anti-tank weapons teams, defeated the attack with help from a strong mobile reserve, the SS Panzer Grenadier Division Das Reich. Close air support helped break apart Soviet units who regardless launched a suicidal attack on Das Reich's potent assembly of armor, anti-tank guns, anti-aircraft guns, and self-propelled artillery. The Germans claim that they left 184 wrecked T-34s strewn across the battlefield. Das Reich's Panther battalion alone claimed the destruction of 53 Soviet tanks from the 24th Guards Tank Brigade's initial strength of 110 T-34s.[50]

The following day, the Red Army attacked again, led by a T-34 wedge numbering in the hundreds. The Germans concentrated all available anti-armor assets to create a wall of fire into which the Soviet tank commanders flung their vehicles. By the day's end, another 154 wrecked Soviet tanks littered the battlefield. That night, the 5th Guards Tank Army's remaining 100 tanks attacked again, and in fierce fighting at ranges down to 100 yards, the Germans once again ripped the Soviet tank army to pieces, with 80 more burned-out hulks visible the next morning. By August 25, only 50 Soviet tanks remained. In addition, German forces in the region had mauled the Soviet 1st Tank Army, which had lost 1,042 tanks, including reinforcements. An offensive beginning with a Soviet advantage of approximately 2,000 tanks over the Germans ended with the Soviet tank armies deploying only 500 tanks in the field—this against the surviving 330 German tanks, from the 500 German tanks, including reinforcements, deployed during the battle.[51]

Table 9.7 Soviet Tank Army Strength Returns Versus SS Panzer Divisions during Soviet Offensive in Kharkov-Belgorod Region during August 1943[1]

Unit	August 3, 1943	August 25, 1943
Tank strength in Red Army Units committed to offensive	2,300	500
1st Tank Army	542	120[2]
5th Guards Tank Army	503	50
Tank strength in defending German Panzer and Panzer grenadier divisions (minus Grossdeutschland)	220	330
2nd SS Panzer Grenadier Division	51[3]	55[4]
3rd SS Panzer Grenadier Division	44	61

[1]David M. Glantz, *From the Don to the Dnepr: Soviet Offensive Operations, December 1941–August 1943* (Frank Cass, 1991), 219–365.
[2]Including reinforcements, lost 1,042 tanks during offensive.
[3]Total includes tanks and assault guns on August 15.
[4]Total includes tanks and assault guns on August 23.

The high Soviet armored losses stemmed from a number of reasons beyond the standard higher casualty tolls endured by an army on the offensive. Spotty combined-arms usage, and the piecemeal nature of assaults, heavily reduced the Red Army's efficacy. In addition, because of the heavy casualties, the Red Army was forced at times to turn to criminals and the borderline mentally handicapped to help crew their tanks. On the other hand, working in the Red Army's favor was that, despite tremendous losses, the Red Army nearly always forced the Germans to give ground. As a result, Russian vehicle repair teams consistently returned many damaged tanks to duty. Consequently, although the battles had seesawed back and forth for well over two weeks, by August 28 the Red Army had recaptured Kharkov. Overall, Soviet casualties during the Belgorod-Kharkov operation totaled 255,566 men against 51,724 casualties in 4th Panzer Army and Army Detachment Kempf during all of August of 1943.[52] Many German infantry divisions lost two-thirds of their strength in these battles.

Overall, the month of August had proved far more disastrous to Germany's position in the Soviet Union than had July and events near Kursk. For instance, Army Group South had suffered 133,000 casualties during August 1943 and yet received only 33,000 men to replace these losses.[53] Moreover, and in yet another indictment of the German senior leadership, German infantry shortages was made all the more grotesque by the fact the Kriegsmarine's increased manpower resulted in the German navy's personnel strength standing at nearly half a million men greater than it had at the start of the war.[54] The infantry-starved German forces in the Ukraine had therefore become horribly overstretched. Consequently, it is no surprise that a massive series of offensive begun on August 26 by the Central, Steppe, and Voronezh fronts split the 4th Panzer Army into three parts, and leveraged a huge gap between it and the German 8th Army, the former Army Detachment Kempf, forcing Army Group South to begin a westward retreat lasting an entire month. At the same time, offensives led by the Southwestern, and Southern fronts had driven the 1st Panzer Army, with three mechanized divisions and eight infantry divisions in its ranks, and the reconstituted German 6th Army into a complementary running retreat to the Dnieper River.[55]

German equipment losses were staggering; Panther-equipped tank battalions in Grossdeutschland, the 2nd SS Das Reich, and the 11th Panzer Division lost 80 Panthers in September alone, most destroyed at German hands after breaking down. This once again illustrated how German economic failings revolved as much around an inability to make equipment that functioned properly as around an inability to make enough equipment in a quantitative sense. These failings were highlighted even more by Soviet tank formations, such as the 56th Guards Tank Brigade from Rylbalko's 3rd Guards Tank Army, that were able to execute 100-mile road marches in mere days and still retain significant numbers of tanks in the field.[56] In comparison, not until the spring of 1944 would Panther-equipped German Panzer battalions average even 50 percent readiness rates in terms of the number of "runners" on hand. Manstein's beleaguered Army Group skidded to a halt only at the Dnieper River, the last great defensive barrier standing between the Red Army and its opportunity to finally evict the Wehrmacht from southern Soviet Union.

The Red Army' success had not been an accident; it had sustained its offensives with extensive logistical support, and coordinated its campaigns with officers enjoying the use of ample quantities of communications equipment sent through Lend-Lease. Creativity in the use of combat arms further helped disrupt German defensive efforts. For instance, repeated para-drops throughout September, though generally resulting in the destruction of the Soviet airborne formations as effective fighting units, led to the reinforcement of local partisan forces, creating a separate set of headaches for the Germans. By September's end, Army Group South's contiguous front ran from north to south as follows: the 4th Panzer Army, the 8th Army, and the 1st Panzer Army. Farther south was the particularly weak 6th Army, which, along with the 17th Army, formed the new German Army Group A under Kleist. The German 17th Army had been finally forced to give up its toehold in southern Russia, and had withdrawn across the Kerch Strait into the Crimea. Soviet efforts to destroy the 17th Army had met with repeated failure, as the Germans had prepared in-depth defensive positions to mask the withdrawal—and created enough reserves to contain Soviet efforts to disrupt the operation.[57]

For its part the Red Army reorganized, and the Voronezh, Steppe, and Southwestern fronts became the 1st, 2nd, and 3rd Ukrainian fronts, respectively, while the Central Front became the Belorussian Front. Throughout October,

SOVIET ADVANCE AUG. TO DEC. 1943

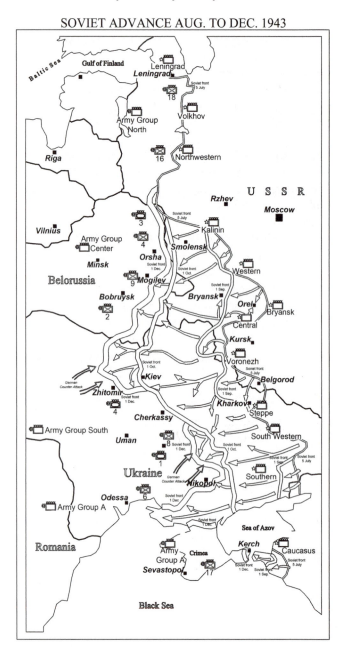

these Soviet fronts, including the newly formed 4th Ukrainian Front, sought to exploit several bridgeheads across the Dnieper, taken during September's great advance, and then take Kiev. But, in contrast to September's successes, they failed miserably. Although Manstein had failed to eliminate the most important Soviet bridgeheads opposing Army Group South, the regular presence of heavy concentrations of German combined-arms armor played a key role in Army Group South's relative defensive successes during October.

For example, the German 4th Panzer Army and the 8th Army, led by the 48th Panzer Corps, held off a particularly massive offensive launched by two armies from the Belorussian Front and six armies from the 1st Ukrainian Front. The 19th Panzer Division, working in conjunction with the 72nd Infantry Division and Luftwaffe close air support, also turned aside heavy assaults on October 21–22 that left 75 Soviet AFVs destroyed on the battlefield.[58] In addition, from October 1 to October 13, the 1st Panzer Army held onto its bridgehead on the east bank of the Dnieper at Zaporozhe and bloodily repulsed the Southwestern Front's best efforts. Only on October 14 did the 1st Panzer Army's newest nemesis, the combined forces of the Soviet 1st Guards Mechanized and 23rd Tank Corps, drive the 40th Panzer Corps from the bridgehead and city. Then on October 15, Konev's 2nd Ukrainian Front split the seam between the 1st Panzer Army and the 8th Army in an offensive launched from bridgeheads captured over the Dnieper south of Kremenchug. Even so, Manstein took the steam out of Konev's move when he reinforced the 1st Panzer Army with the 14th and 24th Panzer Divisions and SS Totenkopf and counterattacked the Soviet spearheads on October 27, destroying the better part of two mechanized corps.

Following October's setbacks, the Red Army in November finally overcame its less-than-stellar performance in a manner that armies have traditionally used to defeat their foes, namely, superior generalship. On November 3, Vatutin's 1st Ukrainian Front surged from the Liutezh bridgehead across the Dnieper River, just to Kiev's north, and quickly shattered German defensive positions. Deception had played the critical role in his success. The Soviet 3rd Guards Tank Army spearheaded the breakout even though just one week earlier this veteran, albeit battered, tank army sat in the Bukrin bridgehead approximately 120 miles south of the Liutezh bridgehead. The 3rd Guards Tank Army had pulled completely from the Bukrin bridgehead, wheeled well over 100 miles to the northwest, and assimilated enough reinforcements to bring its strength up to nearly 70 percent. It accomplished all of this in just three remarkable days. At the same time, the German 8th Army, opposite the Bukrin bridgehead, belatedly believed that the 3rd Guards Tank Army sat before it, a misperception fueled by a November 1 attack. Accordingly, the 19th Panzer Division had been mistakenly sent south. This weakened the 4th Panzer Army's positions at the worst possible time. Only on November 3 did the 4th Panzer Army finally register the 3rd Guards Tank Army's presence, but by then it was too late. Vatutin's moves had fooled Manstein, and on November 6 the Germans subsequently lost Kiev.

The 1st Ukrainian Front, led by the 3rd Guards Tank Army and General Moskalenko's 38th Army, drove further west. Then the arrival of German armored reserves helped turn the region west of Kiev, near Zhitomir and Korosten, into a huge armored battlefield.[59] Initially, the veteran 3rd Guards Tank Army decimated the inexperienced 25th Panzer Division, newly arrived from France.[60] In turn, however, Manstein had ordered the 48th Panzer Corps, the 1st and 7th Panzer Divisions, and the 1st SS Panzer Division Leibstandarte to strike into the 38th Army's flanks. Although Rybalko's men helped in parrying the initial German thrust, the 3rd Guards Tank Army suffered heavy losses and was then forced to give ground under a second effort begun on November 14, one that forced Vatutin's entire front onto the defensive late in November near Fastov. All told, Manstein had brought together six Panzer divisions equipped with 585 tanks, including 70 Panthers and 30 Tigers, in Balck's 48th Panzer Corps. Again, though the heavily armed Panzers knocked out scores of Soviet tanks, German engineering was its own worst enemy. For instance, in nine days of fighting, from November 15 to November 23, Leibstandarte's Panthers destroyed 40 Soviet tanks. Of the 61 Panthers lost in the battle, only seven were destroyed by Soviet gunfire. The remainder fell victim to mechanical breakdown. German attacks in December further pressed the 1st Ukrainian Front, but could accomplish no more.[61] The 1st Ukrainian Front had paid a heavy price for its defensive stand. It lost over 30,000 dead, 9,000 prisoners of war, and 857 tanks from November 8 to December 13 alone.[62]

In the lower Don River region near Nikopol and Krivoi Rog, the German 1st Panzer Army and 17th Army bent, but held off the 2nd, 3rd, and 4th Ukrainian Fronts in a series of battles lasting from November 1943 into 1944. The ferocious fighting near Nikopol, lasting from October 1943 to January 1944, had been marked in particular by Soviet efforts to eliminate two German bridgeheads on the Dnieper's eastern bank, each held in deference to economic needs; particularly the use of the manganese ore mines in the region. Again, armored reserves had proved critical to the German 6th Army's survival. In one instance, Kampfgruppen from the 24th Panzer Division had shuttled from hot spot to hot spot, stopping repeated Soviet attacks and bolstering German infantry that managed to hold the Nikopol bridgehead for over three months.[63] In addition, during the October fighting around Melitopol, the 13th Panzer Division, equipped in part with new Panzer V Ausf. A Panthers, had inflicted dreadful losses on the Soviet 20th Tank Corps and 4th Guards Mechanized Corps. Then, the day after Melitopol fell, the 13th Panzer Division counterattacked the 4th Guards Mechanized Corps and destroyed 35 T-34/76s at Kalinovka. All told, the 13th Panzer Division's Panthers destroyed over 80 Soviet tanks in just two weeks of action. Nonetheless, such impressive results were mitigated not only because they failed to stop the larger offensive, but also because half the available Panthers broke down. Most were then blown up by the Germans because they could not mechanically execute the long road marches during the subsequent retreat west.[64]

Farther north, German Army Groups North and Center still held positions well inside the prewar Soviet Union's western borders, having contained and stopped several enormous Soviet offensives. From October 3 to December 31, 1943, the Red Army had flung itself against Army Group Center's defenses, but, in addition to suffering heavy losses, the Red Army had failed to meet its goals of taking Minsk and ejecting the Germans from Belorussia. In particular, early in 1944, the fight for Vitebsk raged at an intense pace, especially between February 3 to February 8. Nonetheless, the 3rd Panzer Army weathered the best that the 1st Baltic Front could throw at it during these months. This was even though, on January 17, it counted only one Panzer division—the 20th—in its ranks and, other than the assistance provided by the Feldherrnhalle Panzer Grenadier Division, and a few Stug and Hornisse battalions, was largely bereft of AFVs. The Soviet 33rd Army alone suffered over 90,000 casualties in three separate assaults launched between the end of December 1943 and March 1944, with each offensive producing meager gains of roughly one to five miles each. Overall, the Soviet attritional push west was anything but the pinnacle of deep operations as an operational doctrine come to fruition, and speaks to the tentativeness of the qualitative shift occurring on eastern Europe's battlefields. Nevertheless, the Red Army could field 6,394,500 men, 5,800 tanks, 101,400 artillery pieces, and 13,400 aircraft as 1943 came to a close.[65] Two million men fresh conscripts in 1943, an effective replacement system for returning recovered wounded veterans to the front, and the Red Army's ability to recapture significant territory, and thus manpower, enabled the Red Army to grow. As it moved west, the Red Army forcibly conscripted boys as young as 15 and grandfathers well over 50 years old alike. Many conscripts merely received a rifle and transport to the front. The ever-present commissars guaranteed that the new blood did not slip away to return home, for the Red Army had become increasingly cognizant of the limitations on its manpower reserves.

By the end of 1943, the Germans had killed, wounded, or captured 18,872,542 Soviet military personnel. The year 1943 had been the worst yet. The Red Army suffered 7,438,647 casualties in 1943 alone. This included an astonishing 2,864,661 casualties between July 1 and September 30, 1943.[66] Furthermore, these numbers do not include the millions of Soviet civilians deported to death camps, worked to death, or starved to death by the scorched-earth campaigns waged by both sides.[67] To put the Soviet total into perspective, by the end of November 1943, the Wehrmacht had suffered 3,599,000 casualties in all theaters combined since September 1939.[68] The appalling loss in human life, and the need to divert almost all industrial capacity to producing tanks, artillery, and aircraft had crippled the Soviet economy. For example, during the fall harvest, General Rokossovsky had been forced to reassign 27,250 men and officers to help harvest the crops for a nation standing on the brink of mass starvation. Turnaround times at Soviet military

Table 9.8 German Tiger Tank Battalions in World War II[1]

Tiger Battalions	Tiger Losses/In Action[2]	Enemy Tanks Destroyed
14[3]	1,580/713	8,600[4]

[1] Christopher W. Wilbeck, *Swinging the Sledgehammer: The Combat Effectiveness of German Heavy Tank Battalions in World War II* (Combat Studies Institute, 2002), 127.

[2] Tiger crews destroyed/abandoned approximately 41 percent (654 tanks) of all Tigers destroyed. This occurred mostly during long retreats or mechanical failures or because of an inability to recover damaged/broken down tanks. Roman Johann Jarymowycz, *Tank Tactics from Normandy to Lorraine* (Lynne Rienner Publishers, 2001).

[3] Total includes three SS and 11 army battalions.

[4] In action, Tiger battalions lost only one Tiger for every 12.16 enemy tanks destroyed. If total Tiger losses are included (including Tigers lost for mechanical reasons, destroyed during retreats by their own crews, or lost during mass surrenders, such as when Axis forces in Tunisia surrendered in May 1943), then this ratio falls to a still incredible 5.44 enemy tanks for each Tiger destroyed. When considering kill ratios such as this, the fact that the American/British/Soviet coalition outproduced Germany/Italy in tanks/self-propelled guns by a five-to-one ratio during the war becomes less than impressive and more a matter of necessity.

hospitals accelerated in a desperate attempt to fill the army's ranks. Women served the Red Army in increasing numbers; as telephone operators, truck drivers, medical personnel, and so on—all to replace men mowed down at the front. In response, perhaps the most important reform that the Red Army had made had been to steadily increase firepower. This allowed Soviet rifle platoons, companies, and battalions to punish the Germans defenders even as line strengths decreased. Without the Red Army's continual renewal and reorganization, it may not have defeated a German army that, at the operational and tactical levels, had proven far too proficient at dealing out death and destruction to have been defeated by sheer numbers alone. This was true even when fighting grossly outnumbered, as shown by Germany's Tiger tank battalions during the war, which, even though struggling to keep the mechanically fickle Tigers in the field, had grossly disproportionate kill ratios in their own favor.

For example, modern estimates hold that the Wehrmacht had destroyed an estimated 59,100 tanks and self-propelled guns and 62,500 Soviet aircraft by the end of 1943. In 1943, the Germans destroyed 49 percent of all tanks and self-propelled guns sent from Soviet factories to the front, as well as 20 percent of all Soviet combat aircraft manufactured that year. In just two and a half months, from July 5 to September 30, 1943, the Red Army lost 11,703 tanks in eight major operations, though domestic tank production and Lend-Lease aid meant that the Russians replaced their losses.[69]

As for the German army deployed in the Soviet Union, though totaling 26 Panzer and 151 other divisions, it contained only 2,468,500 men, with an additional 706,000 other Axis troops bolstering this total.[70] Furthermore, Panzer battalions equipped with Panther Ausf. D or A models commonly fought at operational readiness rates hardly reaching above 35 percent. This was against the 65 percent operational reliability rates in Panzer IV–equipped tank battalions and the 50 to 70 percent operational readiness rate for Soviet T-34–equipped tank battalions. Considering that the average German tank battalion around late 1943 was assigned roughly 90 tanks, this represented the difference between putting approximately 30 Panthers into the field or twice as many Panzer IVs per battalion. Equipment losses meant that on November 20, 1943, of Army Group South's 14 Panzer divisions, nine had fewer than 30 Panzers each ready for action.[71] On any given day in December 1943, Army Group South could field only 54 Tigers, 80 Panthers, and 350 Panzer III/IVs against roughly 5,000 T-34s. From July to December 1943 of the 493 Panthers lost during the final six months of the year half had come at German hands, after the vehicles had mechanically failed.[72]

As for the infantry, the German replacement system still had not overcome the lingering after effects of Stalingrad. Moreover, between July 1 and September 30, the Wehrmacht's total casualties in the Soviet Union had come to 533,025 men, with only approximately 300,000 men replacing these losses.[73] The Allied invasion of Italy had also played a role here as well. Hitler's need to funnel well over one dozen German divisions into Italy in September and October 1943, following Italian surrender, meant that the Germans could not form a strategic reserve in eastern Europe, or flesh out the weakening armies in the Ukraine being slowly driven west by the Red Army.

THE WINTER OF 1943–1944 AND THE FINAL BATTLES FOR THE UKRAINE

In December 1943, Stavka prepared five campaigns, led by the 1st, 2nd, 3rd, and 4th Ukrainian fronts, designed to eject Manstein's Army Group South and Kleist's Army Group A from the western Ukraine. On December 23, 1943, Vatutin's 1st Ukrainian Front led off, exploding from its bridgeheads 35 miles to the west of Kiev. The presence of relatively strong German armored units inflicted heavy losses on the advancing Red Army.[74] In one instance, German armor helped to forge a Kessel not far from Uman, where the Germans took 13,500 prisoners of war and captured 700 abandoned Soviet AFVs and 680 guns.[75] Nevertheless, Konev's 2nd Ukrainian Front had, along with the 1st Ukrainian Front's efforts, created a German salient centered on the town of Korsun, roughly 100 miles southeast of Kiev and pointing east toward the Dnieper River. Two corps from the German 8th Army defended these exposed positions. For its part, the 8th Army, led by General Otto Wohler, had managed to inflict tremendous losses on the advancing Soviet armies. Between January 5 and January 12 alone, the German 8th Army destroyed 380 Soviet AFVs and

374 guns and anti-tank guns.[76] Regardless, the German 8th Army had been left badly positioned for what was to come. Stavka had ordered the 1st and 2nd Ukrainian fronts to penetrate the salient (from its west and east, respectively), encircle the German defenders, and crush them.

Konev's attack on the German salient's eastern face needed to cover 40 miles and would be led by the 4th Guards and the 53rd Armies. The 5th Guards Tank Army would exploit the anticipated breakthrough even though it could put only about 200 tanks and self-propelled guns into the field.[77] The main weight of Konev's attack would fall on the German 389th Infantry Division's 1,500 frontline combat infantry and the weak 3rd Panzer Division, roughly 20 tanks and five self-propelled guns in running order.[78] Vatutin's attack against the west face of the German salient needed to cover 25 miles to reach its assigned meeting point with Konev's spearheads. It would be led by the 27th and 40th Armies, with the newly formed 6th Tank Army set to exploit the breakthrough's won. In reality, the 6th Tank Army represented little more than a pairing of the 5th Guards Tank Corps and the 5th Mechanized Corps. It deployed only a combined 190 tanks and self-propelled guns, including a substantial complement of Lend-Lease Sherman tanks. All told, Vatutin and Konev were able to gather 451 tanks and 62 self-propelled guns in running order to face 159 operational German tanks, assault guns, and self-propelled anti-tank guns. In addition, the 1st and 2nd Ukrainian fronts held a roughly four- or five-to-one advantage in artillery tubes, mortars, infantry guns, and howitzers in 40 Soviet divisions facing off against 15 German divisions.[79]

Konev's 2nd Ukrainian Front struck from the east on January 24, 1944. Vatutin's 1st Ukrainian Front attacked from the west on January 26. Despite Konev's tremendous numerical advantages, it would take him over two days to break through the defensive zone held by the German 389th Infantry Division and the 3rd Panzer Division, both supported by the arrival of, first, the unimposing 14th Panzer Division and, on the second day, the relatively stronger 11th Panzer Division, with all told approximately 45 tanks and self-propelled guns in the 11th Panzer Division. On January 27, the 11th Panzer Division cut the 5th Guards Tank Army's lines of communication.[80] Despite the arrival of the 18th Tank Corps and the 5th Guards Cavalry Corps, at mid-day the 11th and 14th Panzer Divisions solidified the German position astride the 5th Guards Tank Army's supply lines. In addition, on January 28 the newly arrived I./Pz.Rgt.26, a total of 61 Panthers, joined the German counter-attack.[81] Even so, poor coordination with supporting arms, a general lack of infantry, inadequate intelligence, and a combination of confused leadership, coupled with significant losses in the battalion's senior leadership, meant that the German attack foundered. The best chance to stop the 5th Guards Tank Army's penetration had passed.[82] Meanwhile, on the northwestern face of the German salient, the 104th Rifle Corps and the 6th Tank Army's 5th Mechanized Corps ran into a brick wall in the form of the German 34th

KORSUN POCKET

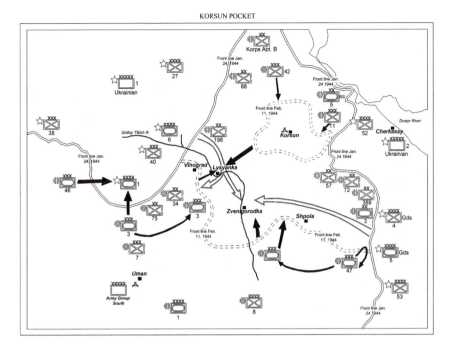

Infantry Division. Nonetheless, secondary attacks launched against the German 88th and 198th Infantry Divisions went better. Vatutin reinforced his successes and on January 28 linked up with Konev's spearhead.[83]

Thus began a tremendous struggle as the Germans attempted to both supply and free the bulk of the German 8th Army's 11th Corps and 1st Panzer Army's 42nd Corps. At the same time, Vatutin and Konev sought to crush the greatest German pocket since Stalingrad. The Germans put the 54,000 to 59,000 men trapped in the pocket under the German 8th Army's command, and designated this force Gruppe Stemmermann after the pocket's highest-ranking officer.

Manstein, fresh off the decimation of the Soviet 1st Tank Army, initially sought to use the pocket as a leverage point for trapping the Soviet 5th Guards and 6th Tank Armies between the relief forces and the pocket itself. Nevertheless, wildly oscillating weather conditions, changing from freezing cold on one day to thaws the next and producing churning seas of mud, helped take away the window of opportunity for the dramatic double envelopment envisioned by Manstein. The two-pronged German relief effort ultimately featured the 1st, 16th, and 17th Panzer Divisions; the 1st SS Panzer Division Liebstandarte Adolf Hitler; and the 503rd Heavy Panzer Battalion from the 1st Panzer Army organized primarily into the 3rd Panzer Corps and located on the southwestern edge of the pocket. On the southeastern edge of the pocket, the 3rd, 11th, 13th, 14th, and 24th Panzer Divisions from the 8th Army, organized into the 47th Panzer Corps under General Nikolaus von Vormann, readied their relief effort.[84] Also participating in the relief effort was Schweres-Panzer-Regiment Bäke, or the 503rd Heavy Panzer Battalion, with eight Panthers and eight Tigers in running order on February 4, and the 506th Heavy Panzer Battalion, with its eight operational Tigers attached to the 16th Panzer Division. Including the 5th SS Panzer Division Wiking trapped in the pocket, this represented one of the larger late-war concentrations of German armor.[85]

Vormann's relief force attacked first. Jumping off at 0600 hours on February 1, the 11th Panzer Division, with the 13th Panzer Division covering its left flank, advanced 12 miles in only five and a half hours. But then it halted at the town of Iskrennoye because a Panther had collapsed the only bridge over the Shpolka River. Vormann was forced to wait for bridging equipment capable of supporting a Panther's weight. The Soviet 29th Tank Corps led an initial Soviet counterattack. Although these attacks were driven off, they helped to further stall Vormann's effort.

Then at 0600 hours on February 4, the 3rd Panzer Corps began its relief effort led by the reinforced 16th and 17th Panzer Divisions. Even so, muddy roads, coupled with the stout resistance put up by the otherwise outgunned Soviet 104th Rifle Corps, caused the 3rd Panzer Corps to bog down. Although the 1st Panzer and 1st SS Panzer Divisions began arriving on February 5, the mud had meant that only portions of each Panzer division were initially ready to join the fight. In the meantime, during the night of February 4–5, Vatutin had brought up the 2nd Tank Army, 6th Tank Army, and 40th Army and launched several strong counterattacks on the 3rd Panzer Corps spearhead. Meanwhile, in spite of repeated Soviet attempts to split and reduce the pocket, Stemmermann's beleaguered command held on. The disintegrating roads under an unseasonable thaw meant that a lack of supplies and reinforcements reaching the front also had greatly hampered Konev's and Vatutin's efforts in both stopping the German relief effort and reducing the pocket.[86]

Within the pocket, Stemmermann shuffled his 72nd Infantry Division and SS Wiking to lead a breakout toward the 3rd Panzer Corps. At the same time, Vormann shifted his Panzer divisions west toward the 3rd Panzer Corps penetration. Konev, sensing that something was afoot, countered Vormann's moves by shifting west the 5th Guards Tank Army and Major General Selivanov's 5th Guards Cavalry Corps. Thus, the main locus of the relief effort remained with Breith's 3rd Panzer Corps.

With most of the 1st Panzer Division and 1st SS Panzer Division having arrived by this time, Breith actually had a far stronger force on February 10 than he did two weeks earlier.[87] Early on the morning of February 11, the 3rd Panzer Corps began its final lunge spearheaded by Bake's 10 operational

Tigers and 32 Panthers, it quickly secured an important bridgehead over the Gniloi Tikich River. At this point, however, the offensive slowed, as fuel and ammunition remained stuck in the mud far behind the Panzer spearheads and also came under attack from bypassed Soviet units.[88] In particular, the Soviet 3rd Guards Airborne Division and 58th Rifle Division launched substantial counterattacks against the 3rd Panzer Corps. In addition, the 3rd Panzer's Corps Kampfgruppe spent much of the day on February 12 completely immobilized by a lack of fuel.[89] The German inability to exploit the initial day's gains was made all the more significant on February 13 when Konev overran Korsun airfield.[90] In turn, Breith's corps desperately thrust forward. Bake's Tigers and Panthers almost immediately ran into the 2nd Tank Army. With timely close air support, however, the Germans managed to destroy 70 tanks and 40 antitank guns against losses of only five Tigers and four Panthers.

Meanwhile, Stemmermann's breakout drive toward 3rd Panzer Corps ran into heavy counterattacks launched by the 5th Guards Cavalry Corps. Then, at 2300 hours on February 16, the final breakout attempt began only four miles from freedom.[91] Most of the 72nd Infantry Division infiltrated right through the Soviet lines, as did the bulk of the 5th SS Wiking Panzer Division.[92] But by then, Soviet blocking forces had swooped in and attacked many of the remaining fleeing German columns.[93] Russian T-34s rampaged up and down the German lines, grinding up men in their treads.[94] Cossacks from the 5th Guards Cavalry Corps, fighting on horseback, sliced apart the German infantry with sabers in an eerie scene reminiscent of the nineteenth century. German soldiers who escaped the carnage and made it to the Gniloi Tikich River were forced to swim the frigid water in freezing weather, with many drowning.[95]

There remains significant debate regarding how many men Germany lost in the pocket. The most reliable estimates hold that the Red Army ended up capturing or killing 19,000 German soldiers, and wounding 11,000 of the 59,000 men initially trapped.[96] The 1st Panzer Army's units involved in the relief operation, mostly 3rd Panzer Corps, lost 160 tanks and assault guns as permanent write-offs, while the 47th Panzer Corps irretrievably lost 80 tanks and assault guns. Overall, German tank and assault gun losses totaled nearly 300 vehicles.[97] Again, most of the tank and assault gun losses came when the vehicles had to be abandoned in the mud, or because of breakdowns.[98] For instance, of the 138 tanks that the 1st Panzer Army wrote off during the Korsun battle, only 35 losses could be attributed to enemy fire and 10 to mines.[99] Of the 1st Panzer Division's 27 Panther losses during the Korsun battle, only nine were due to enemy fire.[100] Of the 503rd Heavy Panzer Battalion's seven lost Tigers, all but one lost to enemy fire were blown up by the Germans during the retreat.[101]

Moreover, on January 27, the 3rd and 4th Ukrainian fronts, led by Generals R. Ia. Malinovsky and F. I. Tolbukhin, respectively, had pounded into Army

Table 9.9 German Army Group South, Sample of Tank Losses by Cause, 1943–1944

Army Group South Tank Losses (Panthers only)[1] 1943 (July–December): 493

Cause	Number and Percent Destroyed
Mechanical failure	493/>50

First Panzer Army Tank Losses (All Models): 1944 (February Korsun Pocket Battle[2]): 138

Cause	Number and Percent Destroyed
Mechanical failure	78/57
Enemy gunfire	35/25
Mines	10/7
Spontaneous engine fire	9/7
Bogging down	5/4
Bridge collapse	1/0.7

[1]Robert Forczyk, *Panther vs. T-34, Ukraine 1943* (Osprey Publishing, 2007), 75.
[2]Niklas Zetterling and Anders Frankson, *The Korsun Pocket: The Encirclement and Breakout of a German Army in the East, 1944* (Casemate, 2008), 286.

Group A and the German 6th Army, captured the vital road and rail junction at Krivoi Rog, and swept German forces from the critical defensive positions offered by the "great bend" in the Dnieper River. For its part, during the Korsun operation, the Red Army incurred 80,188 casualties from the 336,700 men deployed to surround and collapse the German pocket.[102] As for armored losses, some estimates hold that Konev's and Vatutin's fronts lost as many as 850 tanks and self-propelled guns during the Korsun operation. The 1st Ukrainian Front alone lost 569 tanks and assault guns between February 1 and February 20. Given the relative quiet elsewhere on the front, it can be surmised that most of these losses came against the 3rd Panzer Corps.[103]

Regardless, the Red Army launched a massive offensive that began on March 4, 1944, and ran from the Pripet marshes south to the Black Sea. The 2nd Belorussian Front and the 1st, 2nd, and 3rd Ukrainian fronts attacked Army Group South, as the 4th Ukrainian Front under Fyodor I. Tolbukhin looked to sweep the Crimea free of German forces. The fighting took an even more savage twist when Ukrainian guerilla armies fighting primarily the Germans also attacked Russian lines of communication and rear-area units. The fighting in the Ukraine did not end in 1945 either; between February 1944 and May 1946, the Red Army and NKVD (People's Commissariat for Internal Affairs) killed 100,000 people in the Ukraine, and Baltic nations, deporting another 570,826 to the gulags.[104] On February 28, the Red Army had suffered the most militarily significant casualty from this violence when General Vatutin's small convoy, comprising three vehicles, was attacked by nearly 100 Ukrainian guerillas from the Ukrainian Insurgent Army.[105] Vatutin was critically wounded. On April 15, he died from his wounds in a hospital at Kiev. Consequently, on March 1, Stavka Representative Marshall Zhukov personally took command of the 1st Ukrainian Front.

Both Zhukov's 1st Ukrainian Front and the 2nd Ukrainian Front drove Army Group South's entire center and left wings west. German counterattacks failed to staunch the Soviet advance, even though the battered German 8th Army destroyed an estimated 153 Soviet AFVs in front of its left wing in just the first couple of days.[106] Problems that had plagued Germany throughout the war had still not been resolved, a fact best demonstrated on March 10, 1944, when Konev captured Uman, the site of a vast German supply depot. Among the booty were approximately 300 German tanks immobilized by a lack of spare parts, and left behind because of inadequate rail transport. The Luftwaffe was forced to airdrop supplies to German infantry fighting their way west, often completely cut off from friendly lines.[107] In addition, partisan activity took a steady toll on German lines of communication. Late in March, the 14th Panzer Division lost the bulk of its 88-mm guns when partisans destroyed a train's locomotive.[108] Then, during the late March fighting between the Dniester and Pruth Rivers, the 8th Army had been effectively broken into pieces. In one location, four infantry-heavy groupings fought in space separated by gaps of 9 to 12 miles each. Nonetheless, German armor concentrations enabled the defensive hedgehogs to survive, mostly by plugging gaps and counterattacking Soviet penetrations[109] In addition, mostly well-maintained rail connections allowed for the effective replacement of heavy weapons and munitions.[110]

Meanwhile, the Red Army had also exploited a huge gap between Army Groups Center and South that had exposed Tarnopol, a major communications hub for German forces in the region. Prior to the war, Tarnopol had been a thriving Polish city of 35,000 to 40,000 people comprising a mix of ethnic Poles and Ukrainians with a large Jewish population as well. After September 1939, Stalin had deported many of the ethnic Poles, and had extended to the city his brutal campaign against Ukrainian Nationalists. After Barbarossa began, the Germans had largely exterminated the Jewish population.

On March 4, Zhukov's 1st Ukrainian Front, including the 3rd Guards Tank Army and the 4th Tank Army, completely unhinged the German defensive front between the 4th and 1st Panzer Armies. Although struggling at times against fierce German resistance, Zhukov's front flowed past much of the German defenses, including at Tarnopol, which Hitler had declared a Fester Platz, or "fortress." On March 5, Konev's 2nd Ukrainian Front also struck the overstretched German front, this time farther south, and likewise leveraged the 1st Panzer Army away from the 8th Army to its south. While all this was going on, the 3rd Ukrainian Front had pounded into the junction between the German 8th and 6th Armies. By March 12–13, the 1st Ukrainian Front had enveloped Tarnopol and completed the encirclement.[111] In the first half

OPERATIONS IN THE UKRAINE JAN. TO MAY 1944

of April, the 9th and 10th SS Panzer Divisions and a Kampfgruppe from the 8th Panzer Division led the attempts to break through to the city but failed. On April 16, the Russian forces eradicated the pocket. The 4th Panzer Army's 13th Panzer Corps, having retreated west for the better part of March, was hit yet again on March 27 in the Brody region northwest of Tarnopol. The Red Army promptly enveloped this midsize town, designated a Fester Platz by Hitler, sitting astride a key rail line running west to the communications node of Lemberg, where the headquarters of Army Group North Ukraine was located. The Russian forces were unable to completely seal off the Kessel. Thus, throughout the first weeks of April, a back-and-forth struggle for the city ultimately resulted in Zhukov's breaking off his attacks.

In the meantime, on March 25, 1944, the 1st and 4th Tank Armies from the 1st Ukrainian Front met the 40th Army from Konev's 2nd Ukrainian Front, and completed the loose encirclement of the German 1st Panzer Army near the city of Kamenets-Podolsky. All told, 200,000 men in approximately 20 divisions from the strongest German army in the Ukraine had been surrounded. However, the 1st Panzer Army, led by Generaloberst Hans-Valentin Hube, ended up successfully fighting free in one of the most skillfully conducted retreats of the war. Hube organized his men into two huge columns moving in parallel. Assault guns and infantry were in the vanguard while the Panzers guarded the rear. Support came from outside the pocket in the form of the 2nd SS Panzer Corps' 9th and 10th SS Panzer Divisions and the 100th Jaeger and 367th Infantry Divisions. In an operation lasting nearly two weeks, the 1st Panzer Army, while being partially resupplied by the Luftwaffe, moved west over 100 miles. It reached safety on April 6, when its advance elements linked up with the 2nd SS Panzer Corps. Although the 1st Panzer Army was able to bring out only minimal amounts of heavy equipment, Hube lost only 6,000 men.[112]

Farther south yet, on April 7 in Romania, the Red Army crossed the 1941 western Soviet borders for the first time since Germany began the war.[113] The Red Army had ripped Army Group South in half. The new Army Group North Ukraine, under Model's command, featured the 1st and 4th Panzer Armies, which had been forced back into Poland. The southern half of the former Army Group South—Germany's 6th and 8th Armies and the Romanian 3rd and 4th Armies, all pushed into Romania—was renamed Army Group South Ukraine, commanded by Colonel General Ferdinand Schorner. In addition, by May 12, Tolbukhin's 4th Ukrainian Front, under Vasilevsky's oversight, had recaptured the entire Crimean Peninsula, including Sevastopol. According to some, the Red Army captured 21,000 German soldiers; according to others, only about 40,000 Axis soldiers escaped in total from the original 200,000-man 17th Army, yet others state 151,457 German and Romanian soldiers were evacuated of the 230,000 men who made up the 17th Army in April.[114] Soviet success in the Crimea brought further horrors for the local population, including the 600-year-old local Tatar population, an ethnic group descendant from the Scythians, Goths, and Greeks. Stalin ordered 200,000 Tatars collected from the Crimea on May 18, 1944, and shipped east to the gulags, ostensibly as punishment for collaborating with the Germans.[115]

Elsewhere on Germany's Eastern Front, in a tremendous offensive beginning on January 14, and lasting throughout February, the Red Army's 2nd Baltic,

Leningrad, and Volkhov fronts—a total of 1,250,000 men, 1,580 tanks and assault guns, and 1,390 aircraft—had finally pushed Army Group North over 150 miles to the west of Leningrad's approaches, causing Hitler to sack Kuchler on January 29 and replace him with Model. Surprise and creativity proved crucial to the Soviet success; the 2nd Shock Army attacked from the otherwise quiet Oranienbaum salient, and the 42nd Army attacked west from Leningrad to distract the German 18th Army. The Soviet 8th, 54th, and 59th Armies subsequently pounded into the weakened German 18th Army's right flank. Although Soviet casualties were immense, almost 278,000 men against nearly 37,000 German casualties, the Soviet offensive lost steam only late in February when it ran into the German Panther defensive line. There, the heavily outnumbered German 16th and 18th Armies—741,000 men, 385 tanks and self-propelled guns, and 370 aircraft—had sought shelter.

Despite vastly overmatching Army Group North in available manpower, armor, and artillery, Army Group North fielded not a single Panzer division in January 1944, the Red Army, though breaking the siege of Leningrad, had still not managed to engineer any great encirclements. Thus, though battered, Army Group North was able to settle into its new defensive positions. Accordingly, throughout March and well into April, General L. A. Govorov's Leningrad Front and General M. M. Popov's 2nd Baltic Front would continue their offensive, assaulting the Panther line again and again—but to no avail. This fighting in the Baltic states was of a tremendous importance to the German command, mostly because of the Baltic Sea's strategic significance, in terms of acting as a trade route for critical raw materials, including iron ore from Sweden, nickel from Finland, and shale oil from Estonia. Meanwhile, Army Group Center had faced seven major Soviet offensives from December 29, 1943, through March 29, 1944, and although giving some ground, the Soviet Belorussian, 1st Baltic, and Western fronts suffered more than 200,000 casualties for strategically insignificant gains. Consequently, Stavka sacked the Western Front's commander, General V. D. Sokolovsky. Stalin, however, had increasingly stepped back from micromanaging his generals. In contrast, Hitler and his General Staff's meddling had extended firmly into even the tactical realm, circumscribing the freedom of their frontline commanders.[116]

Moreover, further clouding the command situation was the existence of Hitler's SS, Schutzstaffel, or "Protection Echelon," led by Reichsführer Heinrich Himmler, an organization that had in part evolved into an army parallel to the regular German army. The SS comprised four organizations, including the Waffen-SS (SS-VT early in its history), the SS Totenkopf (Death's Head [concentration camp personnel]), Police-SS, and Ordinary-SS. The SS-VT initially served as Hitler's personal guard, organized into the Standarte (regiment) Leibstandarte Adolf Hitler under Sepp Dietrich's command. From these beginnings, the Waffen-SS grew rapidly to 501,049 men by the end of 1943, and by the war's end, the Waffen-SS could field 38 combat divisions.[117] The creation of a parallel army duplicated command structures unnecessarily; in addition, the Waffen-SS tended to hoard the best recruits, helping to cripple Germany's capacity to persecute a war increasingly tilted in its opponent's favor.

For instance, on March 19, Germany had been forced to occupy Hungary to stop it from defecting from the Axis. Eichmann and his minions promptly rounded up and murdered over 300,000 of Hungary's 750,000 Jews.[118] In addition, Marshall Ion Antonescu's government in Romania also teetered on collapse. Meanwhile, Hitler further undermined the army's effectiveness when he removed two of his best remaining field commanders: Field Marshals Manstein and Kleist. At this point in the war, Hitler's hopes for stabilizing Germany's shaky Eastern Front would have to come from elsewhere; increasingly dependent on the outcome of the anticipated Allied invasion of western Europe. For their part, the Allies had aggressively sought to wear down Nazi Germany in preparation for their assault, an effort most prominently made in the skies over Nazi-occupied Europe.

Part III

Chapter 10

A New Perspective for Explaining D-Day's Outcome

While the Red Army spent the spring of 1944 inexorably pushing the Wehrmacht from the Soviet Union, Germany faced, almost unbelievably enough, an even larger crisis. The Anglo-American alliance was finally ready to invade Nazi-occupied western Europe. Moreover, the Allies enjoyed significantly heightened prospects for success. This was in large part because following a back-and-forth aerial war, fought since the war began, they had finally, early in 1944, broken the Luftwaffe's back.

THE ALLIED STRATEGIC BOMBING CAMPAIGN'S IMPACT ON THE WAR

From the war's beginning, the British Royal Air Force (RAF) had, and mostly via its Bomber Command, launched small-scale daylight bombing raids on Germany. These were of limited effectiveness. In large part, this was because unescorted bombers flying during the day were overwhelmingly vulnerable to prowling fighter aircraft. Even escorted German bomber formations subsequently sustained heavy losses flying over daytime England during the Battle of Britain. Thus, since 1940, both the British and the Germans had turned to targeting each other's homeland mainly through nighttime bombing, with the lion's share of the bombing conducted by the RAF in an area bombing campaign against German cities.

In turn, the Luftwaffe focused ever-greater resources toward defending against the RAF's campaign. The Luftwaffe's defensive efforts were less than the model of efficiency. In particular, an overreliance on inefficient anti-aircraft guns had left the Luftwaffe critically shorthanded in fighter aircraft, and absorbed the bulk of German gun tube production.[1] If even a quarter of the anti-aircraft guns defending German cities had been sent to the Eastern Front, or the aluminum needed for producing anti-aircraft gun tubes been redirected in 1940–1943 to manufacture additional fighters, such outcomes may have had a dire impact on the Allied prosecution of the war. Instead, by 1943, the Luftwaffe employed approximately 1 million men and teenagers to man Germany's proliferating flak batteries. This represented nearly twice the men needed to flesh out German infantry formations in eastern Europe. If for no other reason than this deflection of substantial German industrial and military resources from the war against the Soviet Union, one can consider early returns on the RAF's otherwise less-than-spectacular early war strategic bombing campaign to be beneficial to the Allied war effort.

Moreover, Air Marshal Arthur Harris's February 22, 1942, assumption of control over Bomber Command, combined with the RAF's introduction of new directional radars such as GEE, H2S, and Oboe and new tactics, increased the efficacy of area bombing. So did new aircraft, such as modern Lancaster bombers capable of flying great distances with a heavy payload. In addition, the air war over occupied Europe took on a new dimension when in August 1942 the U.S. Army Air Force (USAAF) conducted its first daylight raid against the French city of Rouen. The American B-17 bombers that attacked Rouen belonged to the newly formed U.S. 8th Air Force, commanded by General Carl Spaatz, with General Ira Eaker commanding the heavy bomber wings. In overall command of the USAAF was General Henry "Hap" Arnold, a hard-driving workaholic. USAAF strategic bombing doctrine had long since regarded "precision bombing" during the day as not only possible, but also preferable given the greater chance of hitting specific economic targets and the alleged survivability inherent in the heavily armed American bombers. Most important, USAAF research had determined that 154 targets, not cities, existed within Germany that, if eliminated, would bring Germany to the brink of defeat.[2]

To equip the air fleets envisioned for turning doctrine into practice, the USAAF took delivery of heavily armed and rugged four-engine B-17 and B-24 bombers. Each roughly 10-man bomber crew wielded the bomber's potent defensive firepower, as many as a dozen machine guns, and performed the primary bomb delivery task. Furthermore, the USAAF expected that by flying these airborne battleships in tight formations, the exponentially increased available firepower would prevent the severe losses that had doomed previous daytime bombing campaigns.[3]

Nonetheless, early returns regarding crew survivability proved less than encouraging. The Luftwaffe's defensive efforts proved effective enough that by

Table 10.1 Comparison between Strategic Bombing Campaign's Primary 1943–1945 Heavy Bombers

	Cruising Speed (mph)	Range (miles)[2]	Normal Bomb Load (pounds)	Service Ceiling (feet)	Defensive Armament
Lancaster	211	2,480	13,970	24,492	Nine 7.7-mm MGs
B-17 Flying Fortress	248	3,100	5,995	25,920+	Thirteen 12.7-mm MGs
B-24 Liberator	217	2,170	7,984	32,500	Nine 12.7-mm MGs

[1.]Jim Winchester, gen. ed., *The Aviation Factfile: Aircraft of World War II* (Thunder Bay Press, 2004), 27, 41, 57.
[2.]With a 4,400-pound bomb load for the Lancaster, a 2,200-pound bomb load for the B-17, and a 5,500-pound bomb load for the B-24.

March 1943, the 8th Air Force actually fought significantly weaker than it had in January. For their part, the British directed two-thirds of all raids from March to July 1943 on the Ruhr Valley. There is no doubt that the campaign against the Ruhr hurt the German economy. For instance, steel output fell by 200,000 tons in the first quarter of 1943. Consequently, otherwise recently revived German armaments output stagnated from the spring through the summer of 1943.[4] Despite these results, however, there was little effective Allied follow-up. Meanwhile, the British lost 1,000 bombers and over 7,000 veteran bomber crewmembers during 43 major attacks in the four-month concentrated campaign over the Ruhr. At the same time, the 8th Air Force lost 450 bombers against only 50 German fighters shot down during the day.[5] Considering the huge investment needed in time, training, resources, and infrastructure to maintain even one heavy bomber in the field, as opposed to that needed to maintain a single-engine fighter with one pilot, the Luftwaffe was more than holding its own against the superior resources arrayed by the Allied air forces.[6]

That said, on the night of May 16, 1943, Bomber Command delivered the most spectacular Allied success to date in the air war. A specially trained squadron flying Lancaster bombers conducted the now famous "Dam Buster" raid, destroying the huge dams responsible for the industrial and residential supply of water in the Ruhr Valley. The resultant water flows inundated over 50 factories.[7] In addition, during a massive series of area attacks carried out from July into August 1943, combined British and American efforts destroyed Hamburg, Germany's second-largest city. German armaments production plunged.[8] Göbbels and Speer reacted fearfully to the destruction. It appeared to them that the war in the air had reached a turning point. The Gestapo and the SD both reported that German civilian morale was sinking across the country.

At this point, however, the Germans managed to rebound, mostly by introducing new defensive tactics; and by making more efficient use of their existing fighters to inflict ever-increasing losses on the Allied strategic bombing campaign. Between August 23 and September 4, three major raids by Bomber Command resulted in 125 aircraft shot from the sky of the 1,669 sorties flown, a 7.5 percent loss rate. During the day, the Americans insisted on sending unescorted bombers deep into Europe, paying an enormous price for the damage they were able to inflict on the Axis war effort. For instance, on August 1, 1943, the USAAF attacked the massive, heavily defended Axis oil-refining complex at Ploesti, Romania. Axis forces blew from the sky 73 of the roughly 150 B-24 bombers that made it to the target. For their sacrifice, the bomb crews damaged half the refineries. Nevertheless, within months, Romanian workers had the refineries running again at full production. In the meantime, and during July's last week, the U.S. 8th Air Force lost a third of its operating strength of 300 bombers during a series of raids over Germany. Although several German targets took heavy damage, loss rates such as these did not portend well for what was to come, as the viability of unescorted daylight bombing as a tactic was brought near its breaking point.

Harris and Spaatz sought to destroy the German ball-bearing and aircraft industry in preparation for the anticipated invasion of France the following spring. To that end, they had targeted the strategically important Bavarian cities of Regensburg and Schweinfurt. American bombers were dispatched to hit both cities on August 17, 1943. The 8th Air Force sent out 376 bombers that day; 60 were shot down by German fighters and flak, 11 were scrapped on landing as total losses, and 162 others were damaged. The loss rate totaled 19 percent with 482 casualties, against German losses of only 27 fighters and a like number of pilots.[9] Although the American bomber crews had heavily damaged important German factories, the cost had been prohibitively high. Then, over Stuttgart in September, the Germans destroyed 45 B-17s of 338 sent on the raid. Finally, on October 14, 1943, the 9th Air Force sent 291 bombers to hit the ball-bearing plants at Schweinfurt. After the short-range escort fighters turned back, the Germans pounced once again. They shot 60 bombers from the sky and damaged a further 138, with many of these bombers written off on crash-landing in England. Total American losses reached 77 aircraft, and 600 dead or missing highly trained crew members. Against this devastation, the Luftwaffe lost approximately 40 fighters.[10]

As for the RAF, Air Marshal Harris myopically focused on his newest idea, a joint Anglo-American bombing campaign against Berlin. Although Harris correctly ascertained that many valuable targets existed in and around Berlin, he mistakenly believed that a series of attacks on Berlin would crush German civilian morale. On the night of November 18, 1943, the four-and-a-half-month

Table 10.2 Comparison between Primary Allied versus Axis Fighters in 1944[1]

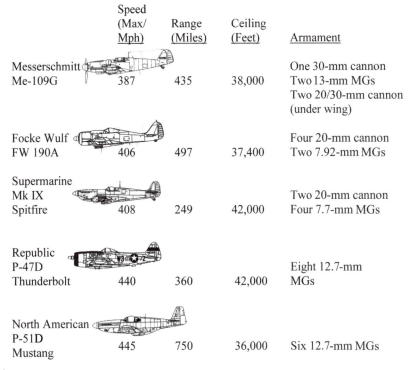

	Speed (Max/ Mph)	Range (Miles)	Ceiling (Feet)	Armament
Messerschmitt Me-109G	387	435	38,000	One 30-mm cannon Two 13-mm MGs Two 20/30-mm cannon (under wing)
Focke Wulf FW 190A	406	497	37,400	Four 20-mm cannon Two 7.92-mm MGs
Supermarine Mk IX Spitfire	408	249	42,000	Two 20-mm cannon Four 7.7-mm MGs
Republic P-47D Thunderbolt	440	360	42,000	Eight 12.7-mm MGs
North American P-51D Mustang	445	750	36,000	Six 12.7-mm MGs

[1]Jim Winchester, gen. ed., *The Aviation Factfile: Aircraft of World War II* (Thunder Bay Press, 2004), 95, 163, 205, and 223.

battle for Berlin began.[11] By the year's end, Berlin had suffered extensive damage, but Bomber Commands' losses remained above 5 percent per mission. German morale remained nowhere near cracking. The worst of it actually came over Nuremberg when, on the night of March 30, 1944, the Luftwaffe shot down a staggering 98 heavy bombers from 795 sent.[12]

In the meantime, the Americans had discovered what turned out to be both technical and operational solutions to the daylight bombing campaign's tactical problems. First, and from a technical perspective, late in 1943 the USAAF began deploying the P-51 "Mustang" single-engine fighter, a timely answer to the USAAF's long-range escort problems. Originally designed as a reconnaissance aircraft for the RAF, the American-built Mustang airframe, when fitted with a powerful British Merlin engine, provided tremendous high-altitude performance and an outstanding 750-mile operational radius. This allowed it to escort bombers over virtually any part of Germany. The Mustang also offered its pilot's great all-around visibility, flew 50 miles per hour faster than the FW-190A or Me-109G, and could outclimb or outdive either German plane.

Table 10.3 Decline in Luftwaffe Pilot Training Hours during the War[1]

Period	Hours
October 1942–June 1943	220
July 1943–June 1944	175
July 1944–May 1945	125

[1]John Ellis, *Brute Force, Allied Strategy and Tactics in the Second World War* (Andre Deutsch, 1990), 205.

The P-51's appearance in the ranks of Allied fighter squadrons allowed the Americans to put in place their biggest adjustment following the Schweinfurt debacle, a focus on defeating the Luftwaffe in the air. Then, with air superiority won, the Americans would not only systematically pound German industrial choke points—but also clear the way for an Allied invasion of France. The key period in the daytime effort to defeat the Luftwaffe began roughly at the same time as the February 1944 American "Big Week" raids. These raids—and the corresponding sustained attritional battle in the sky——caused unsustainable losses to veteran Luftwaffe fighter pilots facing well-trained American fighter pilots flying aircraft superior to almost anything in the Luftwaffe's arsenal. This was far from a one-sided battle. At one point, the Americans lost 244 heavy bombers in just five days, but steady losses in the ranks of Germany's best fighter pilots proved critical to breaking the Luftwaffe's back.[13] The Luftwaffe lost 2,262 irreplaceable fighter pilots from January to June 1944. Over 50 percent of the operational German daytime fighter force fell from the skies on average in each month from March up to D-Day. Then, from July into September 1944, the Luftwaffe lost more fighters in combat against the Anglo-American air forces than it had in the previous two years over the entirety of the German Eastern Front. This represented a staggering rate of attrition mooting a tardy increase in aircraft production that had seen output climb from 930 Me-109 and 380 FW-190 fighters in January 1944 to 1,605 Me-109s and 1,390 FW-190s in September 1944.[14] In addition, and even though by June 1944 Luftwaffe training schools cranked out over 1,000 graduates per month, the belated waves of newly minted pilots had come about mostly because of reduced instructional time. Only half of all pilots within the Luftwaffe even survived their tenth sortie. With veteran Allied pilots facing off against such inexperienced foes, the Luftwaffe's daytime fighter force had been defeated in the air.

Meanwhile, with the Luftwaffe's daytime fighter force marginalized, the Americans and British had turned their attentions to denying the Wehrmacht its most important attribute, namely, the ability to maneuver. Two components existed to this end: destroying infrastructure and crushing the German oil industry. Accordingly, and beginning in May 1944, the Allies systemically annihilated Germany's oil and synthetic fuel industry.

Table 10.4 Strategic Bombing Campaign Bomb Tonnage Dropped Per Year on Germany during the War[1]

Year	Total[2]
1940	14,631
1941	35,509
1942	53,755
1943	226,513
1944	1,188,577
1945	477,051

[1]Helmut Heiber and David Glantz, *Hitler and His Generals Military Conferences 1942–1945: The First Complete Stenographic Record of the Military Situation Conferences, from Stalingrad to Berlin* (Enigma Books, 2003), p. 1073.
[2]In tons.

Germany's available petroleum fell by half in just four months.[15] At the same time, the Allies had considerably ramped up the total bomb tonnage being dropped as they also attacked Germany's transportation network. This effort included a significant mine-laying offensive along the Reich's interior waterways, and a concerted assault on Axis rail networks in France. In May alone, the Allies destroyed 900 locomotives and 16,000 freight cars.[16] By October 1944, the German rail network had met the same fate as the French rail network—and was savaged to such an extent that only one in 50 trains even reached the Ruhr. The scale of destruction proved such that by November 11, 1944, Speer informed Hitler that the Allied bombers had nearly completely isolated the Ruhr from the rest of Germany.[17]

During World War II, the Allied combined bomber offensive failed to break German morale. Nevertheless, it substantially crimped Axis armaments output, undermined the Wehrmacht's mobility, and decimated the Luftwaffe. Moreover, if one does nothing else but examine the scale of German defensive efforts, one can see what the combined bomber offensive had meant to Allied and Soviet successes in other theaters of operations. For instance, at its peak, over half a million of Germany's foreign workers worked exclusively repairing bomb damage. Two million Germans had jobs revolving around anti-aircraft defense. Fifty percent of all German electronic and technical production was devoted to the air war. Thirty percent of gun production went to anti-aircraft artillery, with 55,000 anti-aircraft weapons in service within Germany at the end of 1943.[18] Twenty percent of German ammunition production went to these tens of thousands of high-velocity weapons pointed at the German skies and not wreaking havoc on Allied and Soviet armies.[19] The air war over Europe consequently and ultimately imposed costs on Nazi Germany that played a vital role in paving the way for the decisive events that occurred during the summer of 1944.

THE WEHRMACHT VERSUS THE ALLIES: WHO REALLY HELD THE PRE–D-DAY ADVANTAGE?

Today, the ultimately victorious June 1944 Allied invasion of France, known in the West as D-Day, is often described as a forgone conclusion. The theory is that overwhelming Allied strength defeated an outnumbered, but gamely resisting, German army. In reality, Allied plans for D-Day called for only nine combat divisions to establish the foothold in France. This was to be done against a German army in western Europe totaling 58 divisions. The Allies held a number of important advantages, including unquestioned command of the English Channel and air superiority in the skies over Normandy. Nevertheless, one question lingers, namely, how did nine Allied assault divisions successfully conduct a technically difficult amphibious and airborne assault, consolidate a fragile beachhead, and then, after reinforcement, best a numerically larger German army in western Europe; one enjoying substantial advantages in terrain, tactics, and weaponry?

After all, no other military operation is as fraught with hazard as an amphibious invasion. For instance, during World War I, the British and Commonwealth armies suffered a body blow overcome with only great difficulty after the failed attempts to break out from the beachhead established by the amphibious landings at Gallipoli. During World War II, an American amphibious invasion of Guadalcanal in the Solomon Islands hung in peril

Table 10.5 Allied D-Day Invasion Force[1]

	British Commonwealth	United States
Air landing	British 6th Airborne Division	82nd Airborne Division
		101st Airborne Division
First-wave sea landing	British 3rd Infantry Division	1st Infantry Division
	Canadian 3rd Infantry Division	29th Infantry Division
	British 50th Infantry Division	4th Infantry Division
	2nd Armored Brigade	
	8th Armored Brigade	
	27th Armored Brigade	
Second-wave sea landing	British 51st Highland Division	29th Infantry Division
	British 49th Infantry Division	9th Infantry Division
	British 7th Armored Division	79th Infantry Division
	4th Armored Brigade	90th Infantry Division
	1st Special Brigade	
	4th Special Brigade	

[1]Helmut Heiber and David Glantz, *Hitler and His Generals: Military Conferences 1942–1945: The First Complete Stenographic Record of the Military Situation Conferences, from Stalingrad to Berlin* (Enigma Books, 2003), 967–69.

until late in 1942. This campaign was then followed by costly amphibious assaults that took place across the Pacific against a Japanese foe who inflicted consistently high casualties on U.S. assault troops. Moreover, the Japanese had managed to inflict such serious losses even though they often fought not only completely isolated, but also largely lacking even minimal air and armor support. Meanwhile, the 1942 Dieppe raid had proved a complete Allied disaster. In the Mediterranean, dangerous German counterattacks against Allied beachheads in Sicily, at Salerno, and at Anzio had provided the planners of Operation Overlord, the invasion of Western Europe, even more recent and vivid examples of the vulnerability and fragility inherent in armies landing on hostile shores—even when enjoying near absolute naval and air supremacy.

For instance, at Salerno in September 1943, during the initial U.S. landings in Italy, the German 76th Panzer Corps had nearly split in two the reinforced U.S. 36th and 45th Infantry Divisions. Only timely reinforcements, coupled with the massive firepower of Allied warships, had finally stopped the German counterattack. Then, on January 22, 1944, the Allied 15th Army Group had sought to flank the German fortifications cutting across the Italian peninsula, named the Gustav Line, by landing Major General John P. Lucas and his U.S. 6th Corps' two divisions at Anzio on the coast just south of Rome. Allied reinforcements subsequently poured onto the beaches. The Germans however not only contained the beachhead, but a counterattack delivered by the German 3rd Panzer Grenadier Division on February 18 nearly drove the Allies into the sea. In short, there existed a tremendous body of negative precedent littering the historical landscape, ripe for consideration in weighing the potential success offered by an invasion scheduled against what was anticipated as the strength of the most formidable war machine built in the previous 100 years. In addition, the Allies needed Overlord to be a success. Its defeat would have meant significant delays in launching a second attempt, heavy casualties in men and material, and total losses among the elite airborne troops and Allied special operations forces spearheading the invasion. Moreover, an Allied failure at Normandy would have allowed Hitler to concentrate on the Soviet Union the near full weight of a Wehrmacht backed by a rehabilitated arms industry cranking out more tanks and assault guns per quarter during 1944 than built in any of the first three individual years during the war in total.[20]

Given the stakes involved in Overlord's success, perhaps the most important question initially confronting Eisenhower and his staff was in deciding where to strike. Several overriding concerns shaped any answer to this question. This included the need to find landing beaches that were capable of supporting masses of men and materials and located near adequate deep-water port facilities that were within range of land-based air support from England. As such, planning for D-Day quickly settled on two potential locations, each meeting the previously mentioned criteria. After rejecting an obvious choice, the

Calais region of northeastern France, the narrowest point between the English and the European coasts but perhaps the most heavily fortified region in western Europe, the Allies chose the Normandy region of France, located west of Paris and the Seine River. The second question was when. Allied planners sought a unique combination of tidal and lunar conditions that would maximize the effectiveness of amphibious landings and airborne operations. The first set of such dates revolved around the period from June 5 to June 7, with the next set of appropriate dates not until the third week of June; the Allies ultimately settled on the earlier window of opportunity. Meanwhile, the Germans struggled to coalesce around a viable defensive strategy.

For the Germans the general overall strategy appeared to be one of leveraging interior lines of communication to first stop the Allied invasion attempt, and then redirect the bulk of German forces to crush the Red Army in Eastern Europe. To accomplish the first part of this task, and to direct the German defensive effort in the west, Hitler had turned, in the spring of 1942, to Field Marshal Gerd von Rundstedt. Rundstedt took over a command in France plagued by numerous problems, not the least of which was a firm German belief that the Allies would land at Calais. On March 23, 1942, Hitler had, through his Directive No. 40, laid out his belief that an Allied landing should be met with strong counterattacks to throw the invaders back into the sea before the Allies could dig in. However, Hitler hardly had prioritized the defense of potential landing sites. Moreover, only with Hitler's November 3, 1943, Directive No. 51 did he finally accelerate the buildup of field-ready units in France. In addition, Hitler also appointed Field Marshal Erwin Rommel to prepare the "Atlantic Wall" for repulsing an Allied invasion, with Rommel commanding Army Group B under Rundstedt and with the latter in overall command of the western theater, or Oberbefehlshaber (OB) West. Rommel also believed that events on the beaches would determine German success or failure. As such, Rommel built extensive defensive fortifications and strong points to slow the invaders and, if possible, stop them. Rommel also wanted German armor reserves deployed as close to the beaches as possible, in order to counterattack in force on the first day of an Allied invasion. Nevertheless, Hitler had split the command over Germany's Panzer reserves in western Europe. Rommel commanded a small part of the German reserve, but a significant portion of the armor was in the hands of the OKW (Oberkommando der Wehrmacht, or High Command of the Armed Forces), or under General Baron Leo Geyr von Schweppenburg in command of Panzer Group West.

Rundstedt agreed with Rommel and Hitler as to the importance of stopping the Allies on the beaches, but he also believed that it was necessary for Germany to maintain an armored reserve within the French interior. These beliefs were bolstered by Guderian and Schweppenberg, each convinced that German armored formations could still outmaneuver and defeat the Allies. Rommel, drawing on his experiences in North Africa, believed that maneuvering

Table 10.6 German Divisional Distribution in Western Europe on June 6, 1944[1]

58 Total Divisions (48 infantry divisions,[2] nine Panzer divisions, one Panzer grenadier division)

	Divisions	
Location	Infantry	Panzer
Normandy	6	1 + 2 deep inland
Brittany	9	—
Channel Islands	1	—
Between Seine and Somme Rivers	3	1
Central France, south of Loire River	5	2 + 1 Panzer Grenadier
Pas de Calais	9	1
Belgium and Netherlands	7	1
Mediterranean	8	1

[1]Helmut Heiber and David Glantz, *Hitler and His Generals: Military Conferences 1942–1945: The First Complete Stenographic Record of the Military Situation Conferences, from Stalingrad to Berlin* (Enigma Books, 2003), 968–69.
[2]Many of the infantry divisions were static garrison divisions (including half the divisions in Normandy), Luftwaffe field divisions (three divisions), or in training (seven divisions) and of a poor quality.

armored formations in the face of near absolute Allied air superiority would prove nearly impossible.[21] Hitler resolved the debate inconclusively; by spreading the German armor across all of France and Belgium. Command disagreements such as these proved only the beginning of Germany's troubles. For instance, the Luftwaffe and the Kriegsmarine were largely nowhere to be found. This left the German army to face the Allied invasion largely alone.

Of the 58 Germans divisions deployed in western Europe during the spring of 1944, only 27 represented quality units; 10 Panzer/Panzer grenadier divisions and 17 field-ready infantry divisions capable of both offensive and defensive combat. The rest were training and garrison divisions. Although the infantry were of a decidedly spotty mix, there were still far more veteran infantry divisions than the Allies could expect to initially throw at the Germans. Moreover, the quality of German armor heavy units in western Europe was better yet. Approximately 1,552 tanks, mostly Panzer IVs and Vs, filled out the 10 German armor heavy divisions. Nonetheless, tank strength on hand in the German Panzer divisions encompassed an uneven range. For instance, on June 6, 1944, the 2nd SS Panzer Division deployed a mere 69 tanks and 33 assault guns.[22] Conversely, the Panzer Lehr Division, a skilled formation created from training units, possessed 183 tanks and 40 tank destroyers. The OKW also deployed in western Europe several independent armored battalions. Three Tiger battalions ultimately fought in France: the 101st SS Heavy Tank Battalion with 37 Tigers, the 102nd SS and its 28 Tigers, and the 503rd with 24 Tigers.[23]

Against this imposing mass of armor stood the Anglo-American–led alliance driven mainly by a U.S. Army much smaller than had been initially planned. The Soviet Union's ability to tie down the German army's strength had helped influence American war planners to reduce an originally forecast size of the U.S. Army; down from 215 divisions to 89 divisions, including 16 armored divisions. General George Marshall, U.S. Army chief of staff, believed that American air superiority and strategic bombing would compensate for the lower number of highly mobile army divisions to counter what he perceived to be Axis numerical strength.[24]

Following the Kasserine Pass debacle, the U.S. Army had brought 13 of the 16 US armored divisions formed during the war into a common organizational framework featuring an even ratio of tanks to infantry to artillery. Each armored division included three tank battalions deploying 169 M4 Sherman medium tanks and 77 M5 Stuart "light" tanks. As for infantry, each U.S. armored division deployed three mechanized infantry battalions in 378 M3 half-tracked armored personnel carriers. The U.S. armored division also included 54 self-propelled 105-mm howitzers, known as the "Priest" because of the commander's pulpit, in the three artillery battalions[25] and numerous heavily armed supporting units. Combined arms in the U.S. armored divisions came from its organization into three "combat commands," each approximately brigade sized, but lacking the fluidity of a German Kampfgruppe. The armored division was only one of three types of armored units created by the U.S. Army, the other two being individual tank battalions, equipped with 54 medium tanks, and tank destroyer battalions, frequently attached to specific units as needed. American doctrine held that the tank's role was to act as pursuit weapons, or support the infantry. Tanks were not meant to purposefully fight other tanks as a primary mission. That role was reserved for the tank destroyers.

Unlike U.S. armored divisions, British armored divisions typically deployed by being divided into two brigades—one armored and one infantry—with numerous attached divisional-level regiments and battalions in the supporting combat arms. The armored brigade in a British armored division came equipped with 195 M4 Sherman medium tanks, including a sprinkling of potent Model VC "Firefly" Shermans. In addition, the reconnaissance regiment fielded another 65 Shermans.[26] Outside the armored divisions, the British also deployed independent armored brigades typically assigned to the corps. From there, the brigades were often attached to individual infantry divisions. British armored brigades most often consisted of either Sherman tanks in the cruiser role, or heavily armored Churchill tanks in the infantry support role. All told, the British and Canadians would deploy eight independent armored brigades in Normandy. As for the infantry, the standard British or Canadian infantry division numbered 18,300 men, in contrast to American infantry divisions numbering 14,250 men.[27]

Table 10.7 U.S. Army Mobilization during the War[1]

Date	Number of Men under Arms in U.S. Army
June 1939	187,893[2]
December 31, 1941	1,685,403[3]
June 30, 1945	8,291,336[4]

[1]Trevor N. Dupuy, *Hitler's Last Gamble* (HarperCollins, 1994), app. B.
[2]199,491 more in National Guard.
[3]Including 275,889 in Air Corps.
[4]In 89 divisions and 1,011 independent battalions, with these battalions possessing a combined divisional equivalent strength of 74 divisions. James F. Dunnigan and Albert A. Nofi, *Dirty Little Secrets of World War II* (William Morrow & Company, 1994), 219.

Although Allied armor and infantry combat formations appeared formidable, the German army to this day has held a reputation for superior combat capabilities. The primary reason for this reputation was because the Germans could rely on a well-trained, veteran, officer corps and noncommissioned officer cadre who religiously embraced the use of combined-arms teams as the best tool for defeating their foes. In contrast, Allied leaders frequently failed to completely grasp how best to create, direct, and employ combined-arms teams. Given the U.S. Army's massive expansion from 456,000 men on June 30, 1940, to roughly 20 times that number by June 30, 1945, this is in part understandable.

In addition, the U.S. Army had long since been ill prepared for armored warfare. For instance, during the entire decade of the 1930s, the U.S. Army took delivery of only 321 light tanks. This was at a time when the French, Soviets and Germans built thousands of light, medium, and even heavy tanks.[28] In Normandy, German units further enjoyed a clear-cut technical superiority. For example, the standard German 75-mm PAK 40 anti-tank gun, no less the 88-mm PAK 43 anti-tank gun, hit far harder than Allied towed anti-tank weapons. The standard German 10-man rifle squad also possessed an enormous firepower advantage over the standard 12-man American rifle squad, the latter's main source of firepower coming from a single 20-round clip-fed Browning Automatic Rifle. In contrast, the German rifle squad wielded the belt-fed MG-42 light machine gun with a 1,200-round-per-minute rate of fire, twice that of the Browning or the British Bren gun. In addition, each German squad also equipped three men with 9-mm Schmeisser submachine guns instead of rifles. This provided additional close-range firepower, a lesson learned from facing Soviet squads well equipped with PPSH submachine guns that had frequently outgunned German squads equipped with Mauser rifles.

The German infantry could also count on significant numbers of one- or two-man crewed portable anti-tank rocket launchers the Raketenpanzerbuche 54, or Panzerschreck, and the smaller disposable Panzerfaust. Although the

Americans had pioneered the use of such weapons, with the M9 60-mm anti-tank rocket launcher—best known as the "bazooka;" the German Panzerschreck fired a much more potent 88-mm warhead. The Germans cranked out these weapons, and the shorter-ranged Panzerfaust, by the thousands. The huge numbers of such inexpensive, but effective, anti-tank weapons would knock out thousands of Allied and Soviet tanks alike in World War II's final year, all at a fraction of the cost it took to replace a tank. In addition, the Germans fought with a determination, a belief in victory, and a belief in the abilities possessed by their fellow soldiers, at least at the rifleman's level, beyond all proportion to the reality faced after June 6, 1944. If one were to look only at this, it is obvious why the German army had a reputation for superior combat capabilities, thus often leaving the casual history enthusiast to believe that only superior Allied numbers could have defeated the Wehrmacht. In reality, the Allies held a number of notable qualitative advantages of their own.

Foremost in 1944 was Allied dominance in the air and at sea. In addition, Allied mastery over the intelligence war also paid huge dividends; either in deceiving the Germans where the Allies would strike next or in reading the Axis playbook. Furthermore, although the German army possessed an edge on the battlefield itself, this edge did not flow across the board. For instance, Allied artillery was more effective than any other combatant's artillery arm during World War II. The Americans could flexibly, accurately, and lethally call down heavy, devastating artillery support at will and even when on the move. In large part this was because the Americans deployed the best fire control system in the world, supported by excellent communications technology. Technically, the M1 105-mm howitzer and M1 155-mm howitzer also proved accurate at long ranges. Further enhancing American artillery's effectiveness was its mobility. Every artillery piece was either truck pulled or mounted as self-propelled weapons. Additionally, the U.S. Army fought equipped with the accurate, reliable M1 Garand semi-automatic rifle. This weapon could lay down fire more quickly than the bolt-action German Mauser or British Enfield. Moreover, most U.S. infantry divisions nearly always fought with attached tank battalions or tank destroyer battalions, and were equipped with a plethora of AFVs such that each was really the equivalent of a Panzer grenadier division. Furthermore, the M3 half-track, though not as well protected as the German SdKfz 251, could carry more men and equipment, and had greater horsepower and off-road capability as well as fewer maintenance problems than did its German peer.[29] In addition, the U.S. 1st Infantry Division, 82nd Airborne Division, and 101st Airborne Division were all elite units that would play prominent roles on D-Day. As a whole, the GIs represented America's best human material, while in 1944 Germany scraped the bottom of its manpower barrel.[30]

Moreover, the training, skill, and experience within America's senior combat officer ranks rarely receive their due notice. The U.S. Army fielded 22 combat corps in World War II, ultimately led by 34 different generals.

Twenty-four of these generals attended West Point. Twenty-three served in France during World War I. Sixteen experienced combat in France, while two participated in the postwar fighting in Siberia. Thirty-three graduated from the U.S. Army's Command and General Staff School at Fort Leavenworth, Kansas, and Omar Bradley graduated at the top of his class in 1929. Most went on to further training, and also ended up teaching as well. Moreover, these veteran, well-trained men frequently displayed a strong enthusiasm for maneuver-based warfare, a fact not unnoticed by a German army rapidly losing its own mobility.

General Erich Marks's 84th Corps, under General Dollmann's 7th Army, spearheaded the German defense of Normandy. Marks commanded five mostly garrison divisions, though he did have the reinforced 91st Airlanding Division and one of the 7th Army's few veteran field-capable infantry divisions: the 352nd Infantry. Moreover, in all of Normandy, only one Panzer division awaited the Allies: the 21st Panzer. The OKW controlled, in its reserve, the two other geographically closest Panzer divisions: the 12th SS Panzer Division and Panzer Lehr. Both required Hitler's approval for their release. This is, in part, how a German army in France that possessed substantial initial numerical advantages in men and armor allowed approximately 160,000 Allied soldiers to secure a beachhead in France on June 6, 1944. In addition, a forecast of poor weather had helped cause the Germans to lower their alert status.[31] So too did the German command's neglect of valuable intelligence acquired by the Gestapo in the week prior to D-Day, intelligence showing that the French Resistance had been activated by Allied communications—as well as other such signals indicating that an invasion was near.

Allied plans called for hitting five beaches in Normandy. The American 1st Army, led by General Omar Bradley, would take the westernmost beaches. The U.S. 7th Corps would assault the beach farthest west, located on the eastern coast of the Cotentin Peninsula, code-named Utah Beach. The U.S. 5th Corps, led by the veteran 1st "Big Red One" Infantry Division and the 29th Infantry Division, would land at Omaha Beach east of Utah Beach. The U.S. 82nd and 101st Airborne Divisions were to drop inland and take and hold key road junctions, bridges, and causeways. The British 2nd Army, led by Lieutenant General Miles Dempsey, would come ashore at beaches Gold, Juno, and Sword to the east. The British 6th Airborne Division would land on both sides of the Orne River, and seize bridges, causeways, and road junctions therein. The 21st Army Group, led by Montgomery and comprising British, Canadian, and Polish troops, fielded one airborne division, five armored divisions, another armored division—including customized tanks to penetrate the German fortifications on D-Day itself, and 10 infantry divisions. Bradley's 12th Army Group of American and French troops comprised two airborne divisions, six armored divisions, and 13 infantry divisions. In addition, the Allied assault army was initially supported by over 11,000 aircraft and set sail as part of the largest invasion fleet in history: approximately 5,000 ships.

D-DAY: REVISITING ONE OF HISTORIES GREAT MILITARY TRIUMPHS: DID OVERWHELMING STRENGTH CARRY THE DAY?

The events that occurred on June 6, 1944, are among the most analyzed in the Anglo-American historiography on the war. Most of this analysis has painted a picture of overwhelming Allied strength carrying the day. However, this portrayal of events has shrouded what was a considerable achievement, one wrought by Allied soldiers securing a beachhead in the face of a German army enjoying far greater resources to draw on during the critical first day of the Allied invasion.

As the immense Allied invasion fleet steamed across the English Channel, late on June 5 a fleet of C-47 transport aircraft carrying elite Allied airborne troops flew above in tightly packed formations. Problems cropped up almost immediately given a flight plan calling for the pilots to cross the English Channel at a mere 500-foot altitude, to avoid German radar, and then climb rapidly to avoid German anti-aircraft weapons placed on offshore islands before finally dropping back down to the jump altitude. All this was to be done while maintaining formation with hardly any radio communication. Poor weather and heavy anti-aircraft fire further unraveled the transport's flight plans. This resulted in the main body of the Allied paratroopers at times floating to earth more than 30 miles from their assigned drop zones.[32] Then the equally dispersed glider-borne troops began slamming into hedgerows, trees, farmhouses, and just about any other obstacle in the fields dotting the Norman countryside. In the 82nd Airborne Division alone, 16 percent of the division's glider-borne soldiers became casualties before firing a shot in anger. Nearly 20 percent of the jeeps and anti-tank guns were lost or destroyed during the landings.[33]

D-Day's planners had expected the American 82nd and 101st Airborne Divisions to quickly take and hold the vital causeways, bridges, and towns controlling ingress and egress across the flooded, marshy land behind Utah Beach. Instead, the battered, and badly disorganized, airborne troops needed to find targets that they often were nowhere near within groups of men who were often not even from the same battalion or regiment. Behind the beaches in the British sector, the British 6th Airborne Division faced similar problems and possessed a similarly extensive task list. Its main objectives included capturing the two bridges over the Orne River and the Caen Canal, while destroying other bridges to stop German reinforcements from streaming down on the exposed beachheads. Despite being scattered across the map, the crack British and American airborne troops ultimately secured many of their most important objectives, a testament to their training, skill, and courage.

Meanwhile, German phone lines throughout France lit up with alerts from Normandy.[34] The 21st Panzer Division, equipped with over 100 tanks (albeit many obsolete) and located just behind the British drop zones, began assembling for a counterattack. Then, just after 0300 hours, German radar detected the Allied invasion fleet. Rundstedt ordered the motivated and well-equipped 18,000-man 12th SS Panzer Division toward Caen, and alerted the equally potent Panzer Lehr Division to move as well. Either one of these divisions could have wreaked havoc on any of the invasion beaches, not to mention the devastating results possible if both attacked in conjunction with the 21st Panzer. Nonetheless, at this critical point in the morning, the absurdity in the German command situation became cripplingly real for the German army in Normandy. Rundstedt's orders needed to first get clearance through the OKW and a sound-asleep Adolf Hitler several hundred miles to the east at Berchtesgaden. Consequently, not until 10:00 a.m. did the OKW even release the 12th SS Panzer Division to move toward the coast. Although at 5:00 a.m. the 7th Army headquarters had released the 21st Panzer Division, it wasted valuable time forming up for its counterattack.

At the same time, Eisenhower's huge invasion fleet arrived off the landing beaches supported by 3,467 heavy bombers and 1,645 medium bombers protected by 5,409 fighters. In comparison, only two German aircraft even penetrated the Allied fighter screen over the beaches on D-Day. Of the 113 Allied aircraft lost on D-Day, all fell to German anti-aircraft fire.[35] In addition, six battleships, 23 cruisers, and 104 destroyers roamed freely off the coast, blasting away at will and softening up the five invasion beaches. The first waves of British and Canadian troops hit the three eastern beaches, Gold, Juno, and Sword, at approximately 7:45 a.m. The 50th British Division landed closest to the American beaches: at Gold Beach 10 miles east of Omaha Beach. One mile farther east, the Canadian 3rd Infantry Division took Juno Beach, and five miles east of Juno, the British 3rd Infantry Division seized Sword Beach.

Although the beaches themselves represented insignificant obstacles, hedgerows dominated the terrain behind the beaches to a depth reaching nearly 40 miles. A large open stretch of land just to Caen's southeast provided the first sizable break in the hedgerows. This land, as well as Caen, the primary road junction in the region and the most important objective for the first day's operations, would prove the most hotly contested piece of real estate in France for the better part of the ensuing summer. The German 716th Division, a garrison division filled with second-rate troops, including a number of forced conscripts from eastern European nations, defended the British- and Canadian-targeted beaches. German resistance duly crumbled in the face of several hours of combined aerial and naval bombardment. This was followed up by the first landing waves of infantry, well supported by custom-built DD tanks equipped with floatation kits and dual-drive propulsion systems to allow for forward movement through the water. This crude modification could have meant trouble in the rough waters of the English Channel. Thus, the decision to launch the assault waves from only seven miles offshore helped the DD tanks to successfully negotiate the strong chop. Unfortunately, the Americans would not enjoy such a uniformly smooth landing experience.

The low cloud ceiling and poor weather had resulted in most of the U.S. preinvasion aerial bombardment missing the German coastal defenses. As for what awaited the Americans onshore at Utah Beach on the Cotentin Peninsula's eastern coast, the worst of the obstacles were behind the beaches, where the Germans had flooded the marshy low-lying land, leaving only several elevated causeways leading from the beach. Miles of hedgerows waited deeper in the countryside, along with more marshy land and the Merderet and Douve Rivers. The German 709th Infantry Division, again featuring eastern European "volunteers," only weakly defended Utah Beach. Thus, by mid-morning the Americans had secured the beach and linked up with elements from the airborne divisions. By nightfall, 23,000 men had been deposited onshore.[36]

On the other hand, at Omaha Beach, between Utah Beach to the west and the British beaches to the east, Eisenhower's armies suffered D-Day's greatest difficulties. The 1st Infantry Division, the "Big Red One," had, along with the American 29th Infantry Division, faced the task of taking Omaha. Unfortunately, their opposition was the well-dug-in, combat-experienced German 352nd Infantry Division. In addition, as a landing beach, Omaha left much to be desired. Steep and imposing cliffs bookended a relatively broad beach, but one that ended abruptly in dunes and bluffs rising over 150 feet in height at some places. Moreover, the folds in the land provided extensive cover, hiding defenders from view in the grass-lined slopes, and masking the few cuts in the dunes and bluffs providing egress from the beach. German strongpoints guarded these natural objectives. Making matters even worse for the Americans was that the preinvasion bombardment had largely missed the beach, or failed to penetrate the heavy German concrete gun emplacements.[37] The decision to launch the assault craft and DD tanks nearly 11 miles out to sea proved a disastrous choice. Most of the tanks quickly took on water in the heavy seas; 27 of the first 32 DD tanks launched from Allied shipping quickly dropped to the English Channel's bottom.[38] Amphibious two-and-a-half-ton trucks (DUKW's) carrying artillery pieces similarly foundered and sank. This left only the infantry, the scattered few surviving artillery pieces, and the assault engineers to face veteran German infantry manning largely intact defenses.[39]

German machine guns, mortars, artillery, and other heavy weapons swept a deadly hail of fire across the landing craft. One German 88-mm gun emplacement destroyed three landing craft in a row, one after the other, as if on a shooting range.[40] The Germans annihilated nearly the entire first landing wave, totaling almost 1,500 troops, 96 tanks, 16 tank dozers, and the many assault engineer teams. Within four hours from the first assault wave's landing, the Germans had killed or wounded over 3,000 American soldiers. One brave landing ship officer, in an effort to alleviate the massacre, brought his ship, with its cargo of 16 Sherman tanks, directly onto the beach. Nonetheless, German 75-mm and 88-mm anti-tank weapons blazed away from over half a dozen concrete bunkers, knocking out half the tanks almost immediately. Of the 112 Sherman tanks from the 741st and 743rd Tank Battalions that landed that day, only 41 survived.[41]

General Omar Bradley faced the chilling prospect of calling off the attack on Omaha. This would have left an enormous gap between the three British beaches to the east and isolated Utah Beach to the west. Nevertheless, late in the morning, individual groups of brave American soldiers finally punched through the German strongpoints with support from devastatingly accurate naval gunfire.[42] At 1330 hours, General Bradley received tentative word that the assault waves had secured the bluffs over Omaha. By the day's end over 3,000 Americans had died. But the survivors had secured the beachhead. Despite the slaughter at Omaha Beach, by the evening of June 6 over 150,000 Allied troops had landed on the five beachheads spreading 24 miles along the French coast. For this victory, the Allies endured approximately 10,000 casualties.

Allied success came about mainly because of thorough planning, preparation, and the considerable skill and courage displayed by the Allied assault battalions. Yet German leaders also had made critical errors. Crucially, though the OKW had stationed three Panzer divisions relatively near the Norman coast, only one was under direct 7th Army command, the 21st Panzer, which launched the belated and sole significant German counterattack on D-Day. At 8:00 p.m., a force led by the veteran 192nd Panzer Grenadier Regiment had actually reached the coast, and driven a narrow corridor between Sword and Juno beaches. But shortly thereafter, the 21st Panzer's commander, fearing that his lines of communication would be cut, ordered his battered and isolated units to retreat. Meanwhile, the OKW had failed to release the 12th SS Panzer Division and Panzer Lehr until 1700 hours, or more than 14 hours after Panzer Lehr's commanding officer, General Bayerlein, had prepared his men to move. The dithering at the OKW had meant two things. First, and most important, neither of these powerful formations was available to reinforce 21st Panzer Division's initial success. This means that even if they could not have initially driven Allied forces into the sea, they well could have perhaps fatally weakened the eastern edge of the Allied beachhead—by splitting British and Canadian forces between what would have effectively been an entire Panzer Corps' considerable combat power. Second, with the skies having cleared by the afternoon, two of the German army's most well equipped divisions needed to fight through incessant Allied air attacks just to reach the battlefield.

Having failed to stop the landings on D-Day, the German response was nevertheless adequate enough that the Allies soon found themselves bottled up tightly in the beachhead, so much so as to result in Montgomery's Army Group not even taking his first day's goals, including most notably at Caen, until late in the summer. Meanwhile, to the west, Bradley's efforts to expand the beachhead had quickly degenerated into a slow slogging match, as the Germans settled into defensive positions in the hedgerow country. And all this occurred even though well into the summer Hitler remained worried that the landings in Normandy would prove a diversion, in part thanks to Allied deception efforts, that, far from slacking off after D-Day, had continued unabated. Even as late as June 18, the 20 Allied divisions in the Normandy beachhead faced only 18 of the 58 German divisions in France on D-Day.[43]

Having been outfought on D-Day, and having squandered their massive edge in manpower, the German army in Normandy then managed to contain an Allied beachhead bulging with men and material and supported by massive offshore and air-delivered firepower, doing so, moreover, even though the German forces in Normandy fought grossly outnumbered for much of the summer. This prompts one to wonder how beat-up German formations, remaining in line for weeks on end, could have held out against quantitatively superior forces constantly growing in size and power if sheer material power supposedly served as the determinant for success in World War II. Meanwhile, a Red Army that since the war's first day had maintained enormous quantitative advantages over the German army, and yet had struggled enormously against its smaller foe, had finally attained a position whereby it could deliver a decisive blow.

Chapter 11
Hitler's Greatest Defeat

With the Allies ensconced in France, conventional wisdom today holds that Germany's quantitatively superior enemies simply steamrollered the Wehrmacht during the war's final year. In reality, the story explaining the beginning of the end for Hitler and his vile empire during the great summer battles of 1944 is, in fact, a more nuanced story; one illuminating many of the themes in this book and driving a new understanding regarding why the war ended in German defeat. The war's final year is a tale of the qualitative ascendance of two different armies—one Anglo-American led and the other Soviet while at the same time the Wehrmacht crumbled. This qualitative improvement in Germany's opponents was far from linear, and took varying levels of alternatively superiority, parity, and even lingering inferiority against a German army decidedly in decline. Consequently, during the war's final year, the German army's enduring strengths allowed it to inflict appalling losses on its opponents. It also provided for the Third Reich's survival long past what one would consider reasonable if we had simply analyzed events during the years 1944–1945 strictly by looking at a statistical balance sheet. The explanation as to how this occurred, against overwhelming numerical odds, provides the context for this study as it moves into the war's final year.

Events in eastern Europe during 1943–1944 have poked several big holes in the brute-force thesis for explaining the war's outcome. In addition, even though the 1944-era Red Army would achieve its greatest victories, the same Red Army would also suffer repeated and severe defeats at the hands of its German foe. Perhaps the most salient example discrediting the theory that the Red Army was an unstoppable colossus following Kursk and, moreover, discrediting the steamroller thesis for explaining Soviet victory in the war occurred during the spring of 1944—a time when a failed and often ignored strategic-level Soviet offensive aimed at Romania provides further evidence as to why more than sheer numbers determined World War II's outcome.

THE RED ARMY'S ROMANIAN MISADVENTURE

During April and May 1944, despite fighting heavily outnumbered and underequipped and with armies disorganized after months of relentless combat, Germany's Army Group South Ukraine, comprising the German 6th and 8th Armies and the Romanian 4th and 3rd Armies, defeated multiple strategic-level offensives launched into Romania by the Soviet 2nd and 3rd Ukrainian fronts. On May 1, 1944, few army groups then existing in the world could, on paper, match the strength of Konev's 2nd Ukrainian Front. It included half the Red Army's tank armies, seven additional combined-arms armies, and sizable supporting forces.[1]

Although numerically far stronger than his front's Axis opponents, Konev's weary command was far from ready to act as the spearhead for Stavka's ambitious attempts to drive into the heart of Romania and destroy Army Group South Ukraine. For example, his tank armies could put only half their assigned tank complement into the field. On the other hand, and working in his favor, Konev's tank armies featured some of the Red Army's most experienced tank generals. These men included Lieutenant General S. I. Bogdanov, in command of the 2nd Tank Army; Colonel General P. A. Rotmistrov, leading the 5th Guards Tank Army; and Lieutenant General A. G. Kravchenko, who led the 6th Tank Army.[2] Konev's front was to drive into Romania by attacking along the Tirgu-Frumos axis in the Iasi and Kishniev region.

Meanwhile, to the south Malinovsky's 3rd Ukrainian Front would launch its drive into Romania to the south and southeast, from the Tiraspol region, south of Kishinev, and against Odessa on the Black Sea.[3] On paper, R. I. Malinovsky's 3rd Ukrainian Front also represented a potent offensive force. It comprised six combined-arms armies, including one of the Red Army's elite formations: Colonel General V. I. Chuikov and his 8th Guards Army.[4] Still, Malinovsky's command was thoroughly worn down by April 1944. In addition, he lacked Konev's wealth of armor, fielding only 350 tanks and self-propelled guns. Moreover, though by April 10 Malinovsky's thinly stretched front had captured the Black Sea city and port of Odessa, the battle had left his front poorly organized for the planned follow-up offensive into Romania. In addition, the spring mud and rains only added to the logistical problems facing both Soviet commanders.

In opposition, Army Group South Ukraine was led by one of Hitler's most devoted disciples, the general, future field marshal, and war criminal

Ferdinand Schorner.[5] Schorner had divided his command; the German 8th Army and Romanian 4th Army were responsible for defending northern Romania from the Carpathian foothills south to near Kishniev. This grouping was under the overall command of the 8th Army's commanding officer, Colonel General Otto Wohler, a man whose "accomplishments" during the war included, among other things, frequently aiding and abetting in the mass murder of thousands of innocent civilians.[6] The German 6th Army, under Colonel General Karl Hollidt, and the Romanian 3rd Army defended the remainder of northern Romania, with their southern boundary anchored on the Black Sea. Most of the available German armor fought under Wohler's command, and opposed the 2nd Ukrainian Front. This collection of armor included quite a few run-down Panzer divisions. Nonetheless, it also featured two relatively strong formations.[7] First, the 3rd SS Panzer Division Totenkopf could count 70 to 100 tanks in running condition, or roughly half its authorized strength. Nevertheless, it was well equipped in comparison to its peers. In addition Wohler possessed the elite Panzer Grenadier Division Grossdeutschland, superbly equipped with 160 tanks, including 80 Panthers, 40 Tigers, and 40 Panzer IVs and 40 assault guns, 12 artillery batteries, and four batteries of 88-mm guns. Moreover, Grossdeutschland was led by one of Germany's most outstanding Panzer commanders, General Hasso von Manteuffel.[8] Nonetheless, the 2nd and 3rd Ukrainian fronts outnumbered the German armies by ratios over two to one in infantry, armor, and artillery. Only in aircraft did the Axis approach parity in numbers.

On April 8, 1944, Konev launched the first phase of the offensive. Nevertheless, fierce counterattacks led by Grossdeutschland defeated Konev's shock group, and the 27th Army, 40th Army, and 2nd Tank Army; and brought the offensive to a halt. Then, in conjunction with a Kampfgruppe from 24th Panzer Division, Grossdeutschland and supporting Axis formations parried subsequent Soviet attacks, retook several key objectives, and stabilized the German defensive front.[9] After regrouping and reinforcing his shock armies, Konev attacked again and was defeated again. Although subsequent attacks, lasting until April 23, achieved some limited tactical successes, they utterly failed to achieve the offensive's stated strategic goals.[10] Meanwhile, in fighting against the German 6th Army that lasted throughout April, Malinovsky's 3rd Ukrainian Front had also failed to meet its strategic goals. Nonetheless, it had captured Odessa and cleared Axis forces from the eastern bank of the Dniester River.[11]

Subsequently, both Malinovsky and Konev regrouped. Konev took on considerable reinforcements such that he deployed 491 tanks in his shock armies alone. In addition, he had ordered in the 8th and 13th Guards Tank Regiments as part of the 2nd Tank Army, each regiment equipped with the Red Army's brand-new heavy tank: the Iosef Stalin (or IS-series). Konev launched diversionary attacks beginning on April 24, but the Germans defeated the attacks so quickly as to leave their defenses along Konev's main axis of attack well prepared for what was to come. Meanwhile, from April 25 to April 28, the Romanian 5th Corps organized a series of effective spoiling attacks on Konev's assembly areas.[12] Consequently, though Konev enjoyed substantial numerical advantages over his Axis opponents, his preparations had already been knocked off balance. In addition, the Germans had marshaled strong armored reserves amidst hills and woodlands bolstering defensive positions dug in on relatively narrow divisional frontages. Finally, and most important, the Germans knew that Konev was coming and where he would strike.[13]

At 4:20 a.m. on May 2, 1944, Konev's offensive began with over 1,800 guns and mortars firing for over one hour against German and Romanian defensive positions near Tirgu-Frumos.[14] Nevertheless, dazed survivors of the bombardment slowed the Soviet assault even as it penetrated seven miles into German lines. Savage counterstrokes launched by a Kampfgruppe from Totenkopf played a key role in further blunting the Russian attack.[15] On Grossdeutschland's defensive front, even though the Russians overran Manteuffel's Panzer grenadiers and fusiliers, his 88-mm guns and Panzer regiment took advantage of favorable defensive terrain allowing for generous fields of fire. Mobile German combined-arms teams, well supported by tank-buster aircraft, crushed the Soviet armored penetrations.[16] Even the new IS-2 Stalin tanks had been bested—and not only by firepower but by superior tactics as well. Three IS-2s were lost when otherwise hopelessly outclassed German Panzer IVs had crept up on the hulking Soviet tanks from behind, and destroyed them by firing into the heavy tank's thin rear armor.[17] By the end of the first day, Soviet records show that the 5th Guards Tank Army alone had lost an estimated 180 tanks and assault guns, or half its preassault strength.[18] Konev repeated his assault on May 3 and 4 and again failed. Well-sited teams of Tigers, Panthers, Sturmgeshutze, and anti-aircraft and anti-tank guns ripped his armor apart, though patrolling Soviet Shturmoviks took a toll on the German defenders.[19] Then, from May 5 to May 7, the Germans launched several counterattacks of their own. These inflicted considerable damage on Konev's front, and largely wiped out the minor tactical gains Konev's armies had made in the prior days.[20]

Meanwhile, Stavka had issued a blizzard of orders assigning units and reorganizing existing units so that the 3rd Ukrainian Front was far stronger than it had been in April. With his preparations completed, Malinovsky sought to break out from his bridgeheads across the Dniester River, take Kishinev, and advance 90 to 130 miles southwest to Birlad and Focsani. All of these efforts became moot, however, for in a series of counterstrokes lasting from May 8 to May 30, and as noted by American historian David Glantz, the German 6th Army, relying on well-led and well-structured Kampfgruppen, became the first major Wehrmacht force since 1942 to penetrate and destroy a Soviet bridgehead, actually accomplishing this twice at different points on the front.[21] The German 6th Army delivered defeats on Malinovsky's front so severe as to forestall until August any further Russian offensives in the region.[22] The fighting in April and May 1944 cost the 2nd Ukrainian and 3rd Ukrainian fronts approximately 150,000 casualties. In comparison, the Axis armies suffered 45,000 casualties.[23]

In analyzing the reasons behind the Soviet defeat, the Axis forces had not only known where the Red Army was attacking but also built strong in depth defensive positions. Perhaps most important, the Germans had marshaled mechanized reserves and fought an aggressive mobile combined-arms defense. In contrast, the Soviet armies fought piecemeal, deployed worn-out armies, ineffectively coordinated their combat arms, relied on poorly trained soldiers, and lacked the logistical and communications base to support their ambitious offensives. Finally, the weather, mud, flooding, destroyed regional infrastructure, and favorable defensive terrain also had contributed to Soviet difficulties in organizing and carrying out the assault. These two months in Romania provide a stunning contrast for what was to come in White Russia.

DEEP OPERATIONS IN 1944: WHY THE NUMBERS GAME FAILS TO EXPLAIN THE RED ARMY'S SUCCESS

In 1944 the Red Army had designed its summer offensive around the same overall goals that the previous Soviet frontwide campaigns had sought, namely, to evict German troops from the prewar Soviet borders by applying pressure everywhere to produce a penetration somewhere. The centerpiece in the Soviet summer campaign was code-named Operation Bagration, the second part in a series of offensives scheduled for the summer campaign season. Bagration sought to annihilate Germany's Army Group Center, a task that the Red Army had repeatedly failed to accomplish in preceding months and years.[24] Yet in June 1944, the Red Army held a superb chance to produce and exploit a strategic success against Army Group Center. In large part this was because of the German Army Group's overextended deployment, coupled to a simple but well-thought-out Soviet plan of attack, brilliantly masked in its intent by an enormous deception effort, or *maskirovka*. In particular, the Red Army had reinforced the reorganized Soviet fronts facing Army Group Center with almost everything but the Red Army's powerful tank armies that otherwise all too often gave away aggressive Soviet intentions by their mere presence. In addition, by the summer of 1944, the Red Army finally could meet the immense logistical requirements demanded by deep operations. Furthermore, at the point of contact, Soviet front-level assaults had evolved considerably from the human wave era of 1941–1942, involving the integrated use of partisans and refined uses of indirect weapons so as to rip open select portions of the front rather than pulverize more indiscriminately. Moreover, combined-arms "shock groups" (*udarnyye gruppy*) worked with "delaying groups" (*skovyvayushchiye gruppy*) much more effectively than in years past, holding Axis forces in place and not allowing them to fall back into further defensive lines.[25]

Because the late-war Red Army emphasized firepower and mobility, this meant that the March 1944 *shtat* for a rifle division had fallen to 5,400 men—from 10,566 men in July 1942.[26] Regardless, Soviet riflemen were lavishly supported compared to their 1941–1942 brethren. In 1944, each attacking 100-man rifle company was often assigned two or three tanks or self-propelled guns, two anti-tank guns, two divisional artillery guns, and engineers.[27] In so equipping the assault units, the Soviet front commander could commit the large armored concentrations in a fresh second wave, otherwise known as the "exploitation echelon" (*echelon razvitiya proryva*). To that end, the Red Army had concentrated most of the 2,715 tanks and 1,355 self-propelled guns gathered for Bagration in only eight mechanized or tank corps. In addition, dozens of independent tank and assault gun brigades and regiments also supported the infantry. For further mobility in the marshy and infrastructure-poor Pripet marshes, where much of Army Group Center sat, Stavka had coupled cavalry corps with mechanized units to form two cavalry-mechanized groups (KMGs). These units would play a crucial role in unhinging and defeating German positions during the summer of 1944.[28] In addition, the Red Army also had organized smaller armored elements to range nearly 30 miles from the main armored body. Such units were meant to further deny the German defenders time to respond, and even though aggressive Soviet armored tactics were far from new, in the summer of 1944 seasoned commanders produced better outcomes.

Moreover, to further aid in command and control, by 1944 approximately 80 percent of the T-34/76s had radios installed, making the coordinating of large armored units far easier. In addition, the new T-34/85 had begun equipping frontline units. Equipped with an 85-mm gun firing a standard AP round at a muzzle velocity reaching 899 meters per second, or 2, 950 feet per second, the T-34/85 possessed penetrating power comparable to the Panther. As for its armored protection, the T-34/85 had 75 mm of sloped frontal armor—rather than the sloped 60-mm frontal armor protecting the T-34/76. Finally, a redesigned heavily armored three-man turret reduced some of the inefficiencies characterizing its predecessor's turret. Furthermore, the new 46-ton IS-2 or JS-2 (as the I/JS derivation came from Stalin's name, Iosef/Josef Stalin) had an impressive 160 mm of sloped frontal armor and a 122-mm main gun. Although the IS-2's 122-mm gun produced a muzzle velocity reaching only 747 meters per second, it made up for its comparatively slow muzzle velocity with an enormous 56-pound shell twice as heavy as the 88-mm shell fired by the Tiger. Organizationally, the tank army numbered 620 tanks in 1944, down from 654 tanks in 1943, but each tank army contained substantially more self-propelled guns than before and a greater artillery allotment.[29]

Table 11.1 Changes in Composition of Soviet Tank Corps and Tank Armies during the War[1]

	Tank Corps[2]				Tank Army[3]		
	1942	1943	1944	1945	1943	1944	1945
Tanks	168	208	207	228	500+	600+	700+
Self-propelled Guns	0	49	63	42	25	98+	250
Guns/mortars	30	60	130	150	500+	650+	850+
Personnel	7,000	10,000	12,000	11,788	40,000	48,000	50,000

[1]See William M. Conner, *Analysis of Deep Attack Operations: Operation Bagration, Belorussia 22 June–August 1944* (Combat Studies Institute, 1987), and Roman Johann Jarymowycz, *Tank Tactics from Normandy to Lorraine* (Lynne Rienner Publishers, 2001), 301.
[2]Three tank brigades (in 1944, about65 tanks each).
[3]Two tank corps and sometimes one mechanized corps (in 1944, the standard Soviet Mechanized corps included 16,442 men, 183 tanks, 63 self-propelled guns, and 234 guns/mortars).

As the Red Army continued to reorganize and reequip its combat formations, planning for Bagration evolved. In short, instead of doing the obvious and striking at Army Group Center's flanks, the Red Army prepared to rip apart Army Group Center by attacking the face of the salient that it held, and then surround its component armies.[30] Bagration's northern wing featured the 1st Baltic Front, led by Bagramyan, and 3rd Belorussian Front, led by Chernyakhovskii, initially set to attack northwest and southwest of Vitebsk, encircle the city, and destroy its German defenders. Marshal Vasilevsky coordinated these two fronts' operations. The 1st Baltic Front fielded 359,500 men; 561 tanks; 126 assault guns; nearly 5,000 guns, mortars, and *katyushas*; and 902 aircraft—and could count on 19,537 trucks for providing crucial mobility.[31] The 3rd Belorussian Front's attack was split into two components and, minus the attached 5th Guards Tank Army, the only tank army initially assigned to Bagration, deployed 579,300 men; 1,169 tanks; 641 assault guns; over 6,500 guns, mortars, and *katyushas*; 1,864 aircraft; and 16,208 trucks.[32]

Farther south, Marshal Zhukov held overall command over the 2nd Belorussian Front, under Zakharov, and Rokossovsky's 1st Belorussian Front. Zhukov and Rokossovsky centered the 1st Belorussian Front's main attack near Bobruisk.[33] On the 1st Belorussian Front's southern wing, the German 2nd Army would be pinned in place.[34] The massive 1st Belorussian Front put 1,071,000 men into the field in late June 1944. The potent northern wing of the front featured the bulk of its heavy firepower—883 tanks; 414 assault guns; approximately 8,500 guns, mortars, and *katyushas*; 2,033 aircraft; and 17,177 trucks—to help move its masses of men and munitions. The 2nd Belorussian Front's attack featured the Soviet 49th Army's planned drive to take Mogilev and follow up by driving on to the Berezina River. At the same time, the front's 33rd and 50th Armies held the German defenders in place.

To accomplish its goals, the 2nd Belorussian Front fielded 319,500 men; 102 tanks; 174 assault guns; approximately 4,000 guns, mortars, and *katyushas*; and 528 aircraft.[35] Stavka also assembled extensive reserves to back up these powerful fronts. In addition, the 2nd Baltic Front would seek to pin down German Army Group North. All told, the Red Army had gathered one-third of its striking power for Bagration: 2,331,700 men. In comparison, Army Group Center could put 792,196 men into the field. Still, the force concentrations on the six actual axes of attack would tilt even far more in Soviet favor.[36]

Bagration's design incorporated everything that the Red Army had learned to date at such great expense. Although the constant post-Kursk retreats had hollowed out the German eastern armies, the huge Red Army had failed to inflict on the Wehrmacht the series of catastrophic defeats that the Axis had inflicted on it during 1941–1942. Instead, the Wehrmacht remained within the Soviet Union's prewar borders. Moreover, the Red Army continued to suffer prodigious battlefield losses,[37] in many ways alleviated in large part because of territorial gains. For instance, the 2nd Ukrainian Front received 265,000 men from recently recaptured territories between March and May 1944. During this period, the 3rd Ukrainian Front was able to round up 79,000 men as well.[38]

Given the Red Army's reliance on western movement to help replenish its ranks, if Germany could bottle up the Normandy beachhead, then the Red Army would face a real problem. It would face a reinforced and geographically blessed German army growing more powerful as the front narrowed and the defensive terrain improved. Vast forests filled the northern sector of the front. Great north- and south-running rivers flowed from the heavily forested, wet, and underdeveloped Pripet marshes in the center of the front. To the south, additional north-to-south–running rivers were backed by the Carpathians and Transylvanian Mountains, and the rugged Balkans guarded the southern approaches to the greater Reich. Merely pushing the German army west would not suffice; given the potential for German units to fall back and fortify the stout defensive terrain.

For their part, the decisions made by Hitler and the OKH (Oberkommando der Heer, or Army High Command) in deploying Germany's eastern army groups against the anticipated Soviet summer campaign were influenced by a number of elements. First, even before D-Day, the threat of the Allied invasion and the fighting in Italy had forced Hitler to leave Germany's June 1944 Eastern Front 30 divisions short of its previous year's strength.[39] In addition, when in late June 1944 German army intelligence identified the Soviet tank armies as opposite Army Groups North Ukraine and South Ukraine, the inference was that the next Soviet blow would come between the Dniester and Pripet Rivers near Lvov. Thus, in Hitler's and the OKH's eyes, to the extent that Army Group Center was vulnerable, it would be from Army Group North Ukraine's positions, an impression reinforced not only by the location of the Soviet tank armies but also because the fighting during early 1944 had left Army Group Center's southern front projecting east as part of the salient that it held jutting into Belorussia. Therefore, south of the Pripet marshes, the OKH assembled the strongest armored reserves the German army had mustered since Kursk; 24 of the 30 Panzer and Panzer Grenadier Divisions on the German Eastern Front in June 1944.

Despite German armored dispositions, Army Group Center had not been ignored. During May 1944, the German Replacement Army had sent to Army Group Center 80,000 men, of the 226,000 men ordered to Germany's four eastern army groups that month, a move that brought the majority of Army Group Center's infantry divisions up to near full strength.[40] Furthermore, in June 1944, Army Group Center held the key road and rail junctions controlling movement through the Pripet marshes; running from north to south the cities of Vitebsk, Orsha, Mogilev, and Bobruisk. Moreover, it had done so for some time against major Soviet efforts that had been launched throughout the winter of 1943–1944.[41] Given that these four cities were heavily fortified, and blocked road-bound movement through what they believed to be the otherwise impassable Pripet marshes (at least for mechanized armies), the OKH and Hitler reasoned that a defense based on these cities would prove just as adequate as it had in past months.[42]

Despite the OKH's intelligence assessment, and in spite of Soviet deception efforts, enough intelligence information trickled through to Field Marshal Busch, Army Group Center's commander, for him to realize prior to Bagration that the Red Army had prepared a significant offensive directed at his command. In addition, on the night of June 19, some 140,000 partisans attacked German rail lines linking important cities such as Brest, Minsk, Orsha, Pinsk, and Polotsk, moves further indicative of an impending major offensive.[43]

Thus, many German officers following the war have argued that if Hitler had entrusted any flexibility to Army Group Center's forewarned leadership, particularly in retreating a certain distance just before Bagration began, then Army Group Center would have been saved. Nonetheless, this argument is a weak one from a contextual perspective if for no other reason than the precedent provided by the 1943–1944 German defensive successes in Army Group Center's area of operations. In addition, Army Group Center, running from north to south as follows: the 3rd Panzer Army, the 4th Army, the 9th Army, and the 2nd Army, included nearly one-third more men than the next largest German Army Group.[44] On the other hand, the Army Group's strongest armored units, the 25th Panzer Grenadier Division and the 501st Heavy Panzer Battalion, could field only 45 assault guns and 10 self-propelled 88-mm guns and 29 Tiger tanks, respectively.[45] The presence or absence of strong armored reserves was perhaps the crucial determinant underlying the outcome of major operations on Germany's Eastern Front. Thus, the simplest preventive course for bolstering Army Group Center that could have been taken, again within the context of the day, would have been for the OKH and Hitler to have granted Army Group Center even a few more Panzer divisions. Nevertheless, given the OKH's intelligence assessment expecting an attack on Army Group North Ukraine, Busch's command would have to fight with what little armor it had in late June 1944.

BAGRATION: HITLER'S GREATEST DEFEAT

On June 22 at 5:00 a.m., after a brief 16-minute artillery bombardment, the initial assault battalions from Bagramyan's 1st Baltic Front closed with and penetrated the 3rd Panzer Army's forward positions.[46] The attack's nature, without the usual overwhelming and heavy initial assault, played into Russian hands as the OKH dithered over whether these attacks presaged an important Soviet thrust even as Bagration began in earnest.

North of Vitebsk, the 1st Baltic Front's heavily reinforced, well-equipped, 100,000 man combined-arms 6th Guard Army, under General I. M. Chistyakov,[47] rolled over the 3rd Panzer Army's defenses and moved south to encircle Vitebsk. Meanwhile, the attached 1st Tank Corps, deploying 195 T34/85 tanks and 42 assault guns, zipped through the yawing gaps blown in the German 9th Corps' defenses and headed west.[48] The OKH reacted by ordering the 24th Infantry Division and the 909th Assault Gun Brigade to move south from Army Group North's 16th Army.[49] Hitler rejected Busch's request to pull back, believing that the region's poor road network and German defensive efforts would prove sufficient for thwarting the Soviet offensive.[50] Nonetheless, by June 24, a gap more than 10 miles wide had opened in the German defenses, and 35,000 German soldiers had been surrounded in Vitebsk. Events for the Germans spiraled rapidly downhill from there. The OKH only belatedly ordered the 5th Panzer Division to move north from Army Group North Ukraine, a decision indicative of the abandonment of the principles and doctrine that had previously made the German army so effective. Only several Panzer divisions acting in concert would have been capable of possibly stabilizing the battered 3rd Panzer Army.[51] By June 25, Busch had committed his entire reserve, and still the 3rd Panzer Army was being eviscerated. On June 27, the Vitebsk pocket collapsed. Meanwhile, just south of Vitebsk, another disaster engulfed Army Group Center.

The 3rd Belorussian Front's 39th Army and armor-heavy 5th Army, under General N. I. Krylov, had followed a crushing, nearly two-and-a-half-hour artillery bombardment, supplemented with heavy raids from the Soviet 1st Air Army, by punching through the German 4th Army and moving north to meet the 43rd Army and complete the Vitebsk encirclement. Meanwhile, General N. S. Oslikovskiy's horse-mechanized group—the 3rd Guards

BAGRATION

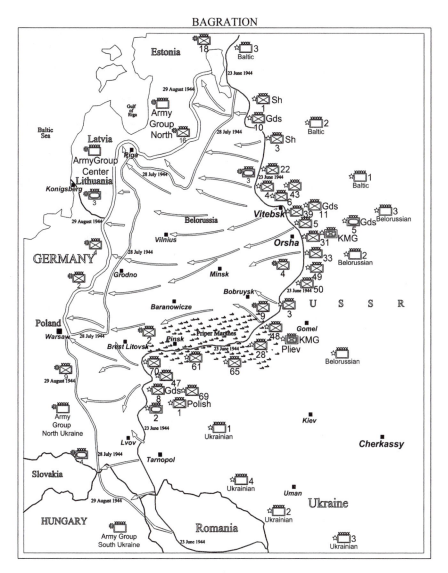

Cavalry Corps and the 3rd Guards Mechanized Corps—raced west deep behind German lines toward Minsk. The 3rd Belorussian Front's southern two armies—the 11th Guards Army and the 31st Army—had also moved south to surround Orsha. All this had occurred despite the fact General Pfeiffer's 6th Corps held down one of Army Group Center's strongest defensive fronts, with three of its four infantry divisions at or near full strength and supported by two assault gun brigades. Nevertheless, Pfeiffer lacked mobile reserves, and the Soviet forces, led by Oslikovskiy's group, poured west through a massive 18-mile-wide gap between the German 6th and 9th Corps, unhinging the 4th Army's defensive front from the 3rd Panzer Army to its north. Then, late in the day on June 25, the 524 tanks and assault guns of the 5th Guards Tank Army added their weight to the attack. Only after having traversed 180 miles between June 22 and July 4 did the 3rd Belorussian Front's spearheads finally run out of steam when they ran into a German defensive line thrown up at the Vilnya River.

Although the 3rd Belorussian Front achieved spectacular success during Bagration, not all had gone according to plan. On June 22, both of the 3rd Belorussian Front's southern armies—the 11th Guards Army under General Galitskiy and the 31st Army under General V. V. Glagolev—had attacked the 78th Assault and 256th Infantry Divisions of General Volker's 27th Corps. Both of the Soviet armies were stopped within the main German defensive lines. The fact that no major breakthrough occurred was on its face shocking given the vast preponderance of Soviet firepower over the German defenders.

For example, the 11th Guards Army put three assault gun regiments, four tank regiments, a tank brigade, and the imposing 2nd Guards Tank Corps' 250 tanks and assault guns into the field.[52] Volcker's 22nd Corps, from the German 4th Army, deployed the strong 260th Infantry Division, the mobile 25th Panzer Grenadier Division, and the potent 78th Assault Division. The latter was a specially reinforced quasi-elite infantry division allotted an over-abundance of heavy weapons (including assault guns) and men. In addition to these veteran formations, Volcker could also rely on support from the Tiger tanks of the 501st Heavy Tank Battalion. In response to the armor-aided German defensive effort, however, Vasilevsky had smoothly and simply rerouted the 3rd Belorussian Front's powerful armored reserves. This flexibility—coupled with the relentless nature of the Soviet attacks, even in the face of heavy casualties and armored losses (the 22nd Corps claimed 116 destroyed Soviet tanks in just three days)—set the stage for a German defeat made inevitable by Hitler's June 24 denial of General Tippelskirch's request to withdraw his still intact 4th Army.[53] For his part, Hitler reasonably believed that there was hardly a chance that his barely mobile infantry-heavy divisions could successfully withdraw without being cut down in the open. But without armored reserves to back them, staying in place meant that their chances for survival proved nonexistent. Thus, Orsha fell on June 27, and German defensive efforts found only sporadic success, such as the 5th Panzer Division's ferocious several-day-long defensive battle against the 5th Guards Tank Army on the road to Minsk.[54] Regardless, by July 3 to July 4, Minsk had been completely surrounded. In addition, the bulk of the 4th Army was trapped on the wrong side of the Berezina River.

While the 1st Baltic and 3rd Belorussian fronts carved up the German defenses east of Mogilev, on June 22 Zakharov's 2nd Belorussian Front's 33rd,

49th, and 50th Armies had met stout resistance. The German 4th Army's combat-seasoned 39th Panzer Corps under General Martinek fielded four veteran infantry divisions. In addition, it had the direct support of the 185th Assault Gun Brigade and the Feldherrnhalle Panzer Grenadier Division from the army general headquarters. Nevertheless, Zakharov's ability to pin down Martinek's command prevented it from posing a threat to the other Soviet fronts to the north or south. As it was, it took the 2nd Belorussian Front's three full armies three bloody days to smash open the 39th Panzer Corps' defensive front, a testament to the effort of the veteran German infantry, but also to the presence of even minimal German armor support. On June 28, Mogilev fell. Only in the first days of July and after the arrival of German reserves did the 2nd Belorussian Front's advance slow to a crawl.[55]

Meanwhile, on June 22 and east of Bobruysk, General Rokossovsky's massive 1st Belorussian Front crushed General Jordan's German 9th Army. On June 23, Rokossovsky's three main assault armies—the 3rd, 48th, and 65th—breached the German defenses. The Soviet 3rd Army then struck north to encircle Mogilev from the south, while the 9th Tank Corps pushed deeper to threaten Bobruysk. South of Bobruysk, the Soviet 28th and 65th Armies ran over General Weidling's thinly spread 41st Corps.[56] Pliev's fast-moving horse-mechanized group, the 4th Guards Cavalry Corps and the 1st Mechanized Corps, drove deep behind German lines to the west. At the same time, the Soviet 1st Guards Tank Corps moved northward to encircle Bobruysk and then drive on Minsk.[57] A critical moment when it may have been possible to save the bulk of 9th Army occurred late on June 25 when Jordan argued for a pullback. But his request was rejected by Hitler, the OKH, and Busch, with the German command again deluding themselves in thinking that the Red Army, even though it deployed ample numbers of Lend-Lease–supplied four-wheel trucks, could not maintain mobility and supply while moving through the marshes.

On June 28, Hitler sacked Busch and replaced him with Field Marshal Model. In addition, Hitler, the OKW (Oberkommando der Wehrmacht, or High Command of the Armed Forces), and the OKH sought to bring relief to Army Group Center's disintegrating order of battle by grabbing divisions from wherever they could and throwing them into the gaping hole blown in the Ostheer's front. From Italy, they requisitioned the Fallshirm-Panzer Grenadier Division Hermann Göring. Two infantry divisions were taken from Norway and the Balkans. In Romania, Army Group South Ukraine gave up the 3rd SS Panzer Division Totenkopf and Grossdeutschland. From Army Group North Ukraine came the 4th Panzer Division, 5th Panzer Division, 7th Panzer Division, 5th SS Panzer Division Wiking, and five infantry divisions. Army Group North gave up the 12th Panzer Division and three infantry divisions. Finally, the Reserve Army sent the 6th Panzer Division, 19th Panzer Division, 25th Panzer Division, 6th Infantry Division, and promised

10 new Volksgrenadier divisions.[58] Had even a quarter of this significant assembly of men and machines been made available to Army Group Center one week earlier, or if it were allowed to assemble together behind German lines and then committed en masse, who knows what would have subsequently happened. Instead, reinforcing divisions were committed to battle in isolation, thus often simply swallowed up by the fast-moving Soviet armies. In addition, those divisions that began arriving in early July were not allowed to wait until their component parts were fully assembled. Great distances traveled meant that transportation issues frequently found Panzer grenadier battalions or Panzer battalions arriving isolated; without the supporting arms that had made the combined-arms Panzer division such an effective weapon. Soviet air and partisan attacks further upset German deployment timetables. Most important, the piecemeal reinforcements could hardly alter the reality that Army Group Center was being liquidated.

From the four initial fortress towns that Hitler had ordered held along Army Group Center's front, by June 29 all had fallen to Soviet armies pouring through the great holes rent in the German lines.[59] The German lack of mobility meant that for much the same reasons that the early war German armies had found success, so too did the Red Army during Bagration. The Soviet fronts had ripped a hole in the German Eastern Front some 200 miles in breadth. Moreover, it had done so while at times fighting in horrible weather, moving a mechanized armored spearhead across swollen rivers, sodden marshes, and massive swamps, all accomplished against a veteran German Army Group of considerable size occupying prime defensive terrain. Overall, Army Group Center lost 350,000 men captured or killed, including 31 of 47 German generals involved in the fighting, and thus the majority of those in 3rd Panzer Division and the 4th and 9th Armies.[60] The German 9th Army, once one of Germany's strongest, had been annihilated. Only 10,000 to 15,000 of its men survived the slaughter.[61] The Red Army had obliterated 28 Axis divisions in a disaster for the German army dwarfing Stalingrad, the surrender in North Africa, or the casualties incurred before Moscow in December 1941.

In comparison, though the Red Army's losses had been manageable during Bagration's initial weeks, they had suffered especially tremendous losses in men and material after German reserves had arrived in the region. For example, the 5th Guards Tank Army began Bagration with a line strength of 524 tanks and assault guns. As late at July 5, and the 5th Guards could still put 307 tanks and assault guns into the field. By July 16, however, following the arrival of German reserves, the once formidable 5th Guards Tank Army could only field 50 tanks.[62] In addition, between June and August 1944, the primary Soviet armies involved in Bagration suffered 770,999 casualties and lost 2,957 tanks, 2,447 artillery pieces, and 822 aircraft. In comparison, the Americans and British suffered 30,000 dead during the June–July Normandy fighting.[63]

ARMY GROUP NORTH UKRAINE PAYS A STEEP PRICE FOR BAGRATION'S SUCCESS

On July 13, the Red Army dealt another massive blow to the German eastern armies but this time against Colonel-General Harpe's Army Group North Ukraine. Harpe's command comprised, running north to south, the 4th Panzer Army, the 1st Panzer Army, and, subordinated to the 1st Panzer Army, the 1st Hungarian Army. Situated just south of the defensive positions formerly held by Army Group Center's 2nd Army, Harpe's men defended most of Galicia from the Pripet marshes south to the Carpathian Mountains. Despite featuring two Panzer armies, Harpe's Army Group did not represent the armored juggernaut it had three weeks prior. In large part, this was because the OKH and Hitler had scattered the Panzer divisions in piecemeal efforts to belatedly help the doomed Army Group Center. That said, Harpe's men were ensconced in well-prepared defensive positions, bolstered by the wealth of natural defensive barriers in the region. In addition, Harpe still had 34 infantry divisions, four Panzer divisions, and one Panzer grenadier division, with approximately 500 armored fighting vehicles (AFVs) between them.[64] Harpe could also ostensibly count on the 2nd Hungarian Panzer Division and 14th Waffen-SS Grenadier Division, though both formations were ill equipped for their grandiose titles, while the 14th-SS was comprised primarily of poorly trained Ukrainian volunteers.[65]

Meanwhile, Konev prepared to strike Army Group North Ukraine with 1,200,000 men, 2,200 tank and self-propelled guns, 14,000 guns and mortars, and 2,806 aircraft; all assembled for what the Red Army termed the Lvov-Sandomierz Strategic Offensive Operations. To meet his objectives Konev created two main axes of advance separated by approximately 45 miles. The 1st Guards Tank Army spearheaded the offensive's northern wing, launched from west of Lutsk, supported by the 3rd Guards Army and 13th Rifle Army and one cavalry mechanized group. The southern wing comprised two rifle armies (the 60th and the 38th) and two tank armies (the 3rd Guards and the 4th), and had orders to attack toward Lvov from just north of Ternopol.[66] Despite German knowledge regarding where the attack was coming, Konev manipulated both the timing of the Soviet offensive and the weight of each assault. Overall, his thorough deception effort effectively threw off German expectations regarding where the main weight of the offensive would fall. Thus, when on July 13 the northern wing of Konev's assault began, it quickly found success.

Nevertheless, farther south and for two full days, Konev's front, the most powerful in the Red Army,[67] was stymied by the Germans in a vicious and unrelenting battle. In response and shifting his effort farther south, on July 15 Konev forced his way through the German 349th Infantry Division but on a frontage so narrow, roughly two miles in width, that his breakthrough forces were pasted by German artillery. Nonetheless, a German counterattack that was supposed to have been led by the 1st and 8th Panzer Divisions working jointly was instead conducted primarily by the 1st Panzer Division. The 8th Panzer Division had taken the wrong route while under constant air attack, and could not effectively support the 1st Panzer's attack. Then, on July 19, what the Germans initially had thought was a Soviet tank corps proved to be Lieutenant General Pavel Rybalko's entire 3rd Guards Tank Army punching through the two- to three-mile hole in the German lines. In the meantime, on Konev's northern wing, his exploitation forces had negotiated a breach in the German lines made by the Soviet 13th Army. Konev's northern and southern armored spearheads then encircled a large pocket of German troops west of Brody, and parried fierce German counterattacks designed to break through to the pocket. Konev's front finally destroyed the pocket on July 22, capturing or killing over 40,000 German soldiers. Having split Army Group North Ukraine in two,[68] Konev's men, led by the 1st Tank Army and the 13th Army, forged bridgeheads across the Vistula River at Baranov.[69] Konev had also taken the key communications center of Lvov; supported by the Polish Home Army, with some 3,000 of its men. They were rewarded for their efforts in typical Soviet fashion. The NKVD (People's Commissariat for Internal Affairs) arrested the Polish officers, and sent the men to replenish the Red Army's ranks.[70]

In revisiting whether Hitler and the OKH could have acted differently to spare Army Group Center's and Army Group North Ukraine's resounding defeat, there is one point that often is not made but must be. The Red Army, in terms of using deception, structuring available military assets to emphasize mobility and concentrated firepower, backing up those assets with adequate logistical support, and exercising flexibility and aggressiveness in leadership, had created a situation so that once Bagration started, it would have been hard for the German army to avoid some kind of defeat. Then, in moving on to the "what-if" game of German mistakes, what was perhaps most surprising was in how much the OKH and Hitler went all in on the bet that the Red Army would mirror the OKH's and Hitler's errors one year before—when they had obligingly attacked Kursk in an entirely obvious manner. That said once Bagration began, had the Germans decided to pull up several Panzer divisions at once from Army Group North Ukraine, then these divisions acting in concert may have been able to mitigate Army Group Center's losses. This latter point was proven when German armored reserves had finally arrived to assist a devastated Army Group Center and stiffened German defenses enough to force the Red Army into spending two costly months advancing a distance roughly equivalent to that previously covered in Bagration's first two weeks.

For instance, in late July 1944, the fast-moving 1st Belorussian Front's offensive had run into a roadblock formed by intense German counterattacks delivered by five half-strength German Panzer divisions that nevertheless, when combined, proved formidable opponents. In this fighting, the

Parachute-Panzer Division Herman Göring, the SS Panzer Division's Totenkopf and Wiking, and the 4th and 19th Panzer Divisions decimated two of the three tank corps making up the Soviet 2nd Tank Army and capped what had been an already expensive Soviet campaign.[71] During August 1944 alone, the 1st Belorussian Front lost 114,400 men and received only 69,215 replacements, with the worst of these losses incurred against the fierce German resistance to Warsaw's east and southeast. These battles—lasting from July through October 1944 and fought, most notably, between the Panzer divisions listed above and the Soviet 2nd Tank Army (but also including other formations from both the German 2nd and the German 9th Armies) and between the 4th Panzer Army and the 1st Belorussian Front and armies from the 1st Ukrainian Front— are worth a longer look. Not only in terms of their role in setting up the 1945 Soviet drive on Berlin, but with the battles fought near Warsaw further illuminating the points driving this larger study, including the following:

A. The German army's dangerous prowess at the tactical and operational level even late in 1944
B. The continued importance that massed mobile armor heavy units played in determining success or defeat in eastern Europe, including the importance that mobile reserves played in general
C. Why qualitative factors continued to outweigh the quantitative in leading to victory on World War II's battlefields
D. The growing importance "Allied" army's played in fleshing out the Red Army's increasingly firepower-heavy, but rifleman-sparse, frontline ranks during the war's final years

The tense battles that would rage outside of Warsaw had been set up by the advance of both Rokossovsky's 1st Belorussian Front's drive west and Konev's 1st Ukrainian Front's drive from farther south. In opposition and situated just east of the Bug River on July 18 sat the German 2nd Army under General Weiss. To its immediate south and just east of the Bug River stood the 8th Corps and the 56th Panzer Corps of Army Group North Ukraine's 4th Panzer Army. The 1st Belorussian Front was the primary opponent of these two German armies, with its northern wing comprised of five rifle armies in direct opposition to the German 2nd Army. The 1st Belorussian Front's southern wing featured, running north to south, the 47th Army, 8th Guards Army, 69th Army, and 7th Guards Cavalry Corps in line with the 2nd Guards Cavalry Corps, 2nd Tank Army, 11th Tank Corps, and 1st Polish Army ready to exploit any breakthroughs amply backed by further mobile reserves. These Soviet armies stood against the 4th Panzer Army's 8th and 56th Corps, which also had to contend with the 1st Ukrainian Front's 3rd Guards Army.[72] The forces assembled on the 1st Belorussian Front's left, or southern, wing totaled 416,000 men; 8,355 artillery pieces, mortars, and rockets; 1,748 AFVs; and the 1,465 combat aircraft in the Soviet 6th Air Army.

The offensive began on July 18, crushing the 4th Panzer Army's left flank as the 1st Belorussian Front completed its linkage with the 1st Ukrainian Front's right flank. This left the German 2nd Army to face the brunt of Rokossovsky's efforts.[73] At this point, however, Stalin intervened and ordered Lublin taken so that Stalin could put Moscow's stamp on Poland's political future. As the Polish Home Army and 2nd Tank Army took Lublin, Konev's 3rd Guards Army and Rokossovsky's men finished destroying the 4th Panzer Army's left flank, sending the survivors scrambling west across the Vistula. Meanwhile, the re-forming German 9th Army, under General Vormann, attempted to fashion a semblance of a defensive front, led by the recently arrived Fallshirm-Panzer Grenadier Division Hermann Göring and its 63 AFVs.[74] At that point, Stavka ordered Rokossovsky to direct his efforts farther west toward Warsaw's suburb of Praga, east of the Vistula, and assist the 2nd Belorussian Front's efforts northeast of Warsaw near the Narew River. Zhukov desperately wanted bridgeheads across the Vistula and Narew Rivers, bracketing Warsaw from the east and the north, as the jumping-off points for the next great campaign.[75]

The weary 2nd Tank Army comprised mostly of the 3rd Tank Corps, 8th Guards Tank Corps, and 16th Tank Corps—spearheaded Rokossovsky's efforts along the Vistula. The fighting between July 18 and July 27 in particular had been costly, having left the 2nd Tank Army left with roughly 586 AFVs on July 27, including 103 Lend-Lease M4A2 Sherman and Mark IV "Valentine" tanks, from the 810 AFVs with which it had begun the offensive.[76] For the Germans, the 39th Panzer Corps, under Lieutenant General Dietrich von Saucken, which initially contained the 70-AFV 19th Panzer Division and the Fallshirm-Panzer Grenadier Division Hermann Göring, moved up as the 3rd SS Panzer Division Totenkopf and 5th SS Panzer Division Wiking fell back from the east. In addition, the 4th Panzer Division redeployed from the northeast with some 78 AFVs in running order. Perhaps as important for the Germans as the gathering concentration of Panzer divisions was the proximity of the nearby 6th Luftflotte. Moreover, the Luftwaffe also redeployed strong anti-aircraft batteries from Warsaw to the front south and east of the city, further bolstering the German infantry in the region.[77]

By July 29, the 8th Guards Tank Corps had closed to within 15 miles of Praga. But German Panzers and the Luftwaffe relentlessly hammered at Rokossovsky's spearhead. Meanwhile, Chuikov's elite 8th Guards Army energetically expanded its bridgehead across the Vistula south of Warsaw.[78] Nevertheless, on August 1, counterattacks launched by the 19th Panzer Division and the Hermann-Göring Panzer Division finally penetrated the 2nd Tank Army's defensive front. They were joined shortly thereafter by elements from the 3rd and 5th SS Panzer Divisions attacking from the east. This cut off the 3rd Tank Corps from the rest of the 2nd Tank Army even as the 8th Guards Tank Corps slammed into the two SS Panzer Divisions from

Table 11.2 German Late-War Panzer/Waffen-SS Panzer Division versus Soviet Tank/Mechanized Corps

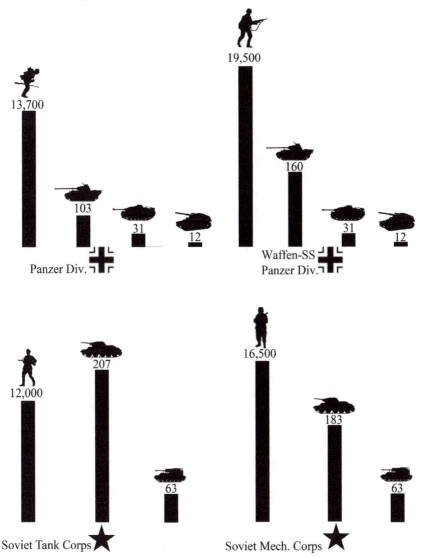

[1]William M. Conner, *Analysis of Deep Attack Operations: Operation Bagration Belorussia 22 June–August 1944* (Combat Studies Institute, 1987); Roman Johann Jarymowycz, *Tank Tactics from Normandy to Lorraine* (Lynne Rienner Publishers, 2001), 301; Keith E. Bonn, ed., *Slaughterhouse: The Handbook of the Eastern Front* (The Aberjona Press, 2005), 392–93, 428, 430.

the south. On August 2, the 4th Panzer Division joined the battle. German attacks on subsequent days finished the decimation of the 2nd Tank Army. Losses on both sides had been heavy.[79]

Although there is some debate as to Soviet losses, the consensus appears to be that the 2nd Tank Army lost approximately 340 AFVs between July 29 and August 6 and a total of 470 AFVs between July 18 and August 6. As for the Germans, they fared better, control over the battlefield allowed the Hermann-Göring Division to report 51 operational tanks on August 6, only 12 fewer than one week earlier. Totenkopf and Wiking reported 56 and 45 tanks in running order respectively, representing roughly one-quarter fewer than their total "runners" from a week earlier.[80] The marshaling of German armored reserves and their employment in coherently planned counterthrusts had therefore cost the Red Army dearly. As it was, of the 2,331,000 men employed by the Red Army from June to July against Army Groups Center and North Ukraine, 178,507 were dead or missing and 587,308 wounded. In addition, the Red Army lost 4,226 tanks and self-propelled guns against the two German Army Groups.[81]

In the meantime, one of World War II's great tragedies unfolded in Warsaw. On August 1, the long-suffering residents of the Polish capital, sensing liberation at hand and led by Polish Brigadier General Bor-Komorowski, rose up against the genocidal German occupation forces.[82] Stalin, having had already presided over the mass murder of 20,000 Poles captured in 1939, and responsible for, along with Beria's brutal NKVD, a record of atrocities playing second fiddle only to Himmler's SS,[83] regarded extending aid to Polish Nationalists as against his own interests. Hitler and Himmler sent in the SS to brutally slaughter everyone in Warsaw and level the once great city. The Poles bravely fought for their survival against SS, police, and other security forces ranking among the war's most despicable criminals. For instance, the SS "Dirlewanger" Division, named after its commander, was filled with convicts on probation. SS Oberfuhrer Bronislav Kaminski's RONA Sturmbrigade also consisted of criminals looking forward to murdering, raping, and looting without abandon.[84] In addition, the German 9th Army's headquarters also committed frontline combat troops, pioneers, and artillery to join the slaughter.[85] Nonetheless, only on October 5 did Komorowski's remaining 17,000 fighters surrender. Estimates regarding the toll in human life vary, but most find that the Germans murdered approximately 180,000 to 250,000 civilians, with an additional 10,000 to 16,000 Polish freedom fighters killed.[86] According to some estimates, the Germans lost 19,000 dead of their own; others hold that as few as 2,000 Germans were killed.[87]

Meanwhile, outside Warsaw, on August 10 Rokossovsky had resumed his attempts to destroy German forces east of the Vistula, especially the 4th SS Panzer Corps, led by the 3rd SS Panzer Division and 5th SS Panzer Division. Although the Soviet assault units enjoyed increasingly effective close air support from waves of Shturmoviks, devastating German artillery positions in particular, the advance had devolved into a brutal slow grind against fanatical resistance.[88] The 4th SS Panzer Corps claimed the destruction of 249 Soviet tanks and self-propelled guns between August 18 and August 22 alone.[89] Then at 10:00 a.m. on September 10 and beginning with a crushing hour-and-a-half artillery barrage, Rokossovsky again sent in the 47th and 70th Armies as well as the 8th Guards Tank Corps and 1st Polish Army against the 4th SS Panzer Corps. Although the initial Russian efforts were met with heavy resistance, Praga fell on September 15. Major General Zygmunt Berling's 1st Polish Army desperately attempted to help their countrymen in Warsaw, but, lacking in critical logistical support, his men failed to make a difference and lost 1,987 dead or missing and 289 wounded.[90]

Then, in October, and after yet another failed offensive against the 4th SS Panzer Corps, Rokossovsky used deception where brute force had failed in the past. He fooled the German command into pulling forces from 4th SS Panzer Corps' area of operations. This finally allowed the Russian 47th Army to force the SS back. The front along the Vistula finally calmed down early in November. Casualties on both sides had been immense. Between August 1 and August 15 alone, the 1st Belorussian Front endured 166,808 casualties. During the same time, the German 2nd and 9th Armies suffered 91,595 casualties.[91] Nothing in this accounting of death and destruction during the several months of battles outside and inside Warsaw is indicative of anything that the Germans could term a victory. Nevertheless, the length of the struggle, and the casualty tolls represented a very different outcome than that created by Bagration's initial weeks; highlighting once again the role that mobile combined-arms teams had played in determining the cost of military success.

As the struggle in Poland had raged on into the fall of 1944, to the south the Slovakians had also attempted a late-summer uprising that, although receiving Soviet support, saw Himmler's SS lead another furious and homicidal response. The Germans left a gruesome wake of mass graves and burned-out villages behind, and many local residents were either murdered outright or shipped off to concentration camps. Meanwhile, the newly formed 4th Ukrainian Front, under Petrov, led the Red Army's march into Slovakia. Army Group North Ukraine's disintegration as a cohesive formation had meant that, while the 4th Panzer Army was pushed over the Vistula, the 1st Panzer Army and 1st Hungarian Army, fighting together under the title of PanzerArmeeoberkommando 1, had spent late July into early August being forced into the Carpathian foothills.[92] On September 7, the 1st Guards Army attacked the 1st Panzer Army in an effort to wrest the Dukla Pass, a key crossing through the mountains, from the Germans. Relying heavily on the favorable defensive terrain, the 1st Panzer Army dueled with the Soviet armies in a constantly flowing battle that saw the Germans temporarily encircle the Soviet 38th Army's 1st Guards Cavalry Corps. In turn, Soviet forces not only escaped the trap on September 24, but also took the Dukla Pass on

October 6. Despite this victory, the 4th Ukrainian Front had lost 442 tanks in the fighting that had lasted from late summer to early fall, and, what's more had suffered such losses even though it, and its supporting forces, had out-numbered the Germans at least four to one in men and heavy weapons.[93] The 4th Ukrainian Front had also suffered over 80,000 casualties,[94] while Konev's 1st Ukrainian Front lost 62,014 killed and wounded in just over a month and a half of desperate fighting in and along the Slovakian moun-tains.[95] Meanwhile, having largely held in the Carpathians, far to the southeast and in the Balkans the German army had suffered yet another epic defeat.

FIGHTING ON THE PERIPHERY: THE RED ARMY IN THE BALKANS AND AT EAST PRUSSIA'S BORDERS

On August 20, 1944, the seemingly indefatigable Red Army turned its atten-tion once again to crushing Army Group South Ukraine. Commanded by Colonel-General Friessner, Army Group South Ukraine comprised over 600,000 soldiers: 24 German divisions, assorted independent units, and Romanian troops, all equipped with 400 tanks and 800 aircraft and deployed across a 350-mile front line, with numerous rivers providing solid defensive barriers. Nevertheless, Army Group South Ukraine had lost its best divisions during June and July, those sent farther north by the OKH and fed into the meat grinder in Poland and Belarus. Moreover, the best defensive positions for Army Group South Ukraine sat in the foreboding Carpathian Mountains and Transylvania, far behind the main Axis positions. From a military perspective, a decision to withdraw and fortify Transylvania and the Carpathians could have allowed the Germans to bog down the Red Army in regions ranking among Europe's wildest. Thus, this would have allowed the Axis to employ as a force multiplier the superb defensive terrain across the Balkans and eastern and cen-tral Europe, channeling the Red Army into narrow offensive fronts with poten-tially dire consequences for Stalin's plans to pour into central Europe. Regardless, and for obvious political reasons, the German armies in Romania would not reset defensively.

The Soviet 2nd and 3rd Ukrainian fronts, led by Malinovsky and Tolbukhin, respectively, carried out the Soviet drive into the Balkans. In contrast to the debacles of the spring, each army was well equipped, possessed ample logistical backing, and was rested. The 2nd Ukrainian Front deployed 11,000 guns and mortars, 1,283 tanks and self-propelled guns, and 900 aircraft. The 3rd Ukrainian put 8,000 guns, 600 tanks, and 1,000 aircraft into the field. Although each front enjoyed superb leadership, the men filling out these fronts included poorly trained forced conscripts, men provided by the Red Army's sweep through the western Ukraine. These sweeps had netted 345,000 men for the 2nd and 3rd Ukrainian fronts. Without such forced conscription and given Bagration's demands, the two fronts would have received only 8,224 men from Red Army reserve pools between April and August.[96]

For their part, the Germans noticed the gathering storm on the Romanian border. Nevertheless, Hitler and the OKH denied Freissner's request to fall back to better defensive positions; given Hitler's focus on grand strategic considerations. Consequently, on August 20, Malinovsky's and Tolbukhin's fronts simply ran over and through Army Group South Ukraine. By August 30, the Red Army had driven through nearly all of Romania, arriving in Ploesti that day; having wiped 22 German divisions off the map and destroying or taking 490 German tanks and 1,500 artillery pieces. On August 23, the Romanian king Micheal removed the fascist prime minister Ion Antonescu from power and surrendered to the Soviet and Romanian soldiers—with the latter having turned on their former German allies. On September 8, Bulgaria left the Axis and joined the Soviets. German troops retreated from Greece and Albania. By October 22, Belgrade fell, with the German army losing another 15,000 killed and 9,000 prisoners of war in a weeklong battle for the Yugoslavian city. Only Hungary hung on as a German ally, and only then because German troops had occupied the country the previous spring, and, in October, had installed in power the brutally anti-Semitic right-wing Hungarian National Socialist Arrow Cross movement.[97] Germany's defeat in Romania, loss of Transylvania, and loss of a significant portion of the Carpathians meant that Hitler had failed to hold the last great defensive barriers protecting central Europe from the north and the east—ironically exposing to the onrushing Red Army the Hungarian plains and oil fields that Hitler sought so desperately to hold on to during the war's final year.

That said, by October 1944 both the Soviet 2nd and 3rd Ukrainian fronts had run out of steam. The entire 6th Tank Army, from the 2nd Ukrainian Front, was down to a mere 130 tanks and 56 self-propelled guns. Operations since April 1944 in Romania alone had cost the Red Army 218,209 casualties, 2,200 tanks lost, 2,000 guns and mortars destroyed, and the loss of 528 aircraft. Although the Red Army had shattered the German armies in Romania, killing or capturing 400,000 Axis troops, a pause in operations became necessary.[98] The Soviet fronts ran so short on manpower that Stalin set aside his standing orders to send surrendering units to the gulags in Siberia. He also allowed entire Romanian and Hungarian units to fight for the Red Army.[99] As the Soviet offensive slowed, the Germans rushed reinforcements to Budapest. Thus, by October, a vicious battle for the city had begun. The numerical odds were staggering. Germany's Army Group South marshaled only 200,000 men in 31 divisions and 293 tanks and assault guns to face the 1,098,200 men in the two Soviet fronts in opposition, and 825 tanks and assault guns in the 2nd Ukrainian Front alone.[100]

The Germans and, at times, the Hungarians fought hard.[101] From October 10 to October 14, a large tank battle raged near Debrecen. There, 11

German and Hungarian divisions, with 227 tanks and assault guns, faced 39 Soviet divisions with 773 tanks and assault guns. On October 22, the Pliev KMG, an arguably elite grouping comprising the 1st Tank and 2nd Guards Cavalry Corps, had done what it did best and had aggressively pushed deep behind the German 8th Army. The Germans quickly counterattacked. The 8th Army moved in from the east, and the 3rd Panzer Corps struck from the west, encircling and massacring Pliev's command. The Red Army had lost 25,000 men and hundreds of AFVs in the encirclement, including 6,662 dead. Of course, the Germans were also hard hit. The fighting left 3rd Panzer Corps a shell of its former already weakened self.[102]

As the German and Soviet armies fought in Hungary, the Hungarian people's future was decided during in Moscow. There, British Prime Minister Winston Churchill met with Stalin and coolly and casually divided southeastern Europe into respective "spheres of influence."[103] Then, on October 28, 1944, Stalin ordered Malinovsky's 2nd Ukrainian Front to take Budapest. For its part, the German army had redeployed several tank-heavy units to the region. These included the 13th, 23rd, and 24th Panzer Divisions; the Feldherrnhalle Panzer Grenadier Division; the Florian Geyer 8th SS Cavalry Division; the 503rd Heavy Panzer Battalion; and several assault artillery battalions—with even more Panzer divisions set to arrive in the coming weeks and months.[104] Nevertheless, Soviet troops had pounded their way into the city's suburbs by early in November. Budapest's size—the city sprawled across both sides of the broad Danube River, the hilly Buda on one side and Pest on the other—assisted the German and Hungarian defensive effort.[105] In addition, the 95,000 German and Hungarian troops, 500 guns, and 220 tanks and assault guns trapped in Budapest defended the city against a Soviet and Romanian force standing at only 177,000 men on December 24, 1944.[106] Accordingly, the Soviet and Romanian forces involved in the siege sought to leverage their superior firepower, but suffered heavy casualties all the same. Only one-third of the men, 75,000, beginning the siege on December 24, 1944, were still in the line when Budapest fell in February 1945.[107]

Nevertheless, in February the Axis forces were massacred when the Budapest garrison commander, SS General Karl Pfeffer-Wildenbrusch, having ignored far better opportunities to break out in early January, for fear of challenging Hitler's inane orders, ordered an attempted breakout on February 11, 1945. Of the Axis soldiers in Budapest, 28,000 took part in the breakout. Only 700 made it safely to German lines. In just four days, the Red Army had killed 17,000 German and Hungarian soldiers and took 22,350 prisoners.[108] The battle for Budapest also cost the Hungarian people dearly, leaving 38,000 civilians dead by February 11, 1945.[109] In addition, some estimate that as many as 50,000 women and girls in and around Budapest were raped by Soviet soldiers.[110] Budapest joined Warsaw and Berlin in the dubious ranks of those European capitals most devastated by the war.

In the meantime, and far to the north, the three Soviet Baltic fronts had battered their way west against Army Group North. However, again, where available, German armor proved to be a benefit out of all proportion to its numerical strength. For instance, the 502nd Tiger Battalion played a crucial role in enabling Army Group North to withdraw under some measure of control, including one notable encounter that resulted in the 502nd losing not one tank against Soviet losses totaling 55 heavy tanks and T-34s.[111] Nevertheless, by July 31, the Red Army's 2nd Baltic Front, 3rd Baltic Front, and Leningrad Front had forced Germany's Army Group North southwest into Lithuania and East Prussia. Only a thin sliver of land connected Army Group North to Army Group Center's remnants. German counterattacks, led by a 3rd Panzer Army temporarily reinforced with six Panzer divisions,[112] had finally slowed the Russians late in the summer but left Army Group North badly battered. Between combat losses and units stripped from Army Group North to help other German forces, the 700,000-man Army Group in June had been reduced to 570,000 men by September 1.[113]

Then, in an offensive beginning on September 14, four Soviet fronts relentlessly pounded into Army Group North yet again.[114] The 1st Baltic and 3rd Belorussian fronts sliced through German lines and reached the Baltic coast. The Red Army had cut off most of German Army Group North, approximately 33 divisions worth of men from the German 16th and 18th Armies, in the Courland peninsula in Latvia.[115] Thereafter, from October 1944 to May 1945, the German armies defending Courland would defeat six full-scale Soviet offensives.[116] Although the German army in Courland suffered heavy casualties during its defensive stand, it also inflicted staggering losses on the Red Army. The Germans were able to hold off the superior Soviet forces for a number of reasons. But, most notably, as late as February 1945, the German armies in Courland deployed 632 tanks and assault guns, including 69 Tiger and Panther tanks.[117]

Meanwhile, after mostly clearing the Baltic states, the 3rd Belorussian Front, led by Cherniakhovsky, had, on October 16, wheeled to the southwest into East Prussia with the 5th and 11th Guards Armies in the vanguard. However, a tremendous German defensive effort led by the 3rd Panzer Army caused the two Soviet armies to slam to a halt. Cherniakhovsky responded by bringing in his 31st and 39th Armies. For four days, an intense battle raged in the first German defensive belt protecting Prussia's frontier. Cherniakhovsky had to bring in further reinforcements, including his 28th Army, spearheaded by the 2nd Guards Tank Corps, to widen his penetration into the German defensive belt. Despite the substantial Soviet effort, the Germans had also brought in their own reinforcements. This led to a massive armored battle near the town of Goldap; one that left 616 Soviet tanks destroyed, the 3rd Belorussian Front's spearhead in tatters, and that, on October 27, had brought the Red Army to a halt.[118] In just two months of fighting, the Red Army suffered 261,946 casualties or, in comparison to events in western Europe, well over one-third the entire casualty total suffered by the Allied armies in northwestern Europe from D-Day to the war's end.[119] Accordingly, late in 1944 and despite an increase in overall manpower as an organization, the bulk of the Red Army's rifle divisions were lucky if they could field more than 5,000 men each. The need for bodies in the rifle divisions proved so pressing that as of September 1944, some 1,030,494 men rotting in the gulags were thrown into "penal battalions" meant to serve as nothing more than pure cannon fodder.[120]

Nonetheless, the Red Army's victories had meant that from June 1, 1944, to November 1944, Germany had lost a stunning 903,000 men in eastern Europe.[121] In addition, though German factories cranked out approximately 1,650 tanks and assault guns during July 1944, the German army lost nearly 2,100 such weapons, well over twice as many tanks and assault guns as Germany had lost during all of July 1943 and including the assault at Kursk.[122] Ethnic Germans also paid a heavy price for the Wehrmacht's failures; 97,484 German men and women from the Balkans were enslaved and sent to replace those dying in droves in Russian factories. As for East Prussia's civilians, Russian soldiers had been primed for bloody vengeance by Germany's genocidal occupation policies, their personal loss, alcohol, and propaganda. On October 22, 1944, the Red Army temporarily overran the German village of Nemmersdorf in East Prussia. As a result, nearly every single female inhabitant of Nemmersdorf was murdered, mutilated, and raped. Men were killed as a matter of course. German civilians would now join other central and eastern Europeans in suffering the wrath of those surviving Hitler's criminal war in eastern Europe. To make matters even worse for Germany's rapidly deteriorating war effort, the Allies had broken the long stalemate in Normandy.

Chapter 12

How the Third Reich Staved Off Total Defeat during the Summer of 1944

Today, the eventual Allied victory following D-Day is often described as a given. After all, once ensconced in their bridgehead, the Allies poured masses of men and war material into Normandy against a portion of the German army's total strength in western Europe. Nonetheless, and at that time, the days and weeks that followed hardly represented an overwhelming Allied success. That is because despite being outfought on D-Day, the German army in Normandy spent the better part of the summer containing an Allied beachhead not only bulging with men and material but also supported by massive offshore and air-delivered firepower. This thus prompts one to wonder how beat-up German formations, remaining in line for weeks on end, could have held out for as long as they did against quantitatively superior forces if sheer material power supposedly served as the determinant for success in World War II.

Part of the answer to that question lies in a further examination of the German army and its performance during the war's final year, a performance that today provides much of the Anglo-American world with it's enduring fascination with a military establishment that allowed the Third Reich to hang on against all conceivable reasons as the world's most powerful nations worked in concert to engineer German defeat. So far, we have partially addressed the paradox presented by German military resilience in the face of overwhelming power by pointing to the Red Army's gradual transformation into a master of the operational art of war as the German army's ability to fight a war of maneuver had concomitantly diminished. But in western Europe, the question remains: How did the Anglo-American army's ultimately best the German army? We

Table 12.1 Allied versus German Buildup in Normandy, June–July 1944, Divisions Only[1]

Date	Allied Forces	German
June 7, 1944	15 divisions[2]	13 divisions
June 18, 1944	20 divisions	18 divisions[3]
July 25, 1944	36 divisions	28 divisions

[1]Helmut Heiber and David Glantz, *Hitler and His Generals: Military Conferences 1942-1945: The First Complete Stenographic Record of the Military Situation Conferences, from Stalingrad to Berlin* (Enigma Books, 2003), 967–69.

[2]The Allies also landed numerous independent brigades and dozens of independent battalions (e.g., the British brought in four armored brigades with approximately 1,000 tanks in the invasion's first two waves). Added up as divisional equivalents, the numerous independent brigades and battalions would more than double the Allied strength in Normandy for each dated listed above.

[3]Unlike the Allies, the Germans only sparsely replenished their existing divisions in Normandy. For example, the 18 divisions listed here on June 18, 1944, had an equivalent strength of only 14 divisions. In addition, the Germans added few independent battalions to their divisions in Normandy (just three heavy Panzer battalions and a couple assault gun/tank destroyer battalions). Roman Johann Jarymowycz, *Tank Tactics from Normandy to Lorraine* (Lynne Rienner Publishers, 2001), 99.

will begin to answer this question by examining the battle for Normandy and the months that followed this battle, shining new light on the European war's final year and how and why it ended as it did.

WAR IN THE BOCAGE

The U.S. Army in Normandy had been built as an army to defeat the early war German army in an anticipated war of movement. Regardless, Normandy's terrain played a role in turning that plan on its head, bolstering the defensive prowess of a relatively immobile German army in Normandy. The bocage that defined the Norman countryside was a network of hedgerowed natural fences. These fences had been built up over the centuries by the local farmers into raised earthen berms, at times the height of a man, and were originally designed for restricting the farmer's animals to specific fields. In addition, a dense covering of trees, shrubs, and other vegetation almost always sat on top of these nearly impenetrable hedgerows. Sunken lanes ran between the fields. The foliage, often arcing overhead, provided excellent cover for German soldiers seeking to avoid the Allies' near absolute air superiority. Moreover, the average field ran no more than 15 acres in size, the majority much smaller.

Thus, these numerous, individually divided fields turned the entire landscape into a checkerboard of defensive strongpoints miles in depth. The Germans had duly converted each field into a miniature killing ground, employing a cornucopia of heavy weapons in taking a fearsome toll of Allied men and machines alike. For instance, the dense cover allowed Panzerfaust-armed German infantry to remain hidden until Allied tanks moved well within this cheap and effective shoulder-fired weapon's killing range. The Germans often dug heavy machine guns and other crew-served weapons into the corners of the fields, so any Allied infantry movement across the field proved nearly impossible without heavy loss of life. In addition, the Germans preregistered artillery and mortars on each field, with mortars proving particularly deadly to the Allied infantry.[1]

In such an environment, movement more than a few miles represented a rare hard-won success for the worn-down GIs. The intimate battlefields, with the opposing forces often separated by fewer than 100 yards, further hindered the Americans' otherwise massive firepower advantages in artillery, naval gunfire, and air support. Although two U.S. armored divisions were in Normandy during much of June (and by the end of July, there were five, bolstered by numerous independent tank and tank destroyer battalions), these powerful mobile formations could not be concentrated in force within the bocage. Allied tank combat attrition rates quickly soared to double what had been anticipated based on the Allied experience in Italy. In turn, greater-than-expected tank losses put an enormous burden on Allied infantry all too often called on to clear out well-dug-in German defensive positions. Nevertheless, the Norman topography only goes so far in explaining the Allied forces' plodding advance. Credit for German defensive successes in Normandy also should go to the veteran German officers and noncommissioned officers who extracted the best from their men, and who, among other things, practiced a nearly religious adherence to the idea of counterattacking their enemies whenever possible. Flexibility, responsiveness, and adaptability at the tactical level thus led to equally strong German defensive efforts in either the seemingly never-ending bocage facing the Americans, or in the more varied terrain facing the British and Canadians.

During this final year in the war, the British also faced a number of problems beyond those posed only by Normandy's terrain and German resistance, particularly a severe manpower crunch, especially in the rifle battalions. By July 1944, the British army's rifle battalions comprised only 14 percent of the 700,000 men they deployed in Normandy. As in the American army, the British army fielded a lengthy logistical tail necessitated by an army prepared for mobile, armored warfare rather than the commitment in infantry needed to defeat an enemy dug into difficult defensive terrain. Overall, the combined strength in the combat arms (including armor, artillery, and so on) in each division in the British army represented only 65.3 percent of the division's total manpower. The remaining men fed, supplied, repaired, and otherwise sustained the division in the field. Although this may seem like an inordinate waste of manpower, it was a product of the fact that most American and British generals preferred to seek their objectives via set-piece attacks employing massive amounts of supporting firepower. For that matter, the British proved combat efficient compared to their American and Canadian allies.

Only 43.5 percent of the American army's and 34.2 percent of the Canadian army's manpower resided in the combat arms.[2]

In terms of raw numbers, this meant that the least efficient Allied army, the Canadian army, needed 93,150 men behind the lines to sustain a combat division in the field. On the other hand, the German army required only 23,000 men to support each combat division in the field. In addition, efficiency related to more than only logistics. For example, German divisional staffs characteristically comprised only 30 officers, whereas the standard American infantry division in World War II included 79 officers.[3] On the other hand, at the strategic organizational level, no other army wasted manpower like the Germans, as exemplified by the Luftwaffe field divisions and the Waffen-SS.[4]

Nevertheless, Allied decisions regarding manpower usage, coupled with the reality that only a few Allied combat units carried the offensive against a German army continually counterattacking, meant that the operational tempo quickly devoured Allied infantry battalions. For instance, British frontline infantry suffered 80 percent of Britain's casualties. This was well beyond the 50 percent limit the British War Office earlier estimated as the breaking point for British manpower in Montgomery's army.[5] To find replacements for combat losses, the British broke up the 59th Infantry Division as well as several independent infantry and armored brigades. The repeated attempts to take Caen took a particularly heavy toll on the British army throughout June and July, with Operations Epsom, Charnwood, and Goodwood standing out in particular for their cost in lives. The American situation in Normandy was better, but still the U.S. Army stripped over 25,000 men from units training in the United States, all done to meet the demand for riflemen in Europe, where American infantry battalions ran astronomical 90 percent casualty rates.[6] As if the infantry-dominated war in the bocage was not bad enough, the Allied armies had to deal with another unpleasant reality provided in particular by the more open land near Caen. There, Rommel's men effectively deployed weapons and tactics tailor-made for exploiting the terrain where Normandy's great tank battles were fought.

TANK VERSUS TANK: WHY GERMAN ARMOR DOMINATED ALLIED ARMOR IN NORMANDY

Allied armored failures in Normandy are today legendary, and have been attributed mainly to the superiority of German armor. That said, by mid-1944, it was hardly a mystery that the Allies would face well-protected, hard-hitting German AFVs in France. Thus, answering the question of why Allied AFV crews had to endure the pounding they did in Normandy requires examining more than simply the technical attributes of German tanks. It first requires looking at the underlying organizational and technical weapons procurement decisions made by high-ranking Allied personnel years prior to Operation Overlord.

For the Allies, a whole host of officers took on intersecting roles in creating a series of tanks unsuited for taking the field in direct opposition to German armor during 1944. Whether we are discussing the Americans or British, each had prepared for combating the German blitzkrieg, even though its days had long since passed by in 1944. This played an important role in the questionable Allied response to the German armor it faced during the war's final two years.

For instance, the U.S. armored force, formed initially at Fort Knox, Kentucky, had been heavily influenced by the cavalry. This meant that early war U.S. armored divisions were heavy on tanks (in replacement of horses) and light on combined arms. Moreover, they were deployed under a doctrine heavily favoring pursuit operations behind enemy lines. In terms of how the U.S. Army developed tanks during World War II, perhaps the greatest influences were the U.S. Army Ordnance Department and General Leslie McNair. McNair was a former artillery man, and the head of U.S. Army ground forces during a crucial period of its World War II development. The Ordnance Department developed a number of superb weapons systems during the war, including world-class field artillery pieces. Nonetheless, throughout the war the Ordnance Department struggled in regard to both tank development and dealing with anticipated future threats. This meant that as tanks and tank armament and protection went through several generational leaps, the Ordnance Department, having come late to the game, remained largely one step behind. As a result, in 1944, and as the German army and Red Army deployed increasing numbers of heavily armed and protected heavy and main battle tanks, the U.S. Army was still equipped mostly with a tank, the M4 Sherman, designed for competing with the 1941–1943 era Panzer III and Panzer IV.

With the armored divisions initially expected to fulfill a cavalry-type role, the American approach to tank-on-tank warfare featured building numerous independent tank-destroyer battalions to combat German tanks, with independent tank battalions to support the infantry. Consequently, initial conceptual frameworks divorcing the tank from possessing an anti-tank role ultimately proved difficult to overcome.[7] On November 27, 1941, the War Department ordered 53 tank-destroyer battalions formed and assigned to the general headquarters level only, with the tank destroyers thus a combat arm independent of armor or infantry.[8] The doctrine developed in the prewar and early war years consequently influenced the development of the primary tank equipping the U.S. armored divisions, the M4 Sherman medium tank.[9] With a turret-mounted 75-mm main gun, sloped frontal armor, and a crew of five, with the commander, gunner, and loader in the turret, the M4 Sherman represented a thoroughly modern design when it began rolling off assembly lines in February 1942. Although it faced numerous teething issues and subsequent changes in its early testing and production models, the Sherman proved a perfectly sound medium tank. It emphasized speed and reliability over armor and armament, and thus met its designated role as a breakout vehicle that spent far more time on the battlefield than it did in repair. In addition, its average weight and size meant that the Americans could easily ship considerable numbers of Shermans to Europe.[10]

Nonetheless, by mid-1944, the Sherman, having remained essentially unchanged since 1942, was showing its age. This was also a product of McNair's "battle-need" criteria for developing new weapons based on reports from the front. Nonetheless, this meant that the U.S. Army's tank and anti-tank weapons were always one step behind the newest generation of weapons fielded, most notably, on Germany's Eastern Front.[11] Moreover, each jump aimed to move ahead—and substantially so, such that the T-34, the premier tank in the world in 1941, was by 1943 obsolete in terms of armament and armored protection. Anti-tank weaponry had similarly moved ahead. Subsequent generations completely outclassed weapons that had been effective only one to two years prior.[12] In addition, the tank destroyer was hardly equal to a tank when used on the attack if for no other reason than that it lacked sufficient armored protection. In comparison, German tanks rarely operated without the support of other combat arms. Thus, the all-too-frequent combination of indirect fire support from artillery, rockets, and mortars provided to German Panzer formations proved particularly lethal to open-topped self-propelled tank destroyers. As for firepower, the most common self-propelled tank destroyer in the American inventory on D-Day was the M10, armed with a 75-mm cannon hardly adequate for defeating German armor. Not until the M36 appeared later in the fall of 1944, mounting a 90-mm gun capable of taking out any German tank, did the tank destroyers possess even adequate armament. In spite of these problems, the US Army fielded 56 tank destroyer battalions in Europe, each comprising 673 officers and men with 36 tank destroyers.[13]

For their part, the British dogmatically clung to the idea of building some tanks for supporting infantry, and building other tanks for the separate role of providing speed and maneuver. Although the British adapted this viewpoint, the problems here were that the British trailed the learning curve set by the Germans, and failed to adequately assimilate significant doctrinal changes into its army. As a result, reform in the British ranks occurred far too slowly despite a renewed emphasis on combined arms. Nevertheless, and more specifically, how exactly did German armor dominate the Norman battlefield?

Roman Johann Jarymowycz, in his study on 1944-era armored warfare in France, lays out a number of critical technical advantages that German tanks possessed over the primary Allied tanks, such as the M4 Sherman and the British Churchill and Crusader series. In addition, and perhaps even more important, the combination of well-trained German tank crews laying in ambush in terrain that they not only had time to get to know, as the defender, but that was also difficult in the extreme for maneuvering large armored formations, meant that the Germans all too often were able to more easily see, engage, and hit their Allied foes. Allied opponents all too often fought at the disadvantage of being the attacker in such an environment playing to the strengths of a generation of Panzers very different than those that had equipped early war Panzer divisions. In what was an undoubtedly difficult situation, the best technical matchup for the Allies was actually between the Sherman and the Panzer IV. For instance, both tanks possessed comparably thick frontal armor. Nevertheless, even here, the Panzer IV maintained distinct advantages in standoff firepower over the Sherman, as the former's main gun could penetrate any Allied tank out to ranges reaching 1,500 meters. Meanwhile, the Sherman needed to close to 1,000 meters for a reasonably successful chance to penetrate the Panzer IV's frontal armor.[14]

For whatever success the Sherman tank crews found against the Panzer IV, the well-trained German tank crews in Normandy that were equipped with the Panzer V Ausf. G model "Panther," enjoyed the attributes of a superb defensive weapon. The Panther's high-velocity 75-mm L/70 gun, low-flash gunpowder, superior optics, superior ability to negotiate mud without bogging down, well-designed commander's cupolas, and thick frontal armor completely outclassed Allied M4 Sherman capabilities.[15] Finally, if the Panzer V Panther dominated the M4 Sherman, then the Panzer VI Tiger proved virtually impervious to almost any Allied tank in Normandy at almost any range. In addition, the Tiger's 88-mm high-velocity cannon penetrated all Allied tanks at ranges in excess of 2,500 meters. The 75-mm-gun–armed Sherman did have a slightly better equipped relative, but the few 76-mm L/52 up-gunned Shermans reaching the European theater of operations were also overmatched by either a Tiger or a Panther at anything but nearly suicidal ranges. In addition, the Sherman had even less of a chance of besting the even newer 70-ton Tiger II (King Tigers) trickling onto the battlefield. Luckily for the Allies, the King Tiger's introduction severely limited the Tiger's availability. If the Germans had merely continued to build Tigers at over 100 per month, instead of switching over to the King Tiger as they did during the summer of 1944, then the Allies would have faced even greater problems in slugging their way through the Norman countryside; as shown by one battle in particular— one that has come to emphasize the Tiger's enduring legend in Normandy.

The British had already attacked Caen numerous times when, on June 13, they attempted to sneak the veteran 7th Armored Division around German defenses with orders to take both the town of Villers-Bocage near Caen and the important high ground outside Villers-Bocage. The 7th Armored resourcefully found a hole in the German lines almost immediately after beginning their attack. Unbeknownst to the British, however, Germany's premier tank "ace," SS Captain Michael Wittman, arrived, leading several Tiger tanks from the 501st SS Heavy Tank Battalion. Wittman quickly destroyed over 25 British tanks and other vehicles. Wittman's platoon followed up his initial success by nearly wiping out the entire lead brigade from the 7th Armored and knocking out 27 tanks from Tank Company A and destroying the division headquarters.[16] Luckily for the British, an overconfident Wittman met his match when he ordered his Tigers into the town without infantry support. They were soon knocked out by British anti-tank guns. Nevertheless, the Germans had defeated the British flanking maneuver in detail, recaptured Villers-Bocage, and forced the famous "Desert Rats" to retreat. Although this engagement was unusual in the extent of its one-sidedness, the British defeat at Villers-Bocage exemplified how badly German tanks outclassed Allied tanks in Normandy. The British alone would lose 1,300 tanks in June and July.[17]

Nevertheless, the British had also discovered a cure to the Allied tank problems. They had found that the 17-pounder L/55 anti-tank gun, when using a higher-than-normal amount of propellant and firing tungsten armor-piercing rounds, possessed tremendous armor-penetrating power.[18] Tungsten anti-tank rounds could penetrate the Panzer IV's frontal armor out to 2,000 yards, a Panther's frontal armor at ranges reaching over 1,200 yards, and a Tiger's at 500 yards. In addition, the existing M4 Sherman could accommodate this weapon.[19] The resulting tank was named the Sherman Vc "Firefly." Some Americans foolishly denigrated this excellent stopgap solution, and McNair was particularly condescending.[20] Accordingly, because of British economic handicaps and American inflexibility, only 109 Fireflies had arrived in Normandy by the end of June.[21] Consequently, by the end of 1944, of 2,579 American, 1,103 British, and 473 Canadian tank losses examined in one study on Allied armor attrition in western Europe during 1944, 51, 59, and 55 percent of the respective nations' losses came from German gunfire.[22] In return, studies done during and after the war have revealed that 40 percent of German tank losses in 1944–1945 came from breakdowns. The high breakdown rate, combined with strong survivability against enemy gunfire to make German control over static battlefields crucial to German success in 1944.[23] All the same, the German army still needed to retain enough flexibility, and mobility, to avoid being fixed in place and destroyed. A task more easily said than done.

By the end of June, Bradley's men had captured the port of Cherbourg at the cost of 2,811 dead, 13,564 wounded, and 5,665 missing against 47,070 German casualties.[24] Then, on June 25, Montgomery began a renewed attempt to take Caen. Although his assault turned into another Allied bloodbath, he had forced the Germans to prematurely commit the newly arrived 2nd SS Panzer Corps to stop the attack—rather than mass with other German armored units for a far more potent counterattack than the relatively ineffective

Table 12.2 German Western Front Sample of Tank Losses by Cause, 1944–1945[1]

Total Tank Losses Sampled during 1944–1945: 1,198 Cause	Number/ Percent Destroyed
Mechanical failure	522/44
Enemy gunfire	520/43
Air attack	91/7.5
Hollow-charge weapons	53/4
Miscellaneous, enemy action	9/0.7
Mines	3/0.2

[1]Roman Johann Jarymowycz, *Tank Tactics from Normandy to Lorraine* (Lynne Rienner Publishers, 2001), 269.

one ultimately ordered up in late June. Meanwhile, even more exasperatingly for Rommel, 24 German infantry divisions, two Panzer divisions, and five Luftwaffe field divisions waited vainly in Calais for the "real" invasion that Hitler expected any day.[25] Regardless, the brutal slugfest in Normandy continued unabated.

ST. LO AND OPERATION GOODWOOD: CHANNELING GALLIPOLI?

By July 1, 1944, the Allied beachhead was at only one-fifth the size that Overlord's planners envisioned prior to the invasion for one month following D-Day.[26] Although abundant reinforcements of men and material were pouring into the Allied beachheads virtually unhindered, a variety of factors, not the least of which being limited space available to the Allies, meant that these resources could hardly be used as intended if the Allies could not create adequate space for maneuvering. Moreover, the fierce storms that swept the English Channel during June's third week had further burdened the Allied supply network. As it was Allied logisticians were straining to meet the thousands of tons of munitions and other such war material needed daily by an Allied army in France totaling just over 850,000 men and 4,100 tanks by the end of June, let alone the vast amounts of such material needing to be stockpiled to fuel a breakout from what was becoming an increasingly crowded lodgment.

Accordingly, if Hitler and the OKW (Oberkommando der Wehrmacht, or High Command of the Armed Forces) had created the preconditions for creating an armored reserve, that is, by releasing the field-capable infantry divisions in the German 15th Army located in Calais, the Germans might have tied down the Allies in Normandy indefinitely. As it was, the 8th and 7th Corps from the American 1st Army, though capably led by Generals Middleton and Collins, respectively, had spent much of July grinding out only meager advances. Five American divisions sustained 11,000 casualties during the two weeks it took to secure the city of St. Lo.[27] Considering Montgomery's losses near Caen, ostensibly tying down the German army's striking power in Normandy, the Americans' progress proved hardly encouraging. Yet another attack on Caen resulted in the British holding only half the city by July 9. Then, another British-led attack on July 18, Operation Goodwood, accomplished little more than tie down German armor, even though, on paper, the balance of forces was tilted in Montgomery's favor.

For Goodwood Montgomery's armies deployed 14 nearly full-strength divisions, four armored divisions, and numerous independent brigades against 12 German divisions and assorted independent battalion-strength units. The Germans, however, had the advantage of fighting from deep, dug-in defensive positions built around terrain constricting armored operations. As a result, in planning Goodwood, Montgomery had deployed his armored divisions on a narrow front: three full armored divisions spearheaded the attack albeit with ample support from the infantry. Montgomery also had scheduled a preattack bombardment from bombers of all size, artillery, and offshore naval fire support. Unfortunately for Montgomery, Rommel not only knew that the attack was coming, but also had deployed his men in multiple defensive lines studded with well-camouflaged combined-arms strongpoints with, most important, an armored reserve to respond as needed.

Nonetheless, Montgomery's massive preassault bombardment virtually annihilated the 16th Luftwaffe Field Division and the remaining 50 tanks from the 21st Panzer Division. All the same, the British armor then failed to exploit this initial success. By the day's end, the attack had faltered. German anti-tank gun nests had been well supported by quick and effective counterattacks led by heavy armored units. Both the 101st and the 503rd Heavy Tiger Battalions were present, with one company of the 503rd equipped with King Tigers firing imperviously from long range to pick off Allied tanks at will, helping to crush the British armored spearhead. Within Goodwood's first three days, the British lost a third of the 877 tanks that the three armored divisions rode into battle.[28] The Germans counterattacked repeatedly and found further success, shattering Canadian infantry cut off from armor support.[29] For the Allies, Goodwood had wearingly represented the pattern of battle existing near Caen since D-Day: inadequate Allied coordination of combat arms against aggressive German commanders fighting from in-depth defensive fronts backed by potent armored concentrations. The Allies had lost well over 400 tanks; though these losses could be replaced, the roughly 5,000 British and Canadian casualties in a 21st Army Group already facing a manpower crisis could not so easily be overcome.

The most notable Allied success that materialized during July's first three weeks occurred on July 17, when Rommel was severely injured by Allied

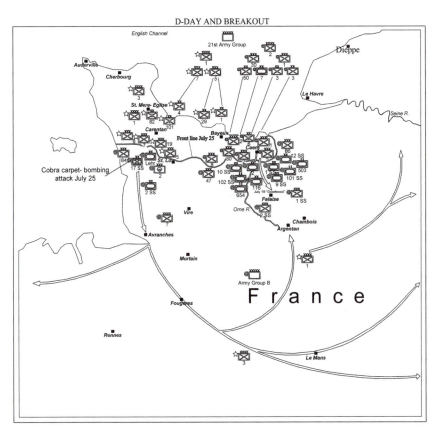

D-DAY AND BREAKOUT

fighter bombers strafing his car. Rommel's injury was followed three days later by the July 20 attempt on Hitler's life, an attempt made by a small group of German generals recognizing that Hitler's command was leading Germany to annihilation. The assassination attempt nearly succeeded, and but for a regrettably heavy table leg, it almost ended Hitler's reign. Instead, the wounded Führer survived. In the ensuing months, he killed over 5,000 suspected conspirators and sent thousands of others to concentration camps. Rommel, fingered as sympathetic to the would-be assassins' cause, was forced by Hitler to commit suicide on October 14, 1944. Of Germany's 18 field marshals during World War II, only two served until the war's end in a remarkably debilitating rate of turnover unmatched by any other major combatant during the war in Europe. Nonetheless, well before Hitler's purges played out and Germany's most driven fanatics consolidated power, the outcome of the German failure to stop the Allied invasion of France on the beaches reached its logical conclusion.

AN ANALYSIS OF THE ALLIED OPERATIONAL ART:
THE BREAKOUT FROM NORMANDY AND THE RACE
ACROSS FRANCE

Operation Cobra, the Allied breakout from the Normandy beachhead, commenced on July 25, 1944. General Omar Bradley's plan was to punch through the German positions just south of St. Lo and reach the more open countryside in central France—land ideal for Allied armies built on mobile warfare. Bradley's plan sought to first break through the German positions, and, second, turn loose General Patton's newly activated 3rd Army to cut off the Brittany peninsula from France. After securing his flanks Patton would race for the Seine River to the east, and then beyond.

Cobra is often cast as a victory engineered chiefly by firepower, and to that point there is no question that Bradley amassed enough weapons and munitions to support Cobra with a massive aerial and artillery bombardment. Nevertheless, for the Allied armies to even think about a breakout, they had needed to rely on far more than existing advantages in deliverable firepower. To that end, the frustrating months in Normandy had not been without benefit. The U.S. Army had gained valuable experience and matured as an organization. In addition, a variety of innovative solutions had been discovered to assist in better integrating the combat arms in practice. For instance, the Americans had learned how to better employ combined-arms teams of infantry, indirect weapons, and armor led by Sherman tanks equipped with heavy steel rams attached on the tanks' frontal armor, nicknamed "Rhino" tanks, to rip through and best the German hedgerow-based defenses. Although the increasing proficiency of the Allied combat arms was important, one cannot discount the role that firepower played in Allied doctrine. To that end, Bradley's use of strategic bombers in a close support role reflected what was becoming a distinctively American approach to war, one dependent in part on firepower and set-piece breakthrough operations designed to wear down and crush, rather than flow past, an enemy's defensive positions.

Consequently, on July 25, Allied bombers of all sizes led off Cobra by pulverizing the German defenses and, regrettably, frontline U.S. soldiers who suffered 750 casualties to ordnance dropped short by the heavy bombers, with the most prominent casualty being General Lesley McNair.[30] As the battered assault battalions moved forward, scattered German survivors still managed to put up a stiff fight from their ruined defensive positions. Nevertheless, General Collins, commanding the heavily reinforced U.S. 7th Corps leading the assault, threw both the 2nd and the 3rd Armored Divisions into the attack as well as the 1st Infantry Division in an effort to forge a breakthrough.[31] Kluge desperately sought help, as the U.S. 7th Corps comprised over 88,000 men in its six combat divisions alone. In response, Hitler released three infantry divisions from the Calais region, but this support came two months too late—the German Seventh Army had been bled dry, and its own internal reports rated the 13 divisions in its ranks as possessing the combat equivalence of five. Most critically, the 7th Army lacked any immediately deployable mobile reserves to speak of amidst a larger paucity of units equipped with heavy weapons in general. Consequently, the initial trickle of American units exploiting Cobra's success quickly turned into a flood of olive-drab GIs in fast-moving mechanized formations pouring out of the bocage into increasingly open terrain. American P-47 fighter-bombers from the U.S. 9th Tactical Air Command mauled the exposed German columns fleeing down roads choked with retreating vehicles.[32] In particular, on July 29 and near the town of Roncey, American fighter-bombers pummeled the retreating Germans while fast-moving U.S. forces closed on the survivors. All told, four German divisions were decimated, with the Americans taking over 8,000 prisoners of war and capturing or destroying several hundred tanks, assault guns, and other vehicles. Both Avranches and Coutances quickly fell to the rampaging American tanks.

In response, Hitler ordered a full-scale counterattack into the seemingly long and exposed American flank that had opened up near Mortain, with his overly ambitious counterstroke codenamed Operation Luttich. The German army in Normandy, however though possessed of a field strength of nearly 300,000 men, or 50,000 men more than on July 1, was not the freewheeling version of years past. Consequently, after much difficulty in assembling forces, on August 6, three weak and run-down Panzer divisions—the 1st SS Panzer, 2nd SS Panzer, and 2nd Panzer—spearheaded the assault with a combined strength of one preinvasion Panzer division, or 145 tanks and 32 assault guns combined. In addition, the relatively fresh 116th Panzer Division participated, but only in part, as it could not easily disengage from ongoing combat in its area of operations, and therefore made its contribution to the counteroffensive in only a piecemeal fashion. Nonetheless, the German Panzers crashed through the American screening battalions and advanced up to seven miles into the Allied flanks. At that point, lacking reserves for exploiting the initial penetration, the attack bogged down against fierce resistance; including most notably from the men of the U.S. 30th Infantry Division's 2nd Battalion of the 120th Regiment.[33]

Meanwhile, Montgomery had ordered up yet another push. On August 8, 1944, Operation Totalize commenced, led by Canadian General Guy Simonds. Simonds deployed nearly the equivalent of four armored divisions in the vanguard—the Canadian 4th Armored Division, the Polish 1st Armored Division, the Canadian 2nd Armored Brigade, and the British 33rd Armored Brigade—and three infantry divisions. The Canadian's primary antagonist, Kurt Meyer's 12th SS Panzer Division, with a newly arrived infantry division in support, stood in Totalize's path. Totalize began somewhat uniquely at night, but like Cobra, it featured the nearly obligatory use of heavy bombers. This allowed the Allied armor spearheads to easily push through the devastated German defensive positions. However, Simonds paused. He seems to have believed that he needed the heavy bombers and artillery to neutralize any further German defensive holdouts. Though these holdouts had invariably been able to hammer the Canadian-led Allied armor, to their credit the Canadians and Poles had done better than any of the previous British-led efforts.

For their part the Germans, despite being heavily outnumbered, had fought a fluid battle group–based defense. As the Allied weight in armor pressed back his initial counterattacks, Meyer responded with strikes into the Allied flanks. Overall, the Allied attacks featured poor coordination and lacked coherence while German armor and anti-tank guns lining the woods also helped Meyer's defensive efforts. That said, although Montgomery's men suffered tremendous losses, losing over 150 tanks within a two-day stretch, the Allies had forced the Germans to give up eight miles of precious real estate. When the bombers reappeared several days later, kicking off the new Operation Tractable on August 14, initial results were less than promising for the Allies; not only did many shorts cause casualties in the Allied ranks, but the Germans yet again launched aggressive counterattacks. Nevertheless, this time the Allies were able to press on against increasingly depleted German forces, with the Allies led by General Stanislaw Maczek's Polish 1st Armored Division; all told 16,000 men and well over 300 tanks charging toward a planned link-up with the Americans. At the same time, the American armored spearheads stormed across the French countryside, and a dangerous noose began forming around the German 7th Army. Falaise fell to Montgomery on August 17. Then, on August 19, the Polish 1st Armored Division's 10th Polish Dragoons Regiment s met elements of the the U.S. 90th Infantry Division near Chambois, 15 miles southeast of Falaise. The Allies had closed the pocket, albeit tenuously—as the isolated and Polish soldiers sat astride a six-mile-wide escape route teeming with fleeing German soldiers desperate to escape. At the same time, the Canadian 3rd Infantry Division and 4th Armored Division moved up to help further tighten the noose on a rapidly shrinking pocket being pounded by Allied artillery and the RAF's 2nd Tactical Air Force. Meanwhile, the Germans launched savage counterattacks against the Polish and American troops holding the pocket closed, with the Poles fighting a particularly epic battle against German forces led by several SS Panzer divisions.

Ironically, and in spite of the speed of the Allied advance, it had not been without several notable flaws in execution. These mistakes, including multiple mistakes of varying scope and timing made by nearly all the senior American commanders involved in the breakout and encirclement operation, meant that had the German forces in Normandy begun withdrawing even as late as August 11, they likely would have had an excellent chance to save most of the infantry, let alone the far more mobile Panzer divisions. Instead, Luttich had been pressed far past the point at which it had inevitably collapsed into failure. It was not until late in the day on August 12 that the Germans began to react to the Allied noose forming around them, in terms of preparing to withdrawal, and it would not be until August 16 that the retreat began in earnest, with the time thus wasted virtually guaranteeing much of the destruction visited on the German forces. Meanwhile, Patton turned toward the Seine across largely undefended open countryside, while the overburdened American 1st Army continued the dirty work of reducing the German pocket.[34] Overall, the entire American-led advance and operational conduct during the breakout reflected a U.S. Army whose operational leadership was only slowly coming of age as practitioners in armored warfare. As had the Germans in the war's early years, nevertheless the U.S. Army gradually gained confidence, responding increasingly well to fluid, ever-changing events and creating battle groups tailored to tasks as needed. For their part, Montgomery's forces also deployed in a less than-an-optimal manner for collapsing a pocket, with much of their efforts resulting in German troops being pushed along toward the pocket's only loosely closed eastern edge. This thereby worked with contemporaneous American mistakes to only further facilitate the escape of the overwhelming bulk of the German manpower in Normandy that otherwise should have been trapped in the Falaise pocket, but whose escape OB West was engineering at a rapid pace.

All told, some 10,000 Germans were killed inside the Falaise pocket and another 40,000 captured. By early September, the 11 Panzer and Panzer grenadier divisions in France could muster only about 100,000 out of the 160,000 men with which they had begun the Normandy defensive campaign. Total German manpower losses from June 6 to September 1, 1944, reached nearly 400,000 men against over 200,000 Allied casualties during the same period. Moreover, Hitler's army in France would ultimately lose 2,100 of the 2,200 tanks they had put into the field on the eve of D-Day, with some 300 AFVs alone destroyed near the positions held by the Poles and Americans along the final German escape routes from the pocket.[35] Some 3 million Allied soldiers streamed east on two axes of advance with Patton's 3rd Army leading the Americans across central France. Montgomery's armies advanced along the English Channel coast. If the fighting in Normandy had seen the worst of the Sherman tank, the rapid Allied advance across France saw the tank demonstrating its best characteristics. Its rugged durability and mechanical reliability powered the Allied army's sweep east. In contrast, Germany's mechanically unreliable Panthers and fuel-thirsty Tigers would have been unable to maintain such a pace even if the chance had existed.

Meanwhile, on August 15, 1944, the Allied 6th Army Group under U.S. Lieutenant General Jacob L. Devers had landed in southern France. The Allied landings forced the 250,000-man German 19th Army, under General Frederich Wiese, to withdraw from southern France or risk being cut off by the Allied armies advancing on the German border from Normandy.[36] By September 12, elements from the U.S. 3rd Army had linked up with the French 2nd Corps (from the U.S. 7th Army led by General Alexander Patch advancing from the south) and thus created a continuous front. In September's first weeks, the British-led armies had liberated the Calais region, the American 1st Army advanced toward the German border north of the Ardennes, and Patton's 3rd Army headed for the Maginot Line. From September 11 to September 13, the American 3rd and 5th Armored Divisions penetrated the prewar German border 10 miles south of the ancient city of Aachen west of the Ruhr Valley and Germany's industrial heartland. At virtually the same time, elements of the U.S. 28th Infantry Division entered Germany at Sevenig, and the U.S. 4th Infantry Division's scouts crossed the Our River into Germany at Hemmeres.[37]

Patton's 3rd Army, in addition to gobbling up great chunks of real estate, had also proven itself an increasingly formidable army during a series of battles fought throughout September in the French province of Lorraine, where Patton's men decisively defeated the best of Germany's hastily assembled reserves in the west. These battles signaled the U.S. Army's maturation into a world-class army, fully capable of holding its own against the late 1944 version of the German army. Notable American commanders making their name during this fighting included General Wood, the American 4th Armored Division's commander, and tank leader and theorist Lieutenant Colonel Creighton Abrams, commanding the 37th Tank Battalion from the 4th Armored's Combat Command A. Wood's 4th Armored Division, the 6th Armored Division, and the 35th and 80th Infantry Divisions made up Major General Manton S. Eddy's 12th Corps.[38] Their men were well-trained and battle-hardened soldiers who had learned much in the months following D-Day.

Opposing the US 3rd Army stood German Panzer General Manteuffel's 5th Panzer Army. It included the veteran 11th Panzer Division, the reconstituted 21st Panzer Division, the 3rd and 15th Panzer Grenadier Divisions, the 17th SS Panzer Grenadier Division, and Panzer Brigades 106-108 and 111-113. A formidable force on paper, in reality the 5th Panzer Army was, for a number of reasons, far from ready to take on the U.S. Army's best mechanized units in the fast pace of operations in Lorraine. One reason for the 5th Panzer Army's lack of readiness was because of Hitler. At Hitler's behest, the German army had hastily formed the Panzer brigades in a serial run of about one dozen. Each brigade was supposed to include anywhere from approximately 36 tanks and 11 tank destroyers each to 90 tanks and 10 tank destroyers each. In reality, many contained only about half their allotment of tanks and tank destroyers, with only three of the four present in Lorraine operating at anywhere close to full strength.[39] As it was, the Panzer brigades were highly unbalanced formations. They lacked the combined-arms flexibility so crucial to the Panzer division's success. Consequently, they matched up poorly against the all-arms American forces, at this time in the war operating at a level of skill, teamwork, efficiency, and quick-hitting fire support unmatched in terms of its responsiveness to anything even the Eastern Front veterans had seen from the Russians.[40] Moreover, because the Panzer brigades were new units, with many new crews, they lacked adequate training, let alone the specialized, extensive and realistic training that had been a hallmark of the Panzerwaffe's elite early war status. One of Hitler's new Panzer brigades actually lost 10 Panthers to poor driving in its initial deployment.

Moreover, even though the heavy Panthers and Tigers had acquitted themselves well in Normandy, there they had not been forced to maneuver over any kind of substantial distances. In contrast, when expected to operate on the counteroffensive in Lorraine, the same tanks broke down with a sickening regularity. The plague of breakdowns had been made all the worse by the German decision to maintain tank production while reducing spare parts output in the face of punishing Allied strategic bombing raids on tank plants and other industrial facilities—60 percent of Allied bomb tonnage dropped on Germany during the war were dropped after July. On the other hand, Lorraine was a logical place for the Germans to challenge the U.S. 3rd Army. Located in eastern France, the province of Lorraine represented a historic Franco-German battlefield. It traditionally offered the best available terrain for invading armies moving either east or west across the Franco-German borders; given the dense forests to the north of Lorraine and imposing mountains to the south. Thus, the Germans had little choice but to engage Patton's divisions, or else risk allowing him to drive into Germany proper.

In the ensuing tank-on-tank battles that swirled across Lorraine, Patton's men simply decimated the 5th Panzer Army. First, on September 7–8, the U.S. 90th Infantry Division pummeled Bake's Panzer Brigade 106. The German brigade lost almost all its equipment, including 21 tanks and tank destroyers.[41] Then, on September 13, the French 2nd Armored Division crushed Panzer Brigade 112, leaving the brigade with only 21 tanks from the 80 with which it had begun the battle. Next, on September 19 in a dense fog near Arracourt, Panzer Brigade 113 was chewed up by the 4th Armored Division's 37th Tank Battalion and the 704th Tank Destroyer Battalion. Fighting at ranges of, at times, less than 150 yards, even a Sherman's 75-mm gun or an M18's 76-mm gun could easily penetrate a Panther. Moreover, the ability of the experienced U.S. tank crews to identify, engage, and hit their targets first proved crucial in their success over the otherwise more heavily armed and armored German Panzers. On the first day of the battle, the Americans destroyed 43 brand-new Panthers against losses of only five Shermans and three tank destroyers. Although American losses mounted on subsequent days, with much-reduced kill disparities, the German Panzer brigades involved in the counteroffensive had been crushed, with over 186 German tanks destroyed or knocked out.[42] Training, experience, and skill at the tactical level continued to hold the edge over measures based largely on technical prowess and numerical superiority.

Although the Allied forces had won a number of engagements at the tactical and operational levels, logistics had quickly reestablished its time-honored role as the ultimate arbiter of military success. Allied supply lines, largely reliant on inefficient trucking, given the pre–D-Day destruction of the French rail network, ran dry and slowed the advance across France. Meanwhile, as the 12th Army Group struggled with its logistical demons, the U.S. 6th Army Group surged northeast at a breakneck pace. In large part, this was because the 6th Army Group was far smaller than the 12th Army Group, it enjoyed the benefits from Devers's close attention to planning and logistical requirements, and could rely on the superb port at Marseilles; which ended the war discharging more cargo than even Cherbourg or Antwerp.[43]

Eisenhower failed to exploit the 6th Army Group's relative mobility. For instance, in an attempt to protect Patton's flank in Lorraine, the Supreme Headquarters Allied Expeditionary Force (SHAEF) had conservatively ordered the 6th Army Group's veteran 6th Corps, under U.S. General Lucian Truscott, to move into the Vosges Mountains. This took pressure off the German 19th Army at a moment when, as later admitted by its commander, it was incapable of otherwise stopping Truscott from driving through the Belfort Gap, which split the mountainous terrain. Such a move would have allowed the Allied 6th Army Group to race across Alsace into Germany across the Rhine River, and may have unhinged the southern half of the German front. However, at this point in the war, the Allied command was perhaps showing the cultural antecedents that had left its component armies at times matching up poorly in relation to its Soviet and German peers as practitioners of the operational art of war.

Although the American army in France in 1944 was incomparably equipped and supported, it had grown from a different culture and society than that which created either the Wehrmacht or the Red Army. In the period between the world wars, as the Wehrmacht and Red Army theorized, trained, and otherwise tackled the unique set of problems cropping up from the revolution in military affairs brought about by the internal combustion engine, the U.S. Army had stagnated.[44] By 1939, the U.S. Army's armored force was actually smaller than that of Poland or Italy. The army's inadequate attention to fighting a land-based war of maneuver is even more remarkable considering American success in the Pacific, where all branches of the American armed forces worked brilliantly, almost seamlessly, across vast geographical spaces dwarfing those in Europe—regularly conducting sophisticated amphibious operations of which not one failed.[45]

Lacking established doctrine and experience, it is not unsurprising that at the operational and tactical levels, the U.S. approach to breakthrough and pursuit operations was slow to develop. The American approach to breaking free of the stalemate in Normandy evinced some similarities to the Red Army, particularly in its use of combined-arms infantry-heavy teams following up massive applications of firepower to break through German defenses and open up the front for breakthrough and exploitation by the armor. Moreover, once the

U.S. breakthrough operations worked during Cobra, the following breakout phase evinced a strong superficial similarity in tactics to the Red Army's own deep operational goals, perhaps befitting the cavalry traditions around which each army based its primary mobile combat units: the tank corps for the Red Army and the armored division for the U.S. Army.

Nevertheless, despite the similarities between Cobra, the Normandy breakout, and the Soviet deep operations breakthrough and exploitation phases, there were also notable differences in execution. For instance, Cobra developed along a single, narrow six-mile front versus the six axes of attack each over six miles in breadth featured in Operation Bagration. Moreover, even though the Russians enjoyed much more geographical space to work with in eastern Europe than did the Allies in Normandy, at no point during Cobra did either American- or British-led armies stand ready to shift reserves across the width of the front to exploit initial penetrations as, for example, Konev did when he dismantled Army Group North Ukraine in July. In further comparison to Soviet operational leadership, and for all his accolades as perhaps the Allies' finest operational leader, Patton, for his part, still unimaginatively planned and directed an offensive through Lorraine, lasting from September through December 1944, during which he spread the 3rd Army's nine divisions across 60 miles of real estate. Patton thus allowed a weaker opposing force to turn his advance into a slowly unfolding bloodbath. Mastering the operational art of warfare requires practice, planning, more practice, planning, and more practice still. To have expected such capabilities from a nation that up until World War II had virtually no tradition of a professional army establishment, in an era of recent revolution in military culture and practice no less, may have been asking a bit much.

Overall, the defeats inflicted on Germany from June 6, 1944, to early September 1944 appeared insurmountable. Allied intelligence briefs determined prior to D-Day that they would not reach the German border until May 2, 1945. Yet in September 1944, the U.S. Army did exactly that as GIs stepped onto German soil following a post-Falaise collapse of the German front in France that lasted for the better part of an entire month and featured the formation and destruction of several German pockets, including one near Mons, Belgium, early in September. The situation was so bad that Rundstedt, having been recalled by Hitler early in September to serve yet again as Commander in Chief West, assessed his 60-plus divisions in Army Groups B and G as having an effective combat strength only half that number. Germany's field army in the west that had been 892,000 men strong on July 1 by September 1 could put only 543,000 men into the field. In Italy, the Allied armies had surged past Rome, pushing well into Tuscany. Over Germany, the Allied air armadas annihilated German domestic fuel production and ripped apart the Reich's infrastructure. In eastern Europe, the German army had lost over 900,000 men since the end of June. Nevertheless, Hitler firmly held on to power. Moreover, the Wehrmacht had resurrected itself from the grave. It was able to accomplish this monumental task for a number of reasons, and, what's more, do so even though Hitler was handicapping the German army's best efforts to reassemble along Germany's western border—as he held back his best divisions in preparation for Wacht am Rhein, a massive planned counterattack against the Allies to be launched through the Ardennes.

One reason the German army was able to stave off total defeat in western Europe during the late summer of 1944 was that Hitler had brought in some of his most seasoned commanders to lead German forces, men such as Rundstedt and Model, with the latter's organizational and defensive skills put to good use in command of Army Group B. Moreover, on September 20, 1944 another proven tank commader, General Hermann Balck, took command of Army Group G, replacing Blaskowitz. In addition, in terms of generating more manpower, Hitler had created the Volksgrenadier divisions ("people's divisions"). These were comprised of men from the Luftwaffe and Kriegsmarine, as well as teenage boys and those previously considered unfit for military service. The Volksgrenadiers combined with the formation of the Volkssturm, a militia, to bring another million men under arms from August to December 1944.[46] Although these men could hardly compare to first-rate frontline divisions, let alone being ready to challenge world-class highly mobile Allied armies on open terrain, they would not have to. The German border region featured terrain deeply hostile to mobile operations, including numerous rivers, ravines, and thickly forested hills, all drenched in autumn rains greatly lessening the effectiveness of experienced Allied combined arms teams.

In addition, while German armies efficiently reorganized on relatively well maintained interior lines of communication, the Allies had to fight at the end of frayed and extended logistical lines. This left the Allies striving to take select towns linking road and rail lines that the Germans had long since recognized as of vital importance for moving through the region. Thus the Germans had long since fortified these communications centers with the bunkers and obstacles of a Siegfried Line that, though far from imposing on paper, could significantly leverage its defenses with the advantages posed by the favorable terrain. All of which allowed the Germans to concentrate their defensive efforts on the few remotely adequate routes of advance into Germany, such as in the Saar and near Aachen.

Furthermore, the German replacement system, Wehrkreise, also proved particularly efficient in rebuilding shattered divisions. A system that divided the German Reich into administrative zones, the Wehrkreise were responsible for training, weapons testing and development, raising home defense armies, and setting up new units or repairing old ones. With a history dating back to military reforms made in the former Prussian kingdom of the seventeenth to nineteenth centuries, the key to Germany's replacement system was in maintaining a constant core around which each division could rebuild. Wounded men returned to their parent units, and replacements who were culturally similar to those who had come before renewed each formation's ranks. Accordingly, the German system for building and maintaining the military establishment guaranteed the loyalty and esprit de corps of its men. Each fought for each other, and for the past reputation of units represented by those family and friends who came generations before. As a result, even as veteran, fast-moving U.S. formations, such as the 1st Infantry Division and 3rd Armored Division, bolstered by the 9th Tactical Air Command, pounded elements of Army Group B in the Mons pocket early in September, not only was the German 7th Army being quickly reconstructed under the command of General Erich Brandenberger, but its largely immobile, mostly half-strength mix of formations were also moving into the superb defensive terrain along the German front near Aachen. There the Germans lack of training, mobility, and armor did not hurt them nearly as much as it should have given the impact of not only the terrain, but also the ability of even the Siegfried Line's relatively weak fortifications to dramatically increase their combat capabilities.

German efforts at reorganization also received tremendous boosts from Allied operational and tactical mistakes. For instance, the blow sustained from losing the huge port at Antwerp to the advancing British army on September 4 was mitigated by Montgomery's colossal failure to clear the approaches to the port in a timely manner. Instead, the German 15th Army escaped encirclement and dug in along the myriad islands, marshes, and flooded land controlling Antwerp's link to the ocean, interdicting prospective Allied shipping and negating any logistical advantage created by taking the port upriver from the sea. In addition to Allied mistakes, there were still other reasons for the Third Reich's survival.

Hitler was not just the German leader, but with the increasing radicalization that had followed the attempt on his life, he had, in effect, become the state. There were hardly any checks on Hitler's rule and, given their role in the Holocaust and thus likely no way out, the vast majority of the Nazi Party, government apparatus, and military and business establishment all lined up behind him for a nihilistic fight to the death. For those who questioned his rule, a massive crackdown on any domestic dissent, with widespread acts of violence and terror against the German population that would only accelerate in the months to come, coupled with an ideological retrenching to ensure there would be no uprising from within the main body of a German people that had increasingly come to hate the Nazi Party.[47] Of course, not all hated the Nazi Party. The Wehrmacht's newest recruits, many of whom were teenage boys, in many ways represented the perfect disciples for Hitler and the Nazi political leadership. After all, they had been raised on little but Nazi ideology; believed in their own perceived racial superiority; believed, like their commanding officers, especially top-ranking generals who showed mostly unswerving loyalty to Hitler to the end, if not in the strength of the will, then in the nationalistic theories that had driven the quest for Lebensraum; and, finally, so feared the "inhuman" Slav as to justify the savage resistance characterizing the war's final year and a driving goal of protecting German soil. And just to make sure there was no misunderstanding regarding expectations for the German army, on September 10, 1944, Himmler issued a directive stating that any soldier surrendering was risking his family's life. This order occurred within the context of a Wehrmacht that executed an estimated 21,000 of its own men during the war, almost entirely to guarantee their commitment to fight. This rate of disciplinary terror occured at a rate unmatched by any other of the European war's major participants, but for the Red Army.[48]

Finally, helping to bolster the Wehrmacht's rejuvenation were German factories reaching their highest output levels in the fall of 1944, easily reequipping retreating soldiers and divisions. Moreover, with preparations for the Ardennes counterattack in full swing, the Western Front held a distinct priority in terms of replenishing equipment stocks over the German Eastern Front. For instance, eight of the Panzer divisions reequipping following the late summer disasters in France would field 416 Panzer Vs by mid-December, let alone their additional complement of Panzer IVs; this from a low of 62 Panzer Vs in these same units early in September. Such output was not only a product of temporarily shunting all tank production to the Western Front after November 1 but also stemmed from the fact that by 1944, Hitler had forced 7,487,000 foreign workers[49] and prisoners of war into the labor force. They represented 20.8 percent of the overall workforce. During the 1943–1944 retreat from eastern Europe alone, the Wehrmacht had dragged at least 400,000 people with it; 67,000, mostly women and children, came from Warsaw alone following the failed uprising,[50] all done at an inhuman cost in lives. For instance, in October 1944, approximately 32,000 slave laborers worked to their deaths at the Mittelwerk industrial complex built into and under the Harz Mountains. They produced Hitler's uselessly deployed and expensive "Vengeance rocket" program; it is estimated that Germany could have built 24,000 more fighter aircraft with the resources used to create the A-4 rocket program.[51] Fifty percent of those sent to work at the Mittelwerk died. Mittelwerk furthermore represented only part of a vast apparatus run by the SS for the benefit of the German war machine. For instance, BMW's 16,600 foreign laborers in and near Munich included those from a camp at Allach, a satellite of the infamous Dachau concentration camp.[52] Corporate profits soared as the numbers of concentration camp workers increased, benefiting firms such as I. G. Farben, Siemens, Krupp, Porsche, Junkers, and others. This aided tremendously in rebuilding a Wehrmacht that also took advantage of a series of crucial Allied operational-level mistakes made during the fall of 1944.

MEASURING PROGRESS IN YARDS: THE 1944 ALLIED FALL OFFENSIVE AND THE BATTLEFIELD REASONS FOR FAILURE

In Operation Market Garden, Montgomery attempted what the German army had sought to do for well over a century, namely, produce an operational answer to a strategic problem. In this case, Montgomery attempted to end the war in Europe before Christmas; to be done by skipping across the Rhine River in the Netherlands and thus allowing Montgomery's Army Group to break free into Germany. With Eisenhower backing him, considerable Allied resources fueled and supported Montgomery's plan to the detriment of the overall Allied cause. In particular, SHAEF's failure to support Truscott's U.S. 6th Corps in the Belfort Gap, or to reinforce the U.S. 5th Corps under Major General Gerow, which had contemporaneously penetrated the German western wall, represented significant missed opportunities.[53] Pursuing Market Garden not only meant reorienting the 21st Army Group ever farther north away from one of the prime avenues of advance into Germany, the Aachen corridor, but also meant that the U.S. 1st Army under Hodges had to shift its efforts farther north. This created a cascade effect as the U.S. 9th Army under Simpson was forced to shore up Hodge's flank. Meanwhile, Patton lost critical logistical support necessary for maintaining the pressure farther south. In addition, this meant the entire U.S. 12th Army Group had been largely split north and south of the Ardennes, and, with its component armies largely incapable of supporting each other, this only further bolstered German defensive efforts[54] Farther south yet, the U.S. 7th Army had been forced to stretch its best assets north to bolster Patton's overextended southern flank. All of this was done on behalf of a plan that called on three reinforced airborne divisions to hold multiple crossroads and bridges along a single raised highway providing egress across the marshy low-lying Dutch plains up to 60 miles behind German lines, and, what's more, to do so until British armor could drive up a single road and reach the isolated paratroopers.

Market Garden auspiciously began on September 17 as Allied paratroopers dropped from the sky in an arc from the southwest to the northeast near Eindhoven (the U.S. 101st Airborne Division), Nijmegen, (the U.S. 82nd Airborne Division), and Arnhem (the British 1st Parachute Division and Polish 1st Parachute Brigade). Meanwhile, on the ground, the British 30th Corps, comprising 30,000 men and 20,000 vehicles, began its drive to link up with the paratroopers. The Allies however, had encountered the enormous misfortune of dropping into the re-forming and refitting area for the 2nd SS Panzer Corps, comprised of the veteran 9th SS and 10th SS Panzer Divisions. Although the SS Panzer divisions represented mere shadows of their former selves, they had more than enough firepower to crush lightly armed paratroopers. As the SS pounded the beleaguered paratroopers, especially in and around Arnhem, only on the assault's fifth day did the British armored columns finally reach to within 10 miles west of the Rhine. Moreover, this advance occurred only after two battalions from the Polish brigade dropped from the sky just south of the Rhine on D+4 to help the surviving 3,000 members from the British 1st Airborne Division break out of Arnhem. Montgomery's plan to slip around the German defenses had failed, leaving

Allied forces in northwestern Europe not only lacking in logistical reserves, with such reserves used up to fuel Market-Garden, but also badly out of position for future efforts to penetrate into Germany. The consequences of this defeat reverberated beyond the Allied military effort. German forces held on to large parts of the Netherlands until the war ended, and over 12,000 Dutch citizens starved to death between November 1944 and May 1945; 35,000 more died in German work camps or captivity, and 23,000 more died from Allied bombing raids on German rocket sites and positions that held out within the Netherlands.[55]

Overall, during the fall of 1944, the Wehrmacht took a fearful toll on the Allied army. Though the Allies had closed up with the German border early in September 1944, they would not break free of the German border region and Siegfried Line until six months later—in March of 1945. In particular, October through December 1944 proved some of the most difficult months that the U.S. Army experienced in the entire twentieth century, if not its entire history. For example, General Hodges's 7th and 5th Corps endured one shattered rifle division after another along the relatively well fortified German border near the medieval city of Aachen, only taken on October 21, and in the primeval Huertgen Forest. Although only 10 miles across and 20 miles deep, this forest bore witness to some of the most brutal fighting during the war in northwestern Europe. Crisscrossed by deep ravines and valleys, this region marked one of the wildest parts of the Ardennes-Eiffel forestland, where Belgium, Germany, and Luxembourg come together. Although Bradley had gathered heavy firepower, including yet another Cobra-style carpet-bombing raid, to support an early November 12th Army Group drive to the Rhine, the U.S. 1st Army had been ordered to first sweep through the Huertgen in what was anticipated as a preliminary move to protect the American's flanks. Nonetheless, for the better part of three months, the US Army measured progress in yards. A number of elements played into the Allied difficulties including; the terrain, the Germans, and because the American leadership committed the veteran American infantry piecemeal against the one part of the front where the weakened German army could easily mount an effective defense.

Despite heroic efforts by American company, platoon, and squad leaders, the American leadership fed one infantry division after another singly into the dreary rain-soaked forest, each chewed up in mere weeks and spit back out of the meat grinder. In only 11 days of fighting and with only two of its three regiments engaged in the forest fighting, the American 9th Infantry Division suffered 4,500 casualties in capturing 3,000 yards of bloody real estate.[56] Then, on November 2, the veteran American 28th Infantry Division, led by Major General Norman D. Cota, received orders to enter the forest, force a breakthrough, and advance on the Rhine River. The 28th Infantry was a powerful division, lavishly equipped with engineers, mortars, artillery, tanks, and tank destroyers and supported by a battery of corps-level artillery, all to facilitate the breakthrough.[57] Unfortunately, the men in the 28th

Infantry Division faced not only the appalling weather, paucity of winter clothing, and claustrophobic fighting conditions in the Huertgen but also a poor plan of attack put together at the corps level. This plan divided Cota's combat elements among multiple objectives with no real chance to provide mutual support for each individual axis of attack. In total, the 28th Infantry Division suffered 6,184 casualties in a battle Charles B. MacDonald describes it as "one of the most costly actions to be fought by a United States division during World War II."[58] American armored units in the region hardly fared better. On the northern edge of the Huertgen, CCB of the 3rd Armored Division was carved up by a combination of German flak guns, artillery, mines, and Panzerfausts. Even the elite U.S. 1st Infantry Division paid a steep price in finally pushing through the forest's final four miles over the course of two weeks; with the loss of 4,000 casualties.

All told, from September 14 to December 13, the U.S. Army committed five infantry divisions, an entire combat command from the 5th Armored Division, and numerous supporting units totaling over 120,000 men to win an advance totaling just over 20 miles. Nearly a third of the men committed to battle were killed, wounded, or captured; suffered debilitating physical illness or mental breakdown; or will never be found.[59] The infantry battalions had played a particularly heavy price, with the U.S. 7th Corps alone suffering over 24,000 casualties from early November to mid-December 1944 alone. Although the Germans had also suffered heavy casualties and material losses in and around Aachen and the Huertgen, for instance, the U.S. 2nd Armored Division, though losing 75 tanks of its own, had destroyed 86 of the 9th Panzer Division's and 15th Panzer Grenadier Division's AFVs in heavy fighting late in November, losses that would later be felt during the Ardennes offensive; the Germans, using minimal resources, had largely managed to stabilize their Western Front. For their part, the Allied armies had struggled across the entire Western Front and even when taking their objectives suffered through horribly blown timetables and brutal casualties.

In the Netherlands, the efforts to clear the Scheldt Estuary meant that 13,000 men, mostly Canadian, fell in clearing the approaches to Antwerp, finally completed on November 26. Far to the south, the fortress city of Metz held out against repeated assaults from Patton's 3rd Army dating back to September 5; only by November 21 had the majority of the fort and city fell to the American attackers. They had been held up mostly by powerful defensive fortifications, but also ones manned by only a couple of poorly trained German infantry divisions and the understrength 17th SS Panzer Grenadier Division. Patton's quest to penetrate into Germany ground to a halt at the western wall after crossing the Saar River early in December. His men had suffered approximately 50,000 casualties during the fall of 1944.

Meanwhile, Devers's Army Group had been forced to protect Patton's flank, rather than take full advantage of the German 19th Army's weakness.

Devers's best corps, Truscott's 6th Corps, had been ordered to attack into the imposing and deeply forested Vosges Mountains. The fighting ground on week after week. The German 19th Army's defenders fell back on seemingly endless forested mountains, hills, and ravines. The effort was exhausting. The intensity of the struggle along the German border sent morale plunging in the Allied armies. Desertion rates soared. By January 1945, the U.S. Army officially recognized that there were approximately 18,000 AWOL (absent-without-leave) Americans, joining the estimated 10,000 British soldiers who had abandoned their duties and went underground in an attempt to escape the conditions at the front.[60] Even more exasperating, when able to break into the open, the U.S. Army was more than a match for the Germans. For instance, in fighting near the Roer River early in December, the U.S. 2nd Armored Division repelled counterattacks from the 9th Panzer Division, the 15th Panzer Grenadier Division, and an entire battalion of Tigers.[61]

Perhaps most tragically, during the carnage of the fall of 1944, it appears as if Eisenhower may have missed a golden opportunity to close out the war in Europe, for, on November 22, the 6th Army Group's French 2nd Armored Division followed up on the success brought by the U.S. 15th Corps' offensive and launched a final drive through Alsace that would see its men taking nearly all of Strasbourg on November 23. The Germans reacted quickly, but the elite U.S. 4th Armored Division defeated the primary German counterattack.[62] The 6th Army Group, having defeated the German 19th Army in Alsace, sat on the Rhine River, the last major geographic barrier protecting Germany from a western invasion. Thus, Devers, Patch, and the rest of the U.S. 6th Army Group must have been stunned when, on reaching the Rhine, their infantry patrols crossed the river and found nothing blocking their way into Germany, the product of a series of mistaken German assumptions regarding the strength of the Vosges Mountains as a defensive barrier, Allied intentions, and Hitler's decision to pull units out of the line to create reserves for mounting a counteroffensive in the Ardennes.[63]

General Devers immediately ordered the U.S. 15th Corps to cross the Rhine.[64] The plan was straightforward: cross the Rhine, establish a defensive bridgehead, pour men and material over the river, and then wheel north 20 miles to Karlsruhe before turning west. This would trap the entire German 1st Army between the 7th Army and Patton's 3rd Army, all of which would allow Patton to break free, capture the Saar industrial region, and sweep north to the Ruhr. Nevertheless, a forewarned Eisenhower canceled the crossings the very day before they were set to begin, a controversial decision for which since no single clear answer has emerged as to why it was made.[65] Devers has to take some blame as well. A bolder general, such as Patton, likely would have crossed first and then told Eisenhower as a fait accompli, exactly what Patton did when he crossed the Rhine in March 1945.[66] In the meantime, Hitler prepared one more German roll of the dice.

Chapter 13

End Game

THE ROLE GERMAN DEFEAT IN THE ARDENNES PLAYED IN THE THIRD REICH'S FINAL DESTRUCTION

By mid-December 1944, the Allies had spent months mired in bloody combat along the western German border. Meanwhile, in eastern Europe, the Red Army's most powerful fronts sat in the same locations they had since early in the fall of 1944—several hundred miles removed from Berlin. Yet by April 1945, or only four months later, Germany's Eastern and Western fronts had collapsed. This final chapter will examine how and why the Allies and Soviet Union engineered the Third Reich's final defeat, illuminating yet again the larger themes discussed in these pages. First, we will return to the late 1944 slugfest on the western German border, and examine what had happened to Allied armies that in September 1944 had been actively discussing ending the war by Christmas.

Despite the reality that the U.S. 1st, 9th, and 3rd Armies all prepared major offensives set to begin in mid-December, a palpable strain wracked the overall Allied army in western Europe, a strain imposed primarily by an ever-growing manpower shortage within the frontline rifle companies. Worst afflicted were the British army and its Commonwealth allies. Nonetheless, the otherwise massive U.S. Army was hardly immune to the same problems. This in large part stemmed from the U.S. Army's method of waging war, not the least of which was the lengthy logistical tail needed to support a nearly completely mechanized field army designed to fight what had been thought would be a highly mobile Wehrmacht.

Meanwhile, combat experience in Italy and Normandy had demonstrated the continued value that infantry held on the battlefield, especially against the immobile German army of 1944 that the Allies faced in reality. As a result, the overstretched and overworked U.S. infantry absorbed a huge percentage of the army's losses. Fully one-third of the 61 U.S. combat divisions in Europe suffered replacement rates over 100 percent, with the U.S. 4th Infantry Division leading the way at a casualty rate of 252.3 percent.[1] By December 1944, the U.S. Army in the European theater of operations was a full 17,000 men understrength in the frontline infantry companies alone.[2] The composition of the average U.S. infantry divisions only made the casualties endured even more prohibitive. A typical U.S. infantry division of 14,000 men comprised 3,240 riflemen. Consequently, when in December 1944 Patton's 3rd Army fought nearly 15 percent understrength in its infantry battalions, these missing 11,000 riflemen would have been enough to flesh out the infantry battalions for an entire corps.

In addition to grappling with inadequate manpower, by December 1944 the world's greatest industrial power had somehow let stocks of important war material, including tanks, decline. Part of the problem had stemmed from the home front, where worker strikes had become an increasingly common response to wages frozen by large corporations enjoying soaring profits. In addition, and in regard to tank output alone, numbers had declined from the demands of Lend-Lease, requests for more tanks in the Pacific theater, and because the U.S. Army had lost in the European theater of operations over 1,000 tanks during the fall of 1944 alone.[3] As early as September 1944, and because of heavier-than-expected tank losses in Normandy, the U.S. Army's armored units in the theater fought some 335 Sherman tanks understrength. This was the rough equivalent of one and a half armored division's worth. By the end of January 1945, this gap had grown to 865 medium tanks, leaving U.S. armored units 30 percent understrength.[4]

Meanwhile, in the fall of 1944, Hitler planned a counteroffensive against the Allies. This plan called for attacking through the Ardennes, driving to Antwerp, and thus cutting off the Allied armies farther north in a rough imitation of the stunning success of 1940. There are several theories as to what exactly Hitler was trying to accomplish. American historian Howard D. Grier has argued that Hitler's offensive was actually part of a comprehensive strategic plan. A plan premised largely on Admiral Karl Doenitz's position that if Germany could protect the Baltic coast and Scandinavia for training German U-boat crews, then he could deliver enough of the modern Type XXI and Type XXIII U-boats to cut the Allied sea-lanes in the Atlantic and starve Britain from the war.

If Hitler's counterstroke in the Ardennes could cripple the Allied armies, it was thought that this would allow Germany to then engineer a massive transfer of military resources east. Hitler could then crush the better part of the Red Army between twin offensives launched by Army Group Center in Prussia and Poland and the remainder of Army Group North trapped in Courland. This would buy time for Doenitz's new U-boats to come online.[5] To that end, on August 19, 1944, Hitler had ordered Speer to study the consequences of territorial losses held by the Germans. On September 5, Speer informed Hitler that Germany could afford to lose the Balkans and suffer the loss of trading with Sweden, Spain, and Portugal because Germany would have enough important raw materials, such as chromium, to support arms production until January 1, 1946. Speer assumed that Germany would hang on to Hungary, Croatia, northern Italy, and the Polish lands conquered in 1939.

In looking at Hitler's subsequent decisions, we see remarkable congruence with Speer's report. Hitler allowed his armies to retreat from southern France and the Balkans. Conversely, he ordered the French ports along the Atlantic held at all costs; he also maintained a large garrison in Norway and Denmark, and refused to allow Army Group North to evacuate from Courland. Moreover, early in 1945, and following the Ardennes debacle, Hitler would send Germany's tank reserves to Hungary, where Germany's best remaining oil source was located. In January 1945, Hitler also let Army Group Center be bottled up in the Baltic ports in East Prussia and Pomerania, to hold open U-boat training areas in the Baltic, rather than fall back to defend Berlin.[6] Grier's position strongly contrasts with the conventional wisdom, encouraged through memoirs such as by Guderian, that Hitler was little more than a raving idiot by the fall of 1944. In addition, there are other, and longer standing, arguments for why Hitler chose to attack in the Ardennes, namely, Hitler's belief in his own destiny; and its parallels with a Prussian history based in part on Frederick the Great's victories against much larger opposing armies at Rossbach and Leuthen—victories that had caused the coalition against Prussia to fall apart.

If we were to assume that Hitler was as heavily influenced by Donitz as has recently been advocated, then a more limited plan, proposed by several of Hitler's key generals, had a far greater chance of accomplishing similar goals. Moreover, in this case, Hitler's generals may have been on to something given the multitude of reasons why it was doubtful that Hitler's armies could reach Antwerp, not the least of which was the unlikelihood of his largely immobile and oil-starved army being able to generate the speed needed to meet his goals. In addition, though the fall fighting in the Huertgen forest had bloodied American forces, it had not left the Germans unscathed. It had decimated half a dozen German divisions and placed the Americans in control of a region that had the Germans been able to have held onto would have made Hitler's plan more feasible. The more narrowly structured plan of the German generals would have therefore more realistically sought to envelop and destroy the 14 American divisions near the Huertgen forest and Aachen. If successful, this would have effectively forced the Allies onto their heels, and thus have allowed Germany to quickly shift ample, relatively fresh resources to fight the Red Army. In addition, under this plan, the shortened distance that German troops would need to traverse stood far more in line with the miniscule German fuel reserves.[7] Reserves, that, as it was, would be stretched to their limits in powering the stocks of heavy German tanks gathered in the Ardennes. What's more, these tanks, even had they possessed the fuel, were unlikely to go very far given the typical German Panther–equipped Panzer battalion on the German Western Front was lucky if it exceeded a 70 percent readiness rate on the eve of the Ardennes offensive. Regardless, Hitler ordered up the more ambitious but risky plan, in a gamble with Germany's entire strategic reserves.

German plans called for Sepp Dietrich's 6th SS Panzer Army to lead the assault through the Ardennes, as the northern army of the three German assault armies. Dietrich first needed to seize Eupen, Stavelot, and Vevries; so that he could establish a strong defensive shoulder for the drive west to the Losheim gap and beyond. Just to the 6th SS Panzer Army's south was Manteuffel's 5th Panzer Army, which first needed to take the important road junctions of Bastogne and St. Vith. After crossing the Meuse River near Namur, the 5th Panzer Army was to provide support and protection for the SS spearhead's southern flank. The Panzer armies deployed a combined armored strength of 900 tanks and 200 self-propelled guns. The all-infantry 7th Army under General Eric Brandenburger provided flank protection for the southern shoulder of the offensive. All told, the German assault force was over 20 divisions strong, including seven Panzer divisions, from 28 total divisions earmarked for the offensive. Despite its size, the assault armies assembled largely concealed from the mostly unsuspecting Allies. Therefore, only four thinly spread infantry divisions in the Ardennes held the line for the Americans, backed up by elements of the U.S. 9th Armored Division. The Germans enjoyed overwhelming local superiority in all arms if not in logistics, time, and leadership. As to the latter point, Hodges, commanding the 1st Army, and Patton, later to play a key role in the battle, ranked as far better officers than Dietrich. On the other hand, the advantage that the Germans enjoyed in achieving near absolute surprise gave them a chance. It was with this chance that the German counteroffensive began early on the cold morning of December 16, 1944.

The Americans were quickly forced to give ground, with many of the early retreats turning into a rout. German success proved ephemeral however, especially for the 6th SS Panzer Army, as Dietrich committed several fundamental errors. For one, he allowed his spearheads to bog down, and endured repeated stiff fights against several American infantry units that did not crumble and, far from it, bought time for reinforcements to pour into the area. In particular, one platoon from the 394th Regiment of the U.S. 99th Infantry Division, ensconced in the village of Lanzerath, fought off a series of desperate assaults launched by elements of the German 3rd Parachute Division. It became the most decorated American platoon for a single action during World War II. In addition, Dietrich had begun his offensive with a crushing artillery barrage that did little more than warn the Americans he was coming, as well-dug-in

BATTLE OF THE BULGE

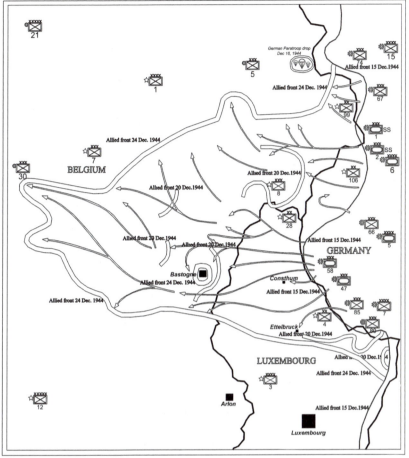

U.S. positions with even modest overhead cover were able to ride out the onslaught. Meanwhile, on December 17, Brigadier General Bruce Clarke's Combat Command B, from the American 7th Armored Division, met the 1st SS Panzer Division on the approaches to the critical communications crossroads at St. Vith, 10 miles behind the original Allied front lines. During eight days of fierce combat, the American armor, surviving elements from the 106th Infantry Division, and a hodgepodge of independent units held off multiple German assaults. Eventually, however, the Germans forced the Americans to withdraw, but only after the GIs had completely upset the German timetable. In response, Model shifted the offensive's weight to the 5th Panzer Army, which by the night of December 17 had penetrated 20 miles following Manteuffel's skillful use of infiltration tactics to facilitate his initial penetrations in the U.S. lines. Nevertheless, Allied reinforcements streamed toward the fighting. Most prominently these included Patton's headquarters staff and an entire corps pulled from the line well south of the Ardennes, and wheeled north to road march approximately 100 miles; a feat that a German Panzer corps would have been hard pressed to accomplish at this stage in the war. Within days, over 60,000 reinforcements had arrived in the U.S. 1st Army's area of operations. These men included the elite U.S. 82nd and 101st Airborne Divisions. Ordered to hold the vital road junction at Bastogne, a mixed bag of encircled airborne and armored troops further delayed the German push west.

Then, on December 23, the skies cleared. Allied aircraft pounded German forces as they ground ahead to reach within four miles of the Meuse River on December 26. Nevertheless, relentless air attacks, lack of fuel, and the defensive efforts led by the American 2nd Armored and 84th Infantry Divisions brought the Germans to a screeching halt. The American 2nd Armored Division almost completely annihilated the German 2nd Panzer Division.[8] Also on December 26, a relief column led by Lieutenant Colonel Creighton W. Abrams's 37th Tank Battalion from the 4th Armored Division had lifted the German siege against Bastogne. Meanwhile, the American 3rd Armored Division stopped the German 2nd SS Panzer Division east of Namur.

Hitler's great counteroffensive had failed, though it would take until January 28, 1945, for the Allies to regain the ground lost to the Germans. Hitler's counterattack in the Ardennes had cost him his strategic reserves: 100,000 casualties against 81,000 American and 1,400 British casualties. The Luftwaffe lost nearly 1,000 aircraft, and the Panzer divisions lost 800 tanks, with yet again as much as 40 percent of German tank losses attributable to mechanical failure. For their part, the Americans had lost 730 tanks and tank destroyers.[9] The German defeat's scope was such that one leading U.S. general, Joe Collins, believed that the Ardennes campaign took six months off the war's length.[10]

GOTTERDAMMERUNG IN THE EAST

In January 1945, the Red Army, the primary beneficiary of Hitler's gamble in the Ardennes, readied an ambitious campaign of its own, one designed to surge across Poland's plains and into Germany, all while conducting additional offensives on the front's northern and southern peripheries. Working against the Red Army was the fact that the breadth of the front had narrowed, and that German defenses had thickened—particularly in East Prussia. On paper, however, the Red Army completely outclassed the thinly spread Wehrmacht.

The 1945 Red Army fielded 6.5 million men in over 500 rifle divisions equipped with 12,900 tanks and self-propelled guns, 15,000 frontline aircraft, and over 100,000 guns and mortars. Although this army had been nearly as massive in 1941 and had been decimated by its Axis foes, it had dramatically matured as the renaissance of operational theories developed and applied in the past had been further refined under the auspices of a cadre of aggressive and relentless leaders. Perhaps most significant, in the Red Army of January 1945 firepower was king. A full 10 percent of the Red Army's men were employed in support and logistical units, stockpiling and delivering the gasoline and munitions needed to power the Red Army's abundant heavy weapons. In addition, in January 1945, another one-sixth of the Red Army's strength was in artillery, compared to only 8 percent in 1941,[11] and in tank-heavy units.[12]

Organizationally, by the war's end the typical Soviet tank army included 50,000 men, 850 to 920 tanks and self-propelled guns, and 800 guns and mortars. The 1945-era tank corps included 212 T-34s and 49 self-propelled guns. All told, the Red Army deployed its 12,900 tanks and self-propelled guns in six tank armies, 14 independent tank corps, seven independent mechanized corps, 27 independent tank brigades, seven self-propelled artillery brigades, and dozens of independent tank and self-propelled gun regiments.[13] The vast numbers of guns available meant that a typical 4,000-man rifle division, really no more than a regiment in any other army of the era, still had the backing of a division's worth of artillery plus ample numbers of automatic weapons.[14] More than ever before, the Red Army's attempts to find manpower meant that greater numbers of White Russians, Ukrainians, and other non-Russian ethnic groups filled out the rifle company's ranks.[15] For instance, of the 2.5 million men in the fronts assigned to clear the Germans from Poland and East Prussia, 200,000 were Polish soldiers.

Stavka deployed this army in a Soviet winter campaign that would begin on the front's southern boundary, in Hungary, with an axis of attack directed toward Vienna. The 2nd and 3rd Ukrainian fronts, with Malinovsky and Tolbukhin in command, respectively, led this offensive. In Poland, the Red Army would begin the main stage of the frontwide offensive with Zhukov's 1st Belorussian Front, set to envelop Warsaw and explode west toward the prewar German border and Berlin. Konev's 1st Ukrainian Front, to Zhukov's south, would penetrate past Krakow and into the vitally important industrial region of Silesia. Just north of the 1st Belorussian Front, the 2nd Belorussian Front, led by Rokossovsky, and the 3rd Belorussian Front, led by Cherniakhovsky, would seek to batter their way through the heavy defensive belts protecting Prussia. Facing Rokossovsky's 2nd Belorussian Front and Chernyakhosvsky's 3rd Belorussian Front were more than 400,000 German soldiers in the 4th and 3rd Panzer Armies as well as innumerable smaller formations. For its part, in January 1945 the 3rd Panzer Army was a shadow of the armored juggernaut it had been earlier in the war, a mere nine infantry divisions. Only the 5th Panzer Division's 50 tanks gave any credence at all to its grandiose name.[16]

Although the Red Army disguised its plans as best possible, there was little mystery regarding what the Wehrmacht faced. Hitler's focus, however, was on the Soviet offensives near Budapest, mostly because of Hitler's desire to protect the western Hungarian oil fields. Of the 18 German Panzer divisions opposing the Red Army in January 1945, seven fought in Hungary, two remained trapped in Courland, four defended East Prussia, and only five sat opposite Konev's and Zhukov's massive collection of men and machines in Poland.[17] Consequently, the battles in Hungary, lasting from January to March 1945, featured the final great armored clashes of the war. The Red Army deployed 2,130 tanks and assault guns in the Carpathian Basin of central and eastern Hungary against 1,050 tanks and assault guns in Germany's Army Group South. Hitler and the OKH, however, deployed the Panzer divisions in a disjointed and piecemeal fashion.[18] They thus foreclosed on the chance to mass the German armor for a single blow that may have resulted in the destruction of the Soviet fronts deployed in Hungary; an outcome that may have forced Stalin to rethink his strategy for ending the war.

Accordingly, and with the Red Army having enveloped and besieged Budapest on December 26, 1944, Hitler first sent to Hungary the 4th SS Panzer Corps comprising 60,000 men and 200 tanks in total.[19] Shortly after the New Year, Hitler dispatched the 6th SS Panzer Army to Hungary. Ultimately, between January 1, 1945, and March 15, 1945, alone, Hitler ordered up five offensives in western Hungary. Some of these offensives were powerful. For instance, on January 18, heavy German attacks launched by the 4th SS Panzer Corps nearly split Tolbukhin's 3rd Ukrainian Front in half. The German attacks crushed the Soviet 7th Mechanized Corps and, but for a lack of infantry, nearly encircled the Soviet 18th Tank Corps and 133rd Rifle Corps plus advanced to within 15 miles of the Axis units trapped in Budapest. In turn, Tolbukhin launched fierce counterattacks of his own, and beat back the German effort.[20] As it was, from October 29, 1944, to February 11, 1945, the Red Army suffered 80,026 dead and 240,056 wounded in the fighting near Budapest, while the 2nd and 3rd Ukrainian fronts lost 1,766 tanks and assault guns, 4,127 heavy artillery pieces, and 293 aircraft during this same period. This was far from a one-sided fight. From October 29, 1944, to February 15, 1945, the Axis armies suffered 137,000 dead, wounded, and captured in the fighting near Budapest.[21]

As German forces dueled with the Red Army in Hungary, two German army groups—Army Group A in southern Poland and, to its north, Army Group Center—awaited the Red Army's main strength. All told, the Germans had gathered 980,000 men, 1,836 tanks and self-propelled guns, and 785 aircraft. Straddling southern Poland and northeastern Czechoslovakia, Army Group A's five armies, running from north to south the German 9th Army, the 4th Panzer Army, the 17th Army, the 1st Panzer Army, and the Hungarian 1st Army, were strung out along a massive, almost uniformly thin defensive front approximately 470 mile wide. They were backed by a mere five and a half mobile divisions.[22] In contrast, the 1st Ukrainian Front had massed 1,700 tanks and assault guns, mostly from the 3rd Guards Tank Army and 4th Tank Army, in the roughly 75-mile-wide and 36-mile-deep bridgehead facing the 4th Panzer Army and part of the 17th Army.[23] In addition, Hitler refused to countenance any anticipatory withdrawals prior to the beginning of the Soviet offensive. Thus, when on January 12 Konev began the offensive with a massive artillery barrage, it killed or wounded nearly one-quarter of the German combat troops lost in the front-line trenches.[24] Following closely behind the artillery, the 1st Ukrainian Front's combined-arms assault echelons simply shattered the 4th Panzer Army's dazed frontline infantry divisions.[25] Konev's breakthrough and exploitation forces, led by the 3rd Guards and 4th Tank Armies, subsequently raced through a gap in the German lines over 20 miles wide and bypassed the majority of the German defensive zone. Then, on January 14, Zhukov's 1st Belorussian Front's 61st Army, 5th Army, and 8th Guards Army, with its exploitation and pursuit forces led by the 1,635 tanks and self-propelled guns in the 1st Guards Tank Army and 2nd Guards Tank Army, ripped into the German 9th Army.[26]

All across the German front in Poland, efforts to stop the Red Army proved hopelessly inadequate. That said, events on the 9th Army's defensive front demonstrated the importance that even weak armored reserves fighting a mobile battle held for the outcome of such seemingly one sided late-war battles. For example, on the evening of the first day, the reinforced 19th Panzer Division actually brought one Soviet spearhead to a halt. Moreover, this had occurred despite the fact that the 19th Panzer Division had itself been attacked by the Soviet assault echelons, destroying 51 Soviet tanks in the process, before it could launch its own counterattack. Still, where armored reserves were either nonexistent or poorly deployed, the Red Army easily punched through the German front. Thus, both the 9th Army's sector and the 4th Panzer Army's sector collapsed. Ironically, prior to the Soviet attack, Army Group A had been forced to give up the 8th and 20th Panzer Divisions to Army Group South for operations in Hungary.[27] The inopportune shuffling of German mobile divisions in the weeks prior to the beginning of the Soviet Vistula-Oder offensive highlights yet again one reason why a formerly qualitatively superior German army was being defeated by more numerically blessed foes that it had otherwise handled quite efficiently earlier in the war, but against whom it could no longer maneuver effectively.

Meanwhile, on Army Group A's southern flank, both the 17th and the 1st Panzer Army gave ground in a more controlled fashion. The OKH (Oberkommando der Heer, or Army High Command) reshuffled its armies so that Army Group A became Army Group Center. Regardless, Konev crossed the Oder River, entered into Silesia, and encircled the towns of

SOVIET VISTULA TO ODER OFFENSIVE

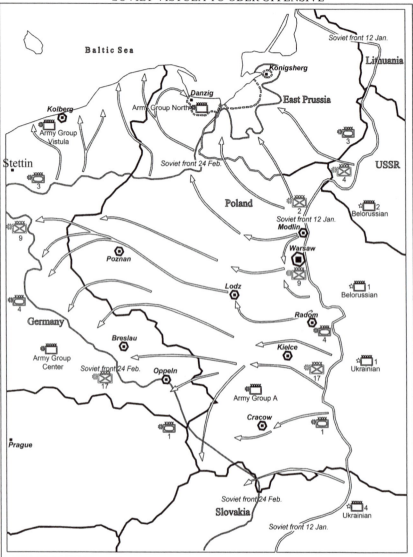

Breslau and Glogau with 35,000 to 50,000 and 4,100 German soldiers, respectively, cut off in each city. Breslau, situated along the Oder River, held out until the end of the war despite being defended by a hodgepodge of German army regulars, Luftwaffe field units, militia (in particular a large contingent of Volkssturm), police, SS, Kriegsmarine, and Hitler Youth.[28] For its part, the 1st Ukrainian Front, having masked Breslau, finally came to a halt in

February on the Neisse River,[29] though it still needed to clear German troops from vast sections of Upper and Lower Silesia.[30] In addition, and in late January, the Red Army liberated Auschwitz, where only a few thousand victims survived from the more than 1 million "processed" through the death camp by Hitler's minions. These few barely clung to life after abandonment in the frigid cold nine days earlier, when the SS had brutally marched the remaining concentration camps victims to the west. This death march was far from unique, and in the final months of the war, approximately 250,000 people would be killed in such forced relocations, as the Third Reich continued its genocidal policies to the very end of its existence.[31]

Meanwhile, in Prussia, the 3rd Belorussian Front's 44 rifle divisions, 3,000 guns, and 800 tanks had slammed into the 3rd Panzer Army's defenses on an axis of advance heading straight for Königsberg. However, General Erhard Raus, leading 3rd Panzer Army, still had a few tricks up his sleeve. Most of the Red Army's preassault artillery bombardment had landed on largely empty lines as Raus, anticipating the January 13 assault date, had withdrawn most of this men out of harm's way. Then Raus counterattacked with his modest armored reserves, destroyed 122 Soviet tanks, and retook his original defensive positions. The Soviet assault completely bogged down in the German defensive zones. Nevertheless, with the Germans lacking the backing and fluidity to take advantage of their initially strong defensive efforts, by January 18 Soviet pressure had forced the Germans to begin falling back on Königsberg. The 5th Guards Tank Army reached Elbing on the Baltic coast late in January, and thus the 3rd Panzer Army, the 4th Army, and part of the 2nd Army were isolated in East Prussia. The 3rd Panzer Army headquarters, 4th Panzer Division, and several infantry divisions were subsequently evacuated out and re-formed the 3rd Panzer Army in Pomerania to the west.[32]

In the center of the front and on January 17, Warsaw fell to Zhukov's 1st Belorussian Front. In the Polish countryside, the reconstituted German 4th Panzer and 9th Armies had simply ceased to exist. Thousands of cutoff German troops fell dozens of miles behind Soviet armored spearheads. Over the ensuing weeks, small groups of German soldiers desperately attempted to infiltrate west past Soviet spearheads and toward relative safety in Germany.[33] On January 22, Zhukov's 1st Belorussian Front, rapidly approaching the prewar German border with Poland, and enveloped but did not seize the important road and rail center at Posen, yet another of Hitler's fortress cities. Some 12,000 German soldiers, militia, and police had taken refuge in Posen, protected by massive nineteenth-century forts, including an inner citadel. It would end up taking parts of Chuikov's elite 8th Guards Army and the 69th Army well over one month to finally take Posen, with the final German surrender occurring only on February 23.[34]

As Zhukov's and Konev's armies rampaged across central Poland, the German 1st Panzer Army had been left far behind in the Tatra Mountains along the Polish-Czech border. The 1st Panzer Army, part of Army Group A in January, was by March part of the re-formed Army Group Center, which also included the 4th Panzer Army and the 17th Army. In a three-week span following January 30, the new Army Group Center actually gave up only about 12 miles against Petrov's 4th Ukrainian Front.[35] Petrov was ultimately replaced by Eremenko, as an offensive beginning on March 10 netted only seven to eight miles in one week of fighting against a stubborn German defense spearheaded by the understrength 8th and 16th Panzer Divisions. For his part, Eremenko fared hardly better.[36] German defensive tactics during these battles again show what a numerically outmatched army could do to a more powerful foe, but mostly only if it retained its flexibility of movement and even remotely adequate armored reserves.[37] For instance, on March 22 the unimposing 8th Panzer Division and Fuhrer-Begleit Division destroyed 101 Soviet tanks. German infantry losses were severe,[38] but one would be hard pressed to find even one example of Anglo-American tank losses approaching such levels in any one single-day engagement during all of 1945. All told, between March 10 and April 4, the Red Army lost 1,423 tanks and assault guns against Army Group Center.[39]

Meanwhile, to the north, on January 26, the 1st Belorussian Front crossed the German prewar border with Poland. From January 31 to February 2, all of Zhukov's lead armies had reached and even crossed the Oder River,[40] which sat only 40 miles east of Berlin and represented the final major geographic barrier protecting Berlin. That said, though the Oder itself was fairly wide, it was not particularly deep. Accordingly, what made the Oder a strong defensive position was the marshy, wet, low-lying land stretching away to its west; land bisected by numerous canals, streams, and other rivers, all of which was flooded and a veritable sea of mud and water in the late winter to early spring of 1945. This difficult terrain for wheeled vehicles ran west some six to nine miles until hitting the Seelow Heights, which granted an additional advantage to the defender in providing observation over the entire region.

Unfortunately for the Germans, Zhukov had established multiple bridgeheads across the Oder. His efforts to link these bridgeheads however, were repeatedly stymied in particular by German forces defending Kustrin. Along with its suburbs, Kustrin sat astride the Oder and Warthe Rivers in an area representing a critical communications junction astride key highway and rail lines running from Berlin. Then, making Zhukov's task more difficult, Stalin had ordered him to dispatch his potent tank armies north into Pomerania. This was to support Rokossovsky's 2nd Belorussian Front against the savage German resistance in Prussia, and to eliminate the questionable threat to Zhukov's extended northern flank posed by the woefully weak German forces in Pomerania. Stalin's decision gave the Germans the time they desperately needed to throw together defenses before Berlin, and to launch further counterattacks against the Soviet bridgeheads over the Oder. These counterattacks ultimately failed, in part because they were all too often launched on an ad hoc basis without effectively concentrating available assets; such as in regard to the counterattacks launched independently by the 21st Panzer Division and the 25th Panzer Grenadier Division.[41]

As the German operational art continued its disintegration, the men of the German army paid the price. In January and February alone, the Red Army had inflicted 603,000 casualties on the Wehrmacht, seized the vital Silesian industrial region (up to that point providing enormous quantities of arms for the German war effort), and driven German forces west to the gates of Berlin. Russian casualties also proved horrendous. From January 12 through February 3, Zhukov's 1st Belorussian and Konev's 1st Ukrainian fronts had suffered 77,342 and 115,783 casualties, respectively.[42] Soviet material losses had again been heavy. Konev reported that he had begun the Vistula-Oder operation on January 12 with 3,648 tanks and self-propelled guns. By February 16, his front could put only 1,289 tanks and self-propelled guns into the field.[43]

In addition, the civilian populations of the region suffered incomparable terrors. Zhukov, Konev, and Rokossovsky cleared Poland, Pomerania, and East Prussia in an absolute orgy of murder and rape. The ideologically driven horrors Germany had perpetrated on the Soviet people were repaid in horrific kind on the people of Poland and Prussia. Millions of German women joined their female brethren raped in Hungary, Romania, Poland, and wherever the Red Army conquered.[44] Refugees desperately fleeing the Red Army died in the hundreds of thousands from malnutrition and exposure, as well as mass murder, in random encounters with the brutalized German and Soviet combatants savaging Europe. Freed Soviet prisoners of war and male forced laborers fared only marginally better. Many were immediately sent, with no training or medical attention, to flesh out the ranks of the Red Army's woefully understrength rifle divisions.[45] The Red Army and NKVD (People's Commissariat for Internal Affairs) also rounded up German civilians by the tens of thousands for use as forced laborers. The enslaved women faced not only backbreaking work, but also constant sexual assault and disease.[46] As the Red Army brought its own unique brand of horrors west, an immense struggle for Prussia had taken center stage on Germany's Eastern Front.

The locus for this battle centered on Königsberg, where an epic siege unfolded. The Soviet siege of Königsberg represented the fifth time in history that the Russian army had attacked the city, including twice before during the Seven Years' War, in the winter of 1812–1813, and during 1914 early in World War I. To help alleviate the pressure brought when Prussia had been cut off from Germany proper, the Germans had launched large-scale counterattacks against Rokossovsky's armies in East Prussia. But the Red Army had smashed the German efforts after several days of ferocious fighting. Meanwhile, from January 23 and on into the war's end, the German navy's remnants had begun evacuating over 2 million people from Prussia and to relative safety in Germany proper. Inevitably, tragedy at sea accompanied the carnage on the ground. A Russian submarine torpedoed the 27,000-ton former German cruise ship *Wilhelm Gustloff* on the night of January 30, resulting in an estimated 7,000 people killed in the greatest maritime disaster in history.[47]

On land, the fanatical German defensive effort simply exhausted Rokossovsky's 2nd Belorussian Front. The average Soviet rifle division fell to the strength of an American regiment, around 3,600 men. By February 1945, the 2nd Belorussian Front fielded only 297 tanks, many of these in dubious mechanical condition.[48] The battles in Prussia continued well into April, with Königsberg itself finally succumbing only on April 9.[49] Tens of thousands were killed on all sides, including at least 25,000 civilians, but that was hardly the end of it. Of an estimated population of 110,000 in Königsberg on April 9, by June only 73,000 were left. This followed waves of murder, suicide, and disease that had swept through the city under Soviet occupation.[50] The battle for East Prussia, although causing immense misery to the civilian population, and resulting in the destruction of the German 4th Army, had also cost the Red Army dearly. Between January and April 1945 alone, the Red Army suffered 584,778 casualties and lost 3,525 tanks and 1,450 planes in taking this single German province. To put the intensity of the combat in East Prussia, and the Red Army's losses in East Prussia, into perspective, the Wehrmacht, in comparison, had suffered 700,000 casualties during Operation Barbarossa's first five months across a front nearly 800 miles deep and well over 1,000 miles in breadth.

As Prussia entered the final stages of its centuries-old existence, the Red Army moved to subjugate eastern Pomerania, shrugging off German counter-attacks begun on February 15 as part of the ill-fated and, as modified, largely doomed Operation Sonnenwende.[51] Zhukov and Rokossovsky responded, the latter attacking westward on February 24 and the former attacking to the north on March 1. By March 4, Zhukov's 1st Guards Tank Army and 1st Polish Army had reached the Baltic Sea. By March 21, Zhukov and Rokossovsky had finished clearing most of eastern Pomerania and had driven the battered 3rd Panzer Army west across the Oder.[52]

Within Pomerania, numerous German towns and cities fought extended sieges against the Soviet armies. For instance, Danzig, the city and the issue exploited more than any other by Hitler as grounds for war nearly six years earlier, on March 15 represented the focal point for six Russian armies determined to capture this key communications center on the Baltic. Danzig was also the gathering point for over 1.5 million refugees streaming into Pomerania from East Prussia. On land, the German 2nd Army fought to protect the teeming masses of refugees. Offshore, the German cruisers *Prince Eugen* and *Leipzig* joined the battleship *Schlesien* and pounded the Soviet attackers relentlessly whenever they came within range of the ship's big guns. Nonetheless, the Red Army inexorably advanced. On March 27, the garrison commander of Danzig ordered the city abandoned. Meanwhile, to the southwest of Danzig, Zhukov's siege of Kustrin, and the German effort to maintain a supply corridor to the city, raged unabated throughout February and March. The battle sapped defender and attacker alike, but on March 28, Kustrin finally fell. Zhukov could unite several bridgeheads and create a 30-mile-wide and four-to six-mile-deep springboard in which to amass his men to begin the final drive on Berlin.[53]

As the Red Army dismantled Hitler's army, the soon-to-be-victorious Stalin, Churchill, and Roosevelt had met at Yalta on February 4, 1945. The November 1943 meeting at Tehran had laid the groundwork for the shape of the postwar world, and the meeting at Yalta confirmed many of the earlier-discussed plans. The United States and Soviet Union planned the boundaries setting the new world order, and Britain struggled to retain its own vast empire. Roosevelt and his advisers attached the most importance to cementing American economic primacy in the world, far outweighing considerations over eastern Europe's fate. In particular, American businessmen, and thus political interests, eagerly lined up to cement their claims on Middle Eastern oil.

At the same time, Budapest fell on February 12 in a brutal orgy of murder and rape. Then, on March 5, 1945, Hitler ordered 400,000 German soldiers and 900 tanks and assault guns to hit Tolbukhin's 3rd Ukrainian Front; still located in Hungary. The German forces included six Waffen-SS divisions along with the 1st and 3rd Panzer Divisions. These divisions represented some of the German army's best in 1945. In some cases, they were very well equipped: the 1st SS included 36 King Tigers, and the 12th SS had an attached battalion of 31 Jagpanzer IVs and 11 Jagdpanthers in addition to its organic tank complement.[54] Nonetheless, thanks to ULTRA intercepts, Tolbukhin knew that the Germans were coming and had prepared a deep and elaborate defensive front. With the assistance of mud bogging down the German heavy armor, the Soviet defenses absorbed the German attack. On March 16, the Red Army counterattacked with 1 million soldiers and 1,699 tanks and assault guns. The Soviet offensive ripped a 20-mile hole in the German lines, and Soviet forces advanced though Bratislava into Austria and took Vienna. The German front had crumbled, albeit at the cost of another 167,940 casualties to the Red Army in 31 days of fierce fighting for Vienna. Nevertheless, the stage was set for the long-awaited direct assault on the German capital.

END GAME

Remarkably, Hitler had prepared only a relatively weak defensive force to assist his last stand. To defend the capital, Army Group Vistula fielded 320,000 men in the 3rd Panzer Army and 9th Army. These armies featured few first-class divisions, and in total the Germans could deploy only 754 tanks to defend Berlin.[55] For instance, the relatively strong "Kurmark" Panzer

Grenadier Division, even though bolstered by the attached 502nd SS Heavy Tank Battalion, could field only 92 tanks, assault guns, and self-propelled guns.[56] All told, the 9th Army deployed only 200,000 men and 512 tanks, assault guns, and self-propelled guns; though it could rely on the substantial firepower brought to the field by 139 flak batteries with 695 guns.[57] In addition, Heinrici had built a deeply echeloned 25-mile-thick defensive front featuring countless field fortifications and strongpoints, taking full advantage of the marshy wetlands west of the Oder. Moreover, to avoid the worst of the anticipated Soviet preattack bombardment, he protected his mainline defenders by leaving only a thin screening force in the forward lines.[58]

In opposition, Stalin pitted Zhukov and Konev against each other in an egotistical race to take the city, with the offensive scheduled to begin on April 16, 1945.[59] Only after seizing Berlin would the Red Army deal with the bulk of Army Group Center in Czechoslovakia. Nonetheless, unlike earlier offensives, the Russian plans faced considerable restrictions imposed by Berlin's looming presence as a huge urban center spreading across the 35 miles separating Berlin's center from the front. The Red Army consequently gathered enormous quantities of fuel and munitions to power Zhukov's 1st Belorussian Front's three primary thrusts on the German capital—to be led by the 47th Army, the 3rd Shock Army, and a separate main axis of advance led by the combined forces of the 5th Shock Army and 8th Guards Army. Each assault army was backed by tremendous artillery fire support in concentrations reaching as high as 345 guns and rocket launchers per kilometer. Standing ready to exploit the assault armies' efforts were the 1st and 2nd Guards Tank Armies, all told 1,373 tanks and self-propelled guns between them both.[60] Including Konev's forces, the two Russian fronts fielded 2.5 million men and 6,250 tanks.[61] In addition, on April 20, Rokossovsky's 2nd Belorussian Front, and its 33 rifle divisions and 951 tanks and assault guns, would seek to cross the Oder to the north of Zhukov against General Manteuffel's mere 105,000 men and 242 armored fighting vehicles in the shattered 3rd Panzer Army.[62]

The battle for Berlin began with Zhukov's intense but brief artillery barrage early in the predawn hours of Monday April 16, 1945. Russian assault infantry surged forward, only to be driven back repeatedly by the fierce German defense. German flak guns and Panzers took a fearful toll on the armor supporting the Soviet assault armies, with one German Panzer battalion reporting that it had destroyed as many as fifty Soviet tanks by the evening of the first day.[63] In an attempt to better bolster his infantry Zhukov had assigned approximately half his armor, or more than 1,400 tanks and self-propelled guns, to units outside his two tank armies. The individual Soviet tank and self-propelled gun units however, often restricted by the waterlogged terrain to the roads running across the flat coverless landscape, paid heavily for each kilometer they advanced. Regardless, Zhukov mercilessly threw his men into the slaughter, and ordered the artillery to pound away even as it cut down

ASSAULT ON BERLIN

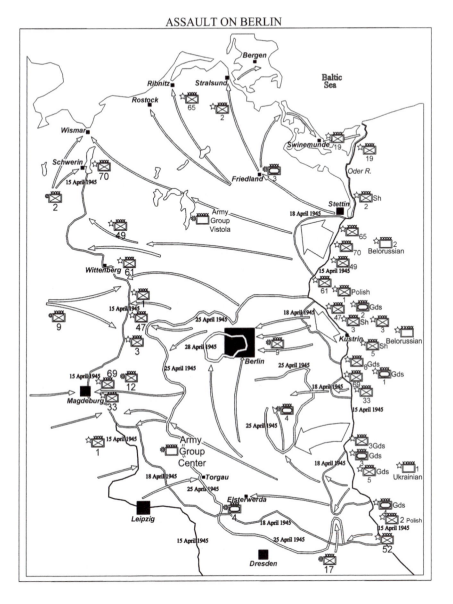

advancing Soviet infantry dying in the thousands. Zhukov, enraged by the delays, early in the afternoon on the first day ordered his two tank armies, totaling six tank corps, forward into the German defenses—this decision being made despite the sodden ground, vast minefields, and the failure of the assault armies to break open a hole in the German defensive front. The battlefield was now hopelessly clogged with Russian men and material. The advance bogged

Table 13.1 Soviet Tank/Self-Propelled Gun Production and Losses during the War[1]

Year	Tank/Self-Propelled Gun Production	Tank/Self-Propelled Gun Losses
1941	4,700	20,500
1942	24,500	15,100
1943	24,100	23,500
1944	29,000	23,700
1945 (January–April)	16,000	13,700
Total	98,300	96,500

[1]David M. Glantz, *When Titans Clashed: How the Red Army Stopped Hitler* (University Press of Kansas, 1995), 306.

down further, and fighting continued without pause throughout the night. Finally, men from Katukov's 1st Guards Tank Army and Chuikov's 8th Guards Army penetrated the German positions, but to a depth of only five miles.[64] Had Heinrici possessed any kind of real armored reserves with which to counterattack Zhukov's front may have been in serious trouble.

Accordingly, Zhukov endured a wrathful call from Stalin, who viciously implied that Konev, who had already ripped the German lines apart farther south, would be allowed to turn toward Berlin. On April 16, Konev's armies had blasted forward behind a 7,700-gun barrage that resulted in established crossings up and down Neisse River by day's end. Although slicing through 4th Panzer Army's defensive front, Konev's men had suffered heavily from German defensive efforts bolstered by local geography, as Konev had to cross two major rivers against frantic counterattacks. Expertly using heavy bridging equipment, however, Konev was able to get the 4th Guards and 3rd Guards Tank Armies in motion, and after shrugging off another counterattack west of Gorlitz, his men were off to the races.[65]

In contrast to Konev's well-executed assault, Zhukov's effort, backed by Antonov and Stalin, against the vastly outnumbered and underarmed German defenders on the Seelow Heights, ranks among one of his more poorly planned and executed operations during the war. It took until the fourth day of the attack, April 19, for Zhukov to fully crack open what was largely a static German defensive front only weakly supported by a paucity of mobile formations. In spite of this, over 30,000 Russian soldiers lost their lives in just three days of combat.[66] Soviet tank crews led the charge into Berlin's suburbs. Fanatic German troops, armed with Panzerfausts, took a heavy toll of the Soviet armor, in a deadly game of cat and mouse, as the Red Army lost 1,997 tanks in the fighting in and around Berlin.[67] Nonetheless, by April 25 the Red Army had enveloped Berlin. Meanwhile, American and Soviet troops met at Torgau on the Elbe River, just southwest of Berlin, with this meeting following a whirlwind Allied advance across western Germany.

ALLIED DRIVE ACROSS GERMANY

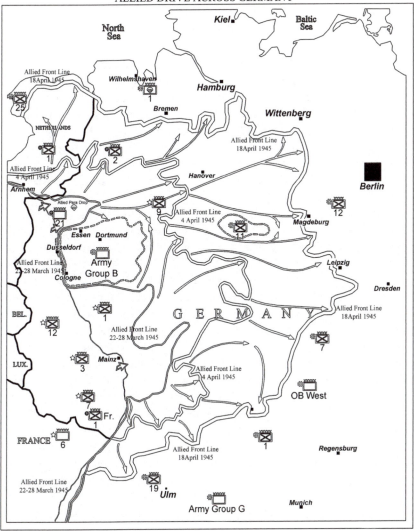

The Allies, after clearing the Bulge, had early in February begun a slow advance on a broad front with nearly 90 divisions and 4.5 million men fighting against stiff German resistance west of the Rhine River.[68] Following the failed German launched New Year's Day Operation Nordwind against Dever's 6th Army Group, Hitler had doubled down on his failure. On January 5, he had thrown the 14th SS Corps into the fray. Then, on January 7, the German 19th Army had attacked north from the Colmar pocket west of the Rhine.

Finally, on January 16, the 10th SS Panzer Division and 7th Falschirmjager Division also had hit the U.S. 6th Corps. Not only did the Americans stop everything the Germans threw at them, but the U.S. 6th Army Group ground down and finally crushed the Colmar pocket. The Germans suffered 22,000 casualties against 18,000 Allied casualties in turn.[69] At the same time, and in the skies above Germany, Allied bombers maintained their relentless assault on the German economy and cities. The Allied attack against Dresden on February 13–14, 1945, conducted by nearly 1,110 British and American bombers, leveled the city and killed an estimated 30,000 to 50,000 people. By the war's end, the Allied bombing campaign had inflicted over 1 million German civilian casualties, with most dying in the war's final year. As the air war over Germany continued unabated, the Allies finally crossed the Rhine River.

On March 7, 1945, a small American battle group from the 9th Armored Division found the Ludendorff railroad bridge intact in Remagan, swiftly crossed, and set up a bridgehead. Although the Remagan Bridge collapsed on March 17, Hodges's 1st Army had rapidly expanded the American position on the Rhine's east bank. Meanwhile, Patch's 7th Army and Patton's 3rd Army enveloped several German armies in a substantial pocket just west of the Rhine. In fighting that lasted from March 13 to March 20, Patton and Patch crushed the German 1st Army, capturing approximately 90,000 German soldiers against 17,000 American casualties.[70] In addition, they had taken Germany's Saar industrial region, an area that produced 10 percent of German steel output and almost half of Germany's chemicals, mostly from a massive I. G. Farben complex at Ludwigshafen. To the north and beginning on the night of March 23, 1945, Montgomery crossed the Rhine in a character-istically elaborate set-piece assault that featured the last major para-drop during the war. Then Bradley engineered the only truly massive Allied forged Kessel of the war. On April 1, the U.S. 2nd and 3rd Armored Divisions linked up near Lippstadt to complete Bradley's grand envelopment of Model's Army Group B in the Ruhr. Bradley's men captured 317,000 German soldiers, Model committed suicide on April 21, and all major German resistance in the west had collapsed.[71]

As the Allied combat armies streamed through Germany, their frontline sol-diers further uncovered the enormity of the Third Reich's crimes against humanity. For instance, following an advance into Thuringia, the Americans came across the sprawling, loosely connected set of work and death camps that made up the Buchenwald complex. In the tunnels of Nordhausen-Dora, some 12,000 people existed in name only, surrounded by 3,000 corpses and dying at the rate of approximately 50 per day.[72] The reaction to Buchenwald, and the uncovering of other Nazi atrocities, would spur what would become a U.S. occupation marked during its early years by a negligence (and at times brutal-ity) largely unknown to this day. As many as 40,000 of 1 million German prisoners of war held by the U.S. Army in camps along the Rhine River would die during the summer of 1945, mostly of starvation.[73] However, that said, this was nothing compared to the horror show behind the Red Army's lines, where over 1 million German prisoners of war would never make it home alive.[74]

Simpson's 9th Army crossed the Elbe River in central Germany on April 11 and built up a large bridgehead less than 60 miles from Berlin, four days prior to the Russian assault on the German capital. However, Eisenhower had previously informed Stalin that he would come no closer to Berlin than the Elbe. On April 25, 1945, men of the American 1st Army's 69th Infantry Division met elements from the 1st Ukrainian Front advancing from the east upstream from the village of Torgau on the banks of the Elbe River. To the southeast, Patton penetrated into Czechoslovakia and US forced also entered Austria. On April 24, the 1st Panzer Army's 8th and 16th Panzer Divisions met the Soviet 6th Guards Tank Army near Austerlitz in the war's last major armored battles. The German and Soviet forces ended up locked in combat near Prague past the official end of the war.[75]

Outside Berlin, the German 9th Army had been encircled in a pocket near Halbe, southeast of Berlin. In a breakout planned by Heinrici; General Busse, the German 9th Army commander; and Wenck, the German 12th Army commander, and carried out from the end of April through the first week of May, the German armies managed to save several thousand soldiers and civilians from Soviet capture. That said, of 140,000 Germans in the pocket, as many as one-third to half were killed.[76] Meanwhile, in Berlin, and following a brief ceremony, Hitler and Eva Braun wed on April 30. Both committed suicide that same day, just after 3:00 p.m., as Russian artillery crashed outside their bunker in Berlin.[77] Karl Doenitz took over as Hitler's successor, and set up his command in Schleswig-Holstein. Berlin surrendered on May 2 after a final cataclysmic spasm of violence. All told the battle for Berlin had cost 125,000 German lives.[78] Konev, Rokossovsky, and Zhukov had lost 352,425 men, with over 100,000 killed in the fighting between April 16 and May 8, 1945.

At Eisenhower's headquarters in Reims, the German surrender was signed on May 7, 1945, and executed at 11:01 p.m. the following day. Fighting on the Eastern Front did not end until one week later. The 1st, 2nd, and 4th Ukrainian fronts actually endured 49,348 casualties between May 6 and May 11.[79] It had taken three of the world's greatest industrial powers working together nearly four years to defeat Hitler's war machine in a war the likes of which the world had never seen nor has seen since.

Although the following sea of statistics cannot possibly convey the scope of human suffering endured during the war, it is still important to understand the cost in lives created by Hitler's quest for Lebensraum and the intense struggle to defeat him. In northwestern Europe alone, between D-Day and VE (Victory in Europe) Day, 488,080 Allied soldiers (including 356,660 Americans) had been killed or wounded or were missing.[80] In addition,

Table 13.2 Axis Permanent Losses[1] during the War against the Soviet Union[2]

German Army Losses (by period)	Total Killed, Disabled, or Missing
September 1939–September 1, 1942	922,000 (over 90% in east)
September 1, 1942–November 20, 1943	2,077,000 (over 90% in east)
November 20, 1943–November 1944	2,957,000 (over 70% in east)[3]
December 30, 1944–April 30, 1945	2,000,000 (67% in east)
Captured during war	3,035,700
Total German Army Losses for above periods	10,991,700 (3,888,000 dead)[4]

Other Axis Losses (by country)	Eastern Front Killed, Disabled, Missing, or Captured
Hungary	863,700 (350,000 dead, disabled, and missing)
Romania	681,800 (480,000 dead, disabled, and missing)
Italy	93,900 (45,000 dead, disabled and missing)
Finland	86,400 (84,000 dead, disabled and missing)
Total other Axis losses	1,725,000
Total Axis losses on Eastern Front	12,483,000 dead, missing, permanently disabled, or captured[5]

[1]Killed, disabled, missing, or captured.
[2]David M. Glantz, *Slaughterhouse: The Handbook of the Eastern Front* (Aberjona Press, 2005), 10–12.
[3]Estimated.
[4]Total German armed forces losses during the war were 13,488,000 with 10,758,000 in eastern Europe.
[5]Against official Soviet Armed forces losses of 28,199,127 killed and 10,008,434 missing or captured.

Britain suffered 60,595 civilian dead during the war.[81] France suffered 350,000 dead, the Dutch 204,000 dead, and the Greeks 430,000 dead.[82] Yugoslavia was in ruins with 10 percent of its prewar population dead, 1.4 million people.[83] Poland lost 5 million people killed between 1939 and 1945.[84] During 1945–1948, another 30,000 Poles would die fighting a guerilla war against the Red Army and the communist regime that Stalin put in power over Poland.[85] As for Germany, the Wehrmacht endured 13,488,000 casualties,[86] with the vast majority, approximately 80 percent, stemming from the war against the Soviet Union.[87] Regarding German civilian deaths, some estimate that at least 1.8 million German civilians had died by May 7, 1945.[88] Then, from 1945 to 1950, the Soviet Union executed an estimated 65,000 to 80,000 more Germans. Mass graves have been found at NKVD camps throughout eastern Germany and at former concentration camps. For instance, Stalin kept Buchenwald up and running until 1950, with more than 7,000 people killed in the camp after the war had officially ended.[89] In addition, an estimated 14 million to 16 million ethnic Germans were expelled from eastern Europe during the war's final months and the following years of Soviet rule, with estimates ranging from hundreds of thousands up to 1.71 million dying of

Table 13.3 Red Army Permanent Losses during the War[1]

Year	Total Killed	Missing or Captured
1941	4,308,094	2,993,803
1942	7,080,801	2,993,536
1943	7,483,647	1,977,127
1944	6,503,204	1,412,335
1945	2,823,381	631,633
Total	28,199,127	10,008,434[2]

[1]David M. Glantz, *Slaughterhouse: The Handbook of the Eastern Front* (Aberjona Press, 2005), 10.
[2]At least 3.3 million Soviet prisoners of war died in German captivity.

starvation, exposure, exhaustion, or murder during the brutal journey to Germany.[90]

For its part, Nazi crimes had risen to a level unmatched in history. An estimated 7 million non-Germans, predominantly Jews, died in the death or work camps, mostly during the years 1941–1944.[91] The greatest absolute loss of life occurred in the Soviet Union—with the overwhelming majority killed because of, or directly from, German activities. The Soviet military suffered 29 million casualties during World War II, including 11,444,100 killed, missing, or captured with 8,668,400 killed in action.[92] Capture had often meant death; of the 5.7 million Soviet soldiers who surrendered to the Axis, 3.3 million were either murdered outright or died in captivity.[93] Including civilians, most estimates indicate that as many as 27 million to 29 million people from the former Soviet Union lost their lives in the war.[94]

Of course, not all died as a result of the Axis alone. Beginning prior to the war and continuing throughout it, together Stalin and Hitler deliberately murdered 14 million eastern Europeans outside of those killed either by violence perpetrated by Hitler's and Stalin's allies or as a result of combat operations.[95] As for violence and repression committed against members of his own military, Stalin was perhaps even more brutal than was Hitler. Of the 1,833,567 prisoners of war returned to the Soviet Union, Stalin sent 1.5 million to forced labor and the gulags. Within the regular Red Army, Stalin resurrected the purges; in 1945 alone, 135,056 Red Army men and officers were convicted of "counterrevolutionary crimes." During the war, 158,000 Soviet soldiers received death sentences.[96] In addition, within eastern Europe and the Soviet Union death was a common occurrence following the war. A poor harvest arising from the devastation in the Soviet Union's best agricultural regions helped cause an estimated 1 million civilian deaths to starvation in 1946.[97] It is now estimated by some that the Soviet Union's 1950 population fell 50 million human beings short of what it should have been had the 1941–1945 war not happened.[98] Most historians agree that the Soviet Union never really overcame the damage done by Hitler's invasion.

CONCLUSION

World War II marked the most violent and horrific restructuring of political power in world history, and was hardly the forgone conclusion it is often treated as today. During the war's first three years, an outnumbered German state and Wehrmacht regularly defeated the most powerful military establishments on the planet after having reestablished a traditional German method for waging war based on maneuver. Moreover, Germany came within a whisker of cementing a European-based empire that, by commonly cited measures of military potential, Germany never should have had even a remote chance of winning; doing so by playing to its qualitative strengths as a continental power and attacking the Soviet Union in 1941.

Although since the end of the war many have used the advantages of hindsight to argue that Hitler's attack on the Soviet Union was his undoing and thus should not have been launched, given the country's great size and the enormous military potential of the Red Army, this not only misses the whole criminal purpose of Hitler's Third Reich in terms of seeking Lebensraum in eastern Europe, and thus completely lacks historical context, but also overlooks the reality that Germany came far closer to attaining hegemony over all of Europe than many have previously realized. Moreover, had Hitler been able to seize the bounty of economic resources accessibly found within the western and southern Soviet Union, the Third Reich could have drawn on these reserves, particularly in terms of addressing its otherwise overwhelming lack of petroleum products, and not only would have dwarfed the Soviet colossus that ultimately emerged from the war to confront the United States in a roughly half-century-long Cold War; but also may have proved undefeatable.

Just as the German way of war paved the way for future success, it also created and exacerbated internal contradictions that undermined the Wehrmacht, and left it vulnerable to enemies with the capacity to adapt and build on potent military traditions of their own. Therefore, Germany's chance to forge a self-sustaining European empire ultimately foundered as its military and political leadership failed to fully understand and exploit the tremendous early war operational success that Germany had enjoyed on Europe's battlefield—and thus maintain and reinforce what had made the Wehrmacht so potent against its numerically superior enemies.

Simply put, Germany lost the war because during 1941–1942 it failed to secure the economic resources needed to fight a long war at the same time the Soviet Union and the Western Allies made substantive qualitative improvements to their armed forces, all while the Wehrmacht lost much of the preexisting qualitative advantages that it held over its enemies. Consequently, arguments defining World War II's outcome as based on the sheer numerical advantages possessed by Germany's foes not only ignores the fact that Germany fought outnumbered throughout the war, but also do a tremendous disservice to the brave men and women who defeated the Third Reich. Moreover, quantitative based arguments also support a plethora of pernicious myths about the war; not the least of which are those enabling the continuing respect and adulation that some grant an outnumbered Wehrmacht whose central role in carrying out some of history's most vile crimes against humanity not only is marginalized or ignored but also misses the point that even though numerically inferior to its opponents, the Wehrmacht as a military organization was far from the pinnacle of operational excellence that it has often been held out to be. In fact, its own failings played perhaps a greater role in its defeat than the numerical strength of its foes. Most importantly, such arguments contribute to a gross misunderstanding as to how and why the most important event in modern human history ended as it did—misunderstandings that this book, it is hoped, has redressed for the reader, at least in part.

Notes

CHAPTER ONE

1. Richard Overy, *The Dictators: Hitler's Germany and Stalin's Russia* (Norton, 2004), 457.

2. Chris Bellamy, *Absolute War: Soviet Russia in the Second World War: A Modern History* (Macmillan, 2007), 2, 9.

3. Robert M. Citino, *Death of the Wehrmacht: The German Campaigns of 1942* (University Press of Kansas, 2007), 3–5.

4. Ibid., 4.

5. Ibid., 255.

6. Robert Kirchubel, *Hitler's Panzer Armies on the Eastern Front* (Pen & Sword, 2009), 1.

7. Geoffrey P. Megargee, *Inside Hitler's High Command* (University Press of Kansas, 2000), 3.

8. Ibid., 8.

9. Ibid., 9.

10. Robert M. Citino, *The German Way of War: From the Thirty Years' War to the Third Reich* (University Press of Kansas, 2005), 52.

11. See Marcel Stein, *Field Marshal von Manstein: The Janus Head: A Portrait* (Helion & Company, 2007), 56.

12. Benoit Lemay, *Erich von Manstein: Hitler's Master Strategist* (Casemate Publishers, 2010), 24–25.

13. Wolfram Wette, *The Wehrmacht: History, Myth, Reality* (Harvard University Press, 2006), 158.

14. James S. Corum, *The Roots of Blitzkrieg: Hans von Seeckt and German Military Reform* (University Press of Kansas, 1992), 47.

15. Robert M. Citino, *Path to Blitzkrieg: Doctrine and Training in the German Army, 1920–1939,* (Lynne Rienner Publishers, 1999), 25.

16. Roman Johann Jarymowycz, *Tank Tactics from Normandy to Lorraine* (Lynne Rienner Publishers, 2001), 58.

17. Corum, *The Roots of Blitzkrieg,* 21–23.

18. Dennis Showalter, *Hitler's Panzers: The Lightning Attacks That Revolutionized Warfare* (Berkley Publishing Group, 2009), 18.

19. Ibid., 19–35.

20. Corum, *The Roots of Blitzkrieg,* 127.

21. Richard L. Dinardo, *Germany's Panzer Arm in WWII* (Stackpole Books, 2006), 90–92.

22. Corum, *The Roots of Blitzkrieg,* 138–39.

23. Paul Deichmann, ed., and Dr. Littleton B. Atkinson, USAF Historical Division Research Studies Institute Air University, *USAF Historical Studies No. 163, German Air Force Operations in Support of the Army* (Arno Press, 1968), 9–10.

24. Keith Bird, *Erich Raeder, Admiral of the Third Reich* (Naval Institute Press, 2006), 2.

25. Ibid., xxii–xxiii.

26. Geoff Hewitt, *Hitler's Armada: The Royal Navy and the Defense of Great Britain April–October 1940* (Pen & Sword Maritime, 2008), 1.

27. Ian Kershaw, *Hitler 1936–1945: Nemesis* (Norton, 2000), xliv.

28. Adam Tooze, *The Wages of Destruction: The Making and Breaking of the Nazi Economy* (Allen Lane, 2006), 167.

29. Ibid., 60–66.

30. Lemay, *Erich von Manstein,* 46–47.

31. Alan Milward, *War, Economy and Society, 1939–1945* (1977, Allen Lane), 314

32. Mark Harrison, *The Economics of World War II: Six Great Powers in International Comparison* (Cambridge University Press, 1998), 126.

33. Tooze, *The Wages of Destruction,* 240–42.

34. Ibid., 198.

35. Harrison, *The Economics of World War II,* 138.

36. Rolf-Dieter Muller et al., Milatargeschichtliches Forshungsamt, *Germany and the Second World War, Volume V/II, Organization and Mobilization of the German Sphere of Power* (Clarendon Press, 2003), 730.

37. Overy, *The Dictators,* 248.

38. Gordon, Martel, *The Origins of the Second World War Reconsidered, A.J.P. Taylor and the historians, Second Edition* (Routledge Publishing, 1999), 188.

39. Showalter, *Hitler's Panzers,* 53.

40. F. M. Von Senger und Etterlin, *German Tanks of World War II* (Stackpole Books, 1969), 22–26.

41. Tooze, *The Wages of Destruction,* 294.

42. Senger und Etterlin, *German Tanks of World War II,* 211.

43. Tooze, *The Wages of Destruction,* 302–3.

44. Megargee, *Inside Hitler's High Command,* 13–14.

45. Lemay, *Erich von Manstein,* 16.

46. Tooze, *The Wages of Destruction,* 58–59.

47. Hewitt, *Hitler's Armada,* 43.

CHAPTER TWO

1. Benoit Lemay, *Erich von Manstein: Hitler's Master Strategist* (Casemate Publishers, 2010), 72.

2. Laurance Rees, *World War II behind Closed Doors: Stalin, the Nazis and the West* (Pantheon Books, 2008), 3.

3. Catherine Merridale, *Ivan's War: Life and Death in the Red Army, 1939–1945* (Picador, 2006), 73.

4. Ian Kershaw, *Hitler 1936–1945: Nemesis* (Norton, 2000), 253, 254–61.

5. Lemay, *Erich von Manstein*, 83.

6. Christopher Shores, *Duel in the Sky: Ten Crucial Air Battles of World War II* (Grubb Street, 1999), 28.

7. Ibid., 22–23.

8. Adam Tooze, *The Wages of Destruction: The Making and Breaking of the Nazi Economy* (Allen Lane, 2006), 340.

9. Geoff Hewitt, *Hitler's Armada: The Royal Navy and the Defense of Great Britain April–October 1940* (Pen & Sword Maritime, 2008), 13.

10. James S. Corum, *The Roots of Blitzkrieg: Hans von Seeckt and German Military Reform* (University Press of Kansas, 1992), 204.

11. Richard Overy, *The Road to War* (Penguin Books, 1989), 124.

12. Richard Vinen, *A History in Fragments: Europe in the Twentieth Century* (De Capo Press, 2000), 178.

13. Franz Kurowski, *Panzer Aces* (Ballantine Publishing Group, 1992), 465–66.

14. Lemay, *Erich von Manstein*, 133.

15. Marcel Stein, *Field Marshal von Manstein: The Janus Head: A Portrait* (Helion & Company, 2007), 20–23.

16. Robert Kirchubel, *Hitler's Panzer Armies on the Eastern Front* (Pen & Sword, 2009), 7.

17. Showalter, *Hitler's Panzers*, 104–5.

18. Kirchubel, *Hitler's Panzer Armies on the Eastern Front* 8.

19. Heinz Guderian, *Panzer Leader* (De Capo Press, 1996), 98.

20. Stein, *Field Marshal von Manstein*, 77.

21. Ibid., 77.

22. Roman Johann Jarymowycz, *Tank Tactics from Normandy to Lorraine* (Lynne Rienner Publishers, 2001), 54–56.

23. Lemay, *Erich von Manstein*, 139.

24. Tooze, *The Wages of Destruction*, 372.

25. Horst Boog, ed., *The Conduct of the Air War in the Second World War: An International Comparison, Proceedings of the International Conference of Historians in Freiburg im Breisgau, Federal Republic of Germany, from 29 August to 2 September 1988* (Berg, 1992), 504.

26. Ibid., 369.

27. Richard L. Dinardo, *Germany's Panzer Arm in WWII* (Stackpole Books, 2006), 13; Tooze, *The Wages of Destruction*, 383–85.

28. Rolf-Dieter Muller et al., Milatargeschichtliches Forshungsamt, *Germany and the Second World War, Volume V/II, Organization and Mobilization of the German Sphere of Power* (Clarendon Press, 2003), 215.

29. Hewitt, *Hitler's Armada*, 10–11.

30. John Ellis, *Brute Force: Allied Strategy and Tactics in the Second World War* (Andre Deutsch, 1990), 15.

31. Tooze, *The Wages of Destruction*, 396; Richard L. Dinardo, *Germany and the Axis Powers: From Coalition to Collapse* (University Press of Kansas, 2005), 5–17.

32. Hewitt, *Hitler's Armada*, 18.

33. Ibid., 34–43.

34. Ibid., 22–33.

35. Ibid., 28.

36. Ibid., 23–24, 60–65, 170.

37. Ibid., 140, 142–45.

38. Ibid., 125–26.

39. Ibid., 130.

40. Ibid., 155–59.

41. Ibid., 131–32, 170–71.

42. Ibid., 139.

43. Keith Bird, *Erich Raeder, Admiral of the Third Reich* (Naval Institute Press, 2006), 159.

44. Richard Overy, *Interrogations: The Nazi Elite in Allied Hands, 1945* (Penguin Group, 2001), 347.

45. Ellis, *Brute Force*, 26.

46. Shores, *Duel in the Sky*, 55; Kenneth K. Koskodan, *No Greater Ally: The Untold Story of Poland's Forces in World War II* (Osprey, 2009), 95–96.

47. Tooze, *The Wages of Destruction*, 425.

CHAPTER THREE

1. Walter S. Dunn Jr., *Hitler's Nemesis: The Red Army 1930–45* (Stackpole Books, 2009), xvi.

2. Mark Harrison and R. W. Davies, "The Soviet Military-Economic Effort under the Second Five-Year Plan (1933–1937)," *Europe East-Asia Studies* 49, no. 3 (1997): 369–406.

3. Horst Boog et al., Milatargeschichtliches Forshungsamt, *Germany and the Second World War, Volume IV, The Attack on the Soviet Union* (Clarendon Press, 1998), 55.

4. Dunn, *Hitler's Nemesis*, 164.

5. Boog et al., *The Attack on the Soviet Union*, 62.

6. Dunn, *Hitler's Nemesis*, 2, 105.

7. Boog et al., *The Attack on the Soviet Union*, 64.

8. Richard Overy, *The Dictators: Hitler's Germany and Stalin's Russia* (Norton, 2004), 194.

9. Richard Overy, *The Road to War* (Penguin Books, 1989), 233.

10. Catherine Merridale, *Ivan's War: Life and Death in the Red Army, 1939–1945* (Picador, 2006), 69. Overy, *The Dictators*, 477.

11. Evan Mawdsley, *Thunder in the East: The Nazi-Soviet War 1941–1945*, (Hodder Headline Group, 2005), 21.

12. David M. Glantz, *Stumbling Colossus: The Red Army on the Eve of World War* (University Press of Kansas, 1998), 29.

13. Boog et al., *The Attack on the Soviet Union*, 71.

14. Ibid., 49.

15. Ibid., 50.

16. Chris Bellamy, *Absolute War: Soviet Russia in the Second World War: A Modern History* (Macmillan, 2007), 79–81.

17. Overy, *The Dictators*, 452.

18. Mawdsley, *Thunder in the East*, 30.

19. Bellamy, *Absolute War*, 175.

20. Dunn, *Hitler's Nemesis*, 116.

21. Rodric Braithwaite, *Moscow 1941: A City and Its People at War* (Alfred A. Knopf, 2006), 43.

22. Boog et al., *The Attack on the Soviet Union*, 77.

23. Merridale, *Ivan's War*, 55–56.

24. Mawdsley, *Thunder in the East*, 31.

25. Dunn, *Hitler's Nemesis*, 113.

26. John Erickson, *The Road to Stalingrad* (Harper & Row Publishers, 1975), 63.

27. Robert Forczyk, *Panther vs. T-34, Ukraine 1943* (Osprey Publishing, 2007), 16.

28. Ibid., 18–20.

29. Ibid., 20.

30. Glantz, *Stumbling Colossus*, 116–18.

31. Mawdsley, *Thunder in the East*, 26.

32. Glantz, *Stumbling Colossus*, 13.

33. Mawdsley, *Thunder in the East*, 28.

34. Glantz, *Stumbling Colossus*, 184.

35. Mawdsley, *Thunder in the East*, 28–29.

36. Boog et al., *The Attack on the Soviet Union*, 78, 93.

37. Boog, *Attack on the Soviet Union*, 120–121.

38. Boog, *Attack on the Soviet Union*, 131.

39. Tooze, 431.

40. Geoffrey P. Megargee, *Inside Hitler's High Command* (University Press of Kansas, 2000), 104.

41. Bellamy, *Absolute War*, 83.

42. Robert Kershaw, *War without Garlands: Operation Barbarossa 1941–1942* (Ian Allen, 2000), 43–45.

43. Megargee, *Inside Hitler's High Command*, 114–15.

44. Boog et al., *The Attack on the Soviet Union*, 270–75.

45. Megargee, *Inside Hitler's High Command*, 124.

46. Adam Tooze, *The Wages of Destruction: The Making and Breaking of the Nazi Economy* (Allen Lane, 2006), 454–55.

47. Mawdsley, *Thunder in the East*, 11.

48. Benoit Lemay, *Erich von Manstein: Hitler's Master Strategist* (Casemate Publishers, 2010), 200.

49. Wolfram Wette, *The Wehrmacht: History, Myth, Reality* (Harvard University Press, 2006), 93.

50. Marcel Stein, *Field Marshal von Manstein: The Janus Head: A Portrait* (Helion & Company, 2007), 272–73, 320–24.

51. Lemay, *Erich von Manstein*, 200.

52. Ibid., 205.

53. Ibid., 206.

54. Geoffrey P. Megargee, *War of Annihilation: Combat and Genocide on the Eastern Front 1941* (Rowman & Littlefield, 2006), 37.

55. Tooze, *The Wages of Destruction*, 469–70.

56. Ibid., 433–37.

57. Tooze, *The Wages of Destruction*, 437–39.

58. Alan Milward, *War, Economy and Society, 1939–1945* (Allen Lane, 1977), 80.

59. Stein, *Field Marshal von Manstein*, 179.

60. Kershaw, *War without Garlands*, 177.

61. Dennis Showalter, *Hitler's Panzers: The Lightning Attacks That Revolutionized Warfare* (Berkley Publishing Group, 2009), 137–38.

62. Dunn, *Hitler's Nemesis*, 116.

63. Boog et al., *The Attack on the Soviet Union*, 219.

64. Dunn, *Hitler's Nemesis*, 116.

65. Mawdsley, *Thunder in the East*, 30–31.

66. Boog et al., *The Attack on the Soviet Union*, 93.

67. David M. Glantz, *Barbarossa: Hitler's Invasion of Russia 1941* (Tempus Publishing, 2001), 22.

68. Boog et al., *The Attack on the Soviet Union*, 93.

69. Lemay, *Erich von Manstein*, 197.

70. Mark Harrison, *The Economics of World War II: Six Great Powers in International Comparison* (Cambridge University Press, 1998), 19, 269.

71. Mawdsley, *Thunder in the East*, 51; Milward, 132–34.

CHAPTER FOUR

1. John Lukacs, *June 1941: Hitler and Stalin* (Yale University Press, 2006), 103.

2. Laurance Rees, *World War II behind Closed Doors: Stalin, the Nazis and the West* (Pantheon Books, 2008), 47.

3. Ibid., 103.

4. Horst Boog et al., Milatargeschichtliches Forshungsamt, *Germany and the Second World War, Volume IV, The Attack on the Soviet Union* (Clarendon Press, 1998), 53.

5. Gabriel Gorodetsky, *Grand Delusion: Stalin and the German Invasion of Russia* (Yale University Press, 1999), 243, 319.

6. Robert Kershaw, *War without Garlands: Operation Barbarossa 1941–1942* (Ian Allen, 2000), 119–21.

7. Boog et al. *The Attack on the Soviet Union*, 764.

8. Kershaw, *War without Garlands*, 125.

9. Evan Mawdsley, *Thunder in the East: The Nazi-Soviet War 1941–1945*, (Hodder Headline Group, 2005), 58.

10. Rees, *World War II behind Closed Doors*, 92.

11. Richard J. Evans, *The Third Reich at War* (Penguin Books, 2008), 197.

12. Richard L. Dinardo, *Germany and the Axis Powers: From Coalition to Collapse*, (University Press of Kansas, 2005), 95–102.

13. Victor J. Kamenir, *The Bloody Triangle: The Defeat of Soviet Armor in the Ukraine, June 1941* (Zenith Press, 2008), 265–81.

14. Ibid., 263–81.

15. Ibid., 37.

16. Ibid., 78–80.

17. Ibid., 161–62.

18. Ibid., 142–43.

19. Kershaw, *War without Garlands*, 181.

20. Chris Bellamy, *Absolute War: Soviet Russia in the Second World War: A Modern History* (Macmillan, 2007), 203.

21. David M. Glantz, *Barbarossa: Hitler's Invasion of Russia 1941* (Tempus Publishing, 2001), 53.

22. Robert Kirchubel, *Hitler's Panzer Armies on the Eastern Front* (Pen & Sword, 2009), 24–26.

23. Bellamy, *Absolute War*, 179.

24. Kershaw, *War without Garlands*, 111–13.

25. Mawdsley, *Thunder in the East*, 60.

26. Kershaw, *War without Garlands*, 206–7.

27. Boog et al., *The Attack on the Soviet Union*, 768.

28. Geoffrey P. Megargee, *War of Annihilation: Combat and Genocide on the Eastern Front 1941* (Rowman & Littlefield, 2006), 64–65.

29. Kirchubel, *Hitler's Panzer Armies on the Eastern Front*, 100.

30. Mawdsley, *Thunder in the East*, 67–68.

31. Glantz, *Barbarossa*, 40, 45.

32. Kershaw, *War without Garlands*, 225.

33. Ibid., 200.

34. Bellamy, *Absolute War*, 243.

35. David M. Glantz, *The Siege of Leningrad 1941–44: 900 Days of Terror* (Cassell, 2001), 7–9.

36. Ibid., 9–11.

37. Kirchubel, *Hitler's Panzer Armies on the Eastern Front*, 133.

38. Ibid., 135.

39. Dennis Showalter, *Hitler's Panzers: The Lightning Attacks That Revolutionized Warfare* (Berkley Publishing Group, 2009), 174.

40. Boog et al., *The Attack on the Soviet Union*, 583.

41. Kershaw, *War without Garlands*, 254.

42. Boog et al., *The Attack on the Soviet Union*, 1098–99.

43. Kershaw, *War without Garlands*, 321–29.

44. Bellamy, *Absolute War*, 247–48.

45. Kershaw, *War without Garlands*, 458–59.

46. Walter S. Dunn Jr., *Hitler's Nemesis: The Red Army 1930–45* (Stackpole Books, 2009), 7.

47. Max Hastings, *Armageddon: The Battle for Germany 1944–45* (Alfred A. Knopf, 2005), 174.

48. Hannes Heer and Klaus Naumann, eds., *War of Extermination: The German Military in World War II, 1941–1944*, (Bergham Books, 2000), 66–67.

49. Wolfram Wette, *The Wehrmacht: History, Myth, Reality* (Harvard University Press, 2006), 98–99, 181; Marcel Stein, *Field Marshal von Manstein: The Janus Head: A Portrait* (Helion & Company, 2007), 261–63, 267, 395.

50. Stein, *Field Marshal von Manstein*, 264.

51. Ibid., 265.

52. Glantz, *Barbarossa*, 84.

53. Boog et al., *The Attack on the Soviet Union*, 567.

54. Ibid., 587–91.

55. Glantz, *The Siege of Leningrad1941–44*, 24–25.

56. Richard Overy, *The Dictators: Hitler's Germany and Stalin's Russia* (Norton, 2004), 94.

57. Mawdsley, *Thunder in the East*, 63; Rodric Braithwaite, *Moscow 1941: A City and Its People at War* (Alfred A. Knopf, 2006), 82.

58. Mawdsley, *Thunder in the East*, 63–64.

59. Bellamy, *Absolute War*, 214–15.

60. Glantz, *Barbarossa*, 60.

61. Kershaw, *War without Garlands*, 250.

62. Catherine Merridale, *Ivan's War: Life and Death in the Red Army, 1939–1945* (Picador, 2006), 96–97.

63. Ibid., 108–9.

64. Glantz, *Barbarossa*, 72.

65. John Lukacs, *June 1941: Hitler and Stalin* (Yale University Press, 2006), 111–12.

66. Ibid., 118.

67. Horst Boog et al., Milatargeschichtliches Forshungsamt, *Germany and the Second World War, Volume VI, The Global War* (Oxford University Press, 2001), 27.

68. Rees, *World War II behind Closed Doors*, 97.

69. Bellamy, *Absolute War*, 252–56.

70. Ibid., 45.

71. Benoit Lemay, *Erich von Manstein: Hitler's Master Strategist* (Casemate Publishers, 2010), 247.

72. Boog et al., *The Attack on the Soviet Union*, 784.

73. Bellamy, *Absolute War*, 262.

74. Antony Beevor, *Stalingrad* (Penguin Books, 1998), 56.

75. Boog et al., *The Attack on the Soviet Union*, 604.

76. Kershaw, *War without Garlands*, 374.

77. Megargee, *War of Annihilation*, 88.

78. Ibid., 23.

79. Kirchubel, *Hitler's Panzer Armies on the Eastern Front*, 78.

80. Ibid., 79.

81. Robert Forczyk, *Panther vs. T-34, Ukraine 1943* (Osprey Publishing, 2007), 9–10.

82. Kirchubel, *Hitler's Panzer Armies on the Eastern Front*, 144.

83. Ibid., 106–7.

84. Bellamy, *Absolute War*, 276.

85. Mawdsley, *Thunder in the East*, 95, 98; Showalter, *Hitler's Panzers*, 185.

CHAPTER FIVE

1. Catherine Merridale, *Ivan's War: Life and Death in the Red Army, 1939–1945* (Picador, 2006), 103.

2. Chris Bellamy, *Absolute War: Soviet Russia in the Second World War: A Modern History* (Macmillan, 2007), 310.

3. Merridale, *Ivan's War*, 118.

4. John Erickson, *The Road to Stalingrad* (Harper & Row Publishers, 1975), 223.

5. Evan Mawdsley, *Thunder in the East: The Nazi-Soviet War 1941–1945*, (Hodder Headline Group, 2005), 59.

6. Walter S. Dunn Jr., *Hitler's Nemesis: The Red Army 1930–45* (Stackpole Books, 2009), 171.

7. Horst Boog et al., Milatargeschichtliches Forshungsamt, *Germany and the Second World War, Volume IV, The Attack on the Soviet Union* (Clarendon Press, 1998), 681.

8. Robert Kershaw, *War without Garlands: Operation Barbarossa 1941–1942* (Ian Allen, 2000), 419–20.

9. Georgi K. Zhukov, *Marshal Zhukov's Greatest Battles* (Harper & Row, 1969), 77–78.

10. Boog et al., *The Attack on the Soviet Union*, 893–94.

11. Dennis Showalter, *Hitler's Panzers: The Lightning Attacks That Revolutionized Warfare* (Berkley Publishing Group, 2009), 187.

12. Kershaw, *War without Garlands*, 452.

13. Horst Boog et al., Milatargeschichtliches Forshungsamt, *Germany and the Second World War, Volume VI, The Global War* (Oxford University Press, 2001), 46.

14. Merridale, *Ivan's War*, 119; Rodric Braithwaite, *Moscow 1941: A City and Its People at War* (Alfred A. Knopf, 2006), 67.

15. Boog et al., *The Attack on the Soviet Union*, 893–94.

16. Mawdsley, *Thunder in the East*, 46.

17. Alexander Hill, "British Lend-Lease Tanks and the Battle for Moscow, November–December 1941—A Research Note," *Journal of Slavic Military Studies* 19, no. 2 (2006): 289–94.

18. Erhard Raus, *Panzer Operations: The Eastern Front Memoir of General Raus, 1941–1945*, (Da Capo Press, 2003), 88.

19. Richard L. Dinardo, *Germany's Panzer Arm in WWII* (Stackpole Books, 2006), 16.

20. Geoffrey P. Megargee, *War of Annihilation: Combat and Genocide on the Eastern Front 1941* (Rowman & Littlefield, 2006), 110.

21. Steven H. Newton, *German Battle Tactics on the Russian Front 1941–1945* (Schiffer Publishing, 1994), 53–54.

22. Rolf-Dieter Muller et al., Milatargeschichtliches Forshungsamt, *Germany and the Second World War, Volume V/II, Organization and Mobilization of the German Sphere of Power* (Clarendon Press, 2003), 1.

23. Boog et al., *The Attack on the Soviet Union*, 817.

24. Kershaw, *War without Garlands*, 476.

25. Benoit Lemay, *Erich von Manstein: Hitler's Master Strategist* (Casemate Publishers, 2010), 212–13.

26. Boog et al., *The Attack on the Soviet Union*, 615–19.

27. Ibid., 619.

28. Ibid., 620.

29. Ibid., 653–54.

30. David M. Glantz, *The Siege of Leningrad 1941–44: 900 Days of Terror* (Cassell, 2001), 60–65.

31. Boog et al., *The Attack on the Soviet Union*, 694.

32. Raus, *Panzer Operations*, 89.

33. Megargee, *War of Annihilation*, 114.

34. Robert Kirchubel, *Hitler's Panzer Armies on the Eastern Front* (Pen & Sword, 2009), 83.

35. Merridale, *Ivan's War*, 138–39.

36. Mawdsley, *Thunder in the East*, 121.

37. Dunn, *Hitler's Nemesis*, 8.

38. Megargee, *War of Annihilation*, 135.

39. David M. Glantz, *Barbarossa: Hitler's Invasion of Russia 1941* (Tempus Publishing, 2001), 188.

40. Robert Forczyk, *Moscow 1941: Hitler's First Defeat* (Osprey, 2006), 89.

41. David M. Glantz, *Red Storm over the Balkans: The Failed Soviet Invasion of Romania, Spring 1944* (University Press of Kansas, 2007), 26–27.

42. Braithwaite, *Moscow 1941*, 38–39.

43. Glantz, *Barbarossa*, 210.

44. Richard Overy, *The Dictators: Hitler's Germany and Stalin's Russia* (Norton, 2004), 496.

45. Braithwaite, *Moscow 1941*, 293.

46. Glantz, *The Siege of Leningrad*, 116.

47. Boog et al., *The Attack on the Soviet Union*, 729–31.

48. Rolf-Dieter Muller et al., Milatargeschichtliches Forshungsamt, *Germany and the Second World War, Volume V/II, Organization and Mobilization of the German Sphere of Power* (Clarendon Press, 2003), 163–65

49. Ibid., 155–66.

50. Mawdsley, *Thunder in the East*, 122.

51. Richard L. Dinardo, *Germany and the Axis Powers: From Coalition to Collapse* (University Press of Kansas, 2005), 134.

52. Megargee, *War of Annihilation*, 140.

CHAPTER SIX

1. Rolf-Dieter Muller et al., Milatargeschichtliches Forshungsamt, *Germany and the Second World War, Volume V/II, Organization and Mobilization of the German Sphere of Power* (Clarendon Press, 2003), 479–515.

2. Ibid., 496.

3. Mark Harrison, *The Economics of World War II: Six Great Powers in International Comparison* (Cambridge University Press, 1998), 156.

4. Adam Tooze, *The Wages of Destruction: The Making and Breaking of the Nazi Economy* (Allen Lane, 2006), 508.

5. F. M. Von Senger und Etterlin, *German Tanks of World War II* (Stackpole Books, 1969), app. 4.

6. Muller et al., *German Sphere of Power*, 339.

7. Harrison, *The Economics of World War II*, 284–86.

8. Horst Boog et al., Milatargeschichtliches Forshungsamt, *Germany and the Second World War, Volume VI, The Global War* (Oxford University Press, 2001), 870–73.

9. Ibid., 870–81.

10. Ibid., 605–6.

11. Ibid., 633–34.

12. Chris Bellamy, *Absolute War: Soviet Russia in the Second World War: A Modern History* (Macmillan, 2007), 470.

13. Richard Overy, *The Dictators: Hitler's Germany and Stalin's Russia* (Norton, 2004), 497.

14. Evan Mawdsley, *Thunder in the East: The Nazi-Soviet War 1941–1945*, (Hodder Headline Group, 2005), 50.

15. Overy, *The Dictators*, 497.

16. David M. Glantz with Jonathan M. House, *To the Gates of Stalingrad: Soviet German Combat Operations, April–August 1942* (University Press of Kansas, 2009), 47.

17. Catherine Merridale, *Ivan's War: Life and Death in the Red Army, 1939–1945* (Picador, 2006), 147.

18. Walter S. Dunn Jr., *Hitler's Nemesis: The Red Army 1930–45* (Stackpole Books, 2009), 44–47.

19. Ibid., 65.

20. David M. Glantz and Jonathan M. House, *The Battle of Kursk* (University Press of Kansas, 1999), 9.

21. Glantz, *To the Gates of Stalingrad*, 34–37.

22. Ibid., 40–45.

23. Bellamy, *Absolute War*, 387–88.

24. Tat'iana Mikhailova Tver', "The Battle of Rzhev: Ideology instead of Statistics," *Journal of Slavic Military Studies* 18, no. 3 (2005): 359–68.

25. Boog et al., *The Global War*, 954–57.

26. Joel S. A. Hayward, *Stopped at Stalingrad: The Luftwaffe and Hitler's Defeat in the East, 1942–43* (University Press of Kansas, 1998), 2.

27. Boog et al., *The Global War*, 897.

28. Glantz, *To the Gates of Stalingrad*, 15.

29. Richard L. Dinardo, *Germany and the Axis Powers: From Coalition to Collapse* (University Press of Kansas, 2005), 138–39.

30. Boog et al., *The Global War*, 882–87.

31. Glantz, *To the Gates of Stalingrad*, 16–18.

32. Ibid., 65–68.

33. Mawdsley, *Thunder in the East*, 147.

34. Glantz, *To the Gates of Stalingrad*, 77.

35. Ibid., 79.

36. Ibid., 83.

37. Ibid., 101.

38. Glantz, *To the Gates of Stalingrad*, 89.

39. John Erickson, *The Road to Stalingrad* (Harper & Row Publishers, 1975), 350–51.

40. Boog et al., *The Global War*, 940–41.

41. Marcel Stein, *Field Marshal von Manstein: The Janus Head: A Portrait* (Helion & Company, 2007), 329.

42. Ibid., 354–73.

43. Glantz, *To the Gates of Stalingrad*, table 10.

44. Ibid.

45. Ibid.

46. Ibid., 103–4.

47. Ibid., table 10.

48. Ibid., table 11.

49. Erickson, *The Road to Stalingrad*, 353.

50. Glantz, *To the Gates of Stalingrad*, 153.

51. Ibid., 155.

52. Robert M. Citino, *Death of the Wehrmacht: The German Campaigns of 1942* (University Press of Kansas, 2007), 173–80.

53. Glantz, *To the Gates of Stalingrad*, 158.

54. Boog et al., *The Global War*, 979.

55. Glantz, *To the Gates of Stalingrad*, 200.

56. Ibid., 171–72.

57. Ibid., 214.

58. Bellamy, *Absolute War*, 503.

59. Boog et al., *The Global War*, 991.

60. Ibid., 989.

61. Glantz, *To the Gates of Stalingrad*, 208–11.

62. Ibid., 204.

63. Mawdsley, *Thunder in the East*, 171.

64. Citino, *Death of the Wehrmacht*, 232.

65. Boog et al., *The Global War*, 1029.

66. Robert Kirchubel, *Hitler's Panzer Armies on the Eastern Front* (Pen & Sword, 2009), 42.

67. Dennis Showalter, *Hitler's Panzers: The Lightning Attacks That Revolutionized Warfare* (Berkley Publishing Group, 2009), 208.

68. Michael K. Jones, *Stalingrad: How the Red Army Triumphed* (Pen & Sword, 2007), 7.

69. Overy, *The Dictators*, 497–500.

70. Antony Beevor, *Stalingrad: The Fateful Siege: 1942-1943* (Penguin Books, 1999), 85.

71. Ibid., 86.

72. Jones, *Stalingrad*, 28.

73. Glantz, *To the Gates of Stalingrad*, 231–47.

74. Ibid., 248–51.

75. Ibid., 254–61.

76. Bellamy, *Absolute War*, 493.

77. Citino, *Death of the Wehrmacht*, 247.

78. Glantz, *To the Gates of Stalingrad*, 393.

79. Beevor, *Stalingrad*, 117.

80. Jones, *Stalingrad*, 20–22.

81. Ibid., 45.

82. Bellamy, *Absolute War*, 511–12.

83. Jones, *Stalingrad*, 23–24.

84. Ibid., 94–95.

85. Beevor, *Stalingrad*, 104–6.

86. Jones, *Stalingrad*, 56–60.

87. Ibid., 70–71.

88. Ibid., 14–15.

89. Ibid., 97–98.

90. Ibid., 99–117.

91. Ibid., 139–44.

92. Merridale, *Ivan's War*, 174.

93. Beevor, *Stalingrad*, 176–177.

94. John A. English and Bruce I. Gudmundsson, *On Infantry*, rev. ed. (Praeger, 1994), 93.

95. Vasili I. Chuikov, *The Beginning of the Road* (Macgibbon & Kee, 1963), 285–94.

96. Jones, *Stalingrad*, 165–67.

97. Chuikov, *The Beginning of the Road*, 71–72.

98. Bellamy, *Absolute War*, 523–24.

99. Merridale, *Ivan's War*, 165.

100. Jones, *Stalingrad*, 194–96.

101. Chuikov, *The Beginning of the Road*, 180–85.

102. Jones, *Stalingrad*, 202–18.

103. Ibid., 238–39.

104. Chuikov, *The Beginning of the Road*, 209–16.

105. David M. Glantz and Jonathan M. House, *Armageddon in Stalingrad, September-November 1942,* (University Press of Kansas, 2009) at page 716.

CHAPTER SEVEN

1. See Joel S. A. Hayward, *Stopped at Stalingrad: The Luftwaffe and Hitler's Defeat in the East, 1942-43* (University Press of Kansas, 1998).

2. Catherine Merridale, *Ivan's War: Life and Death in the Red Army, 1939-1945* (Picador, 2006), 160.

3. Richard Overy, *The Dictators: Hitler's Germany and Stalin's Russia* (Norton, 2004), 498.

4. Horst Boog et al., Milatargeschichtliches Forshungsamt, *Germany and the Second World War, Volume VI, The Global War* (Oxford University Press, 2001), 1048-56.

5. Richard L. Dinardo, *Germany and the Axis Powers: From Coalition to Collapse* (University Press of Kansas, 2005), 150.

6. Ibid., 151.

7. Boog et al., *The Global War*, 1123.

8. Ibid., 1124.

9. Ibid., 1134-37.

10. F. W. Von Mellenthin, *Panzer Battles* (University of Oklahoma Press, 1956), 214.

11. Ibid., 218.

12. Dennis Showalter, *Hitler's Panzers: The Lightning Attacks That Revolutionized Warfare* (Berkley Publishing Group, 2009), 215.

13. Boog et al., *The Global War*, 1177.

14. Antony Beevor, *Stalingrad: The Fateful Siege: 1942-1943* (Penguin Books, 1999), 394.

15. David M. Glantz and Jonathan M. House, *Armageddon in Stalingrad: September-November 1942,* (University Press of Kansas, 2009), 716-717.

16. Laurance Rees, *World War II behind Closed Doors: Stalin, the Nazis and the West* (Pantheon Books, 2008), 255-56.

17. Marcel Stein, *Field Marshal von Manstein: The Janus Head: A Portrait* (Helion & Company, 2007), 167.

18. Ibid., 156, 167. See also Benoit Lemay, *Erich von Manstein: Hitler's Master Strategist* (Casemate Publishers, 2010), 318.

19. Dinardo, *Germany and the Axis Powers*, 154-55.

20. David Glantz, *After Stalingrad: The Red Army's Winter Offensive 1942-1943* (Helion, 2008), 25.

21. David M. Glantz and Jonathan M. House, *When Titans Clashed: How the Red Army Stopped Hitler* (University Press of Kansas, 1995), 347.

22. Glantz, *After Stalingrad*, 41.

23. Ibid., 54.

24. Ibid., 56-57.

25. David M. Glantz, *Counterpoint to Stalingrad: Operation Mars (November-December 1942): Marshal Zhukov's Greatest Defeat* (Fort Leavenworth, Kansas: Foreign Military Studies Office), http://fmso.Leavenworth.army.mil/documents/countrpt/countrpt.htm.

26. Glantz, *When Titans Clashed*, 138-39.

27. Showalter, *Hitler's Panzers*, 222.

28. Glantz, *When Titans Clashed*, 296.

29. Glantz, *After Stalingrad*, 25.

30. Ibid., 95–107.

31. Ibid., 26.

32. David M. Glantz, *From the Don to the Dnieper: Soviet Offensive Operations, December 1941–August 1943* (Frank Cass, 1991), 73–76.

33. David M. Glantz, "The Red Army's Donbass Offensive (February–March 1943) Revisited: A Documentary Essay," *Journal of Slavic Military Studies* 18, no. 3 (2005): 369–503.

34. Glantz, *After Stalingrad*, 27–28.

35. Ibid., 110.

36. Ibid., 110–27.

37. Evan Mawdsley, *Thunder in the East: The Nazi-Soviet War 1941–1945*, (Hodder Headline Group, 2005), 258.

38. Glantz, *After Stalingrad*, 137.

39. Ibid., 139.

40. Ibid., 151–76.

41. Robert Kirchubel, *Hitler's Panzer Armies on the Eastern Front* (Pen & Sword, 2009), 45.

42. Ibid.

43. Mawdsley, *Thunder in the East*, 261. Kirchubel, *Hitler's Panzer Armies on the Eastern Front*, 164.

44. Glantz, *After Stalingrad*, 179–92.

45. Glantz, *From the Don to the Dnieper*, 136–50, 189–92.

46. Glantz, "The Red Army's Donbass Offensive (February–March 1943) Revisited,": 369–503.

47. Glantz, *When Titans Clashed*, 295–96.

48. David M. Glantz and Jonathan M. House, *The Battle of Kursk* (University Press of Kansas, 1999), 13.

49. Glantz, *After Stalingrad*, 198–99.

50. Ibid., 199–225.

51. Ibid., 251–84.

52. Ibid., 328.

53. Walter S. Dunn Jr., *Kursk: Hitler's Gamble, 1943* (Stackpole, 1997), 2–3, 8–9.

54. Glantz, *After Stalingrad*, 284–315.

55. Ibid., 315–33.

56. Ibid., 334–50.

57. Glantz, David M., *The Soviet-German War 1941–1945: Myths and Realities: A Survey Essay*, A Paper Presented as the 20th Anniversary Distinguished Lecture at the Strom Thurmond Institute of Government and Public Affairs Clemson University, October 11, 2001 (Clemson, South Carolina).

58. Dunn, *Kursk*, 14–17.

59. Glantz and House, *The Battle of Kursk*, 14.

60. Kirchubel, *Hitler's Panzer Armies on the Eastern Front*, 86.

61. Glantz, *After Stalingrad*, 376.

62. Ibid., 376–86.

63. Ibid., 375–76.

64. Ibid., 376–77.

65. Rolf-Dieter Muller et al., Milatargeschichtliches Forshungsamt, *Germany and the Second World War, Volume V/II, Organization and Mobilization of the German Sphere of Power* (Clarendon Press, 2003), 352.

66. Glantz, *After Stalingrad*, 386–88.

67. Ibid., 390–410.

68. Chris Bellamy, *Absolute War: Soviet Russia in the Second World War: A Modern History* (Macmillan, 2007), 401–2; David M. Glantz, *The Siege of Leningrad 1941–44: 900 Days of Terror* (Cassell, 2001), 150–77.

69. Mawdsley, *Thunder in the East*, 253–55; Glantz, *After Stalingrad*, 410–33.

70. Franz Kurowski, *Panzer Aces* (Ballantine Publishing Group, 1992), 270.

71. Ibid., 271–72; Christopher W. Wilbeck, *Swinging the Sledgehammer: The Combat Effectiveness of German Heavy Tank Battalions in World War II* (Fort Leavenworth, Kansas: Foreign Military Studies Office, 2002), 20–24.

72. Glantz, *After Stalingrad*, 442.

73. Robert Forczyk, *Panther vs. T-34, Ukraine 1943* (Osprey Publishing, 2007), 22.

CHAPTER EIGHT

1. Stephen Howarth and Derek Law, eds., *The Battle of the Atlantic 1939–1945: The 50th Anniversary International Naval Conference* (Naval Institute Press, 1994), 277.

2. Ibid., 278.

3. Adam Tooze, *The Wages of Destruction: The Making and Breaking of the Nazi Economy* (Allen Lane, 2006), 493–94.

4. Howarth and Law, *The Battle of the Atlantic 1939–1945*, 279.

5. Ibid., 284–91.

6. Ibid., 87–88.

7. Michael Gannon, *Operation Drumbeat* (HarperCollins, 1990), 76, 92–93.

8. Office of Naval Intelligence, Navy Department, *Fuehrer Conferences on Matters Dealing with the German Navy 1942, Volume III* (Office of Naval Intelligence, 1946), Document Reference PG 32187 T-14B, January 12, 1942, 1–9, Annex 2.

9. Howarth and Law, *The Battle of the Atlantic 1939–1945*, 569; Gannon, *Operation Drumbeat*, 176–81.

10. Gannon, *Operation Drumbeat*, 338–39.

11. Howarth and Law, *The Battle of the Atlantic 1939–1945*, 570–71.

12. Office of Naval Intelligence, *Fuehrer Conferences*, 130–60.

13. Gooch, John, *Decisive Campaigns of the Second World War* (Frank Cass & Co. Ltd., 1990), 52.

14. Gannon, *Operation Drumbeat*, 390–91.

15. Zetterling, Niklas, and Tamelander, Michael, *Tirpitz, The Life and Death of Germany's Last Super Battleship,* (Casemate Publishers, 2009), 105.

16. Howarth and Law, *The Battle of the Atlantic 1939–1945*, 61.

17. Ibid., 31.

18. Gannon, *Operation Drumbeat*, 389.

19. Ronald Lewin, *Ultra Goes to War: The First Account of World War II's Greatest Secret Based on Official Documents* (McGraw-Hill, 1978), 25.

20. Ibid., 30–33.

21. Ibid., 204–7.

22. Gannon, *Operation Drumbeat*, 395.

23. Lewin, *Ultra Goes to War*, 216–19.

24. Gannon, *Operation Drumbeat*, 396.

25. Howarth and Law, *The Battle of the Atlantic 1939–1945*, 434–36.

26. Tooze, *The Wages of Destruction*, 612–13.

27. Howarth and Law, *The Battle of the Atlantic 1939–1945*, 383.

28. Howard D. Grier, *Hitler, Donitz, and the Baltic Sea: The Third Reich's Last Hope, 1944–1945* (U.S. Naval Institute Press, 2007), 174–75.

29. Ibid., 182, 205.

30. Richard L. Dinardo, *Germany and the Axis Powers: From Coalition to Collapse* (University Press of Kansas, 2005), 28–29.

31. Ed. Dear, I.C.B., *The Oxford Guide to World War II,* (Oxford University Press, 1995), 460–461.

32. Ibid., 460.

33. Gooch, *Decisive Campaigns,* 86.

34. Dinardo, *Germany and the Axis Powers*, 56–57.

35. Alan J. Levine, *The War against Rommel's Supply Lines, 1942–1943* (Praeger Publishers, 1999), 4.

36. Liddell Hart, *The Rommel Papers* (Harcourt, Brace and Company, 1953), xviii.

37. Robert M. Citino, *Death of the Wehrmacht: The German Campaigns of 1942* (University Press of Kansas, 2007), 117–24.

38. Lewin, *Ultra Goes to War*, 169–70.

39. Levine, *The War against Rommel's Supply Lines, 1942–1943*, 20–21.

40. Dinardo, *Germany and the Axis Powers*, 66–68.

41. Office of Naval Intelligence, *Fuehrer Conferences*, 90–91.

42. Citino, *Death of the Wehrmacht*, 129.

43. Steven Zaloga, *Armored Thunderbolt: The U.S. Army Sherman in World War II* (Stackpole Books, 2008), 29.

44. Citino, *Death of the Wehrmacht*, 129.

45. Ibid., 141–48.

46. Dinardo, *Germany and the Axis Powers*, 162–63.

47. Levine, *The War against Rommel's Supply Lines, 1942–1943*, 26.

48. Zaloga, *Armored Thunderbolt*, 30.

49. Citino, *Death of the Wehrmacht*, 273–77.

50. Ibid., 280–82.

51. Dinardo, *Germany and the Axis Powers*, 167.

52. Levine, *The War against Rommel's Supply Lines, 1942–1943*, 58.

53. Ibid., 85, 112.

54. Rick Atkinson, *An Army at Dawn: The War in North Africa, 1942–1943* (Henry Holt and Company, 2002), 325.

55. Ibid., 378–85.

56. Ibid., 389.

57. Ibid., 390.

58. Ibid., 234.

59. Omar N. Bradley, *A Soldier's Story* (Henry Holt and Company, 1951), 35.

60. Ibid., 35–36.

61. Levine, *The War against Rommel's Supply Lines, 1942–1943*, 147.

62. Atkinson, *An Army at Dawn*, 537.

63. Ibid., 536.

64. Levine, *The War against Rommel's Supply Lines, 1942–1943*, 181.

65. Lewin, *Ultra Goes to War*, 277.

CHAPTER NINE

1. Rolf-Dieter Muller et al., Milatargeschichtliches Forshungsamt, *Germany and the Second World War, Volume V/II, Organization and Mobilization of the German Sphere of Power* (Clarendon Press, 2003), 352.

2. F. M. von Senger und Etterlin, *German Tanks of World War II* (Stackpole Books, 1969), app. 4.

3. Robert Forczyk, *Panther vs. T-34, Ukraine 1943* (Osprey Publishing, 2007), 8–15.

4. Muller et al., *German Sphere of Power*, 608–11.

5. Ibid., 611.

6. Forczyk, *Panther vs. T-34*, 38–43.

7. Robert Kirchubel, *Hitler's Panzer Armies on the Eastern Front* (Pen & Sword, 2009), 184.

8. Muller, *German Sphere of Power*, 667–70.

9. Ibid., 686–87.

10. David M. Glantz and Jonathan M. House, *The Battle of Kursk* (University Press of Kansas, 1999), 15–19.

11. K. Rokossovsky, *A Soldier's Duty* (Progress Publishers, 1970), 182.

12. Benoit Lemay, *Erich von Manstein: Hitler's Master Strategist* (Casemate Publishers, 2010), 370.

13. Ibid.

14. Walter S. Dunn Jr., *Hitler's Nemesis: The Red Army 1930–45* (Stackpole Books, 2009), 195.

15. Ibid., 131–32.

16. Catherine Merridale, *Ivan's War: Life and Death in the Red Army, 1939–1945* (Picador, 2006), 162–63.

17. Evan Mawdsley, *Thunder in the East: The Nazi-Soviet War 1941–1945*, (Hodder Headline Group, 2005), 199.

18. Dunn, *Hitler's Nemesis*, 157.

19. Ibid., 18–19.

20. Glantz and House, *The Battle of Kursk*, 33.

21. Dunn, *Hitler's Nemesis*, 137.

22. Forczyk, *Panther vs. T-34*, 44–45.

23. Mawdsley, *Thunder in the East*, 196–97.

24. David M. Glantz and Jonathan M. House, *When Titans Clashed: How the Red Army Stopped Hitler* (University Press of Kansas, 1995), 163–65.

25. Glantz and House, *The Battle of Kursk*, 52.

26. Franz Kurowski, *Panzer Aces* (Ballantine Publishing Group, 1992), 187–88; Christopher W. Wilbeck, *Swinging the Sledgehammer: The Combat Effectiveness of German Heavy Tank Battalions in World War II* (Foreign Military Studies Office Fort Leavenworth, Kansas, 2002), 64–65.

27. Glantz and House, *The Battle of Kursk*, 93.

28. Kirchubel, *Hitler's Panzer Armies on the Eastern Front*, 166.

29. Forczyk, *Panther vs. T-34*, 77.

30. Kirchubel, *Hitler's Panzer Armies on the Eastern Front*, 166.

31. Glantz and House, *The Battle of Kursk*, 52–54.

32. Ibid., 100–101, 316–19.

33. Forczyk, *Panther vs. T-34*, 51.

34. Glantz and House, *The Battle of Kursk*, 135.

35. Ibid., 147.

36. Ibid., 152.

37. Ibid., 151–52.

38. Ibid., 197–221.

39. For the high-end figure, see ibid., 275–76. For the low-end figure, see Marcel Stein, *Field Marshal von Manstein: The Janus Head: A Portrait* (Helion & Company, 2007), 212.

40. Glantz and House, *The Battle of Kursk*, 280.

41. Dunn, *Hitler's Nemesis*, 160.

42. Ibid., 158.

43. Glantz and House, *The Battle of Kursk*, 51–58.

44. Chris Bellamy, *Absolute War: Soviet Russia in the Second World War: A Modern History* (Macmillan, 2007), 587.

45. Kirchubel, *Hitler's Panzer Armies on the Eastern Front*, 87.

46. Glantz and House, *When Titans Clashed*, 296.

47. Kirchubel, *Hitler's Panzer Armies on the Eastern Front*, 115–16.

48. Muller et al., *German Sphere of Power*, 463.

49. Kirchubel, *Hitler's Panzer Armies on the Eastern Front*, 170–71.

50. Forczyk, *Panther vs. T-34*, 25, 62.

51. David M. Glantz, *From the Don to the Dnieper: Soviet Offensive Operations, December 1941–August 1943* (Frank Cass, 1991), 359–65.

52. Niklas Zetterling and Anders Frankson, *The Korsun Pocket: The Encirclement and Breakout of a German Army in the East, 1944* (Casemate, 2008), 299.

53. Lemay, Benoit, *Erich von Manstein, Hitler's Master Strategist* (Casemate Publishers, 2010), 48.

54. Zetterling, Niklas, and Tamelander, Michael, *Tirpitz, The Life and Death of Germany's Last Super Battleship* (Casemate Publishers, 2009), 193.

55. Kirchubel, *Hitler's Panzer Armies on the Eastern Front*, 49.

56. Forczyk, *Panther vs. T-34*, 64.

57. Rolf Hinze, *Crucible of Combat: Germany's Defensive Battles in the Ukraine 1943–44* (Helion & Company, 2009), 35–36.

58. Ibid., 53.

59. Ibid., 141–61.

60. Ibid., 146.

61. Forczyk, *Panther vs. T-34*, 69.

62. Kirchubel, *Hitler's Panzer Armies on the Eastern Front*, 174.

63. Hinze, *Crucible of Combat*, 97–114.

64. Forczyk, *Panther vs. T-34*, 65.

65. Glantz and House, *When Titans Clashed*, 184.

66. Zetterling and Frankson, *The Korsun Pocket*, 10, 299.

67. Glantz and House, *When Titans Clashed*, 292.

68. Zetterling and Frankson, *The Korsun Pocket*, 10, 299.

69. Rokossovsky, *A Soldier's Duty*, 214–17; Dunn, *Hitler's Nemesis*, 149.

70. Glantz and House, *When Titans Clashed*, 184.

71. Muller, *German Sphere of Power*, 1019.

72. Forczyk, *Panther vs. T-34*, 31–33, 72–75.

73. Zetterling and Frankson, *The Korsun Pocket*, 10.

74. Hinze, *Crucible of Combat*, 164.

75. Ibid., 170–74.

76. Ibid., 176.

77. Zetterling and Frankson, *The Korsun Pocket*, 37–39.

78. Ibid., 37–39, 52–55.

79. Ibid., 37–54.

80. Ibid., 39, 53, 55–74.

81. Ibid., 77, 85.

82. Ibid., 85–96.

83. Ibid., 97–101.

84. Ibid., 153–54.

85. Ibid., 149–54.

86. Ibid., 154–67, 181, 184–85.

87. Ibid., 189–97.

88. Ibid., 199–210.

89. Ibid., 199–216.

90. Ibid., 213–17, 229.

91. Hinze, *Crucible of Combat*, 187–90; Zetterling and Frankson, *The Korsun Pocket*, 244–45.

92. Zetterling and Frankson, *The Korsun Pocket*, 258–69.

93. Ibid., 275.

94. Wilbeck, *Swinging the Sledgehammer*, 82–83.

95. Zetterling and Frankson, *The Korsun Pocket*, 261, 265, 268, 272.

96. Kirchubel, *Hitler's Panzer Armies on the Eastern Front*, 52; Zetterling and Frankson, *The Korsun Pocket*, 277.

97. Zetterling and Frankson, *The Korsun Pocket*, 283–92.

98. Dennis Showalter, *Hitler's Panzers: The Lightning Attacks That Revolutionized Warfare* (Berkley Publishing Group, 2009), 283.

99. Zetterling and Frankson, *The Korsun Pocket*, 286–87.

100. Ibid., 331–33.

101. Ibid., 286, 350.

102. David M. Glantz and Harold S. Orenstein, eds., *The Battle for the Ukraine: The Red Army Korsun'-Shevchenkovskii Operation, 1944 (The Soviet General Staff Study)* (Frank Cass, 2003), 153.

103. Zetterling and Frankson, *The Korsun Pocket*, 284, 293–94.

104. Richard Overy, *The Dictators: Hitler's Germany and Stalin's Russia* (Norton, 2004), 522, 525.

105. Merridale, *Ivan's War*, 253.

106. Hinze, *Crucible of Combat*, 242–45.

107. Ibid., 250–53.

108. Ibid., 256–58.

109. Ibid., 272–79, 280–81.

110. Ibid., 273.

111. Ibid., 308–13.

112. Showalter, *Hitler's Panzers*, 284–86. Kirchubel, *Hitler's Panzer Armies on the Eastern Front*, 54–55.

113. Mawdsley, 279.

114. For the lower figure, see Mawdsley, *Thunder in the East*, 286; For the higher figure, see Richard L. Dinardo, *Germany and the Axis Powers: From Coalition to Collapse* (University Press of Kansas, 2005), 185–86. For the midrange estimate, see Hinze, *Crucible of Combat*, 443–44.

115. Merridale, *Ivan's War*, 260–61.

116. Helmut Heiber and David Glantz, *Hitler and His Generals Military Conferences 1942-1945: The First Complete Stenographic Record of the Military Situation Conferences, from Stalingrad to Berlin* (Enigma Books, 1962), 340–41.

117. Muller et al., *German Sphere of Power*, 1062.

118. Ian Kershaw, *Hitler 1936-1945: Nemesis* (Norton, 2000), 647.

CHAPTER TEN

1. Helmut Heiber and David Glantz, *Hitler and His Generals Military Conferences 1942-1945: The First Complete Stenographic Record of the Military Situation Conferences, from Stalingrad to Berlin* (Enigma Books, 1962), 1070.

2. Robin Neillands, *The Bomber War: The Allied Air Offensive against Nazi Germany* (The Overlook Press, 2001), 158–61.

3. Ibid., 158–61.

4. Adam Tooze, *The Wages of Destruction: The Making and Breaking of the Nazi Economy* (Allen Lane, 2006), 597–98.

5. Neillands, *The Bomber War*, 216–22.

6. Ibid., 224–26.

7. Neillands, *The Bomber War*, 228–33. Martin Middlebrook and Chris Everitt, *The Bomber Command War Diaries* (Viking Books, 1985), 387–88.

8. Tooze, *The Wages of Destruction*, 557.

9. Neillands, *The Bomber War*, 248–55.

10. Ibid., 256–74.

11. Ibid., 283–85.

12. Middlebrook and Everitt, *The Bomber Command War Diaries*, 487.

13. Richard Suchenwirth, USAF Historical Division Research Studies Institute Air University, *USAF Historical Studies No. 189, Historical Turning Points in the German Air Force War Effort* (Arno Press, 1968), 28.

14. W. H. Tantum IV, and E. J. Hoffschmidt, *The Rise and Fall of the German Air Force 1933–1945* (WE Inc. Old Greenwich, 1969), 309.

15. Ronald C. Cooke, *Target: Hitler's Oil, Allied Attacks on German Oil Supplies 1939–1945*, (William Kimber, 1985), 137–139.

16. Department of Military Art and Engineering, U.S. Military Academy, West Point, *The War in Western Europe Part I (June to December 1944)* (U.S. Military Academy, 1952), 61–62.

17. Tooze, *The Wages of Destruction*, 649–51.

18. Mark A. Stoler, Melanie S. Gustafson, *Major Problems in the History of World War II* (Houghton Mifflin Company, 2003), 146.

19. Horst Boog, ed., *The Conduct of the Air War in the Second World War: An International Comparison, Proceedings of the International Conference of Historians in Freiburg im Breisgau, Federal Republic of Germany, from 29 August to 2 September 1988* (Berg, 1992), 46–47.

20. Heiber and Glantz, *Hitler and His Generals Military Conferences 1942–1945*, 314.

21. Samuel W. Mitcham Jr., *The Desert Fox in Normandy: Rommel's Defense of Fortress Europe* (Praeger, 1997), 26.

22. Ibid., 14–16, 57–59; Roman Johann Jarymowycz, *Tank Tactics from Normandy to Lorraine* (Lynne Rienner Publishers, 2001), 96–105.

23. Jarymowycz, *Tank Tactics from Normandy to Lorraine*, 96–105.

24. Horst Boog et al., Milatargeschichtliches Forshungsamt, *Germany and the Second World War, Volume VI, The Global War* (Oxford University Press, 2001), 43.

25. Steven J. Zaloga, *US Armored Divisions The European Theater of Operations, 1944–45*, (Osprey Publishing, 2004), 45.

26. Jarymowycz, *Tank Tactics from Normandy to Lorraine*, 96–105.

27. Ronald Andidora, *Home by Christmas: The Illusion of Victory in 1944* (Greenwood Press, 2002), 29; Trevor N. Dupuy, David L. Bongard, and Richard C. Anderson Jr., *Hitler's Last Gamble: The Battle of the Bulge, December 1944–January 1945*, (HarperCollins, 1994), 407.

28. Steven Zaloga, *Armored Thunderbolt: The U.S. Army Sherman in World War II* (Stackpole Books, 2008), 3.

29. Zaloga, *US Armored Divisions*, 37.

30. Stephen E. Ambrose, *D-Day June 6, 1944 the Climactic Battle of World War II* (Simon & Schuster, 1994), 48.

31. Ibid., 177.

32. Edwin P. Hoyt, *Airborne: The History of the American Parachute Force* (Stein and Day Publishers, 1979), 68.

33. Ambrose, *D-Day*, 221.

34. Paul Carell, *Invasion: They're Coming!* (Bantam Books, 1964), 24.

35. Ambrose, *D-Day*, 251.

36. Omar N. Bradley, *A Soldier's Story* (Henry Holt and Company, 1951), 275.

37. Ambrose, *D-Day*, 269.

38. Bradley, *A Soldier's Story*, 268.

39. Ambrose, *D-Day*, 321.

40. Ibid., 273.

41. Zaloga, *Armored Thunderbolt*, 144.

42. Ambrose, *D-Day*, 387.

43. Heiber and Glantz, *Hitler and His Generals Military Conferences 1942–1945*, 969.

CHAPTER ELEVEN

1. David M. Glantz, *Red Storm over the Balkans: The Failed Soviet Invasion of Romania, Spring 1944* (University Press of Kansas, 2007), 28–29, 379–80.

2. Ibid., 54–59.

3. Ibid., 18–24.

4. Ibid., 32–36.

5. Howard D. Grier, *Hitler, Donitz, and the Baltic Sea: The Third Reich's Last Hope, 1944–1945* (U.S. Naval Institute Press, 2007), 90.

6. Marcel Stein, *Field Marshal von Manstein: The Janus Head: A Portrait* (Helion & Company, 2007), 301–378.

7. Glantz, *Red Storm over the Balkans*, 36–214.

8. Rolf Hinze, *Crucible of Combat: Germany's Defensive Battles in the Ukraine 1943–44* (Helion & Company, 2009), 289.

9. Glantz, *Red Storm over the Balkans*, 52–70.

10. Hinze, *Crucible of Combat*, 289–90.

11. Glantz, *Red Storm over the Balkans*, 110–62.

12. Hinze, *Crucible of Combat*, 291; Glantz, *Red Storm over the Balkans*, 176–88.

13. Glantz, *Red Storm over the Balkans*, 188–207.

14. Hinze, *Crucible of Combat*, 291–92.

15. Glantz, *Red Storm over the Balkans*, 215–26.

16. Hinze, *Crucible of Combat*, 292; Glantz, *Red Storm over the Balkans*, 227–28.

17. Hinze, *Crucible of Combat*, 292.

18. Glantz, *Red Storm over the Balkans*, 228–49.

19. Hinze, *Crucible of Combat*, 295.

20. Glantz, *Red Storm over the Balkans*, 273.

21. Ibid., 291.

22. Ibid., 291–319.

23. Ibid., 378–81.

24. Evan Mawdsley, *Thunder in the East: The Nazi-Soviet War 1941–1945*, (Hodder Headline Group, 2005), 298.

25. Walter S. Dunn Jr., *Soviet Blitzkrieg: The Battle for White Russia, 1944* (Stackpole Books, 2008), 26.

26. Walter S. Dunn Jr., *Hitler's Nemesis: The Red Army 1930–45* (Stackpole Books, 2009), 89–90.

27. Ibid., 13.

28. Chris Bellamy, *Absolute War: Soviet Russia in the Second World War: A Modern History* (Macmillan, 2007), 613.

29. Dunn, *Hitler's Nemesis*, 144.

30. K. Rokossovsky, *A Soldier's Duty* (Progress Publishers, 1970), 233–36.

31. Dunn, *Soviet Blitzkrieg*, 31.

32. Ibid., 31.

33. Mawdsley, *Thunder in the East*, 302.

34. Dunn, *Soviet Blitzkrieg*, 24.

35. Ibid., 31–32.

36. Ibid., 21, 32.

37. Ibid., 64.

38. Dunn, *Hitler's Nemesis*, 85.

39. Dunn, *Soviet Blitzkrieg*, 59.

40. Ibid., 61.

41. Mawdsley, *Thunder in the East*, 300.

42. Dunn, *Soviet Blitzkrieg*, 5.

43. Rolf-Dieter Muller et al., Milatargeschichtliches Forshungsamt, *Germany and the Second World War, Volume V/II, Organization and Mobilization of the German Sphere of Power* (Clarendon Press, 2003), 169.

44. Mawdsley, *Thunder in the East*, 301.

45. Samuel W. Mitcham Jr., *Crumbling Empire: The German Defeat in the East, 1944* (Praeger, 2001), 8–13.

46. David M. Glantz and Jonathan M. House, *When Titans Clashed: How the Red Army Stopped Hitler* (University Press of Kansas, 1995), 204–5.

47. Dunn, *Soviet Blitzkrieg*, 98.

48. Ibid., 95.

49. Ibid.

50. Ibid., 97.

51. Robert Kirchubel, *Hitler's Panzer Armies on the Eastern Front* (Pen & Sword, 2009), 119.

52. Dunn, *Soviet Blitzkrieg*, 141–42.

53. Ibid., 139–47.

54. Ibid., 145–56.

55. Ibid., 153–78.

56. Ibid., 181–85.

57. Ibid., 2–3, 181–85.

58. Norbert Bacyk, *The Tank Battle at Praga July–Sept. 1944: The 4th SS-Panzer-Corps vs the 1st Belorussian Front* (Leandoer & Ekholm Publishing, 2009), 14–15.

59. Mawdsley, *Thunder in the East*, 300.

60. Franz Kurowski, *Panzer Aces* (Ballantine Publishing Group, 1992); 125. Bacyk, *The Tank Battle at Praga July–Sept. 1944*, 14.

61. Bellamy, *Absolute War*, 615.

62. Dunn, *Soviet Blitzkrieg*, 225.

63. Mawdsley, *Thunder in the East*, 308.

64. Dennis Showalter, *Hitler's Panzers: The Lightning Attacks That Revolutionized Warfare* (Berkley Publishing Group, 2009), 304.

65. Rolf Hinze, *to the Bitter End: The Final Battles of Army Groups North Ukraine, A, and Center—Eastern Front, 1944-45* (Casemate, 2010), 17.

66. Ibid., 20.

67. Mawdsley, *Thunder in the East*, 324.

68. Kirchubel, *Hitler's Panzer Armies on the Eastern Front*, 179.

69. Bellamy, *Absolute War*, 619.

70. Laurance Rees, *World War II behind Closed Doors: Stalin, the Nazis and the West* (Pantheon Books, 2008), 274.

71. John Erickson, *The Road to Berlin* (Westview Press, 1983), 246.

72. Bacyk, *The Tank Battle at Praga July-Sept. 1944*, 209.

73. Ibid., 25-27, 210.

74. Ibid., 31-37.

75. Ibid., 38-42.

76. Ibid., 48.

77. Ibid., 53, 64, 84.

78. Ibid., 62, 63.

79. Ibid., 64-77.

80. Ibid., 91-93.

81. Glantz, *When Titans Clashed*, 215.

82. Lynne Olson and Stanley Cloud, *A Question of Honor, The Kosciuszko Squadron* (Vintage Books, 2003), 315-317.

83. Max Hastings, *Armageddon: The Battle for Germany 1944-45* (Alfred A. Knopf, 2005), 121.

84. Rees, *World War II behind Closed Doors*, 290-91.

85. Muller et al., *German Sphere of Power*, 189.

86. Ibid., 190.

87. Ibid. For the high-end figure, see Kenneth K. Koskodan, *No Greater Ally: The Untold Story of Poland's Forces in World War II* (Osprey, 2009), 220

88. Bacyk, *The Tank Battle at Praga July-Sept. 1944*, 94-114.

89. Ibid., 101.

90. Ibid., 143-45.

91. Ibid., 159.

92. Hinze, *To the Bitter End*, 25.

93. Kirchubel, *Hitler's Panzer Armies on the Eastern Front*, 58-59.

94. Hinze, *To the Bitter End*, 60.

95. Hastings, *Armageddon*, 118.

96. Erickson, *The Road to Berlin*, 350-53.

97. Krisztian Ungvary, translated by Ladislaus Lob, *The Siege of Budapest: One Hundred Days in World War II* (Yale University Press, 2005), xiv-xx, 3-4.

98. Erickson, *The Road to Berlin*, 356-66.

99. Ungvary, *The Siege of Budapest*, 320.

100. Ibid., 1-2.

101. Mawdsley, *Thunder in the East*, 349.

102. Mitcham, *Crumbling Empire*, 220.

103. Ungvary, *The Siege of Budapest*, 4-6.

104. Ibid., 35.

105. Rees, *World War II behind Closed Doors*, 321.

106. Ungvary, *The Siege of Budapest*, 70–74, 80.

107. Ibid., 80.

108. Ibid., 255.

109. Ibid., xxv.

110. Rees, *World War II behind Closed Doors*, 327.

111. Showalter, *Hitler's Panzers*, 302.

112. Ibid.

113. Grier, *Hitler, Donitz, and the Baltic Sea*, 47.

114. Bellamy, *Absolute War*, 621.

115. Grier, *Hitler, Donitz, and the Baltic Sea*, 55.

116. Ibid., 81–82.

117. Ibid., 81–107.

118. Kirchubel, *Hitler's Panzer Armies on the Eastern Front*, 125.

119. Hastings, *Armageddon*, 115.

120. Ibid., 129.

121. Glantz, *When Titans Clashed*, 232. Hastings, *Armageddon*, 8.

122. Muller et al., *German Sphere of Power*, 615.

CHAPTER TWELVE

1. Alan J. Levine, *From the Normandy Beaches to the Baltic Sea: The Northwest Europe Campaign, 1944–1945* (Praeger, 2000), 60–61.

2. John A. English and Bruce I. Gudmundsson, *On Infantry*, rev. ed. (Praeger, 1994), 112–15.

3. James S. Corum, *The Roots of Blitzkrieg: Hans von Seeckt and German Military Reform* (University Press of Kansas, 1992), 47.

4. English and Gudmundsson, *On Infantry*, 112.

5. Ibid.

6. G. E. Murray, *Eisenhower versus Montgomery: The Continuing Debate* (Praeger, 1996), 118.

7. Christopher Gabel, *Seek, Strike, and Destroy: U.S. Army Tank Destroyer Doctrine in World War II* (Combat Studies Institute, U.S. Army Command and General Staff College, 1985), 2–5.

8. Ibid., 14–17.

9. Steven Zaloga, *Armored Thunderbolt: The U.S. Army Sherman in World War II* (Stackpole Books, 2008), 20–34.

10. Ibid., 46.

11. Ibid., 46–47, 71–72, 75.

12. Ibid., 74–75.

13. Gabel, *Seek, Strike, and Destroy*, 45.

14. Roman Johann Jarymowycz, *Tank Tactics from Normandy to Lorraine* (Lynne Rienner Publishers, 2001), 258; Ronald Andidora, *Home by Christmas: The Illusion of Victory in 1944* (Greenwood Press, 2002), 58.

15. Jarymowycz, *Tank Tactics from Normandy to Lorraine*, 264–65; Andidora, 58, 264–65, 276.

16. Franz Kurowski, *Panzer Aces* (Ballantine Publishing Group, 1992); 366; Christopher W. Wilbeck, *Swinging the Sledgehammer: The Combat Effectiveness of German Heavy Tank Battalions in World War II* (Fort Leavenworth, Kansas: Foreign Military Studies Office), 96–97.

17. Dennis Showalter, *Hitler's Panzers: The Lightning Attacks That Revolutionized Warfare* (Berkley Publishing Group, 2009), 326.

18. Zaloga, *Armored Thunderbolt*, 99.

19. Walter S. Dunn Jr., *Hitler's Nemesis: The Red Army 1930–45* (Stackpole Books, 2009), 156.

20. Zaloga, *Armored Thunderbolt*, 123–24, 133.

21. Jarymowycz, *Tank Tactics from Normandy to Lorraine*, 258–62.

22. Ibid., 271, app. E.

23. Ibid., 271, 276, app. E.

24. Samuel W. Mitcham Jr., *The Desert Fox in Normandy, Rommel's Defense of Fortress Europe,* (Praeger, 1997), 137.

25. Ibid., 141–42.

26. Andidora, *Home by Christmas*, 42.

27. Mitcham, Jr., *Desert Fox*, 169.

28. English and Gudmundsson, *On Infantry*, 114.

29. Jarymowycz, *Tank Tactics from Normandy to Lorraine*, 119.

30. Andidora, *Home by Christmas*, 69; Omar N. Bradley, *A Soldier's Story* (Henry Holt and Company, 1951), 348.

31. Zaloga, *Armored Thunderbolt*, 162.

32. Jarymowycz, *Tank Tactics from Normandy to Lorraine*, 150; Andidora, *Home by Christmas*, 74–75.

33. Bradley, *A Soldier's Story*, 371. Andidora, *Home by Christmas*, 82–85.

34. Bradley, *A Soldier's Story*, 380.

35. Showalter, *Hitler's Panzers*, 331.

36. David Colley, *Decision at Strasbourg: Ike's Strategic Mistake to Halt the Sixth Army Group at the Rhine in 1944* (Naval Institute Press, 2009), 25–27.

37. Ibid., 44.

38. Christopher R. Gabel, *The Lorraine Campaign: An Overview, September-December 1944* (U.S. Army Command and General Staff College, 1985), 14.

39. Zaloga, *Armored Thunderbolt*, 184–89.

40. Showalter, *Hitler's Panzers*, 333.

41. Zaloga, *Armored Thunderbolt*, 184

42. Steven J. Zaloga, *US Armored Divisions The European Theater of Operations, 1944–45* (Osprey Publishing, 2004), 64.

43. Colley, *Decision at Strasbourg*, 70–74

44. Bruce W. Menning, *Operational Art's Origins* (U.S. Army Command and General Staff College, 1998).

45. Ibid.

46. Howard D. Grier, *Hitler, Donitz, and the Baltic Sea: The Third Reich's Last Hope, 1944–1945* (U.S. Naval Institute Press, 2007), 214.

47. Rolf-Dieter Muller et al., Milatargeschichtliches Forshungsamt, *Germany and the Second World War, Volume V/II, Organization and Mobilization of the German Sphere of Power* (Clarendon Press, 2003), 2.

48. Richard J. Evans, *The Third Reich at War* (Penguin Books, 2008), 501–2.

49. Tony Judt, *Post War: A History of Europe since 1945* (Penguin Books, 2005), 14.

50. Muller et al., *German Sphere of Power*, 242.

51. Ibid., 631.

52. Adam Tooze, *The Wages of Destruction: The Making and Breaking of the Nazi Economy* (Allen Lane, 2006), 519.

53. See Colley, *Decision at Strasbourg*, 56–59, 142–43.

54. Murray, *Eisenhower versus Montgomery*, 74.

55. Max Hastings, *Armageddon: The Battle for Germany 1944–45* (Alfred A. Knopf, 2005), 407–8.

56. Charles B. MacDonald, *The Battle of the Huertgen Forest* (Jove Books, 1983), 85–86.

57. Ibid., 89.

58. Ibid., 95–120.

59. Ibid., 195–96.

60. Hastings, *Armageddon*, 185.

61. Levine, *From the Normandy Beaches to the Baltic Sea*, 138.

62. Colley, *Decision at Strasbourg*, 121–25.

63. Ibid., 179.

64. Ibid., 17–20, 115.

65. Ibid., 85–93.

66. Ibid., 152–53.

CHAPTER THIRTEEN

1. Mark A. Stoler and Melanie S. Gustafson, *Major Problems in the History of World War II* (Houghton Mifflin Company, 2003), 156.

2. Alan J. Levine, *From the Normandy Beaches to the Baltic Sea: The Northwest Europe Campaign, 1944–1945* (Praeger, 2000), 135. Stoler, 157.

3. Max Hastings, *Armageddon: The Battle for Germany 1944–45* (Alfred A. Knopf, 2005) 196.

4. Steven Zaloga, *Armored Thunderbolt: The U.S. Army Sherman in World War II* (Stackpole Books, 2008), 180–81.

5. See Howard D. Grier, *Hitler, Donitz, and the Baltic Sea: The Third Reich's Last Hope, 1944–1945* (U.S. Naval Institute Press, 2007).

6. Ibid., 148–51.

7. Marcel Stein, *Field Marshal von Manstein: The Janus Head: A Portrait* (Helion & Company, 2007), 113–14.

8. Trevor N. Dupuy, David L. Bongard, and Richard C. Anderson Jr., *Hitler's Last Gamble: The Battle of the Bulge, December 1944–January 1945*, (HarperCollins, 1994), 253.

9. Zaloga, *Armored Thunderbolt*, 258.

10. Hastings, *Armageddon*, 235.

11. Walter S. Dunn Jr., *Hitler's Nemesis: The Red Army 1930–45* (Stackpole Books, 2009), 70, 181.

12. Ibid., 71.

13. Ibid., 146.

14. Ibid., 90.

15. Ibid., 72.

16. Robert Kirchubel, *Hitler's Panzer Armies on the Eastern Front* (Pen & Sword, 2009), 125.

17. Hastings, *Armageddon*, 241.

18. Krisztian Ungvary, translated by Ladislaus Lob, *The Siege of Budapest: One Hundred Days in World War II* (Yale University Press, 2005), 188–200.

19. Ibid., 189.

20. Ibid., 197–200.

21. Ibid., 374–75.

22. Rolf Hinze, *To the Bitter End: The Final Battles of Army Groups North Ukraine, A, and Center—Eastern Front, 1944–45* (Casemate, 2010), 85.

23. Ibid., 63–75.

24. Ibid., 87.

25. Kirchubel, *Hitler's Panzer Armies on the Eastern Front*, 180.

26. Hinze, *To the Bitter End*, 88–92.

27. Ibid., 85 104.

28. Ibid., 124.

29. Kirchubel, *Hitler's Panzer Armies on the Eastern Front*, 181.

30. Tony Le Tissier, *Zhukov at the Oder: The Decisive Battle for Berlin* (Stackpole Books, 2009), 104.

31. Antony Beevor, *The Fall of Berlin 1945* (Viking, 2002), 45.

32. Kirchubel, *Hitler's Panzer Armies on the Eastern Front*, 126.

33. David M. Glantz and Jonathan M. House, *When Titans Clashed: How the Red Army Stopped Hitler* (University Press of Kansas, 1995), 245.

34. Tissier, *Zhukov at the Oder*, 31–32.

35. Hinze, *To the Bitter End*, 140.

36. Kirchubel, *Hitler's Panzer Armies on the Eastern Front*, 58–60.

37. Hinze, *To the Bitter End*, 143–47.

38. Ibid., 147–48.

39. Ibid., 150.

40. Tissier, *Zhukov at the Oder*, 32–37.

41. Ibid., 43–61.

42. Hastings, *Armageddon*, 260.

43. Tissier, *Zhukov at the Oder*, 104.

44. Giles MacDonogh, *After the Reich: The Brutal History of the Allied Occupation* (Basic Books, 2007), 25–26.

45. Beevor, *The Fall of Berlin 1945*, 110–11.

46. Ibid., 106.

47. Hastings, *Armageddon*, 285–87.

48. Georgi K. Zhukov, *Marshal Zhukov's Greatest Battles* (Harper & Row, 1969), 278–79.

49. MacDonogh, *After the Reich*, 47.

50. Ibid., 50–51.

51. Tissier, *Zhukov at the Oder*, 101.

52. Ibid., 101–3.

53. Ibid., 81–98.

54. Dennis Showalter, *Hitler's Panzers: The Lightning Attacks That Revolutionized Warfare* (Berkley Publishing Group, 2009), 362.

55. Chris Bellamy, *Absolute War: Soviet Russia in the Second World War: A Modern History* (Macmillan, 2007), 650.

56. Tissier, *Zhukov at the Oder*, 274–75.

57. Ibid., 125.

58. Ibid., 118–22.

59. Evan Mawdsley, *Thunder in the East: The Nazi-Soviet War 1941–1945*, (Hodder Headline Group, 2005), 387.

60. Ibid., 138--43.

61. Hastings, *Armageddon*, 462.

62. K. Rokossovsky, *A Soldier's Duty* (Progress Publishers, 1970), 316–18; Kirchubel, *Hitler's Panzer Armies on the Eastern Front*, 128.

63. Tissier, *Zhukov at the Oder*, 176–77.

64. Hastings, *Armageddon*, 465.

65. Kirchubel, *Hitler's Panzer Armies on the Eastern Front*, 181–82.

66. John Erickson, *The Road to Berlin* (Westview Press, 1983), 563–75.

67. Mawdsley, *Thunder in the East*, 392; Ungvary, *The Siege of Budapest*, 431.

68. Levine, *From the Normandy Beaches to the Baltic Sea*, 171.

69. David Colley, *Decision at Strasbourg: Ike's Strategic Mistake to Halt the Sixth Army Group at the Rhine in 1944* (Naval Institute Press, 2009), 192–93.

70. Levine, *From the Normandy Beaches to the Baltic Sea*, 182–83.

71. Hastings, *Armageddon*, 418–19.

72. MacDonogh, *After the Reich*, 84–86.

73. Ibid., 398–99.

74. Ibid., 421.

75. Kirchubel, *Hitler's Panzer Armies on the Eastern Front*, 59–60; Hinze, *To the Bitter End*, 163–65.

76. Tissier, *Zhukov at the Oder*, 245–50.

77. Beevor, *The Fall of Berlin 1945*, 359.

78. Tony Judt, *Post War: A History of Europe since 1945* (Penguin Books, 2005), 16.

79. Levine, *From the Normandy Beaches to the Baltic Sea*, 200–202; Erickson, *The Road to Berlin*, 637.

80. Hastings, *Armageddon*, 490; 42,042 Canadian military members died during the war.

81. Judt, *Post War*, 82, 235.

82. Ibid., 18, 82, 235.

83. Ibid., 16–18.

84. Ibid., 16–18, 21.

85. Ibid., 34.

86. Mawdsley, *Thunder in the East*, 238.

87. Adam Tooze, *The Wages of Destruction: The Making and Breaking of the Nazi Economy* (Allen Lane, 2006), 672.

88. MacDonogh, *After the Reich*, 1.

89. Laurance Rees, *World War II behind Closed Doors: Stalin, the Nazis and the West* (Pantheon Books, 2008), 385.

90. Tooze, *The Wages of Destruction*, 672.

91. Richard Overy, *The Dictators: Hitler's Germany and Stalin's Russia* (Norton, 2004), 197.

92. Ibid., 526.

93. Hastings, *Armageddon*, 393.

94. Bellamy, *Absolute War*, 2–10.

95. Timothy Snyder, *Bloodlands, Europe Between Hitler and Stalin,* (Basic Books, 2010) at page 409.

96. Mawdsley, *Thunder in the East*, 215.

97. Overy, *The Dictators*, 427–28.

98. Bellamy, *Absolute War*, 2–15.

Selected Bibliography

Given the sheer number of sources referenced in creating this book this is not an exhaustive list. Rather, its purpose is to acquaint the reader with the sources most referenced by this study. For a more complete bibliography go to www.globeatwar.com.

Ambrose, Stephen E. *D-Day June 6, 1944 the Climactic Battle of World War II*. Simon & Schuster, 1994.

Armstrong, Richard N. *Soviet Operational Deception: The Red Cloak*. U.S. Army Command and General Staff College, Combat Studies Institute, 1988.

Atkinson, Rick. *An Army at Dawn: The War in North Africa, 1942–1943*. Henry Holt and Company, 2002.

Bacyk, Norbert. *The Tank Battle at Praga July–Sept. 1944: The 4th SS-Panzer-Corps vs the 1st Belorussian Front*. Leandoer & Ekholm Publishing, 2009.

Bartov, Omar. *The Eastern Front, 1941–1945: German Troops and the Barbarization of Warfare*. St. Martin' Press, 1986.

Bellamy, Chris. *Absolute War, Soviet Russia in the Second World War: A Modern History*. Macmillan, 2007.

Bird, Keith. *Erich Raeder, Admiral of the Third Reich*. Naval Institute Press, 2006.

Boog, Horst, ed. *The Conduct of the Air War in the Second World War: An International Comparison, Proceedings of the International Conference of Historians in Freiburg im Breisgau, Federal Republic of Germany, from 29 August to 2 September 1988*. Berg, 1992.

Boog, Horst, et al. Milatargeschichtliches Forshungsamt, *Germany and the Second World War, Volume IV, The Attack on the Soviet Union*. Clarendon Press, 1998.

Boog, Horst, et al. Milatargeschichtliches Forshungsamt, *Germany and the Second World War, Volume VI, The Global War*. Oxford University Press, 2001.

Bradley, Omar, N. *A Soldier's Story*. Henry Holt and Company, 1951.

Buchanan, Russell A., ed. *The United States and World War II: Military and Diplomatic Documents*. University of South Carolina Press, 1972.

Chuikov, Vasili I., *The Beginning of the Road*. Translated by Harold Silver. Macgibbon & Kee, 1963.

Citino, Robert M., *The Path to Blitzkrieg: Doctrine and Training in the German Army, 1920-1939*. Lynne Rienner Publishers, 1999.

Citino, Robert M. *The German Way of War: From the Thirty Years' War to the Third Reich*. University Press of Kansas, 2005.

Citino, Robert M. *Death of the Wehrmacht: The German Campaigns of 1942*. University Press of Kansas, 2007.

Colley, David. *Decision at Strasbourg: Ike's Strategic Mistake to Halt the Sixth Army Group at the Rhine in 1944*. Naval Institute Press, 2009.

Corum, James S. *The Roots of Blitzkrieg Hans von Seekt and German Military Reform*. University Press of Kansas, 1992.

Dinardo, Richard L. *Germany's Panzer Arm in WWII*. Stackpole Books, 2006.

Dinardo, Richard L. *Germany and the Axis Powers: From Coalition to Collapse*. University Press of Kansas, 2005.

Dunn, Walter S., Jr. *Kursk: Hitler's Gamble, 1943*. Stackpole Books, 1997.

Dunn, Walter S., Jr. *Soviet Blitzkrieg: The Battle for White Russia, 1944*. Stackpole Books, 2008.

Dunn, Walter S., Jr.*Hitler's Nemesis: The Red Army 1930-45*. Stackpole Books, 2009.

Echevarria, Antulio J., II. "Moltke and the German Military Tradition: His Theories and Legacies." *Parameters*, Spring 1996.

Eisenhower, Dwight D. *Crusade in Europe*. Doubleday & Co., 1948.

Ellis, John, *Brute Force: Allied Strategy and Tactics in the Second World War*. Andre Deutsch, 1990.

English, John A., and Bruce I. Gudmundsson. *On Infantry*, Rev. ed. Praeger, 1994.

Erickson, John. *The Road to Stalingrad*. Harper & Row Publishers, 1975.

Erickson, John. *The Road to Berlin*. Westview Press, 1983.

Evans, Richard J. *The Third Reich at War*. Penguin Books, 2008.

Gabel, Christopher. *Seek, Strike, and Destroy: U.S. Army Tank Destroyer Doctrine in World War II*. Combat Studies Institute, U.S. Army Command and General Staff College, 1985.

Glantz, David M. *From the Don to the Dnepr: Soviet Offensive Operations, December 1941-August 1943*. Frank Cass, 1991.

Glantz, David M. *Kharkov 1942: Anatomy of a Military Disaster through Soviet Eyes*. Ian Allan Publishing, 1998.

Glantz, David M. *Stumbling Colossus: The Red Army on the Eve of World War*. University Press of Kansas, 1998.

Glantz, David M. *Barbarossa: Hitler's Invasion of Russia 1941*. Tempus Publishing, 2001.

Glantz, David M. *The Siege of Leningrad 1941-44: 900 Days of Terror*. Cassell, 2001.

Glantz, David M., and Jonathan M. House. *When Titans Clashed: How the Red Army Stopped Hitler*. University Press of Kansas, 1995.

Glantz, David M. *The Battle of Kursk*. University Press of Kansas, 1999.

Glantz, David M. *Red Storm over the Balkans; The Failed Soviet Invasion of Romania, Spring 1944*. University Press of Kansas, 2007.

Glantz, David M. *Armageddon in Stalingrad: September–November 1942.* University Press of Kansas, 2009.

Glantz, David M. *Armageddon in Stalingrad, September–November 1942.* University Press of Kansas, 2009.

Glantz, David M., and Harold S. Orenstein. *The Battle for Kursk 1943.* The Soviet General Staff Study. Frank Cass Publishers, 1999.

Glantz, David M. *The Battle for the Ukraine: The Red Army Korsun'-Shevchenkovskii Operation, 1944 (The Soviet General Staff Study).* Frank Cass, 2003.

Glantz, David M. "The Red Army's Donbass Offensive (February-March 1943) Revisited: A Documentary Essay." *Journal of Slavic Military Studies* 18, no. 3 (2005): 369–503.

Glantz, David M. "The Red Army's Lublin-Brest Offensive and Advance on Warsaw (18 July–30 September 1944): An Overview and Documentary Survey." *Journal of Slavic Military Studies* 19, no. 2 (2006): 401–41.

Glantz, David M. *Counterpoint to Stalingrad, Operation Mars (November–December 1942): Marshal Zhukov's Greatest Defeat.* Fort Leavenworth, Kansas: Foreign Military Studies Office. http://fmso.Leavenworth.army.mil/documents/countrpt/countrpt.htm.

Glantz, David M. "Prelude to German Operation Blau: Military Operations on Germany's Eastern Front, April–June 1942." *Journal of Slavic Military Studies* 20, no. 2 (2007): 171–234.

Grier, Howard D. *Hitler, Donitz, and the Baltic Sea: The Third Reich's Last Hope, 1944-1945.* U.S. Naval Institute Press, 2007.

Guderian, Heinz. *Panzer Leader.* Da Capo Press, 1996/

Harrison, Mark. *The Economics of World War II: Six Great Powers in International Comparison.* Cambridge University Press, 1998.

Harrison, Mark, and R. W. Davies. "The Soviet Military-Economic Effort under the Second Five-Year Plan (1933–1937)." *Europe East-Asia Studies* 49, no. 3 (1997): 369–40.

Hart, Liddell, B. H. *The Rommel Papers.* Harcourt Brace, 1953.

Hastings, Max. *Armageddon: The Battle for Germany 1944-45.* Alfred A. Knopf, 2005.

Heer, Hannes, and Klaus Naumann. *War of Extermination: The German Military in World War II, 1941-1944.* Berghahn Books, 2000.

Hinze, Rolf. *Crucible of Combat: Germany's Defensive Battles in the Ukraine 1943-44.* Helion & Company, 2009.

Hinze, Rolf. *To the Bitter End: The Final Battles of Army Groups North Ukraine, A, and Center—Eastern Front, 1944-45.* Casemate, 2010.

Howarth, Stephen, and Derek Law. *The Battle of the Atlantic 1939-1945: The 50th Anniversary International Naval Conference.* Naval Institute Press, 1994.

Humpert, David M. "Viktor Suvorov and Operation Barbarossa: Tukhachevskii Revisited." *Journal of Slavic Military Studies* 18, no. 1 (2005): 59–74.

Jacobsen, Hans-Adolf, and Jurgen Rohwer. *Decisive Battles of World War II: The German View.* Andre Deutsch, 1965.

Jacobsen, Hans-Adolf and Arthur L. Smith Jr. *World War II: Policy and Strategy, Selected Documents and Commentary.* Clio Books, 1979.

Jarymowycz, Roman Johann. *Tank Tactics from Normandy to Lorraine.* Lynne Rienner Publishers, 2001.

Jones, Michael K. *Stalingrad: How the Red Army Triumphed.* Pen & Sword, 2007.

Keithly, David M., and Stephen P. Ferris. "*Auftragstaktik*, or Directive Control, in Joint and Combined Operations." *Parameters.* U.S. Army War College Quarterly, Autumn 1999.

Kershaw, Ian. *Hitler 1936–1945: Nemesis.* Norton, 2000.

Kershaw, Robert. *War without Garlands: Operation Barbarossa 1941–1942.* Ian Allen, 2000.

Kipp, Jacob W. *Mass, Mobility, and the Red Army's Road to Operational Art 1918–1936*, Foreign Military Studies Office, 1988.

Kirchubel, Robert. *Hitler's Panzer Armies on the Eastern Front.* Pen & Sword, 2009.

Lemay, Benoit *Erich von Manstein: Hitler's Master Strategist.* Casemate Publishers, 2010.

Levine, Alan J. *The War against Rommel's Supply Lines, 1942–1943.* Praeger, 1999.

Levine, Alan J. *From the Normandy Beaches to the Baltic Sea: The Northwest Europe Campaign, 1944–1945.* Praeger, 2000.

Lewin, Ronald. *Ultra Goes to War: The First Account of World War II's Greatest Secret Based on Official Documents.* McGraw-Hill, 1978.

Lisitskiy, P. I., and S. A. Bogdanov. "Upgrading Military Art during the Second Period of the Great Patriotic War." *Military Thought* 14, no. 1 (January–March 2005): 191.

Lukacs, John. *Five Days in London, May 1940.* Yale University Press, 1999.

MacDonogh, Giles. *After the Reich: The Brutal History of the Allied Occupation.* Basic Books, 2007.

Manstein, Erich von. *Lost Victories.* Presidio, 1982.

Mawdsley, Evan. *Thunder in the East: The Nazi-Soviet War 1941–1945.* Hodder Headline Group, 2005.

Megargee, Geoffrey P. *Inside Hitler's High Command.* University Press of Kansas, 2000.

Megargee, Geoffrey P. *War of Annihilation: Combat and Genocide on the Eastern Front 1941* (Rowman & Littlefield, 2006).

Mellenthin, F. W. *Panzer Battles.* University of Oklahoma Press, 1956.

Menning, Bruce W. *Operational Art's Origins.* U.S. Army Command and General Staff College, 1998.

Merridale, Catherine. *Ivan's War: Life and Death in the Red Army, 1939–1945.* Picador, 2006.

Middlebrook, Martin, and Chris Everitt. *The Bomber Command War Diaries.* Viking Books, 1985.

Mikhailova Tver' (formerly Kalinin), Tat'iana. "The Battle of Rzhev: Ideology instead of Statistics." *Journal of Slavic Military Studies* 18, no. 3 (2005): 359–68.

Military Intelligence Service War Department. *The German Armored Army.* Special Series No. 2, August 10, 1942. Unclassified July 13, 1987.

Milward, Alan. *War, Economy and Society, 1939–1945.* Allen Lane, 1977.

Muller, Rolf-Dieter, et al. Milatargeschichtliches Forshungsamt, *Germany and the Second World War, Volume V/II, Organization and Mobilization of the German Sphere of Power.* Clarendon Press, 2003.

Office of Naval Intelligence, Navy Department. *Fuehrer Conferences on Matters Dealing with the German Navy 1942, Volume II.* Office of Naval Intelligence, 1947. Conference with Fuehrer on September 17, 1941, 37, Annex 1.

Office of Naval Intelligence, Navy Department. *Fuehrer Conferences on Matters Dealing with the German Navy 1942, Volume III.* Office of Naval Intelligence, 1946. Document Reference PG 32187 T-14B.

Office of Naval Intelligence, Navy Department. *Fuehrer Conferences on Matters Dealing with the German Navy 1942, Volume III.* Office of Naval Intelligence 1946. Document Reference PG 332651 T-79, April 13, 1942.

Overy, Richard. *The Road to War.* Penguin Books, 1989.

Overy, Richard. *Interrogations: The Nazi Elite in Allied Hands 1945.* Penguin Group, 2001.

Overy, Richard. *The Dictators Hitler's Germany and Stalin's Russia.* Norton, 2004.

Raus, Erhard. *Panzer Operations: The Eastern Front Memoir of General Raus, 1941–1945.* Da Capo Press, 2003.

Rees, Laurance. *World War II behind Closed Doors: Stalin, the Nazis and the West.* Pantheon Books, 2008.

Reese, Roger R. *Stalin's Reluctant Soldiers: A Social History of the Red Army 1925–1941.* University Press of Kansas, 1996.

Rokossovsky, K. *A Soldier's Duty.* Progress Publishers, 1970.

Senger und Etterlin, F. M. von. *German Tanks of World War II, The Complete Illustrated History of German Armoured Fighting Vehicles 1926–1945,* (Stackpole Books, 1969).

Showalter, Dennis. *Hitler's Panzers: The Lightning Attacks That Revolutionized Warfare.* Berkley Publishing Group, 2009.

Sontag, Raymond James, and James Stuart Beddie. *Nazi-Soviet Relations 1939–1941: Documents from the Archives of the German Foreign Office.* U.S. Department of State Publication, 1948.

Speer, Albert. *Inside the Third Reich.* Galahad Books, 1970.

Stein, Marcel. *Field Marshal von Manstein: The Janus Head: A Portrait.* Helion & Company, 2007.

Tissier, Tony. *Zhukov at the Oder: The Decisive Battle for Berlin.* Stackpole Books, 2009.

Tooze, Adam. *The Wages of Destruction: The Making and Breaking of the Nazi Economy.*Allen Lane, 2006.

Trevor-Roper, H. R. *Blitzkrieg to Defeat Hitler's War Directives 1939–1945.* Holt, Rinehart and Winston, 1964.

Ungvary, Krisztian. *The Siege of Budapest: One Hundred Days in World War II.* Yale University Press, 2005.

Vinen, Richard. *A History in Fragments: Europe in the Twentieth Century.* Da Capo Press, 2000.

Warlimot, Walter. *Inside Hitler's Headquarters 1939–45.* Presidio Press, 1964.

Watson, James. *Documentary Background of World War II, 1939–1941,* (University Microfilms Inc., Ann Arbor, 1966).

Weinberg, Gerhard L., et al. *Hitler and His Generals Military Conferences 1942–1945: The First Complete Stenographic Record of the Military Situation Conferences from Stalingrad to Berlin.* Enigma Books, 2002.

Wette, Wolfram. *The Wehrmacht: History, Myth, Reality.* Harvard University Press, 2006.

Wilbeck, Christopher W. *Swinging the Sledgehammer: The Combat Effectiveness of German Heavy Tank Battalions in World War II.* Foreign Military Studies Office, Fort Leavenworth, Kansas, 2002.

Zaloga, Steven. *Armored Thunderbolt: The U.S. Army Sherman in World War II.* Stackpole Books, 2008.

Zetterling, Niklas, and Anders Frankson. *The Korsun Pocket: The Encirclement and Breakout of a German Army in the East, 1944.* Casemate, 2008.

Zhukov, Georgi K. *Marshal Zhukov's Greatest Battles.* Harper & Row, 1969.

Index

Note: Page numbers followed by an *m* refer to maps. Page numbers followed by a *t* refer to tables.

About the Author

STEVEN D. MERCATANTE is the founder and editor in chief of The Globe at War, a website focused on exploring World War II. Since its launch in August 2008 The Globe at War has acquired a reputation for insightful analysis and has established the author's name as a respected authority on World War II. He received his BA from the University of Michigan, has a teaching certificate in history and political science from Eastern Michigan University, and a JD from Michigan State University College of Law; graduating with a concentration in international law. He is a a corporate tax attorney, member of the State Bar of Michigan, and is the founder and principal of TIR Consulting LLC, a consulting firm specializing in international, federal, state, and local tax compliance. His published works include many writings in the legal, financial, and historical fields, including the 2008 journal article *The Deregulation of Usury Ceilings, Rise of Easy Credit and Increasing Consumer Debt* published by the South Dakota Law Review.